Research Anthology on Agile Software, Software Development, and Testing

Information Resources Management Association
USA

Volume IV

Published in the United States of America by
    IGI Global
    Engineering Science Reference (an imprint of IGI Global)
    701 E. Chocolate Avenue
    Hershey PA, USA 17033
    Tel: 717-533-8845
    Fax: 717-533-8661
    E-mail: cust@igi-global.com
    Web site: http://www.igi-global.com

Library of Congress Cataloging-in-Publication Data

Names: Information Resources Management Association, editor.
Title: Research anthology on agile software, software development, and
  testing / Information Resources Management Association, editor.
Description: Hershey, PA : Engineering Science Reference, [2022] | Includes
  bibliographical references and index. | Summary: "This reference book
  covers emerging trends of software development and testing, discussing
  the newest developments in agile software and its usage spanning
  multiple industries, covering topics such as global software
  engineering, knowledge management, and product development"-- Provided
  by publisher.
Identifiers: LCCN 2021040441 (print) | LCCN 2021040442 (ebook) | ISBN
  9781668437025 (h/c) | ISBN 9781668437032 (eISBN)
Subjects: LCSH: Agile software development. | Computer programs--Testing.
Classification: LCC QA76.76.D47 R468 2022 (print) | LCC QA76.76.D47
  (ebook) | DDC 005.1/112--dc23/eng/20211021
LC record available at https://lccn.loc.gov/2021040441
LC ebook record available at https://lccn.loc.gov/2021040442

British Cataloguing in Publication Data
A Cataloguing in Publication record for this book is available from the British Library.

The views expressed in this book are those of the authors, but not necessarily of the publisher.

For electronic access to this publication, please contact: eresources@igi-global.com.

List of Contributors

Table of Contents

Section 2
Development and Design Methodologies

Volume II

Section 3
Tools and Technologies

Volume III

**Section 4
Utilization and Applications**

Volume IV

Section 6
Managerial Impact

Chapter 102

Abdulkadir Seker, Sivas Cumhuriyet University, Turkey
Banu Diri, Yıldız Technical University, Turkey
Halil Arslan, Sivas Cumhuriyet University, Turkey
Mehmet Fatih Amasyalı, Yıldız Technical University, Turkey

Preface

As organizations grow to require new and innovative software programs to improve processes, there is a need for the science of software development to constantly evolve. Agile practices have shown great benefits for improving the effectiveness of software development and its maintenance due to their ability to adapt to change. It is essential for organizations to stay current with the developments in agile software and software testing to witness how it can improve business operations.

Staying informed of the most up-to-date research trends and findings is of the utmost importance. That is why IGI Global is pleased to offer this four-volume reference collection of reprinted IGI Global book chapters and journal articles that have been handpicked by senior editorial staff. This collection will shed light on critical issues related to the trends, techniques, and uses of various applications by providing both broad and detailed perspectives on cutting-edge theories and developments. This collection is designed to act as a single reference source on conceptual, methodological, technical, and managerial issues, as well as to provide insight into emerging trends and future opportunities within the field.

The *Research Anthology on Agile Software, Software Development, and Testing* is organized into seven distinct sections that provide comprehensive coverage of important topics. The sections are:

1. Fundamental Concepts and Theories;
2. Development and Design Methodologies;
3. Tools and Technologies;
4. Utilization and Applications;
5. Organizational and Social Implications;
6. Managerial Impact; and
7. Critical Issues and Challenges.

The following paragraphs provide a summary of what to expect from this invaluable reference tool.

Section 1, "Fundamental Concepts and Theories," serves as a foundation for this extensive reference tool by addressing crucial theories essential to understanding the concepts and uses of agile software, software development, and testing in multidisciplinary settings. The first chapter of this section, "Challenges and Trends of Agile," by Prof. Jorge Marx Gómez of Carl von Ossietzky Universität Oldenburg, Germany and Prof. Fayez Salma of Carl von Ossietzky Universität Oldenburg, Germany, studies agile methodologies and different challenges with suggested solutions generated from agile philosophy itself. The last chapter of this section, "A Historical and Bibliometric Analysis of the Development of Agile," by Profs. Sathiadev Mahesh, Kenneth R. Walsh, and Cherie C. Trumbach of University of New Orleans, USA, summarizes the traditional approaches and presents the conditions that led to agile approaches such as product complexity, shortened life cycle of the market, and eventually to the widespread acceptance of Scrum.

Section 2, "Development and Design Methodologies," presents in-depth coverage of the design and development of agile software for their use in different applications. The first chapter of this section, "Software Effort Estimation for Successful Software Application Development," by Prof. Syed Mohsin Saif of Islamic University of Science and Technology, India, explains different types of software applications, software estimation models, the importance of software effort estimation, and challenges faced in software effort estimation. The last chapter of this section, "A Simulation Model for Application Development in Data Warehouses," by Prof. Nayem Rahman of Portland State University, Portland, USA, presents a simulation model of a data warehouse to evaluate the feasibility of different software development controls and measures to better manage a software development lifecycle and improve the performance of the launched software.

Section 3, "Tools and Technologies," explores the various tools and technologies used in the implementation, development, and testing of agile software for various uses. The first chapter of this section, "Use of Qualitative Research to Generate a Function for Finding the Unit Cost of Software Test Cases," by Prof. Mark L. Gillenson of University of Memphis, Memphis, USA; Prof. Thomas F. Stafford of Louisiana Tech University, Ruston, USA; Prof. Yao Shi of University of Memphis, Memphis, USA; and Prof. Xihui "Paul" Zhang of University of North Alabama, Florence, USA, demonstrates a novel use of case research to generate an empirical function through qualitative generalization. This innovative technique applies interpretive case analysis to the problem of defining and generalizing an empirical cost function for test cases through qualitative interaction with an industry cohort of subject matter experts involved in software testing at leading technology companies. The last chapter of this section, "Metastructuring for Standards: How Organizations Respond to the Multiplicity of Standards," by Prof. Ronny Gey of Friedrich Schiller University Jena, Germany and Prof. Andrea Fried of Linköping University, Sweden, focusses on the appearance and implementation of process standards in software development organizations.

Section 4, "Utilization and Applications," describes how agile software is used and applied in diverse industries for various technologies and applications. The first chapter of this section, "Social Capital and Knowledge Networks of Software Developers: A Case Study," by Prof. VenuGopal Balijepally of Oakland University, Rochester, USA and Prof. Sridhar Nerur of University of Texas at Arlington, Arlington, USA, examines the structural and relational dimensions of developers' knowledge networks, identifies the specific actionable knowledge resources accessed from these networks, and explores how entry-level and more experienced developers differ along these dimensions. The findings from the qualitative analysis, backed by limited quantitative analysis of the case study data, underpin the discussion, implications for practice, and future research directions. The last chapter of this section, "A Game Theoretic Approach for Quality Assurance in Software Systems Using Antifragility-Based Learning Hooks," by Profs. Vimaladevi M. and Zayaraz G. of Pondicherry Engineering College, India, proposes an innovative approach which uses a fault injection methodology to perform the task of quality assurance.

Section 5, "Organizational and Social Implications," includes chapters discussing the impact of agile software on society and shows the ways in which software is developed in different industries and how this impacts business. The first chapter of this section, "Media Richness, Knowledge Sharing, and Computer Programming by Virtual Software Teams," by Profs. Idongesit Williams and Albert Gyamfi of Aalborg University, Denmark, concludes, based on the case being investigated, that rich media does not fit the task characteristics of a software programmer. It further concludes that media richness does affect knowledge sharing in these virtual teams. This is because the current lean media actually enables knowledge sharing as it fits the core characteristics of the software programming process. The last chapter of this section, "On the Rim Between Business Processes and Software Systems," by Profs. Ricardo J. Machado and Maribel Yasmina Santos of Universidade do Minho, Portugal and Prof. Maria Estrela Ferreira da Cruz of Polytechnic Institute of Viana do Castelo, Portugal, uses the information existing in business process models to derive software models specially focused in generating a data model.

Section 6, "Managerial Impact," presents the impact of agile software within an organizational setting. The first chapter of this section, "Boosting the Competitiveness of Organizations With the Use of Software Engineering," by Prof. Mirna Muñoz of CIMAT, A. C. Unidad Zacatecas, Mexico, provides a research work path focused on helping software development organizations to change to a continuous software improvement culture impacting both their software development process highlighting the human factor training needs. Results show that the implementation of best practices could be easily implemented if adequate support is provided. The last chapter of this section, "Measuring Developers' Software Security Skills, Usage, and Training Needs," by Prof. Daniela Soares Cruzes of SINTEF Digital, Norway; Prof. Tosin Daniel Oyetoyan of Western Norway University of Applied Sciences, Norway; and Prof. Martin Gilje Gilje Jaatun of SINTEF Digital, Norway, presents a survey instrument that can be used to investigate software security usage, competence, and training needs in agile organizations.

Section 7, "Critical Issues and Challenges," presents coverage of academic and research perspectives on challenges to using agile software in different methods, technologies, and techniques in varied industry applications. The first chapter of this section, "Towards a Security Competence of Software Developers: A Literature Review," by Prof. Nana Assyne of University of Jyväskylä, Finland, utilises a literature review to identify the security competences of software developers. Thirteen security competences of software developers were identified and mapped to the common body of knowledge for information security professional framework. The last chapter of this section, "Open Source Software Development Challenges: A Systematic Literature Review on GitHub," by Prof. Abdulkadir Seker of Sivas Cumhuriyet University, Turkey; Prof. Banu Diri of Yıldız Technical University, Turkey; Prof. Halil Arslan of Sivas Cumhuriyet University, Turkey; and Prof. Mehmet Fatih Amasyalı of Yıldız Technical University, Turkey, reviews the selected 172 studies according to some criteria that used the dataset as a data source.

Although the primary organization of the contents in this multi-volume work is based on its seven sections, offering a progression of coverage of the important concepts, methodologies, technologies, applications, social issues, and emerging trends, the reader can also identify specific contents by utilizing the extensive indexing system listed at the end of each volume. As a comprehensive collection of research on the latest findings related to agile software, the *Research Anthology on Agile Software, Software Development, and Testing* provides software developers, software engineers, computer engineers, IT directors, students, managers, faculty, researchers, and academicians with a complete understanding of the applications and impacts of agile software and its development and testing. Given the vast number of issues concerning usage, failure, success, strategies, and applications of agile software in modern technologies and processes, the *Research Anthology on Agile Software, Software Development, and Testing* encompasses the most pertinent research on the applications, impacts, uses, and development of agile software.

Chapter 76
Systematic Review of Risks in Domestic and Global IT Projects

Franciane Freitas Silveira
UFABC, São Bernardo do Campo, Brazil

Rosária de F. S. Macri Russo
UNINOVE, São Paulo, Brazil

Irapuan Glória Júnior
UNINOVE, São Paulo, Brazil

Roberto Sbragia
Universidade de São Paulo (USP), São Paulo, Brazil

ABSTRACT

The development of information technology projects is no longer limited to the domestic sphere. This study identifies the differentiation of risk categories between global and domestic projects through an exploratory research carried out by means of a systematic literature review. 1367 risks were identified in 37 articles and classified within 22 categories. The major concern regarded in domestic project management was the client (external risk) and scope (internal risk) and, in global project management, the psychic distance (external) and coordination and control (internal). The main difference between the risk categories for each project type refers to the psychic distance category, which was identified almost exclusively in global projects, thus making the external risks more relevant than those in domestic projects. On the other hand, it makes risks such as client, supplier and stakeholders be underestimated. The results indicate that project managers should focus on different risks depending on the type of IT project: global or domestic.

DOI: 10.4018/978-1-6684-3702-5.ch076

INTRODUCTION

In order to gain competitive advantage, organizations use globalization for developing IT projects, introducing new challenges that are peculiar to this type of project. The characteristics of global projects are geographically dispersed teams, having members with different cultures and enabled by the IT infrastructure (Lee-Kelley & Sankey, 2008). There are many differences between the attributes in domestic and global projects. While domestic projects involve a single or limited number of organizations, global projects have multiple organizations and departments involved, each with their own different interests and cultures. While legislation is known and well understood in domestic projects, in global projects the comprehension is difficult and needs interpretation (Lientz & Rea, 2003).

Global Information Technology [IT] projects aim at assisting organizations to quickly meet their demands (Sommerville, 2015). Technology dependence is a characteristic of IT projects that generates uncertainty during execution, producing a high level of failure among organizations (Sauser, Reilly, & Shenhar, 2009). Uncertainties in the projects can impact positively or negatively the objectives of the projects (PMI, 2012). The knowledge area within project management [PM] that handles risk in a systematic way is the Risk Management [RM].

Many studies focus on the risks in domestic IT projects regarding information systems (Hwang et al., 2016), software (Jiang & Klein, 2000), Enterprise Research Planning [ERP] (Sumner, 2000) and Outsourcing (Bunker, Hardy, Babar & Stevens, 2015). Other articles focus on the risks of global IT projects related to ERP (Aloini, Dulmin, & Mininno, 2012), outsourcing (Kliem, 2004) and software (Perrson et al., 2009; Verner, Brereton, Kitchenham, Turner & Niazi, 2013). However, few studies look into the difference between the risks in both of them. The exception was Nakatsu and Iacovou (2009), who, nevertheless, focus on the main risk factors in outsourcing projects.

This situation leads to the following question: "What is the difference between the categories of risks commonly presented in global and domestic IT projects?" This question will be answered through a systematic review of literature in order to recognize such distinction and generate a complete list of risk categories. The results of this research will produce practical implications for IT managers, who should be aware of what the main risk categories are and how to manage them. With the evolution of organizations and globalization, a manager of domestic IT projects may be required to manage a global project without notice, and might need help to deal with the situation at hand.

CONCEPTUAL BACKGROUND

IT projects are classified into system and infrastructure development projects. In the former, delivery is a computational system. In infrastructure projects, on the other hand, deliveries are related to servers, communications, and other several possibilities, thus having specific risks for each type (Sommerville, 2015). In this study, we will focus on computational systems. It is common to use offshore teams in this type of project (Kliem, 2004), constituting what is known as a global project, which uses distributed teams (Ebert, 2011).

Global projects are those that involve individuals, teams, groups and organizations from multiple locations (Lientz & Rea, 2003), cultures and business units and functions (Anantatmula & Thomas, 2010). There are unique challenges in this new context, such as language and communication barriers, cultural differences, distributed teams, and different government regulations from one country to another. The trend of involving different countries in such projects is due to the use of each country's competitive advantages, which can be explained specifically by two factors: the marketing factor, in which there is the need for access to markets and use of distribution channels, responding to local needs and increasing client intimacy, and the technology factor, related to the recruitment of qualified personnel, access to foreign talents, the existence of lower wages and differentiated technologies (Chiesa, 1995).

Specifically, global IT development projects promise improvements in the time to market, "round-the-clock" development, client proximity and access to cheaper skilled labor (Carmel, 1999; Holmstrom, Conchúir, Ågerfalk & Fitzgerald, 2006) and thus to gain and maintain competitive advantage (Kommeren & Paiviainen, 2007). However, in addition to bringing benefits to the projects, this new reality introduces new challenges to their management due to the distance aspects known as geographical distance, temporal distance (time zone difference), and socio-cultural distance. These characteristics are usually termed as "global distance" (Noll, Beecham, & Richardson, 2010).

All these challenges must be dealt with through RM. They are another aspect that becomes predominant within the overall project scope and, if ignored, can increase the likelihood of project failure (Ropponen & Lyytinen, 2000; Jalali & Wohlin, 2010). It can be seen as a combination of probability of occurrence and alternate impacts, including perceived importance for the stakeholders (Treasury, 2004). Thus, it involves uncertainty and it is an opportunity, if positive, or a threat, if negative. (PMI, 2012,) and "specific unknown risks cannot be managed proactively, which suggests that project teams should create a contingency plan" (PMI, 2009). Although RM is a continuous process, Nikander and Eloranta (2001) state that it occurs practically in the initial phase of the project, emphasizing the importance of identification of the early signs of environment change during the project.

IT risks are related to systems development, support infrastructure, peopleware and information security (Sommerville, 2015). Many risk factors come from outside the project, the company and its environment, so the project manager should promote favorable effective communication and collaboration between all stakeholders, a particularly important condition for the early detection of risk and its management (Thamhain, 2013). The user is one of the most important stakeholders, because they are the primary source of requirements for the system (Schmidt, Lyytinen, Keil, & Cule, 2001). Risks events can serve as input information for knowledge management in projects (Alhawari, Karadsheh, Talet, & Mansour, 2012) to organizational learning. Prikladnicki and Yamaguti (2004) affirm that RM must not only be adapted to the configuration of global software development projects, as it also becomes more important in this context than in the context of domestic projects.

RESEARCH PROCEDURES

This paper summarizes a literature review about risks in global and domestic IT projects with an evidence-based approach (Tranfield, Denyes & Smart, 2003). As research strategy, we used systematic literature review. It differs from usual and narrative reviews because it uses a "replicable, scientific and transparent process" (Tranfield et al., 2003, p. 209). Our original inclusion criteria were (1) studies from the IT sector; (2) those that addressed global or domestic projects; (3) those that had empirical research; (4) those that listed the risks of these projects; and (5) those written in English.

To explore the literature, we used the first nine steps defined by Petticrew and Roberts (2008). We also made use of one step not defined by the authors for performing a statistical evaluation of the results. These steps are detailed in Figure 1. The committee (step 2) consisted of four researchers, two experts in RM and two global PM specialists; every step was made by one researcher and reviewed by another. Conflicts were discussed in committee meetings for consensus. The protocol (step 3) was defined toward research and analysis, which was followed in the subsequent steps.

Figure 1. Systemic review development flow in 10 steps (Source: Authors)

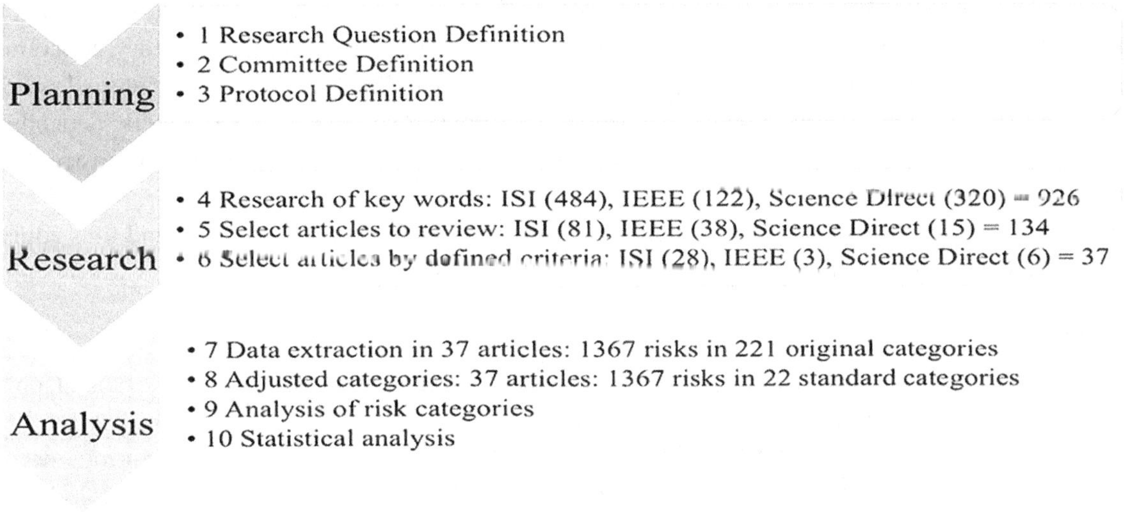

Planning
- 1 Research Question Definition
- 2 Committee Definition
- 3 Protocol Definition

Research
- 4 Research of key words: ISI (484), IEEE (122), Science Direct (320) = 926
- 5 Select articles to review: ISI (81), IEEE (38), Science Direct (15) = 134
- 6 Select articles by defined criteria: ISI (28), IEEE (3), Science Direct (6) = 37

Analysis
- 7 Data extraction in 37 articles: 1367 risks in 221 original categories
- 8 Adjusted categories: 37 articles: 1367 risks in 22 standard categories
- 9 Analysis of risk categories
- 10 Statistical analysis

For the research (step 4), we used three tools to access information: Institute for Scientific Information [ISI], Science Direct and Institute of Electrical and Electronics Engineers [IEEE]. We searched for the words "risk", "project", "global project", "international project", "information technology", "information systems", "ERP" and "software"; whenever possible, the research scope was defined within the areas "Business" and "Computer Science". With this method, we were able to conduct the research in various types sources, including conference proceedings and industry. In this step, we selected 926 articles.

In the following step (5), the abstracts were assessed and the five inclusion criteria were applied, resulting in 134 complete articles to be analyzed. Reading these articles in the following step (6) led to the exclusion of 97 of them, which either were duplicated in the bases, or dealt with the same projects, or presented only risk categories, or were theoretical or did not meet the inclusion criteria completely. We made a quality assessment of internal validity of each article and some were excluded when the resulting list of risks was not object of analysis.

In the following step (7), we extracted the lists of risk items and their respective risk categories. Seven articles did not categorize the risks. We classified projects as global or domestic projects and by the type of IT. We also identified the source of the information in the articles, regarding the risk list as empirical research, when the list of risks was originated in the research of the article, or as literature, when the list was generated based on literature searches. In order to identify relevant outcomes, we extracted the objectives, keywords, methodological procedures applied, outcomes and contributions. We then conducted another quality assessment of internal validity of each article to identify the impact factor and number of citations as well. The result was a database with 1367 risks, another with their 221 original categories and the classification of 37 articles.

Aiming at consolidating the original categories, we reclassified them in the subsequent step (8). First, the database with original categories was compared with standard categories based on the initial risk factor lists of RM standards established in the Protocol (Committee of Sponsoring Organizations of the Treadway Commission [COSO] (2007); Higuera & Haimes, 1996; Office of Government Commerce [OGC], 2005; PMI, 2012; Treasury, 2004). Some of these standards refer to these lists as risk categories, a term that is also used in this study.

A risk can be external or internal. The external risk factors, arising from outside the organization, can only be mitigated, but cannot be managed. They can be classified as political, regulatory, economic, social, technology, environment, and suppliers. The internal risk factors related to the internal operations of the organization refer to providing capacity and competence. They can vary greatly depending on the product, the project and the organization. In general, they can be classified into: infrastructure, staff, process and technology.

Those categories, however, have shown to be insufficient for proper classification and thus adjustments have been made, resulting in 22 categories, called adjusted categories:

A. External categories:
    ◦ External standard categories were maintained - political, regulatory, economic, social, environmental, supplier and technological
    ◦ The client, psychic distance and stakeholder classes were included due to various occurrences in the articles that did not fit in the standard categories
B. Internal categories:
    ◦ The default category staff was maintained
    ◦ The internal category called process was subdivided into categories related to product-complexity, product process, technology and Project Management acquisition, communication, coordination and control, cost, scope, staff management, quality and time
    ◦ The infrastructure category was absorbed by the technology category
    ◦ A category related to the internal organizational environment was included

After that, we evaluated the classification of each risk under the adjusted categories. At times, we needed to reread the original article to get a deeper understanding of each risk in order to classify it in the correct category. In some cases, it was necessary to transfer the risk to another category, as when the original category was referring to a specific phase of the life cycle of the project. Then, a comparative framework was generated based on adjusted categories. Although client, supplier and staff were considered stakeholders, we decided to split them into various categories, given the large number of risk items related to each one of them.

The analysis (step 9) was made using differences and similarities between risk categories (internal and external) and the categories of domestic and global projects. The literature was accessed to validate our findings. Step 10 (statistically evaluate the results) was not indicated by Petticrew and Roberts (2008) as advisable, but was included in order to validate the hypothesis of a difference in the treatment of risks among the authors of articles related to global and domestic projects. For the verification of independence between the two groups of articles, the chi-square statistical test was applied, and the significance level (or error rate) was set at 5% in the statistical analysis (Siegel & Castellan, 1988).

RESULTS AND ANALYSIS

Analysis of Selected Articles

Table 1 features 37 selected papers, 13 pertaining to global projects, 23 articles related to domestic projects and only 1 article covering the two types of projects. Among the selected references, 2 articles evaluated ERP projects, 3 articles evaluated Information System projects, 6 evaluated Outsourcing and the majority referred to Software development. The vast majority applied a qualitative research to deal with the risks. Among those, 12 articles were exclusively based on the risks described in literature. Aundhe and Mathew (2009) used the grounded theory and Liu, Zhang, Keil and Chen (2010) applied the Delphi method to compare the difference in perception between project managers and sponsors. Eleven articles obtained their list of risks through empirical surveys. Kliem (2004) is an experienced consultant who builds a list of risks based on his experience. Although that article was not academic, we decide to use it because it built an in-depth list of global IT projects.

Table 1. References selected in the systematic review of literature INDEXa: SJR (ISI Web of Knowledge) INDEXb: JCR (SCOPUS)

Id	Reference	Project Type	It Project	Research Type	INDEX (2015)
1	Ahmed et al., 2014	Global	Outsourcing	Mixed	0,473a
2	Aloini et al., 2012	Global	ERP	Qualitative	1,269a
3	Aundhe & Mathew, 2009	Global	Outsourcing	Qualitative	1,437a
4	Baccarini et al., 2004	Domestic	Software	Quantitative	1,278a
5	Brookfield et al., 2014	Domestic	Software	Quantitative	0,458a
6	Bunker et al., 2015	Domestic	Outsourcing	Qualitative	0,100b
7	Dwivedi et al., 2015	Domestic	Information Systems	Qualitative	1,197a
8	Ebert et al., 2008	Global	Software	Qualitative	0,254b
9	Elzamly et al., 2016	Domestic	Software	Quantitative	0,000b
10	Gheni et al., 2016	Global	Software	Mixed	0,170b
11	Han, 2014	Domestic	Software	Quantitative	1,393a
12	Hijazi et al, 2014	Domestic	Software	Qualitative	0,262b
13	Hwang et al., 2016	Domestic	Information Systems	Qualitative	1,148a
14	Jiang & Klein. 2000	Domestic	Software	Quantitative	3,243a
15	Kliem, 2004	Global	Outsourcing	N/A	0,638b
16	Lee & Baby, 2013	Global	Software	Qualitative	1,183a
17	Liu & Wang, 2014	Domestic	Outsourcing	Quantitative	2,885a
18	Liu et al., 2010	Domestic	Software	Qualitative	2,522a
19	Lopez & Salmeron, 2012	Domestic	Software	Qualitative	0,134b
20	Lu et al., 2013	Domestic	Software	Qualitative	0,644a
21	Nakatsu & Iacovou, 2009	Both	Outsourcing	Qualitative	2,163a
22	Neves et al., 2014	Domestic	Software	Qualitative	2,885a

continues on following page

Table 1. Continued

Id	Reference	Project Type	It Project	Research Type	INDEX (2015)
23	Nurdiani et al., 2011	Global	Software	Qualitative	0,122b
24	Perrson et al., 2009	Global	Software	Qualitative	1,454a
25	Rodriguez et al., 2016	Domestic	Software	Qualitative	2,981a
26	Samantra et al., 2016	Domestic	Software	Quantitative	0,556b
27	Sarigiannidis & Chatzoglou, 2014	Domestic	Software	Quantitative	2,885a
28	Schmidt et al., 2001	Global	Software	Quantitative	3,036b
29	Sharma & Gupta, 2012	Domestic	Software	Mixed	2,885a
30	Shrivastava & Rathod, 2015	Global	Software	Qualitative	2,981a
31	Smite, 2006	Global	Software	Quantitative	0,317b
32	Sonchan & Ramingwong, 2014	Domestic	Software	Qualitative	0,100b
33	Sumner, 2000	Domestic	ERP	Qualitative	4,775a
34	Verner et al, 2014	Global	Software	Qualitative	1,569a
35	Vrhovec et al., 2015	Domestic	Software	Qualitative	2,885a
36	Wallace & Keil, 2004	Domestic	Software	Quantitative	1,910b
37	Ziemba & Kolasa, 2015	Domestic	Information Systems	Qualitative	0,200b

Source: Authors

Regarding the measurement of the selected journals' reputation, the impact factor was used to measure its degree of importance. The impact factor is often used as a proxy to measure the relative importance of a journal within its field; journals with higher impact factors are often considered more important than those with minors. According to Table 1, some journals were evaluated by the Journal Citation Report (JCR), when someone were not indexed in JCR, the SJR (SCOPUS) was used. In the list of 37 articles selected, the journal with the greatest impact factor is the Journal of Information Technology - 4.77 (JCR). Another publication with relevant impact factor is the International Journal of Project Management with 4 articles selected 2,885 (JCR).

The researched papers bring us different points of view regarding the risks, as clients (Nakatsu & Iacovou, 2009), managers (Dwivedi et al., 2015), project managers (Smite, 2006), service providers (Ahmed et al., 2014), experts and practitioners (Shrivastava & Rathod, 2015); team members (Hwang et al., 2016). Few articles explore more than one point of view: senior executives and project manager (Liu et al., 2010), client and vendor (Bunker et al., 2015) and managers and software developers (Neves et al., 2014).

Analysis of Risk Categories

External Risks

Table 2 summarizes the external risk items identified from 37 references, classifying them according to different categories, project type and references. Moreover, it is noteworthy that most external risks were cited in articles pertaining to global projects. This result reveals a greater concern with external risks in global projects. Lu, Yu, Chang & Su (2013) and Samantra et al. (2016) did not mentioned external risks.

Table 2. External risks, by categories and by reference

References	Client	Psychic Distance	Economic	Supplier	Environment	Political	Regulatory	Stakeholders	Technological	Total
Domestic	**83**	**3**	**8**	**22**	**4**	**1**	**5**	**13**	**6**	**145**
%	**57%**	**2%**	**6%**	**15%**	**3%**	**1%**	**3%**	**9%**	**4%**	**100%**
Baccarini et al., 2004			3	1				1		5
Brookfield et al., 2014	3								2	5
Bunker et al., 2015	5	2		14	4		1	3	3	32
Dwivedi et al., 2015	7	1		1		1			1	11
Elzamlyet al., 2016	2		1	1			1			5
Han, 2014	1		1	1			1			4
Hijazi et al, 2014	2									2
Hwang et al., 2016	3									3
Jiang & Klein 2000	13									13
Liu & Wang, 2014	5									5
Liu et al., 2010	7		3	2				2		14
López & Salmeron, 2012	5									5
Nakatsu & Iacovou, 2009	3									3
Neves et al., 2014	2									2
Rodriguez et al., 2016	1									1
Sarigiannidis & Chatzoglou, 2014	5						1			6
Sharma & Gupta, 2012	1							1		2
Sonchan & Ramingwong, 2014							1			1
Sumner, 2000	2									2
Vrhovec et al., 2015	2							6		8
Wallace & Keil, 2004	7			2						9
Ziemba & Kolasa, 2015	7									7
Global	**28**	**79**	**13**	**17**	**1**	**7**	**11**	**10**	**0**	**166**
%	**17%**	**48%**	**8%**	**10%**	**1%**	**4%**	**7%**	**6%**	**0%**	**100%**
Ahmed et al., 2014			8	1		2	2			13
Aloini et al., 2012	1			2						3
Aundhe & Mathew, 2009	15		2			1	3			21
Ebert et al., 2008		1	1	1			1			4
Gheni et al., 2016		5								5
Kliem, 2004		3	1			1	1			6
Lee & Baby, 2013		2			1		1	1		5
Nakatsu & Iacovou, 2009	2	3		2		2				9
Nurdiani et al., 2011		36	1				1	2		40

continues on following page

Table 2. Continued

References	Client	Psychic Distance	Economic	Supplier	Environment	Political	Regulatory	Stakeholders	Technological	Total
Perrson et al., 2009		5						3		**8**
Schmidt et al., 2001	9			3				1		**13**
Shrivastava & Rathod, 2015	1	1		2				1		**5**
Smite, 2006		9								**9**
Verner et al, 2014		14		6		1	2	2		**25**
GENERAL TOTAL	**111**	**82**	**21**	**39**	**5**	**8**	**16**	**23**	**6**	**311**
%	**36%**	**26%**	**7%**	**13%**	**2%**	**3%**	**5%**	**7%**	**2%**	**100%**
% of Total Risks	8%	6%	2%	3%	0%	1%	1%	2%	0%	**1367**
Domestic	9%	0%	1%	2%	0%	0%	1%	1%	1%	**941**
Global	7%	19%	3%	4%	0%	2%	3%	2%	0%	**426**

Source: Authors

Note: The authors of each reference are detailed in Table 1

The global and domestic projects showed a relative concern with the client category of risks, although, in percentage terms, the domestic projects have shown a slightly higher concern. Risks related to system users were also included in this category. From the 37 authors investigated, two of them did not list any kind of client-related risk in domestic projects and nine in global ones. In domestic projects, the main types of risks found were related to the failures in managing client expectations and lack of commitment, support and participation of users, as Jiang and Klein (2000) discussed in detail. In addition to the fact that these same risks have been found in global projects, risks related to the difficulty in managing conflicts of major clients, changes in the structure (like mergers and acquisitions), CEO/top management change, and processes specific to bigger clients have also been noted.

The psychic distance is defined as the sum of the factors that affect the flow of information between countries whose companies perform certain trading activities. Thus, the greater the difference between the home country and the foreign country in terms of development, educational content and level, language, culture, economy, political system, market structure, among others, the greater the level of uncertainty involved in the business (Carlson, 1975). Even in domestic projects, some authors (Bunker et al, 2015, Dwivedi et al., 2015) highlighted the risks when the project involves different organizations in a team. Nurdiani, Jabangwe, Smite & Damian (2011) extensively explored this kind of risks in global projects in three dimensions: temporal, as time-zone differences; geographical, which limits face-to-face meeting; and socio-cultural, which includes language, values and work process. These risks can result in a decrease in communication frequency, access and richness. Difficulty in creating mutual trust and cohesion between team members due to physical distance was also reported. It was expected that this risk category would be significantly different between global and domestic projects, as Table 2 shows. This category is very significant and represents 48% of the external risks on global projects.

Few risks were related to the economic category, which shows low concern from domestic and global projects with this kind of risk. These risks are related to currency fluctuation, macroeconomic instability (such as inflation), high exchange rate and competitors' actions, which were the main factors reported. Apart from these risks, Ahmed et al. (2014) cited new competitors that may affect both the organization and offshore outsourcing projects. The major importance given by researchers of global projects, based on the higher percentage of risks identified, can be explained by the novelty of the context that this type of project will be faced with, and the likely consequent lack of knowledge of the new market and competitors.

The risks covered by the supplier category are related to the performance and behavior of suppliers, which can hardly be anticipated or controlled. Despite the slight difference in quantity of risks in global and domestic projects, it cannot be considered significant. Articles from both projects mention risks relating to non-compliance with deliveries agreed upon, lack of cooperation and integration between suppliers or between them and the client, infrastructure incompatible with the requirements, opportunistic or unethical behaviors and hidden costs. Bunker et al. (2015) highlights the hazard of reputational damage caused because of this category of risks.

Risk events related to the environment category are linked to the requirements or restrictions imposed by nature. Only five risks were mentioned: one related to global projects and the others to domestic projects: they were related to the lack of disaster recovery practices, both for the project and for the business. This indicates that there is little concern about risks related to the environment for both project types.

Global projects are more concerned about political risks from hostile societies (such as terrorism, demonstrations, insurrection, riots, revolutions and civil wars) and interstate (such as economic sanctions and wars) than risks related to a government, expropriation, confiscation, restrictions, and taxation. The risks cited in researched articles were: tension between countries, war, disorder, terrorism, corruption, protectionism laws, and political instability of the destination countries. Some authors jointly addressed the political and regulatory risks as they are closely linked.

The regulatory risk category is reported mainly in articles pertaining to global projects. Issues related to lack of knowledge or understanding of the law, differentiation of agreements, protection of patents and intellectual property, including concerns about private property.

The stakeholder category includes generic risks to any external stakeholder of the project and those that could not be classified into the supplier or client/user categories. Internal organization stakeholders (sponsor, representatives of other departments) were classified in the organizational environment category. The risks cited in global and domestic projects relate to an excessive external dependence, lack of commitment and trust, and failure to identify all stakeholders. In domestic projects, the concern was focused on conflicts between users and developers and withholding of information.

Obsolescence and emergence of new technologies risks may rise due both to the opportunity to find a more suitable technology and to the increased cost to find new technological options. Bunker et al. (2015) classified them in strategy risks, which included ROI and reputational damage risks, while Brookfield et al. (2014) considered the appropriateness of choice of technology and its impacts as cost. It is surprising that only articles about domestic projects cited this kind of risks. The cited authors considered more relevant the risk to deal with technology internally than the change in technology itself.

Regarding the social category that encompasses risks related to external issues such as language and culture, no occurrences were found. This allows us to infer that project management is still far from addressing more structural and deeper issues of the external environment.

Internal Risks

The internal risks are presented in Table 3 classified into thirteen categories. Each of the risk categories will be detailed to identify the differentiation between global and domestic IT projects. It has been observed that internal risks were mentioned more in articles pertaining to domestic projects than to global projects.

Table 3. Internal risks, by category and by reference

References	Org. Environment	Acquisition	Complexity	Communication	Coord. and Control	Cost	Scope	Staff Management	Staff	Product Process	Quality	Technology	Time	Total
Domestic	98	32	44	16	102	17	135	93	58	107	34	39	21	**796**
%	12%	4%	6%	2%	13%	2%	17%	12%	7%	13%	4%	5%	3%	100%
Brookfield et al., 2014	4		1	1	6		10	2	3	4	2	3	4	**40**
Bunker et al., 2015	7	27		2	12	8	5	10	1	3	26	2	1	**104**
Dwivedi et al., 2015	12		2		7		1	3	2	4	1	4		**36**
Elzamly et al.,2016	3	1		1	10		11	5	2	11		1		**45**
Han, 2014	1				4		3	1		4		2	1	**16**
Hijazi et al, 2014				1	1	3	25	1		66			1	**98**
Hwang et al., 2016	4		2	1	2		4	1	4			1		**19**
Jiang & Klein 2000			8		2		2	19				5		**36**
Liu & Wang, 2014	6		3	1	5		4		4	4		1		**28**
Liu et al., 2010	8	1	2	1	5		11	3	5	1		3	3	**43**
Lopez & Salmeron, 2012	5		5	1	5		7	4	7	1	1	1	4	**41**
Lu et al., 2013	5		1		2		3	6	2			3		**22**
Nakatsu & Iacovou, 2009	3		2		1	1	3	4						**14**
Neves et al., 2014	1				1		4	1					1	**8**
Rodriguez et al., 2016	2		3		3		1		3	2				**14**
Samantra et al., 2016	3		1		6	2	3	1	3	1	1		1	**22**
Sarigiannidis & Chatzoglou, 2014	4	2	4	1	9		4	2	10		1			**37**
Sharma & Gupta, 2012	1				1	1	5	7	1	2	1	1	1	**21**
Sonchan & Ramingwong, 2014	3		1	1	1	1	3	1	3	1	1	2	1	**19**
Sumner, 2000	3		1		3		2	1	4			2		**16**
Vrhovec et al., 2015	5				1									**6**
Wallace & Keil, 2004	7		5	1	4	1	9	12	1			3	1	**44**
Ziemba & Kolasa, 2015	8		3	4	6		8	7	2	3		2	2	**45**
Global	24	24	6	21	37	8	22	38	23	21	3	29	4	**260**
%	17%	17%	4%	14%	26%	6%	15%	26%	16%	14%	2%	20%	3%	100%

continues on following page

Table 2. Continued

References	Org. Environment	Acquisition	Complexity	Communication	Coord. and Control	Cost	Scope	Staff Management	Staff	Product Process	Quality	Technology	Time	Total
Ahmed et al., 2014	1													1
Aloini et al., 2012	1		1	1	3	1	4	3				2		16
Aundhe & Mathew, 2009		6												6
Ebert et al., 2008		1			1			2	2					6
Gheni et al., 2016			1					1				2		4
Klein, 2004	1		1	3	2	1	3	4	3	3		3		24
Lee & Baby, 2013	2				1			2				2		7
Nakatsu & Iacovou, 2009	2	10				1						3		16
Nurdiani et al., 2011						1	4	3				2		10
Perrson et al., 2009					6			2	1			6	1	16
Schmidt et al., 2001	7		1		4	4	8	6	3	3		2	2	40
Shrivastava & Rathod, 2015	6			4	7	1	2	3	4	9	2	2		40
Smite, 2006	2				3			2	5			2		14
Verner et al, 2014	2	7	2	13	10		4	9	2	6	1	3	1	60
GENERAL TOTAL	**122**	**56**	**50**	**37**	**139**	**25**	**157**	**131**	**81**	**128**	**37**	**68**	**25**	**1056**
%	12%	5%	5%	4%	13%	2%	15%	12%	8%	12%	4%	6%	2%	100%
% of Total Risks	9%	4%	4%	3%	10%	2%	11%	10%	6%	9%	3%	5%	2%	1467
Domestic	10%	3%	5%	2%	11%	2%	14%	10%	6%	11%	4%	4%	2%	941
Global	6%	6%	1%	5%	9%	2%	5%	9%	5%	5%	1%	7%	1%	426

Source: Authors

Among the internal risks of the organization, the organizational environment category stands out. This category was cited by 22 authors, who focused on domestic projects, such as Lu et al. (2013), who identified that this subtype is more influential to experts from a medium scale technology enterprise and a software development company. The risks cited are very similar in both projects. This category can be subdivided into 2 subtypes: issues related to culture and organizational processes and those related to internal stakeholders. As for the first subtype, the following were cited: the distinction of business tradition among organizations, the lack of project value for the business, change conditions and organizational structure. As for the stakeholders, the instability of the organizational environment arising from the change of sponsors and the opposition to the IT department were both cited. The same subdivision can be applied to risks in domestic projects. Regarding the organizational processes and culture, the following were cited: the changing environment, including its priorities and instability, lack of experience of the organization with the project type, lack of organizational structure to support the project, projects generated for political reasons, lack of maturity. As for the stakeholders, certain conflicts between departments were cited, such as lack of support and commitment of sponsors. The lack of executive (sponsor) involvement and support was unanimous among authors.

While the supplier category contains risks that do not depend on the performing organization, the acquisition category contains risks that can be managed by the project team, as part of one of the traditional Project Management knowledge areas. In a series of workshops involving client and vendor representatives, Bunker et al. (2015) identified 27 risks in domestic projects, which involve contracts, as risks arising from the choice of agreement, choice of consultants and outsourcing, false sense of risks being mitigated or transferred. The risks related to global projects present more details on these risks, including supplier selection, the most suitable type of agreement, the inclusion of specific clauses, such as one relating to intellectual property and confidential information, including the lack of learning and control. Therefore, a greater concern has been noted on risks in global projects regarding the acquisition process and the performance of suppliers. It is important to remark the concern conveyed by Nakatsu and Iacovou (2009) on this category only in global projects, when they analyzed the two kinds of projects.

Only a few risks were cited in the complexity category for global projects (6 risks by 5 authors), however, this category was relatively well cited in the domestic projects category (44 risks by 16 authors). While the risks in global projects were more focused on the complexity that results from the interaction with several organizations that impacted project control and communication, domestic projects focused instead on project size, large number of departments or units involved, on the great number of technological interfaces with other systems, on the number of features to be developed and on the technological level required. One could say that these risks relate more to complicated projects than to complex projects, because complexity arises from the interplay of variables. However, some authors (Liu & Wang, 2014; Wallace & Kell, 2004) suggested reducing or managing the complexity because it may amplify a risk's impact.

The communication category presented more risks caused by misunderstandings due to the absence and/or poor communication between project teams. Few authors (17 of 37) reported these risks, although they are mentioned more as a problem in project management. As expected, the risks reported related more to global projects. This is due to the fact that communication in dispersed teams always generates a challenge to global projects. In domestic projects, the poor and inefficient communication with project stakeholders stood out, while in global projects, the lack of synchronous communication and lack of properly designed communication planning were the ones with most detail. Therefore, preventing communication from being minimized between geographically dispersed teams is one of the main challenges of the project, especially when it comes to distributed projects (Perrson, Mathiassen, Boeg, Madsen & Steinson, 2009; Smite, 2006).

Authors have highlighted both in domestic and in global projects the coordination and control category. The leader's role is also emphasized in this category, which was the second most mentioned. The vast majority of risks listed in this category refer to problems in or lack of project managing methodologies, lack of maturity in Project Management, lack of application of management, including RM, and lack of planning, coordination and control. In global projects, strategic thinking and planning were mentioned, as well as problems caused by asymmetry in processes, policies and standards. In addition, some authors mentioned creating, capturing and sharing knowledge (Lee & Baby, 2013; Perrson et al., 2009).

Only seven authors cited the **cost** category generally linked to domestic projects. Such risks focus on measurement, inadequate budget and cost management. In turn, the risks of global projects are more detailed, such as the risks for early definition of costs without detailed definition of the project, assessment of costs of passing from transition to operation, failure to use appropriate tools to calculate the cost, and lack of reserves. It can be said that they relate to the accuracy of projects cost estimates. This category and the time category had the lowest percentage among all internal risk categories.

The scope category had the highest number of occurrence among all others and was mentioned by all but one author in articles related to domestic projects. This category is mainly linked to poorly designed requirements or omissions, including business requirements, failure to meet expected results, mismanaged change requests, lack of freezing changes, erroneous development of features, gold plating (including unsolicited features). Although there is a great difference in the number of risks cited between the two project types, the risks cited for global projects are also classified as specifically formulated for domestic projects. Neves et al. (2014) concluded that unclear or misinterpreted scope and objectives is the main risk factor for domestic projects in incubated technology-based firms.

The staff management category is mainly related to problems with the distribution of roles and re-sponsibilities among team members. This was the third most mentioned category. It was well balanced between the authors and between global and domestic project types. It refers to problems in the distribu-tion of resources, to the lack of qualified personnel, lack of training, turnover, improper distribution of roles and responsibilities, conflict management, negative attitudes by development team, and different levels of knowledge among team members. Jiang and Klein (2000) detailed many kinds of lack of ex-pertise of team members and lack of clarity in role definitions. The distinction in global projects risks is the difficulties in coordination of multisite development (Verner et. al., 2014) and delegation (Klein, 2004). Few studies focus on virtual teams (Gheni et al., 2016) and distributed teams (Nurdiani et al., 2011; Smite, 2006).

Risks relating to personal characteristics of the project team, project manager and members, were grouped in the staff category. It was not as listed as the staff management category. It was well balanced between the authors and between global and domestic project types. The most frequently reported risks pertaining to that category were: lack of expertise, experience, skill and competence; behavioral attitudes such as lack of commitment, trust and collaboration; diversity of styles. Focusing on domestic projects, Baccarini, Salm and Love (2004) identified this risk category as the most present based on interviews with 18 IT managers.

The category that covers all risks related to the specific project product development was named product process. This category was listed by four authors of global projects and 14 authors of domestic projects. The risks referred to errors in the development strategy and product configuration, flaws in software development processes (architecture, analysis, design, coding, and integration). These risks are mentioned in both project types. Some authors (Hijazi, Alqrainy, Muaidi, & KhdourIdentifyin, 2014; Elzamly, Hussin, Saleh, 2016) analyzed in detail the risks of each phase of the life cycle of software project, which can explain the high number or risks in this category.

The risks of the quality category refer mainly to the low quality of tests conducted, as well as their lack of planning. It is perceived that there was little concern for quality in domestic projects (8 articles) and even less in global projects (two articles). The high number of risks generated by Bunker et al. (2015) in this category refers to the risks that may arise regarding the SLA (Service Level Agreement).

The risks related to technology in both types of projects referred mainly to the tools, infrastructure and technologies required to develop the product of the project and transition it into operations. The differentiated risks of global projects were related to the infrastructure of communication and security, cited by Kliem (2004), Nakatsu and Iacovou, (2009), Verner et al. (2014), Shrivastava & Rathod (2015), and Smite (2006).

The time category was also reported in few researched articles. The most prominent risks concerned the estimates of unrealistic deadlines. Moreover, it is noticed that the domestic projects are more concerned about risks related to time, as only three authors of global projects reported risks in this category. Herbsleb and Mockus (2003) concluded that global projects take, on average, more than twice the time required for a domestic project of equal content.

DISCUSSION

In Table 2 and 3, we present the quantity and percentage of risks by category. As the chi-square test requires the number of zeroed cells to be at a minimum, the environment and technological categories were excluded due to the low number of risks identified in each of them, accounting for 18 degrees of freedom. The chi-square statistical test was significant ($p < 0.0001$) (Siege & Castelan, 2006), rejecting the null hypothesis and accepting the alternative in which, according to the authors, there are differences in the treatment of risks between global and domestic projects. In the perceptual of Risks lines in Table 2 and 3, we highlighted the percentage cells of the risk categories with the highest disparity between the projects, with a difference of more than 2%, in order to show differences and similarities between them.

By differentiating global projects from domestic, it is possible to highlight the deeper concern about external risks in global projects when compared to domestic projects. Such risks are hardly controlled directly by the organization; nevertheless, they should be identified and monitored by the company. As Nikander and Eloranta (2001) state, at least managers and team must be aware of changes in the environment to proactively manage the situation.

The greater presence of economic, political and regulatory categories in global projects also demonstrates concern about the instability of governments and regulations that underpin the competitive advantages of such projects. As highlighted by Chiesa (2000), obtaining economies of scale and protection of technological rights are relevant criteria for achieving the purposes of global projects.

It is natural that psychic distance has strong presence in global projects, as it encompasses the differences between the home country and the foreign country. Of the seven specific risk events of global projects identified by Nakatsu and Iacovou (2009), five also fall into this category: the language barrier in communication, cultural differences between nations, restrictions due to different time zones, lack of familiarity with the agreements and laws of the destination country, as well as its political instability. Therefore, it can be mentioned that many risks related to supplier, client, and stakeholder in global projects were included in psychic distance, for instance, the language barrier will not only impact the team elements, but also suppliers, clients, users, interpretation of the law, etc.

Also noteworthy is the lack of concern with external risks in the social, and environment categories for both types of projects. Note, however, that global projects also add complexity to internal management processes, such as processes related to communication (which have their frequency and efficiency diminished), to technology (which is not always compatible with the technology of the foreign units), to the time for project development (which can be two and a half times longer than the time of a domestic project (Herbsleb & Mokus, 2003), among other internal aspects. This concern was in fact verified in the research, since the internal risks of the global projects also stood out with strong occurrence in the researched literature. Thus, it is clear that the effort to manage such internal risks in global projects must be redoubled in practice by project managers. The lack of risks in the technological category in global projects and the small number in domestic projects show that the obsolescence and emergence of new technologies does not concern many practitioners. It is surprising that only articles about domestic projects cited this kind of risks. The cited authors considered more the risk to deal with technology internally than the change in technology outside.

With respect to internal risks, it was observed that the authors mentioned the scope, coordination and control, and the staff management categories the most. The global projects accounted for the minority of risks cited. However, three major risks are noteworthy: acquisition, communication and technology. As well as the supplier external category, the acquisition was presented with more details in global projects, mainly because of the need for including specific clauses such as intellectual property. Another consideration is that communication in global projects should be the focus of most attention, through technology and control being used in ensuring proper flow of information, with the restrictions and peculiarities of this type of project. Allen (2007) and Chiesa (1995) argue that communication becomes more difficult and reduced among teams dispersed worldwide. It is known that problems in communication between teams will cause rework, misunderstandings and will even increase project development time. Virtual and distributed teams used in global project require technology to overcome the distance and support communications (Lee-Kelley & Sankey, 2008; Gheni et al., 2016, Nurdiani et al., 2011), which brings a high level or risks to the project.

It must be clear that a risk list can help identify the occurrence of risks, but as the uncertainties are located precisely in the lack of knowledge, merely listing several factors does not ensure their identification. The team can use such list to get insight about some aspects that differentiate the project so as to be careful about them, as well as obtain more information and perceive early signs of change in the environment, as Nikander and Eloranta (2001) suggested.

CONCLUSION AND CONTRIBUTIONS AND FINAL REMARKS

In response to the purpose of this study, which aimed to identify differences in risk categories between global and domestic IT projects, based on a survey of the relevant theory, the findings will be presented in four points:

1. Categories with more emphasis in global projects: the percentage of risks in global projects in the external category shows that, given its greater focus, the psychic distance plays a rather important role in these projects. The second most important was the supplier category, evidently because language and cultural differences increase management difficulty. It is also noteworthy that the political, economic and regulatory risk categories were more cited in global projects because such projects must deal with political systems and the specific laws of each country involved. The most conspicuous categories related to internal risks were technology, acquisition and communication. Although there are no percentage-related remarks in other categories, some of them show differences in the type of risk involved within the category. The focus of the complexity category differs by being involved in global projects of various organizations, often large corporations; which also led to minor differences in deepening the risks of the client, stakeholder, coordination and control categories. Besides these, it is noted that important aspects of the management of internal risks such as clients and suppliers had little relative occurrence in the global projects compared to the domestic projects. Such lack of concern is probably due to the concern with the risks related to the category of psychic distance.

2. Categories with greater emphasis in domestic projects: internal risks were prevalent. The idea is that these projects also include greater concern with primordial aspects of management, such as the risks related to the organizational environment, complexity, scope, product process, quality and time.

3. Similarities between the categories of the two types of project: environmental and social risks have few citations by authors, and show the stage of IT Management regarding sustainability issues. Technological risks deserve little concern, probably because of the proximity with the technology market of these projects or overconfidence in their criteria to choose the right technology. With regard to external risks, the client and stakeholder categories, and to the internal risks, coordination and control, cost, staff management, staff, and time have similar levels of citation percentage. They are basic areas in PM and show that managers must observe these risks in the same way, regardless of the kind of project.

Thus, the main theoretical contribution of this article was the identification of differences in risk categories between global and domestic IT projects. Additionally, the following contributions stand out: 1) the identification and consolidation of a list of risk categories classified as internal and external risks; 2) the identification of the relevance of these categories in terms of risk occurrences based on the researched literature (1367 risks) derived exclusively from an empirical source; 3) the classification of the relevance of the categories according to the type of project (global and domestic).

The practical contribution indicates that the project managers should focus on different risks depending on the type of IT project, global or domestic. This study relates to the indication of risk categories that must be stressed in managing global and domestic projects. The categories presented in the description of the respective risk events can be an initial list of risks becoming the basis for identifying risks in such projects, in order to get more information or raise awareness of early signs of change in the environment. Moreover, according to the scenario of risks and project needs, the IT project manager can evaluate the skills required for the team, leading it and managing stakeholders so as to mitigate the most likely risks and those with higher impact on the objectives of their project. Also, based on the conclusions above, it is possible to observe the importance of interpersonal competence, communication, cultural and political awareness of global project managers, due to the psychic distance generated mainly related to the personal and cultural aspects, showing that deficiencies in that area may compromise project success.

The risk categories defined by this work summarize the perceptions and experiences of various academics, experts and managers, which has updated the theory of RM in IT projects. This article integrates this theory with the organizational internationalization theory, thus identifying important features for global projects, differentiating them from domestic ones. Its contribution becomes more relevant as, given the literature on internationalization, the specific category of psychic distance could be identified in global projects, as well as its influence on other categories. It should also be remarked that a gap was identified in the RM of both global and domestic projects, with regard to the environmental and social aspects. These categories (external) are essential to meet the increasing demand of society for socially responsible companies. Problems in these areas may not only impact the image and reputation of the project, but also of the entire organization. The heightened focus on external risks to the detriment of internal risks, equally important for the management of global projects was another gap identified by the study, allowing to suggest to practitioners a need for closer attention to the internal aspects of management of global projects.

As a suggestion for future research, there are at least two main paths. The first refers to the generation of an overview of the 1367 risks identified in order to generate a consolidated list of risks for global and domestic IT projects, as well as an evaluation of each type of IT project separately (software, outsourcing, information systems and ERP). This list of risks could be now evaluated by means of case studies or field research to identify their impact on global projects and ways to minimize them. Ultimately, the external categories less cited as environmental, political, social and technological should be the focus of further studies to deepen the understanding of the risks of these categories and identify potential mitigations.

REFERENCES

Ahmed, F., Capretz, L. F., Sandhu, M. A., & Raza, A. (2014). Analysis of risks faced by information technology offshore outsourcing service providers. *IET Software*, *8*(6), 279–284. doi:10.1049/iet-sen.2013.0204

Alhawari, S., Karadsheh, L., Talet, A. N., & Mansour, E. (2012). Knowledge-based risk management framework for information technology project. *International Journal of Information Management*, *32*(1), 50–65. doi:10.1016/j.ijinfomgt.2011.07.002

Allen, T. J. (2007). Architecture and communication among product development engineers. *California Management Review*, *49*(2), 23–41. doi:10.2307/41166381

Aloini, D., Dulmin, R., & Mininno, V. (2012). Risk assessment in ERP projects. *Information Systems*, *37*(3), 183–199. doi:10.1016/j.is.2011.10.001

Anantatmula, V., & Thomas, M. (2010). Managing global projects: A structured approach for better performance. *Project Management Journal*, *41*(2), 60–72. doi:10.1002/pmj.20168

Aundhe, M. D., & Mathew, S. K. (2009). Risks in offshore IT outsourcing: A service provider perspective. *European Management Journal*, *27*(6), 418–428. doi:10.1016/j.emj.2009.01.004

Avritzer, A., Paulish, D., Cai, Y., & Sethi, K. (2010). Coordination implications of software architecture in a global software development project. *Journal of Systems and Software*, *83*(10), 1881–1895. doi:10.1016/j.jss.2010.05.070

Baccarini, D., Salm, G., & Love, P. E. D. (2004). Management of risks in information technology projects. *Industrial Management & Data Systems*, *104*(4), 286–295. doi:10.1108/02635570410530702

Brookfield, D., Fischbacher-Smith, D., Mohd-Rahim, F., & Boussabaine, H. (2014). Conceptualising and responding to risk in IT projects. *Risk Management*, *16*(3), 195–230. doi:10.1057/rm.2014.10

Bunker, D., Hardy, C., Babar, A., & Stevens, K. (2016). Exploring practitioner perspectives of sourcing risks: Towards the development of an integrated risk and control framework. In *Proceedings of the Australasian Conference on Information Systems*, Adelaide, South Australia.

Carlson, S. (1975). *How foreign is foreign trade: a problem in international business research*. Uppsala: Uppsala University Press.

Carmel, E. (1999). *Global software teams: collaborating across borders and time zones*. Prentice Hall PTR.

Chiesa, V. (1995). Globalizing R & D around centers of excellence. *Long Range Planning, 28*(6), 19–28. doi:10.1016/0024-6301(95)00048-N

Chiesa, V. (2000). Global R&D project management and organization: A taxonomy. *Journal of Product Innovation Management, 17*(5), 341–359. doi:10.1016/S0737-6782(00)00049-7

Colomo-Palacios, R., Casado-Lumbreras, C., Soto-Acosta, P., Misra, S., & García-Penalvo, F. J. (2012). Analyzing human resource management practices within the GSD context. *Journal of Global Information Technology Management, 15*(3), 30–54. doi:10.1080/1097198X.2012.10845617

Committee of Sponsoring Organizations of the Treadway Commission [COSO]. (2007). *Gerenciamento de risco corporativo – estrutura integrada*. Recovered on January 26, 2011 from http://www.coso.org/documents/COSO_ERM_ExecutiveSummary_Portuguese.pdf

Dwivedi, Y. K., Wastell, D., Laumer, S., Henriksen, H. Z., Myers, M. D., Bunker, D., & Srivastava, S. C. (2015). Research on information systems failures and successes: Status update and future directions. *Information Systems Frontiers, 17*(1), 143–157. doi:10.100710796-014-9500-y

Ebert, C. (2011). *Global software and IT: A guide to distributed development, projects, and outsourcing*. NY: Wiley-IEEE Computer Society Press. doi:10.1002/9781118135105

Ebert, C., Murthy, B. K., & Jha, N. N. (2008). Managing risks in global software engineering: principles and practices. In *Proceedings of the IEEE International Conference on Global Software Engineering ICGSE '08* (pp. 131-140). 10.1109/ICGSE.2008.12

Elzamly, A., Hussin, B., & Salleh, N. (2016). Top Fifty Software Risk Factors and the Best Thirty Risk Management Techniques in Software Development Lifecycle for Successful Software Projects. *International Journal of Hybrid Information Technology, 9*(6), 11–32. doi:10.14257/ijhit.2016.9.6.02

Gheni, A. Y., Yusmadi, Y. J., Marzanah, A. J., & Norhayati, M. A. (2016). Factors affecting global virtual teams' performance in software projects. *Journal of Theoretical and Applied Information Technology, 92*(1), 90–97.

Han, W. M. (2014). Validating differential relationships between risk categories and project performance as perceived by managers. *Empirical Software Engineering, 19*(6), 1956–1966. doi:10.100710664-013-9270-z

Herbsleb, J. D., & Mockus, A. (2003). An empirical study of speed and communication in globally distributed software development. *Software Engineering. IEEE Transactions on Software Engineering, 29*(6), 481–494. doi:10.1109/TSE.2003.1205177

Higuera, R., & Haimes, Y. (1996). *Software risk management*. Pittsburgh: Carnegie Mellon, Software Engineering Institute.

Hijazi, H., Alqrainy, S., & Muaidi, H., & Khdour, T. (2014). Causality relation between software projects Risk Factors. *International Journal of Software Engineering and Its Applications, 8*(2), 51–58.

Holmström, H., & Conchúir, Ó., E., Ågerfalk, P. J., & Fitzgerald, B. (2006, October 16-19). Global software development challenges: A case study on temporal, geographical and socio-cultural distance. In *Proceedings of the International Conference on Global Software Engineering* (ICGSE2006), Costão do Santinho, Florianópolis, Brazil. 10.1109/ICGSE.2006.261210

Hwang, C., Hsiao, B. H. G., & Chern, C. C. (2016). Multiphase assessment of project risk interdependencies: Evidence from a university ISD Project in Taiwan. *Project Management Journal, 47*(1), 59–75. doi:10.1002/pmj.21563

Jiang, J. J., & Klein, G. (2000). Software development risks to project effectiveness. *Journal of Systems and Software, 52*(1), 3–10. doi:10.1016/S0164-1212(99)00128-4

Kliem, R. (2004). Managing the risks of offshore IT development projects. *Information Systems Management, 21*(3), 22–27. doi:10.1201/1078/44432.21.3.20040601/82473.4

Kommeren, R., & Paiviainen, P. (2007). Philips experiences in global distributed software development. *Empirical Software Engineering, 12*(6), 647–660. doi:10.100710664-007-9047-3

Lee, O. K., & Baby, D. V. (2013). Managing dynamic risks in global it projects: Agile risk-management using the principles of service-oriented architecture. *International Journal of Information Technology & Decision Making, 12*(6), 1121–1150. doi:10.1142/S0219622013400117

Lee-Kelley, L., & Sankey, T. (2008). Global virtual teams for value creation and project success: A case study. *International Journal of Project Management, 26*(1), 51–62. doi:10.1016/j.ijproman.2007.08.010

Lientz, B. P., & Rea, K. P. (2003). *International project management*. San Diego, California: Academic Press.

Liu, S., & Wang, L. (2014). Understanding the impact of risks on performance in internal and outsourced information technology projects: The role of strategic importance. *International Journal of Project Management, 32*(8), 1494–1510. doi:10.1016/j.ijproman.2014.01.012

Liu, S., Zhang, J., Keil, M., & Chen, T. (2010). Comparing senior executive and project manager perceptions of IT project risk: A Chinese Delphi study. *Information Systems Journal, 20*(4), 319–355. doi:10.1111/j.1365-2575.2009.00333.x

López, C., & Salmeron, J. L. (2012). Risks response strategies for supporting practitioners decision-making in software projects. *Procedia Technology, 5*, 437–444. doi:10.1016/j.protcy.2012.09.048

Lu, S. T., Yu, S. H., Chang, D. S., & Su, S. C. (2013). Using the Fuzzy Linguistic Preference relation approach for assessing the importance of risk factors in a software development project. *Mathematical Problems in Engineering*.

Milewski, A. E., Tremaine, M., Kobler, F., Egan, R., Zhang, S., & OSullivan, P. (2008). Guidelines for effective bridging in global software engineering. *Software Process Improvement and Practice, 13*(6), 477–492. doi:10.1002pip.403

Nakatsu, R. T., & Iacovou, C. L. (2009). A comparative study of important risk factors involved in offshore and domestic outsourcing of software development projects: A two-panel Delphi study. *Information & Management, 46*(1), 57–68. doi:10.1016/j.im.2008.11.005

Neves, S. M., da Silva, C. E. S., Salomon, V. A. P., da Silva, A. F., & Sotomonte, B. E. P. (2014). Risk management in software projects through Knowledge Management techniques: Cases in Brazilian Incubated Technology-Based Firms. *International Journal of Project Management, 32*(1), 125–138. doi:10.1016/j.ijproman.2013.02.007

Nikander, I. O., & Eloranta, E. (2001). Project management by early warnings. *International Journal of Project Management, 19*(7), 385–399. doi:10.1016/S0263-7863(00)00021-1

Noll, J., Beecham, S., & Richardson, I. (2010). Global software development and collaboration: Barriers and solutions. *ACM Inroads, 1*(3), 66–78. doi:10.1145/1835428.1835445

Nurdiani, I., Jabangwe, R., Smite, D., & Damian, D. (2011, August). Risk identification and risk mitigation instruments for global software development: Systematic review and survey results. In *Proceedings of the 2011 Sixth IEEE International Conference on Global Software Engineering Workshop (ICGSEW)* (pp. 36-41). IEEE 10.1109/ICGSE-W.2011.16

Office of Government Commerce [OGC]. (2005). *Managing successful projects with Prince2* (4th ed.). London: The Stationery Office.

Persson, J. S., Mathiassen, L., Boeg, J., Madsen, T. S., & Steinson, F. (2009). Managing risks in distributed software projects: An integrative framework. *IEEE Transactions on Engineering Management, 56*(3), 508–532. doi:10.1109/TEM.2009.2013827

Petticrew, M., & Roberts, H. (2008). *Systematic reviews in the social sciences: A practical guide*. John Wiley & Sons.

Prikladnicki, R., & Yamaguti, M. (2004). Risk management in global software development: a position paper. In *Proceedings of the Third International Workshop on Global Software Development (GSD '04)*, Stevenage, UK. 10.1049/ic:20040306

Project Management Institute [PMI]. (2009). *Practice Standard for Project Risk Management*. Newton Square: PMI.

Project Management Institute [PMI]. (2012). *PMBOK Guide – A guide to the Project Management Body of Knowledge* (5th ed.). Newton Square: PMI.

Rodríguez, A., Ortega, F., & Concepción, R. (2016). A method for the evaluation of risk in IT projects. *Expert Systems with Applications, 45*, 273–285. doi:10.1016/j.eswa.2015.09.056

Ropponen, J., & Lyytinen, K. (2000). Components of software development risk: How to address them? A project manager survey. S*oftware Engineering. IEEE Transactions on Software Engineering, 26*(2), 98–112. doi:10.1109/32.841112

Samantra, C., Datta, S., Mahapatra, S. S., & Debata, B. R. (2016). Interpretive structural modelling of critical risk factors in software engineering project. *Benchmarking: An International Journal, 23*(1), 2–24. doi:10.1108/BIJ-07-2013-0071

Sarigiannidis, L., & Chatzoglou, P. D. (2014). Quality vs risk: An investigation of their relationship in software development projects. *International Journal of Project Management, 32*(6), 1073–1082. doi:10.1016/j.ijproman.2013.11.001

Sauser, B. J., Reilly, R. R., & Shenhar, A. J. (2009). Why projects fail? How contingency theory can provide new insights – A comparative analysis of NASAs Mars Climate Orbiter loss. *International Journal of Project Management, 27*(7), 665–679. doi:10.1016/j.ijproman.2009.01.004

Schmidt, R., Lyytinen, K., Keil, M., & Cule, P. (2001). Identifying software project risks: An international Delphi study. *Journal of Management Information Systems, 17*(4), 5–36. doi:10.1080/07421222 .2001.11045662

Sharma, A., Sengupta, S., & Gupta, A. (2011). Exploring risk dimensions in the Indian software industry. *Project Management Journal, 42*(5), 78–91. doi:10.1002/pmj.20258

Shrivastava, S. V., & Rathod, U. (2015). Categorization of risk factors for distributed agile projects. *Information and Software Technology, 58*, 373–387. doi:10.1016/j.infsof.2014.07.007

Siegel, S., & Castellan, N. J. Jr. (1988). *Nonparametric Statistics for the Behavioral Sciences*. New York: McGraw-HiU Book Company.

Šmite, D. (2006). Global software development projects in one of the biggest companies in Latvia: Is geographical distribution a problem? *Software Process Improvement and Practice, 11*(1), 61–76. doi:10.1002pip.252

Sommerville, I. (2015). *Software Engineering*. Pearson Education.

Sonchan, P., & Ramingwong, S. (2014, May). Top twenty risks in software projects: A content analysis and Delphi study. In *Proceedings of the 2014 11th International Conference on Electrical Engineering/ Electronics, Computer, Telecommunications and Information Technology (ECTI-CON)* (pp. 1-6). IEEE. 10.1109/ECTICon.2014.6839820

Sumner, M. (2000). Risk factors in enterprise-wide/ERP projects. *Journal of Information Technology, 15*(4), 317–327. doi:10.1080/02683960010009079

Thamhain, H. (2013). Managing risks in complex projects. *Project Management Journal, 44*(2), 20–35. doi:10.1002/pmj.21325

Tranfield, D., Denyer, D., & Smart, P. (2003). Towards a methodology for developing evidence informed management knowledge by means of systematic review. *British Journal of Management, 14*(3), 207–222. doi:10.1111/1467-8551.00375

Treasury, H. M. S. (2004). *The Orange Book: management of risk–principles and concepts*. London: HM Treasury.

Verner, J. M., Brereton, O. P., Kitchenham, B. A., Turner, M., & Niazi, M. (2014). Risks and risk mitigation in global software development: A tertiary study. *Information and Software Technology*, *56*(1), 54–78. doi:10.1016/j.infsof.2013.06.005

Vrhovec, S. L., Hovelja, T., Vavpotič, D., & Krisper, M. (2015). Diagnosing organizational risks in software projects: Stakeholder resistance. *International Journal of Project Management*, *33*(6), 1262–1273. doi:10.1016/j.ijproman.2015.03.007

Wallace, L., Keil, M., & Rai, A. (2004). How software project risk affects project performance: An investigation of the dimensions of risk and an exploratory model. *Decision Sciences*, *35*(2), 289–321. doi:10.1111/j.00117315.2004.02059.x

This research was previously published in the Journal of Global Information Management (JGIM), 26(1); pages 20-40, copyright year 2018 by IGI Publishing (an imprint of IGI Global).

Chapter 77
Test Suite Optimization Using Firefly and Genetic Algorithm

Abhishek Pandey

University of Petroleum and Energy Studies, Dehradun & Birla Institute of Technology, Mesra-Ranchi, India

Soumya Banerjee

Conservatoire Nationale des Arts et Metiers & INRIA Paris ex-visiting CNRS INSA de Lyon, Paris, France

ABSTRACT

Software testing is essential for providing error-free software. It is a well-known fact that software testing is responsible for at least 50% of the total development cost. Therefore, it is necessary to automate and optimize the testing processes. Search-based software engineering is a discipline mainly focussed on automation and optimization of various software engineering processes including software testing. In this article, a novel approach of hybrid firefly and a genetic algorithm is applied for test data generation and selection in regression testing environment. A case study is used along with an empirical evaluation for the proposed approach. Results show that the hybrid approach performs well on various parameters that have been selected in the experiments.

INTRODUCTION

Software testing is the most expensive and time-consuming task among all other activities that are performed in software engineering (Myers, Sandler & Badgett, 2011; Korel, 1992). The first idea of software testing is probably due to Turing (Turing, 1949). The first mention of software optimization of any kind is due to Ada Augusta Lovelace in 1842 (Harman, 2010). The first application of optimization techniques in software testing is due to the seminal work of James King (King, 1969). Search based software engineering is an emerging area of research to optimize various software engineering processes.

DOI: 10.4018/978-1-6684-3702-5.ch077

Search-based software engineering reformulates software-testing problem as an optimization problem (Harman & Jones, 2001). Search based methods (SBMs) also applied in various testing problems such as test data generation, test suite minimization, test case selection and test case prioritization in the literature (Harman, Jia & Zhang, 2015). Software module clustering and software refactoring problem are good candidates for the application of search-based techniques (Harman, Mansouri & Zhang, 2012). Regression testing is performed in the software maintenance phase of the software development life cycle. The whole software undergoes retesting whenever any modification occurs during regression testing. Regression test case selection techniques strive to increase the testing quality based on the test adequacy criteria, such as effort, coverage, and fault detection.

Various new software development paradigms impose many restrictions on regression testing. Retesting is necessary in these cases. In this case, regression testing must be performed using the available computing resources judicially. Regression testing problem can thus be seen as a combination of test suite minimization, test suite selection, test suite prioritization problem in order to save computing resources (Rothermel & Harrold, 1996). The present work is an attempt to optimize the regression testing process and to evaluate the performance of newly proposed nature-inspired algorithms such as hybrid firefly and genetic algorithm for test case selection. In this paper, we are proposing a new hybrid algorithm for test case selection problem. Initially, a case study based on the available test suite is performed for regression testing and simulation results are shown. Results shows the better performance of hybrid approaches when compared to some popular swarm intelligence-based algorithms.

Rest of the paper is organized as related work, problem formulation, proposed methodology, experimental evaluation, results and conclusion.

RELATED WORK

Agrawal & Kaur (2018) compares the performance of two metaheuristics namely ant colony and hybrid particle swarm optimization exclusively for test cases selection problem. The quality parameters in this research are execution time and fault coverage. Experiments were performed using Matlab. This article demonstrates the significance of hybrid algorithms for test cases selection problem in software engineering.

De Oliveira Neto et al. (2018) evaluates similarity-based test case selection on integration level tests. The results confirm the existing strong evidence that similarity-based test case selection is the major candidate for test optimization.

Choudhary, Agrawal & Kaur (2018) presents an effective method for test case selection using Pareto based multi-objective harmony research. Fors et al. (2019) present a safe regression test case selection for Modelica using static analysis.

Nogueira et al. (2019) discuss model-based testing using natural language description of use cases. It is important to note that formal description of use cases using mathematical notation poses challenges in test case generation and selection process. To overcome this issues, use cases are described in natural language that is easily understandable to the testing team.

Arrieta et al. (2019) describes a search-based approach for prioritizing the test cases in cyber physical system (CPS). Wang et al. (2019) proposes a location-based test case prioritization for embedded software using law gravitation.

Shin et al. (2019) discusses empirical evaluation of various test case prioritization techniques in a recent research study. Sahoo & Ray (2018) presents a comprehensive review of various search-based techniques for test case generation and selection in recent study. Subashini & Mala (2017) proposes an efficient technique for test suite reduction and fault detection using data mining technique. Di Nardo et al. (2015) presents a case study of coverage-based regression testing technique on an industrial system. Panichella et al. (2015) proposes a new approach of injecting diversity in genetic algorithm for multi objective test case selection.

Many test suite minimization techniques suffer from the drawback that discarded test case can still detect a fault, but though some guarantee that fault detection capability does not affect. Search based methods are efficient in finding the solutions to tough non-linear problems. Not all efficient meta-heuristics are good in providing the global optimum. Moreover, these algorithms are very good at providing local optimum solutions (Yang, 2012).

Various chaos-enhanced meta-heuristics have shown good optimization performance in test cases selection in many studies (Xiang, 2007; Gandomi et al., 2013). Moreover, chaotic tunneling is used with various algorithms such as particle swarm optimization (Alatas et al., 2009), bat algorithm (Gandomi & Yang, 2014), artificial immune optimization (Guo & Wang, 2005) and Imperialist competitive algorithm for test case selection problem (Talathari et al., 2012).

Bat algorithm is a recent swarm intelligence-based algorithm. This new metaheuristic method is based on the echolocation properties of bats. After the tremendous applications of Firefly-algorithm and harmony-search algorithm, a new metaheuristic bat algorithm also shows good efficiency in test case generation and selection in various studies (Fister et al., 2013).

The test suite minimization problem is NP-complete. Therefore, the exact solution of these types of problem may not be computable using traditional methods. The NP-completeness of Test suite minimization problem is basic motivation in applying heuristics (Harder, Mellen, & Ernst, 2003; Schroeder & Korel, 2000; Singh, Kaur & Suri, 2010).

Kazmi et al. (2017) presents a systematic literature review for effective regression test case selection in a research study.

BACKGROUND

Firefly Algorithm

Firefly algorithm is a recent metaheuristic that employs a simulated model of social fireflies. This is based on the flashing behavior of Firefly. Some of the flashing characteristics of fireflies can be idealized to formulate an algorithm. Following assumption are taken in the formulation of firefly algorithm.

1. All fireflies are unisex.
2. Attractiveness is proportional to brightness. Both are inversely proportional to the distance of any two fireflies. If no brighter fireflies are present, then fireflies will move randomly.
3. The brightness of the firefly is determined by the landscape of the objective function.

Algorithm 1. Generic Firefly Algorithm
  1. Objective function f(x), $x = (x_1, ..., x_d)^T$
  2. Generate initial population of fireflies x_i (i = 1,2, ..., n)
  3. Light intensity Ii at xi is determined by f(xi)

4.   Define light absorption coefficient γ
5.   while (t <MaxGeneration)
6.   for i =1: n all n fireflies
7.   for j =1: i all n fireflies
8.   if (Ij > Ii), Move firefly i towards j in d-dimension; end if
9.   Attractiveness varies with distance r via exp[−γr]
10. Evaluate new solutions and update light intensity
11. end for j
12. end for i
13. Rank the fireflies and find the current best
14. end while
15. Postprocess results and visualization

Comparison of Various Evolutionary Algorithms

Comparison of various evolutionary algorithms are shown in table 1 below. This comparison is shown to have a clear understanding of some popular evolutionary algorithms and their important properties.

Table 1. Comparison of various evolutionary algorithm

Characteristic of Algorithm	Genetic Algorithm	Evolutionary programming	Evolutionary strategies	Genetic programming	Differential evolution
Algorithm Types	Genotypic/ Phenotypic	Phenotypic	Phenotypic	Phenotypic	Phenotypic
Developed by	Holland	Fogel	Rechenberg Schwefel	Koza	Storn and Price
Basic principle	Natural selection or survival of the fittest	Survival of the fittest	Survival of the fittest	Survival of the fittest	Survival of the fittest
Solution representation	Binary/ real-valued	Finite state machines	Float valued vectors	Expression trees	Real-valued
Fitness	Scaled objective value	Payoff function value	Objective function value	Scaled objective value	Objective function value
Selection	Probabilistic preservative	Probabilistic extinctive	Probabilistic extinctive	Probabilistic extinctive	Deterministic extinctive
Evolutionary operators	Mainly cross over other mutation	Mutation recombination	Mutation cross over	Cross over and mutation	Mainly mutation, cross over

PROBLEM FORMULATION

Test suite optimization problem has an analogy with the firefly algorithm. Flashing behaviour of firefly algorithm capture the fitness value representing test adequacy criteria such as branch coverage. The flashing behavior of fireflies is the primary motivation to construct a fitness function. The bioluminescence process produces these flashes. The primary function of this light is believed to be debating. The flashing light can be formulated in such a way that it is associated with the fitness value. In this case fitness function is branch coverage of a particular test case. In our proposed model, artificial fireflies represent test cases. The intensity of fireflies is represented by the branch coverage of a particular test case.

Reformulation of test data generation problem as an optimization problem would require an objective function. Various studies of test data generation suggest the use of branch distance as an objective function (Korel, 1990). Fitness function captures the test adequacy criteria that has to be improved over different iterations. Let the initial test case is a set of n test data $\{t_1, t_2, t_3....t_n\}$. Calculation of fitness is based on the following branch distance function (which has to be minimized in order to increase branch coverage. Branch coverage is still the most acceptable test adequacy criteria. It is defined as the ratio of nodes traversed by the test data (n) through a control flow graph and a total number of nodes (k).

$$\text{branch cov} = f(t) = \frac{n}{K} \times 100 \tag{1}$$

$$b(i) = \begin{cases} 0, & \text{if branch is covered} \\ k, & \text{if branch is not covered} \end{cases} \tag{2}$$

Since the maximum value of branch distance is not known, normalized branch distance is used otherwise.

$$normalize(branch\ distance) = 1 - 1.001^{-branch\ distance} \tag{3}$$

Approach level is a measure of untraversed nodes of the control flow graph (α) with respect to the target path (p).

Following equation represents the approach level:

$$approach\ level(xi) = \frac{\alpha(xi)}{P(t)} \tag{4}$$

Fitness Function Formulation

The fitness function is based on three parameters such as approach level, controlling parameter (ε) and branch distance (Table 2).

$$f(t) = \left(\varepsilon + approach\ level + \sum_{i=1}^{b} w(i).normalize\ b(i) \right)^{-1} \tag{5}$$

Now we observe the analogy between the test cases and the firefly in the context of search-based testing (Table 3).

Table 2. The objective function for branch predicates

Branch Predicates	Branch function F	rel
E1 > E2	E2- E1	<
E1>= E2	E2- E1	<=
E1< E2	E1- E2	<
E1 <= E2	E1- E2	<=
E1= E2	Abs (E1-E2)	=
E1 ≠ E2	Abs (E1-E2)	≠

Table 3. The analogy between firefly behavior and test cases optimization

Parameters	Parameters of Firefly Algorithm	Parameters of Test case optimization
Representation	Real values representing the location of fireflies in the objective function	Test cases are represented by real values associated with the branch predicates
Fitness function	The intensity of light forms the fitness function(I)	Intensity will represent the test adequacy criteria that is branch coverage metric
Operators used	Fireflies movement towards other fireflies based on Intensity of light	Test case movement towards other test case based on the test adequacy criteria
Solution	Fireflies converged to the optimized solution	Test cases converged to the optimized solution

PROPOSED METHODOLOGY

Test suite minimization is concerned to generate optimized test data, which ensures 100% branch coverage in minimal time. In this proposed work test suite selection problem is modelled in the framework of the firefly algorithm and GA. This is the first application of Hybrid firefly algorithm and genetic algorithm for search-based software testing. In this research study 4 benchmark laboratory "C" programs are taken as a data set on which experiments are performed. Also, genetic operators are incorporated to improve local search capability and exploration of firefly algorithm. Initial population of test data (fireflies) are initialized. Firefly parameters concerning attractiveness (β), the absorption coefficient (γ) and randomization parameter are set.

Table 4. List of benchmark programs for experiments

Serial no.	Program name	No. of variables	Cyclomatic complexity
1.	Triangle classification problem	3	8
2.	Even Odd	1	3
3.	Quadratic equation	3	4
4.	Largest of three numbers	3	3

Table 4. shows the list of the program under test for applications of search-based techniques. It has two parameters against each program under test (PUT). Variables have their usual meaning in programming. Cyclomatic complexity also is known as Mc.cabes complexity and depicts the total number of independent test paths in the program

Algorithm 2. Proposed algorithm

1. Input test program
2. Generate a control flow graph
3. 3. Define the Objective function:

$F(x) = I$

I— statement coverage of test case(i)/total number of statements*100, $x = (T_1, T_2, ..., T_n)$;

4. Generate an initial population of test cases T_i (i= 1,2,3…, k); randomly
5. Calculate fitness value as Intensity (statement coverage of CFG) of test cases I. so that it is associated with f(x) or I = f(x)
6. Define absorption coefficient $\gamma = 0.15$ and r = 1;
7. While (t < Max Generation);
8. for (i = 1; i< n; i++); for (j= 1;j<:n;j++)
9. If $(I_j > I_i)$
10. Move test case t_i towards t_j according to the equation
   $t_j = t_i + \beta_0 e^{-\gamma r^2}(t_j - t_i) + \alpha.rand(0,1)$ *where α is randomization parameter 0 < α < 1*
11. Replace test case j to the position of i.
12. Update attractiveness by exponential($-\gamma r^2$);
13. Apply crossover, mutation, selection operators
14. Repeat.

CASE STUDY

We evaluate the performance of the proposed algorithm on the following dataset (Tables 5-6)

Binary encoding of test cases: bit representation 1 when the respective statement is covered otherwise 0 starting from the leftmost bit (Table 7).

Now 10 fireflies are initialized that would select the test cases and their statement coverage will be associated as brightness at the origin. In our methodology fitness function is directly proportional to the coverage criteria. In addition, to have a better analogy with firefly algorithm coverage criteria is directly proportional to the brightness of the fireflies. Considering all these analogies following table 8 is represented. Initial brightness at time '0' is the same as statement coverage also the value of decay coefficient is set as 0.15. Therefore, we have the following values of brightness of initialized fireflies. Any two selections by fireflies will operate according to OR gate. This is analogous to crossover. Finally, mutation operator is applied and any two bit positions are flipped.

Table 5. Data set for a case study

Test case	S_1	S_2	S_3	S_4	S_5	S_6	S_7	S_8	S_9
T_1		×	×	×			×		
T_2			×	×	×	×		×	
T_3	×	×			×		×		×
T_4	×			×		×	×	×	×
T_5	×		×			×		×	
T_6	×					×		×	
T_7	×	×	×			×			×
T_8	×	×		×	×		×	×	
T_9	×			×			×		×
T_{10}	×		×		×			×	×

Table 6. Test cases with their respective coverage and execution time

Test cases	Number of statements covered	Execution time(msec.)
T_1	4	6
T_2	5	7
T_3	5	4
T_4	6	8
T_5	4	3
T_6	3	9
T_7	5	1
T_8	6	6
T_9	4	4

Table 7. A logical representation of test case

Test cases	Binary representation
T_1	011100100
T_2	001111010
T_3	110010101
T_4	100101111
T_5	101001010
T_6	100001010
T_7	111001001
T_8	110110110
T_9	100100101
T_{10}	101010011

Movements of Fireflies During the First Iteration of the Proposed Algorithm

Movement of fireflies is based on the generic firefly algorithm movement equation in which less bright fireflies will be moved towards more bright fireflies and then performs cross over and mutation operation. Based on the objective function less bright fireflies will move towards the brighter fireflies. These two fireflies will perform crossover and mutation and based on the objective function new fireflies will be selected. For example, based on the algorithm, FF6 will move towards FF4 and perform the Genetic operations. Similarly, in all iterations, new generation of fireflies will emerge.

100001010 OR 100101111 = 100101111
Mutated binary sequence 110101111

Table 8. Fireflies and associated brightness values

Fireflies	Brightness at origin (t = 0)	Brightness ($\beta= \beta_0 e^{-\gamma r^2}$)	Execution time (Sec.)
FF_1	4	3.4453	6
FF_2	5	4.3066	7
FF_3	5	4.3066	4
FF_4	6	5.1679	8
FF_5	4	3.4453	3
FF_6	3	2.5839	9
FF_7	5	4.3066	1
FF_8	6	5.1679	6
FF_9	4	3.4453	4
FF_{10}	5	4.3066	3

As we can observe that this binary sequence will now cover 7 statements. So, this firefly will be selected. Similarly, in each iteration, we can get an optimized set of fireflies in a lesser number of iterations. In the next section, we attempt the simulation of our algorithm.

Table 9. Movement of fireflies during the first iteration

Movements	Test cases selection	Statement coverage	Modified brightness	New firefly emerged
FF1 ----FF2	T1, T2	7	6.8654	yes
FF2----FF4	T2, T4	9	8.1643	yes
FF3----FF8	T3, T8	7	6.8654	yes
FF_6----FF_7	T_6, T_7	6	5.7865	yes
FF_9----FF_{10}	T_9, T_{10}	7	6.5656	yes

As we can see in the table 9 that during the first iteration itself five new fireflies emerged that overall increase the mean statement coverage of the testing case study taken. Also, further it should be noted that full statement coverage is achieved in the first iteration itself. But we will perform further iteration because the termination criteria chosen is a maximum number of generations. Now, these new fireflies will form a new population of test cases as shown in the tables 10 and 11.

The outcome of Case study: Full coverage achieved during the first iteration itself. Also, during the second iteration, a gradual increase of coverage has been observed (Figures 1 and 2).

Table 10. The emergence of new fireflies

Fireflies	Test cases	Statement coverage	Brightness ($\beta = \beta_0 e^{-\gamma r^2}$)
F_1	T_1	4	3.4453
F_2	T_2	5	4.3066
F_3	T_3	5	4.3066
F_4	T_4	6	5.1679
F_5	T_5	4	3.4453
F_6	T_6	3	2.5839
F_7	T_7	5	4.3066
F_8	T_8	6	5.1679
F_9	T_9	4	3.4453
F_{10}	T_{10}	5	4.3066
F_{11}	T_{11}	7	6.8654
F_{12}	T_{12}	9	8.1643
F_{13}	T_{13}	7	6.8654
F_{14}	T_{14}	6	5.7865
F_{15}	T_{15}	7	6.6756

Table 11. Movements of fireflies during the second iteration

Movements	Test cases selection	Statement coverage	Modified brightness
F_{11}----F_{12}	T_{11}, T_{12}	9	7.9465
F_{14}-----F_{13}	T_{14}, T_{13}	8	7.9465
F_{15}—F_{11}	T_{15}, T_{11}	9	7.9465
F_{10}—F_{12}	T_{10}, T_{12}	8	7.9465
F_9—F_{12}	T_9, T_{12}	8	7.9465

EXPERIMENTAL EVALUATION

A case study has already presented in the previous section. In this section, the experimental settings of the proposed algorithm are discussed. Four benchmark test programs are used for experiments. These four test programs are triangle classification problem, even odd, quadratic equation and largest of three numbers.

- **Triangle Classification Problem**: The program checks whether the triangle exists and if formed classify it into the type such as scalene, equilateral or isosceles.
- **Even Odd Problem:** The program checks whether the input number is even or odd.
- **Quadratic Equation:** It computes the roots of the quadratic equation.
- **Largest of Three Numbers:** It computes the largest of three inputs.

Figure 1. Graphical illustrative representation of fireflies during first iteration

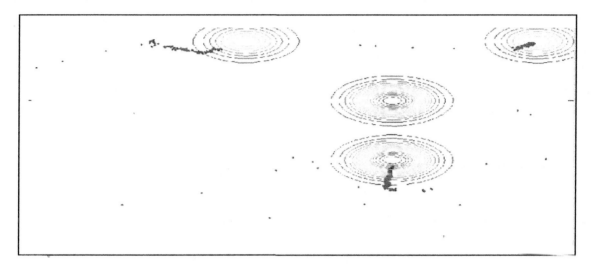

Figure 2. Graphical illustrative representation of fireflies during the second iteration

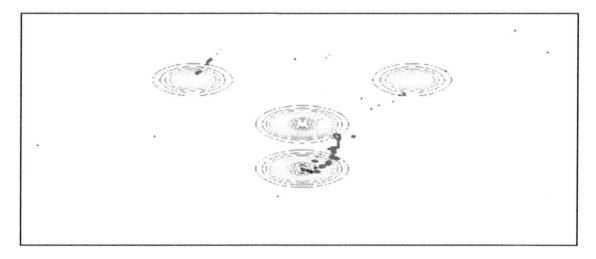

To compare the performance of the various evolutionary algorithm with the proposed algorithm the common parameters, which are consistent in all the experiments, are maximum evolutionary generation is set to 100. Population size was set to 40. All experiments were performed on Microsoft Windows 10 pro with Intel Core™ 6006 U CPU @ 2.0000GHz. Internal memory 4 GB system type 64-bit operating system. All algorithms are implemented on Matlab.

RESULTS AND ANALYSIS

In this section simulation results of the proposed algorithm are presented and analyzed. For the purpose of performance comparison, some evolutionary algorithm such as genetic algorithm, ant colony optimization and artificial bee colony optimization are also employed in this research work. Evaluation metrics are also defined to assess the quality of test suite optimization.

Evaluation Metrics

In this study, two-assessment quality parameter are used. First one is the quality of test suite generated and the second one is the speed of test data generation. Therefore, the following quality-based evaluation metrics are defined (Tables 12-14).

- **Average Branch Coverage:** This metric is the main quality indicator as it represents the average branch coverage over the different run of the algorithms.
- **Success Rate:** Probability of coverage of all branches by the generated test data.
- **Average Convergence Generation:** Average number of generations in which 100% coverage was achieved.
- **Average Convergence Speed:** This metric indicates the average test data generation speed.
- **Average Execution Time:** Average execution time for all the branches to cover by the generated test data.

Table 12. Parameter selection

Algorithms	Parameter	Value
GA	Selection technique Cross over probability Mutation probability Max Gen	Gambling wheel 0.90 0.12 100
ACO	Number of ants Search domain Maximum radius Initial pheromone (ρ_0) Max gen Pheromone evaporation parameter Global stochastic search probability	40 $\mathfrak{R}$ 6 0 100 0.50 0.40
ABC	Initialization probability Employee bee probability Scout bee search	Boundary value analysis 0.67 $(1-\alpha)\sigma$, where α is search probability and σ is Gaussian probability distribution
Hybrid firefly-GA algorithm	Initial no. of fireflies Brightness at the origin (β_0) Brightness (β) Absorption coefficient r crossover probability mutation probability max generation No. of run	40 Same as statement coverage at t=0 $\beta = \beta_0 e^{-\gamma r^2}$ $\gamma = 0.15$ 1 0.50 0.10 100 1000

Table 13. Comparison of performance of four algorithms on average branch coverage evaluation metric

Programs	Average branch coverage GA ABC ACO Firefly -GA				Success rate GA ABC ACO Firefly-GA			
TCP	73.74	98.84	96.34	100	70.48	97.34	96.45	100
Even-odd	72.83	98.23	95.45	100	70.47	96.84	94.34	100
Quadratic equation	59.45	98.34	95.84	99.12	56.84	97.47	94.83	99.93
Largest of three numbers	89.37	99.83	98.32	100	87.93	98.43	98.34	100

Table 14. Comparison of performance of four algorithms on average convergence generation evaluation metric

Programs	Average convergence generation GA ABC ACO Firefly-GA				Average execution time(msec.) GA ABC ACO Firefly-GA			
TCP	52.32	18.89	21.73	10.52	10.21	2.29	13.27	2.73
Even-odd	31.83	16.38	19.38	14.32	25.61	2.63	1.44	1.21
Quadratic equation	36.83	12.54	14.12	14.23	13.82	1.21	3.83	1.36
Largest of three numbers	42.84	21.83	18.48	11.52	8.26	1.93	1.42	1.98

STATISTICAL ANALYSIS

To gain confidence in the results a good statistical analysis is necessary. In this study ANOVA (Analysis of variance) is used to validate the statistical results. Statistical results also show the significance of the proposed algorithm when compared to others. ANOVA performance testing is also used to demonstrate the effectiveness of particular experiments during different runs statistically. In this section, statistical analysis of the performance of various evolutionary algorithms with respect to various problems is discussed (Tables 15 and 16).

In the experiments, the performance of hybrid firefly-GA outperforms GA, ACO and ABC algorithms for the metric average branch coverage for all the test problems. Test data generated through Hybrid firefly-GA yields 100% branch coverage calculated as an average.

Table 15. ANOVA test on coverage of four algorithms with significant level 0.05

Programs	Firefly-GA(x) vs GA(y)		Firefly-GA(x) vs ABC(z)		Firefly-GA(x) vs ACO(w)	
	x-y(%)	p-value	x-z(%)	p-value	x-w(%)	p-value
TCP	1.62	1.7391E-12	0.92	0.15	2.83	1.8731E-19
Even-Odd	1.82	1.7635E-14	0.88	0.12	1.48	1.8736E-18
Quadratic equation	4.72	4.8372E-7	0.93	1.7631E-9	1.73	0.08
Largest of three numbers	0.92	1.7632E-9	0.73	0.07	0.06	1.7673E-17

Table 16. ANOVA test on average convergence generation of four algorithms with significant level 0.05

Programs	Firefly-GA(x) vs GA(y)		Firefly-GA(x) vs ABC(z)		Firefly-GA(x) vs ACO(w)	
	x-y(%)	p-value	x-z(%)	p-value	x-w(%)	p-value
TCP	1.73	1.3652E-9	0.57	3.8732E-8	0.47	0.1922
Even-Odd	1.62	2.8635E-7	1.76	0.9637E-24	0.02	0.2812
Quadratic equation	3.82	0.6732E-18	1.36	0.1272	0.89	0.2831
Largest of three numbers	0.82	1.8773E-4	0.57	1.2688	0.02	0.8372

CONVERGENCE AND STABILITY ANALYSIS

Generally, stability analysis is an analytic method to show the effectiveness of an algorithm. It is also a method to analyze the stability of convergence of the algorithms. Here convergence refers to the achievement of 100% branch coverage during different runs and generations of the evolutionary algorithms. For the stability analysis, 300 trials of the experiments were performed. In order to search for the most stable behaviour of the algorithms, stability analysis is performed (Table 17).

Table 17. Stability analysis of coverage metric

Programs	Full Coverage Failures				Worst Coverage			
	GA	ABC	ACO	Firefly-GA	GA	ABC	ACO	Firefly-GA
TCP	74	6	12	0	43	70	76	99.73
Even-odd	89	9	18	0	45	75	74	100
Quadratic equation	120	12	16	4	49	78	55	98.33
Largest of three numbers	55	0	19	0	47	80	34	100

CONCLUSION

Software engineering methods are evolving continuously and often requires satisfying opposing criteria. Software engineering relies on various metrics for quality assessment and timely progression of software projects. Search based strategies help in finding the optimal solutions for a software engineering problem. In this paper, heterogeneous approaches are evaluated for the test case selection problem. Search based testing formulates the testing problem as a search problem. Branch coverage metrics of software engineering are the ideal candidate for fitness function. In most studies branch coverage is taken as a fitness function where branch distance becomes the branch function. Results shows that the performance of hybrid approaches are better than individual approaches such as GA, ABC and ACO.

REFERENCES

Agrawal, A. P., & Kaur, A. (2018). A comprehensive comparison of ant colony and hybrid particle swarm optimization algorithms through test case selection. In *Data Engineering and Intelligent Computing* (pp. 397–405). Singapore: Springer. doi:10.1007/978-981-10-3223-3_38

Alatas, B., Akin, E., & Ozer, A. B. (2009). Chaos embedded particle swarm optimization algorithms. *Chaos, Solitons, and Fractals*, *40*(4), 1715–1734. doi:10.1016/j.chaos.2007.09.063

Arrieta, A., Wang, S., Sagardui, G., & Etxeberria, L. (2019). Search-Based test case prioritization for simulation-Based testing of cyber-Physical system product lines. *Journal of Systems and Software*, *149*, 1–34. doi:10.1016/j.jss.2018.09.055

Choudhary, A., Agrawal, A. P., & Kaur, A. (2018). An effective approach for regression test case selection using pareto based multi-objective harmony search. In *Proceedings of the 11th International Workshop on Search-Based Software Testing* (pp. 13-20). ACM. 10.1145/3194718.3194722

de Oliveira Neto, F. G., Ahmad, A., Leifler, O., Sandahl, K., & Enoiu, E. (2018). Improving continuous integration with similarity-based test case selection. In *Proceedings of the 13th International Workshop on Automation of Software Test* (pp. 39-45). ACM. 10.1145/3194733.3194744

Di Nardo, D., Alshahwan, N., Briand, L., & Labiche, Y. (2015). Coverage-based regression test case selection, minimization and prioritization: A case study on an industrial system. *Software Testing, Verification & Reliability*, *25*(4), 371–396. doi:10.1002tvr.1572

Fister, I., Jr., Fister, D., & Yang, X. S. (2013). A hybrid bat algorithm. arXiv:1303.6310

Fors, N., Sten, J., Olsson, M., & Stenström, F. (2019). A Safe Regression Test Selection Technique for Modelica. In *Proceedings of The American Modelica Conference* 2018, October 9-10, Somberg Conference Center, Cambridge MA (pp. 131-137). Linköping University Electronic Press. 10.3384/ecp18154131

Gandomi, A. H., & Yang, X. S. (2014). Chaotic bat algorithm. *Journal of Computational Science*, *5*(2), 224–232. doi:10.1016/j.jocs.2013.10.002

Gandomi, A. H., Yun, G. J., Yang, X. S., & Talatahari, S. (2013). Chaos-enhanced accelerated particle swarm optimization. *Communications in Nonlinear Science and Numerical Simulation*, *18*(2), 327–340. doi:10.1016/j.cnsns.2012.07.017

Garousi, V., Özkan, R., & Betin-Can, A. (2018). Multi-objective regression test selection in practice: An empirical study in the defense software industry. *Information and Software Technology*, *103*, 40–54. doi:10.1016/j.infsof.2018.06.007

Guo, Z. L., & Wang, S. A. (2005). The comparative study of performance of three types of chaos immune optimization combination algorithms. *Acta Simulata Systematica Sinica, 2*.

Harder, M., Mellen, J., & Ernst, M. D. (2003). Improving test suites via operational abstraction. In *Proceedings of the 25th international conference on Software engineering* (pp. 60-71). IEEE Computer Society.

Harman, M. (2010). Why source code analysis and manipulation will always be important. In *2010 10th IEEE Working Conference on Source Code Analysis and Manipulation* (pp. 7-19). IEEE. 10.1109/SCAM.2010.28

Harman, M., Jia, Y., & Zhang, Y. (2015). Achievements, open problems and challenges for search based software testing. In *2015 IEEE 8th International Conference on Software Testing, Verification and Validation (ICST)* (pp. 1-12). IEEE. 10.1109/ICST.2015.7102580

Harman, M., & Jones, B. F. (2001). Search-based software engineering. *Information and Software Technology*, *43*(14), 833–839. doi:10.1016/S0950-5849(01)00189-6

Harman, M., Mansouri, S. A., & Zhang, Y. (2012). Search-based software engineering: Trends, techniques and applications. *ACM Computing Surveys*, *45*(1), 11. doi:10.1145/2379776.2379787

Holland, J. H. (1992). *Adaptation in natural and artificial systems: an introductory analysis with applications to biology, control, and artificial intelligence*. MIT Press. doi:10.7551/mitpress/1090.001.0001

Kazmi, R., Jawawi, D. N., Mohamad, R., & Ghani, I. (2017). Effective regression test case selection: A systematic literature review. [CSUR]. *ACM Computing Surveys*, *50*(2), 29. doi:10.1145/3057269

King, J. C. (1969). A Program Verifier [PhD thesis]. Carnegie Mellon University.

Korel, B. (1992). Dynamic method for software test data generation. *Software Testing, Verification & Reliability*, *2*(4), 203–213. doi:10.1002tvr.4370020405

Korel, B., Tahat, L. H., & Vaysburg, B. (2002). Model based regression test reduction using dependence analysis. In *International Conference on Software Maintenance 2002 Proceedings*. (pp. 214-223). IEEE. 10.1109/ICSM.2002.1167768

Myers, G. J., Sandler, C., & Badgett, T. (2011). *The art of software testing*. John Wiley & Sons.

Nogueira, S., Araujo, H., Araujo, R., Iyoda, J., & Sampaio, A. (2019). Test case generation, selection and coverage from natural language. *Science of Computer Programming*. doi:10.1016/j.scico.2019.01.003

Panichella, A., Oliveto, R., Di Penta, M., & De Lucia, A. (2015). Improving multi-objective test case selection by injecting diversity in genetic algorithms. *IEEE Transactions on Software Engineering*, *41*(4), 358–383. doi:10.1109/TSE.2014.2364175

Rothermel, G., & Harrold, M. J. (1996). Analyzing regression test selection techniques. *IEEE Transactions on Software Engineering*, *22*(8), 529–551. doi:10.1109/32.536955

Sahoo, R. R., & Ray, M. (2018). Metaheuristic Techniques for Test Case Generation: A Review. *Journal of Information Technology Research*, *11*(1), 158–171. doi:10.4018/JITR.2018010110

Schroeder, P. J., & Korel, B. (2000). Black-box test reduction using input-output analysis. ACM SIGSOFT Software Engineering Notes, 25(*5),* 173–177.

Shin, D., Yoo, S., Papadakis, M., & Bae, D. H. (2019). Empirical evaluation of mutation-based test case prioritization techniques. *Software Testing, Verification & Reliability*, *29*(1-2), e1695. doi:10.1002tvr.1695

Singh, Y., Kaur, A., & Suri, B. (2010). Test case prioritization using ant colony optimization. *Software Engineering Notes*, *35*(4), 1–7. doi:10.1145/1811226.1811238

Subashini, B., & Mala, D. J. (2017). An Effective Approach to Test Suite Reduction and Fault Detection Using Data Mining Techniques. *International Journal of Open Source Software and Processes*, *8*(4), 1–31. doi:10.4018/IJOSSP.2017100101

Talatahari, S., Azar, B. F., Sheikholeslami, R., & Gandomi, A. H. (2012). Imperialist competitive algorithm combined with chaos for global optimization. *Communications in Nonlinear Science and Numerical Simulation*, *17*(3), 1312–1319. doi:10.1016/j.cnsns.2011.08.021

Tallam, S., & Gupta, N. (2006). A concept analysis inspired greedy algorithm for test suite minimization. *Software Engineering Notes*, *31*(1), 35–42. doi:10.1145/1108768.1108802

Turing, A. M. (1949). Checking a large routine. In *Report of a Conference on High Speed Automatic Calculating Machines*, Cambridge, England, University Mathematical Laboratory (pp. 67 69).

Wang, X., Zeng, H., Gao, H., Miao, H., & Lin, W. (2019). Location-Based Test Case Prioritization for Software Embedded in Mobile Devices Using the Law of Gravitation. In *Proceedings of Mobile Information Systems 2019*.

Xiang, T., Liao, X., & Wong, K. W. (2007). An improved particle swarm optimization algorithm combined with piecewise linear chaotic map. *Applied Mathematics and Computation*, *190*(2), 1637–1645. doi:10.1016/j.amc.2007.02.103

Yang, D., Li, G., & Cheng, G. (2007). On the efficiency of chaos optimization algorithms for global optimization. *Chaos, Solitons, and Fractals*, *34*(4), 1366–1375. doi:10.1016/j.chaos.2006.04.057

Yang, X. S. (2010). *Nature-inspired metaheuristic algorithms*. Luniver press.

Zeller, A. (1999). Yesterday, my program worked. Today, it does not. Why? *Software Engineering Notes*, *24*(6), 253–267. doi:10.1145/318774.318946

This research was previously published in the International Journal of Software Science and Computational Intelligence (IJSSCI), 11(1); pages 31-46, copyright year 2019 by IGI Publishing (an imprint of IGI Global).

Chapter 78
Machine Learning Classification to Effort Estimation for Embedded Software Development Projects

Kazunori Iwata

Department of Business Administration, Aichi University, Nagoya, Japan

Toyoshiro Nakashima

Department of Culture-Information Studies, Sugiyama Jogakuen University, Nagoya, Japan

Yoshiyuki Anan

Process Innovation H.Q, Omron Software Co., Ltd., Kyoto, Japan

Naohiro Ishii

Department of Information Science, Aichi Institute of Technology, Nagoya, Japan

ABSTRACT

This paper discusses the effect of classification in estimating the amount of effort (in man-days) associated with code development. Estimating the effort requirements for new software projects is especially important. As outliers are harmful to the estimation, they are excluded from many estimation models. However, such outliers can be identified in practice once the projects are completed, and so they should not be excluded during the creation of models and when estimating the required effort. This paper presents classifications for embedded software development projects using an artificial neural network (ANN) and a support vector machine. After defining the classifications, effort estimation models are created for each class using linear regression, an ANN, and a form of support vector regression. Evaluation experiments are carried out to compare the estimation accuracy of the model both with and without the classifications using 10-fold cross-validation. In addition, the Games-Howell test with one-way analysis of variance is performed to consider statistically significant evidence.

DOI: 10.4018/978-1-6684-3702-5.ch078

INTRODUCTION

The growth and expansion of our information-based society has resulted in an increasing number of information products. In addition, the functionality of these products is becoming ever more complex (Hirayama, 2004; Takagi 2003). Guaranteeing the quality of software is particularly important, because this relates to reliability. It is, therefore, increasingly important for corporations that develop embedded software to realize efficient methods while guaranteeing timely delivery, high quality, and low development costs (Boehm, 1976; Komiyama, 2003; Nakashima, 2004; Ogasawara & Kojima, 2003; Takagi 2003; Tamaru, 2004; Ubayashi, 2004; Watanabe, 2004). Companies and divisions involved in the development of such software are focusing on a variety of improvements, particularly in their processes. Estimating the amount of effort (man-days cost) required for new software projects and guaranteeing product quality are especially important, because the amount of effort is directly related to cost and the product quality affects the reputation of the corporation. In the field of embedded software, there have been various studies on development techniques, management techniques, tools, testing techniques, reuse techniques, real-time operating systems, and other elements. However, there has been little research on the relationships among the scale of the development, amount of effort, and number of errors based on data accumulated from past projects. Previously, we investigated the estimation of total effort and errors using an artificial neural network (ANN), and showed that ANN models are superior to regression analysis models for estimating effort and errors in new projects. We proposed a method to estimate intervals for the number of errors using a support vector machine (SVM) and an ANN. These models were created with data that excluded outliers. The outliers can be identified in practice once the projects have been completed, and so they should not be excluded during the creation of models and when estimating the effort required. This paper presents classifications for embedded software development projects based on whether the amount of effort is an outlier or not using an ANN and an SVM. After the classification stage, we establish effort estimation models for each class using linear regression (LR), an ANN, and ε-support vector regression (ε-SVR). Evaluation experiments are carried out to compare the estimation accuracy of the model both with and without classification using 10-fold cross-validation and by applying the Games-Howell test with one-way analysis of variance (ANOVA).

The rest of this paper is organized as follows. First, we explain the related works. Second, we show datasets used in this paper. After that, we place our work and evaluation experiments. As a result, we conclude the paper.

RELATED WORKS

Support Vector Regression

SVR uses the same principles as SVM for classification, albeit with a few minor differences. The ε-SVR (Alex & Bernhard, 2004) regression method uses an ε-insensitive loss function to solve regression problems. This approach attempts to find a continuous function in which as many data points as possible lie within the ε-wide insensitivity tube. ε-SVR is used to estimate the amount of effort required for software projects (Oliveira, 2006). This approach has been tested using the well-known NASA software project dataset (John & Victor, 1981; Shin & Goel, 2000). However, these studies did not investigate the parameters of ε-SVR. The effectiveness of the SVM (and SVR) using the resulting continuous function depends on the kernel parameter (γ) and soft margin parameter (C) (Cortes & Vapnik, 1995). In addition, the value of ϵ affects the estimations given by ε-SVR.

We proposed a three-dimensional grid search to find the most appropriate combination of these parameters (Iwata, Liebman, Stone, Nakashima, Anan & Ishii, 2015). Our method improved the mean magnitude of relative error (MMRE, see Equation (3) in the section "Evaluation Criteria") from 0.165 (Cortes & Vapnik, 1995) to 0.149 using leave-one-out cross-validation (Shin & Goel, 2000).

Artificial Neural Networks

In earlier papers, we showed that ANN models are superior to regression analysis models for estimating the effort and errors in new projects (Iwata, Nakashima, Anan & Ishii, 2008). In addition, we proposed a method for reducing the margin of error (Iwata, Nakashima, Anan & Ishii, 2010; Iwata, Liebman, Stone, Nakashima, Anan & Ishii, 2015). However, outliers are excluded during the creation of the models, because they may be detrimental to performance. These outliers can be identified in practice once the projects have been completed, and so they should not be excluded from the model creation process or when estimating the amount of effort.

Our Contribution

The above algorithms have a certain level of estimation accuracy for data in which outliers are excluded. The outliers negatively affect the estimation, but cannot be detected before the projects have been completed. Therefore, in this paper, we propose a two-step method for reducing the estimation errors using an ANN and an SVM. Projects are classified according to whether the amount of effort is an outlier, with attributes that can be measured before the projects start used for the classification. After the classification stage, we establish effort estimation models for each class using LR, an ANN, and ε-SVR. We have studied the methods and states in Iwata, Nakashima, Anan & Ishii (2016). This paper is the extended version of the paper.

DATASETS AND OUTLIERS

Original Datasets

Using the following data from a large software company, we created models to estimate the amount of planning effort (E*ff*).

Eff: "The amount of effort," which indicates the cost, in man-days, of the review process for software development projects.

V_{new}: "Volume of newly added," which denotes the number of steps in the newly generated functions of the target project.

V_{modify}: "Volume of modification," which denotes the number of steps modified or added to existing functions to use the target project.

V_{survey}: "Volume of original project," which denotes the original number of steps in the modified functions and the number of steps deleted from the functions.

V_{reuse}: "Volume of reuse," which denotes the number of steps in a function that confirm an external method and are applied to the target project design without confirming the internal content.

Detection of Outliers

This paper examines the classification of outliers in terms of the amount of effort required in a project. Figure 1 shows the distribution of the amount of effort, and Figure 2 is a boxplot of this metric. The lowest datum of the boxplot is within 1.5 times the interquartile range (IQR) of the lower quartile, and the highest datum is within 1.5 IQR of the upper quartile. The outliers are denoted by circles. The Y coordinate values of the outliers have no meaning. The varying the values is used to improve understanding the distribution of the outliers. Of the total of 1416 data points, 146 are outliers. Each value of the boxplot is shown in Table 1.

Figure 1. Distribution of the Amount of Effort in Intervals 500

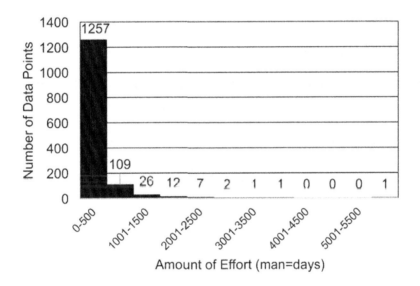

Figure 2. Boxplot of the Amount of Effort

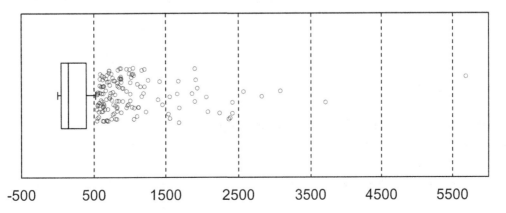

Table 1. Detailed Information of the Boxplot in Figure 1

	Value
IQR	197.070
Minimum	0.000
Lower quartile	49.430
Median	98.500
Upper quartile	246.500
Maximum	542.105

EFFORT ESTIMATION MODELS

The effort estimation models have two steps-classification and estimation

Model Creation

The data are divided into two groups of normal values and outliers on the basis of the amount of effort. The classification methods are created using an ANN and an SVM. The estimation methods are established for both normal values and outliers using LR, the ANN, and ε-SVR. Figure 3 illustrates the process of model creation.

Figure 3. Model Creation

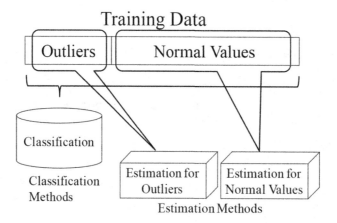

Effort Estimation

As the first step in estimating the amount of effort in a project, the data are classified using the classification methods. The step divides the date between candidates for normal values and for outliers. The amount of effort is then estimated using the method corresponding to the classification result (Figure 4). The volumes described in the section "Original Datasets" are used to classify a project and to estimate the amount of effort.

Figure 4. Effort Estimation

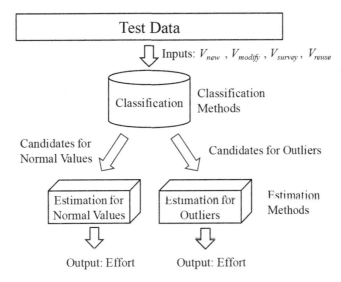

EVALUATION EXPERIMENT

Data Used in Evaluation Experiment

To evaluate the performance of the proposed technique, we performed 10-fold cross-validation on data from 1416 real projects. The original data were randomly partitioned into 10 equally sized subsamples (with each subsample having data from 141 or 142 projects). One of the subsamples was used as the validation data for testing the model, while the remaining nine subsamples were used as training data. The cross-validation process was repeated ten times, with each of the ten subsamples used exactly once as validation data. An example of 10-fold cross-validation is shown in Figure 5.

Figure 5. Ten-Fold Cross-Validation

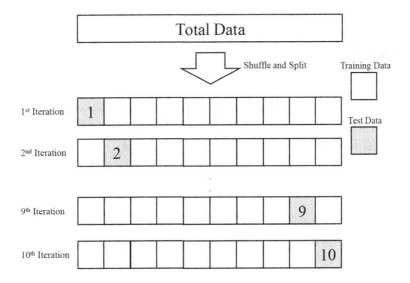

Classification Accuracy

The accuracy of the classification is affected by the estimation model used. The results of classification by ANN and SVM are shown in Tables 2 are 3, respectively. The values in the table represent the aggregate over 10 experiments. The diagonal values in the tables indicate the successfully classified projects. ANN classification achieved a 94.35% (= (1236 + 100) / 1416) success rate, and SVM classification attained a 95.34% (= (1247 + 103) / 1416) success rate. These results illustrate that the SVM gives slightly better results, but the difference is not significant. Therefore, both methods can be used to classify the projects.

Table 2. Classification Results by ANN

| | | Expected Classes | | |
		Normal Values	Outliers	Total
True Classes	Normal Values	1236	34	1270
	Outliers	46	100	146
	Total	1282	134	1416

Table 3. Classification Results by SVM

| | | Expected Classes | | |
		Normal Values	Outliers	Total
True Classes	Normal Values	1247	23	1270
	Outliers	43	103	146
	Total	1290	126	1416

Models for Experiments

We compared the accuracy of the following models in estimating the amount of effort required in the projects. Models 1) - 3) do not use the proposed classification methods, and estimate the amount of effort involved in a project directly. In contrast, models 4) - 6) divide the projects into two groups according to the ANN classification results. Models 7) - 9) divide the projects into two groups according to the SVM classification results.

Model 1) LR model without classification (LR w/o CL)
Model 2) ANN model without classification (ANN w/o CL)
Model 3) ε-SVR model without classification (ε-SVR w/o CL)
Model 4) LR model with ANN classification (LR w/ ANN)
Model 5) ANN model with ANN classification (ANN w/ ANN)
Model 6) ε-SVR model with ANN classification (ε-SVR w/ ANN)
Model 7) LR model with SVM classification (LR w/ SVM)
Model 8) ANN model with SVM classification (ANN w/ SVM)
Model 9) ε-SVR model with SVM classification (ε-SVR w/ SVM)

Evaluation Criteria

The following six criteria were used as performance measures for the effort estimation models (Shin & Goel, 2000). *PRED(p)* is the prediction level in Equation (5) (Conte, Dunsmore & Shen, 1986). For the measures 1) and 3), smaller values of the evaluation criterion indicate higher relative accuracy. In contrast, a larger value of *MPRED(25)* implies higher relative accuracy. The value of $\dfrac{X - \hat{X}}{X}$ is regarded as 1 if *X* is equal to 0 in the calculation of *MMRE* and *SDRE*. The actual value is expressed as X, while the predicted value is expressed as $\hat{X}$.

1. Mean of absolute errors (*MAE*).
2. Standard deviation of absolute errors (*SDAE*).
3. Mean magnitude of relative errors (*MMRE*).
4. Standard deviation of relative errors (*SDRE*).
5. *MPRED(25)* is the mean of *PRED(25)*.
6. *SDPRED(25)* is the standard deviation of *PRED(25)*.

$$MAE = \frac{1}{n}\sum \left| X - \hat{X} \right| \tag{1}$$

$$SDRE = \sqrt{\frac{1}{n-1}\sum \left(\left| X - \hat{X} \right| - MAE \right)^2} \tag{2}$$

$$MMRE = \frac{1}{n}\sum \left| \frac{X - \hat{X}}{X} \right| \tag{3}$$

$$SDRE = \sqrt{\frac{1}{n-1}\sum \left(\left| \frac{X - \hat{X}}{X} \right| - MMRE \right)^2} \tag{4}$$

$$PRED(q) = \frac{k}{n} \tag{5}$$

where for the set of *n* estimates, let *k* denote the number of estimates for which the magnitude of relative errors is less than or equal *q*%.

RESULTS AND DISCUSSION

For each model, the experimental results for all projects using 10-fold cross-validation are presented in Tables 4, 5 and 6.

Tables 7, 8 and 9 give the experimental results for projects considered to have normal values. The projects for models were detected using the classification methods. In contrast, the projects for models 1), 2) and 3) were extracted from the full dataset according to the true classes. Tables 10, 11 and 12 present the experimental results for projects considered to be outliers. These outlier projects were detected in a similar manner to the projects with normal values.

Table 4. Experimental Results of Absolute Errors (AE) for All Data

Models	# of Projects	MAE	SDAE	95% Confidence Interval
LR w/o CL	1416	115.795	206.506	[105.030, 126.560]
ANN w/o CL	1416	114.347	239.777	[101.848, 126.847]
SVR w/o CL	1416	129.110	265.647	[115.262, 142.958]
LR w/ ANN	1416	126.488	218.713	[115.086, 137.889]
ANN w/ ANN	1416	111.713	218.951	[100.300, 123.127]
SVR w/ ANN	1416	105.209	222.991	[93.584, 116.833]
LR w/ SVM	1416	123.919	225.216	[112.179, 135.660]
ANN w/ SVM	1416	109.504	236.506	[97.175, 121.833]
SVR w/ SVM	1416	**101.623**	233.828	[89.433, 113.812]

Table 5. Experimental Results of Relative Errors (RE) for All Data

Models	# of Projects	MMRE	SDRE	95% Confidence Interval
LR w/o CL	1416	1.886	5.789	[1.584, 2.188]
ANN w/o CL	1416	1.220	3.010	[1.063, 1.377]
SVR w/o CL	1416	0.948	1.789	[0.855, 1.042]
LR w/ ANN	1416	1.844	5.597	[1.552, 2.136]
ANN w/ ANN	1416	0.958	2.358	[0.835, 1.081]
SVR w/ ANN	1416	0.944	2.331	[0.823, 1.066]
LR w/ SVM	1416	1.834	5.596	[1.542, 2.126]
ANN w/ SVM	1416	0.951	2.361	[0.828, 1.074]
SVR w/ SVM	1416	0.933	2.333	[0.812, 1.055]

Table 6. Experimental Results of MPRED (25) for All Data

Models	# of Projects	MPRED(25)	SDPRED(25)	95% Confidence Interval
LR w/o CL	1416	0.258	0.037	[0.256, 0.260]
ANN w/o CL	1416	0.293	0.056	[0.290, 0.296]
SVR w/o CL	1416	0.303	0.040	[0.301, 0.305]
LR w/ ANN	1416	0.221	0.047	[0.218, 0.223]
ANN w/ ANN	1416	0.299	0.055	[0.296, 0.302]
SVR w/ ANN	1416	0.331	0.049	[0.329, 0.334]
LR w/ SVM	1416	0.222	0.043	[0.219, 0.224]
ANN w/ SVM	1416	0.302	0.054	[0.299, 0.305]
SVR w/ SVM	1416	0.342	0.042	[0.339, 0.344]

Table 7. Experimental Results of Absolute Errors (AE) for Normal Values

Models	# of Projects	MAE	SDAE	95% Confidence Interval
LR w/o CL	1270	79.983	110.539	[73.899, 86.069]
ANN w/o CL	1270	76.798	139.113	[69.140, 84.456]
SVR w/o CL	1270	88.400	139.778	[80.705, 96.095]
LR w/ ANN	1282	87.716	119.111	[81.190, 94.243]
ANN w/ ANN	1282	73.462	108.244	[67.531, 79.393]
SVR w/ ANN	1282	71.460	117.921	[64.998, 77.921]
LR w/ SVM	1290	91.605	156.889	[83.036, 100.175]
ANN w/ SVM	1290	77.549	159.690	[68.827, 86.272]
SVR w/ SVM	1290	74.590	166.990	[65.468, 83.711]

Table 8. Experimental Results of Relative Errors (RE) for Normal Values

Models	# of Projects	MMRE	SDRE	95% Confidence Interval
LR w/o CL	1270	2.057	6.089	[1.722, 2.392]
ANN w/o CL	1270	1.312	3.164	[1.138, 1.486]
SVR w/o CL	1270	1.008	1.877	[0.905, 1.112]
LR w/ ANN	1282	1.921	5.821	[1.602, 2.240]
ANN w/ ANN	1282	**0.996**	2.462	[0.861, 1.131]
SVR w/ ANN	1282	0.954	2.364	[0.824, 1.083]
LR w/ SVM	1290	1.913	5.804	[1.596, 2.230]
ANN w/ SVM	1290	0.992	2.455	[0.858, 1.126]
SVR w/ SVM	1290	0.948	2.358	[0.819, 1.076]

Table 9. Experimental Results of MPRED (25) for Normal Values

Models	# of Projects	MPRED(25)	SDPRED(25)	95% Confidence Interval
LR w/o CL	1270	0.249	0.039	[0.247, 0.251]
ANN w/o CL	1270	0.286	0.055	[0.283, 0.289]
SVR w/o CL	1270	0.303	0.047	[0.300, 0.306]
LR w/ ANN	1282	0.213	0.029	[0.211, 0.214]
ANN w/ ANN	1282	0.296	0.028	[0.294, 0.297]
SVR w/ ANN	1282	0.327	0.032	[0.325, 0.328]
LR w/ SVM	1290	0.211	0.029	[0.209, 0.212]
ANN w/ SVM	1290	0.295	0.028	[0.293, 0.296]
SVR w/ SVM	1290	0.332	0.026	[0.331, 0.334]

Table 10. Experimental Results of Absolute Errors (AE) for Outliers

Models	# of Projects	MAE	SDAE	95% Confidence Interval
LR w/o CL	146	427.306	447.521	[354.104, 500.508]
ANN w/o CL	146	440.973	521.440	[355.680, 526.267]
SVR w/o CL	146	483.228	613.902	[382.810, 583.646]
LR w/ ANN	134	497.420	466.666	[417.681, 577.159]
ANN w/ ANN	134	477.673	496.549	[392.828, 562.519]
SVR w/ ANN	134	428.093	526.561	[338.120, 518.066]
LR w/ SVM	126	454.755	444.836	[376.324, 533.186]
ANN w/ SVM	126	436.656	500.036	[354.864, 518.448]
SVR w/ SVM	126	378.389	494.845	[291.141, 465.637]

Table 11. Experimental Results of Relative Errors (RA) for Outliers

Models	# of Projects	MMRE	SDRE	95% Confidence Interval
LR w/o CL	146	0.391	0.253	[0.349, 0.432]
ANN w/o CL	146	0.408	0.338	[0.353, 0.463]
SVR w/o CL	146	0.417	0.336	[0.362, 0.472]
LR w/ ANN	134	1.106	2.488	[0.681, 1.531]
ANN w/ ANN	134	0.591	0.767	[0.460, 0.722]
SVR w/ ANN	134	0.852	1.987	[0.513, 1.192]
LR w/ SVM	126	1.021	2.500	[0.580, 1.462]
ANN w/ SVM	126	0.528	0.853	[0.389, 0.668]
SVR w/ SVM	126	0.785	2.056	[0.423, 1.148]

Table 12. Experimental Results of MPRED(25) for Outliers

Models	# of Projects	MPRED(25)	SDPRED(25)	95% Confidence Interval
LR w/o CL	146	0.327	0.082	[0.314, 0.340]
ANN w/o CL	146	0.354	0.092	[0.339, 0.369]
SVR w/o CL	146	0.295	0.081	[0.282, 0.308]
LR w/ ANN	134	0.298	0.126	[0.276, 0.319]
ANN w/ ANN	134	0.334	0.158	[0.307, 0.361]
SVR w/ ANN	134	0.379	0.124	[0.358, 0.400]
LR w/ SVM	126	0.331	0.112	[0.311, 0.351]
ANN w/ SVM	126	0.379	0.159	[0.353, 0.405]
SVR w/ SVM	126	0.439	0.112	[0.419, 0.458]

We compared the accuracy of the models using the Games-Howell test. This is a post hoc method for one-way ANOVA with unequal group sizes and unequal variances. The test is based on Welch's t-test and uses the studentized range statistic (q-distribution). This distribution is similar to the t-distribution from the t-test. If the p-value is less than or equal to the significance level, the null hypothesis is rejected. The null hypothesis in our experiment can be interpreted as "there is no difference between the means of the estimation errors in the pair of models being compared". The results of the one-way ANOVA prior to the Games-Howell test reveals that the Games-Howell test for outliers AE is not warranted and should not be carried out at a significance level of 0.05.

The results of the Games-Howell test are given as underlined values in Tables 4-12. They indicate statistically significant differences between with and without a classification, and illustrate the effect of classification on estimating the amount of effort. In addition, the tests indicate that the ANN w/ ANN, ANN w/ SVM, SVR w/ ANN and SVR w/ SVM can estimate the amount of effort more accurately than LR. However, Tables 10, 11 and 12 suggest that the classification process does not affect the estimation of the amount of effort in outliers. This is because the number of outliers is so small that there can be no statistically significant differences between model pairs.

CONCLUSION

This paper has examined the effect of classification in estimating the amount of effort required in software development projects. Embedded software development projects have been classified according to whether the amount of effort is an outlier using an ANN and an SVM. After the classification stage, effort estimation models for each class were created using LR, an ANN, and ε-SVR.

Evaluation experiments were conducted to compare the estimation accuracy of the models both with and without the classification step using 10-fold cross-validation. The results show that the classification process has a positive effect. In addition, the Games-Howell test was performed to identify statistically significant evidence. The results indicate statistically significant differences between certain pairs of models.

In future research, we will investigate the following:

- Having implemented a model to estimate the final amount of effort required in new projects, we plan to estimate the partial effort at various stages (e.g., halfway) in the project development process.
- We intend to consider a more complex method, such as a Bayesian network, to improve the accuracy of the proposed technique.
- More data are needed to further support our work. In particular, data for projects including outliers are essential to ameliorate the models.

ACKNOWLEDGMENT

This work was supported by JSPS KAKENHI Grant Number JP16K00310.

REFERENCES

Akaike, H. (1973). Information theory and an extension of the maximum likelihood principle. In B. N. Petrov, & F. Csaki (eds.), *Proceedings of the 2nd International Symposium on Information Theory* (pp. 267-281).

Alex, J. S., & Bernhard, S. (2004). A Tutorial on Support Vector Regression [Kluwer Academic Publishers.]. *Statistics and Computing, 14*(3), 199–222. doi:10.1023/B:STCO.0000035301.49549.88

Aoki, S. (2007). In testing whether the means of two populations are different (in Japanese), Retrieved from http://aoki2.si.gunma-u.ac.jp/lecture/BF/index.html

Boehm, B. W. (1976). Software engineering. *IEEE Transactions on Software Engineering, C-25*(12), 1226–1241.

Conte, S. D., Dunsmore, H. E. & Shen, Y. E. (1986). Software Engineering Metrics and Models: Benjamin-Cummings Publishing Co., Inc.

Cortes, C., & Vapnik, V. (1995). Support-Vector Networks. *Machine Learning, 20*(3), 273–297. doi:10.1007/BF00994018

Hirayama, M. (2004). Current state of embedded software (in Japanese). *Journal of Information Processing Society of Japan, 45*(7), 677–681.

Iwata, K., Liebman, E., Stone, P., Nakashima, T., Anan, Y., & Ishii, N. (2015). Bin-Based Estimation of the Amount of Effort for Embedded Software Development Projects with Support Vector Machines. In L. Roger (Ed.), *Computer and Information Science 2015, Studies in Computational Intelligence* (Vol. 614, pp. 157–169). Springer International Publishing. doi:10.1007/978-3-319-23467-0_11

Iwata, K., Nakashima, T., Anan, Y., & Ishii, N. (2008). Error Estimation Models Integrating Previous Models and Using Artificial Neural Networks for Embedded Software Development Projects, *In Proceedings of 20th IEEE International Conference on Tools with Artificial Intelligence ICTAI '08* (pp. 371-378). IEEE Press.

Iwata, K., Nakashima, T., Anan, Y., & Ishii, N. (2010). Improving Accuracy of an Artificial Neural Network Model to Predict Effort and Errors in Embedded Software Development Projects. In L. Roger (Ed.), *Software Engineering, Artificial Intelligence, Networking and Parallel/Distributed Computing 2010, Studies in Computational Intelligence* (Vol. 295, pp. 11–21). Springer Berlin Heidelberg. doi:10.1007/978-3-642-13265-0_2

Iwata, K., Nakashima, T., Anan, Y., & Ishii, N. (2011-08), Clustering and Analyzing Embedded Software Development Projects Data using Self-Organizing Maps, In L. Roger (Ed.), Software Engineering, Artificial Intelligence, Networking and Parallel/Distributed Computing 2011, SCI (Vol. 377, pp. 47-59). Springer Berlin Heidelberg.

Iwata, K., Nakashima, T., Anan, Y., & Ishii, N. (2016), Effort Estimation for Embedded Software Development Projects by Combining Machine Learning with Classification. *Proceedings of 3rd ACIS International Conference on Computational Science/Intelligence and Applied Information CSII '16* (pp. 265-270). IEEE Press. 10.1109/ACIT-CSII-BCD.2016.058

Iwata, K., Nakashima, T., Anan, Y., & Ishii, N. (2011-11), Effort Prediction Models Using Self-Organizing Maps for Embedded Software Development Projects. *Proceedings of 23rd IEEE International Conference on Tools with Artificial Intelligence ICTAI '11* (pp. 142-147). IEEE Press.

John, W. B., & Victor, R. B. (1981). A meta-model for software development resource expenditures. *Proceedings of the 5th international conference on Software engineering ICSE '81* (pp. 107-116). IEEE Press, Piscataway, NJ, USA.

Komiyama, T. (2003). Development of foundation for effective and efficient software process improvement (in Japanese). *Journal of Information Processing Society of Japan, 44*(4), 341–347.

Nakamoto, Y., Takada, H., & Tamaru, K. (1997). Current state and trend in embedded systems (in Japanese). *Journal of Information Processing Society of Japan, 38*(10), 871–878.

Nakashima, S. (2004). Introduction to model-checking of embedded software (in Japanese). *Journal of Information Processing Society of Japan, 45*(7), 690–693.

Ogasawara, H., & Kojima, S. (2003). Process improvement activities that put importance on stay power (in Japanese). *Journal of Information Processing Society of Japan, 44*(4), 334–340.

Oliveira, L. I. A. (2006). Estimation of software project effort with support vector regression. *Neurocomputing, 69*(13-15), 1749–1753. doi:10.1016/j.neucom.2005.12.119

Shapiro, S. S., & Wilk, M. B. (1965). An analysis of variance test for normality (complete samples). *Biometrika, 52*(3-4), 591–611. doi:10.1093/biomet/52.3-4.591

Shin, M., & Goel, L. A. (2000). Empirical data modeling in software engineering using radial basis functions. IEEE Transactions on Software Engineering, 26(6), 567-567.

Boehm, B. W., Madachy, R., & Steece, B. (2000). Software Cost Estimation with Cocomo ii. NJ: Prentice Hall.

Student. (1908). The probable error of a mean. *Biometrika, 6*(1), 1-25.

Takagi, Y. (2003). A case study of the success factor in large-scale software system development project (in Japanese). *Journal of Information Processing Society of Japan, 44*(4), 348–356.

Tamaru, K. (2004). Trends in software development platform for embedded systems (in Japanese). *Journal of Information Processing Society of Japan, 45*(7), 699–703.

Ubayashi, N. (2004). Modeling techniques for designing embedded software (in Japanese). *Journal of Information Processing Society of Japan, 45*(7), 682–692.

Watanabe, H. (2004). Product line technology for software development (in Japanese). *Journal of Information Processing Society of Japan, 45*(7), 694–698.

Welch, B. L. (1947). The generalization of student's problem when several different population variances are involved. *Biometrika, 34*(28). PMID:20287819

This research was previously published in the International Journal of Software Innovation (IJSI), 5(4); pages 19-32, copyright year 2017 by IGI Publishing (an imprint of IGI Global).

Chapter 79

Knowledge Management in University–Software Industry Collaboration

Marcello Chedid
https://orcid.org/0000-0003-0435-6568
University of Aveiro, Portugal

Leonor Teixeira
https://orcid.org/0000-0002-7791-1932
IEETA / DEGEIT, University of Aveiro, Portugal

ABSTRACT

The university-software industry collaboration relationship has been represented a key resource, to the extent that together they can more easily promote technological development that underpins innovation solutions. Through a literature review, this chapter aims to explore the concepts and the facilitator or inhibitor factors associated with the collaboration relationships between university and software industry, taking knowledge management into account. This chapter is organized as follows. In the first section, the authors briefly introduce university, software industry, and knowledge management. The following section, based on the literature reviewed, provides a critical discussion of the university-software industry collaboration relationship, knowledge management in knowledge intensive organizations or community, and knowledge management in collaboration relationship between these two types of industries. Finally, in the rest of the sections, the authors point to future research directions and conclude.

INTRODUCTION

The current environment that characterizes the software industry is extremely dynamic and somewhat complex demanding high-performance solutions, rapid development and cost efficiency. The collaboration relationship with universities has been represented a key resource, to the extent that together more easily can promote technological development that underpins innovation solutions. In addition, several

DOI: 10.4018/978-1-6684-3702-5.ch079

studies point out knowledge sharing as an important and strongly influential factor in a collaboration relationship.

Organizations belonging to the software industry, as well as higher education institutions designated in this work as universities are recognized as organizations based on intensive knowledge. Given the knowledge intensive nature of the two types of organizations, the collaboration strategy requires the integration of specialized knowledge dispersed between each of the members of the work teams, usually multidisciplinary. The highly specialized knowledge, both tacit and explicit, is created and shared in the different phases of the relationship (Boyarchuk, Kharchenko, & Sklyar, 2018; Salavisa, Videira, & Santos, 2009). However, tacit knowledge becomes more important to the relations between these types of organizations (Ryan & O'Connor, 2013). Edmondson et al. (2012) add that the true value of a collaboration relationship is often associated with the tacit knowledge that is shared. This implies that possible solutions that aim at the sustainability and success of the relationship should be examined through knowledge management (Gill, 2002; Philbin, 2008).

In this study, the term "university-software industry collaboration relationship" is defined as an activity that involves the interaction between teams composed of people from academia (teachers, researchers and students) and software industry professionals. The objective of this collaboration is to create and share knowledge and technology, with neither party being relegated to a simple case study (Daria & Kostiantyn, 2018). This collaboration is expected to benefit the related members and teams (teachers, researchers, students and professionals), the organizations that establish the relationship and, consequently, the surrounding society (Boyarchuk, Kharchenko, & Sklyar, 2018). As suggested by Wholin (2013, p. 43), when universities enter into a collaboration relationship with the industry, they should not see it as just a place to study, but rather as a partner to do the study with.

Through a literature review, this chapter aims to explore the concepts and the facilitator or inhibitor factors associated with the collaboration relationships between university and software industry, taking knowledge management into account.

This chapter is organized as follows. In the next section, the authors briefly introduce university, software industry and knowledge management. The following section, based on the literature reviewed, provides a critical discussion of the university-software industry collaboration relationship and knowledge management in knowledge intensive organizations or community. Finally, in the remainder sections, the authors point future research directions, and conclude.

BACKGROUND

In this section, this chapter outlines a brief theoretical foundation of the study. The first part covers the context of the study. The second part presents the knowledge management.

The Context of the Study

About the University

Universities (or higher education institutions) are complex and heterogeneous organizations (Bozeman & Boardman, 2013), fragmented into different knowledge domains, structured through communities (e.g. pedagogical, scientific, and institutional) with inviolable values of freedom and academic autonomy based on traditions and histories (Tippins, 2003). The various communities assume their own culture within a symbolic context, making it difficult to establish a culture with a rational management process and strategic vision (Dill, 1982). Currently, the high level of specialization also contributes to the existence of subcultures within their own universities. Their integration into a single institutional culture is a great challenge that universities have been facing for years (Sporn, 1996). This specialization, according to Dill (1982, p. 312), may result "in declining involvement in institutional requirements and a lessening of social ties with disciplinary and institutional colleagues". Encouraging a higher level of social interactions can be a facilitator in leading to the unification of the various subcultures of the different communities around a main culture (Dill, 1982).

The structuring of the university based on different areas of knowledge also leads to the formation of several subcultures that overlap with the institutional culture (Howell & Annansingh, 2013). Subculture usually exert a strong influence on the behavior and how each member of the institution acts. On the other hand, Howell and Annansingh (2013) define subculture as a set of meanings shared by members of a group, determining how they taught, develop researches and interact with others members of the institution; regardless of whether they are peers, employees or students.

Kerr (1987) suggests that, although the university is one of the sectors of society that can most be affected by political, economic, social and technological changes, unlike other sectors of society, the university has not yet been subjected to any great challenge and "the faculty members continue to operate largely as individual craftsmen" (Kerr, 1987, p. 184). However, Duderstadt (2001, p. 7) stresses that in the current context, we are faced with a "technology that has evolved so rapidly and relentlessly, increasing in power by a hundred-fold or more every decade, obliterating the constraints of space and time, and reshaping the way we communicate, think, and learn".

It should also be noted that universities nowadays suffer from the impact of: (i) life cycles associated with technological innovations (Gill, 2002); (ii) economic and cultural globalization; (iii) the educational needs of an increasingly knowledge-driven society; and (iv) the training needs for high-performing professional activities (Bruckmann & Carvalho, 2014; Duderstadt, 2001). Solutions to these factors — which constitute major reasons for change in higher education institutions around the world — may be found in a collaboration relationship with the software industry.

About the Software Industry

The history of software has evolved significantly in the last 30 years and its increasing relevance and criticality is well documented in several studies in the literature (Druffel, 2017). Looking back at the history of software, it can be divided into two important phases: a first phase where software was exclusively associated with technology. More recently, in a second phase, the emphasis has been put on applications and social changes brought about by software-based innovation processes, with increasingly significant changes in all societal contexts (Campbell-Kelly, 2007).

"Modern society is increasingly more dependent on software that offers quality and reliability" (Mead, Seshagiri, & Howar, 2016, p. 28), since these represent cross-cutting solutions for diverse products, services and processes that are part of everyday life in society. Currently, software represents a critical building element for the main types of systems (Druffel, 2017) and remains a fundamental resource for their connectivity and interoperability. This leads companies in this industry to rely heavily on the ability to discover opportunities and create innovative products, devices and solutions, so they can succeed in their marketplaces.

Taking into account the fact that software is present in all domains, being widely used in several areas, the software industry assumes a fundamental role in the economy and distinguishes itself as a type of business with increasing economic importance (Aurum, Daneshgar, & Ward, 2008; Lippoldt & Stryszowski, 2009).

In today's economy, it is difficult to define the boundaries of the software industry, as its limits are increasingly extended, and the profile of the professionals working in this area increasingly complex. In this context, and needing professionals with this profile, we have the most diverse business areas, such as companies dedicated exclusively to software development, companies from other business areas which also use and produce software to integrate their products (e.g. automotive industry), public institutions such as schools and universities, non-governmental organizations, to name a few (Lippoldt & Stryszowski, 2009). In fact, a significant part of software developed by the software industry is not a final product, but rather an integral component of products from other industries (Lippoldt & Stryszowski, 2009). In 2006, Michael Tiemann (2006, p. 3), vice-president of the world's leading provider of open source solutions *Red Hat*, argued that, "the battle of the next 10-15 years will be about who gets to control the ways in which software can be developed, sold, and used". The market for this type of software has been growing rapidly and has taken on an important role outside the traditional software sector (Lippoldt & Stryszowski, 2009).

Nearly two decades ago Watts Humphrey (2002, p. 1), recognized as the 'father' of quality in software and of CMMI (Capability Maturity Model Integration), wrote that "every business is a software business". He stated that although some managers do not recognize this software criticality in their business, almost all, regardless of type, use software directly or indirectly. Humphrey (2002, p. 4) cites the speech from a vice-president of a bank as an example of the importance of software in business: "we are a software business masquerading as a bank". Recently, Bill Ford, the Chairman of the Board of Directors of the centennial automotive Ford company, aware of this context, stated that the future of the automotive industry, particularly in the assembly sector, goes through a paradigm shift, transforming into a software industry (Kevin, 2017). Bill Ford added that the automotive industry should pay attention to start-ups and technology companies, considering that nowadays, they are the real competitors. Similarly, the General Electric Company (GE), the 13th largest company in the world and traditional industry, presented in its 2013 Annual Report (General Electric, 2014), the Shareholder Letter of its CEO Jeffrey Immelt where he clearly states that in the coming years, all companies of the industrial sector will become software industry companies. In pursuit of this strategy, the GE Digital was created in 2015 with the goal of being one of the 'top ten' software companies in 2020. In the 2017 Annual Report (General Electric, 2018), the GE Digital had already accumulated US$ 4.0 billion in annual revenue.

Given the scope associated with the practice of the software industry, this study uses the broad definition adopted by Lippoldt e Stryszowski (2009, p. 41): "the traditional 'software industry' (i.e. companies or institutions that primarily deal with development of software), as well as the parts of other industries that are involved in software development".

The software industry is characterized as being a "high technology, knowledge intensive, highly mutable industry – with weak entry-barriers and short innovation cycles – which demands continuous adaption, learning and access to knowledge" (Salavisa et al., 2009, p. 1). However, most of the existing companies in this sector are small and medium-sized, operating in a resource scarce scenario, with limited access to finance, specialized personnel and knowledge networks; facing competition from large national and international companies (Lippoldt & Stryszowski, 2009). Many of these companies have been created in the last decades as start-ups or spin-offs from universities, and a significant portion of these still maintains this link (Salavisa et al., 2009). The current technological complexity, resulting from the wide range of economic activities, goods and services, requires extended competences and a constant update in terms of knowledge on the part of work teams; making this aspect one of the most challenging when managing this type of industry (Druffel, 2017; Lippoldt & Stryszowski, 2009). It should be noted that this industry is highly dependent on the availability and access to human resources.

As such, one of the biggest challenges that this industry has been facing for some years now is precisely the scarcity of resources with adequate software skills (quantity) and the lack of preparation in critical and emerging areas (quality) (Lippoldt & Stryszowski, 2009). It is believed that by 2020 there will be a shortage of more than 900 thousand professionals in the European Union (OECD, 2017). During the 2006-2016 period, the number of professionals in the market with information and communication technology skills (ICT) increased 39.5%, representing a 10-fold increase in total employment during the same period (3.6%). Among ICT activities, 'IT and other information services' and 'software publishing' are the ones with the highest employment growth in the sector. The European Statistical Office (Eurostat), as well as the Organisation for Economic Co-operation and Development (OECD), define ICT specialists as workers who have the capacity to develop, operate and maintain ICT systems and for which ICT constitutes the main part of their activity. Among the various functions of the ICT specialist, are developers and software and multimedia analysts, database specialists and system administrators, etc.

In the meantime, despite this environment and the evolution of new software development organizational arrangements (e.g. outsourcing, global software development, and open source) Aurum et al. (2008) considered that software development still needs to achieve a higher level of maturity. On the other hand, the software development process is a collective, complex and creative effort that varies according to the organization, the type of software and the members of the teams involved in the process (Ryan & O'Connor, 2013). Additionally the software development process consists of a set of activities, which in turn are based on the intensive use of knowledge, through the processing of a large volume of know-how of different domains and technological competencies (Aurum et al., 2008; Mehta, Hall, & Byrd, 2014). This endows knowledge management an important role in software industry operations (Fehér & Gábor, 2006).

The Knowledge Management

Currently, the factors that lead to the success of businesses are not limited to the financial capital, labor and raw material. Knowledge has, for some years, become the most valuable resource for companies — the only one that can raise companies to the level of innovation and, as such, enhance competitive advantage (Gloet & Terziovski, 2004). Through knowledge, organizations can improve development by creating new business opportunities (Pekka-Economou & Hadjidema, 2011). On the other hand, increasing access to knowledge has made the innovation process complex within organizations, making the innovation process strongly dependent on said knowledge (Gloet & Terziovski, 2004).

Given this context, Peters (1992, p. 382) asks the following question: "if knowledge is the source of most value-added, how do organizations accumulate it?". However, according to Drucker (1994) the great challenge is not how to accumulate knowledge, but how to manage it in order to makes it productive, thus emerging the concept of knowledge management.

According to Prusak (2001), knowledge management, as a field of study, had the conference held in Boston in the year 1993 as its initial milestone, which was specifically dedicated to the theme and organized by him and other colleagues. Some 25 years later, the meaning, application and the comprehensiveness of the concept of ' knowledge management ' are still under discussion (Girard & Girard, 2015). According to Girard and Girard (2015, p. 15), "knowledge management has developed from a premature concept into a mainstream organizational necessity". At present, all scholars of systems, practices and models associated with knowledge management recognize their complexity and, at the same time, their multidimensional and evolutionary nature.

Although knowledge management is a holistic combination of measures involving people, processes and technology management, the literature indicates that organizations in the past have not been consistent in their knowledge management approach. Generally, the efforts to implement this concept into organizations focused on the development of technologies to support knowledge management activities, while not giving due attention to the integration of people and consideration of processes (Gloet & Terziovski, 2004; Grover & Davenport, 2001). However, Smith (2001, p. 319) suggests that "each organization has its unique way to handle knowledge". Variables such as "degree of maturity of the organization, type of business, core competences, culture, infrastructure and marketplace competition" affect how knowledge is used.

Several authors highlight the important role of knowledge management in the creation of new knowledge and innovation process (e.g. Inkinen, 2016). They point out the need of knowledge management practices in organizations since, "knowledge can be likened to a living system, growing and changing as it interact with the environment." (Davenport & Prusak, 1998, p. 8).

Figure 1. Knowledge management 'umbrella'

There are several definitions of the knowledge management in the literature that bring with them the concepts of the domains in which they are applied. In Rowley's view (2000, p. 327), "knowledge management is a complex process which will be understood differently in different contexts". Girard and Girard (2015), in their work entitled 'Defining knowledge management: Toward an applied compendium', relate more than 100 different definitions in 23 distinct domains. McKellar (2015) adds that, currently, knowledge management is like an 'umbrella' under which are other disciplines such as business intelligence, collaboration, big data, business process management, relationship management/customer experience, competitive intelligence, etc., Figure 1.

Although knowledge management relies on three different pillars — technology, people and process — and aims at achieving the objectives of organizations (Davenport & Prusak, 1998), a special dedication to technology has been verified in practice (by organizations). There were substantial investments in highly structured knowledge management solutions, and little attention to knowledge creation processes (Grover & Davenport, 2001). Gill (2002, p. 255) observed that "an increasing tendency of excluding human participation, interpretation and mediation from all sorts of processes and systems in the name of notions such as efficiency, objectivity, transparency and certainty". Technology, by itself, is not a knowledge creator, but can become a process accelerator if used correctly (Malhotra, 2005). According to Webber (1993), the location of knowledge is not in technology, but in the human mind.

UNIVERSITY-SOFTWARE INDUSTRY COLLABORATION RELATIONSHIP

In a rapidly changing scenario with increasingly disruptive innovation processes, the software industry needs more technology-based solutions to ensure its competitiveness (Wohlin et al., 2012). Companies in this industry have generally sought collaborations with universities, in order to have access to specific knowledge, which allows them to complement the skills that they already possess (Ehrismann & Patel, 2015). On the other hand, universities driven by technological progress and social pressure have also sought solutions to some of their problems by establishing collaboration relationships with the software industry (Coccoli, Stanganelli, & Maresca, 2011). It should be noted, that businesses and universities have faced a common problem related to the lack of professionals in emerging technological fields. This is happening at a time when the paradigm is to migrate to industry 4.0 solutions. This problem is exacerbated by the mismatch/misalignment between the profiles that the market demands and the qualifications that graduates obtain from their university education (Mead et al., 2016). According to Mead (2016, p. 29), this mismatch is currently "too high, with significant adverse consequences for employers and jobseekers".

Given this scenario, Boyarchuck (2018, p. 667) states that, "successes in this field are impossible without the fruitful collaboration between universities and the software industry". However, several authors believe that the traditional models of collaboration relationships are not adequate to the dynamics of these types of industries (Boyarchuk et al., 2018; Coccoli et al., 2011). This reinforces the importance of studies based on empirical data, on factors that may be the origin and that sustain a collaboration relationship between these two types of industries. The importance of factors related to new collaboration strategies, with new approaches based on the convergence of technologies, teaching and research, as well as on the increasing importance of knowledge, are also highlighted (Boyarchuk et al., 2018).

Although it seems obvious and that the parties involved recognize the need for collaboration, the difference between their individual expectations may make the opportunity for collaboration impossible, and/or even eliminate it completely (Wohlin, 2013). Rodríguez et al. (2014) also point out that one of the challenges of this type of collaboration relationship is that many software industry professionals view academic research as theoretical and of little value in practical applications (product development). On the other hand, researchers often complain that they do not have access to industry data and practical problems needed to develop their applied research (Rodríguez et al., 2014). A collaboration relationship between these industries can help address these challenges by bridging their interests and converging the expected objectives and benefits. In Ehrismann and Patel's point of view (2015, p. 2), "a clear understanding on common, but also diverging interests is the most truthful and realistic negotiation basis"; which may lead to a successful collaboration relationship. The same authors also point out that understanding and respecting one's organizational culture and combining existing intellectual and technological resources to respond to emerging issues can accelerate and improve the quality of their collaboration relationship (Ehrismann & Patel, 2015).

Figure 2 summarizes the main outcomes and challenges of the university-software industry collaboration relationship.

Figure 2. Main outcomes and challenges of the university-software industry relationship

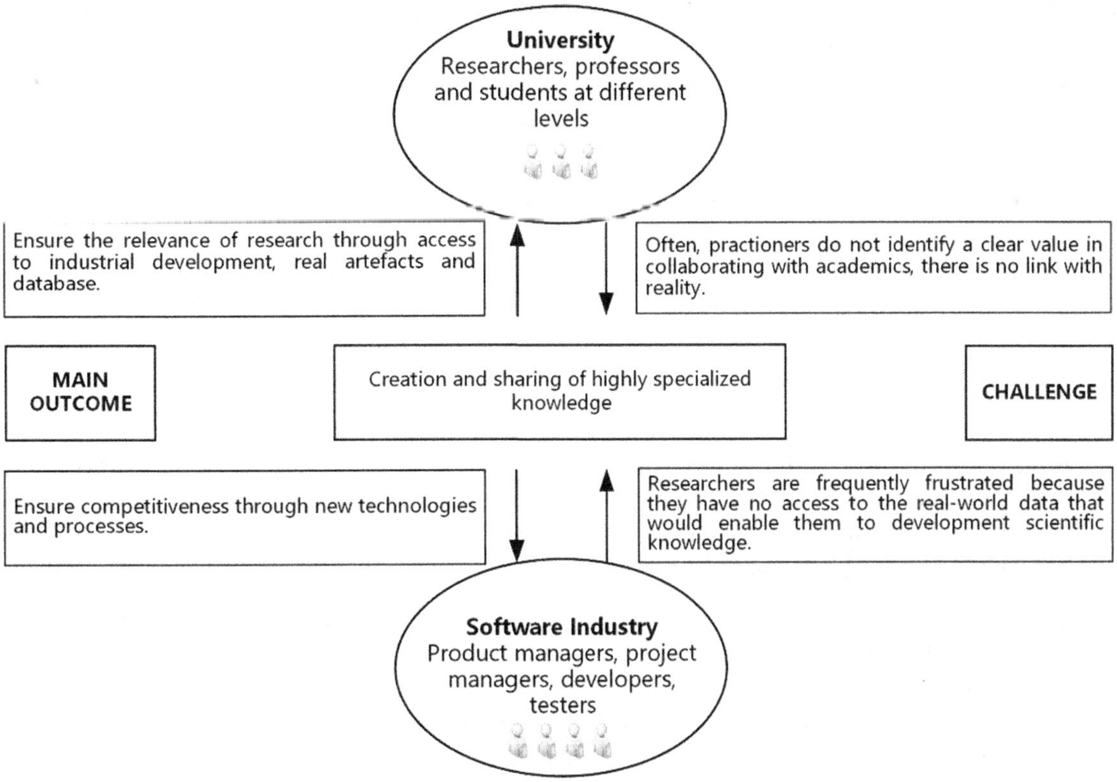

This relationship is characterized by the creation and sharing of highly specialized knowledge; this enables the industry to ensure competitiveness in an increasingly demanding market and provides the university the relevance of its investigations based on the real world. However, in order for this relationship to be successful, the university should seek to understand the real needs of the industry in such a way that the industry professionals attribute their real value to this relationship. Similarly, the industry should be aware of the importance of facilitating access to the existing knowledge base related to its business to the university, which will enable it to create knowledge and solutions that are ever closer to the needs of the industry.

KNOWLEDGE MANAGEMENT IN KNOWLEDGE INTENSIVE ORGANIZATIONS OR COMMUNITIES

According to Swart and Kinnie (2003), the term 'knowledge intensive' can be used to characterize three contexts: (i) knowledge-intensive activities; (ii) knowledge workers and; (iii) knowledge-intensive organizations.

Knowledge-intensive organizations are those where knowledge is of more importance than other inputs. Their main activity is intellectual in nature, and therefore knowledge workers constitute the largest part of their teamwork (Alvesson, 2001; Drucker, 1994; Starbuck, 1992). The absence of formal hierarchical structures and teamwork, where collaboration is fundamental, are the main characteristics of these organizations (Starbuck, 1992). This type of organization generally presents a robust ability to solve complex problems through creative and innovative solutions (Wong, 2005), as well as producing good results during collaboration activities with external specialists (Alvesson, 2001). Typical examples of this type of organization are consulting firms, research centers, engineering firms, high-tech companies, universities, software development companies, etc. (Aurum et al., 2008; Howell & Annansingh, 2013; Lindvall, Rus, & Sinha, 2003; Mehta et al., 2014).

Knowledge-intensive organizations have an important stock of knowledge that result of the sum of the different expertise of each member of their team and of their daily activities supported by knowledge sharing (Bosua & Scheepers, 2007). This inventory has extraordinarily complex combinations of different layers, requiring the development of strong personal and team relationships, so that it is possible to share and leverage these competencies at a project and organizational levels (Mehta et al., 2014). Personal relationship events involve explicit and tacit knowledge and play an important role in knowledge sharing and creation, and in interaction with other specific mechanisms, including technology. This makes the knowledge of these organizations more dynamic, which requires that each member of the team is kept up to date, avoiding the obsolescence of their knowledge (Aurum et al., 2008; Bjørnson & Dingsøyr, 2008). According to Lindvall et al. (2003, p. 137), "knowledge intensive organizations have realized that a large number of problems are attributed to un-captured and un-shared knowledge, as well as the need to know 'who knows what' in the organization".

Given that the solutions are increasingly multidisciplinary and that, for this reason, each team member has a different specialization, the creation and sharing of knowledge are increasingly fundamental processes within knowledge-intensive organizations (Lauring & Selmer, 2012). In general, specialized knowledge is tacit, which makes knowledge sharing more important in this type of environment (Ghobadi, 2015). The best use of tacit knowledge can guarantee a process of creating more efficient and effective solutions (Bierly, Damanpour, & Santoro, 2009).

According to their characteristics and their activities, it is fundamental that knowledge-intensive organizations define a knowledge management strategy (Lee-Kelley, Blackman, & Hurst, 2007). The knowledge management strategy can be developed based on different approaches; however, several studies in the literature regarding knowledge management of this type of organization, have suggested the codification and personalization approaches (Fehér & Gábor, 2006; M. T. Hansen, Nohria, & Tierney, 1999).

Codification is a 'knowledge conversion' approach to document knowledge, focusing on the use of technology. In this case, the knowledge is properly codified and stored in knowledge bases, so that anyone in the organization can access and reuse it. This approach is closely associated with explicit knowledge. On the other hand, personalization is a 'person-to-person' approach; meaning that knowledge is closely related to the person who developed or holds it and is shared through face-to-face contact. The aim is to facilitate exchanges by creating networks and encouraging face-to-face communication between individuals and teams through informal contacts, conferences, workshops, communities of practice, brainstorming, individual sessions, etc. This approach is more closely associated with tacit knowledge. Technology, given the characteristics of these organizations, plays an important role in supporting these approaches (Bosua & Scheepers, 2007; M. T. Hansen et al., 1999). Hansen et al. (1999) suggest three questions that may help define the main strategy to be adopted: (i) does the organization offer standardized or personalized products? (ii) does the organization have a mature or innovative product? and; (iii) do the teams of this organization depend, mostly, on explicit or tacit knowledge to develop new solutions?

Fehér and Gábor (2006) warn that the choice of one or another strategy is not a precondition for success. Hansen et al. (1999) add that organizations that achieve success are those that focus on one of the strategies and use the other as a support. In other words, they find a balance according to the type and use of the prevailing knowledge in each organization. The same authors add that organizations that try to excel in both approaches risk failing in both as well (M. T. Hansen et al., 1999).

KNOWLEDGE MANAGEMENT IN UNIVERSITY-SOFTWARE INDUSTRY COLLABORATION RELATIONSHIP

Given the intensive knowledge nature of these two types of organizations, the collaborative strategy requires the integration of specialized knowledge, often multidisciplinary, and highly specialized, dispersed throughout each member of the work teams (Boyarchuk et al., 2018; Hermans & Castiaux, 2007). Hansen et al. (2017) and Mehta et al. (2014) add that it is not enough to simply save the results of collaborative projects, but rather that it is necessary to transform the results into knowledge and make it accessible. This is in order to be reusable in new and future projects, and to recognize and capitalize on the specific knowledge of each community and its diversity, so to strengthen the relationship and the social network. According to (Hermans & Castiaux, 2007), the knowledge obtained from a collaboration relationship can represent an excellent starting point for new collaborative projects. Gill (2002, p. 263) states that "it is the sharing of a common knowledge base that, continuously builds upon local knowledge bases which, is at the heart of a collaborative process". These facts, evidenced by the literature, indicate that possible solutions aimed at the sustainability of university-software industry collaboration relationships should be explored and evaluated from a knowledge management standpoint (Philbin, 2008).

Although knowledge management and collaboration are complementary, given that they have common, mutually interdependent purposes and practices (Qureshi, Hlupic, & Briggs, 2004), the few existing studies on knowledge management in collaboration relationships focus on outcomes or structures of success of the relationship (I.-E. Hansen et al., 2017), on reports of lessons learned (Bjørnson & Dingsøyr, 2008). Some authors have also pointed out that studies, in a general manner, identify universities as the only providers of knowledge and technology. Besides that, the focus is very centered on the research and development issues rather than on creating a collaboration environment in a holistic way. There is a lack of evidence about the university's role as the recipient of knowledge created by the industry (Bozeman & Boardman, 2013; Jongbloed, 2015). In addition, the scientific community has paid little attention to the role of knowledge in collaboration relationships and the consequent impact on the promotion of innovation and on society (I.-E. Hansen et al., 2017).

Thus, knowledge management assumes an important role for organizations in delivering the best performing solutions (Tippins, 2003). Particularly in the case of tacit knowledge, which requires considerable managerial resources, its value can ensure a more efficient and effective solution creation process, and the ability to manage such knowledge will define the difference between a good and a better performance (Bierly et al., 2009; I.-E. Hansen et al., 2017).

FUTURE RESEARCH DIRECTIONS

Although the literature suggests that this theme as quite relevant, there is an evident lack of empirical studies that properly investigate the factors that can contribute to the sustainable promotion of this type of collaboration relationship (Feng, Zhang, Du, & Wang, 2015). Additionally, there are few studies that address knowledge management in collaboration relationships (I.-E. Hansen et al., 2017).

CONCLUSION

The changes in the software industry have been ever more rapid and more substantial. Toward that scenario, it is possible suppose that the collaboration relationship between university and software industry will become increasingly important for both organizations. This collaboration relationship offers numerous benefits for both parties. As a result of this mutually beneficial relationship, software industry firms can achieve solutions for most of their problems, since university offers firms a wide knowledge base of different scientific domains (pedagogical and scientific), specialists (teachers and researchers), training, etc. On the other hand, university can get involved with specialized professionals and the real world of this industry, which can help its research and educational processes. These potential benefits reinforce the importance and the need to encourage and structure such collaboration.

As shown in the framework in Figure 3., the university and the software industry are organizations that present different cultures with different objectives, needs and competencies. However, if this cultural diversity poses a challenge when establishing and conducting of a collaboration relationship (Du Chatenier, Verstegen, Biemans, Mulder, & Omta, 2009), the knowledge-intensive characteristic relevant to each of these organizations also represents an excellent source of creativity and innovation.

Given the knowledge intensive nature of the two types of organizations, the collaborative strategy requires the integration of specialized knowledge dispersed between each of the members of the work teams, usually multidisciplinary. The highly specialized knowledge, both tacit and explicit, is created and shared in the various phases of the relationship (Boyarchuk et al., 2018; Salavisa et al., 2009). This implies that possible solutions that aim at the sustainability of the relationship should be examined through the knowledge management (Philbin, 2008). This view is also shared by Vasconcelos et al. (2017, p. 1502), who understand that in knowledge-intensive environments "knowledge management processes fit like a glove".

Figure 3. Different objectives, needs and competencies of the university and the software industry

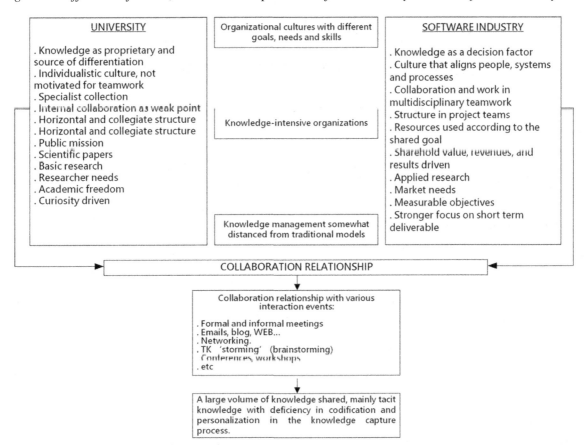

REFERENCES

Alvesson, M. (2001). Knowledge work: Ambiguity, image and identity. *Human Relations, 54*(7), 863–886.

Aurum, A., Daneshgar, F., & Ward, J. (2008). Investigating knowledge management practices in software development organisations – An Australian experience. *Information and Software Technology, 50*(6), 511–533.

Bierly, P. E., Damanpour, F., & Santoro, M. D. (2009). The application of external knowledge: Organizational conditions for exploration and exploitation. *Journal of Management Studies, 46*(3), 481–509.

Bjørnson, F. O., & Dingsøyr, T. (2008). Knowledge management in software engineering: A systematic review of studied concepts, findings and research methods used. *Information and Software Technology, 50*(11), 1055–1068.

Bosua, R., & Scheepers, R. (2007). Towards a model to explain knowledge sharing in complex organizational environments. *Knowledge Management Research and Practice, 5*(2), 93–109.

Boyarchuk, A., Kharchenko, V., & Sklyar, V. (2018). Models and cases for sustainable university-industry cooperation in IT sector. In *2018 IEEE 9th International Conference on Dependable Systems, Services and Technologies (DESSERT)* (pp. 667–671). IEEE.

Bozeman, B., & Boardman, C. (2013). Academic faculty in university research centers: Neither capitalism's slaves nor teaching fugitives. *The Journal of Higher Education, 84*(1), 88–120.

Bruckmann, S., & Carvalho, T. (2014). The reform process of Portuguese higher education institutions: From collegial to managerial governance. *Tertiary Education and Management, 20*(3), 193–206.

Campbell-Kelly, M. (2007). The history of the history of software. *IEEE Annals of the History of Computing, 29*(4), 40–51.

Coccoli, M., Stanganelli, L., & Maresca, P. (2011). Computer Supported Collaborative Learning in software engineering. In *2011 IEEE Global Engineering Education Conference (EDUCON)* (pp. 990–995). IEEE.

Davenport, T. H., & Prusak, L. (1998). *Working knowledge: How organizations manage what they know.* Harvard Business School Press.

de Vasconcelos, J. B., Kimble, C., Carreteiro, P., & Rocha, Á. (2017). The application of knowledge management to software evolution. *International Journal of Information Management, 37*(1), 1499–1506.

Dill, D. D. (1982). The management of academic culture: Notes on the management of meaning and social integration. *Higher Education, 11*(3), 303–320.

Drucker, P. F. (1994). The age of social transformation. *Atlantic Monthly, 274*(5), 53–80.

Druffel, L. (2017). *A technical history of the SEI.* Carnegie-Mellon University (Vol. CMU/SEI-20). Retrieved from http://www.dtic.mil/dtic/tr/fulltext/u2/1046656.pdf

Du Chatenier, E., Verstegen, J. A. A. M., Biemans, H. J. A., Mulder, M., & Omta, O. (2009). The challenges of collaborative knowledge creation in open innovation teams. *Human Resource Development Review, 8*(3), 350–381.

Duderstadt, J. J. (2001). The future of the university in the digital age. In *The Glion III Conference* (pp. 1–26). Retrieved from http://milproj.dc.umich.edu/publications/jjd_glion_iii/jjd_glion_iii.pdf

Edmondson, G., Valigra, L., Kenward, M., Hudson, R. L., & Belfield, H. (2012). *Making industry-university partnerships work: Lessons from successful collaborations. Science\Business Innovation Board AISBL.* Retrieved from www.sciencebusiness.net/innovationboard

Ehrismann, D., & Patel, D. D. (2015). University-industry collaborations: Models, drivers and cultures. *Swiss Medical Weekly, 145*(February), 1–6. PMID:25658854

Fehér, P., & Gábor, A. (2006). The role of knowledge management supporters in software development companies. *Software Process Improvement and Practice, 11*(3), 251–260.

Feng, F., Zhang, L., Du, Y., & Wang, W. (2015). Visualization and quantitative study in bibliographic databases: A case in the field of university–industry cooperation. *Journal of Informetrics, 9*(1), 118–134.

General Electric. (2014). *GE 2013 Annual Report.* Retrieved from https://www.ge.com/ar2013/pdf/GE_AR13.pdf

Ghobadi, S. (2015). What drives knowledge sharing in software development teams: A literature review and classification framework. *Information & Management, 52*(1), 82–97.

Gill, K. S. (2002). Knowledge networking in cross-cultural settings. *AI & Society, 16*(3), 252–277.

Girard, J., & Girard, J. (2015). Defining knowledge management: Toward an applied compendium. *Online Journal of Applied Knowledge Management, 3*(1), 1–20.

Gloet, M., & Terziovski, M. (2004). Exploring the relationship between knowledge management practices and innovation performance. *Journal of Manufacturing Technology Management, 15*(5), 402–409.

Grover, V., & Davenport, T. H. (2001). General Perspectives on Knowledge Management: Fostering a Research Agenda. *Journal of Management Information Systems, 18*(1), 5–21.

Hansen, I.-E., Mork, O. J., & Welo, T. (2017). Knowledge management of university-industry collaboration in the learning economy. In *2017 2nd International Conference on Knowledge Engineering and Applications (ICKEA)* (pp. 173–177). Academic Press.

Hansen, M. T., Nohria, N., & Tierney, T. (1999). What's your strategy for managing knowledge? *Harvard Business Review, 72*(2), 106–116. PMID:10387767

Hermans, J., & Castiaux, A. (2007). Knowledge creation through university-industry collaborative research projects. *Electronic Journal of Knowledge Management, 5*(1), 43–54.

Howell, K. E., & Annansingh, F. (2013). Knowledge generation and sharing in UK universities: A tale of two cultures? *International Journal of Information Management, 33*(1), 32–39.

Humphrey, W. (2002). *Winning with software: An executive strategy.* Pearson Education, Inc.

Inkinen, H. (2016). Review of empirical research on knowledge management practices and firm performance. *Journal of Knowledge Management, 20*(2), 230–257.

Jongbloed, B. (2015). Universities as hybrid organizations. *International Studies of Management & Organization, 45*(3), 207–225.

Kerr, C. (1987). A critical age in the university world: Accumulated heritage versus modern imperatives. *European Journal of Education, 22*(2), 183–193.

Kevin, R. (2017). *Can Ford turn into a tech company?* Retrieved February 9, 2018, from https://www.nytimes.com/interactive/2017/11/09/magazine/tech-design-autonomous-future-cars-detroit-ford.html

Lauring, J., & Selmer, J. (2012). Knowledge sharing in diverse organisations. *Human Resource Management Journal, 22*(1), 89–105.

Lee-Kelley, L., Blackman, D. A., & Hurst, J. P. (2007). An exploration of the relationship between learning organisations and the retention of knowledge workers. *The Learning Organization, 14*(3), 204–221.

Lindvall, M., Rus, I., & Sinha, S. S. (2003). Software systems support for knowledge management. *Journal of Knowledge Management, 7*(5), 137–150.

Lippoldt, D., & Stryszowski, P. (2009). *Innovation in the software sector*. OECD Publishing.

Malhotra, Y. (2005). Integrating knowledge management technologies in organizational business processes: Getting real time enterprises to deliver real business performance. *Journal of Knowledge Management, 9*(1), 7–28.

McKellar, H. (2015). 100 COMPANIES That matter in knowledge management. *KM World*. Retrieved from https://www.kmworld.com/Articles/Editorial/Features/KMWorld-100-COMPANIES-That-Matter-in-Knowledge-Management-102189.aspx

Mead, N. R., Seshagiri, G., & Howar, J. (2016). Meeting Industry Needs for Secure Software Development. In *2016 IEEE 29th International Conference on Software Engineering Education and Training (CSEET)* (pp. 28–36). IEEE.

Mehta, N., Hall, D., & Byrd, T. (2014). Information technology and knowledge in software development teams: The role of project uncertainty. *Information & Management, 51*(4), 417–429.

OECD. (2017). *OECD Digital Economy Outlook 2017*. Paris: OECD Publishing. Retrieved from https://www.oecd-ilibrary.org/science-and-technology/oecd-digital-economy-outlook-2017_9789264276284-en

Pekka-Economou, V., & Hadjidema, S. (2011). Innovative organizational forms that add value to both organizations and community: The case of knowledge management. *European Research Studies, 14*(2), 81–95.

Peters, T. (1992). Liberation Management: Necessary Disorganization for the Nanosecond Nineties. New York: Alfred A. Knopf, Inc.

Philbin, S. (2008). Process model for university-industry research collaboration. *European Journal of Innovation Management, 11*(4), 488–521.

Prusak, L. (2001). Where did knowledge management come from? *IBM Systems Journal, 40*(4), 1002–1007.

Qureshi, S., Hlupic, V., & Briggs, R. O. (2004). On the convergence of knowledge management and groupware. In *International Conference on Collaboration and Technology* (pp. 25–33). Berlin: Springer-Verlag.

Rodríguez, P., Kuvaja, P., & Oivo, M. (2014). Lessons learned on applying design science for bridging the collaboration gap between industry and academia in empirical software engineering. *Proceedings of the 2nd International Workshop on Conducting Empirical Studies in Industry - CESI 2014*, 9–14.

Rowley, J. (2000). Is higher education ready for knowledge management? *International Journal of Educational Management, 14*(7), 325–333.

Ryan, S., & O'Connor, R. V. (2013). Acquiring and sharing tacit knowledge in software development teams: An empirical study. *Information and Software Technology, 55*(9), 1614–1624.

Salavisa, I., Videira, P., & Santos, F. (2009). Spin-offs in the software industry : The role of networks, universities and incubators. In *7th Triple Helix International Conference - Triple Helix as a Basis for Science, Technology and Innovation Capacity Building or The Third Mission of Universities* (pp. 1–9). Glasgow, UK: Academic Press.

Smith, E. A. (2001). The role of tacit and explicit knowledge in the workplace. *Journal of Knowledge Management, 5*(4), 311–321.

Sporn, B. (1996). Managing university culture: An analysis of the relationship between institutional culture and management approaches. *Higher Education, 32*(1), 41–61.

Starbuck, W. H. (1992). Learning by knowledge-intensive firms. *Journal of Management Studies, 29*(6), 713–740.

Swart, J., & Kinnie, N. (2003). Sharing knowledge in knowledge-intensive firms. *Human Resource Management Journal, 13*(2), 60 75.

Tiemann, M. (2006). Software industry vs. software society: Who wis in 2020? In *STS Forum Position Paper* (p. 3). Retrieved from http://people.redhat.com/tiemann/STS-Forum-Tiemann-2006.pdf

Tippins, M. J. (2003). Implementing knowledge management in academia: Teaching the teachers. *International Journal of Educational Management, 17*(7), 339–345.

Webber, A. M. (1993). What's so new about the new economy? *Harvard Business Review, 71*(1), 24–42.

Wohlin, C. (2013). Empirical software engineering research with industry: Top 10 challenges. In *2013 1st International Workshop on Conducting Empirical Studies in Industry (CESI)* (pp. 43–46). IEEE.

Wohlin, C., Aurum, A., Angelis, L., Phillips, L., Dittrich, Y., Gorschek, T., ... Winter, J. (2012). The Success Factors Powering Academia Collaboration. *IEEE Software, 29*(2), 67–73.

Wong, K. Y. (2005). Critical success factors for implementing knowledge management in small and medium enterprises. *Industrial Management & Data Systems, 105*(3), 261–279.

ADDITIONAL READING

Balandin, S. (2010). Experience and vision of open innovations in russia and baltic region: The FRUCT program. In *2010 IEEE Region 8 International Conference on Computational Technologies in Electrical and Electronics Engineering (SIBIRCON)* (pp. 5-10). IEEE.

du Plessis, M., & du Plessis, M. (2007). The role of knowledge management in innovation. *Journal of Knowledge Management, 11*(4), 20–29.

Edwards, J. S. (2003). Managing Software Engineers and Their Knowledge. In *Managing Software Engineering Knowledge* (pp. 5–27). Springer Berlin Heidelberg.

Garousi, V., Petersen, K., & Ozkan, B. (2016). Challenges and best practices in industry-academia collaborations in software engineering : A systematic literature review. *Information and Software Technology, 79*, 106–127.

Johanyak, Z. C. (2016). Real-world software projects as tools for the improvement of student motivation and university-industry collaboration. In *2016 International Conference on Industrial Engineering, Management Science and Application (ICIMSA)* (pp. 1–4). IEEE.

Richardson, I., & Von Wangenheim, C. (2007). Guest editors' introduction: Why are small software organizations different? *IEEE Software, 24*(1), 18–22.

Savolainen, P., & Ahonen, J. J. (2015). Knowledge lost: Challenges in changing project manager between sales and implementation in software projects. *International Journal of Project Management, 33*(1), 92–102.

Schofield, T. (2013). Critical success factors for knowledge transfer collaborations between university and industry. *The Journal of Research Administration, 44*(2), 38–56.

Teixeira, S. J., Veiga, P. M., & Fernandes, C. A. (2019). The knowledge transfer and cooperation between universities and enterprises. *Knowledge Management Research and Practice,* ●●●, 1–12.

Tzortzaki, A. M., & Mihiotis, A. (2014). A review of knowledge management theory and future directions. *Knowledge and Process Management, 21*(1), 29–41.

KEY TERMS AND DEFINITIONS

Codification Approach: Codification is a 'knowledge conversion' approach to document knowledge, focusing on the use of technology. This approach is closely associated with explicit knowledge.

Knowledge Intensive Organizations: Organizations that are characterized by a high proportion of highly qualified workers and where knowledge is of more importance than other inputs.

Multidisciplinary Team: A group composed of members with varied but complimentary experience, qualifications, and skills that contribute to the achievement of specific objectives.

Personalization Approach: Personalization is a 'person-to-person' approach; meaning that knowledge is closely related to the person who developed or holds it and is shared through face-to-face contact. This approach is more closely associated with tacit knowledge.

Software Industry: It comprises the traditional organizations that primary deal with software development, as well as the parts of other industries that are involved in software development.

University: An academic community, made up of schools, departments/colleges, research units, research laboratories and interface units (e.g. technology transfer units, university-company relationship units).

University-Industry Collaboration: Bi-directional relationship between university and industry organizations, established to enable the diffusion of creativity, ideas, skills and people with the aim of creating mutual value over time.

This research was previously published in the Handbook of Research on Modern Educational Technologies, Applications, and Management; pages 114-130, copyright year 2021 by Information Science Reference (an imprint of IGI Global).

Chapter 80
Migrating Software Towards Mobile Technologies

Liliana Maria Favre

(iD) https://orcid.org/0000-0003-1370-1861

Universidad Nacional del Centro de la Provincia de Buenos Aires, Argentina & Comisión de Investigaciones Científicas de la Provincia de Buenos Aires, Argentina

ABSTRACT

New paradigms such as pervasive computing, cloud computing, and the internet of things (IoT) are impacting the business world. Smartphones are at the core of these paradigms by allowing us interaction with the world around us. In light of this, it is imperative to migrate a lot of existing non-mobile software to adapt it to the new technological reality. The main challenge to achieve this goal is the proliferation of mobile platforms. An integration of ADM (Architecture Driven Modernization), cross-platform development and formal metamodeling to face this kind of migration is described. The proposal was validated with the migration of object-oriented software to different mobile platforms through the multiplatform language Haxe. A comparison of the approach with traditional migration processes and the description of existing challenges in real projects of the scientific and industrial field are included.

INTRODUCTION

Today, the use of technology is central to the business world. Organizations need to redesign their processes and models so as not to be left out of the market in the near future. The adoption of new digital technologies offers a competitive advantage and performs as a market differentiator. In particular, new paradigms such as Pervasive Computing, Cloud Computing and the Internet of Things (IoT) are impacting the business world. Smartphones are at the core of these paradigms, letting us locate and easily interact with the world around us. With the Smartphone through Wi-Fi and the 5G, we will handle all kinds of objects connected to the network. Just as smartphones have already displaced the camera, the GPS, the music player, and the wallet, they will be on-ramp for a new IoT revolution. In this scenario, humans and things act synergistically as a whole and smartphones will continue to play a crucial role due to they are the main interface connecting people to the Internet (Stancovik, 2014) (Islam and Want, 2015).

DOI: 10.4018/978-1-6684-3702-5.ch080

Smartphones are being transformed into a service center for different platforms in science, medicine, and education. Hossain et al. (2019) analyze the effects of variety-seeking intention by mobile phone usage on university students' academic performance.

In this context, most challenges for the competitive software industry are related to the problems caused by the proliferation of mobile platforms. New applications must support them as possible to remain profitable. Software applications can take full advantage of platforms only when they are built using native codebase. To address this problem a possible solution is to have different teams of developers who are fluent in a specific programming language to port an application to a specific platform. Instead of this traditional approach, organizations can use multiplatform or multi-paradigm cross-compiler based languages. The term "multiplatform" is used to refer source-source compilation, that is to say, the source code of these languages can be compiled into the source code of another programming language. Haxe is a good example of multiplatform languages. It allows using the same code to deploy an application on multiple platforms such as iOS, BlackBerry or Android. Specifically, it is an open-source high-level multiplatform programming language and compiler that can produce applications and source code for many different platforms from a single code-base (Haxe, 2019).

Frequently, the development of software component and applications aligned to mobile technologies requires adapting existing non-mobile software to different mobile platforms. For instance, there exist valuable software components and libraries implemented in C/C++or Java that need to be adapted for mobile developments. There is the need to define systematic, reusable migration processes with a high degree of automation that reduce risks, time and costs of the cross-platform development. Novel technical frameworks for information integration, tool interoperability, and reuse can help to achieve these goals. Specifically, Model- Driven Engineering (MDE) is a software engineering discipline which emphasizes the use of models and model transformations to raise the abstraction level and the degree of automation in software development (Brambilla et al., 2017). Productivity and some aspects of software quality such as maintainability or interoperability are goals of MDE.

Model Driven Developments (MDD) refer to forward engineering processes that use models as primary development artifacts. A specific realization of MDD is the Model-Driven Architecture (MDA) proposed by the Object Management Group (OMG) (MDA, 2019). Models, metamodels and model transformations play a major role in MDA. The MDA processes can be seen through a sequence of model transformations at different abstraction levels. A transformation is a process of converting a source model that conforms to a source metamodel in a target model that conforms to a target metamodel. The essence of MDA is Meta Object Facility (MOF), an OMG standard for defining metamodels that provides the ability to design and integrate semantically different artifacts in a unified way (MOF, 2016).

The OMG Architecture-Driven Modernization Task Force (ADMTF) is developing a set of specifications and promoting industry consensus on modernization. ADM is defined as "*the process of understand and evolve existing software assets for the purpose of software improvement, modifications, interoperability, refactoring, restructuring, reuse, porting, migration, translation, integration, service-oriented architecture deployment*" (ADM, 2019).

MDE progresses in the direction of achieving to develop software as reliable as any other engineering product, however, its impact on the software industrialization is limited. The main reasons are due, on the one hand, to a lack of repositories that contain reliable metamodels of the programming languages, and transformations between the different metamodels. It is worth considering that, MDE developers, instead of needing CASE tools to support the development on specific platforms, need to reuse metamodels and transformations. The incipient degree of progress in the specification of them requires that the developer, in general, must build them from scratch. This implies additional costs and time involved in these activities that must be compared with the total benefit. In addition, it is important to note that the construction of a metamodel should be considered critical development since the instances of a metamodel (models) must be reliable but currently, it is not focused in this way.

On the other hand, Model-driven approaches were broadcast emphasizing on processes viewed as a sequence of transformations between metamodels defined through the official standards. However, it is convenient to have a more flexible vision of MDE that allows integrating software developed from other frameworks or tools that have been tested through its use for several years and software developers prefer to continue using them. For example, software developers prefer to use multiplatform languages over model-driven developments that require defining metamodels and transformations for all multiple mobile platforms. Integrating multiplatform languages to MDE developments for the modernization of software would not imply defining metamodels and transformations for all the platforms it supports, but only for the multiplatform language.

Metamodeling is crucial in Model-Driven processes. It is important to formalize and reason about MOF metamodels and we propose to exploit the strong background achieved by the community of formal methods. Formal methods provide systematic and rigorous techniques to reduce ambiguities and inconsistencies in software development. Within the next few decades, tools based on verification will be as useful and widespread for software development as they are today in critical systems (Beckert and Hahnle, 2014). Behind the specifications and formal methods exists a community that has developed theories, languages, methods, and tools, but the software industry does not take advantage of them, in particular, to effectively address the software crisis . There is already a substantial body of research, tools and case studies demonstrating that it is possible to develop software as reliable as any other engineering product. To enhance the software industry, artifact analysis tools that support novel combinations of code analysis techniques, model checking, testing and theorems provers are emerging (Beckert & Hahnle, 2014).

In this chapter, we describe a lightweight MDE approach based on the ADM standards. In this context, a lightweight process is the one that leaves open the possibility to fall back to the traditional methodology without model-driven standards. It is based on the integration of cross-platform frameworks, and formal methods with ADM. First, an infrastructure for the definition of reliable metamodels that integrates semi-formal and formal specifications based on algebraic specifications of metamodels is analyzed. Next, an integration of ADM standards with cross- platform development for the migration of desktop software to mobile platforms through the multiplatform language Haxe is described. A repertory of new metamodels and transformation necessary to adapt object-oriented software to different mobile platform through Haxe is presented. Besides, the chapter compares MDE software migration versus traditional migration processes as well as it describes the existing challenges to achieve the results in real projects in the scientific and industrial field.

BACKGROUND

Model Driven Engineering (MDE) is a software development approach that focuses on the use of models to define software development processes with a high degree of automation starting from reusable transformations between models that conform to metamodels. The underlying idea in MDE is that software development can be broken down into standardized, highly automated activities that can mass produce software applications reducing costs, development time and risks.

Different acronyms are associated with model- driven developments: MBE (Model Based Engineering), MDE (Model Driven Engineering), MDD (Model Driven Development), MDA (Model-Driven Architecture), MDSM (Model Driven Software Modernization) and ADM (Architecture Driven Modernization).

MBE is the branch of software engineering in which software models play an important role, being the basis of development. However, there is no direct link between the models and the generated software precisely defined through transformations.

MDE can be viewed as a subset of MBE. It is the branch of software engineering in which processes are driven by models, i.e. models are the primary artifacts of different software processes. MDE has emerged as a new software engineering discipline which emphasizes the use of models and model transformations to raise the abstraction level and the degree of automation in software development. Productivity and some aspects of the software quality such as maintainability or interoperability are goals of MDE.

MDD refers to forward engineering processes that use models as primary development artifacts. A specific realization of MDD is MDA (MDA, 2014). The outstanding ideas behind MDA are, separating the specification of the system functionality from its implementation on specific platforms, managing the software evolution from abstract models to implementations. Models play a major role in MDA, which distinguishes at least:

- Computation Independent Model (CIM), a model that describes a system from the computation independent viewpoint
- Platform-Independent- Model (PIM), a model with a high level of abstraction that is independent of any independent technology,
- Platform-Specific-Model (PSM) a tailored model to specify the system in terms of the implementation constructs available in one specific platform

The Unified Modeling Language (UML) combined with the Object Constraint Language (OCL) is the most widely used way for writing PIM and PSMs.

An MDA process focuses on the automatic transformation of different models that conform to MOF metamodel, the standard for defining metamodels in the context of MDA (MOF, 2016). It provides the ability to design and integrate semantically different languages such as general-purpose languages, DSLs and modeling languages in a unified way. MOF can be considered the essence of MDA allowing different kinds of artifacts from multiple technologies to be used together in an interoperable way. MOF provides two metamodels EMOF (Essential MOF) and CMOF (Complete MOF). EMOF favors the simplicity of implementation over expressiveness. The OMG standard related to model transformation is the MOF 2.0 Query, View, Transformation (QVT) metamodel (QVT, 2016).

In the context of ADM, a set of modernization specifications is developed. ADMTF is developing a set of standards of which we are interested in KDM (Knowledge Discovery Metamodel) and ASTM (Abstract Syntax Tree Metamodel) (ASTM, 2019) (KDM, 2019). KDM is a metamodel for knowledge discovery in software that allows representing information related to existing software assets, their associations, and operational environments regardless of the implementation programming language and runtime platform. KDM is the foundation for software modernization representing entire enterprise software systems, not just code. ASTM is a specification for modeling elements to express abstract syntax trees. KDM and ASTM are two complementary modeling specifications. KDM establishes a specification that allows representing semantic information about a software system, whereas ASTM establishes a specification for representing the source code syntax by means of AST (Abstract Syntax Tree) in a representation that is sharable among multiple tools. ASTM acts as the lowest level foundation for modeling software within the OMG ecosystem of standards, whereas KDM serves as a gateway to the higher-level OMG models.

MDSM is a particular form of reengineering for the technological and functional evolution of legacy systems that begins to be identified in the early 21st century (Brambilla et al., 2017). It is based on model-driven processes of reverse engineering, restructuring and forward engineering. Software reengineering distinguishes different levels of analysis and provides foundations for logical transformations at different abstraction levels, especially for transformations that can be of different types: T2M (Text-to-Model), M2M (Model-to-Model), or M2T (Model-to-Text).

The Eclipse Modeling Framework (EMF) was created for facilitating system modeling and the automatic generation of Java code (EMF, 2019) (Steinberg et al., 2009). EMF started as an implementation of MOF resulting Ecore, the EMF metamodel comparable to EMOF. EMF has evolved starting from the experience of the Eclipse community to implement a variety of tools and to date is highly related to MDD. In this context, the subproject Model to Model Transformation (MMT), hosts model-to-model transformation languages. Transformations are executed by transformation engines that are plugged into the Eclipse Modeling infrastructure. For instance, Atlas Transformation Language (ATL) is a model transformation language and toolkit that provides ways to produce a set of target models from a set of source models (ATL, 2019). Another subproject is Acceleo, which is an implementation of the Model-to-Text (M2T) transformation standard of the OMG for EMF-based models (Acceleo, 2019). Acceleo is used in forward engineering processes.

Today, the most complete technology that support ADM is MoDisco, which provides a generic and extensible framework to facilitate the development of tools to extract models from legacy systems and use them on use cases of modernization. As an Eclipse component, MoDisco can integrate with plugins or technologies available in the Eclipse environment (Modisco, 2019) (Bruneliere et al., 2014). In particular, the ASTM specification mainly includes the following metamodels:

- Generic Abstract Syntax Tree Metamodel (GASTM), a generic set of language modeling elements common across numerous languages establishes a common core for language modeling.
- Language Specific Abstract Syntax Tree Metamodels (SASTM) for particular languages such as Ada, C, Fortran and Java, that are modeled in MOF or MOF compatible forms.
- Proprietary Abstract Syntax Tree Metamodels (PASTM), that express ASTs for languages such as Ada, C and COBOL modeled in formats that are not consistent with MOF, the GSATM, or SASTM and define the minimum conformance standards needed to support model interchange.

In particular, C++ is one of the most commonly used programming language in science and engineering domains and numerous legacy software components written in C++ require to be modernized. EMF4CPP is the first step at providing a set of tools for MDD in C++ as an alternative to the Eclipse tools for Java (EMF4CPP, 2016). It is a C++ implementation and type mapping for the EMF core, the Ecore metamodel. The main facilities provided by EMF4CPP are to generate C++ code from Ecore metamodels and to parse and serialize models and metamodels from and into XMI documents (Jäger et al., 2016). However, an implementation of a MOF-compliant C++ metamodel is necessary for other MDE processes, in particular ADM (e.g., reverse engineering or software modernization).

Multiplatform Development

Today, one of the major challenges for software developers is dealing with the rapid proliferation of mobile platforms that entails the high cost, technical complexity, and risk of targeting development to a wide spectrum of platforms. Taking into account the diversity of platforms, which are also in a dizzying evolution, it is practically intractable defining as many metamodels and transformations as mobile platforms exist. To address this problem a possible solution is to have different teams of developers who are fluent in specific programming language to port an application to a specific platform. Instead of this traditional approach, organizations can use multiplatform or multi-paradigm cross-compiler based languages. In this context, the term "*multiplatform*" is used to refer source-source compilation, that is to say, the source code of these languages can be compiled into source code of other programming language. In this direction, the Haxe language emerges as an open-source high-level multiplatform programming language and compiler that can produce applications and source code for many different platforms from a single code-base.

The Haxe programming language is a high level programming language that mixes features of object oriented languages and functional ones. It is similar (but not pure) to object-oriented languages. Haxe includes a set of common functions that are supported across all platforms, such as numeric data types, text, arrays, binary and some common file formats (Haxe, 2019).

To date, Haxe supports nine target languages which allow for different use-cases: JavaScript, Neko, PHP, Python, C++, ActionScript3, Flash, Java and, C# and test your app on each platform. The Haxe language can be used in a variety of domains such game development, web development and mobile development. In particular, it facilitates mobile development sharing code between key platforms and accessing native functionality without sacrificing performance. The idea behind Haxe is to allow developers choose the best platform for a specific development. To achieve this, it provides a standardized language, a standard library that works the same on all platforms and platform specific libraries that allow accessing the full API for a given platform from Haxe.

Related Work

The first results that address MDE and mobile developments are specifically linked to MDD. A survey of MDD approaches for mobile applications is presented in (Umuhoza and Brambilla, 2016). Various authors describe the challenges of mobile software development. A DSL (Domain Specific Language), named MobDSL, to generate applications for multiple mobile platforms is described in (Kramer, Clark and Oussena, 2010). They perform the domain analysis on two cases in the Android and iPhone platforms. This analysis allows inferring the basic requirements of the language defined by MobDSL. From another angle, Dehlinger and Dixon (2011) highlight creating user interfaces for different kinds of mobile devices, providing reusable applications across multiple mobile platforms, designing context-aware applications and handling their complexity and, specifying requirements uncertainty. On the other hand, a proposal for supporting mobile application development by using models as inputs to an emulator is outlined at (Bowen and Hinze, 2011). The authors describe an MDD-based emulator for using in the design of graphical interfaces and interactions. They propose to transform functional behavior and requirement models with design restrictions into emulated applications. From another perspective, Acerbis et al.(2015) describe a comprehensive tool suite called WebRatio Mobile Platform for model-driven development of mobile applications. It is based on an extended version of OMG standard language called IFML (Interaction Flow Modeling Language) empowered with primitives tailored to mobile systems that enable specification of mobile-specific behaviors.

The following authors show integration of reverse engineering MDE. Favre (2010) describes a reverse engineering approach that fits with MDD. A framework to integrate different techniques that come from compiler theory, metamodeling and formal specification is presented. It emphasizes the use of static and dynamic analysis for generating MDA models. Fernández Candel et al. (2019) describe a model-driven reengineering approach for migrating PL/SQL triggers to Java-based on KDM to represent legacy code and traditional techniques to complement ADM. Test Driven Development (TDD) is used to incrementally develop model transformations that were written in Java instead of using some transformation language like ATL or QVT imperative. A systematic literature review on model-driven reverse engineering approach may be found at (Raibulet et al., 2017)

The following authors relate smartphones and mobile development with new technologies such as Cloud Computing and IoT. Islam and Want (2014) describes major trends affecting future smartphone design and use such as personal computers, the IoT, multimedia delivery, low power operation, wearable computing and context awareness. On the other hand, Ejarque, Miccsik and Badia (2015) present a solution for facilitating the migration of applications to the cloud, inferring the most suitable deployment model for the application and automatically deploying it in the available Cloud providers. The findings of experiments carried out to understand the impact of application characteristics, cloud and architecture and the android emulator used, on application performance when the application is augmented to the cloud, are shown at (Joshi et al., 2015). Gonzalez Garcia et al. (2015) define a domain-specific language (DSL) that allows specifying the coordination and communication between different types of smart objects.

Several works highlight research directions and challenges on the IoT. The spectrum of research needed to achieve IoT on a large scale requires research along with many different directions. Stankovic (2014) identifies five prominent research communities that involve the smart vision of the world: IoT, mobile computing, pervasive computing, wireless sensors, networks, and cyber-physical systems. Zanella et al. (2014) present a discussion of the IoT for smart cities. The authors describe a general reference framework for the design of an urban IoT. An implementation of an urban IoT that has been realized in the city of Padova is described. Key research topics are enumerated and research problems within these topics are discussed. Miranda et al. (2015) propose an infrastructure that supports the evolution from the "Internet of Things" to the "Internet of People" (IoP). The IoP is used in the sense of bringing the IoT closer to people, for easily integrate them and exploit its benefits.

The following articles are directly related to the chapter proposal. A reengineering process that integrates traditional reverse engineering techniques such as static and dynamic analysis with MDA is presented at (Améndola and Favre, 2013). The article describes a case study that shows how to move CRM (Customer Relationship Management) applications from desktop to mobile platforms. The proposal was validated in the open source application platform Eclipse, EMF, EMP, ATL, and Android platform. Diaz Bilotto and Favre (2016) describe a migration process from Java to mobile platforms through the multiplatform language Haxe. A framework for modernizing desktop software based on MDE is presented at (Favre, 2018).

INTEGRATING MDE WITH FORMAL METHODS AND CROSS-PLATFORM DEVELOPMENT

This section describes the main focus of the article: the construction of metamodels starting from the integration of MOF-compliant metamodels and formal specification, and a migration process of non-mobile software to different mobile platforms based on MDE, ADM, and Cross-Platform Development.

Formalizing MOF-Compliant Metamodels

An essential aspect to apply this approach is to have reliable definitions of metamodels. It is important to formalize and reason about MOF metamodels and we propose to exploit the strong background achieved by the community of formal methods. It is important to remark that the instantiation of a metamodel produces models, which in turn are instantiated. So, having errors in a metamodel leads to having errors in its model instances. Besides, a model can be well-formed but still be incorrect. A combination of MOF metamodeling and formal specification can help metadesigners to address these issues.

A major obstacle for specifying metamodels MOF or Ecore is that they must master two different languages: UML for expressing class diagram that capture the structure of the domain and the OCL language for expressing associated semantic (OCL, 2014). Cadavid et al. (2015) observe that, in general, the metamodels concentrate the specifications in a subset of concepts, most of them are loosely coupled to the underlying structure. Most MDE semiformal metamodels do not have support for typing metamodels and the notion of polymorphism at the metamodel level is imprecise due to the type of a metamodel is not defined. These are important limitations regards to the generation of valid instances to test models transformations and to reuse models, metamodels and model transformations.

To address these problems, a formal metamodeling language called Nereus' was defined. Formal methods offer rigor and precision while reducing ambiguity and inconsistency. Nereus allows specifying MOF or Ecore metamodels and reasoning about them. A detailed description of Nereus may be found at (Favre, 2009) (Favre and Duarte, 2016). A set of Nereus tools to make formal metamodeling feasible in practice was developed. The semantic of Nereus was given in the CASL language that can be linked with Automatic Theorem Provers (ATP) provided by Hets (Mossakowski, Maeder, and Codescu, 2019).

The process of meta-model construction is based on the analysis of fragments of models (examples of concrete instances) from which a metamodel is induced. These fragments focus on some interest aspects of the metamodel. In a first step, they are represented as an Ecore metamodel complemented with textual specifications in *OCLinEcore* Editor that overcomes some limitations of the Ecore Editor, for instance, Ecore does not detect syntactic and semantic errors in OCL constraints. Another advantage is that *OCLinEcore* works with text representations instead of using *XMI* (XML Metadata Interchange), allowing greater modifiability, readability and better integration with versioning tools. A metaclass is created for each object of a different type (if it does not exist) and the attributes and operations and their restrictions are identified. Then, the different relationships between metaclasses are identified. The metamodel is subsequently transformed into a Nereus metamodel. The formal specification is analyzed by using the analyzer of Nereus and is modified according to the results of the translation process with the goal of obtaining a syntactically correct specification that, through its integration with CASL could be formally validated.

The typical flow with formal tools that is applied to analyze the specifications of metamodel is shown in Figure 1. In the first step, a semiformal metamodel is transformed into a Nereus specification. The formal specification is analyzed and modified according to the results of the translation process. The goal is to obtain a syntactically correct specification that, through its integration with CASL language can be formally validated. Nereus allows us to experiment both defining metamodels for DSLs from scratch, and analyzing fragments of already defined metamodels, detecting inconsistencies and proposing solutions.

Figure 1. Constructing metamodels

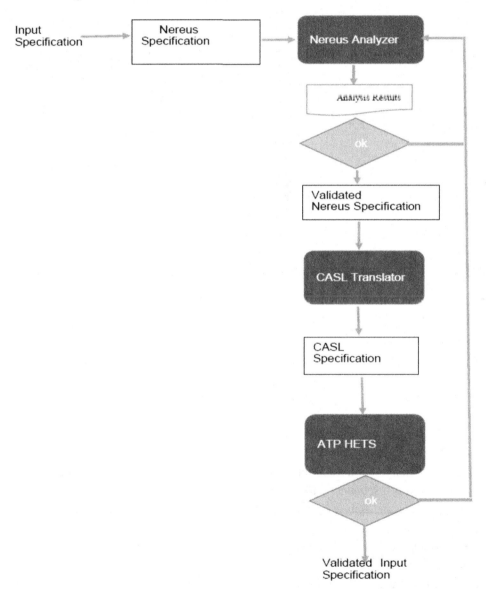

In the context of this work, the Haxe metamodel and C/C++ metamodel were defined. Figure 2 partially shows the C / C ++ metamodel (on the left) and the Haxe metamodel (on the right).

Figure 2. C/C++ and Haxe Metamodels

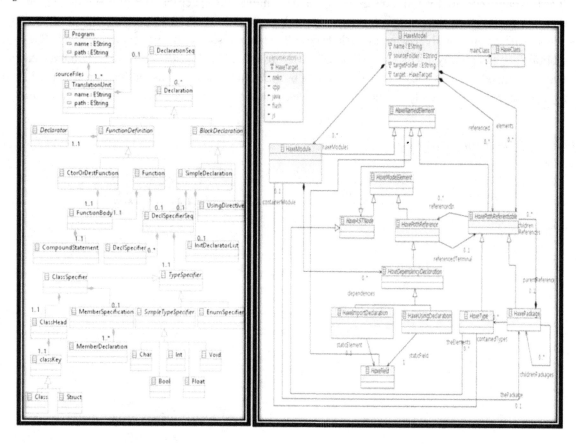

The C++ metamodel conforms to Ecore. The root metaclass is *Program* that represents a C++ program, which owns source files, instances of *TranslationUnit*. A translation unit contains declarations such as block declaration, function definitions, template declarations, among others. A *SimpleDeclaration*, instance of *Block-Declaration*, has a *DeclSpecifierSeq* that is a sequence of *DeclSpecifiers* which refers to a declaration specifiers and a type specifier. In addition, a simple declaration has an *InitDeclaratorList* containing a variable declaration list that is a list of specifiers and the name of a variable and its corresponding initialization. A *FunctionDefinition* has a *Declarator* containing the function identifier and the parameter list. *Function* and *CtorOrDestFunction*, instances of *FunctionDefinition*, have a body that contains compound statements such as declarations, iterations, and selections. In addition, a *Function* has a *DeclSpecifierSeq* that is a sequence of *DeclSpecifiers* such as function specifiers and a type specifier. *TypeSpecifier* subclasses are *SimpleTypeSpecifier*, *ClassSpecifier* and *EnumSpecifier* among others. A *ClassSpecifier* has a *ClassHead* containing the class key (class or struct) and a *MemberSpecification* that contains *MemberDeclarations* such as variables, function declarations, function definitions, constructors, destructor and template members.

Also, the Haxe metamodel was defined in Ecore. The main metaclasses of the Haxe metamodel are those that allow specifying an application using Haxe as language. One of the main metaclasses of the metamodel is *HaxeModel* that serves as element container used to describe an application and store additional information on it, for example, some options of compilation and different metaclasses for modeling such as modules, classes and packages. The metaclasses used directly by *HaxeModel* are *HaxeModule* and *HaxePathReferentiable*. Starting from the relations *HaxeModules, referenced* and *elements*, the class *HaxeModel* allows storing different information. Relation *HaxeModules* allows accessing the different Haxe modules used in the project. Through relation *elements,* it is possible to access the different elements of the package tree. Relation *referenced* provides access to elements which are referenced in the project but are not defined completely. In the case of relations and referenced elements, the type used is *HaxePathReferentiable*, which is the parent type of metaclasses such as*HaxeType and HaxePackage*. The Haxe language includes different kind of types such as class (the type's class and interface), function, abstract type, enumeration, and anonymous structures. A full description of both, the C/C++ and Haxe metamodels may be found at (Duthey and Spina, 2016).

Migrating Software to Mobile Platforms

A process to migrate legacy code to different mobile platforms based on ADM standards and cross platform development is described. The migration process follows model-driven development principles: all artifacts involved in the process can be viewed as models that conform to Ecore meta-metamodel, the process itself can be viewed as a sequence of model-to-model transformations and the extracted information is represented in a standard way through Ecore metamodels. For each transformation, source and target metamodels are specified. A source metamodel defines the family of source models to which transformations can be applied. A target metamodel characterizes the generated models. Different kind of transformations such as T2M, M2M, and M2T are distinguished in the steps of reverse engineering, refactoring/restructuring, and forward engineering. Figure 3 summarizes the proposed process.

The first step is the reverse engineering of source code to obtain the abstract syntax tree of the code and consists of two stages:

- Generating the first model of the code by using a model injector. This model conforms to the source code metamodel, such as C++ and Java. The obtained model could be refactored to reorganize and modify the syntactic elements and to improve the design. The refactoring is implemented as a model-to-model transformation whose source and target models are instances of source code metamodel.
- Generating the abstract syntax tree model, instance of the GASTM metamodel, from the model obtained in the previous stage by an ATL model-to-model transformation.

In this first step of the process, an injector and a transformation to obtain the GASTM model must be implemented for each language, whereas the sequence of transformations involved in the followings steps of the migration process is independent of the language of the legacy code.

The second step generates the KDM model. This process is carried out by means of an ATL model-to-model transformation that takes as input a model conforming to the GASTM metamodel and produces a model conforming to the KDM metamodel.

The advantage of this intermediate step is that starting from the KDM model it is possible to obtain high-level models such as UML class diagrams, activity diagrams and use cases diagrams. These models could be refactored and be the starting point for generating code. This step is common for each source language.

Figure 3. The migration process

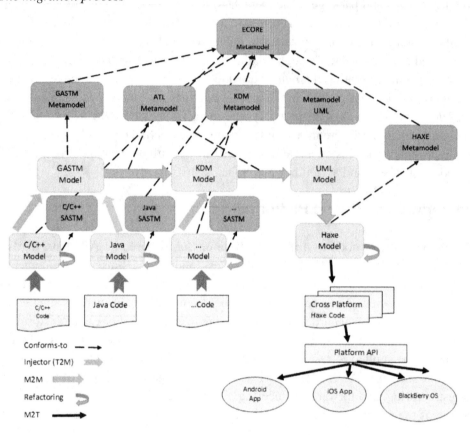

UML models generated from KDM are transformed to UML models for the Haxe platform from which it is possible to generate Haxe code using M2T transformations expressed in Acceleo (Acceleo, 2019).

Given that Modisco provides T2M transformations for Java, we will discuss the stages for the migration of C ++ code to different mobile platforms.

The first transformation extracts an AST model specific to C++ from code. To carry out this task, we constructed a model injector by using EMFText (EMFText, 2019). To generate this injector, EMFText requires the language metamodel and the concrete syntax specification. In our approach, to generate the injector we first specified the C++ metamodel based on the C++ grammar. Then, we specified the concrete syntax that defines the textual representation of all metamodel concepts. Taking these specifications, the EMFText generator derives an advanced text editor that uses a parser and printer to parse language expressions to EMF models or to print EMF models to languages expressions respectively.

The second transformation takes as input the model obtained in the previous step and release a generic AST model conforming to the GASTM metamodel. This transformation specifies the way to produce GASTM projects (target) from C++ programs (source). The previous transformations are dependent on the legacy code language, that is, the model injector and the transformation to obtain the generic AST model are dependent on C++. In contrast to the previous stage, the sequence of transformations from GASTM models to Haxe models is independent of the language.

Haxe allows writing mobile applications that target all major mobile platforms in a straightforward way. The generated code is syntactically correct, although, it does not compile on other platforms without doing changes due to the code refers to proprietary technologies of C++. To run on mobile environments, these technologies can be replaced with OpenFL and HaxeUI (that is an open-source, multi-platform application-centric user interface framework designed for Haxe and OpenFL) (OPEN FL, 2019)

SOLUTIONS AND RECOMMENDATIONS

The previous sections describe two main contributions:

- The migration of object-oriented software to various platforms based on the integration of ADM with Haxe.
- The construction of metamodels based on the integration of semiformal and formal specifications.

With respect to the first contribution, it is possible to migrate the logic of software applications and run them on mobile platforms without having to completely rewrite them. Due to the fact that the objective of the migration is not only "compile" an application in a mobile platform but also to create a fully functional version of the application using quality criteria, small adjustments had to be made.

MDE approach based on ADM provides benefits with respect to ad-hoc migration. One of the benefits is to increase productivity in software development due to the automation that is introduced in the generation of artifacts. In MDE migration projects is more cost-effective when the same process must be repeated frequently as the case of migrations to different platforms.

Another benefit of the process is its independence from source and target technologies. In our approach, the intermediate models act as decoupling elements between source and target technologies. Independence is achieved with injectors and, M2M and M2T transformations. Besides, in a transformation sequence, models could be an extension point to incorporate new stages, for instance, to connect with different multiplatform languages. Model transformations allow developers to concentrate on conceptual aspects of the relations between models and then to delegate most of the migration process to the transformation rules, whereas in the brute-force redevelopment, developers need to migrate by hand the legacy systems, making over and over again the same task.

In the context of our proposal, Haxe allows using the same code to deploy an application on multiple mobile platforms. The migration of object-oriented software to mobile platforms is achieved through the definition of a metamodel for Haxe and a single M2M transformation, delegating the integration with different mobile platforms to Haxe, that is, the evolution of existing platforms or the integration of new mobile platforms is considered a goal of Haxe.

The following limitations our approach were observed. The set of metamodels and discovers that can be used is limited. In our approach, it was necessary to define metamodels for the C / C ++ and Haxe languages and, a discoverer for C/C ++. However, the cost of preliminary activities could be recovered in later developments.

With respect to the second contribution, a metamodeling framework based on MOF and the algebraic formalism that focuses on automatic proofs and tests was provided. The central components of our approach are the definition of the formal language Nereus closed to MOF and the development of tools for formal metamodeling: the Nereus analyzer and the Nereus-to-CASL translator.

FUTURE RESEARCH DIRECTIONS

Figure 3 shows the essential activities to migrate non-mobile software to various mobile platforms. The different stages were validated in medium-scale developments. However, each stage requires more research and experimentation to show the real impact on larger scale developments.

A semiautomatic tool that takes as its starting point a C++ project and produces one written in Haxe, in addition to the generated intermediate files, was developed to prove model transformations. The tool is semi-automatic because it requires additional actions on the Haxe code to make it fully functional (Duthey and Spina, 2016). It is also still a challenge to migrate the visual part if the graphical interfaces are linked to specific libraries. The tool has been used in the migration of games such as Tetris and medium-scale software applications.

Also, it remains to analyze the generation of Haxe code from UML models more deeply. Considering that from KDM it is possible to generate UML models at the PIM level and that currently, CASE MDA / UML tools do not support multiplatform languages it is necessary to move from the stage of validation of transformations through prototypes to a real integration with existing CASE tools, either commercial or free.

An important contribution was to achieve an infrastructure to define metamodels rigorously. It remains to be completed the integration between formal metamodels and Ecore metamodels through the automatic generation of Ecore metamodels from Nereus metamodels.

CONCLUSION

An ADM approach for migrating non-mobile software to different mobile platforms was described. It takes advantage of tools emerged in the cross-platform and formal methods communities. The transformation to different platforms is achieved with the definition of a metamodel for Haxe. It is important to note that was not necessary to define metamodels for all the languages and platforms supported by it, as it would have been necessary in order to realize a "pure" MDE development.

An infrastructure for the definition of metamodels based on the integration of semi-formal and formal specifications was described. It was validated with the definition of two metamodels: the Haxe metamodel and C/C++ metamodel, previously non-existent.

Another contribution to the MDE community is the definition of a set of T2M, M2M and M2T transformations that support the migration process and can be reused in other MDE processes. Considering that mobile application developers need frequently adapt software components and applications developed in languages such as Java or C/C++, the model-driven migration processes could be reused and the cost of preliminary activities would be recovered.

REFERENCES

Acceleo. (2019). *Obeo. Acceleo Generator*. Retrieved July 25, 2019 from http://www.eclipse.org/Acceleo/

Acerbis, R., Bongio, A., Brambilla, M., & Butti, S. (2015). *Model-Driven Development Based on OMG's IFML with WebRatio Web and Mobile Platform. In Engineering the Web in the Big Data Era* (Vol. 9114). Springer-Verlag.

ADM. (2019). *Architecture-driven modernization task force*. Retrieved July 25, 2019 from http://www.adm.org

Améndola, F., & Favre, L. (2013). Adapting CRM Systems for Mobile Platforms: An MDA Perspective. *International Journal of Computer & Information Science*, *14*(1), 31–40.

ASTM. (2011). *Abstract Syntax Tree Metamodel*, version 1.0, OMG Document Number: formal/2011-01-05. Retrieved July, 25, 2019 from http://www.omg.org/spec/ASTM

ATL. (2019). *Atlas Transformation Language Documentation*. Retrieved July 25, 2019 from http://www.eclipse.org/atl/documentation/

Beckert, B., & Hahnle, R. (2014, Jan.). Reasoning and Verification: State of the Art and Current Trends. *IEEE Intelligent Systems*, 20–29.

Bowen, J., & Hinze, A. (2011). Supporting mobile application development with model-driven emulation. *Journal of the ECEASST*, *45*, 1–5.

Brambilla, M., Cabot, J., & Wimmer, M. (2017). *Model-Driven Software Enginneering in Practice. In Synthesis Lectures on Software Engineering* (2nd ed.). Morgan & Claypool Publishers.

Bruneliere, N., Cabot, J., Dupé, G., & Madiot, F. (2014). MoDisco: A Model Driven Reverse Engineering Framework. *Information and Software Technology*, *56*(8), 1012–1032. doi:10.1016/j.infsof.2014.04.007

Cadavid, J., Combemale, B., & Baudry, B. (2015). An analysis of metamodeling practices for MOF and OCL. *Computer Languages, Systems & Structures*, *41*, 42–65. doi:10.1016/j.cl.2015.02.002

Dehlinger, J., & Dixon, J. (2011). Mobile application software engineering: Challenges and research directions. In *Proceedings of the Workshop on Mobile Software Engineering* (pp. 29-32). Berlin: Springer-Verlag.

Diaz Bilotto, P., & Favre, L. (2016). Migrating JAVA to Mobile Platforms through HAXE: An MDD Approach. In A. M. Cruz & S. Paiva (Eds.), *Modern Software Engineering Methodologies for Mobile and Cloud Environments* (pp. 240–268). IGI Global. doi:10.4018/978-1-4666-9916-8.ch013

Duthey, M., & Spina, C. (2016). *Migrating C/C++ to mobile platforms through MDD* (Undergraduate Thesis). Computer Science Department, Universidad Nacional del Centro de la Provincia de Buenos Aires, Argentina.

Ejarque, J., Micsik, A., & Badia, R. (2015). Towards Automatic Application Migration to Clouds. In *Proceedings IEEE 8th Int. Conf. on Cloud Computing (CLOUD)* (pp. 25-32). New York: IEEE.

EMF4CPP. (2016). *What is EMF4CPP?* Retrieved July 25 from https://code.google.com/archive/p/emf4cpp/

EMF. (2019). *Eclipse Modeling Framework (EMF)*. Retrieved July 25, 2019 from http://www.eclipse.org/modeling/emf/

EMFText. (2019). Retrieved July 25, 2019 from www.emftext.org

Favre, L. (2009). A Formal Foundation for Metamodeling. In *Proceedings of 14th Ada-Europe International Conference. Lecture Notes in Computer Science* (Vol 5570, pp.177-191). Berlin: Springer-Verlag. 10.1007/978-3-642-01924-1_13

Favre, L. (2010). *Model Driven Architecture for Reverse Engineering Technologies: Strategic Directions and System Evolution. Hershey, PA*: IGI Global. doi:10.4018/978-1-61520-649-0

Favre, L. (2018). A Framework for Modernizing Non-Mobile Software: A Model-Driven Engineering Approach. In *Protocols and Applications for the Industrial Internet of Things* (pp. 192–224). IGI Global. doi:10.4018/978-1-5225-3805-9.ch007

Favre, L., & Duarte, D. (2016). Formal MOF Metamodeling and Tool Support. In *Proceedings of the 4th International Conference on Model-Driven Engineering and Software Development. MODELSWARD 2016* (pp. 99-110). Roma, Italy: SCITEPRESS.

Fernández Candel, C. J., García Molina, J., Bermúdez Ruiz, F. J., Hoyos Barceló, J. R., Sevilla Ruiz, D., & Cuesta Viera, B. J. (2019). Developing a model-driven reengineering approach for migrating PL/SQL triggers to Java: A practical experience. *Journal of Systems and Software, 151*(May), 38–64. doi:10.1016/j.jss.2019.01.068

González García, C., & Espada, J. (2015). MUSPEL: Generation of Applications to Interconnect Heterogeneous Objects Using Model-Driven Engineering. In V. G. Díaz, J. M. C. Lovelle, & B. C. P. García-Bustelo (Eds.), *Handbook of Research on Innovations in Systems and Software Engineering* (pp. 365–385). IGI Global. doi:10.4018/978-1-4666-6359-6.ch015

Haxe. (2019). *The Haxe Language*. Retrieved July 25, 2019 from https://Haxe.org/

Hossain, S. F. A., Nurunnabi, M., Hussain, K., Saha, S. K., & Wang, S. (2019). Effects of variety-seeking intention by mobile phone usage on university students' academic performance. *Cogent Education, 6*(1), 1574692. doi:10.1080/2331186X.2019.1574692

Islam, N., & Want, R. (2014). Smarthphones: Past, present and future. *Pervasive Computing, 13*(4), 82–92. doi:10.1109/MPRV.2014.74

Jäger, S., Maschotta, R., Jungebloud, T., Wichmann, A., & Zimmermann, A. (2016). An EMF-like UML Generator for C++. In *Proceedings of the 4th International Conference on Model-Driven Engineering and Software Development (MODELSWARD 2016)*, (pp. 309-316). SCITEPRESS. 10.5220/0005744803090316

Joshi, P., Nivangune, A., Kumar, R., Kumar, S., Ramesh, R., Pani, S., & Chesum, A. (2015). Understanding the Challenges in Mobile Computation Offloading to Cloud through Experimentation. In *2nd ACM Int. Conf. on Mobile Software Engineering and Systems (MOBILESoft),* (pp. 158-159). Florence, Italy: ACM. 10.1109/MobileSoft.2015.43

KDM. (2016). *Knowledge Discovery Meta-Model (KDM), OMG Document Number: formal/2016-09-01.* Retrieved July, 25, 2019 from http://www.omg.org/spec/KDM/1.4

Kramer, D., Clark, T., & Oussena, S. (2010). MobDSL: A domain specific language for multiple mobile platform deployment. In *Proceedings of IEEE Int. Conf. on Networked Embedded Systems for Enterprise Applications (NESEA),* (pp. 1-7). Perth, Australia: IEEE. 10.1109/NESEA.2010.5678062

MDA. (2019). *The Model-Driven Architecture.* Retrieved July 25, 2019 from www.omg.org/mda/

Miranda, J., Makitalo, N., Garcia-Alonso, J., Berrocal, J., Mikkonen, T., Canal, C., & Murillo, J. (2015). From the Internet of Things to the Internet of People. *IEEE Internet Computing, 19*(2), 40–47. doi:10.1109/MIC.2015.24

MoDisco. (2019). *Model Discovery.* Retrieved July 25, 2019 from https://eclipse.org/MoDisco/

MOF. (2016). *Meta Object Facility (MOF) Core Specification, Version 2.5, OMG Document Number: formal/2016-11-01.* Retrieved July 25, 2019 from http://www.omg.org/spec/MOF/2.5.1/

Mossakowski, T., Maeder, C., & Codescu, M. (2019). *Hets User Guide, version 0.99.* Retrieved July 25, 2019 from http://www.informatik.unibremen.de/agbkb/forschung/formal_methods/CoFI/hets/

OCL. (2014). *OMG Object constraint language (OCL), version 2.4. OMG Document Number: formal/2014-02-03.* Retrieved July, 25, 2019 from http://www.omg.org/spec/OCL/2.4

OPEN FL. (2019). *OPEN FL 4.7.* Retrieved July 25, 2019 from http://www.openfl.org/

QVT. (2016). *QVT: MOF 2.0 query, view, transformation: Version 1.3.* OMG Document Number: formal/2016-06-03. Retrieved July 25, 2019 from http://www.omg.org/spec/QVT/1.3

Raibulet, C., Arcelli Fontana, F., & Zanoni, M. (2017). Model-Driven Reverse Engineering Approaches: A Systematic Literature Review. *IEEE Access: Practical Innovations, Open Solutions, 5,* 14516–14542. doi:10.1109/ACCESS.2017.2733518

Stankovic, J. (2014). Research Directions for the Internet of Things. *IEEE Internet of Things Journal, 1*(1), 3–9.

Steinberg, D., Budinsky, F., Paternostro, M., & Merks, E. (2009). *EMF: Eclipse Modeling Framework* (2nd ed.). Addison-Wesley.

Umuhoza, E., & Brambilla, M. (2016). Model Driven Development Approaches for Mobile Applications: A Survey. In *Proceedings of Mobile Web and Intelligent Information Systems - 13th International Conference, MobiWIS 2016* (pp. 93-107). Berlin: Springer. 10.1007/978-3-319-44215-0_8

Zanella, A., Bui, N., Castellani, A., Vangelista, L., & Zorzi, M. (2014). Internet of Things for Smart Cities. *IEEE Internet of Things Journal, 1*(1), 22–32. doi:10.1109/JIOT.2014.2306328

KEY TERMS AND DEFINITIONS

ADM (Architecture Driven Modernization): The process of understanding and evolving existing software assets of an existing system in the context of MDA.

ATL (Atlas Transformation Language): A model transformation language and toolkit developed on top of the Eclipse platform that provides ways to produce target models from source models.

Ecore Metamodel: The de-facto reference implementation of EMOF (Essential Meta-Object Facility), a subset of MOF. It is the core metamodel of EMF.

Haxe: An open-source toolkit based on a modern, high level, strictly typed programming language, a cross-compiler, a complete cross-platform standard library and ways to access each platform's native capabilities.

KDM (Knowledge Discovery Metamodel): The core metamodel of ADM, a language-independent metamodel for representing assets of software legacy.

Metamodeling: The process of generating a "model of models"; the essence of Model Driven Development approaches.

Mobile Technology: The technology used for cellular communication.

Model Transformation: A mechanism for automatically creating target models based on information contained in existing source models

Model-Driven Architecture (MDA): An initiative of the OMG for the development of software systems based on the separation of business and application logic from underlying platform technologies. It is an evolving conceptual architecture to achieve cohesive model-driven technology specifications.

Model-Driven Engineering: Software engineering discipline that emphasizes the use of models and model transformations to raise the abstraction level and the degree of automation in software development.

Software Migration: A kind of modernization for moving from the use of one operating environment to another operating environment that is, in most cases, thought to be better.

This research was previously published in the Encyclopedia of Information Science and Technology, Fifth Edition; pages 887-903, copyright year 2021 by Engineering Science Reference (an imprint of IGI Global).

Chapter 81
A Game Theoretic Approach for Quality Assurance in Software Systems Using Antifragility-Based Learning Hooks

Vimaladevi M.
Pondicherry Engineering College, India

Zayaraz G.
Pondicherry Engineering College, India

ABSTRACT

The use of software in mission critical applications poses greater quality needs. Quality assurance activities are aimed at ensuring such quality requirements of the software system. Antifragility is a property of software that increases its quality as a result of errors, faults, and attacks. Such antifragile software systems proactively accepts the errors and learns from these errors and relies on test-driven development methodology. In this article, an innovative approach is proposed which uses a fault injection methodology to perform the task of quality assurance. Such a fault injection mechanism makes the software antifragile and it gets better with the increase in the intensity of such errors up to a point. A software quality game is designed as a two-player game model with stressor and backer entities. The stressor is an error model which injects errors into the software system. The software system acts as a backer, and tries to recover from the errors. The backer uses a cheating mechanism by implementing software Learning Hooks (SLH) which learn from the injected errors. This makes the software antifragile and leads to improvement of the code. Moreover, the SLH uses a Q-Learning reinforcement algorithm with a hybrid reward function to learn from the incoming defects. The game is played for a maximum of K errors. This approach is introduced to incorporate the anti-fragility aspects into the software system within the existing framework of object-oriented development. The game is run at the end of every increment during the construction of object-oriented systems. A detailed report of the injected errors and the actions taken is output at the end of each increment so that necessary actions are incorporated into the actual software during the next iteration. This ensures at the end of all the iterations, the software is

DOI: 10.4018/978-1-6684-3702-5.ch081

immune to majority of the so-called Black Swans. The experiment is conducted with an open source Java sample and the results are studied selected two categories of evaluation parameters. The defect related performance parameters considered are the defect density, defect distribution over different iterations, and number of hooks inserted. These parameters show much reduction in adopting the proposed approach. The quality parameters such as abstraction, inheritance, and coupling are studied for various iterations and this approach ensures considerable increases in these parameters.

1. INTRODUCTION

Software applications are becoming more complex day by day and it is difficult to maintain code quality and manage the cost of the software development. Some of the factors that make this quality-cost balance a challenging task needs further discussion. They are the growing pressure on the software organizations, rise of the developmental costs, need to get the product to market quickly and accelerated development schedules. The most effective way to keep the development cost down is the minimization and the introduction of defects. The software bug cost of United States economy has increased from $59.5 billion to $1.1 trillion from 2002 to 2016. This increase in cost is due to the loss in revenue due to the software being unusable, payments to developers for bug fixing, loss in shareholder value, etc. Also, there are some indirect financial costs arising due to the problem of brand reputation and customer loyalty. The bug fixing process even interferes with other developments and enhancements for new functionality addition that ultimately affect the project schedule. It is critical to catch the defects early since, the cost of fixing the defects increases exponentially as the software progresses through the life cycle phases. From the report of National Institute of Standards and Technology (NIST), the increase in the bug fix follows the trend as shown in Table 1 (National Institute of Standards and Technology, 2002). Here, X is the normalized unit of cost and can be expressed in terms of person-hours.

Table 1. Cost of defect fixing

Design	1X
Implementation	5 X
Integration Testing	10 X
Customer Beta Testing	15 X
Post Product Release	30 X

Hence, there is an important need for proactive approaches to improve the overall quality and decrease the software development cost. This research work discusses such an arrangement to proactively detect defects by building antifragile characteristics into an object-oriented software within the existing software development framework. But this defect prevention is a challenging task. The operating environment and the kinds of failure and recovery of a software system are highly uncertain and are open ended. For example, an information report states that the Eclipse development environment runs on at least 5 million different machines. The developer foreseeing all possible failures is nearly impossible, so as the hard coding of all possible failure conditions, recovery conditions and recovery strategies. The programming style needs to be changed in order to overcome these unforeseen errors or surprises, called as Black swans (Taleb, 2008). The software systems are constantly exposed to randomness, shocks, disorders and stressors. There are lots of works that have come over the decade to ensure quality in critical software systems that make majority of the systems resilient and robust. But with much of the evolution and advancements in the software programming and the development methodologies, it is time to take the art of software development to the next level. The property called *Antifragility*, explained by Taleb in (Taleb, 2012), is explored in this work, which takes the software to one more step ahead in addition to resilience and robustness. A resilient resist the shock and stays the same; whereas the antifragile resists and gets better with such disorders. The antifragile loves disorder and learns from it to improve itself. This requirement poses a lot of challenges in programming such a system, which can learn from failures. Also, it is much better to incorporate this property into the software within the existing successful developmental model such as the Agile methods. This is preferred instead of designing a new process model, since these models are almost mature with its processes and standards in place. Thus, the research question RQ1 can be formulated as:

RQ1: How the "Antifragility" aspect can be introduced in software development within the existing Object-Oriented framework?

A game is a structured form of play played for an achievement or reward or sometimes purely for entertainment. A game can be used as a design tool in research methods to achieve certain goals. Game Theory applies mathematical models to study the strategies the players can make in a gaming environment. It is popularly used in fields such as economics, politics, and biology and in computer science. In computer science, game theory is widely used in Cloud Computing, network security, recommendation systems, and machine learning. Even though it has already been successfully applied in fields such as economics, the application of Game Theory to Software engineering problems is relatively new. The games are of different types such as two-player and N-player games, cooperative and non-cooperative games, simultaneous and sequential games, constant sum, zero sum, and non-zero sum games, etc. Considering the aim of making software antifragile, a two-player game theoretic approach is proposed which makes the software to learn from errors that are injected into the software system. Thus, the research question RQ2 is put forth as:

RQ2: How successfully the concepts of "Game Theory" can be used to build an Antifragile Object Oriented Software?

In order to upgrade to antifragility and achieve the strengths of game theory, a two-player game model is designed with a Stressor and Backer entities, which act as the players of the game. The stressor is interested in introducing errors into the system, whereas the backer defends those and learns from the introduced errors. The Stressor uses the architectural information of the software and the graph metrics to generate crucial defects. The Backer accomplishes its tasks by executing software Learning Hooks (SLH) which implements a Q-Learning algorithm. Even though, this type of approach can be considered one of the test-driven methodologies, it is different from the traditional testing phase, in which the testing is performed to validate specific, well-formed and small failures. Usually these types of antifragile stressors are designed to be incorporated in the production environment. But, in the proposed approach, they are introduced during development phase of object-oriented software, before the release of every increment. The game is run for all the iterations and the report of the errors introduced and actions taken are output for every run. This is helpful to plan for the next iteration. In case of any modification required in the code the developer reviews and makes decision before any changes is applied to the code. This approach is followed foreseeing the risk whether the system can fully recover from such disturbances and this method can outperform the losses. This proposal thus aims in introducing Antifragility within the existing framework of object-oriented software development. The Antifragile Software Manifesto (Russoa & Ciancarinia, 2016), is still in the inception, invites discussion from the software engineering community for its successful application.

To test the constructive benefits of the research questions RQ1 and RQ2, the proposal need to be validated for a sample project for increase in quality and reduction in the defects. Hence, the parameters need to be validated is twofold. The increase in quality need to be tested using major quality attributes namely abstraction, inheritance, and coupling. The important defect related parameters are defect density, defect distribution and number of hooks inserted per iteration. A considerable decrease in the defect related parameters is favored.

The rest of the article is organized as follows: Section 2 presents the motivation and related work. Section 3 gives the details of the proposed game structure. Section 4 furnishes the details of the simulation, results obtained and discussion on the results. Section 5 lists the contributions of this research work and Section 6 lists various threats to the validity of the work. Section 7 concludes the paper.

2. MOTIVATION

There are numerous techniques that are available for quality improvement in various stages of the software life cycle. Any quality assurance technique strives to achieve zero errors post release. In spite of all these constant and effective techniques, there are still some failures in the software that makes the software difficult to survive. There are various factors that make the software obsolete such as changes in the requirements and the operating environment, inefficient calculations and data, difficulty in using, understanding and maintaining the software, ageing of the software, market conditions, etc. (Leach, 2016). There are countless research techniques and ideas that are proposed to overcome these issues to some extent. Every technique has its own advantages and disadvantages. Irrespective of all these efforts, failures still exist in software products which are difficult to predict and avoid completely. Hence, there is a need to find an intelligent solution to counter and cope with these errors. In order to enable the software live with these uncertainties, an innovative methodology needs to be designed, which reinvents the process of software development and its usage.

Antifragility is such an emerging issue in software engineering which is beyond building robust and resilient systems. A system which is robust is resilient to errors to a certain threshold but will remain the same. An antifragile system is one, in addition to being robust, tries to improve when exposed to errors. The Antifragile Software Manifesto proposed in (Russoa & Ciancarinia, 2016) discusses some of the principles and the processes of an antifragile system. This research work is a step towards incorporating the concepts of antifragility into the existing framework of Object-Oriented Software Development. In this work, Anti-Fragility is also proposed as an Anti-Ageing solution to software systems. Fragile, Robust and Antifragile are defined as a triad in explaining the desirable properties of software. A fragile is one which is easily breakable to any disturbance. A robust system resists and withstands such shocks to some extent, but it remains the same. Antifragility is beyond resilience or robustness. The concepts of an Antifragile System are explained meticulously in (Taleb, 2012).

Antifragility is the negative of fragility. An antifragile system gets better by exposure to disorder, shock or uncertainties. An antifragile system is able to evolve its identity by learning from the disorder and by improving itself.

Game theory is becoming popular in the decision-making process in a cooperative or a competitive environment. It has been successfully applied in computer science in network security, scheduling problems, robotics, and interactions in cloud environment and in project management process to arrive at an optimal decision making. However, so far, its application is less in the field of software engineering and it is being widely studied and applied in solving optimization problems. In (Huang, Peled, schewe, & Wang, 2016), a game theoretic approach is proposed in order to validate the resilience of a software system against k dense errors. The authors have designed a two-player concurrent game model with the application of alternating-time μ-calculus (AMC) with an extension. An AMC is a special type of labeled transition systems, called concurrent game structures, where each transition is a result of set of decisions a player takes. The analysis has been modeled as a model checking problem for the software to be resilient to utmost k dense errors.

In (Kumar & Prabhakar, 2009), the authors applied game theory to find an optimal solution for software architecture design with conflicting quality attributes by applying the concepts of Nash equilibrium and Pareto optimality. Mehdi, Raza, & Hussain (2017), presents a game theory based trust model for VANETs by designing a two player attacker and defender model. The outcome of the game is presented using a payoff matrix and Nash equilibrium (NE) is applied to arrive at an optimal strategy for the attacker-defender scenario. Nash Equilibrium is a solution concept in game theory. Each player in a non-cooperative game settles on a strategy; such that no player has anything to gain by merely changing his own strategy constitutes a Nash Equilibrium (Jiang & Brown, 2009). Game Theory is a well studied area of mathematical modeling which finds its origin back in 1944 by John Van Neumann. The modern game theory was developed actively by John Nash during 1950 (Nash, 1951), who introduced the criterion for players' strategies popularly known as Nash Equilibrium. Since then, this topic has been regarded as an important tool and extensively studied in the field of economics.

In (Deng et al., 2014), a game theory framework is designed for a multi-criteria decision-making process in a competitive environment. This work employs Dempster – Shafer Theory (DST) to deal with uncertain information. DST is an approach of combining the degrees of belief from each independent evidence and provides a reasoning to calculate the overall probability of an event. A prisoner's dilemma situation in software development using extreme programming has been analyzed by Hazzan & Dubinsky (2005). Prisoner's dilemma is a popular example in game theory to illustrate the non-cooperative nature of two rational players.

As mentioned earlier, Game Theory models are being applied to identify solutions for decision making and optimization processes in computer science. Among which, the notable few works that applied Game Theoretic concepts to Software Engineering are discussed in this section. Software Refactoring is an important activity in software maintenance which helps in the improvement of the internal structure of the code, without modifying the external visible properties. In (Bavota et al., 2010), the authors apply the game theory solution for the Extract Class refactoring, by modeling as a two-player non-cooperative game. They proved the applicability of the game theory concepts for a refactoring problem.

In this research work, the characteristics of antifragility are introduced into the software using fault injection mechanism. This idea of fault injection in production has been used for a long time to ensure the reliability and thus to trust the system. In (Basiri et al., 2016), the authors explain a practice called "Chaos engineering" to verify the reliability of a distributed system with complex behavior and failure modes. Traditional software testing approaches are not sufficient to identify the potential failures of such complex distributed systems. The server and the clients are overloaded to test the different failure modes. Allspaw (2012) discusses a GameDay exercise that injects faults in production to anticipate similar behavior and understand the effects in future. This exercise forces failures to happen and even designing systems to fail to uncover the risks in the business.

Monperrus (2017) discusses the novel concept of called "software antifragility". The foundations of software antifragility, from classical fault tolerance to the most recent advances on automatic software repair and fault injection in production are explained. The concept of introducing antifragility into the software is viewed as the dream of building reliable system from unreliable components. In this paper also, the test-driven development is insisted in order to uncover the impact of the errors.

The summary of the literature so far is only the beginning of antifragile software engineering. It urges to devise a technique to build effective antifragile software within the existing developmental models. This would make the proposed method to be easily adopted for improved quality and reduced risk. Hence, the application of game theory for building antifragile software would be the most appropriate choice worth exploring.

3. SOFTWARE QUALITY GAME MODEL

To facilitate the explanation of the antifragility-based game theoretic approach, we start by reviewing the concepts of game theory. A software game can be played between two or more players. The game model designed in this research work is a two-player concurrent game. In a concurrent game, all the involved players make their moves simultaneously. The outcome of the game is jointly determined by the moves taken by all the players. Such a game model is significant in expressing a software system. The two players involved in the game designed in this work are the stressor and the backer entities. The stressor is responsible for injecting errors into the software system. The strategy of the stressor is to crash the system by injecting a greater number of errors by selecting critical modules of the software system. The software system acts as the backer, which tries to defend by catching the errors injected by the stressor and invoking appropriate error handlers. The game ends whenever the system crashes or a maximum of K errors are reached. When the system crashes, the backer fails and the stressor wins. In contrast to existing software, in which the error handlers are hard coded, the backer designed in this work executes a special function, called the Software Learning Hooks (SLH). For any uncaught errors, the backer executes these software Learning Hooks by cheating the stressor and improvises the software by making it immune to such type of errors in the future. Since the backer invokes SLHs for the unknown errors encountered, the software learns and improves continuously. Hence, the probability of the system crashing due to a greater number of different types of unknown errors is extremely less. This probability also depends on flooding a greater number of errors arriving at frequent intervals. This game model is run for k number of errors at the end of every iteration, before release to the customer. The SLH modifies the software at runtime temporarily in order to counter the effects of the injected errors. The SLH takes certain actions depending upon the type and nature of the incoming errors, by learning using Q-learning algorithm. The Q-leaning algorithm is a Reinforcement Learning (RL) algorithm, which learns by receiving a reinforcement or reward from the interacting environment. These RL algorithms are predominantly applied in game playing and control problems. This Q-learning algorithm used here is explained in detail in Section 3.2. Once the game is successfully run, a detailed report of the injected errors and the actions taken are output for the developers to perform the quality analysis and make decisions on whether any change in the code is required. This approach is followed instead of actually modifying the code, foreseeing the risk whether the system can completely handle the injected errors, any degradation that may occur due to changes done by the SLH, whether the changes over perform the cost of the software, etc. Hence, the decision is left to the developer of the software to make any changes, if required by analyzing the detailed report. The overall design and working of the game components are depicted in Figure 1.

Figure 1. Flow chart of the software game model

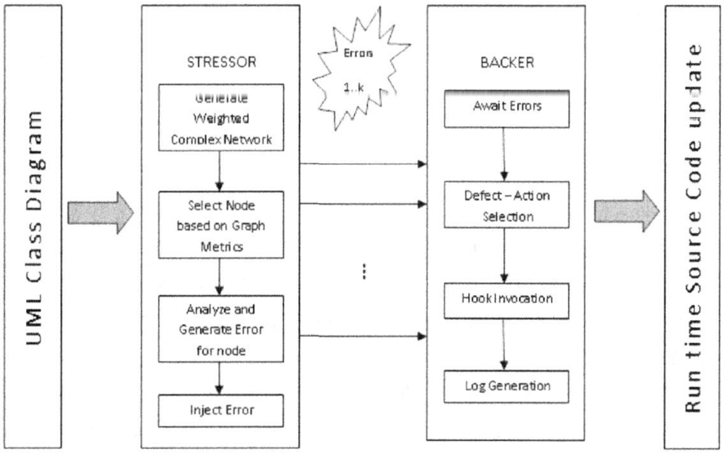

3.1. Stressor Design

In general, the component of stress is important for any system to operate and improve. From the perspective of biology, certain types of stress improve the state of the organism. All stressors are not treated equally, and some stresses certainly make an organism stronger. "Hormesis" as explained in biology is a condition where, a low dosage of toxin leads to beneficial effect of immunization to that toxin. As elucidated in (Taleb, 2012), Hormesis is close to Antifragility. The software is exposed to a series of stressors in order to make them immune against these types of perturbations. In order to achieve this task, a versatile design for the stressor is necessary. An UML class diagram is an important artifact in any software development where, various classes and their relationships are picturized. These UML class diagrams are converted into a weighted complex network. A weighted approach is chosen in order to preserve the information of the classes and the semantics of the relationships that exist between them. The weights are calculated based on the QMOOD (Bansiya & Davis, 2002) metrics of the class using LCOM4 and WMC and the relationships that exist between the classes are given a weightage based of an ordinal scale from 1 to 10 depending on the type of relationship between the participating classes (Chong & Lee, 2015; Pan, 2011). The approach used in (Chong & Lee, 2015) is adopted here for modeling a complex Object-Oriented Software System.

A sample complex network that consists of five classes with the weights assigned as per the relationships between the classes is shown in Figure 2.

Figure 2. A sample conversion of UML class diagram to complex network

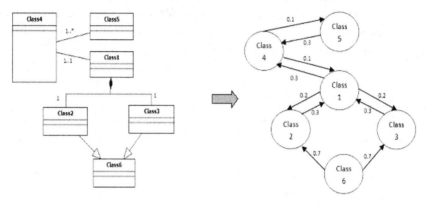

Once the software is modeled as a complex network, the application of Graph level metrics is much beneficial in exploiting the structural characteristics of the software system. These structural characteristics of a software network thus generated are closely related to the quality of the software system (Chong & Lee, 2015). The stressor is designed to select the classes based on its importance in the structure of the software and to introduce errors that cause defects. The classes are chosen based on the graph level metrics and its importance in fulfilling the requirements of the overall software. Metrics such as Average Weighted Degree, Average Shortest Path length and Betweenness Centrality are chosen to identify the most significant classes in the software and the error injection among these classes is given higher weightage.

A graph consists of a set of nodes and edges and represented as G(V,E). The degree of node is the total number of edges connected to the node. The in-degree is the number of incoming edges for a node, whereas, out-degree is the number of outgoing edges emanating from a node. The average degree of a network represents the average degree of the entire nodes in the network. For a weighted complex network, it is denoted as average weighted degree. The average shortest path length is the distance measure of a source to all other reachable destinations of the network. The betweenness centrality of a node measures the number of shortest paths that passes through a given node (Albert & Barabasi, 2002).

The operating states of the selected classes are analyzed in a fine-grained level for the injection of the error. The error generation rate of the stressor follows Poisson distribution. Poisson's process is one of the most widely used processes for modeling the probability of occurrence of random events at certain rate (Ross, 2009). The Poisson process is a random process which counts the number of random events that have occurred up to some point t in time. The random events must be independent of each other and occur with a fixed average rate. The probability mass function of a Poisson distribution with a random variable X and rate λ is given below:

$$P\left(X = k\right) = \frac{e^{-\lambda}\lambda^{k}}{k!}, where, k = 0,1,2,\ldots$$

The algorithm for the Stressor module is presented below.

Stressor Algorithm

Step Computation Details

1 Start Stressor

2 Input the source code zip format

Input UML files XML format

Initialize max error count k

3 Generate Graph parsing the UML file

4 Calculate graph metrics for every node in the graph

5 Prioritize the node list based on graph metric values

6 If error count reaches k; Goto Step 11

7 Select the prioritized class from list

Analyze class members and relationships

Generate defect data

8 Generate Poisson Defect event with defect data

Instantiate class with defect data

9 Log the error generated details

10 Increment error count; Goto Step 6

11 Exit Stressor

The prioritization of the nodes is done based on the graph metrics such as average weighted degree, average shortest path length and Betweenness centrality. These three-graph metrics are chosen since these provide the importance of a node in a network. The higher value of these metrics explains that the nodes are vital in the operation of a network. From the software perspective, erroneous operation of a node with high values of these metrics poses greater chances of failure of the software. Hence, it is important to validate the efficiency of operation and error handling in these priority nodes. The Stressor design ensures more types of errors are injected involving these nodes.

3.2. Backer Design

The function of the Backer entity is to act upon the errors injected by the Stressor. These errors have to be captured by the error handlers provided in the software. This game play ensures frequent invocation of these error routines, which prevent code rusting, making the software more robust against these categories of errors. However, the error handlers provided in the software will not be sufficient to handle all the errors generated by a versatile stressor as explained earlier since foreseeing and hard coding of all these error cases is highly impossible. Hence, the Backer designed here is able to capture the unknown and unexpected errors and record the fine-grained information about the incoming errors. This fine-grained information is required to analyze and learn from the errors to aid in the process of making the software antifragile in the successive increments.

This functionality of the Backer is achieved by a cheating mechanism by implementing hooks, called as Software Learning Hooks (SLH). These hooks incorporate a reinforcement learning algorithm to learn from the incoming errors. The Q-learning algorithm used here is helpful in selecting the most efficient action for the defects encountered. This builds antifragility into the software when the code is updated in successive iterations with knowledge gained from the game run.

Reinforcement learning is a type of unsupervised learning, where a software entity learns by receiving a reward from the environment in return of executing an action. Based on the reward, the software dynamically learns to operate perfectly in a particular environment (Singh, Lewis, Barto, & Sorg, 2010). The hooks designed in this model follow a "cause and effect" idea. The purpose of the SLH is to select an action for the defects injected by the Stressor. For selection of this action, the Backer uses this SLH, which implements a Q-Learning algorithm. Q-Learning is a Temporal Difference (TD) learning approach of machine learning to predict a quantity based on differences in predictions over some time steps (Poole & Mackworth, 2017). This algorithm learns to arrive at an optimal policy for selecting the actions based on reinforcement called reward. The Q-Learning algorithm usually receives and learns from the reward received from the environment upon which the action is taken. However, this reward function need not be extrinsic always. For example, in a biological environment, certain animals perform some action merely for enjoyment of the task or out of curiosity. In these situations, the reward function can also be a function of the internal state of the agent, in which case it is considered as an intrinsic reward (Singh, Lewis, Barto, & Sorg, 2010). The Q-Learning algorithm designed here uses a combination of both intrinsic and extrinsic reward functions. This hybrid reward model is used because, the extrinsic reward, which is calculated from the changes in the quality attributes may not be always sufficient in calculating the reward. The intrinsic reward is calculated based on the defect salience. Defect salience denotes the severity and the priority of the defects. The extrinsic reward is calculated based on the quality functions such as Abstraction, Inheritance and Coupling measured from the source where the hooks are inserted. A weighted sum of software metrics is used in calculating the extrinsic reward. The source code metrics used for calculation of the quality attributes are adopted from Mohan, Greer and McMullan (2016).

The operational detail of the Backer module is explained in the following algorithm.

Backer Algorithm

Step Computation Details
    1 Initialize reward functions // for quality attribute calculation
Load Defect-Action policy lookup file
Initialize τ, α, γ
    2 For each incoming unhandled defect D^i; Goto Step 3
    3 Analyze the defect data
Select Action A^i from Defect-Action policy
Add a runtime hook
    4 Invoke the hook
    5 Log the defect-action details
Capture the core and memory dump
    6 Calculate intrinsic reward $r^i = \tau\,[1 - P(D^i)]$
    7 Calculate reward functions
Calculate extrinsic reward r^e = cumulative reward function values
    8 Calculate the Q-Value using

$$Q(D,A) \leftarrow Q(D,A) + \alpha[r^i + r^e + \gamma \cdot max\; Q(D',A') - Q(D,A)]$$

9 Update the Defect-Action Policy; Goto Step 2

Here,

$\alpha \rightarrow$ The learning rate, $(0 < \alpha \le 1)$

$\gamma \rightarrow$ The discount factor, $(0 < \gamma \le 1)$

$r^i \rightarrow$ Intrinsic reward based on defect salience

$r^e \rightarrow$ Extrinsic reward based on quality attributes

$\tau \rightarrow$ A constant multiplier

$P(D^i) \rightarrow$ Probability model for defect D^i

$Q(D,A) \rightarrow$ Q-value of a Defect – Action pair

The Q-value of a Defect – Action pair estimates the goodness of the action taken or the extent to which the results of the action taken is expected to be. These value functions are represented using notation $Q(D,A)$ –which represents the value of taking action A for the defect D under certain policy. This policy ensures that the expected value of the reward return of the actions taken is to the maximum achieved. The functional design of a Backer module representing the hybrid reward model is diagrammatically represented using Figure 3.

Figure 3. Functional diagram of SLH

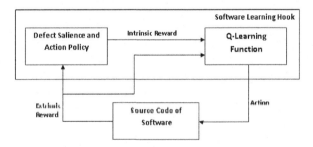

By performing the above method, the hook learns over a period of time about the actions to be taken for the incoming types of defects. Hence, operating upon a considerable number of defects, the hooks help in the betterment of the performance of the software to certain type of repeated defects.

3.3. Evaluation Parameters

The effectiveness of the proposed technique is analyzed using two categories of performance parameters, namely the defect related and quality related attributes. These parameters are evaluated at every iteration and at the end of the all the iterations to facilitate the comparison of improvements. The details of these game evaluation parameters are given in Table 2.

Defect Density is an important and fundamental metric in Software Engineering. The metric is calculated from the total number of defects discovered divided by the size of the software. Size can be expressed in terms of Function Points (FP) or Lines of Code (LOC). This metric gives a picture of the overall quality of the software and decides whether the product is ready for release. Many research works in literature uses defect density as a vital software metric for quality investigation and defect prediction

(Cartwright & Shepperd, 2000; Koru, Zhang, Emam, & Liu, 2009; Yadav & D. Yadav, 2015). Defect Distribution gives the categorization of the defects based on type, root cause priority, test type, environment, etc. Studying the defect distribution chart is helpful in understanding and identifying the areas to target for defect removal and the components that requires the application of quality improvement techniques. Researchers use this defect distribution analysis to gain understanding on the technique they applied and its outcome (Cartwright & Shepperd, 2000; Li, Li, & Sun, 2010; Beller, Bholanath, McIntosh, & Zaidman, 2016). The Hooks per Increment metric gives the trend of the number of unknown defects and hence, it is important to arrive at a logical conclusion for the reduction in the number defects in the source code. Apart from these defect related parameters, this study uses quality related parameters, namely the quality attributes such as Abstraction, Inheritance and Coupling. These attributes are used in most of the quality analysis literature and applied in majority of the software engineering problems such as architectural analysis, code quality analysis and improvement, refactoring, etc. These quality attributes are measured using standard well-defined software metrics. As mentioned earlier, QMOOD metrics proposed by Bansiya and Davis (2002) is used in this research.

Table 2. Details of the performance parameters

Category	Parameter	Context	Desired Value
Defect related	Defect Density	The number of defects per thousand lines of code	Low
	Defect Distribution	The number of different types of defects in each iteration	Low
	Hooks per Increment	The number of hooks that are executed in each iteration	Low
Quality related	Abstraction	Easiness with which the system can be extended, suppressing the more complex details	High
	Inheritance	The mechanism of creating new classes from existing classes	High
	Coupling	The measure of dependency between classes	Low

4. RESULTS AND DISCUSSION

The experiment is conducted using a sample open source Java project with 236 classes, namely the OpenFAST. OpenFAST is an open source Java implementation of the FAST protocol (OpenFAST, 2013). The classes are prioritized based on the graph metrics and the experiment is conducted with 12 iterations. The initial iterations are planned with the important classes and the other classes are integrated incrementally with the number of iterations. The software quality game model designed here is executed for every iteration and the game parameters are studied. The detailed report of the defects and the hooks that are inserted are analyzed and the changes in the code, if required, are performed in the next successive iterations. This is done after the review confirmation from the developer in order to avoid any adverse effect that may be caused by the execution of hooks. Moreover, the hooks are only temporary alterations to the code in runtime. Hence, the changes have to be studied before making any actual changes to the code. This process as explained earlier pushes the software towards antifragility. The following graphs explain the details of the results achieved.

Figure 4 shows the defect density values in various iterations with and without the proposed game theoretic approach. From the graph, there is reduction in the number of defects when the proposed technique is applied. This is due to the fact that the defects that are injected in the iterations are learned by the SLHs and the changes are made in the code to capture these categories of defects. In the existing method, these defects still exists which leads to the increased number of defects. Hence, with the successive iterations, there is a reduced defect count by using the proposed technique, whereas the defect count is still high in existing method. A similar inference can be made for the number of hooks inserted over iterations (Figure 5), which reduces over iterations. There are only few hooks required to handle the injected defects and the majority of the defects are captured by the code itself, which is modified in earlier iterations based on the learning information gained by the SLHs. The defect distribution chart is given in Figure 6, which gives the categories of defects occurred over different iterations. From this chart, it can be inferred that the majority of the defects during the initial phases of iteration were the defects related to memory, user data entry and environment. Even though there is reduction in the defects related to user data entry over iterations, memory and environment related defects contribute more, which needs special attention in the software design process. Much of the semantics and concurrency related defects are uncovered during earlier iterations and there is reduction in these categories of defects. It has to be noted that here the error injection rate by the Stressor is unaltered and only the number of uncaught or unforeseen errors are reduced.

Figure 4. Defect density over number of iterations

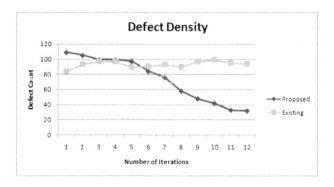

Figure 5. Number of hooks executed over number of iterations

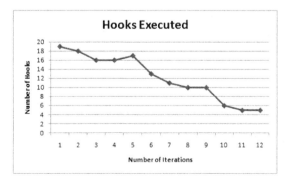

Figure 6. Defect distribution by cause chart over number of iterations

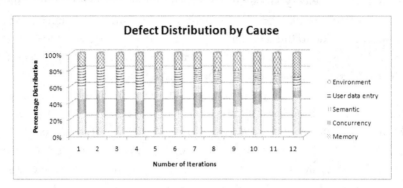

Figures 7, 8 and 9 shows the improvement in the quality attributes, namely the Abstraction, Inheritance and coupling respectively. The values of these quality attributes are compared with and without the proposed game theoretic approach. The improvement shown here is due to the modification done in the code by the development team based on the details of the defect-action report output by the Backer. As such the execution of SLH does not contribute to the improvement of the code; it is the effectiveness of the learning gained by the SLHs. From the Figures 7, 8, and 9, even though there is improvement in the quality attributes, the proposed technique does not increase them to a greater extent. But from Figure 4, there is drastic decrease in the defect density by using the proposed game model. Hence the proposed technique can be very well applied to reduce the defect density of any object-oriented software.

Figure 7. Improvement in abstraction over number of iterations

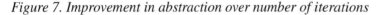

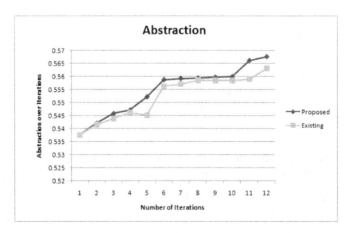

Figure 8. Improvement in inheritance over number of iterations

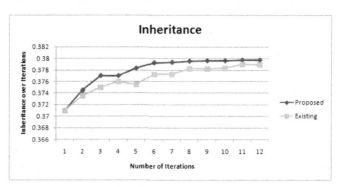

Figure 9. Improvement in coupling over number of iterations

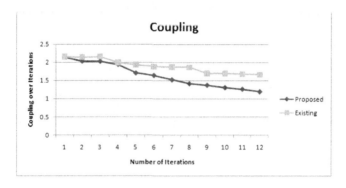

5. CONTRIBUTIONS

The proposed model enhances the quality of operation of the software system by following a novel approach for the development process. Within the existing traditional way of development and quality assurance, an innovative lateral approach has been introduced in this work. The summary of our contributions are as follows:

1. Introduction of game theoretic approach for quality enhancement of the software system by using the stressor and backer entities;
2. Following an innovative lateral approach by using cheating methods (via, software leaning hooks) to achieve positive benefits;
3. Antifragility is a rising issue in Software Engineering. This work provides a good start on achieving antifragility within the existing framework of software development methodology;
4. Apart from the existing error models, which inject errors at random, our model uses an intelligent and more realistic error model. This is achieved by modeling the software system as weighted complex networks and making use of the graph level metrics such as Betweenness Centrality, Average weighted degree of the nodes and Average Shortest Path Length;
5. Application of Q-Learning reinforcement function with a hybrid reward function that predicts the actions to be taken for the injected errors;

6.   A better result in terms of reduced defect density and improved quality attributes.

6. EMPIRICAL VALIDATION

The threats to the validity of the study are discussed with respect to the design viewpoint of the Stressor and the Backer modules. Firstly, even though the Stressor uses a versatile design using graph metrics, the generation of defects varies for different class and highly depends on the design of the class. This means that the type of attributes, the type of relationship of the class and role of the class in the overall structure of the software plays a vital role and differ from project to project. Hence, the technique has to be applied for wide range of real time projects and experience need to be gained in order to arrive at a mature logic for defect generation. Secondly, the software learning hooks used in the backer design needs more attention which poses security concerns. The hooks are only the temporary alterations to the code at runtime and hence require caution while using and also, the execution time of the proposed method increases with the number of hooks running at a time. The next viewpoint is based on the defect-action policy used by the backer. This again requires testing on a greater number of projects. The last viewpoint is the logging of fine-grained information about the incoming defects and the action taken by the hooks. The log must provide required information for the developer to carry out the analysis and hence the level of details logged must be satisfying. The core dump and the memory dump need to be captured for each generated defect that put forth storage constraints of the output files.

7. CONCLUSION

The increase in the complexity of software systems mandates the use of innovative technologies to cope with the increased number of software defects. Antifragility is a most desired property of software in current trends. This property makes the software immune to unknown and unexpected defects, the called Black swans. It prepares the software to learn from the errors. Antifragility is a breakthrough and the binding property of the future software development. This research work is motivated in incorporating antifragility into the existing framework of object oriented software development, thereby increasing the quality of operation of the software. Hence, to build this property in any software, the system must be exposed to a number of disorders; in the software perspective, the defects that occur during the operation of the software.

Usually, this type of technique in applied in a production environment as a routine of defect driven approach. In contrast to this method, in our work, the proposal is applied during the development phase of the software life cycle. This approach is combined with the concepts of Game Theory, by designing a two-player quality game. Player 1 called the Stressor injects errors into the software and the Software acting as Player 2 resists and learns from these errors. The Stressor uses the intelligence gained through the graph metrics measured from the architecture of the software for defect generation. The defects are introduced at intervals following a Poisson's distribution up to a maximum of 'k' defects. The Backer acts upon these errors and its primary concern is to avoid crashing of the system. To achieve this, the Backer uses a cheating mechanism using hooking techniques to defend against the errors. These software learning hooks incorporate reinforced learning algorithms, to progressively gain insight into the type of defect and selecting appropriate action to take to handle these errors. The hooks are introduced at run time into the software to make temporary changes into the software. At the end of the game run, a detailed report of defect-action information is output for the developer to analyze and make actual modifications in the code to handle the possible errors. Since hooks are only temporary modifications to the code at runtime, these changes have to be validated by the development team before incorporating into the actual source code. This step is used as a precaution to avoid any adverse effect of the code changes. This process is repeated for various iterations of the project, making the software develop its antifragility asset.

The proposed method is validated using an open source Java project with 236 classes. The results are studied with a two-fold category of parameters, namely, the defect related and quality related sort. The defect related parameters give the insight of the number and the category of the defects that can be uncovered from the system. By following the proposed approach leads to reduced defect density compared to the existing method of developments. The results of the quality related parameters, namely, abstraction, inheritance and coupling measured using QMOOD metrics shows stable improvement.

Even though there are certain challenges that need further insights and improvements as explained in the Empirical validation section, this approach is a step towards building antifragility into the software development methods. Thus, the research questions RQ1 and RQ2 set in Section 1 are tested and asserted, proving the applicability of Game Theory in building Antifragile Software Systems. Some future research directions include, (i) Examining the cases where the continuous improvement of the system leads to changes in the operational profiles of the software, (ii) Security issues when hooking techniques are used and analysis of alternate techniques instead of hooks, (iii) Selection of better learning algorithms for the learning hooks, and (iv) Analyzing the usage of other techniques such as Meta Programming and Self Modifying code instead of hooks to overcome performance issues.

ACKNOWLEDGMENT

This research work is funded by the Quality improvement Programme (QIP) launched by All India Council for Technical Education (AICTE), Government of India.

REFERENCES

Albert, R., & Barabasi, A. L. (2002). Statistical mechanics of complex networks. *Reviews of Modern Physics*, *74*(1), 47–97. doi:10.1103/RevModPhys.74.47

Allspaw, J. (2012). Fault injection in production. *Communications of the ACM*, *55*(10), 48–52. doi:10.1145/2347736.2347751

Bansiya, J., & Davis, C. G. (2002). A hierarchical model for object-oriented design quality assessment. *IEEE Transactions on Software Engineering*, *28*(1), 4–17. doi:10.1109/32.979986

Basiri, A., Behnam, N., Rooij, R., Hochstein, L., Kosewski, L., Reynolds, J., & Rosenthal, C. (2016). Chaos engineering. *IEEE Software*, *33*(3), 35–41. doi:10.1109/MS.2016.60

Bavota, G., Rocco, O., Lucia, A. D., Antoniol, G., & Guéhéneuc, Y. G. (2010). Playing with refactoring: Identifying extract class opportunities through game theory. In *Proceedings of the IEEE International Conference on Software Maintenance*. IEEE Press. 10.1109/ICSM.2010.5609739

Beller, M., Bholanath, R., McIntosh, S., & Zaidman, A. (2016). Analyzing the State of Static Analysis: A Large-Scale Evaluation in Open Source Software. In *Proceedings of the 23rd IEEE International Conference on Software Analysis, Evolution, and Reengineering* (pp. 470-481). IEEE Press. 10.1109/SANER.2016.105

Cartwright, M., & Shepperd, M. (2000). An Empirical Investigation of an Object-Oriented Software System. *IEEE Transactions on Software Engineering*, 26(8), 786–796. doi:10.1109/32.879814

Chong, C. Y., & Lee, S. P. (2015). Analyzing maintainability and reliability of object-oriented software using weighted complex network. *The Journal of Systems and Software, Elsevier, 110*, 28–53. doi:10.1016/j.jss.2015.08.014

Deng, X., Zheng, X., Su, X., Chand, F. T. S., Hu, Y., Sadiq, R., & Deng, Y. (2014). An evidential game theory framework in multi-criteria decision making process. *Applied Mathematics and Computation, Elsevier, 244*, 783–793. doi:10.1016/j.amc.2014.07.065

Hazzan, O., & Dubinsky, Y. (2005). Social Perspective of Software Development Methods: The Case of the Prisoner Dilemma and Extreme Programming. In *Proceedings of the International Conference on Extreme Programming and Agile Processes in Software Engineering* (pp. 74–81). Springer. 10.1007/11499053_9

Huang, C. H., Peled, D., Schewe, S., & Wang, F. (2016). A Game-Theoretic Foundation for the Maximum Software Resilience against Dense Errors. *IEEE Transactions on Software Engineering*, 42(7), 1–1. doi:10.1109/TSE.2015.2510001

Jiang, A. X., & Leyton-Brown, K. (2009). A tutorial on the proof of the existence of Nash equilibria. Univ. British Columbia.

Koru, A. G., Zhang, D., Emam, K. E., & Liu, H. (2009). An Investigation into the Functional Form of the Size-Defect Relationship for Software Modules. *IEEE Transactions on Software Engineering*, 35(2), 293–304. doi:10.1109/TSE.2008.90

Kumar, K., & Prabhakar, T. V. (2009). Quality Attribute Game: A Game Theory Based Technique for Software Architecture Design. In *Proceeding of the 2nd annual conference on India software engineering conference* (pp. 133–134). ACM. doi:10.1145/1506216.1506244

Leach, R. J. (2016). *Introduction to Software Engineering* (2nd ed.). CRC Press.

Li, N., Li, Z., & Sun, X. (2010). Classification of Software Defect Detected by Black-Box Testing: An Empirical Study. In *Proceeding of the 2010 Second World Congress on Software Engineering* (pp. 234-240). Academic Press. doi:10.1109/WCSE.2010.28

Mehdi, M. M., Raza, I., & Hussain, S. A. (2017). A game theory based trust model for Vehicular Ad hoc Networks (VANETs). *Computer Networks: The International Journal of Computer and Telecommunications Networking, 121*, 152–172. doi:10.1016/j.comnet.2017.04.024

Mohan, M., Greer, D., & McMullan, P. (2016). Technical debt reduction using search based automated refactoring. *Journal of Systems and Software, Elsevier, 120*, 183–194. doi:10.1016/j.jss.2016.05.019

Monperrus, M. (2017). Principles of Antifragile Software. In Programming '17. ACM Press.

Nash, J. (1951). Non-Cooperative Games. *The Annals of Mathematics. Second Series, 54*(2), 286–295. doi:10.2307/1969529

National Institute of Standards and Technology. (2002). The Economic Impacts of Inadequate Infrastructure for Software Testing.

OpenFAST reference. (2013). Retrieved from http://openfast.sourceforge.net/

Pan, W. (2011). Applying Complex Network Theory to Software Structure Analysis. *World Academy of Science, Engineering and Technology, 60*, 1636–1642.

Poole, D., & Mackworth, A. (2017). *Artificial Intelligence: Foundations of Computational Agents* (2nd ed.). Cambridge University Press. doi:10.1017/9781108164085

Ross, S. (2009). *A First Course in Probability* (8th ed.). Prentice Hall.

Russoa, D., & Ciancarinia, P. (2016). A Proposal for an Antifragile Software Manifesto. *Procedia Computer Science, 83*, 982–987. doi:10.1016/j.procs.2016.04.196

Singh, S., Lewis, R. L., Barto, A. G., & Sorg, J. (2010). Intrinsically Motivated Reinforcement Learning: An Evolutionary Perspective. *IEEE Transactions on Autonomous Mental Development, 2*(2), 70–82. doi:10.1109/TAMD.2010.2051031

Taleb, N. N. (2008). *The black swan: the impact of the highly improbable* (2nd ed.). London: Penguin.

Taleb, N. N. (2012). *Antifragile: Things That Gain From Disorder*. USA: Random House Publishing Group.

Yadav, H. B., & Yadav, D. K. (2015). A fuzzy logic based approach for phase-wise software defects prediction using software metrics. *Information and Software Technology, 63*, 44–57. doi:10.1016/j.infsof.2015.03.001

This research was previously published in the Journal of Cases on Information Technology (JCIT), 22(3); pages 1-18, copyright year 2020 by IGI Publishing (an imprint of IGI Global).

Section 5
Organizational and Social Implications

Chapter 82
Media Richness, Knowledge Sharing, and Computer Programming by Virtual Software Teams

Idongesit Williams
https://orcid.org/0000-0002-5398-3579
Aalborg University, Denmark

Albert Gyamfi
https://orcid.org/0000-0002-3839-4178
Aalborg University, Denmark

ABSTRACT

Software programming is a task with high analyzability. However, knowledge sharing is an intricate part of the software programming process. Today, new media platforms have been adopted to enable knowledge sharing between virtual teams. Taking into consideration the high task analyzability and the task characteristics involved in software development, the question is if the media richness of the current media platform is effective in enabling knowledge sharing among these virtual teams? An exploratory research was conducted on a software company in Denmark. The data was gathered was analyzed qualitatively using narrative analysis. This paper concludes, based on the case being investigated, that rich media does not fit the task characteristics of a software programmer. It further concludes that Media richness does affect knowledge sharing in these virtual teams. This is because the current lean media actually enables knowledge sharing as it fits the core characteristics of the software programming process.

DOI: 10.4018/978-1-6684-3702-5.ch082

INTRODUCTION

This chapter explores how media richness influences knowledge sharing activities in virtual teams involved in software programming. The task of interest is the process of programming or coding of the software. In recent times, large corporations have been involved in the decentralization of the operational aspects of their companies. Such corporations include SAP, IBM and General etc. (Lepsinger, 2015). The facilitation of their virtual operations has been enabled by the opportunities enabled by globalization and the evolution of the Internet. Based on our previous knowledge of the first author in software development and a brief practice in the trade, it was intriguing to learn that software development companies have been embracing virtual teams (Ramesh & Dennis, 2002). These companies have different software developers in different locations collaborating online to implement or programme software. This, of course, was not the intriguing part. That was because software development has always been developed with computers. So having such collaborative development effort with different computers connected to each other over the Internet was not that exciting. What was exciting though was how media richness enabled knowledge sharing within a virtual software development team as they implement or code the software. In a software development team domicile in a particular location, knowledge sharing is not difficult. Knowledge could be shared via face-to-face interaction using a device with rich media; placing comments in a programming code to explain a code in the software, documentation of daily team meetings, one on one tutorials in a company training session and codes and other relevant materials stored in repositories (see examples (Ramesh & Dennis, 2002; Ying, Wright, & Abrams, 205; DeRosa, 2014)). In this way, various members of the team are able to learn something new from one another. The new knowledge will help them implement their codes. If this scenario is transposed online, the need for this kind of knowledge sharing activities will still exist.

But knowledge sharing, as a result of the complexity in communication programming languages outside the software designed for it, might be challenging. This will definitely be the case in a scenario where two remote software developers working on the same project for the same company run into challenges on how to implement the codes. Depending on the level of information richness they need from each other in order to collaborate, different media platforms can be used. However, the more they try to unravel how to solve a programming code, rich media platforms may not be helpful. But lean media platforms might be helpful because they could read each other's codes, ponder on it and possibly verbalize their thoughts. A media platform used for such an activity should be able to enhance knowledge sharing in less ambiguous and equivocal manner. But in a situation where the software developers are discussing the requirement specifications they were given or they are presenting their thoughts in a scrum meeting. The nature of information being transmitted may not necessary be complex. The other team members will not only be interested in hearing what their colleague says, they will want to take not of non-verbal gestures. Here they can sense if they are on the same page or there are minor differences in opinion. In such a situation, rich media will be helpful. Therefore the media needs for the transmission of different forms of information by the team will differ. The fact that knowledge sharing in software teams, and by extension virtual software teams, require different set of media is supported in literature. The literature states that no media tool supports every facet of the operational dynamics in the development of a software (see (Bindrees, Pooley, Ibrahim, & Taylor, 2014)). For example, virtual teams use collaborative platforms such as GitHub to share programming codes and other media platforms such as WebEx, adobe connect or GoToMeeting, to support their daily tasks (DeRosa, 2014). Therefore one cannot dispute the use of multiple media platforms by these virtual software teams. But this raises a question. Does the media richness in the existing media platforms used by virtual software development teams for their core task support knowledge sharing?

In order to gain some insight into this phenomena, an inductive qualitative exploratory study was conducted. A Danish software company with 200 employees was chosen as a source for identifying a case. They are present in about seven countries and they possess virtual software teams. Data was gathered from a software engineer employed in this company. Narrative analysis was used to analyse the data. Inferences were drawn from the narrative analysis to draw conclusions. Based on the inferences drawn, it was clear that knowledge sharing activities via the media platforms used by the virtual teams did occur. However, it did not happen with rich media platforms, rather it occurred with lean media platforms. This was because the lean media platforms were tailored to fit the task characteristics identified in the task of the programmers.

The organization of the chapter are as follows. This section is the introduction of the chapter. This is followed by the background concepts guiding the chapter. These are the concepts of Software development, media richness and knowledge sharing. The purpose for identifying these background concepts is to explain how they relate within the context of this chapter. The next section is the presentation of the context of discussion in the chapter. This is the context of virtual software development teams and the collaborative media platforms they use. This explanation is followed by the research method by which this research was conducted; the findings and the analysis of the findings; and finally by the discussion and conclusion sections. The findings in this chapter are not generalizable. They are meant to inspire more research into the context.

SOFTWARE DEVELOPMENT, MEDIA RICHNESS, AND KNOWLEDGE SHARING

In this section, the concepts used in this paper and how they relate are described. The development of a software has a lot of processes. The process of interest to this chapter involves software engineer from remote locations implementing various code aspects of a particular software. However, before discussing virtual software teams, it was important to provide a background to this chapter. The foundation of this discussion is the interplay between software development, media richness and knowledge sharing. Knowledge in this chapter is defined as "Justified personal belief" (King, 2009). And knowledge sharing here implies "less focused dissemination of knowledge, such as through a repository (ibid). Knowledge sharing in this chapter is examined as a potential effect of the interaction between media platforms and the software development process. These media platforms are believed to enhance knowledge sharing as it becomes richer (See (Andres, 2002)). The implication is that the richness of the platform serves as a motivation to adopt the platform for knowledge sharing. Therefore in this chapter, an overview on the role of media richness in software development and an overview on the implication of the media richness theory on the knowledge sharing process in the development of software are discussed. To aid this discussion, an overview of the Media richness theory is also presented.

The Role of Media in Software Development

There has always been a fundamental interplay between software development and the media. This is because software is now developed on platforms with access to the media, enabled by the Internet. These media platforms enable knowledge sharing. These platforms exist for independent developers.

An example is the Sun's online forum support for Java programmers (Rus, Lindvall, & Sinha, 2001). Here java software programmers can use this repository to gain knowledge on how to deal with their daily tasks. It also exists within software companies. The natural tool is the code base. The company's codebase is the collection of source code used to build a particular software (Ying, Wright, & Abrams, 205). Software developers working on that software are able to access that codebase to modify it and improve on it. Within these codes, there are comments explaining the functions of the codes. Here newer developers are able to learn new ways of working with that programming language.

Although this relationship did exist, it existed away from the influence of the mass media. In a way one would say that the advancement in software development did create a rippling effect that ended up affecting the trade as well. This is because advances in software development has resulted in the evolution of the mass media. The coincidental evolution in Broadband technology has resulted in the convergence between the mass media, telecommunications and the software development industry. Hence using the personal computer, a software developer using the internet can code a software in a remote server in a country he or she has never visited.

But for software programmers, these evolutions has presented an opportunity for enhanced knowledge sharing. This involves knowledge sharing that is transferred offline to the Internet. This is because the Internet has enabled Media platforms that could support the activities of Software developers to be able to deliver rich information.

THEORETICAL BACKGROUND

The underlying theory in this chapter is the Media richness Theory. In this section, an overview of the theory as it relates to knowledge sharing in virtual software teams is explained.

Overview of Media Richness Theory

The concept of information richness can be explained using the Media Richness Theory. The media richness theory was introduced by Daft and Lengel (1986). Their aim was to understand why organization process information (Daft & Lengel, 1986). They identified that information is required to perform the daily tasks within the organization. However for the information to be received successfully, the information should contain a low degree of uncertainty and equivocality. Hence there has to be debates, and clarification in the communication process until the parties concerned can understand each other perfectly. Within this process the information is made rich as the frame of reference is synchronized and ambiguity is reduced (ibid). This they referred to as information richness. However for an information to be rich, the medium of conveying the information should enable immediate feedback and provide an accurate picture of how both parties verbally and non-verbally interpret the information. They identified 5 medium of communication and how they affect information richness. These forms of media include face-to-face communication, telephone, personal documents such as letters or memos, impersonal written documents, and numeric documents (Daft & Lengel, 1986). The level of richness of each media, from the highest to the lowest, ranges as listed from face-to-face communication to impersonal written documents, and numeric documents. The closer the form of media to face-to-face communication, the greater its ability to enable information richness. In this chapter, this scale is used later on to grade the level of media richness of platforms adopted in the software company studied based on the frequency of usage of the platform for the core task.

Media Richness Theory and the Task Characteristics in Software Programming

In order to determine the level of media richness needed for task, an important issue to take into consideration is the task characteristics (Daft & Lengel, 1986). Task characteristics can be classified into extrinsic and intrinsic task characteristics (Kim & Soergel, 2006). The intrinsic task characteristic implies the intrinsic nature of the task (ibid). The extrinsic characteristics *"originate from outside the task"* (ibid). Kim & Soergel (2006) identify the intrinsic and extrinsic task characteristics as seen in Table 1.

Table 1. Types of task characteristics

	Intrinsic Task Characteristics	Extrinsic Task Characteristics
1	Task Analysability	Task Frequency
2	Task variety	Task imposition
3	Task difficulty	Locus of the task
4	Task Routines	Task autonomy
5	Task complexity	Task significance
6	Task Structuredness	Task urgency
7		Task risk
8		Task reward

Source: Kim & Soergel (2006).

From the Media Richness Theory standpoint, the task characteristics of interest to this chapter are the task variety and the task analysability (Daft & Lengel, 1986). These was so to create a delimitation on our scope of investigation. However the task frequency, which is an extrinsic characteristics of the task will be used to simulate the frequency at which knowledge is shared on media platforms.

In the Media Richness Theory, the variety of the task is determined by the "frequency of unexpected and novel events" while the task analysability refers to the way people in organizations respond to problems (Daft & Lengel, 1986). Based on the theory, if a task is unanalysable and its task variety is low, rich media can be used to resolve the unanalysable issues. If the task is unanalysable and possesses a high task variety, rich media is still needed to solve the unanalysable issues. However, if the task analysability is low the task variety is low, lean media is needed because ambiguity and equivocality is reduced due to the standardized nature of the information. But if a task analysability is high and the task variety is high, leam media is still needed. This is because the data or information transferred is rich to enable decisions being taken.

In the programming of a software, each programming language possess standardized syntax and logic which cannot be interpreted otherwise. Therefore there is an objective way of solving challenges within the software coding process. Therefore the task is highly analysable. In the same vain it is a task with a high variety. This is because business in the software industry is created from ideas. The ideas could be internal or external ideas. These ideas have to be converted into a set of requirement specifications and handed over to the software developers to develop the software. The software developer has to engage in a mind mapping process to develop a flowchart and identify the necessary algorithms needed to implement the software. These software programming or coding process begins, once the software developer has an idea of the syntax needed to implement the software. The programmer then has to run the code on a compiler till he has no errors. It is in this process, that the programmer goes in search for knowledge on how to correct the errors. Therefore the programmer encounters a lot of unexpected events in this process until he or she has could get a solution. Hence due to the unexpected events, which sometimes occur in creating novel solutions, software programming has a high task variety.

Therefore, the level of richness of a media platform chosen by the programmers, as proposed in the theory, will depend the task analysability and task variety. These task characteristics are constant and it will be the same if the software programming is conducted by virtual teams or otherwise.

Implication of Media Richness Theory on the Knowledge Transfer Process in Software Development

The media richness theory explains more of a knowledge transfer process and not too much of a knowledge sharing process. This is because when the theory was proposed, the forms of media and their capabilities were limited. But in recent times, it is safe to say that the theory is also valid for knowledge sharing. This is because, although so far no one has perfectly simulated face-to-face interactions, the technologies today possess a greater level of media richness. It is a matter of time before an almost face-to-face interaction is made possible using technology. And current platforms used for knowledge transfer, even in software industries, support knowledge storage. In addition currently there are researches documenting the potential of media richness in various sectors of the economy (see (Baehr, 2012; Gyamfi, 2016)).

However, based on the Media Richness Theory and the concept of Information richness, independent software developers can assess online software development platforms such as Atom, Cloud9ide and Eclipse PHP developer tools etc. These portals are designed to enable the core task analysability and task variety features in the programming of software. The media richness on this portal is not so much about having access to their remote software development editors, debuggers and compilers for the programmers. Rather, it is also about the support provided to the programmers on these platforms to have access to a knowledgebase for knowledge sharing, collaborative work spaces and an interactive dashboard. However, one cannot say that the media richness on these platforms are high based on the media hierarchy created by Daft and Lengel (1986). But the level of richness they possess enables knowledge sharing. Information on these platforms can be stored and accessed later by relevant parties. In software companies, similar portals exist. Although these media platforms have the ability to enhance knowledge sharing, the software developers still have need for additional rich media platforms to share knowledge on issues supporting the core tasks, such as verbal interactions etc. An example of platforms that can aid these supporting tasks are Skype and Adobe connect etc.

In the next section, an overview of virtual software development teams and the collaborative media platforms they used will be explained.

VIRTUAL SOFTWARE DEVELOPMENT TEAMS AND COLLABORATIVE MEDIA PLATFORMS

This section provides an overview on the contexts by which the concepts of media richness, knowledge sharing within software development was investigated. It provides an insight into virtual teams and why they exist. It further provides a brief overview on virtual software development teams, why they exist and their mode of operation and what enables them collaborate remotely. In that discussion, the role of media platforms in the coordination of the virtual team is mentioned. In the last bit of this section, collaborative media platforms used by virtual software development teams are analysed.

Virtual Teams

Virtual teams are knowledge workers that collaborate on varieties of tasks, but members of the team are geographically distributed (Warkentin, Sayeed, & Hightower, 1997) From a general perspective, different academics do have different view of why virtual teams exist. One perspective is that virtual teams are seen as innovations that are suitable in turbulent business environments (Workman, Kahnweiler, & Bommer, 2003). Another perspective is that virtual teams are viewed as a consequence of technological developments and internationalization (Klitmøller & Lauring, 2013). There are still others, who view virtual teams as a means of organizations gaining competitive advantage over their competitors. Here organizations are able to rapidly respond to the needs of remote customers (Bergiel, Bergiel, & Balsmeier, 2008). There will obviously be more reasons why virtual teams exist in a plethora of industries within any sector within the economy of a nation.

Virtual Teams and Software Development

However, if one narrows these reasons down toward software development, the emergence of virtual teams are identified as a result of globalization, competition, evolution of technological possibilities, access to skilled resources, reduction in operational cost (see (Herbsleb & Moitra, 2001)). These reasons are evident in the creation of virtual teams to assist different operations in the development of software. Such operations include communication, project management, process engineering, knowledge transfer and the enhancement of technical abilities (Casey & Richardson, 2006). In each of the aforementioned operations, different forms of Media platforms can be adopted to connect the remote teams. Thereby creating an opportunity for visibility in coordination, communications and cooperation to take place in the software development process (Casey & Richardson, 2006). In this chapter, the focus is on the actual coordination and cooperation in an aspect of process engineering. This aspect is the actual programming, implementation or coding of the software by the software engineers.

Collaborative Media Platforms Used by Virtual Software Development Teams

Currently for software programmers, there are media platforms used by virtual software programming teams. These platforms can be grouped into two categories namely the main task (core task) supporting media platforms and the complimentary task-supporting media platforms.

- **Main Task-Supporting Platforms:** These are media platforms that support the task of programming the software. These platforms could be owned by the software company or it could be a third party platform. Examples of how such platforms work is GitHub, BitBucket, GitLab, CodePlex (owned by Microsoft), BeanStalk etc. Aside Codeplex, these are third party platforms used by software development companies and independent software developers. On these platforms, software programming teams operating virtually can remotely cooperate and coordinate the development of a software or webpage development for their firm. These platforms enables them to develop, store, transmit and reuse programming codes. In this manner, knowledge transfer occurs as the software developers within the team learn from each other as they work together. These collaborative platforms are mostly text based and they do not require instant feedback and gestures. Programming languages are also text based According to the Media Richness Theory, this a lean media.

These platforms are greatly patronized. An example is GitHub. Currently a lot of software development teams globally patronize GitHub. The owners of the platform claim that 22 million developers and 117 thousand companies use the platform to store, share and reuse the programmed codes for developing software (GitHub, 2017). Some of these companies listed on the GitHub portal are known to use virtual teams in their software development process. Such companies include SAP, IBM and Google (ibid). The same platform also hosts 61 million repositories (ibid). Most of these repositories are open source repositories. This implies that aside internal collaborative software development activities, software companies are also beneficiaries of codes provided by independent software developers. The reverse is unfortunately not the case, as most software companies develop proprietary and not open source software.

- **Complementary Task-Supporting Platforms:** These are media platforms that support tasks that does not involve the programming of the software. Such tasks include, the attendance of remote meetings with other software developers in the company and the presentation of reports to the team etc. Media platforms such as Skype, Google hang out, Adobe connect are often adopted for meetings. The platforms used for live meetings possess various media functionality with varied degrees of media richness. If the meeting is less formal, the chat functionalities of the media platform is used. But if the meeting is formal, a media platform that would support at least voice communication is used. Hence a functionality with medium media richness, according to the Media hierarchy proposed by daft & Lengel (1986), is used.

On the other hand email and Google documents are often used for the presentation of reports to the team. These are platforms with low level of media richness and the task is not performed on real time.

Therefore, one would say that software programmers have various media tools at their disposal to perform their tasks. Each of these tools possess different levels of media richness. Apart from the code repositories such as GitHub, which encourages knowledge sharing, do other media platforms with various levels of media richness encourage knowledge sharing? This is the question this chapter hopes to answer based on the case being investigated. In the next section, the methodology and findings from the case study is presented.

Methodology

This is a qualitative study. The exploratory research approach was adopted to investigate the case. The case were the virtual software development teams in a Danish company in about six locations. The unit of analysis was the team involving the respondent. The respondent requested anonymity as he had not requested permission from his bosses to speak. He preferred to be off the record. The respondent was chosen via purposive sampling. The interview was a face-to-face interview and it lasted for one hour. He was asked open-ended questions with respects to the issues bothering on organizational learning, knowledge sharing and media richness. The context of these questions were on the virtual software teams operating in their company. Although there were guiding concepts to the open-ended questions, the idea behind the open-ended question was not to receive immediate answers to questions. It was rather aimed at deriving enough data to aid in understanding the role rich media played in knowledge sharing activities in these teams. The data gathered from the interviews were recorded using a voice recorder. It was transcribed and narrative analysis was used in analysing the data. The choice of narrative analysis was informed by the need to have a full picture on the media platforms used by software developers in the company; how they share knowledge on these platforms and how they share knowledge offline. Based on the narrative outcome, inferences could be drawn on the type of media platform used; the amount of information richness the platform permits; the level of media richness of the medium; the type of task the medium is used for; and the identifiable level of knowledge sharing permitted by the medium. The narrative analysis was supplemented with a thematic approach towards coding the data.

FINDINGS AND ANALYSIS

This section is divided into two. The first section provides the outcome of the narrative analysis. The second section provides an inference derived from the narrative analysis. The inferences are aimed at providing answers to the main question posed by this chapter. That question was aimed at investigating if the media richness of current media platforms used by virtual software developers for their task are effective for knowledge sharing within their context.

Outcome of Narrative Analysis

In this subsection, findings on the profile of the case company and knowledge sharing procedures in the company are outlines. The finding on knowledge sharing are presented under two headings. These are their online knowledge sharing activities and their offline knowledge sharing activities.

Overview of Case

The case studied was a Danish medium sized company involved in software development. It is business to business company that provides a platform for the delivery of business process products online to companies. They serve both Danish and international clients and they have offices in 7 location outside Denmark. About 100 software developers work for this company. These developers are scattered in the 7 locations. The operational process for the development of the software is the same in the 7 locations. Initially, products developed by the company occurred via the collaboration between virtual teams. Now, products developed at each location are owned by the engineers at that location. However, all developers in the company work on the same kind of code base on the same platform. This enables developers working remotely to have access to other codes from other teams. Also in some cases remote developers still work together.

Table 2. Overview of the company

	About the Company
Type of company	Software development
Activity of company	Handle Business processes
Number of software developers	100
Number of remote locations	7 locations

Knowledge Sharing Procedure

Online Knowledge sharing procedure:

1. **Company's Code Base:** For other developers in the remote teams to access the code, you commit your code to the code base. This process is accompanied by a message and time. Other developers will see the code and the message accompanying it
2. **GitHub:** The developer further pushes the code to GitHub. A developer can access the code here, modify the code and others will see the changes.
3. **Ownership of Code Lines:** In order to identify who added which code, a software is used to identify the developer, who modified and recommitted the code to GitHub, as the owner of those lines. Remote developers gain inspiration from each other using this process.
4. **Comments:** Developers leave comments on the codes stored in GitHub. This helps other developers learn and understand the codes.
5. **Use of VoIP:** Skype and google hangout is used to meet with members of remote teams. Sometimes these tools are used to drop messages for the remote team member. An example is informing the remote team member that a task has been performed. But these meeting are not regular.
6. **Wiki-Page:** The Company has an internal Wikipedia page where new developers can learn about the company's software product and how they were developed. But it is only used as a source of reference to understand the original intention of the product developer.

Offline knowledge sharing procedure:

1. **Team Reshuffling:** Although each location owns each product, developers are often shuffled to allow them familiarize themselves with what other teams are working on. This helps the company to quickly replace a team member if one team member is fired or resigns. The downside is the lack of product ownership by a set of engineers. It is impossible to blame a certain engineer if the product fails.

2. **Team Manager Reshuffling:** Each new team manager comes with a new idea from previous teams. The manager comes with knowledge gathered from clients. The downside is the subtle clash of ideas between the team and the new manager.
3. **Team Manager to Development Team:** The team also receives knowledge of the product from the manager based on requirement specifications developed by the manager in daily scrum meetings.
4. **Documentation:** Initially engineers did provide documentation on their codes. This was because the product development turnout was slow and the company was new. As the company expanded and the product turn out increased documentation was encouraged. Documentation was to help the developers' fine tuning the codes to understand the intent of the previous developer. Else, the new developer will have challenges understanding the code.
5. **Mentorship:** New employees are made to undertake a code programming challenge. A mentor is assigned to new employees within this period. The codes are derived from the company's code base. The mentor reviews the codes and shows the new employees how the codes should be handled for the product.
6. **Sprint Meetings:** The developers meet with the scrum master, project manager every day to discuss the previous day's task. Each developer receives feedback from members of the team. They also share the problems they encountered in their task and decide what they will do next. Knowledge is also shared via casual conversations on a project related issue after each meeting.

Inference From Findings

Below is an attempt to make sense of the data extracted from the narrative analysis. The first thing was to identify each media platform, its level of media richness and the task supported by the platform. This is represented in Table 3.

Table 3. Amount of information richness on the media platforms identified in the case

	Platform	Amount of Information Richness It Allows	Level of Media Richness	Type of Task
1	GitHub	low	Low	Main task
2	Codebase	low	Low	Main task
3	Wikipedia	low	low	Complementary task
4	VoIP	High	High	Complementary task

The second thing was to identify the frequency at which knowledge sharing occur on each media platform. Software developers have various ways of communicating, as they commit codes to the pool every day. Here the members of the virtual team will access these codes and also use it to update their work. The software developers, as thy work, insert comments in the codes, drop messages and notes which will alert the other team member on real time on when they commit their codes to the pool. Hence Knowledge sharing occurs frequently during the day. Based on this backdrop, the frequency of knowledge sharing on the codebase and Github are deemed high.

But on a platform where knowledge is shared once a product is developed and delivered to a Knowledge storing device, the frequency of knowledge sharing is deemed medium. Hence Knowledge sharing on Wikipedia for this case is deemed to occur is deemed medium. On a platform where more of information than knowledge on the core task is shared, and knowledge on the core task is shared occasionally, the level of knowledge sharing is deemed low. Based on this criteria, the level of knowledge sharing in each medium is presented in Table 4.

Table 4. Frequency of knowledge sharing on each media platform

	Platform	Frequency of Knowledge Sharing	Type of Task
1	GitHub	High	Main task
2	Codebase	High	Main task
3	Wikipedia	Medium	Complementary task
4	VoIP	low	Complementary task

Inference 1

Based on the findings, the use of lean media made knowledge sharing effective in the context of the case studied. The reason for this was not the media platform in itself. This was because the media platform with lean media such as the company's codebase and GitHub had the following characteristics:

1. **The Task-Fit of the Media Platform:** As programmers and people who implement codes, GitHub and the code base did fit the task of programming. The programmers could fetch new codes or be inspired by the codes in GitHub or codebase. The programmers were also obliged to commit their codes to these platforms. So programmers from every location working on the same software are synchronized.
2. **The Nature of Programming Languages:** Programming languages are text based and highly explicit, making lean media most suitable for knowledge sharing. Therefore, the best media platform that would enable knowledge sharing had a lean media.
3. **The Transposition of Offline Knowledge Sharing Attributes:** The placements of comments in a code is one way software programmers communicate with each other. This makes the task of software programming highly analysable, hence prompting the use of lean media. In addition, platforms such as GitHub and the code base protects the integrity of the codes. Thus preserving the high analysability characteristics of the software codes. This is one of the main reasons lean media fits the task characteristics of the core task in software programming.

Wiki is lean media as well, but it was not used as much as the company's codebase or GitHub. This was because it did not necessary fit into the task characteristics. However, it was utilized more than the VoIP solutions. This was not because of the media richness of wiki. It was rather because, it was a constant reference material, where other developers will find out how each product works. This was valuable in the reshuffling process as new developers take up new products they did not build to improve on it. This then leads to the next inference.

Inference 2

Rich media was not used in knowledge sharing activities in the core task of programming. This is because it did not fit the task characteristics of the core task, which is highly analysable. Rather the closer the support activity the media platform provided to the main task, the more likely the company being investigated would be adopted a media platform. It did not matter how rich the media was. However, from a theoretical standpoint. Media richness did matter. That was what led the company to choose a lean media which would support the task characteristics of their core task, in which inherent knowledge sharing processes are embedded.

Based on these inferences, it was necessary to find out from the respondent what would make rich media compatible with their line of work. The response was not positive. This was because software developers were already using media rich platforms such as Youtube to gain more knowledge about their trade on an individual basis. They have to continue to update their knowledge as their trade is quite dynamic. But trying to transpose the professional development activities into their firm to enhance knowledge sharing would be an overkill. This is because of 2 reasons.

1.   **Information Overload:** The developers do not only access information needed to help them develop their codes, they also receive other relevant information not related to programming. This includes information gathered from attending meeting, reading reports and performing other tasks. Hence rich media will not enhance their work.
2.   **Developer Apathy:** Developers feel that most information they receive is noise and not needed. An example given in the interview is the desire to introduce a new programming language to the team. In some cases the team spends six to eight months to study the language which becomes obsolete by the time they are done studying. The company decided to change that approach and encourage the introduction of new programming languages. But the aim was not to replace the existing language used by the teams, but to try their hands on a new product with a new team to see how it will fare in the market. Hence, the respondent felt that most new knowledge was noise and rich media platforms will enhance that noise, which may not result in productivity.

Therefore this findings indicates that media richness in media platforms does influence knowledge sharing in virtual software development teams when implementing codes.

DISCUSSION

As the media richness of media platforms evolved, so has the need to use media platforms to enhance knowledge sharing within virtual teams (see (Klitmøller & Lauring, 2013; Gibbs, Kim, & Boyraz, 2017; Batarseh, Usher, & Daspit, 2017)). This need is also identified in the software development industry. This has led to investigations on how collaboration using media platforms can be enhanced in virtual teams in software firms (Storey, Zagalsky, & Filho, 2016). It has also led to investigations on how socio-cultural factors and knowledge sharing affect virtual teams among other investigations (see (Vornanen, 2017). This implies that research within this context will be on the increase as richer media platforms evolve.

However, in setting the conceptual scene to this chapter in section, it was alluded to that as the media richness of media platforms evolves, so will the need to share knowledge on that platform by computer programmers. But the reverse seems to be the case, based on the findings of this chapter. In the implementation of software codes, the task characteristics involved in software coding only permits lean media.

But the findings opens up opportunities into the need for a more micro- level analysis in evaluating the role of media richness in enhancing knowledge sharing for virtual software teams. At the moment research into software development teams are focused on the different aspects of the macro level of the team (see (Woodward & Vongswasdi, 2017; Andres, 2002)). The macro level here implies the software development team as a whole. In a particular team, without mentioning the team leader and the scrum master, there are personnel involved in drafting the requirement specifications, designers of the software (this includes interaction designers), those implementing or coding the software (these are front enders and back enders) and the and user experience professions (involved in testing the software). In some cases the software developer or the personnel implementing the software tests the software using a special programme. Each of these group of professionals have different task characteristics which define their sub-teams. Aside the user experience professionals, each of the other group of professionals can operate with other virtual teams conducting the same tasks. They will utilize different media platforms tailored to their task and their dynamics for working together will be different. There, the independent research into these groups, which is referred to as the micro level here, would be a very beneficial. The analysis should not only be on how they share knowledge but the impact of the knowledge sharing on the improvement of their tasks.

CONCLUSION

This chapter was driven by the need to understand the effectiveness of current media platforms used by virtual software teams to share knowledge as they programme software. The outcome of this research was that in the case studied, media richness did enable knowledge sharing. However, it was the lean media platform that facilitated the core task characteristics in software programming that was adopted. Rich media did not fit the core task characteristics. Therefore it was not used for knowledge sharing in the course of the core task. It served as a support for complementary task. The findings in this chapter cannot be generalized due to its small sample size. In order to make a generalization, a quantitative research with a large sample size will be needed.

REFERENCES

Andres, H. P. (2002). A comparison of face-to-face and virtual software development teams. *Team Performance Management: An International Journal, 8*(1/2), 39–48. doi:10.1108/13527590210425077

Baehr, C. (2012). Incorporating user appropriation, media richness, and collaborative knowledge sharing into blended e-learning training tutorial. *IEEE Transactions on Professional Communication, 55*(2), 175–184. doi:10.1109/TPC.2012.2190346

Batarseh, F. S., Usher, J. M., & Daspit, J. J. (2017). Collaboration cpapbility in virtual teams:Examining the influence on diversity and innovation. *International Journal of Innovation Management, 21*.

Bergiel, B. J., Bergiel, E. B., & Balsmeier, P. W. (2008). Nature of virtual teams: A summary of their advantages and disadvantages. *Management Research News*, *31*(2), 99–110. doi:10.1108/01409170810846821

Bindrees, M. A., Pooley, R. J., Ibrahim, I. S., & Taylor, N. K. (2014). Re-Evaluating Media Richness Theory in Software Development Settings. *Journal of Computer and Communications*, *02*(14), 37–51. doi:10.4236/jcc.2014.214004

Casey, V., & Richardson, I. (2006). Uncovering the reality within Virtual software teams. *GSD '06 Proceedings of the 2006 international workshop on Global software development for the practitioner*, 66-72.

Daft, R. L., & Lengel, R. H. (1986). Organizational Information requirements, Media Richness and Structural design. *Management Science*, *32*(5), 554–571. doi:10.1287/mnsc.32.5.554

DeRosa, D. (2014, November 21). *5 Tools every virtual leader needs*. Retrieved from Onpoint consulting: http://www.onpointconsultingllc.com/blog/2014/11/5-tools-every-virtual-leader-needs

Gibbs, J. L., Kim, H., & Boyraz, M. (2017). Virtual teams. In C. R. Scott, L. Lewis, R. L. Barker, J. Keyton, T. Kuhn, & P. Turner (Eds.), The International Encyclopedia of Organizational Communications (pp. 1-14). Wiley. doi:10.1002/9781118955567.wbieoc215

GitHub. (2017). *Guthub*. Retrieved from Github: https://github.com

Gyamfi, A. (2016). The Impact of Media Richness on the Usage of Web 2.0 Services for Knowledge Transfer. *International Journal of E-Services and Mobile Applications*, *8*(2), 21–37. doi:10.4018/IJESMA.2016040102

Herbsleb, J. D., & Moitra, D. (2001). Globalization and Software. *IEEE Software*, *18*(2), 16–20. doi:10.1109/52.914732

Kim, S., & Soergel, D. (2006). Selectng and measuring task characteristics as indpendent variables. The American Society of Information Science and Technology, 42(1).

King, W. R. (2009). Knowledge Management and Organizational Learning. *Annals of Information Systems, 4*.

Klitmøller, A., & Lauring, J. (2013). When global virtual teams share knowledge: Media Richness, cultural difference and language commonality. *Journal of World Business*, *48*(3), 398–406. doi:10.1016/j.jwb.2012.07.023

Lepsinger, R. (2015, April 27). *3 Companies with High-performing virtual teams*. Retrieved from Linkedin: https://www.linkedin.com/pulse/3-companies-high-performing-virtual-teams-rick-lepsinger

Ramesh, A., & Dennis, A. R. (2002). The Object-Oriented Team: Lessons for Virtual Teams from Global Software Development. *Proceedings of the 35th Hawaii International Conference on System Sciences (HICSS-35'02)*. IEEE. 10.1109/HICSS.2002.993876

Rus, I., Lindvall, M., & Sinha, S. S. (2001). *Knowledge Management in Software Engineering:A DACS State-of-the-Art Report*. Fraunhofer Center for Experimental Software Engineering Maryland and The University of Maryland.

Storey, M., Zagalsky, A., & Filho, F. F. (2016). How Social and Communications channels Shape and Challenge a Participatory Culture in Software development. *IEEE Transactions and Software, 43*(2).

Vornanen, M. (2017). *The impact of socio-cultural factors and knowledge sharing to the success of global software development*. Tampere: University of Tampere.

Warkentin, M. E., Sayeed, L., & Hightower, R. (1997). Virtual teams versus face-to-face teams: An exploratory study of a Web based conference system. *Decision Sciences, 28*(4), 975–996. doi:10.1111/j.1540-5915.1997.tb01338.x

Woodward, I. C., & Vongswasdi, P. (2017). *More that unites than divides: Intergenerational communication preferences in the workplace. In Communication Research and Practice*. Taylor and Francis.

Workman, M., Kahnweiler, W., & Bommer, W. (2003). The effects of cognitive style and media richness on commitment to telework and virtual teams. *Journal of Vocational Behavior, 63*(2), 199–219. doi:10.1016/S0001-8791(03)00041-1

Ying, A. T., Wright, J. L., & Abrams, S. (2005). Source code that talks: an exploration of Eclipse task comments and their implication to repository mining. *Proceedings in MSR '05 Proceedings of the 2005 international workshop on Mining software repositories* (pp. 1-5). St. Louis, MO: ACM.

This research was previously published in Evaluating Media Richness in Organizational Learning; pages 115-134, copyright year 2018 by Business Science Reference (an imprint of IGI Global).

Chapter 83

Planned Investment in Information Technology Companies:
Innovative Methods of the Management in IT

Edilaine Rodrigues Soares
Planned Invesment, Brazil

ABSTRACT

Planned investment has become indispensable for strengthening the management in IT companies. In this chapter, the authors present three innovative methods in a cycle of causes and effects, where the second method is effect of the first and the third is cause of the first and effect of the second method. The first method aims to motivate the human resources with organizational learning and the growth in the professional career. The second method aims to measure the performance, the productivity, the organizational learning, and the growth in the professional career. The third method aims to estimate the anticipation of the costs for the construction of the software project and analysis of planned investment for the better decision making. This motivator scenario, with effect of anticipative and strengthening that aligns methods in a cycle of causes and effects, enabling the analysis of planned investment for the better decision making in the IT companies, provides the government, generates revenue, moves the economy, and generates more wealth for Brazil.

BACKGROUND

This chapter aims to present three essential innovative methods for strengthening of information management in the information technology companies, among them the most important is the professional career plan linked to the quality of the software development process in the IT companies, in the following, the metrics the career plan and then the financial statement of the software project.

DOI: 10.4018/978-1-6684-3702-5.ch083

The three innovative methods are aligned in a cycle of causes and effects that enable the analysis of planned investment for better decision making in the IT companies, as shown the Figure 1.

Figure 1. Cycle of causes and effects of the innovative methods planned investment
Source: Prepared by the authors, 2016

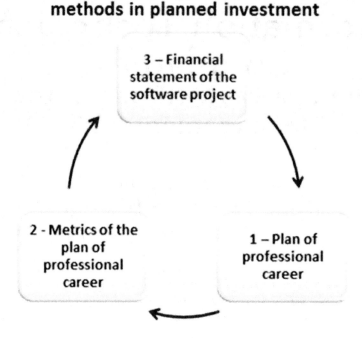

Contextualising the Figure 1, the second method is effect of the first method and the third method is cause of the first method and effect of the second method, enabling the analysis of planned investment in the IT companies.

According to Soares, Zaidan and Jamil (2013), the professional career plan is an interactive dynamic and productive of learning and growth, incremental, in the professional career and aims to motivate the human resources with organizational learning and the growth in the professional career, besides to meeting the needs and expectations of the company and the customer with the continuous improvement in the construction of the contracted service.

The the same authors (2014), the metrics of the professional career plan were defined in a PDCA cycle with based on the percentage of execution of each task. The objective is to measure the performance and the productivity of human resources, how much construction of the contracted service, organizational learning and the growth in the professional career.

For Soares, Zaidan (2016), the financial statement of the software project was defined based on the metrics of the professional career plan, in order to anticipate the factors that threaten the achievement of the expected results, as well as reduce costs and maximize profits.

The authors claim that this method aims to estimate, with antecedence, the cost required to build the software development project and analysis of planned investment for better decision making in the IT companies.

For Costa (2007), the performance evaluation compares the perception between the immediates superiores, subordinate, customers, suppliers and the perception of the occupant of the position has of himself. The main objectives of the Performance Evaluation System are: provide a feedbak objective and careful; identify skills; improve the communication between the people; obtain relevant information for the promotion of employees; cause changes in the culture of the company; search of the continuous improvement.

According Amboni, Andrade (2009), Taylor said there should be planning and apply scientific methods in the development of the work, making them more experienced in what they do and realizing faster and more efficient the production.

In consonance with Ching (2014), the capacity of company to innovate, learn and improve is aligned with maximizing its value.

According to Campos (2004), the strategic business management is a way to add new elements of reflection and action continuous and systematic, in order to evaluate the situation, develop projects of strategic change and also monitor and manage the steps of Implementation.

This chapter has the following approaches to explain the three methods: in the first section, is presented the method that allows motivate human resources with organizational learning and growth in the professional career, in addition to meeting the needs and expectations of the company and of the customer with the continuous improvement in the construction of the contracted service.

In a second section, is presented the method which allows to measure the performance and the productivity of human resources, how much the construction of the contracted service, organizational learning and growth in the professional career. Finally, in the third section, is presented the method which allows to anticipate the costs necessary for the construction of software development project and analysis of the planned investment for the better decision making in the IT companies.

This chapter is aligned in a cycle of causes and effects of innovative methods:

- Plan of professional career linked to the quality of the process of software development in the IT companies;
- Metrics of the plan of professional career linked to the quality of the software development process in the IT companies;
- Financial Statement of software project in the IT companies.

With this motivator scenario, with effect of anticipative and strengthening that aligns methods in a cycle of causes and effects, enabling the analysis of planned investment for the better decision making in the IT companies, provides the government, generate revenue, move the economy and generate more wealth in Brazil.

Plan of Professional Career Linked to the Quality of the Process of Software Development in the IT Companies

This method aims to motivate the human resources with organizational learning and the growth in professional career, in addition to meeting the needs and expectations of the company and the customer with the continuous improvement in the construction of the contracted service.

For Soares, Zaidan and Jamil (2013), the plan of the professional career is a structure of the human resources, defined hierarchically through the attributes of each function, how much the validation and preparation of documents. It consists of a dynamic three (3) human resources that interact each other throughout the process of software development in the IT companies, as shown the Figure 2.

Figure 2. Dynamics of three (3) human resources aligned to the organizational learning X professional career
Source: Prepared by the authors, 2013

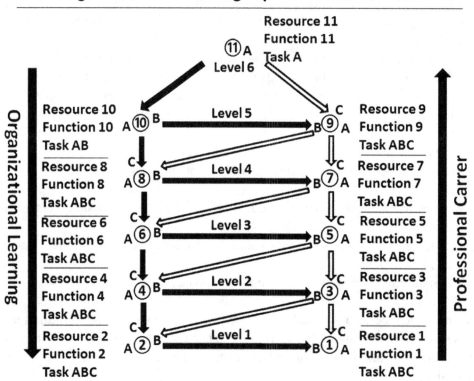

Dynamics of three (3) human resources aligned to the organizational learning X professional career

The Human Resource (1) has the task (A) to prepare the documentation, corresponding to its function (1);

The Human Resource (1) has the task (B) to validate the documentation, corresponding to the function (2), prepared by the human resource (2);

The Human Resource (1) has the task (C) to validate the documentation, corresponding to the function (3), prepared by the human resource (3).

The Human Resource (2) has the task (A) to prepare the documentation, corresponding to its function (2);

The Human Resource (2) has the task (B) to validate the documentation, corresponding to the function (3), prepared by the human resource (3);

The Human Resource (2) has the task (C) to validate the documentation, corresponding to the function (4), prepared by the human resource (4).

The Human Resource (3) has the task (A) to prepare the documentation, corresponding to its function (3);

The Human Resource (3) has the task (B) to validate the documentation, corresponding to the function (4), prepared by the human resource (4);

The Human Resource (3) has the task (C) to validate the documentation, corresponding to the function (5), prepared by the human resource (5).

The same analogy is applied to other human resources with the aim of promoting the dynamics between three human resources.

The authors highlight out that the favorable factors to this dynamic of three (3) human resources are:

- Motivate teams of workers in the exercise of their duties;
- Improve the quality of the product / service;
- Improve the performance;
- Increase the productivity;
- Promote the organizational learning;
- Promote the growth in the professional career;
- Meet the needs and expectations of the company and the customer.

Metrics of the Plan of Professional Career Linked to the Quality of the Process of Software Development in the IT Companies

According to Soares, Zaidan and Jamil (2014), the metrics of the plan of professional career have been defined in a PDCA cycle, based on the percentage of execution of each task during the process of software development in the IT organizations. The objective of the metrics of the plan of professional career is to plan, measure, monitor and evaluate the execution of the tasks, how much the quality, time, cost, performance, productivity, organizational learning and the growth in professional career.

The Balanced Scorecard in a PDCA cycle of the metrics of the plan of professional career consists of the following guidelines: plan, measure, monitor, evaluate and to apply the organizational learning and the growth in the professional career, as shown in Figure 3.

The authors highlight out that the favorable factors to this method are:

- Plan the execution of the tasks (software project management);

- Measure the quality, time, cost, performance, productivity, organizational learning and the growth in the professional career (measures management);
- Monitor the evolution of organizational learning (indicators management);
- Evaluate the organizational learning and apply the growth in the professional career (career management).

Figure 3. Balanced scorecard in a PDCA cycle in IT organizations
Source: Prepared by the authors, 2014

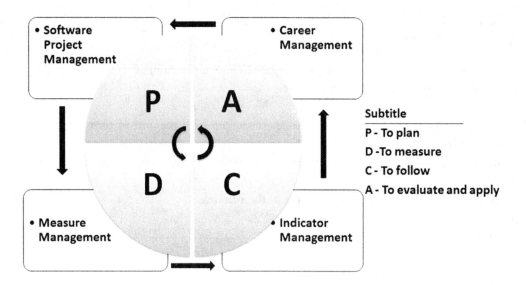

According to Klapan & Norton (1997), the Balanced Scorecard translates the mission and strategy into objectives and measures. It is organized according to four different perspectives: financial, customer, internal processes, learning and growth. The "scorecard" creates a structure, a language, to communicate the mission and strategy and uses indicators to inform employees about the vectors of the current and future success.

For Scartezini (2014), the PDCA cycle was originally developed in the decade of 1930, in the labs of Bell Laboratories in the USA, by the statistical Walter A. Shwhart. It was defined as a cycle of statistical control of processes that can be applied to any type of process or problem.

This author says that PDCA cycle can be defined as a valuable method of control and improvement of organizational processes, through the continuous flow of the cycle in an increasing spiral of improvement, in which the process or pattern can always be reassessed and a new one or a improved process can be promoted.

For Campos (1990), the troubleshooting method, also called by the Japanese of "QC STORY, is a key part of quality control that can be provided. As the quality control via PDCA is the management model for every person in the entire company, this troubleshooting method must be mastered by all.

Campos (1990) says that the management of PDCA cycle is a strategic method to increase the company's competitiveness.

During the measuring process of the professional career plan are established norms, values and attitudes, and expectations shared in individual and group level identify the aspects of excellence and grace points, gaps and adding some knowledge to employees.

This quantifier and qualifier scenario, enabling the construction of the contracted service of software, organizational learning and the growth in the professional career, can be revealed through of the application the metrics of the plan of professional career, as shown in the Figure 4.

Figure 4. Application of the metrics of the plan of professional career of information technology
Source: Prepared by the authors, 2015

Professional career plan
❶ Human resource

Human resource	Function	Level	Position
Human resource 1	Function 1	Level 1	1
Human resource 2	Function 2	Level 1	2
Human resource 3	Function 3	Level 2	3

Metrics of the professional career plan of information technology

Indicators	❶·❶ Tasks	❶·❷ Quality	❶·❸ Time	❶·❹ Cost
Elaborate document				
Note	5	5	5	5
Requisite	Answered	Answered	Answered	Answered
%	100%	100%	100%	100%
Concept	Optimum	Optimum	Optimum	Optimum
Result indicators	❷ Performance	❸ Productivity	❹ Learning	❺ Professional Career
Note	5,00	5,00	5,00	5,00
Obtain	Yes	Yes	Yes	Yes

The quantification and qualification of the metrics of the plan of professional career can be revealed through of the following elements:

1. Human Resources
   a. **Task:** Presents the note corresponding to the percentage of the task performed
   b. **Quality:** Presents the note corresponding to the percentage of quality applied in the task executed
   c. **Time:** Presents the note corresponding to the percentage of the time of the task executed
   d. **Cost:** Presents the note corresponding to the percentage of the cost of the task executed
2. Performance
3. Productivity
4. Learning

5. Professional career

Soares, Zaidan and Jamil (2015) defined the professional career plan metrics based on the parameters of *the dimensions of the software development process in information technology companies*, as shown in Table 1.

Table 1. Parameters for measuring the dimensions of the software development process in information technology companies – PCTI

Dimension	Concept	Requirements	Note
Scope (task) 40% Time 20% Cost 10% Quality 30%	Great	Answered 100%	5
	Good	Answered 80%	4
	Regular	Answered 60%	3
	Bad	Answered 40%	2
	Insufficient	Answered 20%	1
		Not answered	0

Source: Prepared by the authors, 2014

For Soares, Zaidan and Jamil (2014), these parameters are used to classify and measure the scope, time, cost and quality of the metrics of the professional career plan.

In summary, the employee receives from their colleagues the information and the knowledge necessary to perform his task and to obtain the learning for professional growth.

In order to motivate teams and workers, managers need to get some feedback of the tasks performed and, for that, it will be necessary, through the parameters to obtain the measurement of metrics of the professional career plan.

For Soares, Zaidan and Jamil (2014), the following parameters were defined based on the percentage of execution of each task. Each percentage has its score. Each score has its references. Each reference has its concept that will be used to classify the evolution of learning and growth, incremental, in professional career during the software development cycle, as shown in Table 2.

Based on these parameters, it is possible to measure and obtain the feedback of the effort and the result of each worker in the exercise of their function.

For Soares, Zaidan and Jamil (2014), it is necessary that, the greater the weight, the greater the effort; The smaller the note, the greater the effort; The smaller the weight, the better the result; The higher the score, the better the outcome for learning and professional career growth.

Financial Statement of the Software Project in the IT Companies

This method aims to estimate with antecedence the necessary cost to build the software development project and analysis of planned investment for the better decision making in the IT companies.

According to Soares, Zaidan (2016), the financial statement of the software project was defined based in the metrics of the plan professional career, in order to anticipate the factors that threaten the achievement of the expected results, as well as reduce costs and maximize profits.

Table 2. Measurement parameters of the metrics of the professional career plan linked to the quality of the process of software development at IT companies

Function								
Function 9	Function 8	Function 7	Function 6	Function 5	Function 4	Function 3	Function 2	Function 1
Percentage executed task			Note executed task		Reference	Concept		Requirements
100%			5		≥ 5	Great		Answered 100%
80%			4		$\geq 4 < 5$	Good		Answered 80%
60%			3		$\geq 3 < 4$	Regular		Answered 60%
40%			2		$\geq 2 < 3$	Bad		Answered 40%
20%			1		$\geq 1 < 2$	Insufficient		Answered 20%
0%			0		$\geq 0 < 1$			Not answered
Function 10								
Percentage executed task			Note executed task		Reference	Concept		Requirements
100%			5		$\geq 7,5$	Great		Answered 100%
80%			4		$\geq 6 < 7,5$	Good		Answered 80%
60%			3		$\geq 4,5 < 6$	Regular		Answered 60%
40%			2		$\geq 3 < 4,5$	Bad		Answered 40%
20%			1		$\geq 1,5 < 3$	Insufficient		Answered 20%
0%			0		$\geq 0 < 1,5$			Not answered
Function 11								
Percentage executed task			Note executed task		Reference	Concept		Requirements
100%			5		≥ 15	Great		Answered 100%
80%			4		$\geq 12 < 15$	Good		Answered 80%
60%			3		$\geq 9 < 12$	Regular		Answered 60%
40%			2		$\geq 6 < 9$	Bad		Answered 40%
20%			1		$\geq 3 < 6$	Insufficient		Answered 20%
0%			0		$\geq 0 < 3$			Not answered

Source: Prepared by the authors, 2014

The authors highlight out that the favorable factors to this method are:

- Provide the anticipation of the factors that threaten the achievement of expected results;
- Provide the analysis of cost reduction and profit maximization;
- Provide the estimate of the execution time of the software development project;
- Provide the estimate of the measurement of the software development project per function point (FP);
- Provide the estimate of the sales value of the software development project;
- Provide the estimate of the value of the financial revenue of the next month;
- Build the customer portfolio.

For Seleme (2014), it is necessary that managers increasingly seek a holistic view of the business, seeking viable alternatives to reduce costs and obtain a maximization of profits, without affecting the quality of their products or services.

Gropelli and Nikbakht (1998) state that, when making investment decisions, financial administrators consider the effects of changes in demand conditions, offers and prices on the company's performance.

Understanding the nature of these factors, helps the administrators take more advantageous operational decisions. In addition, the administrators can determine the propitious moment of issuing actions, bonds or other financial instruments.

According to the authors, the knowledge of economic principles may be useful in generating the highest possible sales. Understanding and properly responding to changes in demand, allow administrators to take all the advantages from the financial market conditions.

The best managers, in order to get that, develop and adopt reliable and executable statistical techniques which can predict the demand and point when sales direction changes should be made.

Gropelli and Nikbakht (1998) state that companies still use statistics to detect when it is expected changes in economic activities, and therefore, when it is better to apply or to fundraise, refinancing a debt or increasing working capital and expand capacity. With the statistic, a company can calculate the seasonal pattern of sales, using the information to budget effectively, the provisional annual needs of floating capital, the date of purchase of raw materials and the increase or reduction of inventories.

The authors stress that administrators should learn to deal with the statistical techniques to establish the period and predict, as accurate as possible, changes in macroeconomic and micro basic factors.

They must make good use of the accountants who prepare financial statements, thus helping administrators monitor the development of the company. In other words, the best managers know how to use all the available tools and how to combine all sources of information to carry out the goals and more effective investment strategies for the company.

According to Gitman (1997), the activities of the manager may be related to the basic financial statements of the company. Their primary activities are: performing analysis and financial planning. Transforming the financial data, so they can be used to monitor the financial situation of the company; assess the need to increase, or reduce the productive capacity and determine increases or reductions of funding required.

For Soares, Zaidan & Jamil (2015), these factors favor the application of the method for better decision making, and are aligned in 13 indicators relevant and pertinent, integrating the areas of human resources, financial and administrative, accounting, statistics, commercial, business strategy, infrastructure and software project in the IT companies, as shown in figure 5.

The thirteen (13) indicators relevant and pertinent were defined based on the position/function and salary of each human resource allocated in the team of the software development project, as follows:

1. **Nominal Salary Value (Month)**: The value corresponding to the nominal salary (month) of the human resources allocated in the team of the contracted service.
2. **Fixed Value About Value of the Nominal Salary (Month)**: It is the valuecorresponding to the charges, provisions and benefits over the value of the nominal salary (month) of the human resources allocated in the team of the contracted service.
3. **Execution Time (Month):** The time (month) corresponding by the execution of the contracted service.
   a. *Time Per Delay (Day):* The time corresponding to the contracted service delay.

b. *Time Per Addition (Day):* The time corresponding to the addition in the contracted service.
c. *Start Date (Useful Days):* The date corresponding to the start date of the contracted service.

4. **Time Per Function Point (Month):** The time corresponding by the execution of the contracted service per point function.
   a. *And Date (Useful Days):* The date corresponding to the and date of the contracted service.
5. **Cost Per Function Point**: The cost corresponding to the time of the execution of the contracted service per function point.
6. **Variable and Fixed Cost:** The cost corresponding to the costs fixed and variable of the contracted service.
7. **Total Cost**: The cost total corresponding to all costs fixed and variable of the contracted service.
8. **Profitability**: The total value plus the value of the profitability of the contracted service.
9. **Return on Investment:** The value of the profitability of the contracted service.
10. **Cost Per Addition (Days)**: The cost corresponding to the time added in the contracted service.
11. **Cost Per Delay (Days):** The cost corresponding to the time that exceeded the contracted service
12. **Liquid Margin of Sale of the Product_Service:** The value of the liquid margin corresponding to the contracted service.
    a. *Tax Margin of Sale of the Product_Service:* The value of the tax margin corresponding to the contracted service.
13. **Gross Margin Of Sale Of The Product_Service**: The value of the gross margin corresponding to the contracted service.

Figure 5. Application of the estimated of the result financial in IT
Source: Prepared by the authors, 2015

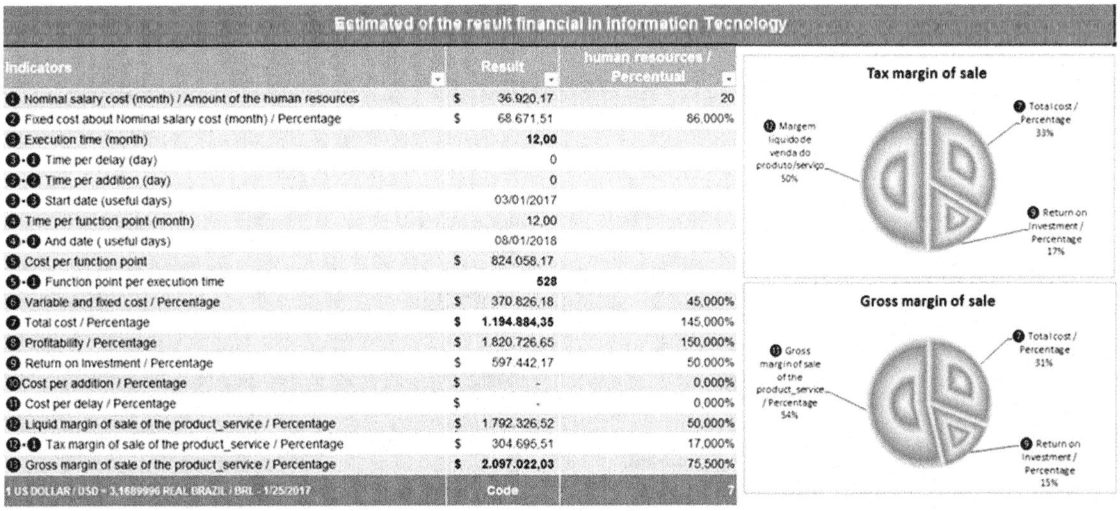

Estimated of the result financial in Information Tecnology

Indicators	Result		human resources / Percentual
1 Nominal salary cost (month) / Amount of the human resources	$	36.920,17	20
2 Fixed cost about Nominal salary cost (month) / Percentage	$	68.671,51	86,000%
3 Execution time (month)		**12,00**	
3-1 Time per delay (day)		0	
3-2 Time per addition (day)		0	
3-3 Start date (useful days)		03/01/2017	
4 Time per function point (month)		12,00	
4-1 And date (useful days)		08/01/2018	
5 Cost per function point	$	824.058,17	
5-1 Function point per execution time		**528**	
6 Variable and fixed cost / Percentage	$	370.826,18	45,000%
7 Total cost / Percentage	$	**1.194.884,35**	145,000%
8 Profitability / Percentage	$	1.820.726,65	150,000%
9 Return on investment / Percentage	$	597.442,17	50,000%
10 Cost per addition / Percentage	$	-	0,000%
11 Cost per delay / Percentage	$	-	0,000%
12 Liquid margin of sale of the product_service / Percentage	$	1.792.326,52	50,000%
12-1 Tax margin of sale of the product_service / Percentage	$	304.695,51	17,000%
13 Gross margin of sale of the product_service / Percentage	$	**2.097.022,03**	75,500%
1 US DOLLAR / USD = 3,1689996 REAL BRAZIL / BRL - 1/25/2017	Code		7

In short, sum up all the costs of the contracted service, applies the percentage of profitability that you want to get of return on investment, gets the liquid value of the contracted service, applies the percentage corresponding to taxes and gets the gross value of the contracted service.

With this liquid value of the product or service of software development, obtained in advance, it is possible, after the analysis of the planned investment, subtract the percentage of 25% of profitability and apply on the capital market, as shown in the future research directions.

FUTURE RESEARCH DIRECTIONS

This chapter allows to present future studies of research that strengthen the integration between IT organizations and the financial market, as follows.

Consortium of Nominative Planned Actions in the Financial Market

This section consists to present a model of the information management that strengthens the financial market with the participation of the small and medium IT companies.

For Soares et al. (2017), this model of the information management, aligned to the financial statement of the software development project in the IT organizations, aims to promote the consortium of planned actions nominative in the financial market.

For Soares et al. (2015), the objective of the management information model is to strengthen the financial market, promoting the participation of 33 small and medium IT companies, as shown in Figure 6.

Figure 6. Consortium of nominative planned actions in the financial market
Source: Prepared by the authors, 2015

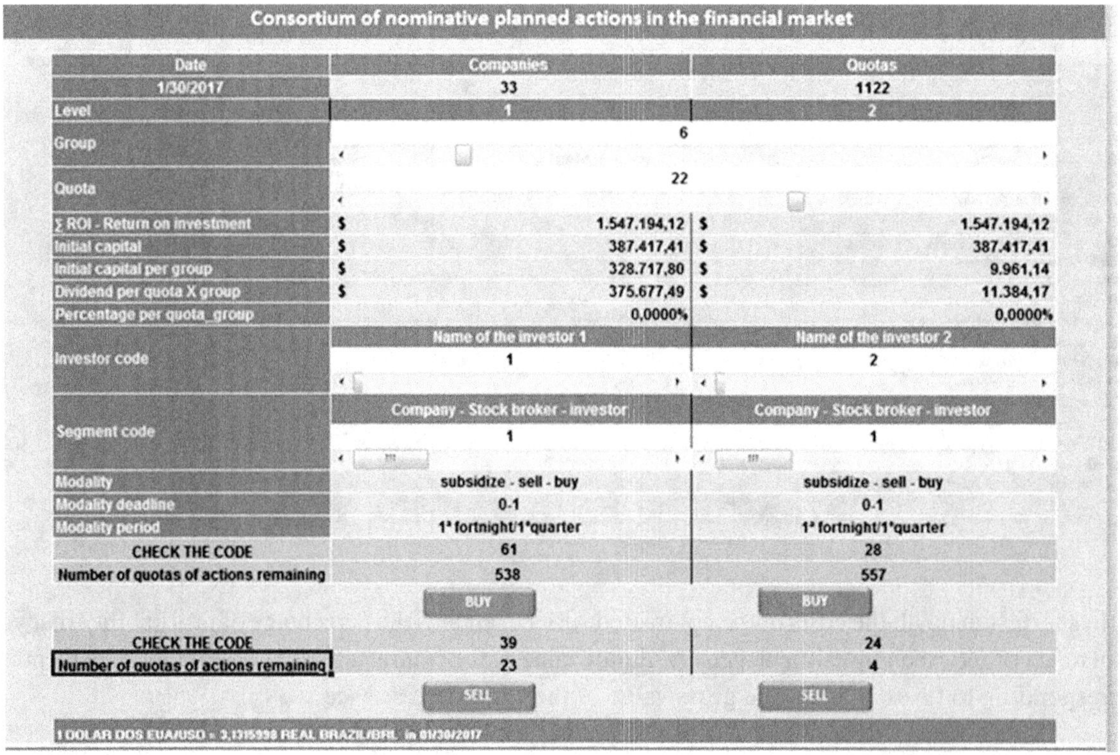

Consortium of nominative planned actions in the financial market		
Date	**Companies**	**Quotas**
1/30/2017	33	1122
Level	1	2
Group	6	
Quota	22	
Σ ROI - Return on investment	$ 1.547.194,12	$ 1.547.194,12
Initial capital	$ 387.417,41	$ 387.417,41
Initial capital per group	$ 328.717,80	$ 9.961,14
Dividend per quota X group	$ 375.677,49	$ 11.384,17
Percentage per quota_group	0,0000%	0,0000%
	Name of the investor 1	**Name of the investor 2**
Investor code	1	2
	Company - Stock broker - investor	**Company - Stock broker - investor**
Segment code	1	1
Modality	subsidize - sell - buy	subsidize - sell - buy
Modality deadline	0-1	0-1
Modality period	1ª fortnight/1ºquarter	1ª fortnight/1ºquarter
CHECK THE CODE	61	28
Number of quotas of actions remaining	538	557
	BUY	BUY
CHECK THE CODE	39	24
Number of quotas of actions remaining	23	4
	SELL	SELL
1 DOLAR DOS EUA/USD = 3,1315998 REAL BRAZIL/BRL in 01/30/2017		

The Table 3 presents the concepts of the elements that make up the consortium of nominative planned actions in the financial market.

Table 3. Description of the elements of the consortium of nominative planned actions

Description of the elements of the consortium of nominative planned actions	
Elements	Concepts
Date	corresponds the date of start of purchase or sale of actions.
Companies	corresponds the number total of companies participating in the consortium of nominative planned actions.
Quotas	corresponds the number total of quotas negotiable in the consortium of nominative planned actions.
Level	corresponds to the level of the amount to be invested.
Group	corresponds to group of 33 small and medium IT companies participating in the consortium of the nominative planned actions.
Quota	corresponds the quota of the group of 33 small and medium IT companies participating in the consortium of nominative planned actions.
ROI – Return on investment	corresponds to the return on investment of 33 small and medium IT companies participating in the consortium of the nominative planned actions.
Initial capital	corresponds to the value of 25% of the return on investment of 33 small and medium IT companies participating in the consortium of the planned actions nominative, more the rates of purchase or sale of actions.
Initial capital per group	corresponds to the value of 25% of the return on investment of 33 small and medium IT companies per group.
Dividend per quota x group	corresponds to the dividend per quota x group.
Percentage per quota and group	corresponds to the percentage per quota and group chosen by the investor for the purchase or sale of actions of 33 small and medium IT companies participating in the consortium of the nominative planned actions.
Investor code	corresponds to the code of interested people in invest part of their profit in the buy and sell of actions.
Segment cod	corresponds to the code of the segment where it will be negotiated the purchase and sale of actions.
Modality	corresponds to the negotiation modality (subsidy, sell, buy).
Modality deadline	corresponds to the deadline of the negotiation modality (subsidy, sell, buy).
Modality period	corresponds to the period of the negotiation modality (subsidy, sell, buy).
Check the code	corresponds to the code of the buy or sell of quotas of actions.
Number of quotas of actions remaining	corresponds to the number of quotas of actions remaining.

Source: Prepared by the authors, 2016

Chronology of Consortium of Nominative Planned Actions in the Financial Market

This section consists in present the chronology of the consortium of nominative planned actions.

For Soares et al. (2017), this chronology corresponds to the study of the time that determines the period of purchase and sale of actions of the consortium of nominative planned actions.

For Soares et al. (2016), this consortium allows to plan, negotiate, investigate and evaluate the purchase and sale of actions of 33, small and medium, IT companies, of the brokerage of values and investors, starting from the anticipation of 25% of profitability of the monthly billing of software project obtained by analysis of the financial statement in software project, as shown in Figure 7.

Figure 7. Chronology of the consortium of nominative planned actions in the financial market
Source: Prepared by the authors, 2016.

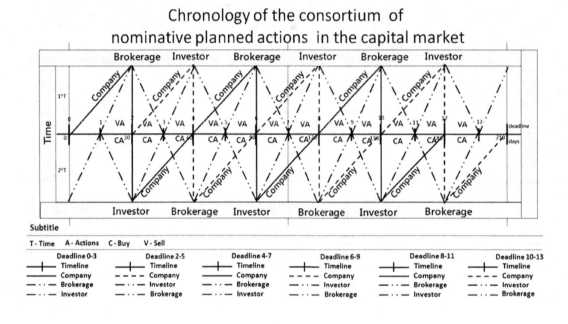

The cycle of the chronology of the consortium of nominative planned actions, can be interpreted, as shown in Tables 4, 5 and 6.

Table 4. Cycle of the chronology of the consortium of nominative planned actions in 90 days per events, 1ˢᵗ time

Cycle of the chronology of the consortium of nominative planned actions in 90 days per events							
Time Pillars	**1ˢᵗ time**						**Deadline Events Cycle**
	Days	**Deadline**	**Events**	**Days**	**Deadline**	**Events**	**Total (days)**	
Company IT	15	0-1	Subsidizes titles of emission	-	-	-	15	Plan
Brokerage of value	30	1-3	Opens for the buy of actions	30	3-5	Opens to the sale of actions	60	Negotiate
Investors			Buy actions			sale actions		
Brokerage of value	-	-	-	15	5-6	Investigate the result	15	Investigate And
Total (days)	45	-	-	45	-	-	90	Evaluate

Source: Prepared by the authors, 2016

Table 5. Cycle of the chronology of the consortium of nominative planned actions in 90 days per events, 2st time

Time Pillars	Cycle of the chronology of the consortium of nominative planned actions in 90 days per events							
	2st time						Total (days)	Deadline Events Cycle
	Days	Deadline	Events	Days	Deadline	Events		
Company IT	15	2-3	Subsidizes titles of emission	-	-	-	15	Plan
Brokerage of value	30	3-5	Opens for the buy of actions	30	5-7	Opens to the sale of actions	60	Negotiate
Investors			Buy actions			sale actions		
Brokerage of value	-	-	-	15	7-8	Investigate the result	15	Investigate And Evaluate
Total (days)	45	-	-	45	-	-	90	

Source: Prepared by the authors, 2016

Table 6. Summary of the cycle of the chronology of the consortium of nominative planned actions in 90 days

Times Pillars	Summary of the cycle of the chronology of the consortium of nominative planned actions				
	1st time		2st time		Deadline Cycle
	Days	Deadline	Days	Deadline	
Company IT	15	0-1	15	2-3	Plan
Brokerage of value/ Investors	60	1-5	60	3-7	Negotiate
Brokerage of value	15	5-6	15	7-8	Investigate and evaluate
Total (days)	90	0-6	90	2-8	

Source: Prepared by the authors, 2016

In a market vision, the consortium of nominative planned actions in the financial market can be used by the brokerages of value to link IT organizations in the financial market, with the participation of investors, as shown in Figure 8.

Soares et al. (2017) also point out that the factors that strengthen the financial market are:

- Small and medium IT companies subsidize actions in the financial market;
- Small and medium IT companies hire more people, purchase machinery;
- Small and medium IT companies generate more revenue for the government;
- Financial market sale and purchase shares to the people (investors);
- Financial market subsidize financial resources for small and medium IT companies;
- People purchase and sale actions;
- People consume goods and services;
- People generate revenue for the government;
- Government build roads, schools, hospitals;

- Brazil move the economy;
- Brazil export and import supplies and products.

Figure 8. Chain of planned investment in the financial market
Source: Prepared by the authors, 2015

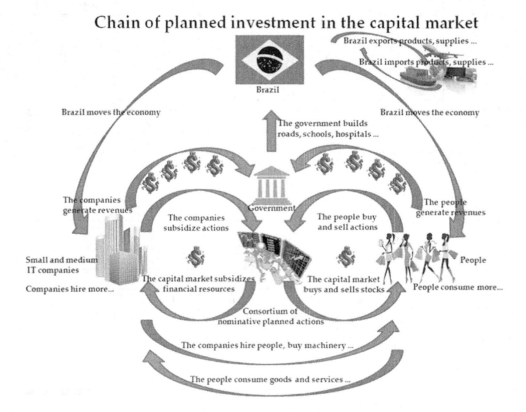

CONCLUSION

This chapter emphasizes that is favorable to align the cycle of causes and effects of innovative methods, enabling the analysis of planned investment to strengthen the management in information technology companies.

The favourable methods are the plan of professional career, the metrics of the plan professional career and the financial statement of the project of software development in the IT companies.

These methods, in addition to anticipate the necessary costs for the construction of the project of software development and analysis of the planned investment, allowing to maximize profits and reduce costs for the better decision making, aimed at motivation and measurement of the human resources for performance, productivity, organizational learning and growth in the professional career. They also meet the needs and expectations of the company and the customer with the continuous improvement in the building of the contracted service of the project of software development in the IT companies.

With this motivator scenario, with effect of anticipative and strengthening that aligns innovative methods in a cycle of causes and effects, enabling the analysis of planned investment for the better decision making in the IT companies, provides the government, generate revenue, move the economy and generate more wealth in Brazil.

REFERENCES

Amboni, N., & Andrade, R. O. B. (2009). *General theory of the administration*. Rio de Janeiro: Elsevier.

Campos, V. F. (1990). Total quality management: strategy to increase competitive brazilian company competitiveness. Belo Horizonte: Christiano Foundation Ottoni. UFMG's engineering school, Rio de Janeiro, Bloch Ed.

Campos, V. F. (2004). *Routine management of day-to-day work* (8th ed.). Belo Horizonte: INDG Technology and Services Ltda.

Ching, H. Y. (2014). *Measuring and managing activities: ABC models and balanced scorecard*. Retrieved from http://www.portaladm.adm.br/af/aof31.pdf

Costa, C. E. (2007). *The Processes of People Management*. Available in http://www.administradores.com.br/informe-se/producao-academica/os-processos-de-gestao-de-pessoas/519/

Gitman, L. J. (1997). *Principles of financial management*. São Paulo: Harbra.

Gropelli, A. A., & Nikbakht. (1998). *Financial administration*. São Paulo: Saraiva.

Kaplan, R. S., & Norton, D. P. (1997). *The strategy in action: Balanced Scorecard* (4th ed.). Rio de Janeiro: Campus.

Scartezini, L. M. B. (2014). *Analysis and improvement of processes*. Retrieved from http://www.aprendersempre.org.br/arqs/GE%20B%20-%20An%E1lise-e-Melhoria de-Processos.pdf

Seleme, R. B. (2014). *Guidelines and practices of financial management and tax guidelines*. Retrieved from http://ava.grupouninter.com.br/tead/hyperibook/IBPEX/protegidos/ DIRETRIZES_E_PRATICA_-_IBPEX_DIGITAL.pdf

Soares, E. R., & Zaidan, F. H. (2016). Information Architecture and Business Modeling in Modern Organizations of Information Technology: *Professional Career Plan in the IT Organizations*. In *Handbook of Research on Information Architecture and Management in Modern Organizations*. IGI Global. doi:10.4018/978-1-4666-8637-3.ch020

Soares, E. R., & Zaidan, F. H. (2016). Defensive Strategies in Organizations of Information Technology: *Financial Statement of Software Project associate to the metrics of the Career Plan Professional*. In *Defensive strategies: Ensuring Competitive Advantages already Conquered*. Rio de Janeiro, RJ: Novaterra.

Soares, E. R., & Zaidan, F. H. (2017). Composition of the Financial Logistic Costs of the Organizations of Information Technology, linked to the Financial Market:*Financial Indicators of the Software Development Project*. In *Handbook of Research on Information Management for Effective Logistics and Supply Chains*. IGI Global; doi:10.4018/978-1-5225-0973-8

Soares, E. R., Zaidan, F. H., & Jamil, G. L. (2013). *Professional career plan linked to the quality of the software development process in IT companies*. Annals & Abstracts: 10th CONTECSI International Congress of Technology Management and Information System, TECSI-FEA USP, São Paulo, SP, Brazil. doi 10.5748/9788599693094-10contecsi/rf-377

Soares, E. R., Zaidan, F. H., & Jamil, G. L. (2014). *Metrics of professional career plan linked to the quality of the software development process in IT companies*. Annals & Abstracts: 11th CONTECSI International Congress of Technology Management and Information System, TECSI-FEA USP, São Paulo, SP, Brazil. doi 10.5748/9788599693100-11contecsi/ps-687

Soares, E. R., Zaidan, F. H., & Jamil, G. L. (2015). *Financial statement of software project associated with the metrics of professional career plan linked to the quality of the software development process in the IT companies*. Annals & Abstracts: 12th CONTECSI International Congress of Technology Management and Information System, TECSI-FEA USP, São Paulo, SP, Brazil. doi 10.5748/9788599693117-12contecsi/rf-1909

Soares, E. R., Zaidan, F. H., & Jamil, G. L. (2015). Consortium of Nominative Planned Actions on the Stock Exchange associated with the Financial Demontrativo in the IT Organizations. In *Spanish-Brazilian Workshop on Corporate Governance Technologies Information, 2015 Santander / Spain. GETI 2015*. Santander, Spain: Editorial University of Cantabria.

Soares, E. R., Zaidan, F. H., & Jamil, G. L. (2016). *Chronology of the consortium of nominative planned actions in the financial market associated with the financial demonstrative in the IT organizations*. Annals & Abstracts: 13th CONTECSI International Congress of Technology Management and Information System, TECSI-FEA USP, São Paulo, SP, Brazil. 10.5748/9788599693124-13CONTECSI/MS-4117

KEY TERMS AND DEFINITIONS

Balanced Scorecard: Methodology of performance management focused on the dimension of the learning and growth.

Chronology: The study of the time and its divisions, with the objective of distinguish the order of occurrence of events.

Companies Plaintiffs: The companies that hire the services of information technology.

Consortium: An association of two or more individuals, companies, organizations, or governments with the objective of participate in a common activity or of resource sharing to achieve a common goal.

Deadline: The deadline of purchase and sale of actions in the financial market, through of the consortium of nominative planned actions.

Financial Statement: Document that representing the financial statement of the company, through financial indicators.

Function Point (FP): Technique for the measurement of the project of software development.

Information Technology: Systems, software, devices, and its associated management tools, which offer technological services for numberless organizational applications.

Knowledge Management: Managerial definitions oriented to deal with organizational knowledge, approaching its production, sharing, valuation, storing, and processing for final applications.

Motivation: Impulse that makes with that the human resources act to achieve their goals.

Organizational Learning: Interactive dynamics to acquire knowledge.

PDCA: Iterative method of management in four steps, plan, do, check, and act, used for the control and continuous improvement of the processes and products.

Pillars: They are companies and financial institutions participating in the consortium of nominative planned actions in the financial market.

Planned Investment: It is the process of planned investment that allows to align the methods in building of the association between IT organizations and the financial market.

Process: A definition of a complete task that can be managed in parts or in its whole conception, including the relationship of its internal phases.

This research was previously published in the Handbook of Research on Strategic Innovation Management for Improved Competitive Advantage; pages 192-210, copyright year 2018 by Business Science Reference (an imprint of IGI Global).

Chapter 84

Intuitionistic Fuzzy Decision Making Towards Efficient Team Selection in Global Software Development

Mukta Goyal

https://orcid.org/0000-0001-6726-3073

Jaypee Institute of Information Technology, India

Chetna Gupta

Jaypee Institute of Information Technology, India

ABSTRACT

For successful completion of any software project, an efficient team is needed. This task becomes more challenging when the project is to be completed under global software development umbrella. The manual selection of team members based on some expert judgment may lead to inappropriate selection. In reality, there are hundreds of employees in an organization and a single expert may be biased towards any member. Thus, there is a need to adopt methods which consider multiple selection criteria with multiple expert views for making appropriate selection. This article uses an intuitionistic fuzzy approach to handle uncertainty in the expert's decision in multicriteria group decision making process and ranking among the finite team members. An intuitionistic fuzzy Muirhead Mean (IFMM) is used to aggregate the intuitionistic criteria's. To gain confidence between criteria and expert score relationship, the Annova test is performed. The results are promising with p value as small as 0.02 and one-tail t-test score equals to 0.0000002.

DOI: 10.4018/978-1-6684-3702-5.ch084

1. INTRODUCTION

Delivering right product within allocated time and budget is both critical and challenging in today's competitive time-to-deliver market. Successful software projects face number of challenges during development life time ranging from understanding stakeholder, changing requirements, software complexity, optimistic schedules, time to deliver pressure, situational factors, managing right skilled people required for each project's unique demands. Due to advancement in Information Technology (IT), there is a steep decline in internet access cost which has resulted in a shift from centralized development work culture to distributed development culture. As a result, organizations have realized the importance of virtual world networks which provide advantages like efficient time management, lower development cost, decline in travel costs, access to larger skilled team members for choosing right skilled people and closer proximity to market and customers (Lee-Kelley, 2006). This aspect of globalization is well captured and utilized by many organizations for software development and is broadly categorized as Global Software Development (GSD).

Global Software Development has numerous benefits in overcoming barriers of different time zones and of multi-site development at various geographical locations with reduction in overall cost of development (Binder,2009; Kern & Willcocks, 2000).The literature has reported several benefits associated with GSD adoption such as, greater availability of human resources and multi-skilled workforce, lower costs, shorter time-to-market cycles (separated Conchuir etal., 2009; Milewsk et al., 2008; Smite et al., 2010; Kommeren et al., 2007; Soora et al., 2008) to name few. This geographically collaborative effort makes adoption of GSD complex in itself and presents a number of challenges ranging from planning and managing of task allocation, coordination and inter-site communication, knowledge sharing, interpersonal relationships, individual technical experience skills, team roles and responsibilities, efficiency, trust among team members, to coordination and inter-site communication barriers in various project management issues (Avritzer et al., 2010; Casey et al., 2009; Garcia-Crespo et al., 2010; Colomo-Palacios et al., 2012; Hernandez-Lopez et al., 2010a; Islam et al., 2009; Deshpande et al., 2012; Ebert, 2010). Research in past has shown that there is a need to address various challenges, issues and risks of adopting GSD (Keshlaf & Riddle, 2010).

Hence, this research aims at selection of software project team members across the globe having different configurations in terms of knowledge, skill, communication and management. Stevens (1998) have discussed how a good configured team has positive impact on team performance, productivity and success of software system. One of the challenging tasks in identification and selection of team members in global software engineering environment is to decide who among the people from the teams (separated geographically) are to be selected for developing a particular project under GSD umbrella. There exist hundreds of individuals in an organization with varied excellences and skills to support various dimensions of a particular project globally. But the reality is that, all individuals cannot be selected to represent the core team for a particular project. This process of identification and selection of core team members for GSD is in fact, a complex multi-criteria decision-making process. The foremost challenge here is to define the most appropriate target criterion for ranking individuals so that the best from the pool of people can be selected. If a single criterion is taken into consideration then it becomes easier to decide the ranking of a given individual, but if there are more than one criteria's, then the decision becomes far more difficult, because a wrong decision can result in extra cost to the organization and the impact of same can be manifolds.

Numerous models have been proposed which emphasize on importance of team composition but till date there is no such technique that researchers and industry has found effective in yielding positive results (Šmiteet al., 2010; Kankanhalli et al., 2004; Gilal et al., 2016; Carmel & Agarwal, 2001; Braun, 2007; Pichle, 2007; Cataldo et al., 2009; Smithet al., 2002; Lee-Kelley et al., 2008; Ebertet al., 2008;Casey & Richardson, 2006; Hofner & Mani, 2007; Lacity et al., 2008). (Bello et al., 2018) have used ant colony optimization, a metaheuristic algorithm to select team by two employers from a set of candidates that is common to both. The imprecise description of the applicant's competence and existence of several experts makes the selection of the candidate a difficult task. Thus, fuzzy set is a suitable tool to attain the maximum possible information from vague and imprecise data (Canós et al., 2014). Fuzzy set consists of only of membership degree whereas intuitionistic fuzzy set (IFS) consists of membership degree as well as non-membership degree. Thus, IFS is a more suitable way to deal vagueness when compared to fuzzy set (Boran et al., 2011). Therefore, due to uncertainty and imprecision of identification and selection of geographically separated team members in multi-attribute decision making environment with respect to GSD, an intuitionistic fuzzy approach is proposed to enhance the productivity and performance as an outcome of the whole identification and selection process.

This paper uses the concept of intuitionistic fuzzy muirhead mean (MM) aggregation operator to handle one of the challenges of selecting optimal team members for GSD. We explore the use of multi criteria decision support system to perform effective selection of the team members. The first objective of this paper is to identify prime criteria's that influence individual selection for global software development projects. The identification of these prime criteria's for individual selection will help management in ensuring that important factors pertaining to success of project are not missed while making selection. For supporting the multi criteria decision support system this paper uses a likert scale to express the expert's preferences for each individual on prime criteria. An intuitionistic fuzzy approach is used to aggregate opinion of various experts. The Muirhead mean is capable of handling interrelationships among any number of arguments assigned by a variable vector to process the intuitionistic fuzzy numbers (IFNs) and then to solve the multi-attribute decision making (MADM) problem. MAGDM provides the ranking results for the finite alternatives or select best choice from them according to the attribute values of different alternatives (Li, 2014). This will help in selecting right skilled people for a particular project without making compromise in productivity and success of software under development. Main contributions of this research are summarized as follows:

- Proposal of multi criteria intuitionistic fuzzy approach to select team members for software development separated globally.
- Efficient handling and management of multi-attribute decision making with multiple experts to attain the objective of this research.
- Proposal of dynamic intuitionistic fuzzy expert weight method to handle issue of priority assignment over one another.

The rest of the paper is organized as related work, preliminaries about intuitionistic fuzzy and muirhead mean operator. Section 3 describes the methodology to compute the performance of team members and ranking among them. Last section describes the result.

2. RELATED WORK

Over the past few decades researchers have shifted their focus from developing software and software technologies to human side of software engineering (Stevens, 1998; Dymova & Sevastjanov, 2016; Zhang & Xu, 2015). According to (Dugenci, 2016) researchers have explored domains aiding teambuilding, promote teamwork, personality composition of team members and foster communication, coordination, and collaboration (Nguyen, 2015; Li& Ren, 2015) have discussed how human aspects such as personalities and cultural identities influence software development life cycle and productivity. Galton (2003) in his work has pointed out that for success of GSD software systems, team members must collaborate efficiently, take responsibility as individuals, work as one team and must have positive attitude towards responsibilities required while performing integration of specific tasks into a larger system. Parker (2000) has stated very clearly that "Not every group is a team, and not every team is effective"; hence there is a need to device mechanism to choose best people from the pool of people available around the globe for building successful projects while minimizing various issues and challenges. This "people factor" is well supported by Bohner & Mohan (2009), stating that human factor is the main ingredient for successful project. Study conducted in (Liu & Jin, 2012) demonstrated that software productivity is influenced by the development environment attributes, system product attributes, and project team members' attributes.

Literature supports that there is still no recipe for successful and efficient performance in globally distributed software engineering (Smite et al., 2010). For multi criteria support researchers have also explored the uses of fuzzy preference relations to represent the opinion of group of experts/decision makers as an effective tool to aggregate decision makers preferences though various preference relations such as multiplicative preference relations (Saaty, 1980), linguistic preference relations(Alonso et al.,2009; Cabrerizo et al., 2009), and intuitionistic fuzzy preference relations(Liao and. Xu, 2014; Szmidt & Kacprzyk, 2003;Wu & Chiclana, 2014) to aggregate opinion of different decision makers. Intuitionistic fuzzy sets have been used in many dimensions to solve the MADM problems highlighted in various papers (Montajabiha, 2016; Li et al., 2015; Liu, 2014; Gifford, 2003; John et al., 2005; Gorla et al., 2004; Cunha, et al., 2009; De Souza et al., 2009; Kitchenham & Mendes, 2004)

3. PRELIMINARIES

The generalization of fuzzy sets was proposed by Atanassov (1986) in the form of intuitionistic fuzzy sets (IFS), which incorporate the degree of hesitation, called hesitation margin. Hesitation margin is defined as 1 minus the sum of membership and non-membership degree. The applications of intuitionistic fuzzy sets are decision making, medical diagnosis, pattern recognition, market prediction, facility location selection and other real-life applications. Due to the flexibility of IFS in handling uncertainty, the tools developed based on it are more consistent for human reasoning, under imperfectly defined facts and imprecise knowledge. This section discusses the definition of IFS, some operation on intuitionistic fuzzy sets and the intuitionistic fuzzy Muirhead mean operator.

Definition 1: An IFS A in X is an object having the following form:

$$A = \{ \left(x, \mu_A\left(x\right), \nu_A\left(x\right)\right) | x \in X \},$$

which is characterized by a membership function μA and a non-membership function νA, where

$$\mu_A : X \to [0,1], x \in X \to \mu_A(x) \in [0,1],$$

$$\nu_A : X \to [0,1], x \in X \to \nu_A(x) \in [0,1],$$

with the condition: $\mu_A(x)+\nu_A(x) \leq 1$ for all $x \in X$ for each IFS A in X, if

$$\pi_A(x) = 1 - \mu_A(x) - \nu_A(x),$$

for all $x \in X$, $\pi_A(x)$ is called the degree of indeterminacy of x to A. It is a hesitancy degree of x to A which is equal to $0 \leq \pi_A(x) \leq 1$ for all $x \in X$.

3.1. Basic Relations and Operations on Intuitionistic Fuzzy Sets

Some operations on two intuitionistic fuzzy sets A and B are defined as (Atanassov, 1986):

[Inclusion] $A \subseteq B \leftrightarrow \mu_A(x) \leq \mu_B(x) and \nu_A(x) \geq \nu_B(x) \forall x \in X.$

[Equality] $A = B \leftrightarrow \mu_A(x) = \mu_B(x) and \nu_A(x) = \nu_B(x) \forall x \in X.$

[Complement] $A^c = \{\langle x, \nu_A(x), \mu_A(x) \rangle : x \in X \}.$

[Union] $A \cup B = \{ < x, \max(\mu_A(x), \mu_B(x)), \min(\nu_A(x), \nu_B(x)) > \ : x \in X \}.$

[Intersection] $A \cap B = \{ < x, \min(\mu_A(x), \mu_B(x)), \max(\nu_A(x), \nu_B(x)) > \ : x \in X \}.$

[Addition] $A \oplus B = \{ < x, (\mu_A(x) + \mu_B(x) - \mu_A(x)\mu_B(x)), (\nu_A(x).\nu_B(x)) >: x \in X \}.$

[Multiplication] $A \otimes B = \{ < x, (\mu_A(x).\mu_B(x)), (\nu_A(x) + \nu_B(x) - \nu_A(x).\nu_B(x)) > \ : x \in X \}.$

[Difference] $A - B = \{ < x, \min(\mu_A(x), \mu_B(x)), \max(\nu_A(x), \nu_B(x)) >: x \in X \}.$

[Symmetric difference]
$\{A \Delta B = \{x, \max[\min(\mu_A, \nu_B), \min(\nu_A, \mu_B)], \min[\max(\frac{1}{2}, \mu_B), \max(\nu_B, \mu_A)] >: x \in X\}.$

[Cartesian product] $A \times B = \{\langle \mu_A(x).\mu_B(x), \nu_A(x).\nu_B(x) \rangle : x \in X\}.$

Definition 2: Let $a=(\mu,v)$ be an intuitionistic fuzzy number. The score function S of a is defined as

$$S\left(a\right)=\mu-vS\left(a\right)\in\left[-1,1\right].$$

Definition 3: Let $a=(\mu,v)$ be an intuitionistic fuzzy number, an accuracy function H of a can be represented as

$$H\left(a\right)=\mu+vH\left(a\right)\in\left[0,1\right].$$

The two intuitionistic fuzzy numbers can be compared based on the score function and accuracy function.

Definition 4: Let $a_1=(\mu_1,v_1)$ and $a_2=(\mu_2,v_2)$ be two intuitionistic fuzzy numbers, $S(a_1)=\mu_1-v_1$ and $S(a_2)=\mu_2-v_2$ be the score functions of a_1 and a_2, respectively, and let $H(a_1)=\mu_1-v_1$ and $H(a_2)=\mu_2+v_2$ be the accuracy functions of a_1 and a_2, respectively, then:

If $S(a_1)<S(a_2)$, then a_1 is smaller than a_2, denoted by $a_1<a_2$;
If $S(a_1)=S(a_2)$, then
    1) if $H(a_1)<H(a_2)$, then a_1 is smaller than a_2, denoted by $a_1<a_2$;
    2) if $H(a_1)=H(a_2)$, then a_1 and a_2 represent the same information, denoted by $a_1=a_2$.

3.2. Intuitionistic Fuzzy Muirhead Mean Operator

Definition 5: Let $\alpha_i=(u_i,v_i)(i=1,2,..n)$ be a collection of IFNs and $P=(p_1,p_2,....,p_n)\in R_n$ be a vector of parameters. If

$$IFMM^{p}\left(\alpha_1,\alpha_2,....\alpha_n\right)=\left(\frac{1}{\angle n\sum_{\vartheta\in S_n}\prod_{j=1}^{n}\alpha_{\vartheta(j)}^{P_j}}\right)^{\frac{1}{\sum_{j=1}^{n}P_j}} \tag{1}$$

Then we call *IFMM^P* the intuitionistic fuzzy MM(IFMM), where $\vartheta(j)(j=1,2,...,n)$ is any a permutation of $(1, 2, ..n)$, and S_n is the collection of all permutations of $(1, 2, ..n)$ (Liu & Li, 2017).

Theorem 1. Let $\alpha_i=(u_i,v_i)(1,2,..n)$ be a collection of the IFNs, then, the aggregation result from definition is still an IFN, and it can be obtained that

$$IFMM^{p}\left(\alpha_1,\alpha_2,...\alpha_n\right)=\left(\left(1-\left(\prod_{\vartheta\in S_n}\left(1-\prod_{j=1}^{n}\mu_{\vartheta(j)}^{P_j}\right)\right)^{\frac{1}{n}}\right)^{\frac{1}{\sum_{j=1}^{n}P_j}},1-\left(1-\left(\prod_{\vartheta\in S_n}\left(\left(1-\prod_{j=1}^{n}\left(1-v_{\vartheta(j)}\right)^{P_j}\right)\right)^{\frac{1}{n}}\right)^{\frac{1}{\sum_{j=1}^{n}P_j}}\right)\right) \tag{2}$$

The next section explains the methodology to select the suitable team members having different features in global software development environment by various experts.

4. METHODOLOGY

This section explains the selection of competitive team member measured on different parameters by various experts. Suppose that there are n experts $[EX_1, EX_2, EX_3,...,EX_n]$ to evaluate m teammates $[t_1, t_2, ...,t_m]$ with respect to n attributes $[A_1, A_2, A_3,...,A_n]$ in a global software development process, where the weight vector of the attribute is $w_1, w_2,...,w_n$ satisfying $w_j \geq 0$ where (j=1,2,...n), $\sum_{j=1}^{n} w_j = 1$ and weight vector of experts is $w=(w_1, w_2,...,w_n)$ and satisfying $w_k \geq 0$, $k=1,2,...,q$. Here the attributes are represent in terms of knowledge, skill, communication and management. Thus, foremost step in this direction is to identify prime criteria's that influence individual selection for Global software development projects.

4.1. Identification of Prime Criteria's for Individual Assessment

Different skill set, different knowledge is required to develop a software project in a global environment. One should have good communication skills to communicate with different people from other countries. Thus, it is important to choose the right person for a specific project according to their skills, knowledge in a global environment. The attributes of a team member have been considered through performance assessment/evaluation system. Every organization does performance assessment/evaluated independently annually in the form of appraisals for each and every employee by project managers or managers. This is a systematic way of examining how well an employee has performed in his or her assigned project/ assignment over a period of time. These performance evaluations are maintained in central repositories. A central repository is a computer storage place which is used to keep and maintain aggregation of data in an organized way. It can be used to view specific files or documents or perform selective extraction of data. Accurate information is absolute critical component required while assessing individuals for global team selection in ensuring that important factors pertaining to success of project are not missed while making selection. For this purpose, this research has identified 19 prime criteria's for a team member given in Table 1. These are divided into three major categories namely, individual past experience, individual performance based on old/historic projects and team work related assessment. Each of these three categories has individual criteria's (C1 to C19) as shown in Table 1. Experts can use data stored in central repository as reference to rank individuals on identified criteria's given in Table 1. Experts are project managers or managers under whom the individuals have worked for specific projects in past. This way of collecting historic information of performance assessment about knowledge, skill, communication and management about an individual will help in making accurate decision on identified prime factors of Table 1.

Each team member is evaluated for all 19 criteria's listed above on total ordered discrete linguistic label set such that, S = S_1 - not at all, S_2 - very little, S_3 - little, S_4=medium, S_5 -Quite well, S_6 - very well, S_7 - extremely well S_8. – Perfect.Here {S_1, S_2, S_3... represented as 1, 2, 3..., respectively}. After defining the parameters, experts have to rank each individual using these linguistic variables. Next section describes the selection process.

Table 1. Prime criteria's

Criteria's	Categorization	Remarks
C1		Programmer experience in project domain
C2		Language and tool experience
C3	Individual Past Experience	Use of software tools
C4		Contribution to team effort
C5		Completion of assigned or agreed-upon responsibilities
C6		Completion of assigned or agree-upon tasks on time
C7		Completing tasks fully and on time
C8		Independence of thought and action
C9	Individual performance based on old projects	Creativity in approach to problem
C10		Scientific attitude
C11		Determination and effort
C12		Contributing to discussions
C13		Accepting criticism gracefully
C14		Communicate clearly and with civility with team
C15		Communicate clearly and with civility with stakeholders
C16	Team Work Related	Collaborative work friendly
C17		Effective use of time
C18		Leadership
C19		Ability to understand concepts and views

4.2. Selection Process

Figure 1 presents the architecture of the selection process which is divided into 5 main steps. The process starts with conversion of expert score computed in above section into intuitionistic fuzzy score. In step 2 weight of each expert corresponding to each individual is computed. Thereafter aggregation of weighted score of each expert is computed in step 3 followed by aggregation of criteria's in step 4. In step 5 ranks are computed for all team members based on the final score computation. The detailed discussions of the steps followed in selection process are explained below.

4.2.1. Step 1: Conversion of Expert Decision into Intuitionistic Fuzzy Set

The initial expert decision values for each individual on different parameters are received as a crisp set. These crisp set are mapped into intuitionistic fuzzy set value using equation (3), (4), (5) Equation 3 represent as non-membership value, equation 4 represent as hesitation margin and equation 5 represent as for membership values (Tripathy et al., 2016).

Figure 1. Selection process flow

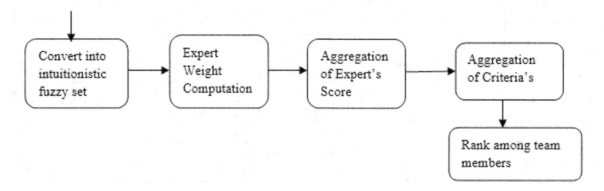

$$N\left(m\left(x\right)\right) = \frac{1 - m\left(x\right)}{1 + \lambda_m\left(x\right)} \quad \text{where } \lambda > 0, N(1) = 0, N(0) = 1 \tag{3}$$

For hesitation margin,

$$\pi(m\left(x\right)) = \frac{\left(1 - m\left(x\right)\right) - \left(1 - m\left(x\right)\right)}{1 + \lambda_m\left(x\right)} \tag{4}$$

For membership value

$$\mu_A(x) + v_A(x) \leq 1 \tag{5}$$

Step 2 describes the computation of weight of each expert corresponding to each individual.

4.2.2. Step 2: Estimation of Dynamic Expert Weight

It is difficult to decide who among the experts are more important than others and who's score value should be given more priority. To address this issue, this paper proposes a dynamic intuitionistic fuzzy expert weight method in which score is calculated for each team member, for each criterion and average score is assigned as weight of the expert. Figure 2 explain the estimation of dynamic expert weight.

Step 3: In step 3, aggregation of all expert's corresponding to all criteria's is calculated using equation 2 for each individual. Here $R^k(k=1,2,\ldots,q)$ represent for each expert matrix convert into a collective matrix by intuitionistic fuzzy muirhead mean operator (IFWMM).

$$r_{ij} = IFWMM\left(r^1_{ij,} r^2_{ij,} \ldots r^n_{ij,}\right) \tag{9}$$

Figure 2. Calculation of dynamic expert weight

Algorithm 1: Estimation of dynamic expert weight

Consider for each expert and team member corresponding to every criteria (E_i, T_j, C_k) where $\{E_i, T_j, C_k \in S\}$

Here, E_i represent the expert from i=1 to 4 whereas T_j represent the team member of the project and criteria C_k represent the attribute value of the team member.

S is score for each team memeber j = 1 to n

for each criteria k=1 to n

Calculate $S_j(a) = \max(0, |\mu_j - v_j|)$;   (6)

$j = j + 1$;

$k = k + 1$;

end;

end;

/* calculate the weight of each Expert

$W_i = \sum_{k=1}^{n} \frac{S_k(a)}{n}$;   (7)

$i = i + 1$;

end

If ($\sum E_i$ is > 1) then

$W_i = \frac{E_i}{\sum_{i=1}^{n} E_i}$;   (8)

else

$W_i = 1$;

Here $S(a) = (\mu, v)$, is an intuitionistic fuzzy number where μ is the membership value and v is the non-membership value.

E_i is expert (i=1 to 4), $w = (w_1, w_2, \ldots \ldots w_n)^T$ is the weight vector of criteria C_k(k=1,2,……..n) and $w_i > 0$ and $\sum_{i=1}^{n} w_i = 1$.

After aggregating expert opinion to rank among each individual, aggregation of each criteria's value is required, this is processed in Step 4.

Step 4: Equation 10 is used to aggregate criteria's for each team member. The criteria's represent as r_{ij}(j=1,2,…,n) values are converted into comprehensive value R_i, by IFWMM operator

$$z_i = IFWMM\left(r_{i1}, r_{i2}, \ldots, r_{in}\right) \tag{10}$$

Step 5 - Ranking Process: In step 5 rank among the team members are computed based on the score function and accuracy which is defined by definition 4.

5. EXPERIMENTAL RESULTS AND DISCUSSION

This section discusses the results of proposed algorithm. As stated above the success of any project depends upon the productivity and performance of team member. Therefore, the productivity metrics must be based on the factors related to team performance, usage of software tools, experience and other relevant parameters. Thus, these criteria's becomes the important feature of the team member. The proposed algorithm provides comprehensive performance evaluations based on 19 criteria's by considering weights of all experts that may reasonably comment on each individual. To reduce the uncertainty and improves precision in decision of expert's an intuitionistic fuzzy approach is used. This technique present significant relationships with performance predictors and has been shown to be a reliable and valid measure of team member performance.

5.1. Data Collection

To conduct this study, a total of 4 experts, 10 individuals (team member) are selected. Experts were asked to rank each team member using Likert scale. This score is converted into intuitionistic fuzzy score using equation (3), (4) and (5) as explained in section 4.2, step 1. Correlation among each expert and between team member is calculated using Pearson correlation [ref]. Figure 3 (a)-(j) presents correlation values between different experts and each team member. Positive value indicates that two experts are closer to rate the team member whereas negative value indicate that there is a difference in experts opinion for a particular team member on different parameter. Referring Figure 3(a) and (c), if we compare the score for Expert-1 (E1) and Expert 2 (E2), it is noted that team member- 1 has a value 0.308 and team member -3 has a value -0.408. This concludes that team member-1 has rated almost similar by expert-1 and expert-2 whereas for teammemebr-3 there is difference of opinion between expert-1 and expert-2.

5.2. Result Analysis and Discussion

This section discusses the results after applying step 2, 3, 4 and 5 of section 4.2. Step 2 calculates weight of each expert from intuitionistic fuzzy data set using equation 2. Table 2 represents the weight of the each expert used in this study. For this study we have taken weights of experts as follows: Expert-1 has given the weight of 0.24, Expert-2 has 0.27, Expert-3 has 0.23 and Expert-4 is 0.26. The sum of all expert weight is 1. These weights have been used in step 3 to aggregate each criterion's score corresponding to per experts by using equation 9.

Table 3 represent the aggregation result in form of mean and standard deviation for each expert corresponding to each criterion after applying step 3 and aggregation. After analysis the table 3 it is easily seen that expert 2 is more liberal than other experts to score each individual for criteria-1(c1).

Table 4 presents aggregated score values of each expert for each individual according to step 4 of section 4.2. It can be seen that different experts have different ranked different teams members as top rankers. It can be seen that Expert -1 has ranked team member-7 with highest score value of 0.097 as compared to team member 1 with score of 0.026 by Expert-2 and likewise from expert 3 and 4.

Collective mean and variance of expert's for each team member is computed (refer Table 5) to rank each team member. The score is arranged in descending order to their mean values for the purpose of ranking. It is seen that team member (TM)-7 has highest score i.e. 0.762191, so he will be ranked first followed by TM-7, TM-10, TM-6, TM-9 and so on.

Figure 3. Correlation between different Experts for different team members (TM)

Correlation values for TM - 1

	E1	E2	E3	E4
E1	1.000			
E2	0.308	1.000		
E3	0.404	0.282	1.000	
E4	0.159	0.354	0.628	1.000

(a)

Correlation values for TM 2

	E1	E2	E3	E4
E1	1			
E2	0.072	1		
E3	-0.02	-0.052	1	
E4	0.537	-0.112	0.254	1

(b)

Correlation values for TM 3

	E1	E2	E3	E4
E1	1			
E2	-0.1316	1		
E3	0.1794	-0.177	1	
E4	0.2578	0.0587	0.3711	1

(c)

Correlation values for TM 4

	E1	E2	E3	E4
E1	1			
E2	-0.01	1		
E3	-0.03	0.04	1	
E4	-0.64	0.15	0.1699	1

(d)

Correlation values for TM 5

	E1	E2	E3	E4
E1	1			
E2	-0.408	1		
E3	-0.32	0.291	1	
E4	-0.233	0.611	0.0449	1

(e)

Correlation values for TM 6

	E1	E2	E3	E4
E1	1			
E2	-0.22	1		
E3	0.101	0.0994	1	
E4	-0	0.2835	-0.175	1

(f)

Correlation values for TM 7

	E1	E2	E3	E4
E1	1			
E2	0.1552	1		
E3	-0.3087	-0.019	1	
E4	-0.1417	0.1018	-0.287	1

(g)

Correlation values for TM 8

	E1	E2	E3	E4
E1	1			
E2	-0.06	1		
E3	0.007	0.57	1	
E4	0.205	0.07	-0.018	1

(h)

Correlation values for TM 9

	E1	E2	E3	E4
E1	1			
E2	-7E-04	1		
E3	0.389	0.419	1	
E4	0.294	0.408	0.5847	1

(i)

Correlation values for TM 10

	E1	E2	E3	E4
E1	1			
E2	0.106	1		
E3	0.214	0.1522	1	
E4	-0.31	-0.284	-0.386	1

(j)

Table 2. Expert weight

Expert-1	Expert-2	Expert-3	Expert-4
0.24	0.27	0.23	0.26

Table 3. Descriptive statistics per experts for each criterion

Criteria's	Expert-1		Expert-2		Expert-3		Expert-4	
	Mean	Standard Deviation	Mean	Standard Deviation	Mean	Standard Deviation	Mean	Standard Deviation
c1	-0.140	0.442	0.217	0.422	0.015	0.452	-0.052	0.450
c2	-0.253	0.345	-0.054	0.367	-0.275	0.330	0.307	0.386
c3	-0.071	0.532	0.023	0.656	-0.030	0.394	-0.088	0.671
c4	0.107	0.518	0.063	0.538	0.130	0.533	-0.107	0.743
c5	0.239	0.401	-0.115	0.537	-0.166	0.300	-0.164	0.364
c6	-0.050	0.500	-0.112	0.629	-0.223	0.604	0.016	0.471
c7	-0.180	0.560	-0.048	0.566	-0.315	0.471	-0.095	0.464
c8	0.194	0.415	0.219	0.491	-0.052	0.432	-0.003	0.581
c9	-0.004	0.550	-0.006	0.498	0.015	0.422	-0.045	0.640
c10	-0.055	0.299	-0.311	0.567	-0.023	0.611	-0.162	0.465
c11	-0.073	0.471	0.042	0.573	-0.073	0.481	0.268	0.605
c12	0.198	0.539	-0.142	0.374	0.020	0.574	0.107	0.509
c13	0.084	0.492	-0.362	0.340	-0.005	0.519	-0.027	0.528
c14	-0.208	0.374	-0.097	0.387	0.064	0.573	-0.249	0.468
c15	-0.069	0.585	-0.243	0.658	-0.160	0.490	0.265	0.514
c16	0.107	0.500	-0.404	0.410	-0.205	0.478	0.241	0.464
c17	-0.229	0.435	-0.221	0.647	0.176	0.561	-0.049	0.517
c18	0.355	0.480	0.108	0.526	0.107	0.511	0.238	0.338
c19	-0.449	0.326	-0.095	0.489	-0.027	0.528	0.173	0.465

Table 4. Descriptive statistics per experts for each person

Team Member's	Expert-1		Expert-2		Expert-3		Expert-4	
	Mean	Standard Deviation	Mean	Standard Deviation	Mean	Standard Deviation	Mean	Standard Deviation
T1	-0.245	0.417	0.026	0.524	0.071	0.441	0.107	0.461
T2	-0.058	0.439	0.025	0.472	-0.013	0.393	-0.091	0.516
T3	-0.032	0.525	-0.253	0.541	-0.140	0.446	-0.020	0.531
T4	-0.103	0.507	-0.291	0.415	-0.115	0.484	-0.124	0.562
T5	-0.103	0.492	-0.241	0.530	-0.220	0.486	-0.136	0.575
T6	0.075	0.566	-0.030	0.593	0.154	0.442	0.037	0.477
T7	0.097	0.535	0.111	0.571	-.088	0.605	0.052	0.574
T8	-0.012	0.439	-0.008	0.540	-.161	0.523	0.057	0.362
T9	0.024	0.453	-0.009	0.504	-.124	0.548	0.333	0.460
T10	0.096	0.474	-0.139	0.464	0.095	0.461	0.088	0.592

Table 5. Collective mean of experts for each team member

Groups	Average (Mean)	variance
TM- 1	0.690439	0.022935
TM-2	0.688352	0.010898
TM-3	0.668507	0.019253
TM- 4	0.641908	0.019691
TM- 5	0.622706	0.031449
TM- 6	0.740629	0.012692
TM- 7	0.762191	0.005524
TM- 8	0.691266	0.014878
TM- 9	0.717261	0.027978
TM- 10	0.742766	0.005737

5.3. Emperical Validation

To validate proposed approach, this study uses a simple mean algorithm (Terr, D.,2010) to compare results of experimentation where both, proposed and weighted mean approach are applied to same data set. Table 6 summarizes the results obtained from both algorithms. It is seen that non-intuitionistic fuzzy approach (weighted mean approach) results have duplicate ranks thereby making task of selection difficult. These duplicate entries need to be handled appropriately before a final rank can be generated for actual use. Thus, it can be seen that proposed algorithm using intuitionistic fuzzy muirmean (IFWMM) operator produces conflict free result to select the efficient team members with different criteria's as evaluated by several experts.

Table 6. Comparison of score values between intuitionistic fuzzy approach and non- intuitionistic fuzzy approach

Intuitionistic fuzzy approach			Non- intuitionistic fuzzy approach	
Score	IFWMM	Rank using IFS	Mean Algorithm	Rank using weighted mean
T1	0.690439	6	0.724	5
T2	0.688352	7	0.724	5
T3	0.668507	8	0.700	6
T4	0.641908	9	0.676	7
T5	0.622706	10	0.667	8
T6	0.740629	3	0.762	2
T7	0.762191	1	0.776	1
T8	0.691266	5	0.720	4
T9	0.717261	4	0.750	3
T10	0.742766	2	0.762	2

5.4. Performance Evaluation

To measure the performance of proposed approach statistical approach, Analysis of Variance (ANOVA) test is applied (Pfaffl, M. W., et.al.,2002). ANOVA test is used to compare the mean of criteria's corresponding to different team members. A t-test is conducted to compare the mean of proposed algorithm using intuitionistic fuzzy approach and non-fuzzy approach. For this purpose, two hypotheses have been proposed to analyze whether there is a significant relationship between IFWMM score or mean score or there is significant relationship between criteria's and team members score. Hypothesis-1 is to find the relevance between the criteria's and team member so that the appropriate task can be assigned to individual team member. Table 7 shows the result of ANOVA test whereas table 8 shows the result of t-test. According to ANOVA test as p value is measured at 95% confidence level. In first hypothesis p value is achieved 0.02 which is less than 0.05. In second hypothesis, the mean of proposed algorithm with non fuzzy algorithm is compared using t-test. Here also p value is measured at 95% confidence level. In this case p value is achieved .000002 which is less than 0.05. Details are explained in result analysis. Thus we reject the null hypothesis that there is significant relationship between IFWMM algorithm and mean algorithm.

Table 7. ANOVA test

ANOVA						
Source of Variation	*SS*	*df*	*MS*	*F*	*P-value*	*F crit*
Between Groups	0.080084	9	0.008898	2.237563638	0.021589	1.932205
Within Groups	0.715818	180	0.003977			
Total	0.795903	189				

Table 8. t-test: Paired between IFWMM score and Mean score

	Expert score	**Final Score**
Mean	0.696603	0.724813416
Variance	0.002019	0.001362642
Observations	10	
Pearson Correlation	0.993971	
Hypothesized Mean Difference	0	
P(T<=t) one-tail	2.28E-06	
t Critical one-tail	1.833113	

6. CONCLUSION

This paper presents an approach which deals with one the challenging tasks of identification and selection of team members in global software engineering environment. Deciding who among the people from teams (separated geographically) are to be selected for developing is in fact is a complex multi-criteria decision-making process. Research in past have shown that intuitionistic fuzzy muirhead mean (MM) aggregation operator are capable of handling interrelationships among any number of arguments assigned by a variable vector to process the intuitionistic fuzzy numbers (IFNs) and then to solve the multi-attribute group decision making (MAGDM) problem. This paper explores the use of multi criteria decision support system to perform effective selection of team members by first identifying prime criteria's that influence individual selection of team members under GSD and later rank them using intuitionistic fuzzy to aggregate opinion of various experts in expressing their preference for each individual on prime criteria's. The whole process is supported with the help illustrative example to show feasibility and validity of presented approach and with non-intuitionistic fuzzy approaches. Results of experimentation shows that there exists a good relationship between criteria and expert score computed using ANNOVA test yielding a small p-value of 0.02 and to validate the expert score and aggregation score paired T-test is done where one tail t-test score yields value equals to 0.0000002.

REFERENCES

Alonso, S., Cabrerizo, F. J., Chiclana, F., Herrera, F., & Herrera-Viedma, E. (2009). Group decision making with incomplete fuzzy linguistic preference relations. *International Journal of Intelligent Systems*, *24*(2), 201–222. doi:10.1002/int.20332

Atanassov, K. T. (1986). Intuitionistic fuzzy sets. *Fuzzy Sets and Systems*, *20*(1), 87–96. doi:10.1016/S0165-0114(86)80034-3

Avritzer, A., Paulish, D., Cai, Y., & Sethi, K. (2010). Coordination implications of software architecture in a global software development project. *Journal of Systems and Software*, *83*(10), 1881–1895. doi:10.1016/j.jss.2010.05.070

Binder, J. (2009). Global project management: communication, collaboration and management across borders. *Strategic Direction*, *25*(9).

Bohner, S., & Mohan, S. (2009). Model-Based Engineering of Software: Three Productivity Perspectives. In *Proceedings of the 33rd Annual IEEE Software Engineering Workshop*. IEEE. 10.1109/SEW.2009.19

Braun, A. (2007). A framework to enable offshore outsourcing. In *Proceedings of the Second IEEE International Conference on Global Software Engineering ICGSE 2007* (pp. 125-129). IEEE.

Cabrerizo, F. J., Alonso, S., & Herrera-Viedma, E. (2009). A consensus model for group decision making problems with unbalanced fuzzy linguistic information. *International Journal of Information Technology & Decision Making*, *8*(01), 109–131. doi:10.1142/S0219622009003296

Carmel, E., & Agarwal, R. (2001). Tactical approaches for alleviating distance in global software development. *Softw. IEEE*, *18*(2), 22–29. doi:10.1109/52.914734

Casey, V., & Richardson, I. (2006). Project management within virtual software teams. In *Proceedings of the International Conference on Global Software Engineering ICGSE'06* (pp. 33-42). IEEE. 10.1109/ICGSE.2006.261214

Casey, V., & Richardson, I. (2009). Implementation of global software development: A structured approach. *Software Process Improvement and Practice, 14*(5), 247–267. doi:10.1002pip.422

Cataldo, M., Shelton, C., Choi, Y., Huang, Y. Y., Ramesh, V., Saini, D., & Wang, L. Y. (2009). Camel: A tool for collaborative distributed software design. In *Proceedings of the Fourth IEEE International Conference on Global Software Engineering ICGSE 2009* (pp. 83-92). IEEE. 10.1109/ICGSE.2009.16

Colomo-Palacios, R., Casado-Lumbreras, C., Soto-Acosta, P., Misra, S., & García-Penalvo, F. J. (2012). Analyzing human resource management practices within the GSD context. *Journal of Global Information Technology Management, 15*(3), 30–54. doi:10.1080/1097198X.2012.10845617

Conchuir, E. O., Holmstrom-Olson, H., Agerfalk, P. J., & Fitzgerald, B. (2009). Benefits of global software development: Exploring the unexplored. *Software Process Improvement and Practice, 14*(4), 201–212. doi:10.1002pip.417

Cunha, A., Canen, A., & Capretz, M. (2009). *Personalities, Cultures, and Software Modeling: Questions, Scenarios and Research. In Proceedings of the Directions CHASE'09 - ICSE'09 Workshop*, Vancouver, Canada. IEEE.

De Souza, R., Sharp, H., Singer, J., Cheng, L., & Venolia, G. (2009). Cooperative and Human Aspects of Software Engineering. *IEEE Software, 26*(6), 17–19. doi:10.1109/MS.2009.176

Deshpande, S., Beecham, S., & Richardson, I. (2011). Global software development coordination strategies-a vendor perspective. In *New Studies in Global IT and Business Service Outsourcing* (pp. 153-174). Academic Press.

Dugenci, M. (2016). A new distance measure for interval valued intuitionistic fuzzy sets and its application to group decision making problems with incomplete weights information. *Applied Soft Computing, 41*, 120–134. doi:10.1016/j.asoc.2015.12.026

Dymova, L. & Sevastjanov, P. (2016). The operations on interval-valued intuitionistic fuzzy values in the framework of Dempster-Shafer theory. *Information Sciences, 360*, 256-272.

Ebert, C., Murthy, B. K., & Jha, N. N. (2008). Managing risks in global software engineering: principles and practices. In *Proceedings of the IEEE International Conference on Global Software Engineering ICGSE 2008* (pp. 131-140). IEEE.

García-Crespo, A., Colomo-Palacios, R., Soto-Acosta, P., & Ruano-Mayoral, M. (2010). a qualitative study of hard decision making in managing global software development teams. *Information Systems Management, 27*(3), 247–252. doi:10.1080/10580530.2010.493839

Gifford, S. S. (2003). A Roadmap for a Successful Software Development Team Assembly Model Using Roles [Doctoral dissertation]. Virginia Tech.

Gilal, A.R., Jaafar, J., Omar, M., Basri, S., Waqas, A. (2016). A rule-based model for software development team composition: team leader role with personality types and gender classification. *Inf. Softw. Technol., 74*, 105-113.

Gorla, N., & Lam, Y. (2004). Who Should Work with Whom? Building Effective Software Project Teams. *Communications of the ACM, 47*(6), 79–82. doi:10.1145/990680.990684

Herna'ndez-Lo'pez, A., Colomo Palacios, R., Garcıa Crespo, A., & Soto-Acosta, P. (2010a). Trust building process for global software development teams. *A review from the Literature. International Journal of Knowledge Society Research, 1*(1), 65–82.

Hofner, G., & Mani, V. S. (2007). TAPER: A generic framework for establishing an offshore development center. In *Proceedings of the Second IEEE International Conference on Global Software Engineering ICGSE 2007* (pp. 162-172). IEEE.

Islam, S., Joarder, M. M. A., & Houmb, S. H. (2009). Goal and risk factors in offshore outsourced software development from vendor's viewpoint. In *Proceedings of the Fourth IEEE International Conference on Global Software Engineering ICGSE 2009.* (pp. 347-352). IEEE.

John, M., Maurer, F., & Tessem, B. (2005). Human and social factors of software engineering. In *Proceedings of the 27th international conference on Software engineering* (pp. 686-686). ACM.

Kankanhalli, A., Tan, B. C. Y., Wei, K.-K., & Holmes, M. C. (2004). Cross-cultural differences and information systems developer values. *Decision Support Systems, 38*(2), 183–195. doi:10.1016/S0167-9236(03)00101-5

Kern, T., & Willcocks, L. (2000). Exploring information technology outsourcing relationships: Theory and practice. *The Journal of Strategic Information Systems, 9*(4), 321–350. doi:10.1016/S0963-8687(00)00048-2

Keshlaf, A. A., & Riddle, S. (2010). Risk management for web and distributed software development projects. In *Proceedings of the 2010 Fifth International Conference on, Internet Monitoring and Protection (ICIMP)* (pp. 22-28). IEEE.

Kitchenham, B., & Mendes, E. (2004). Software Productivity Measurement Using Multiple Size Measures. *IEEE Transactions on Software Engineering, 30*(12), 1023–1035. doi:10.1109/TSE.2004.104

Kommeren, R., & Parviainen, P. (2007). Philips experiences in global distributed software development. *Empirical Software Engineering, 12*(6), 647–660. doi:10.100710664-007-9047-3

Lacity, M. C., & Rottman, J. W. (2008). The impact of outsourcing on client project managers. *Computer, 41*(1), 100–102. doi:10.1109/MC.2008.31

Lee-Kelley, L. (2006). Locus of control and attitudes to working in virtual teams. *International Journal of Project Management, 24*(3), 234–243. doi:10.1016/j.ijproman.2006.01.003

Lee-Kelley, L., & Sankey, T. (2008). Global virtual teams for value creation and project success: A case study. *International Journal of Project Management, 26*(1), 51–62. doi:10.1016/j.ijproman.2007.08.010

Li, D. F. (2014). *Decision and game theory in management with intuitionistic fuzzy sets*. Berlin: Springer.

Li, D. F., & Ren, H. P. (2015). Multi-attribute decision making method considering the amount and reliability of intuitionistic fuzzy information. *Journal of Intelligent & Fuzzy Systems*, *28*(4), 1877–1883.

Li, M., Wu, C., Zhang, L., & You, L. N. (2015). An intuitionistic fuzzy-TODIM method to solve distributor evaluation and selection problem. *International Journal of Simulation Modelling*, *14*(3), 511–524. doi:10.2507/IJSIMM14(3)CO12

Liao, H., & Xu, Z. (2014). Automatic procedures for group decision making with intuitionistic fuzzy preference relations. *Journal of Intelligent & Fuzzy Systems*, *27*(5), 2341–2353.

Liu, P. (2014). Some Hamacher aggregation operators based on the interval-valued intuitionistic fuzzy numbers and their application to group decision making. *IEEE Transactions on Fuzzy Systems*, *22*(1), 83–97. doi:10.1109/TFUZZ.2013.2248736

Liu, P., & Jin, F. (2012). Methods for aggregating intuitionistic uncertain linguistic variables and their application to group decision making. *Information Sciences*, *205*, 58–71. doi:10.1016/j.ins.2012.04.014

Liu, P., & Li, D. (2017). Some muirhead mean operators for intuitionistic fuzzy numbers and their applications to group decision making. *PLoS One*, *12*(1), e0168767. doi:10.1371/journal.pone.0168767 PMID:28103244

Liu, P., & Liu, Y. (2014). An approach to multiple attribute group decision making based on intuitionistic trapezoidal fuzzy power generalized aggregation operator. *International Journal of Computational Intelligence Systems*, *7*(2), 291–304. doi:10.1080/18756891.2013.862357

Liu, P., & Wang, Y. (2014). Multiple attribute group decision making methods based on intuitionistic linguistic power generalized aggregation operators. *Applied Soft Computing*, *17*, 90–104. doi:10.1016/j.asoc.2013.12.010

Milewski, A. E., Tremaine, M., Kobler, F., Egan, R., Zhang, S., & O'Sullivan, P. (2008). Guidelines for effective bridging in global software engineering. *Software Process Improvement and Practice*, *13*(6), 477–492. doi:10.1002pip.403

Montajabiha M. (2016). An extended PROMETHE II multi-criteria group decision making technique based on intuitionistic fuzzy logic for sustainable energy planning. *Group Decision and Negotiation*, *25*(2), 221-244.

Nguyen H. (2015). A new knowledge-based measure for intuitionistic fuzzy sets and its application in multiple attribute group decision making. *Expert Systems with Applications*, *42*(22), 8766-8774.

Parker, G., Zielinski, D., & McAdams, J. (2000). *Rewarding Teams: Lessons From the Trenches San Francisco*. California: Jossey-Bass Inc.

Pfaffl, M. W., Horgan, G. W., & Dempfle, L. (2002). Relative expression software tool (REST) for group-wise comparison and statistical analysis of relative expression results in real-time PCR. *Nucleic Acids Research*, *30*(9), e36–e36. doi:10.1093/nar/30.9.e36 PMID:11972351

Pichler, H. (2007). Be successful, take a hostage or "outsourcing the outsourcing Manager." In *Proceedings of the Second IEEE International Conference on Global Software Engineering ICGSE 2007* (pp. 156-161). IEEE.

Saaty, T. L. (1980). The analytic hierarchy process: planning. New York: McGraw-Hill.

Smite, D., Wohlin, C., Gorschek, T., & Feldt, R. (2010). Empirical evidence in global software engineering: A systematic review. *Empirical Software Engineering, 15*(1), 91–118. doi:10.100710664-009-9123-y

Smith, P. G., & Blanck, E. L. (2002). From experience: Leading dispersed teams. *Journal of Product Innovation Management, 19*(4), 294–304. doi:10.1016/S0737-6782(02)00146-7

Sooraj, P., & Mohapatra, P. K. J. (2008). Modeling the 24-h software development process. *Strategic Outsourcing, 1*(2), 122–141. doi:10.1108/17538290810897147

Stevens, K. (1998). *The effects of roles and personality characteristics on software development team effectiveness* [Doctor of Philosophy]. Virginia Tech. .

Szmidt, E., & Kacprzyk, J. (2003). A consensus-reaching process under intuitionistic fuzzy preference relations. *International Journal of Intelligent Systems, 18*(7), 837–852. doi:10.1002/int.10119

Terr, D. (2010). Weighted Mean. *MathWorld-A Wolfram Web Resource.* Retrieved from http://mathworld. wolfram. com/WeightedMean.html

Tripathy, B. K., Goyal, A., & Patra, A. S. (2016). Clustering Categorical Data Using Intuitionistic Fuzzy K-mode. *International Journal of Pharmacy and Technology, 8*(3), 16688–16701.

Wu, J., & Chiclana, F. (2014). Multiplicative consistency of intuitionistic reciprocal preference relations and its application to missing values estimation and consensus building. *Knowledge-Based Systems, 71*, 187–200. doi:10.1016/j.knosys.2014.07.024

Zhang, Z., & Xu, Z. S. (2015). The orders of intuitionistic fuzzy numbers. *Journal of Intelligent & Fuzzy Systems, 28*(2), 505–511.

This research was previously published in the Journal of Information Technology Research (JITR), 13(2); pages 75-93, copyright year 2020 by IGI Publishing (an imprint of IGI Global).

Chapter 85

The Cultural and Institutional Barrier of Knowledge Exchanges in the Development of Open Source Software

Ikbal Maulana

https://orcid.org/0000-0002-3727-3809

Indonesian Institute of Sciences, Indonesia

ABSTRACT

Open source software (OSS) gives developing countries inexpensive or free alternatives to proprietary software. It gives them the opportunity to develop software and software industry without starting from scratch. This chapter discusses the diffusion and development of OSS in Indonesia especially after the government took "Indonesia, Go Open Source" (IGOS) initiative. This initiative united government organizations, communities, R&D institutions, and universities. While the government's concern was to tackle piracy by replacing illegal software with OSS, the others sought to develop their own OSS. However, the openness of their software is only in terms of that they were developed using OSS development tools, while their mode of development remained closed, which was caused by cultural barrier and institutional incompatibility between government's regime of project administration and the governance of OSS development.

INTRODUCTION

Industry has developed to be increasingly relying on technology rather than on workers. In the past or today in craftsmanship traditions, technology is manifested as tools that are only useful in hands of skillful workers, whereas in modern production systems workers "becomes a mere appendage to an already existing material condition of production" (Marx, 1906, p. 421). As machineries becoming more sophisticated, because knowledge which was previously possessed by workers is increasingly embedded into them, they can be operated by much less skillful workers. This development allows capitalists to better

DOI: 10.4018/978-1-6684-3702-5.ch085

control their production systems and even transport their machineries to any developing country to find low-cost labors to operate them. The transfer of sophisticated machineries to developing countries does not automatically lead to the transfer of knowledge of production. When the machineries are moved to other countries, the workers' involvement in production does not develop necessary skills that allow developing countries to make the same production. Their skills of operating machineries apparently are necessary but easily replaceable parts of production process.

Software industry has given new promises to developing countries, because software can be produced on inexpensive machines. Software programmers can develop their skills by experimenting on widely available computers. Software industry, as part of information and communication technology (ICT) industries, seems to give the sense of promise because it periodically experiences transformation caused by the emergence of, what Christensen (Christensen, 2000) calls, disruptive technology. The disruption of technology demands industry players to play with new knowledge and technology, because the old one is not only irrelevant, but can be a liability to those who use it. It also explains why the innovations that direct this industry has been created by young people who have no significant experience in business and industry. This fact seems to give hope to entrepreneurs in developing countries as well. "Although it is dominated by firms based in major industrialized countries of the world, it continues to offer great prospects for economic growth and industrial development within developing economies" (UNCTAD, 2002, p. 3).

The strong reliance on knowledge rather than on technology may deceive people to underestimate the complexity of the development of software industry, as if knowledge can be easily acquired through simple learning and softwares can be easily produced through mere thinking in front of a computer. The intangibility of software gives them the illusions that the development of software and software industry are easy and inexpensive, and that both developed and developing countries have the same opportunities because this industry does not rely on expensive production capital. Indeed, if every country has the same opportunity, then the competition must be very high, and even higher for software industry, which produces products that are "costly to *produce* but cheap to *reproduce*" (Shapiro & Varian, 1999, p. 3), and can be inexpensively distributed throughout the world. Consequently, having the capability to create a working software is not sufficient, competition demands producers to create it better than similar products competing in the same marketplace. India has often been mentioned as the best exemplar of a developing country that can take advantage of the opportunity in global software industry (Nagala, 2005), but most of other developing countries can only dream of that achievement.

Opportunities in software industry for developing countries have become elusive if we see that the market leaders, which are from advanced countries, can make their clients dependent on them, because users of software "are notoriously subject to switching costs and lock-in: once you have chosen a technology, or a format for keeping information, switching can be very expensive" (Shapiro & Varian, 1999, p. 11). And as current softwares are also very complex, consisting of thousands to hundred thousand of codes which require time consuming, hence expensive, development and testing, it becomes more difficult for new software companies to challenge market leaders. So proprietary software industries from advanced countries have erected a high barrier for new entrants from developing countries.

The above barrier is irrelevant in the development of open source software (OSS). One of the basic tenets of OSS is that you do not have to develop anything from scratch, because it is legal for you to modify what others have developed, and, hence, "open source developers enjoy a great productivity gain from code reuse" (DiBona, 2006, p. 22). In OSS development, you do not need to reinvent the wheel, rather use the wheel invented by others and modify it when it is necessary. This principle is practiced by any OSS developer, including developers working for large corporations. "You can still build platforms today, of course, but for practical considerations, it only makes sense to build them on top of open source infrastructure. Amazon and Google are familiar platform businesses (one for retailing, the other for advertising), built on cheap or free open source building materials" (Polese, 2006, p. xi).

Adopting OSS will benefits developing countries because it is "a means of reducing licensing costs and of promoting indigenous technological development by having access to the source code of these products" (Câmara & Fonseca, 2007, p. 121). This claim is also supported by the reports of United Nations, by adopting OSS developing countries can prevent themselves to be the hostage of proprietary software (UNCTAD, 2004), and by having access to the source code, they can advance knowledge more quickly (UNCTAD, 2003), or adapt existing OSS to their needs, and further the adoption may lead to the development of their software industries (Weerawarana & Weeratunge, 2004).

The benefits of and opportunities from OSS for developing countries have often been mentioned, how to realize the benefits and opportunities is not always clear and easy, even when it is supported by government policy, such as what has happened in Indonesia. This chapter will discuss the barriers that limit the success of OSS diffusion and development in Indonesia by using various perspectives, from knowledge to cultural to institutional perspectives.

LITERATURE REVIEWS

The Role of Software in Economic Development

The utilization of software, together with other elements of ICT, has become unavoidable for any country, including developing countries (Avgerou, 2010). Many businesses and government administrations cannot be carried out without ICT. The increasing complexity and pace of production systems cannot be managed without ICT (Beniger, 1986). The progress of a country depends on how best they can allocate their resources, which in turn depends on how best they utilize various information and knowledge about the resources which is not given to anyone in its totality (Hayek, 1945, p. 520). The performance of a country, therefore, depends on the quality and flow of information from one element to another in their national system of production, which necessitates the utilization of ICT (Stiglitz, 2002). In today's world ICT cannot be ignored, because it is a major driving force of the globalization of economy. "More than any other technology ICTs drive economic and financial globalization as they facilitate rapid transactions and global market transparency" (Miranda et al., 2007, p. 17).

The potentials of ICT in modern economy has promised great opportunities, but with accompanying complex policy challenges in realizing those opportunities. Without having to develop their own ICT industry sector, but by effectively utilizing ICT in any part of their economy, they can boost the productivity of the other industry sectors (Arora & Athreye, 2002). "As every sector of the global economy and nearly every facet of modern society undergoes digital transformation, the ICT industry community is focused on opportunities that spur not only the development of ICT innovations but also, and more importantly, their adoption and use throughout the economy" (Martin, 2016, p. 24). The utilization of ICT requires more than just the implementation of technology, but also demands the changing of business processes or even organizational forms. Many people in developing countries view ICT as magic bullet for development. They are enthusiast to adopt e-government and expect their public administration will run effectively just by putting technology in their offices. However, effective e-government implementation requires bureaucratic reform (Cordella, 2007), which is unlikely to happen voluntarily due to organizational inertia. Effective ICT utilization demands more than just the use of technologies, but the reorganization of internal and interorganizational information flows (Cordella, 2007), which will significantly affect culture, structure and power relations within organization.

Effective utilization of software in other economic sectors is no simpler than the development of software industry. The success of Singapore, a tiny country, which has become one of the most important financial service and economic hubs in the world, is due to the systematic integration of ICT into its government and economic activities (Angelidou, 2014). The incorporation of ICT into various business and government processes were carefully and systematically crafted, and seriously implemented in Singapore's 10-year masterplan entitled Intelligent Nation 2015 (iN2015 Steering Committee, 2006). So, developing countries can take advantage from either the utilization or development of software. Neither is easier than the other. Utilization and development pose different challenges that need to be addressed differently by government policy. OSS reduces the investment cost burdening developing countries, also reveal the algorithmic secret of sophisticated softwares and give economic and engineering benefits of reusable open source codes. That is why "Within the last decade, more than 60 countries and international organizations have developed nearly 275 policy documents related to the use of an open-source approach in the public sector" (Dener, Watkins, & Dorotinsky, 2011, p. 78).

Software as Knowledge

Technology is not merely material objects, but also embeds particular knowledge that enables it to perform particular functions. Therefore, it can be viewed as "a form of knowledge created by humans" (Parayil, 1991a, p. 235), or "as the organization of knowledge for practical purposes" (Mesthene, 1997, p. 74). Technology can also be seen "as a spectrum, with ideas at one end and techniques and things at the other, with design as a middle term" (Layton Jr, 1974, pp. 37–38). If this view is applied to software technology then the spectrum ranges from ideas to designs to softwares, all of which are different kinds of information. While ideas are information that guide people what they should do, softwares are information that dictate computers what they have to do. The development of software can be seen as a translation of human knowledge into the knowledge understood by computers.

Translating human knowledge into software is not easy, not only because a computer speaks different language from human, but it also needs to be told step by step what to do. Developing software is more than just making human knowledge explicit, but also utilizing it to tackle specific problem in systematic and step-wise ways. There is additional complexity, the knowledge that needs to be translated may not be available in one single mind. Currently many softwares have to deal with complex business processes, of which no single individual comprehends the whole processes in their entirety. Before being translated into computer program, a set of human knowledge need to be negotiated and integrated. The common challenge to deal with complex knowledge is how "to make sensible use of what knowledge we think we have, to find ways of combining it effectively with the knowledge that we think other people have, and to protect ourselves against the consequences of our own and other people's ignorance" (Loasby, 1999, p. 7). What makes it difficult is that knowledge is not a mental commodity that can be easily codified and exchanged between individuals (Visser, 2010), and also it is difficult to recognize our own lack of knowledge.

OSS development is an open, and mostly also virtual, collaboration among people who might not know each other personally. The openness and virtuality of the collaboration create opportunities as well as challenges in integrating knowledge and ideas. While richness of knowledge and ideas might flow in from all around the world, transforming that richness into a working OSS is of a great challenge, because not every suggestion can be accommodated. What has to be attempted by OSS project leaders is that while they should keep encourage people's contributions, they also have to prevent chaotic situation due to the unmanageability of crowded involvements. An institution, rule of the game (North, 1990), has to be established to structure the collaboration, to make it more manageable (Parayil, 1991b), even though the collaborative structure of a community of voluntary developers will be different from and more complex than that of a business organization.

The Nature of OSS Development

OSS is open in two senses. First, by definition and in practice, the source code of OSS is open to be examined by anyone with knowledge of programming. The openness of OSS allows people who can read software codes to see the internal working of OSS, which not only allows them to find bugs and propose suggestions, they can also revise it by themselves, modify it, or even develop something else on top of it. Second, an OSS project can be made open to volunteers from any stage of its development, even from the beginning before starting to write any code. Currently, there are many OSS projects that are open for anyone's participation even from the very beginning of ideas which are hosted by SourceForge, GitHub, Google Source Code and many others. Each of these sites can host from as many as thousands to millions of OSS projects. SourceForge claims to host more than 430,000 projects; whereas GitHub claims to host millions of OSS projects (Slashdot Media, 2018; GitHub, 2018). OSS is a model of global peer production, sharing, revision, and review (Vaidhyanathan, 2005).

For popular and complex OSS, such as operating system or office suite, which can be acquired for free, it is common that there are communities of users and developers around the softwares. Since they are free, consequently, there is no vendor that is responsible to help you when you face any problem with that free OSS. Therefore, you must rely on the help of communities of OSS users and developers. It is common practice that users assist each other to utilize OSS (Câmara & Fonseca, 2007). Adopting OSS will encourage users to share more knowledge among themselves than if they use commercial propriety softwares. Not only users are willing to help each other, even some developers are eager to listen and help users. Problems faced by users or suggestion given by users are sources of ideas of improvement for OSS developers. That is why that "The open source development process is somewhat reminiscent of the type of `user-driven innovation' seen in many other industries" (Weber, 2004, p. 3).

Software is different from tangible products. When someone creates the same bicycle as what another person has made, mostly the latter does not mind, because it takes a lot of effort to create that same bicycle. But, it is different for software, making a copy of a software that took weeks or months to create requires just a few mouse clicks, therefore, it is easy for software developers to quickly occupy the whole market with their products, whereas producers of tangible products need to firstly invest in machineries before increasing the production. The nature of software production and reproduction and its market potential makes proprietary software adherents prefer to impose strong IPR protection on software.

The institutionalization of proprietary software development, which has been so intense and influential since 1980s, makes people consider this as the only way of developing software (Vaidhyanathan, 2005). In fact, OSS development was the only way of developing software in the early history of computing. Just as what has been told by one of its pioneers, Richard Stallman, "When I started working at the MIT Artificial Intelligence Lab in 1971, I became part of a software-sharing community that had existed for many years. Sharing of software was not limited to our particular community; it is as old as computers, just as sharing of recipes is as old as cooking" (Stallman, 1999, p. 53).

OSS is certainly not the first type of open innovation. In the past, or even now in traditional society, innovation has been developed openly to public, "…. throughout most of human history all information technologies and almost all technologies have been open source. And we have done pretty well as a species with tools and habits unencumbered by high restrictions on sharing, copying, customizing, and improving" (Vaidhyanathan, 2005, p. 342). Anyone can see what others have developed and improve it without worrying of being complaint about intellectual property right. Even in the beginning of software development, it was very common that software was developed openly and people learned from each other and developed upon what had been developed by others. "The practice of sharing source code is not an entirely novel feature in the software industry. The first "intensive" users of mainframe computers were universities and corporate research laboratories. In that environment, computer programs were eminently seen as research tools, and it was seen as a normal practice to share code with other developers" (Nuvolari, 2005). Sharing source code of a program, which is a manifestation of technical knowledge, was perceived as normal as sharing any kind of knowledge which is until now common in universities.

The Culture of OSS Development

In a global software industry dominated by proprietary softwares, open source mode of development might be considered as a strange way of software development, contradicting common economic reasoning (Nuvolari, 2005). Many people perceive that OSS is developed by a community of altruistic programmers having no commercial interests. This is considered as the only rational explanation of their willingness to sacrifice an enormous amount of time to develop products that later can be freely distributed by other people. What puzzles them is the fact that many large corporations, including IBM and Google, have also participated in OSS development. Indeed, there are many voluntary developers actively contribute to the development of software that can compete against proprietary ones, which shows that the altruistic side of OSS development community, however "altruism is neither the only nor the most important motivation" (DiBona, Cooper, & Stone, 2006, p. xxx).

Modern market economics will find it difficult to comprehend that thousands of top-notch programmers dispersed in many loosely organized virtual community contribute freely to the development of a public good (Lerner & Tirole, 2002, p. 198). And the beneficiaries of their contribution are not only "poor users" from developing countries, but also large corporations in advanced countries. OSS developers are no different from other innovators, many of them are also selfish individuals. "The apparent paradox rests on the assumption that acts of charity necessarily conflict with acts of self-interest. From the point of view of a modern market economy, it often appears that charity and self-interest do conflict against each other. What drives the open source developer, however, is clearly self-interest—even if it is based on an older notion of self-interest not easily captured by modern market economics" (DiBona et al., 2006, p. xxx).

DiBona et al (2006), argue that the paradox can be explained away if reputation is regarded as important currency as money. By becoming important contributors to OSS projects, people can gain reputation among OSS communities as well as in ICT industry in general. Indeed, OSS activists and evangelists, such as Linus Thorvalds and Richard Stallman can never gain wealth as the leaders of proprietary software corporations, but their reputation will provide them with survival resources, their OSS accomplishments could provide them with the opportunities to earn a living from their expertise.

The development of OSS is not always smooth, peaceful and successful. The openness of OSS allows "open development and decentralized peer review to lower costs and improve software quality" (Raymond, 2001, p. xi), but it can also lead to be chaotic and full of conflict and result in dysfunctional softwares. To be successful, certain level of order must be established in OSS project. Therefore, the process of a successful OSS project "is not a chaotic free-for-all in which everyone has equal power and influence. And it is certainly not an idyllic community of like-minded friends in which consensus reigns and agreement is easy. In fact, conflict is not unusual in this community; it's endemic and inherent to the open source process" (Weber, 2004, p. 3).

The ideas proposed by the initiators of OSS project were not immediately understood or accepted by joining volunteers. During the period of development of complex software, a loosely group of independent developers, who are not bound by contract of employment and might have never seen and developed close and warm friendship with each other, would have to struggle to reach consensus. Intensive and harsh discussion were often being carried out before actual codes have been written. "One of the common and most misleading fallacies about the open source process is that it involves like-minded geeks who cooperate with each other in an unproblematic way because they agree with each other on technical grounds" (Weber, 2004, p. 81). Sometimes the discussions were not easy to manage, because it can range from discussion about bugs that give false result, new ideas that need to be incorporated, to conspiracy theory of the intervention of proprietary software industry into OSS projects. Since the discussions were carried out in mailing-lists, the proto-form of social media we know today, people were not constrained by ethics and norms, so the discussions may go wild and lead to interpersonal conflicts.

OSS project is different from what is generally understood as community of practice. In the latter, "knowledge exchange is motivated by moral obligation and community interest rather than by narrow self-interest" (Wasko & Faraj, 2000, p. 155). It is assumed that individuals can submit to community interest without expecting "intangible returns such as reputation and self-esteem" (2000, p. 159). While in OSS projects, ego is considered as the driving force of active participation. "In trying to create a legacy as a great programmer, many developers believe deeply that "scientific" success will outstrip and outlive financial success" (Weber, 2004, p. 140).

The different role of ego in an OSS project and a community of practice can be understood from different commitment and involvement demanded by the two. In the community of practice, people just share knowledge and help one-another with their advices, which do not need to be followed, and hence the competition among members of the community is relatively low. That is why members of the community can easily look good to one another, or at least they do not need to show their ego or self-interest. In an OSS project, developers do not just share their technical knowledge, they also compete and fight to make their technical contribution accepted by others. An OSS project often grows to be a competition for creating memorable legacy. The problem is that there is a limited space that cannot adopt all those legacies. Therefore, criticism against each others' codes is a common game in any OSS project. "The norm in the open source community is to criticize the code, not the individual who wrote it, which may reduce a little bit how badly it hurts. But because code is precisely identified with an author, a virtuous circle of ego-boosting can easily become a much messier status competition, in which one person's ego boost becomes another person's insult" (Weber, 2004, p. 141).

Probably, because what OSS developers pursue is not financial, but the intangible and unmeasurable reputation, the knowledge sharing in OSS projects is more politically complicated than any other form of software development or knowledge sharing. Leaders of OSS projects have to balance the conflicting interests against the progress of OSS development. It is not easy when they have to deal with developers' ego who work voluntarily. "If egos can be boosted, they can also be damaged, which raises the question of what kinds of behavior will follow. The person with the hurt ego has choices: She can leave the project, she can fork the code, she can retaliate against the leader or against other developers" (Weber, 2004, p. 141). Success OSS development requires leadership that can deal with the social dynamic of a loosely group, of which norms and cultures are strongly shaped by the different norms and cultures of participating volunteers as well as by the virtual nature of their interactions. This unprecedented and unique way of doing OSS projects makes this practice not easily transferable to different communities having different values and cultures.

THE INTRODUCTION OF ICT IN INDONESIA

Personal computers were introduced in the early 1980s to Indonesian people when proprietary software had already dominated global software industry. People did not mind to be dependent on proprietary softwares, because they could easily use the illegal copy of any software, which cost just a little more than the the cost of the floppy disk on which the software was recorded. They did not have the sense that it was illegal, because the shops that sold illegal software were open to public, not hiding from law enforcement institutions. The widespread availability of pirated softwares made people not interested in public domain, or free and open source softwares.

Even though piracy had prevented the development of mass market software industry, people had high expectation in ICT professions, including software developers. Many ICT higher educations were established, probably because they attracted a lot of students and were very inexpensive to establish compared to other engineering educations. The education institutions only needed to provide class rooms and computer labs, and even increasingly more students preferred to use their own computers rather than to use their university's computers. Today there are 354 ICT departments belong to universities, and 388 departments belong to ICT specialized higher education institutions (Utami, 2018). What belong to ICT departments are computer engineering, information system, and informatics (software development). Many of the above education institutions have become the fertile ground for the growth of OSS communities. The difficulty of installing and modifying OSS is an attractive challenge for showing off the geekiness of OSS activists.

Government's Commitment on ICT

Formally, ICT has taken special position in Indonesian government since two decades ago. Except the current president, all the previous five presidents had established a council to give advice or formulate ICT-related policy to the president. That the council had never delivered significant policy recommendation was probably due to the fact that the core members of the teams were ministers who actually had already had heavy tasks in their specific areas of duties. While business leaders and top academics who were appointed to assist them were also already busy with their own duties.

The proliferation of ICT educations indicates that government and society regard software development as important capability for the nation. Yet, the strong protection of intellectual property right (IPR) which is required for the development of software industry has never entered public discourse, hence, has never been their concern. While Indonesian government have long sought to formally promote ICT utilization and development, their commitment to protect software copyright has been the target of criticism from overseas until today. Even though copyright law has a history of over a century, for it was introduced by the Dutch colonial government in 1912 (Susanti, Nurjaya, Safaat, & Djatmika, 2014). Indeed, the enactment of this law was for the interest of the colonizers rather than the colonized. Not long after the independence from the Dutch colonialism, in 1950 Indonesia ratified Bern Convention, an international agreement governing the protection of copyright. However, they seemed to see this law just gave the young country unnecessary limitation. In 1958 they abandon their membership to this convention for the reason of promoting national interest in education, namely, to allow local book publishers to print foreign books without paying royalty (Susanti et al., 2014).

The lack of, or weak protection of copyright and other intellectual property rights does not only disadvantage foreign businesses, but also many Indonesian, from authors, musicians, to film producers. Representing only a tiny fraction of Indonesian people, they could neither give sufficient pressure to the government nor effectively raise their concern in public arena.

Indonesia has not reached IPR-based economy, that is the level of economy where local players can derive commercial benefits from their IPR. Currently the IPR system is seen as burden instead of opportunity. Therefore, it was not due to the local interest to protect IPR, but due to the pressure by developed countries. In 1997, Indonesia ratified Bern Convention again through Presidential Decree Number 18. However, until now the protection of copy right is still disappointing many parties. For example, in Indonesia, according to the joint study by Business Software Alliance (BSA) and the International Data Corporation (IDC), the commercial value of illegal software installed on personal computers reached $1.32 billion in 2010, and the illegal users were not just personal users but also companies, which seemed not to realize that they used illegal softwares (Ratri Adityarani, 2011).

Indeed, there have been pressures on Indonesian government to take strong measures against software piracy. In 1995 two US industry associations, the Business Software Alliance (BSA) and the International Intellectual Property Alliance (IIPA), called for the office of United States Trade Representative (USTR) to impose trade sanctions against Indonesia, which they reiterated in the following year (Rosser, 2012). At that time, the source of concern was not only software piracy, but also other informational goods, from books to musics. In May 1996, the USTR responded to this call by moving Indonesia from its 'watch list' to 'priority watch list,' and made the country just one step away from being hit by trade sanctions. Since the US was its major trading partner, Indonesia had no choice but to move ahead with copyright law reform, at least by imposing the use of legal software among its ministries and state-owned enterprises.

The OSS Movements in Indonesia

Since the mid-1990s, the beginning of widespread diffusion of the Internet, many Linux user groups were established in Indonesian cities where there were universities having computer science departments. But membership of the groups soon expanded beyond the confines of the computer departments and universities. Linux and its various tools were attractive because they could be readily used to develop Internet servers and applications. The success stories of American Internet based companies in the second half of the 1990s also got wide coverage in Indonesian media and might inspire Indonesian software developers and businesses to imitate their success.

Virtual interactions among Linux enthusiasts were probably much more intensive than were their off-line interactions. Virtual interactions could engage people nationwide, but also encouraged further formation of Linux user groups in many other cities. Through virtual interactions which were sometimes continued by face-to-face meeting, some people have emerged as Linux evangelists who gained nation-wide popularity among Indonesian Linux communities. In 2005 the Linux user groups were spread over 35 cities. Some activists were not satisfied just expanding the user base of Linux, they also aimed to develop their own versions of Linux. Some versions, namely, WinBI and IGOS Nusantara, were funded and developed by government institutions. While the others, such as BlankOn, Trustix Merdeka, RimbaLinux, were developed by communities or private companies. The Linux communities later promoted the term "open source" to refer to the expansion of their interests which were no longer limited to the operating system.

Among government institutions, the Agency for the Assessment and Application of Technology (BBPT) has been most active in OSS development. Their active role was probably because they were headed by Minister of Research and Technology who was actively promoting high technology industries, such as aircraft and ship building industries. Prior to year 2000, ICT was not perceived as priority by the government which regarded sophisticated technology only tangible and expensive products, such as aircraft technology. In the era when people could easily used illegal softwares, it was difficult to sense the urgency of developing their own softwares. Around 2000s ICT and other buzzwords such as ecommerce, ebusiness and egovernment entered public discourse, national as well as international. The head of BPPT, who was also the Minister of Research and Technology, often accompanied the president to go overseas, which probably made him exposed to the popular awareness of the importance of ICT. Therefore, he increased the budget of software development, which was used to develop the first Indonesian Linux Distro, named WinBi, which literally means Windows in Indonesian language. BPPT has also developed applications that have been widely used by local governments, such as Kantaya (virtual office) and applications for serving local governments' one-stop service. BPPT also saw that the slow diffusion of ICT due to the expensive cost of computer hardwares. In order to decrease the cost of computers and use legal software, BPPT developed a system consisted of a set of old, and therefore cheap, computers and one new computer used as server. The cheap computers were used as terminals, connecting to the server where all data were stored. This system was named KOMURA, the abbreviation of Indonesian phrase which means "cheap computers". This system was intended to be used at school or universities.

Strong pressure on Indonesian government from overseas to respect copy right, had been used by OSS proponents from both inside and outside government institutions to push government to take a major OSS initiative. The IPR regime of OSS gives developing countries chances to free themselves from the market power and monopolistic conditions imposed by large proprietary software firms. Either as users or developers, people from developing countries can benefit from the abundant stock of existing OSS. The reduction of IT investment cost, but without violating IPR protection law, is regarded as the reason that gather the momentum in the utilization of OSS in developed and developing countries (Weerawarana & Weeratunge, 2004, p. 7). The availability of many off-the-shelf OSS that could be used legally for free was often communicated by OSS proponents to the government and society, even though they knew that OSS is not necessarily free (zero cost), because some of them were developing OSS and providing OSS services as their sources of income. The idea of using legal but free software increasingly attracted the government which could not find effective way to tackle software piracy. In 2000s two ministries had been the strong supporters of OSS, namely ministry of research and technology and ministry of communication and information. Ultimately, on June 30, 2004, five ministries declared "Indonesia, Go Open Source" (IGOS) initiative, which was then being followed by various government programs promoting the utilization of OSS. By adopting OSS, at least government institutions can use legal software without spending a lot of money.

To many proponents, the OSS movement was ideological, not just mere technical replacement of proprietary softwares. In many IGOS events, the narrative of nationalism, "OSS for national independence" was occasionally stated. OSS developers, in both communities and government research institutions, wanted more than just promoting the utilization of OSS. They wanted to develop their own OSS. Local Linux distros and various open source applications have been developed by communities as well as government institutions. And rather than using already existing Linux distro, government developed its own Linux distro, namely, IGOS Nusantara. The openness of OSS enables Indonesian developers to dwell into the complexity of sophisticated source code, whereas in proprietary software industry, the source code has become the secret of the company which owns it.

As part of IGOS initiative, supporting organizations were established to help general users to smoothly adopt OSS. Government institutions that committed to adopt OSS established help desk teams in their offices. OSS Empowerment Centers (POSS) were established by a number of major universities to promote OSS, and IGOS Centers were established as business activities to help people or organizations, who previously used proprietary software, to migrate to OSS. Then the support of government was strong, but to be sustainable, both government and OSS activists were aware that OSS movement also needed business supports (Maulana & Handoko, 2006). OSS based industry needed to be developed.

Government's OSS policy to deal with software piracy did not make the critics happy, because it did not recover their losses. Microsoft's strong responses was apparent. When in 2005 ministry of research and technology held IGOS Open House which consisted of lectures and exhibitions of open source companies and communities, Microsoft took part in the exhibition, even though this corporation did not exhibit any open source product. Ironically, its booth became the most crowded, because it gave door prize of some Xbox game consoles to audiences. The participation of Microsoft in this open source event actually surprised many activists. But, in the same year, when some government institutions and communities sought to bundle their efforts to promote OSS, the Indonesian President Yudhoyono met Bill Gates in the United States, and in the following year Indonesian government signed Memorandum of Understanding (MoU) with Microsoft, which became a contract that required the government to buy over 35 thousand licenses of Microsoft Windows and over 177 thousand licenses of Office Suites. In terms of price, Indonesia got big discounted prices, but it was estimated at $40 millions and payment would be due in June 2007 (Oxford Business Group, 2007). It was a very high cost which OSS proponents regarded as unnecessary. This MoU was also criticized by the Business Competition Supervisory Agency (KPPU), which regarded that the MoU contradicted a number of government organizations' initiative to adopt OSS. After the MoU was signed by the Indonesian Ministry of Communication and Information, Sofyan Djalil, who was before a strong supporter of OSS, some OSS activists sought to meet and demand him to give the explanations. They also met Kusmayanto Kadiman, Minister of Research and Technology, who had been successful in forcing his ministry to adopt OSS. It seems that there were conflicting views or interests within the government. However, despite some disappointment, good relationship between government and OSS communities still continued.

Proponents of OSS within government institutions and communities continued to support one another. They established Indonesian Association of Open Source (AOSI) in June 2009 to further push OSS movement. Even though government officials actively support the establishment of the association, formally they kept distance from it to allow strong initiatives from communities and private sectors. Betti Alisjahbana, former country general manager of IBM, was appointed as the first chairperson. Within the same year, in November 2008, they held Asia-Africa Conference on Open Source, which was actively supported by the government.

Some elements in government still showed their support for OSS as a way to reduce software copy right violation. In March 2009, the Ministry of Administrative Reform (MenPAN) issued Circular Letter No. 1 of 2009 to all government organizations and State-owned enterprises, endorsing the adoption and use of OSS. But, it made International Intellectual Property Alliance (IIPA) not happy and regarded that it "will create additional trade barriers and deny fair and equitable market access to software companies" (IIPA, 2010, p. 51). IIPA responded to it by recommending that Indonesia remain on the Priority Watch List.

THE ACHIEVEMENTS AND FAILURES OF OSS INITIATIVES

The Adoption of OSS After the End of Formal Campaign

Through the IGOS initiative the government expected that by the end of December 2011 all government institutions would have adopted OSS. To further stimulate the use of OSS among government organizations and communities, Ministry of Communication and Information presented Indonesia Open Source Award (IOSA) to government organizations, educational institutions, individuals and communities. Despite the lively ceremonies of many OSS events as well as formal promotion of OSS, proprietary softwares could easily sneak into government organizations through the procurement of computers, which usually have been installed with proprietary operating systems. Beside that, the MoU between the government and Microsoft was regarded as the permission to allocate budget to procure proprietary softwares which were considered more user-friendly than OSS. The MoU had weakened government's messages of support for OSS.

Today, there is no longer any program that explicitly support the diffusion and development of OSS. The government organizations that were in the past actively promoting OSS, have switched their attentions to something else, for example, creative industry, mobile technologies, Internet of Things or the fourth industrial revolution. OSS is no longer an attractive terrain. Communities of Linux Users and AOSI do still exist, even though they are not as active or enthusiast as a decade ago. The current development of technologies and ICT industry have posed different challenges. Mobile technologies and businesses based on those technologies attract more attentions. Fighting for OSS seems to be out of fashion in the current technological discourse.

However, several local governments have successfully maintained their adoption of OSS, either of off-the-shelf applications or of specially developed applications for egovernment services. Even though their ICT skills are relatively lower than central government organizations, but when their leaders show strong visions and commitments, employees of local governments seem to be relatively easier to lead to adopt OSS. BPPT, a technology development state organization, have strongly supported these local governments in developing their back-office applications. But BPPT admitted that most of the ideas came from their local government partners which interacted with them intensively. Without strong commitment from the management, the complexity of massive OSS migration at organizational scale might be unbearable and unsustainable. Since there was no vendor that could provide post-sale services, then the organization that adopted OSS must establish their own help desks. In fact, part of the IGOS initiative was the setting up of various supporting institutions, from help desks at the organizational level, to Linux or OSS communities to commercial supporting units. But the establishment of such supporting units and making them sustainable were quite a challenge. Many local government could not establish their own help desks, while the cooperations with communities were often difficult to establish due to the institutional and cultural incompatibility between the former and the latter. OSS communities relied on voluntarism which gave their members freedom, while dealing with government organizations required them to go through administrative and bureaucratic hurdles.

As the government's formal supports of OSS ceased and then ended, OSS seemed to be immediately forgotten in many places. Except in several local governments, OSS has returned to their previous positions, the toys and tools of geeks and computer enthusiasts. The ideological narrative of OSS proponents that OSS could make the country technologically more independent and advanced failed to spread throughout society and government.

Cultural and Institutional Incompatibility of OSS Development

Government's supports for both OSS and e-government should consequently stimulate the growth of an exciting and vibrant OSS industry, not just of hobbyists' activities. There have been many open source applications being developed, however, most of them are OSS in the sense that they were developed using OSS development tools, such as PHP, Python, etc and running on Linux operating system. Their mode of development was as closed as the development of proprietary softwares. The three proceedings of national conferences of OSS held by Indonesian Institute of Science (LIPI) in 2006, 2007 and 2009 shows the papers describing OSS developed by universities and research organizations which did not engage people outside their organizations to contribute and did not provide links to the source codes of the applications. Even, the major work of developing two Linux distros were carried out as closed activities by two separate government R&D organizations. They took advantages of the available OSS but did not apply OSS as a mode of development, which opened the process of development to public. OSS as a governance structure of software development (Jensen & Scacchi, 2010) was not adopted.

There has never been any specific policy to promote and deal with the complexity of OSS development. The intangibility of softwares might deceive people to underestimate the complexity of its development. Regardless of the level of complexity, from a few lines of code to a complex operating system, the skill to develop software is called programming, and it just looks like typing on a computer, without any visible sophistication like working in a laboratory or in manufacturing plant. OSS development is much more than just knowledge sharing, such as what happens in virtual discussion forums or Wikipedia. In discussion forums each member can have different opinions without affecting each other's opinions, in Wikipedia people seek to produce a coherent article, but the system allows incoherency and contradiction, whereas in OSS, any part of the code can affect the working of the whole system, therefore even a small error in any part of the software cannot be tolerated and must be corrected.

Coordinating collaboration of software development is very complicated due to the intangibility of the product they seek to produce. The more people involved in software development, the more difficult to reach the consensus in determining the architecture of a software, identifying its building blocks, and implementing it in programming language. Therefore, OSS production could be more complicated than the closed production of a proprietary software, but this complication could be compensated by the voluntary contributions of enthusiast and experienced programmers from any part of the world (Rusovan, Lawford, & Parnas, 2005).

The involvement of programmers from around the world can give the projects access to abundance of technical knowledge, however, it can also pose severe problems. Besides the increasing complexity of managing those people and incorporating their contributions, online communication can lead to unfriendly interactions. "Successful collaboration among these highly talented people is not simple.

Conflict is customary. It will not do to tell a story about the avoidance of conflict among like-minded friends who are bound together by an unproblematic technical rationality, or by altruism, or exchanges of gifts" (Weber, 2004, p. 88). From the Indonesian cultural perspective, there is a paradox in an OSS project. The project has a noble goal, that is to deliver a software that can be used by anyone. But, in the process of developing the software, conflict is often unavoidable. For many Indonesian people who generally seek to maintain harmony at work, participating in voluntary work full of conflict is just unacceptable. However, the conflict can be much reduced if the goal of the project is clear, the design of technical solutions has been clearly established. So, the initiators of the project should have already solved their design problems before inviting others to contribute to the project.

It can be claimed that there have been a number of successful OSS applications being developed and funded by the government, but the OSS as a mode of development has been failed to develop. Besides culture, the other cause of the failure is institutional incompatibility. Government funded OSS projects were usually carried out by a small team from single government organizations or universities without engaging external communities, because the regime of administration of government projects did not give sufficient flexibility to engage OSS communities that would contribute voluntarily. According to the administration, everything – the number of people who would participate, what would be delivered, the time it would be finished, and the budget being allocated, should be clearly specified in detail and in advance. IGOS initiative, which was formally aimed at promoting the development of OSS, did not address the inflexibility of the administration regime. So the incompatibility of government administration and OSS development governance remained unaddressed and hence unsolved.

There are different opportunities from OSS each of which poses different challenges. The opportunity mostly taken by the government was of the least resistance, namely, diffusing generic applications that would be widely used by end-users, such as operating system and office suite. They were already available, well-proven and widely used by OSS-familiar users. Adopting them at organizational scale could relieve government from great expenses, as has been shown by a number of local governments. OSS proponents wanted the government to do more than just the diffusion of existing OSS. The opportunity was there, because the OSS initiative went simultaneously with the e-government initiative. Together, both initiatives would trigger local OSS development. Given the e-government budget of all government organizations, it should be enough to boost local OSS industry. Unfortunately, OSS based companies are mostly small and could not participate to bid in government projects. While rhetorically the government and others often mention about encouraging startup companies, they did not address the problem of how to engage OSS businesses in government's projects.

People tended to focus on overcoming technical problems and underestimating the rest. Technology was not the only determining factor in the development and diffusion of innovation. To be sustainable, the initiative should develop a well-functioning industry. What the OSS providers should deliver is not a mere product, but solution. When their clients are organizations/businesses, not individual users, the complex utilizations of software often demanded the creation of innovative business models, to make their products/services more flexible and affordable for their clients. "In a commodity world, technologists need to think about innovating in their business models as much as (if not more than) innovating in their technology. Of course, it's a natural trap for the technologist to think about technology alone, but technology is but a small part of the technology business" (Murdock, 2006, p. 102).

CONCLUSION

OSS gives computer users inexpensive or even free alternatives to proprietary softwares. OSS also removes the wall that constrains developing countries to enter into developing their own software industry. The openness of OSS allows software developers to examine the internal working of softwares as well as to freely modify and distribute it. The openness does apply for all, hence the benefits given by OSS is widely and equally distributed, rather than concentrated on a few business players. Different policy approaches are needed to take the advantages of OSS, because the development and business of OSS have different nature from that of proprietary softwares.

Indonesian government has taken major OSS initiative, the IGOS initiative, which was intended to support the diffusion and development of OSS. This initiative allowed the government to combine their power and resources with the knowledge and creativity of communities, R&D organizations and higher educations. While the major concern of government was to overcome the problem of widespread software piracy by replacing illegal softwares with OSS, the others wanted more than just the diffusion of OSS, but also the development of local OSS.

The IGOS initiative soon triggered unhappy responses from overseas businesses, which was suspected to cause the government's signing an MoU with Microsoft. This MoU has weakened the government's messages of support for OSS and made others raise question about the commitment of the government in supporting OSS. Nevertheless, some government organizations have actively organized events and implemented programs to promote the diffusion and development of OSS. But after all these were over, OSS seems to be forgotten in many government organizations, except in few local governments where OSS has strong presence to support not only routine office or administrative works but also back office applications that underly their public services.

Many OSS have been developed and funded by the government. But, they are only open in the sense that they were developed using OSS development tools, while the governance of development itself remain closed, preventing the involvement of volunteers that is usual in common OSS projects. The development of OSS demands for the adoption of special norms and cultures, but also the openness toward the behaviors that violate any norm and culture. It is culturally challenging for society that are used to seek harmony among themselves, especially among people who participate in voluntary works, such as OSS projects. Another source of constraint that prevented open mode of development was the incompatibility between the rigid administration regime of government's project and the open participation of volunteers in common OSS projects.

OSS is the product of people who are not only willing to share their knowledge, but also confront their ideas with one another, and struggle to reach the agreement on technical solutions. All volunteers may bring their own ideas/solutions into an OSS project, for the used ideas/solutions must logically and technically fit with one another, there is high possibility that many ideas/solutions would be abandoned. The involvement in OSS projects can be intellectual, emotional as well as political struggle. Managing OSS projects and being involved in an OSS project demands more than just knowledge and programming skills, but also attitudes and mental toughness, because the norms and cultures of virtual OSS project can be very harsh and totally different from those faced people in their daily life.

REFERENCES

Angelidou, M. (2014). Smart city policies: A spatial approach. *Cities (London, England)*, *41*, S3–S11. doi:10.1016/j.cities.2014.06.007

Arora, A., & Athreye, S. (2002). The software industry and India's economic development. *Information Economics and Policy*, *14*(2), 253–273. doi:10.1016/S0167-6245(01)00069-5

Avgerou, C. (2010). Discourses on ICT and Development. *Information Technologies and International Development*, *6*(3), 1–18.

Beniger, J. R. (1986). *The Control Revolution: Technological and Economic Origins of the Information Society*. Cambridge, MA: Harvard University Press.

Câmara, G., & Fonseca, F. (2007). Information Policies and Open Source Software in Developing Countries. *Journal of the American Society for Information Science and Technology*, *58*(1), 121–132. doi:10.1002/asi.20444

Christensen, C. M. (2000). *The Innovator's Dilemma*. New York, NY: HarperBusiness.

Cordella, A. (2007). E-government: Towards the e-bureaucratic form? *Journal of Information Technology*, *22*(3), 265–274. doi:10.1057/palgrave.jit.2000105

de Miranda, A., Peet, D.-J., Mulder, K. F., Berkman, P. A., Ruddy, T. F., Pillmann, W., & Bijker, W. E. (2007). ICT for Development: Illusions, Promises, Challenges, and Realizations. In W. Shrum, K. R. Benson, W. E. Bijker, & K. Brunnstein (Eds.), *Past, Present and Future of Research in the Information Society* (pp. 13–31). New York, NY: Springer. doi:10.1007/978-0-387-47650-6_2

Dener, C., Watkins, J. A., & Dorotinsky, W. L. (2011). *Financial Management Information Systems: 25 Years of World Bank Experience on What Works and What Doesn't*. Washington, DC: The World Bank. doi:10.1596/978-0-8213-8750-4

DiBona, C. (2006). Open Source and Proprietary Software Development. In C. DiBona, D. Cooper, & M. Stone (Eds.), *Open Sources 2.0: The Continuing Evolution*. Sebastopol, CA: O'Reilly.

DiBona, C., Cooper, D., & Stone, M. (2006). Introduction. In C. DiBona, D. Cooper, & M. Stone (Eds.), *Open Sources 2.0: The Continuing Evolution 2.0*. Sebastopol, CA: O'Reilly.

GitHub. (2018). *The Largest Open Source Community in the World*. Retrieved from https://github.com/open-source

Hayek, F. A. (1945). The Use of Knowledge in Society. *The American Economic Review*, *35*(4).

IIPA. (2010). *2010 Special 301: Indonesia. iN2015 Steering Committee. (2006)*. Singapore: Innovation. Integration. Internationalisation.

Jensen, C., & Scacchi, W. (2010). Governance in Open Source Software Development Projects: A Comparative Multi-level Analysis. In P. Ågerfalk, C. Boldyreff, J. M. González-Barahona, G. R. Madey, & J. Noll (Eds.), *Open Source Software: New Horizons: 6th International IFIP WG 2.13 Conference on Open Source Systems, OSS 2010, Notre Dame, IN, USA, May 30 -- June 2, 2010. Proceedings* (pp. 130–142). Berlin: Springer Berlin Heidelberg. 10.1007/978-3-642-13244-5_11

Layton, E. T. Jr. (1974). Technology as Knowledge. *Technology and Culture, 15*(1), 31–41. doi:10.2307/3102759

Lerner, J., & Tirole, J. (2002). Some Simple Economics of Open Source. *The Journal of Industrial Economics, L*(2).

Loasby, B. J. (1999). *Knowledge, Institutions and Evolution in Economics*. London: Routledge. doi:10.4324/9780203459096

Martin, C. (2016). Shaping the Industry Agenda. In *Annual Report 2015-2016*. Geneva: World Economic Forum.

Marx, K. (1906). *Capital: A Critique of Political Economy*. New York, NY: Random House.

Maulana, I., & Handoko, D. (2006). Tantangan dalam Pengembangan Industri OSS. In Prosiding Seminar Nasional Strategi Pemasyarakatan Open Source Software di Indonesia. Academic Press.

Mesthene, E. G. (1997). The Role of Technology in Society. In K. S. Shrader-Frechette & L. Westra (Eds.), *Technology and Values* (pp. 71–86). Lanham, MD: Rowman & Littlefield Publishers, Inc.

Murdock, I. (2006). Open Source and the Commoditization of Software. In C. DiBona, D. Cooper, & M. Stone (Eds.), *Open Sources 2.0: The Continuing Evolution*. Sebastopol, CA: O'Reilly.

Nagala, S. V. (2005). India's Story of Success: Promoting the Information Technology Industry. *Stanford Journal of International Relations, 6*(1). Retrieved October 21, 2017 from https://web.stanford.edu/group/sjir/6.1.05_nagala.html

North, D. (1990). *Institutions, Institutional Change and Economic Performance*. Cambridge, MA: Cambridge University Press. doi:10.1017/CBO9780511808678

Nuvolari, A. (2005). Open source software development: Some historical perspectives. *First Monday, 10*(10). doi:10.5210/fm.v10i10.1284

Oxford Business Group. (2007). *The Report: Emerging Indonesia 2007*. Author.

Parayil, G. (1991a). Technological Change as a Problem-Solving Activity. *Technological Forecasting and Social Change, 40*(3), 235–247. doi:10.1016/0040-1625(91)90054-J

Parayil, G. (1991b). Technological Knowledge and Technological Change. *Technology in Society, 13*(3), 289–304. doi:10.1016/0160-791X(91)90005-H

Polese, K. (2006). Foreword: Source Is Everything. In C. DiBona, D. Cooper, & M. Stone (Eds.), *Open Sources 2.0: The Continuing Evolution* (pp. ix–xii). Sebastopol, CA: O'Reilly.

Ratri Adityarani. (2011). *Indonesia Ranks As The 11th Worst Pirating Nation*. Retrieved August 21, 2017, from https://www.techinasia.com/indonesia-pirating-nation

Raymond, E. S. (2001). *The Cathedral and the Bazaar: Musings on Linux and Open Source by an Accidental Revolutionary* (Revised Edition). Sebastopol, CA: O'Reilly.

Rosser, A. (2012). *The Politics of Economic Liberalization in Indonesia: State, Market and Power*. Abingdon, UK: Routledge.

Rusovan, S., Lawford, M., & Parnas, D. L. (2005). Open Source Software Development: Future or Fad? In J. Feller, B. Fitzgerald, S. A. Hissam, & K. R. Lakhani (Eds.), *Perspectives on Free and Open Source Software*. Cambridge, MA: The MIT Press.

Shapiro, C., & Varian, H. R. (1999). *Information Rules: A Strategic Guide to the Network Economy*. Boston, MA: Harvard Business School Press.

Slashdot Media. (2018). *SourceForge*. Retrieved from https://sourceforge.net/about

Stallman, R. (1999). The GNU Operating System and the Free Software Movement. In C. DiBona, S. Ockman, & M. Stone (Eds.), *Open Sources: Voices from the Open Source Revolution*. Sebastopol, CA: O'Reilly.

Stiglitz, J. E. (2002). *Globalization and Its Discontents*. London: Allen Lane.

Susanti, R. D. I., Nurjaya, I. N., Safaat, R., & Djatmika, P. (2014). The Problem of Copyright for Traditional Cultural Expression in Indonesia: The Example of the "Malang Masks." *Journal of Law, Policy and Globalization*, *29*, 57–71.

UNCTAD. (2002). Changing Dynamics of Global Computer Software and Services Industry: Implications for Developing Countries (UNCTAD/ITE/TEB/12). New York: UNCTAD.

UNCTAD. (2003). E-commerce and development report (No. UNCTAD/SIDTE/ECB/2003/1). New York: UNCTAD.

UNCTAD. (2004). Road maps towards an information society in Latin America and the Caribbean (No. LC/G.2195/Rev.1-P). Santiago, Chile: UNCTAD.

Utami, M. S. (2018). *28 Universitas Jurusan Kompter Teknik Informatika Terbaik di Indonesia*. Retrieved from http://www.ban-pt-universitas.co/2015/04/universitas-jurusan-komputer-teknik-informatika-terbaik-di-indonesia.html

Vaidhyanathan, S. (2005). Open Source as Culture - Culture as Open Source. In C. Brandt (Ed.), *Open source annual*. Berlin: Technische University. Retrieved November 4, 2017 from https://ssrn.com/abstract=713044

Visser, M. (2010). Constructing organisational learning and knowledge socially: An interactional perspective. *International Journal of Knowledge and Learning*, *6*(4), 285–294. doi:10.1504/IJKL.2010.038650

Wasko, M. M., & Faraj, S. (2000). "It is what one does": Why people participate and help others in electronic communities of practice. *The Journal of Strategic Information Systems*, *9*(2-3), 155–173. doi:10.1016/S0963-8687(00)00045-7

Weber, S. (2004). *The Success of Open Source*. Cambridge, MA: Harvard University Press.

Weerawarana, S., & Weeratunge, J. (2004). *Open Source in Developing Countries*. Sida.

KEY TERMS AND DEFINITIONS

Copyright: The exclusive legal right, given to an author, a creator, or an assignee to print, publish, perform, film, or record literary, artistic material, or software, and to authorize others to do the same.

Intellectual Property Rights: The rights given to persons over their creations, which are different from those having been created before. The rights give the persons an exclusive right over the use of their creations for a certain period of time, and encompass a collection of rights that include copyrights, trademarks, and patents.

Linux: An operating system that was initially created by Linus Torvalds as a personal project, and then being made open to contributions from thousands of other programmers.

Open Mode of Development: A process of software development which is open to anyone to participate in writing and testing codes, writing manuals, or just giving suggestions and comments. People having Internet access, if they have the necessary skills and knowledge, can participate in open mode of development. Most of open source softwares have been developed through open mode of development.

Open Source Software: A software that is distributed with source code that anyone can read, modify, and compile into a new open source software.

Operating System: A computer software that is running underneath all other softwares on a computer, manages computer hardware and software resources, and provides common services requested by other softwares.

Proprietary Software: A commercial software that is the opposite of open source software, its source code is kept secret by the developers or company that developed it.

Source Code: A text listing of commands written in a programming language to be compiled or assembled into an executable computer program. A source code is understood by human programmers and cannot directly be executed by computers. In order for a source code to be executable by computers, it has first to be converted into a machine executable code.

This research was previously published in The Role of Knowledge Transfer in Open Innovation; pages 139-157, copyright year 2019 by Information Science Reference (an imprint of IGI Global).

Chapter 86
Task Assignment and Personality:
Crowdsourcing Software Development

Abdul Rehman Gilal
Sukkur IBA University, Pakistan

Muhammad Zahid Tunio
Beijing University of Posts and Telecommunication, China

Ahmad Waqas
Sukkur IBA University, Pakistan

Malek Ahmad Almomani
https://orcid.org/0000-0002-3890-9792
University Technology PETRONAS, Malaysia

Sajid Khan
Sukkur IBA University, Pakistan

Ruqaya Gilal
Universiti Utara Malaysia, Malaysia

ABSTRACT

An open call format of crowdsourcing software development (CSD) is harnessing potential, diverse, and unlimited people. But, several thousand solutions are being submitted at platform against each call. To select and match the submitted task with the appropriate worker and vice versa is still a complicated problem. Focusing the issue, this study proposes a task assignment algorithm (TAA) that will behave as an intermediate facilitator (at platform) between task (from requester) and solution (from worker). The algorithm will divide the tasks' list based on the developer's personality. In this way, we can save the time of both developers and platform by reducing the searching time.

DOI: 10.4018/978-1-6684-3702-5.ch086

INTRODUCTION

Crowdsourcing has become an emerging trend for the quick software development due to the parallel and micro-tasking. It is also cost efficient based on the knowledge of the crowd or "wisdom of the crowd". CSD uses an open call format. This process involves three kinds of roles: 1) requester, 2) platform (i.e., the service provider) and 3) crowd-source developer (i.e., the person for coding and testing). This type of call format enables large numbers of task accessibility and self-selection. On the platform, a number of developers can register and choose a task from available set. Once after the submission of the task from developers, the platform is required to evaluate the submission to decide for the best solution from developers, to pay the rewards. Based on the Ke Mao et al. studies (Mao, Capra, Harman, & Jia, 2017; Mao, Yang, Wang, Jia, & Harman, 2015), selection of an appropriate task to reward from the extensive large set of tasks is a very hectic work for the developers. Besides, it is also a tiring and time-consuming job for the platform to evaluate thousands of submitted tasks from developers. Ye Yang and M.C Yuen (Yang, Karim, Saremi, & Ruhe, 2016; Yuen, King, & Leung, 2011) mentioned that from the task requester perspective, it is very hard to match the developer with the task and it is also very difficult to monitor the risk of the reliability of the CSD developers.

In the same view, Chilton and Eman Aldhahri (Aldhahri, Shandilya, & Shiva, 2015; Chilton, Horton, & Miller, 2010) continued to claim that matching of the improper task to improper CSD developer may not only decrease the quality of the software deliverables but it also overburdens both platform and developers. They further mentioned that most workers view a minimum number of recent tasks that are posted at the platform because tasks are posted in hundreds. By considering the low level of skills and expertise level of the crowdsourced software developers, unrealistic matching of CSD worker and the task may have an effect on the software quality. Latoza et al. (Latoza & Hoek, 2015) also emphasized on the matching of workers with their expertise and knowledge and to get maximum benefit from the CSD worker is an issue. Similar is the case is discussed in the (Geiger & Schader, 2014; Gilal, Jaafar, Omar, Basri, & Din, 2016; Gilal, Jaafar, Omar, Basri, & Waqas, 2016; Gilal, Omar, & Sharif, 2013; Tunio et al., 2017) studies that while keeping extrinsic and intrinsic choice of CSD workers self-identification principle for individual contributors to select those tasks which are the best match with their psychological preferences (i.e., personality). Psychological is an important factor to compliance with the choice and individual capabilities with the respective task requirements. Moreover, to choose a few best submissions out of thousand submissions is really a hectic job at CSD platform level. Every CSD worker is not supposed to give the best solution for each task (Dang, Liu, Zhang, & Huang, 2016). More seriously, malicious workers can also submit the tasks for reviews to increase the complexity at the platform (Carmel, de Souza, Meneguzzi, Machado, & Prikladnicki, 2016; Carpenter & Huang, 1998; Nawaz, Waqas, Yusof, Mahesar, & Shah, 2017; Nawaz, Waqas, Yusof, & Shah, 2016; Waqas, Yusof, Shah, & Khan, 2014; Waqas, Yusof, Shah, & Mahmood, 2014). Keeping it in view, Leticia Machado, et al.(Howe, 2006) stated that CSD model does not only deal with technology issues but economic as well as personal issues that make the model more complex.

According to (Fernando Capretz, 2014; Gilal, Jaafar, Basri, Omar, & Abro, 2016; Gilal, Jaafar, Basri, Omar, & Tunio, 2016; Gilal, Jaafar, Omar, Basri, & Waqas, 2016; Gilal, Omar, et al., 2017; Tunio et al., 2018), the key complexities pertinent to the development of software are concerned with human aspects from their social and cognitive point of view. According to Martínez et al., (Martínez, Rodríguez-Díaz, Licea, & Castro, 2010), though the technical aspects maintain principal importance to obtain good performance in a software development process but the human or soft aspects (i.e., personality types) cannot be ignored. Personality refers to internal psychological patterns such as feelings and thoughts that carve the behavior of a person (Fu, Chen, & Song, 2015). Personality can create healthy behavior of an employee that can lead the overall project to success. On the other side, it can also cause damages within project development if it is improperly managed. Numerous studies have been carried out in the past that applies many theoretical frameworks adopted from the domain of psychology to better understand the personality of software developers (Basri et al., 2017; Gilal, Jaafar, Omar, Basri, & Waqas, 2016; Tunio et al., 2017). Thus, human aspects should be emphasized to cope up with the challenges while developing projects under the umbrella of software engineering.

The aim of this study is to propose and formulate a Crowdsourcing software development task assignment algorithm (TAA) based on the type of task and personality types. This study would extend the literature and guidelines for the researchers who are willing to contribute to improve the crowd source algorithms for software development in which human factor is involved. By applying the discussed advancements, future algorithms can reduce the task selection burdens from developers and platforms.

RELATED WORK

There are different dimensions of human factors in software engineering. Studies have been conducted from different perspectives (Capretz & Ahmed, 2010b; Hazzan & Hadar, 2008) such as the investigation of human factors in different phases of software life cycle, the effect of team work in software development, how can a personality profile suit a particular task like code review, or about some other miscellaneous issues. The word personality has been the center of discussion for many psychologists and the number of definitions has been suggested in the past to elaborate this word. Due to its abstract nature, different psychologists have defined this word differently. However, personality is often defined with two classical definitions that have widely accepted among psychologists. The first definition is given by Allport (1961) in which he defines personality as person characteristics that consist of dynamic of behavior, thought and feelings. The second most important definition is given by Child (1968), which refers personality as internal factors that differentiate a person's behavior for particular situations. It can be inferred from these two definitions given by Allport and Child that personality is solely internal process that carves and mold the attitude of people. Though the personality has been considered and discussed under the umbrella of psychology, but the recent finding of the research studies reveal the fact that personality is also shaped and molded due to the biological and genetic inheritance. In the same vein, Child defines personality as stable or relatively stable that does not bring radical change in weeks but it takes time that can be predicated.

The main difference between these two definitions given by Child and Allport is that the first definition reveals consistency within individuals, and difference between individuals, whereas later definition emphasizes characteristic patterns that show the nature of behaviour within individuals. In a nutshell, both definitions shows that personality forms our actions, feelings, thoughts and consistence and it also varies from person to person for different people maintain different attitude and temper having different personalities.

In the conclusion, this study follows the definition of personality given by Allport and Child. In which personality is defined that ——the personality is solely internal process that carves and molds the attitude of people.

For the last 50 years, the Myers-Brigs Type Indicator (MBTI) (Myers, McCaulley, Quenk, & Hammer, 1998) has been used as a source for identification of personality preferences and personality type of an individual. This personality type indicator is used for making theories of Jung applicable and useful in everyday life. An individual's personality type in MBTI is assessed on four dimensions: social interaction (extroversion (E) and introversion (I)), decision making (thinking (T) and feeling (F)), information gathering (sensing (S) and intuition (N)), and dealing with the external world (judging (J) and perceiving (P)). Both Katharine Cook Briggs and her daughter, Isabel Briggs Myers are considered as pioneer of MBTI who not only extensively studied the work of Jung but they also explored and inter-related different theories of human behavior i.e., theory of psychological types into practical use.

The MBTI test allows individual personality type preferences to be classified according to the 16 types with the results reported as a combination of four dimensional pairs, which are Introversion (I) and Extroversion (E); Thinking (T) and Feeling (F); Sensing (S) and Intuitive (N) ; and Judging (J) and Perceiving (P). The 16 possible personality combinations are formed from these four dimensions. Table 1 shows 16 combinations of personality types based on MBTI.

Table 1. MBTI 16 personality types

ISTJ	ISFJ	INFJ	INTJ
ISTP	ISFP	INFP	INTP
ESTP	ESFP	ENFP	ENTP
ESTJ	ESFJ	ENFJ	ENTJ

A person can be classified into one of the 16 personality types based on the largest score obtained. For example, a person scoring higher on Introversion (I) than Extroversion (E); Sensing (S) than Intuition (N); Thinking (T) than Feeling (F); and Judging (J) than Perceiving (P), would be classified as an ISTJ.

Personality is a backbone that carves either negative or positive behaviour of individual towards different things. There are number of personality traits exhibited by people on different occasions influenced by different factors as well. These factors have been illuminated by Goldberg (1990), which are profusely followed and admitted. These factors are put into five broad categories: Extraversion, Neuroticism, Agreeableness, Openness to experience and conscientiousness. Though these five factors can be taken into account to form team for software engineering, but there is also another factor (Block, 1995) i.e., cognitive ability that is also very crucial and important whose importance cannot be denied while forming software engineering team that ensures good results.

The cognitive faculty of an individual covers abstract thinking, mindset, visualization capability and analytic and so on. Though five factors described by Goldberg (1990) are profusely used for the personality assessment in teamwork in software engineering, but the inclusion of cognitive faculty into these five factors prove to be lucrative to assess and point out an ideal personality suitable for SE team group (Block, 1995).

Neuroticism refers to the negative aspects of an individual's emotions that can be highlighted in the form of anxiety, depression, hostility, impulsiveness and self- consciousness. The opposite of neuroticism can be defined with self-control and emotional stability that one maintains despite of facing toughness in terms of working in an environment against to one's nature. People who suffer from this factor in abundance expose following features: they lose cognitive power due to facing constant pressure and depression emerging from surroundings or they commit errors and mistakes in numbers for having anxiety while performing assigned tasks.

This personality trait refers to the recreational aspects of individual who love to enjoy working with people and enjoy their company. Extrovert individuals are sociable, energetic, assertive, enthusiastic, adventurous, and they also show warmth in performing tasks. People who develop extraversion expose following features: they do not like the monotony for being sensitive. Thus, they love working under changing environment-having variety of works. Moreover, the people having an element of consciousness appear to be law abiding, dutiful, showing acute self-discipline and they also strive harder for achievements. These people show following features: they do not hesitate to make thorough decisions to benefit organization. Similarly, the people having this personality trait show much flexibility and compassions for others and they never become antagonist with any one. Such people exhibit tolerance, tactfulness, trust, respect, modesty and sympathy. These people also show following features: they are generally easy to be worked with.

People having this personality trait are more inclined to welcome new learning so as to enhance their experience and ideas. Such people are mostly curious, imaginative, broadminded, cultured and unconventional. These people also show following features: they are curious and immensely interested in learning. Additionally, they love to make improvisations and experimentations while performing assigned tasks. For the requirement of software engineering, cognitive ability factor and its importance cannot be nullified at any point. People having strong cognitive ability show following features: they possess high level of abstract thinking that begets novel ideas and concepts without being involved practically performing the things.

In addition, there are studies conducted in order to investigate the relationship between human skills and the software life cycle phases and indeed human is the key determinant of success to software development (Almomani, Basri, & Gilal, 2018). Human beings' activities for instance analyzing, thinking, decision making, designing, collaborating, communicating, implementing and even personnel morale swing etc. are consisted a lot in the software development. Variety of engineering methodologies to solve the software crisis and each with its own recognized strengths and weaknesses have evolved over years for decades. As a matter of fact, one software development methodology framework is not necessarily applicable to be used by all projects. Thus, researchers and practitioners have jumped into conclusion that there is no silver bullet for software engineering (Hazzan & Hadar, 2008). Over a century, with mobile development technologies and a boom of cloud-based application (Waqas, Gilal, et al., 2017; Waqas, Rehman, Gilal, & Khan, 2016; Waqas, Rehman, et al., 2017), as well as the appearance of e-commerce which brings people's daily life to cyberspace, human factor research has become a crucial topic in software engineering research especially for the field of software development. Similarly, Karn and Cowling (2006) emphasized that decision making process and group processes are always influenced by the personalities of the members involved in team. Additionally, personality can be measured keeping in account the traits and the types of individuals. Defining the traits and the types of individuals, Karen and Cowling also maintain that traits are associated with behaviour of individuals that can be seen through characteristics exposed into different and variety of situations. Whereas, type can be narrated as a category of fixed patterns of traits that reveal the actual characteristics of one's personality.

To recommend Crowdsourcing software development task, a content-based technique was used by Ke Mao, Capra et al., (Mao et al., 2017). This approach used a historical record of registration and winning for the CSD for automatically matching the task and developer. Snow et al., (Snow et al., 2008) proposed bias correction in crowd data in the form of modeling. They used a gold standard data set to estimate the CSD workers model accuracy. However, this method is used in micro-tasking. Ambati et al., (Ambati, Vogel, & Carbonell, 2011) used an implicit model based on skills and interest of CSD worker to recommend the classification based task. Yuen et al. (Yuen et al., 2011) mentioned and proposed an approach based on task matching which will encourage CSD workers to do a task on the continuous and long run. This approach is focused on the recommendation of the tasks to be best matched with the workers. Sheng et al., (Sheng, Provost, & Ipeirotis, 2008) stated that, for a task matching, labeling is used as a technique but it also evident a limitation. Whitehall et al., (Whitehill, Ruvolo, Wu, Bergsma, & Movellan, 2009), and Raykar et al., (Raykar, 2009) used EM algorithm to calculate the accuracy of the CSD worker, and answer matrix to relate and mapping the quality of the CSD worker. Determination of single labeling is focused on these studies (Capretz & Ahmed, 2010a; Dawid & Skene, 2006; Dempster, Laird, & Rubin, 2018; Gentle, McLachlan, & Krishnan, 2006; Gupta, 2011). According to (Howe, 2006), by ignoring the task requirements and the relationship between CSD worker's non-technical skills these approaches may get undesired results. Therefore, a new approach is needed to relate the human skills with the technical skills of the CSD workers. A comparison of other author's work and TAA is presented in 2.

Table 2. Comparison of TAA with other techniques

Authors	Techniques Used	TAA
Ke Mao, Capra et al., (Mao et al., 2017).	This approach used a historical record of registration and winning for the CSD for automatically matching the task and developer	TAA for Crowdsourcing software development algorithm will match the past task preferences and personality types to update the selection list for the developer or other way around for platform. As a result, the quality and efficiency of software deliverables will be increased with minimum efforts.
Snow et al., (Tratz et al., 2016)	Used a gold standard data set to estimate the CSD workers model accuracy. However, this method is used in micro-tasking	
Ambati et al., (Ambati et al., 2011)	Used an implicit modeling based on skills and interest of CSD worker to recommend the task.	
Sheng et al., (Sheng et al., 2008)	For a task matching, labeling is used as a technique.	
Liu et al., (Liu et al., 2012) Whitehall et al., (Whitehill et al., 2009), and Raykar et al., (Raykar, 2009).	Used EM algorithm to calculate the accuracy of the CSD worker, by using EM algorithm and answer matrix to relate and mapping the quality of the CSD worker	

The Existing model of crowdsourcing software development is working on open call format

As shown in Figure 1, initially the requester requests the platform to post the problem. The platform then sort out the problems and made its micro-tasking to post. CSD developers register themselves to participate in the various tasks. They are required to submit their solutions to the platform before deadlines. The platform initiates the review process over the submissions as soon the deadlines ended. After reviewing the submissions, platform publishes the results of prize-winning tasks. Moreover, developers also have the right of appeal against the rejection of their submission. At the end, the reward is given to the winner of submission.

Figure 1. Existing CSD process

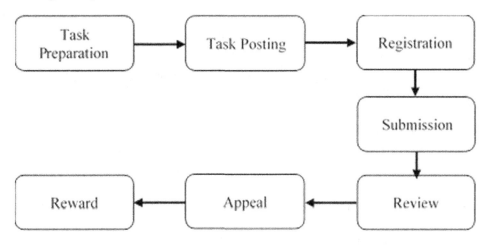

RESEARCH METHODOLOGY

The proposed approach will work the same as the open call format but the proposed task assignment CSD model includes the personality based categorization. Once, after the requester prepared a request for the task, the platform shortlists the posts of tasks for competition based on personality types. In this case, the registration of developer requires the personality measurement test to know the type of personality of developers. Meanwhile, this proposal also suggests that the task should also be included with a specific explanation that can be used to define the required traits of personality for the task. For example, the social networking based tasks may require a developer with the extrovert trait. Since the extrovert developer can understand and work on the task with interest as they involve themselves in social activities. Hence, the task will be directly available for the developers, if the developers are already registered with the platform along with their personality types (i.e., by using MBTI). The classification of individual personality types is classified on the MBTI test that allows the combination of four-dimensional pairs and from those four combinations, there are the 16 possible personality combinations that are already discussed in Table 1. To evaluate a personality of the CSD worker, this study, will use MBTI personality type as an instrument because this instrument is widely used in the research of software engineering (Almomani et al., 2018; Gilal, Jaafar, Abro, et al., 2017; Gilal, Jaafar, Omar, et al., 2017; Jaafar et al., 2017; Kazai, Kamps, & Milic-Frayling, 2011).

This study devised the CSD task assignment algorithm based on personality types and three categories of tasks: design, development and testing. To describe better CSD task matching domain the relationships among the CSD developer, the task, the requester, and platform are to be defined. Following is the definition of the relationships which are basically adapted from the study of Yuen et al.,(Yuen et al., 2011). The mathematical description of TAA is used to sort the available tasks to best matching, sorting and assigning the tasks to developers.

TAA in CSD consists of 5 kinds of tuple {L, M, O, P, Q}

1. Where L: L= {lx\x =1 ….. U_N} is a set of CSD requester who wants to post the tasks on the platform.
2. Where M: M= {my\y=1 …..M_N} is a set of developers on CSD platform and M_N is the maximum number of the CSD developer.

3. Where O: $O = \{oi \backslash i = 1 \ldots O_N\}$ is a set of categories of CSD task available on CSD platform for example (development, design, f2f) whereas O_N is a maximum number of categories of the task.

4. Where P: $P = \{pi \backslash i = 1 \ldots P_N\}$ is a set of personality traits of the CSD developer. Where P_N is the total number of personality types.

5. Where Q: $Q = \{qi \backslash i = 1 \ldots Q_N\}$ is a set of the task in all categories of CSD, whereas, the Q_N is the total number of the task in each category.

The following attributes are in A task category Oi:

r i,j is the requester of the task Q1, Q2 where $ri,j = \exists_L x \in L$.

$Dij = \{d,i,j,k \backslash k = 1 \ldots Dn\}$ is a set of CSD developers who haveparticipated on task q1,q2..qn j, and

DN is the number of developers who participate on task q1,q2.qn where Di, jk $= \exists My \in M$.

e i,j is the personality types of worker wi, k to

mi,j is the reward by the platform r i, j for developer D ij k to complete task Qij

```
Algorithm
Procedure Match the Task (Developer my, personality record PR(my))
{run when CSD developer my log into the CSD platform}
Input: Q, the set of available tasks in all categories
ON, the number of task categories
QN, the number of available tasks in category qi
Algorithm: for i = 1 → O_N do
  for j = 1 → Q_N do
Based on Q and PR(My)
Compute   PR of each available developer for my
  j ← j + 1
  end for i ← i + 1
end for
 Output: the available tasks with personality type matching in all categories
will be sorted for developers.
```

We carried out empirical experiments to collect data on the final year students of bachelors program of Computer Systems Engineering at Dawood University of Engineering and Technology Karachi, Pakistan. Students were taught the fundamental concepts of crowdsourcing in the initial classes. Later, they were required to create an account on the prototype developed for the experiment that replicated the crowdsourcing environment (i.e., Topcoder). The prototype recorded participants' personality and choices. There were 91 students involved in the experiment; 49 were male and 42 were female.

Two rounds of experiments were carried out. In the first round, participants selected tasks based on their own choice from the random list of total 100 small tasks. After the first round, the tasks were computed based on the given algorithm above to evaluate the results. The first round helped us to 1) compute the initial results for the comparison with second round and 2) use the results to update the user profile for second round list. However, in the second round, the task list was shown to the participants based on their technical skills and personality types.

RESULTS AND DISCUSSION

Based on the results, it was found that results from round 2 were better than round 1. For instance, out of total 91 submitted tasks of round 1 only 37 were appeared effective. Whereas, total 61 tasks were classified into effective class in round 2. It could have happened due to a huge list of tasks in round 1. However, optimized task list have surely shown effective choices made by the same participants. Figure 2 shows the comparison between both classes.

Figure 2. Effective and ineffective submissions in both rounds

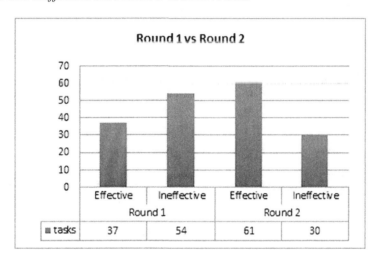

It was further observed from the results of round 1 that developers selected the tasks from the top 20-30 and bottom 80-100 visible tasks from the list. This is mentioned due the reason that only few 5 tasks were selected between 30-80. Figure 3 shows the overall distribution of the selection style of the participants.

However, by applying the selected algorithm on the task list based on the task type and personality in round 2, the task selection behavior of the participants appeared quite different. Each participant got different task list based on his or her skills. Therefore, the submitted tasks fulfilled the requirements effectively.

Moreover, based on the effective results, it was found that each category of task is appealing different type of personality. For instance, ESFP and ENFJ personality types were more attracted towards designing tasks. Similarly, ISFJ, INFJ, INFP and INTP were completely invisible to be working effectively on design projects. Table 3 summarizes the results of all types of tasks against each personality types.

In the same vein, ISTJ, ESTJ and ENTJ personality types were classified effective in both rounds. Capretz and Faheem (Capretz & Ahmed, 2010a) also produced similar results for the programmer personality. In the very study, ISTJ was the most frequent personality type for programmer role whereas our study also denotes "TJ" pair with I or E is effective. Moreover, INTJ, INFP, ENTP and ENFJ were not found in the effective development projects. Lastly, INFP and ESFJ were prominent personality types in both effective rounds. Whereas, ISFJ, INFJ, ISTP, INTP, ESFP, ENFP, ENTP and ESTJ were as disappeared as zero. Figure 4 summarizes the personality types in the effective submissions.

Figure 3. Round 1 selected tasks out of 100

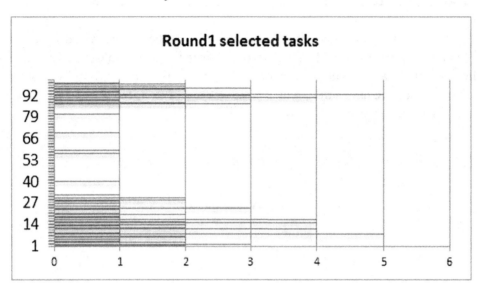

Table 3. Tasks and personality in effective class of both rounds

	Design	Development	Testing
ISTJ	1	11	1
ISFJ	0	2	0
INFJ	0	1	0
INTJ	2	0	3
ISTP	2	1	0
ISFP	1	2	2
INFP	0	0	8
INTP	0	2	0
ESTP	1	3	3
ESFP	9	1	0
ENFP	3	1	0
ENTP	2	0	0
ESTJ	1	5	0
ESFJ	1	1	5
ENFJ	9	0	4
ENTJ	3	6	1

At the end, ISTJ, ENFJ, ESFJ and ESFP personality types were found most frequent in the experiment.

Figure 4. Effective tasks and personality types

Personality types and effective frequency

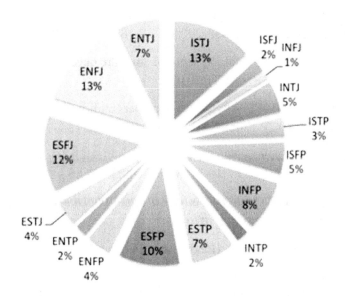

CONCLUSION

Crowdsourcing business approach is still facing crucial challenges in terms of assessing and selecting appropriate tasks as solution. Available techniques, methods or algorithms in CSD are yet to obtain the satisfactory outcomes. Technical requirements of the task along with personality preferences can sort the task list at the developer end for efficient selection. This way cannot only reduce the burden from platform but also increases the effectiveness in the submissions.

REFERENCES

Aldhahri, E., Shandilya, V., & Shiva, S. (2015). Towards an effective crowdsourcing recommendation system: A survey of the state-of-the-art. *Proceedings - 9th IEEE International Symposium on Service-Oriented System Engineering, IEEE SOSE 2015*. 10.1109/SOSE.2015.53

Allport, G. W. (1961). *Pattern and growth in personality*. Academic Press.

Almomani, M. A., Basri, S., & Gilal, A. R. (2018). Empirical study of software process improvement in Malaysian small and medium enterprises: The human aspects. *Journal of Software: Evolution and Process*. doi:10.1002/smr.1953

Ambati, V., Vogel, S., & Carbonell, J. (2011). Towards Task Recommendation in Micro-Task Markets. *Human Computation AAAI Workshop*.

Basri, S., Omar, M., Capretz, L. F., Aziz, I. A., Jaafar, J., & Gilal, A. R. (2017). Finding an effective classification technique to develop a software team composition model. *Journal of Software: Evolution and Process*. doi:10.1002/smr.1920

Block, J. (1995). A contrarian view of the five-factor approach to personality description. *Psychological Bulletin*, *117*(2), 187–215. doi:10.1037/0033-2909.117.2.187 PMID:7724687

Capretz, L. F., & Ahmed, F. (2010a). Making sense of software development and personality types. *IT Professional*, *12*(1), 6–13. doi:10.1109/MITP.2010.33

Capretz, L. F., & Ahmed, F. (2010b). Why do we need personality diversity in software engineering? *Software Engineering Notes*, *35*(2), 1. doi:10.1145/1734103.1734111

Carmel, E., de Souza, C. R. B., Meneguzzi, F., Machado, L., & Prikladnicki, R. (2016). *Task allocation for crowdsourcing using AI planning*. doi:10.1145/2897659.2897666

Carpenter, B., & Huang, Z. (1998). *Multilevel bayesian models of categorical data annotation*. Unpublished Manuscript. doi:10.1023/A:1009769707641

Child, I. L. (1968). Personality in culture. Handbook of Personality Theory and Research, 82–145.

Chilton, L. B., Horton, J. J., & Miller, R. C. (2010). Task search in a human computation market. *Proceedings of the ACM SIGKDD Workshop on Human Computation*, 1–9. 10.1145/1837885.1837889

Dang, D., Liu, Y., Zhang, X., & Huang, S. (2016). A Crowdsourcing Worker Quality Evaluation Algorithm on MapReduce for Big Data Applications. *IEEE Transactions on Parallel and Distributed Systems*, *27*(7), 1879–1888. doi:10.1109/TPDS.2015.2457924

Dawid, A. P., & Skene, A. M. (2006). Maximum Likelihood Estimation of Observer Error-Rates Using the EM Algorithm. *Applied Statistics*. doi:10.2307/2346806

Dempster, A. P., Laird, N. M., & Rubin, D. B. (2018). Maximum Likelihood from Incomplete Data Via the EM Algorithm. *Journal of the Royal Statistical Society. Series B. Methodological*. doi:10.1111/j.2517-6161.1977.tb01600.x

Fernando Capretz, L. (2014). Bringing the human factor to software engineering. *IEEE Software*, *31*(2), 104. doi:10.1109/MS.2014.30

Fu, Y., Chen, H., & Song, F. (2015). STWM: A solution to self-adaptive task-worker matching in software crowdsourcing. Lecture Notes in Computer Science. doi:10.1007/978-3-319-27119-4_27

Geiger, D., & Schader, M. (2014). Personalized task recommendation in crowdsourcing information systems - Current state of the art. *Decision Support Systems*, *65*(C), 3–16. doi:10.1016/j.dss.2014.05.007

Gentle, J. E., McLachlan, G. J., & Krishnan, T. (2006). The EM Algorithm and Extensions. *Biometrics*. doi:10.2307/2534032

Gilal, A. R., Jaafar, J., Abro, A., Umrani, W. A., Basri, S., & Omar, M. (2017). Making programmer effective for software development teams: An extended study. *Journal of Information Science and Engineering*. doi:10.6688/JISE.2017.33.6.4

Gilal, A. R., Jaafar, J., Basri, S., Omar, M., & Abro, A. (2016). Impact of software team composition methodology on the personality preferences of Malaysian students. *2016 3rd International Conference on Computer and Information Sciences, ICCOINS 2016 - Proceedings*. 10.1109/ICCOINS.2016.7783258

Gilal, A. R., Jaafar, J., Basri, S., Omar, M., & Tunio, M. Z. (2016). Making programmer suitable for team-leader: Software team composition based on personality types. *2015 International Symposium on Mathematical Sciences and Computing Research, iSMSC 2015 - Proceedings*. doi:10.1109/ISMSC.2015.7594031

Gilal, A. R., Jaafar, J., Omar, M., Basri, S., Aziz, I. A., Khand, Q. U., & Hasan, M. H. (2017). *Suitable Personality Traits for Learning Programming Subjects: A Rough-Fuzzy Model. International Journal of Advanced Computer Science and Applications*.

Gilal, A. R., Jaafar, J., Omar, M., Basri, S., & Din, I. (2016). Balancing the Personality of Programmer: Software Development Team Composition. *Malaysian Journal of Computer Science*, *29*(2), 145–155. doi:10.22452/mjcs.vol29no2.5

Gilal, A. R., Jaafar, J., Omar, M., Basri, S., & Waqas, A. (2016). A Rule-Based Model for Software Development Team Composition: Team Leader Role with Personality Types and Gender Classification. *Information and Software Technology*, *74*, 105–113. doi:10.1016/j.infsof.2016.02.007

Gilal, A. R., Omar, M., Jaafar, J., Sharif, K. I., Mahesar, A. W., & Basri, S. (2017). Software Development Team Composition: Personality Types of Programmer and Complex Networks. In *6th International Conference on Computing and Informatics (ICOCI-2017)* (pp. 153–159). Academic Press.

Gilal, A. R., Omar, M., & Sharif, K. I. (2013). Discovering personality types and diversity based on software team roles. In *International Conference on Computing and Informatics, ICOCI 2013* (pp. 259–264). Academic Press.

Goldberg, L. R. (1990). An alternative" description of personality": The big-five factor structure. *Journal of Personality and Social Psychology*, *59*(6), 1216–1229. doi:10.1037/0022-3514.59.6.1216 PMID:2283588

Gupta, M. R. (2011). Theory and Use of the EM Algorithm. *Foundations and Trends® in Signal Processing*. doi:10.1561/2000000034

Hazzan, O., & Hadar, I. (2008). Why and how can human-related measures support software development processes? *Journal of Systems and Software*, *81*(7), 1248–1252. doi:10.1016/j.jss.2008.01.037

Howe, J. (2006). *The Rise of Crowdsourcing. Wired Magazine*.

Jaafar, J., Gilal, A. R., Omar, M., Basri, S., Abdul Aziz, I., & Hasan, M. H. (2017). A Rough-Fuzzy Inference System for Selecting Team Leader for Software Development Teams. In *Advances in Intelligent Systems and Computing* (Vol. 661, pp. 304–314). Cham, Switzerland: Springer.

Karn, J. S., & Cowling, A J. (2006). Using ethnographic methods to carry out human factors research in software engineering. *Behavior Research Methods, 38*(3), 495–503. Retrieved from http://www.ncbi.nlm.nih.gov/pubmed/17186760

Kazai, G., Kamps, J., & Milic-Frayling, N. (2011). *Worker types and personality traits in crowdsourcing relevance labels*. doi:10.1145/2063576.2063860

Latoza, T. D., & Van Der Hoek, A. (2015). A Vision of Crowd Development. *Proceedings - International Conference on Software Engineering.* 10.1109/ICSE.2015.194

Liu, X., Lu, M., Ooi, B. C., Shen, Y., Wu, S., & Zhang, M. (2012). Cdas: A crowdsourcing data analytics system. *Proceedings of the VLDB Endowment International Conference on Very Large Data Bases, 5*(10), 1040–1051. doi:10.14778/2336664.2336676

Mao, K., Capra, L., Harman, M., & Jia, Y. (2017). A survey of the use of crowdsourcing in software engineering. *Journal of Systems and Software, 126,* 57–84. doi:10.1016/j.jss.2016.09.015

Mao, K., Yang, Y., Wang, Q., Jia, Y., & Harman, M. (2015). Developer recommendation for crowdsourced software development tasks. *Proceedings - 9th IEEE International Symposium on Service-Oriented System Engineering, IEEE SOSE 2015.* 10.1109/SOSE.2015.46

Martínez, L. G., Rodríguez-Díaz, A., Licea, G., & Castro, J. R. (2010). Big five patterns for software engineering roles using an ANFIS learning approach with RAMSET. In *Advances in Soft Computing* (pp. 428–439). Springer. doi:10.1007/978-3-642-16773-7_37

Myers, I. B., McCaulley, M. H., Quenk, N. L., & Hammer, A. L. (1998). *MBTI manual: A guide to the development and use of the Myers-Briggs Type Indicator* (Vol. 3). Palo Alto, CA: Consulting Psychologists Press.

Nawaz, N. A., Waqas, A., Yusof, Z. M., Mahesar, A. W., & Shah, A. (2017). WSN based sensing model for smart crowd movement with identification: An extended study. *Journal of Theoretical and Applied Information Technology.*

Nawaz, N. A., Waqas, A., Yusof, Z. M., & Shah, A. (2016). WSN based sensing model for smart crowd movement with identification: a conceptual model. *Multi Conference on Computer Science And Information Systems 2016.*

Raykar, V. (2009). *Supervised Learning from Multiple Experts : Whom to trust when everyone lies a bit.* doi:10.1145/1553374.1553488

Sheng, V. S., Provost, F., & Ipeirotis, P. G. (2008). *Get another label? improving data quality and data mining using multiple, noisy labelers.* doi:10.1145/1401890.1401965

Snow, R., Connor, B. O., Jurafsky, D., & Ng, A. Y. (2008). Cheap and Fast - But is it Good? Evaluating Non-Expert Annotations for Natural Language Tasks. *Proceedings of EMNLP.* 10.3115/1613715.1613751

Tratz, S., Hovy, E., Nulty, P., Costello, F., Verhoeven, B., Daelemans, W., … Han, J. (2016). *Cheap and fast - but is it good? Evaluation non-expert annotations for natural language tasks.* doi:10.3115/1119282.1119287

Tunio, M. Z., Luo, H., Cong, W., Fang, Z., Gilal, A. R., Abro, A., & Wenhua, S. (2017). Impact of Personality on Task Selection in Crowdsourcing Software Development: A Sorting Approach. *IEEE Access: Practical Innovations, Open Solutions, 5,* 18287–18294. doi:10.1109/ACCESS.2017.2747660

Tunio, M. Z., Luo, H., Wang, C., Zhao, F., Gilal, A. R., & Shao, W. (2018). Task Assignment Model for crowdsourcing software development: TAM. *Journal of Information Processing Systems.* doi:10.3745/JIPS.04.0064

Waqas, A., Gilal, A. R., Rehman, M. A., Uddin, Q., Mahmood, N., & Yusof, Z. M. (2017). C3F: Cross-Cloud Communication Framework for Resource Sharing amongst Cloud Networks: An Extended Study. *International Journal of Computer Science and Network Security*, *17*(8), 216–228.

Waqas, A., Rehman, M. A., Gilal, A. R., & Khan, M. A. (2016). CloudWeb: A Web-based Prototype for Simulation of Cross-Cloud Communication Framework (C3F). *Bahria University Journal of Information & Communication Technology*, *9*(2), 65–71.

Waqas, A., Rehman, M. A., Gilal, A. R., Khan, M. A., Ahmed, J., & Yusof, Z. M. (2017). A Features-based Comparative Study of the State-of-the-Art Cloud Computing Simulators and Future Directions. *International Journal of Advanced Computer Science and Applications*, *8*(8), 51–59. doi:10.14569/IJACSA.2017.080807

Waqas, A., Yusof, Z. M., Shah, A., & Khan, M. A. (2014). ReSA : Architecture for Resources Sharing Between Clouds. In *Conference on Information Assurance and Cyber Security (CIACS2014)* (pp. 23–28). Academic Press. 10.1109/CIACS.2014.6861326

Waqas, A., Yusof, Z. M., Shah, A., & Mahmood, N. (2014). Sharing of Attacks Information across Clouds for Improving Security: A Conceptual Framework. In *IEEE 2014 International Conference on Computer, Communication, and Control Technology* (pp. 255–260). IEEE. 10.1109/I4CT.2014.6914185

Whitehill, J., Ruvolo, P., Wu, T., Bergsma, J., & Movellan, J. (2009). Whose Vote Should Count More: Optimal Integration of Labels from Labelers of Unknown Expertise. *Advances in Neural Information Processing Systems*.

Yang, Y., Karim, M. R., Saremi, R., & Ruhe, G. (2016). Who Should Take This Task?: Dynamic Decision Support for Crowd Workers. *Proceedings of the 10th ACM/IEEE International Symposium on Empirical Software Engineering and Measurement*. 10.1145/2961111.2962594

Yuen, M. C., King, I., & Leung, K. S. (2011). Task matching in crowdsourcing. *Proceedings - 2011 IEEE International Conferences on Internet of Things and Cyber, Physical and Social Computing, iThings/CPSCom 2011*. 10.1109/iThings/CPSCom.2011.128

This research was previously published in Human Factors in Global Software Engineering; pages 1-19, copyright year 2019 by Engineering Science Reference (an imprint of IGI Global).

Chapter 87
On the Rim Between Business Processes and Software Systems

Maria Estrela Ferreira da Cruz
Polytechnic Institute of Viana do Castelo, Portugal

Ricardo J. Machado
Universidade do Minho, Portugal

Maribel Yasmina Santos
Universidade do Minho, Portugal

ABSTRACT

The constant change and rising complexity of organizations, mainly due to the transforming nature of their business processes, has driven the increase of interest in business process management by organizations. It is recognized that knowing business processes can help to ensure that the software under development will meet the business needs. Some of software development processes (like unified process) already refer to business process modeling as a first effort in the software development process. A business process model usually is created under the supervision, clarification, approval, and validation of the business stakeholders. Thus, a business process model is a proper representation of the reality (as is or to be), having lots of useful information that can be used in the development of the software system that will support the business. The chapter uses the information existing in business process models to derive software models specially focused in generating a data model.

INTRODUCTION

Organizations are constantly being challenged with new demands imposed by markets and must respond to new requirements imposed by governments. Organizations need to have a clear notion of their internal processes to increase their efficiency and the quality of their products or services, enhancing the benefits for their stakeholders (Schmiedel & vom Brocke, 2015; van der Aalst, 2015). Business Process

DOI: 10.4018/978-1-6684-3702-5.ch087

Management allows organizations to know themselves and to be prepared to fight new challenges and easily adapt to new situations (Batoulis et al., 2015).

BPM is considered key for innovation helping companies and organizations in the simulation of possible scenarios (Schmiedel & vom Brocke, 2015). For this and other reasons, business process management and modeling is being increasingly used by organizations (Batoulis et al., 2015).

A business process (BP) is a set of activities, their logical ordering, data, and organizational responsibilities, executed to achieve a business goal. BP models allow organizations to improve, control, automatize, and measure their processes (Weske, 2012). There are several languages that can be used to model the BPs. The Business Process Model and Notation (BPMN) language is being used in this research because it is an increasingly used and disclosed standard among companies and is already considered the default language used in business process modeling (Weske, 2012), besides it is a complete language, easy to learn and to use (Kocbek et al., 2015).

One of the main software quality objectives is to assure that a software product meets the business needs (Jalote, 2008). For that, the software product requirements need to be aligned with the business needs, both in terms of business processes (BPs) and in terms of the informational entities those processes deal with. This drives us to the question: Why not use this information, which is already modeled in business process models, to get the software models to the supporting software system? That is the main objective of the work being presented here.

Usually an organization (or company) deals with many BPs, so a supporting software system, typically, supports many BPs. Consequently, to generate complete and useful software design models for the development of software that will support the business, it is necessary to work and aggregate all the information existent in the set of processes that comprise a business.

This work presents and discusses two approaches to derive a data model from a set of business process models: a direct approach, which generates a data model by piecing together information from a set of business process models; and an indirect approach, which generates a data model by adapting the 4SRS (Four Step Rule Set) (Machado et al., 2006) method to generate a logical software architecture from business process models and extending it to derive the data model from the logical software architecture. Thus, the indirect approach generates several software models considering different software perspectives, namely the data model, use case model (including use case descriptions) and software logical architecture. The research steps are presented in Figure 1, where the solid arrows represent new steps created during the present research work, and the dashed arrows represent existing steps that are adapted in this research work.

An approach to obtain the data model directly from a set of interrelated business process models (arrow 1 in Figure 1) has been previously published in (Cruz et al., 2015b) and is revisited in chapter "Deriving a Data Model Directly from a Set of Business Process Models". An approach to obtain a complete use case model, aggregating a set of business process models (arrow 2 in Figure 1), has been published in (Cruz et al., 2014a, Cruz et al., 2015a). The approach is summarized in chapter "From Business Process Models to Use Case Models". An approach to generate the data model based on the previously obtained complete use case model (arrows 3 in Figure 1) has been published in (Cruz et al., 2016) and is briefly described in chapter "Deriving A Data Model from Logical Software Architecture". This approach, adapts and extends 4SRS. The 4SRS is an iterative method that incrementally verifies and validates the elicited requirements modeled as use cases, and creates a logical software architectural model (Machado et al., 2006).

The 4SRS has proved to be able to deal with complexity (Ferreira et al., 2012) and allows detecting and completing lacking information. The main contribution of this article is to present all the steps together, polishing some of the defined rules, and integrating them to capture the big picture of deriving the data model from an organization's BP models, compare the approaches and identify scenarios in which each of the approaches is more suitable than the other to apply.

Figure 1. Main research phases

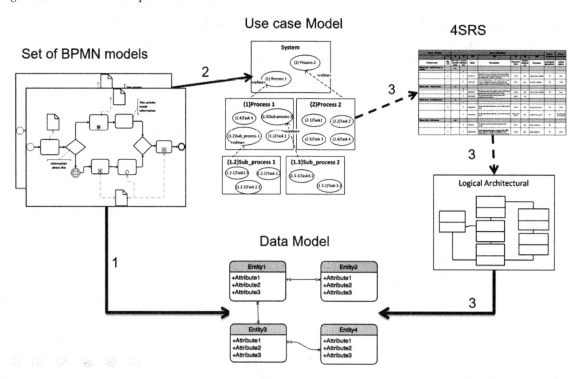

The remainder of this article is structured as follows. The next section describes the direct approach for data model creation based on a set of BPs. The application of the presented approach is then illustrated through a demonstration case. The approach for generating a use case model aggregating a set of BPs is presented in the subsequent section. The following section describes how the 4SRS has been extended to be able to generate a data model based on the previously generated use case model, and then the approach is applied to a demonstration case. After that, the results are compared and analyzed, and related work is presented. Finally, some conclusions are drawn.

DERIVING A DATA MODEL DIRECTLY FROM A SET OF BUSINESS PROCESS MODELS

This section presents an approach to get the data model based on a set of interrelated BPs, modeled in the BPMN language.

During a business process execution, resources and/or data are used and produced. In fact, the information about the data that flows through the process is very important to the software development. The data received, send, created or used during a process execution can be represented by it message flows or data associations as shown in Table represented in Figure 2. Data that flows through a process are represented by *data objects*. Persistent data are represented by *data stores*. Persistent data are the ones that remain beyond the process life cycle, or after the process execution ends (OMG, 2011). The transfer of data, received, created or used during a process execution can be represented by *message flows* or *data associations*. A *message flow* connects two pools, representing the message exchange between two participants (OMG, 2011). *Data associations* connect activities to *data objects* or *data stores* (OMG, 2011).

Figure 2. The data handling

Graphical representation	Description
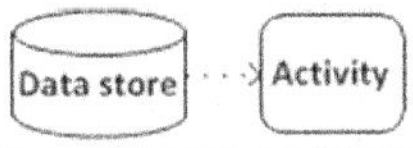 Data store ⋯> Activity	The activity reads information from the data store.
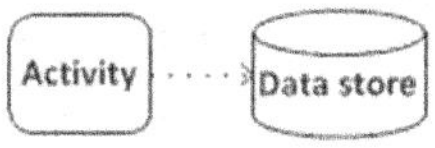 Activity ⋯> Data store	The activity writes information in the data store.
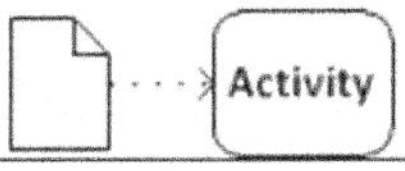 ⋯> Activity	The activity receives a data object.
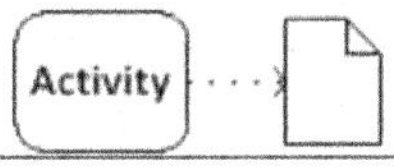 Activity ⋯>	The activity sends a data object.
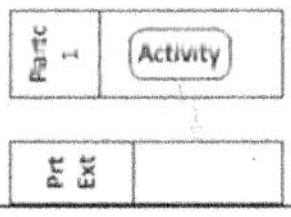 Partc 1 / Activity — Prt Ext	The participant, during the activity execution, sends a message to an external participant.
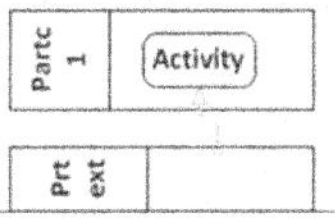 Partc 1 / Activity — Prt ext	The participant, during the activity execution, receives a message from an external participant.

In software development different models are usually used to represent different perspectives. The data model is one of the most important models for designing software applications, representing and organizing data, how it is stored and accessed, and the relationships among different entities.

To generate a data model, it is necessary to identify the entities, the relationship between entities and the entities attributes. An entity is something identifiable, or a concept in the real world that is important to the modeling purpose (Weske, 2012). The information, or the properties, about an entity are expressed through a set of attributes (Weske, 2012). A relationship between two entities is represented through an association between those entities (Chen, 1976). A relationship between two entities can be characterized according to two aspects, Cardinality and Optionality. Both terms are used to denote the number of attributes in a relation. Cardinality represents the maximum number of instances (one or many) of an entity in relation to another entity. Relationship optionality represents the minimum number of elements that exist on that side of the relationship. It may be 1 (the relation is mandatory) or 0 (the relation is not mandatory). In what concerns to cardinality, three types of relationships can be identified (Chen, 1976): mappings (1:n), (m:n) and (1:1).

A set of fourteen rules, summarized next, has been defined to systematically generate a data model from a set of business process models (Cruz et al., 2015b). The first group, constituted by five rules, identifies the data model entities:

R1: A data store, belonging to one of the selected business process models, is represented by an entity (with the same name) in the data model.

R2: Data stores with the same name, involved in several BPs, are represented by the same entity in the data model.

R3: Each participant involved in one of the selected business process models originates an entity in the data model.

R4: Participants with the same name will be represented by the same entity in the data model.

R5: Participants with the same name as data stores will be represented by the same entity in the data model.

Three rules have been created to identify the entities attributes. One to identify the attributes of the entities that represent the participants and another to identify the attributes of the entities that represent the data stores:

R6: A data store is an *"Item-Aware element"*, so the data structure definition of these elements could be specified as a XML file (OMG, 2011). The definition of the structure will be used to identify each item that belongs to the data store. Each item identifies an attribute of the entity that represents the data store.

R7: The initial attributes of an entity that represents a participant (involved in one, or several BPs) are *id* and *name*.

R8: When an entity represents a participant and a data store, the entity will aggregate all the attributes.

The last group, constituted by six rules, identifies the relationships between entities. The relationships between entities are derived from the information exchanged between participants and the activities that store information in data stores and from the information that flows through the process. The rules are summarized next:

R9: When a participant is responsible for carrying out an activity that stores information in a data store, the entity that represents the participant must be related with the entity that represents the data store. Each participant can perform the same process (and the same activity) several times, so the relationship between the entity that represents the participant and the entity that represents the data store, by default, will be (1:n).

R10: When an activity that handles a data store, exchanges information with an External Participant (represented in another pool), the entity that represents the data store is related with the entity that represents the participant in the following situations:

- ◦ The activity receives information from the participant and writes information in a data store (see Figure 3 a)). In this case, it is assumed that the information stored is provided by the participant.
- ◦ The activity reads information from a data store and sends the information to an external participant (see Figure 3 b)). It is assumed that the read information is provided to the participant.
- ◦ The activity writes information in a data store and sends information to the participants. It is assumed that the same information is stored and sent to the participant (as for example a receipt or a certificate).

Figure 3. Exchanging information with external participants

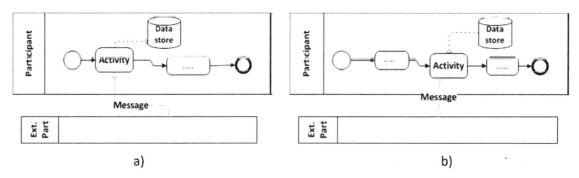

a)   b)

By default, the relationship type is (1:n) from the entity that represents the participant to the entity that represents the data store. The relationship is mandatory on the side of the entity that represents the participant because the activity always interacts with someone playing that role. On the side of the entity that represents the data store it is not mandatory, because this process may never be executed by a specific participant.

R11: When, during a process, an activity writes information in a data store and, in a same process, a previous activity (or the same activity) reads information from another data store (see Figure 4), it is assumed that the read and the written information are related. Consequently, the two entities (representing the two data stores) are related.

Figure 4. Relating two data stores

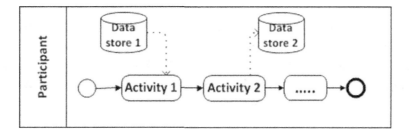

By default, the relationship type is (1:n) from the entity that represents the read data store to the entity that represents the written data store. By default, the relationship is mandatory on both sides. But, if the activity that writes information is performed after a merging gateway (not a parallel join) (Figure 5 a)), then the relationship is not mandatory on the side of the entity representing the read data store because the activity that reads the data store may not be executed. If the execution of the activity that writes the information depends on a condition, for example an exclusive decision gateway (see example in Figure 5 b)), then the relationship is not mandatory on the side of the entity representing the written data store.

Figure 5. Exclusive gateway example

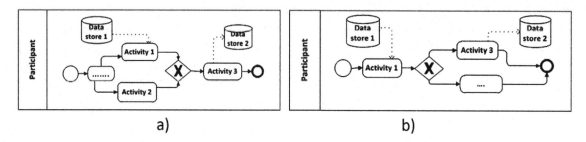

a)   b)

R12: All relationships derived from the several business processes must be preserved in the data model.

A data store may be manipulated by several activities belonging to distinct (or to the same) business processes, giving origin to different relationships. To prevent the loss of information all the relationships must be represented in the generated data model (for further evaluation).

R13: If, between two entities, there are different relationship types, the relationship type with higher cardinality prevails.

R14: If, between two entities, there are relationships with different mandatory types, the not mandatory type prevails.

Some of the derived relations are redundant, so the generated domain model needs to be analyzed by a software engineer to detect and eliminate redundant relations. The complete set of rules, details and explanations can be found in (Cruz, 2016).

Demonstration Case: Direct Approach

In this section, a well-known example of a School Library System is used as a demonstration case, where a group of five related business process models have been selected to be presented here. The selected BPs are: Register User (represented in Figure 5), Lend a Book (Figure 6), Reserve a Book (Figure 7), Renew a Loan (Figure 8) and Return a Book (Figure 9). The Return a Book business process model includes a sub-process, Penalty treatment, represented in Figure 10.

Figure 6. Register User business process model

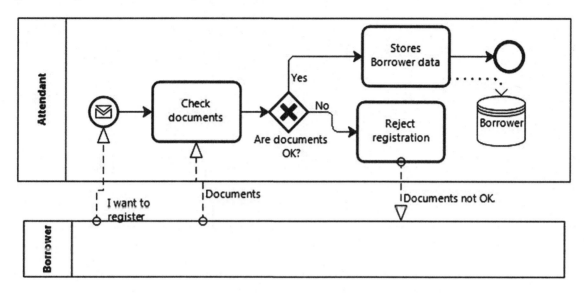

Figure 7. Lend a Book business process model

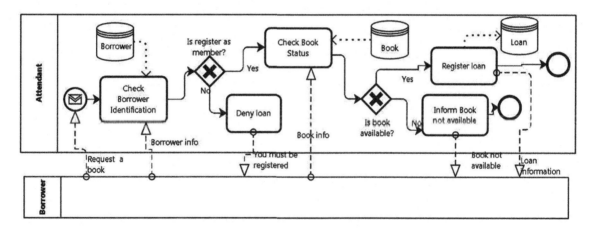

Figure 8. Reserve a Book business process model

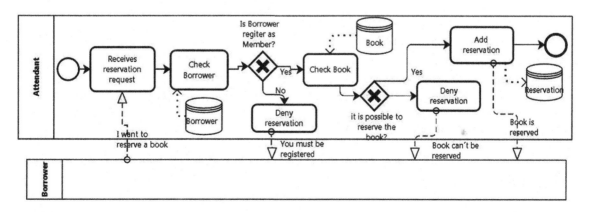

Figure 9. Renew a Loan business process model

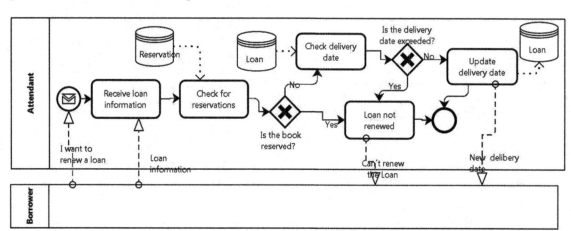

Analyzing the five BPs selected, it can be seen that the participants involved in all BPs are the same: Borrower and Attendant. The two corresponding entities, with the same name, must be represented in the resulting data model.

Figure 10. Return a Book business process model

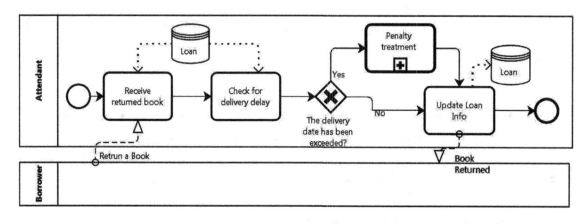

The data stores involved in the selected BPs are: Borrower, Book, Loan, Reservation and Receipt.

All identified entities (originated by participants and data stores) and the relationships identified in each process are presented in Table 1.

The resulting data model is shown in Figure 11. In this model the relations are represented according to Chen (1976) terminology. Focusing in one side of a relationship, and considering the optionality and cardinality together, there are the following combinations: 0 or 1 (represented as 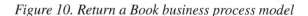), 1 (represented as), 0 to many (represented as) and 1 to many (represented as).

Figure 11. Penalty treatment business process model

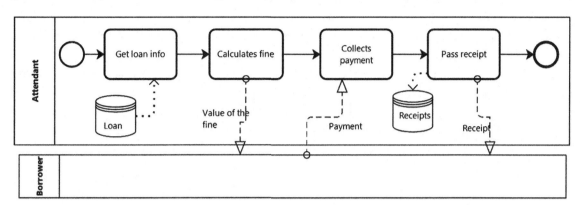

Table 1. Entities and relationships

Business Process	Entities	Relationship
Register User	Attendant, by R1 Borrower, by R5	Attendant-Borrower(1:n), by R9
Lend a Book	Attendant, by R1 Borrower, by R5 Book, by R2 Loan, by R3	Attendant-Loan(1:n), by R9 Borrower-Loan(1:n), by R10 Book-Loan(1:n), by R11
Reserve a Book	Attendant, by R1 Borrower, by R5 Book, by R3 Reservation, by R3	Attendant-Reservation(1:n), by R9 Borrower-Reservation(1:n), by R10 Book-Reservation(1:n), by R11
Renew a Loan	Attendant, by R1 Borrower, by R5 Loan, by R3 Reservation, by R3	Attendant-Loan(1:n), by R9 Borrower-Loan(1:n), by R10
Return a Book + Penalty treatment	Attendant, by R1 Borrower, by R5 Loan, by R3 Receipt, by R3	Attendant-Loan(1:n), by R9 Attendant-Receipt(1:n), by R9 Borrower-Receipt(1:n), by R10 Loan-Receipt(1:n), by R10

Analyzing the generated data model, it may be said that from a group of interrelated business process models, it is possible to generate a complete data model identifying all the entities involved, attributes and all the relationships between the entities. However, to obtain a complete data model, the business process model must contain all relevant information about data involved in the BPs including the identification of the persistent data.

The approach presented in this section allows getting a complete data model aggregating all the information about persistent data that can be extracted from a set of business process models, serving as a basis for the development of the software that will support the business.

The set of business processes internal to an organization usually complemented each other, meaning that the information written by one process is, most of the times, used in the same, or in another business processes. Consequently, joining all the existent information in the set of business processes it is possible to get a complete data model. However, to enable the ulterior obtainment of the data model, it is necessary that the business process modeling is made taking data into account, i.e. the modeler must monitor the data throughout the process. Moreover, it is necessary to identify the activities that write or make use of the information stored in the data store, and ensure that the roles responsible for performing those activities are identified.

The indirect approach, presented in the next section, starts by generating a use case model aggregating the information that exists in a set of BP models.

Figure 12. The resulting data model

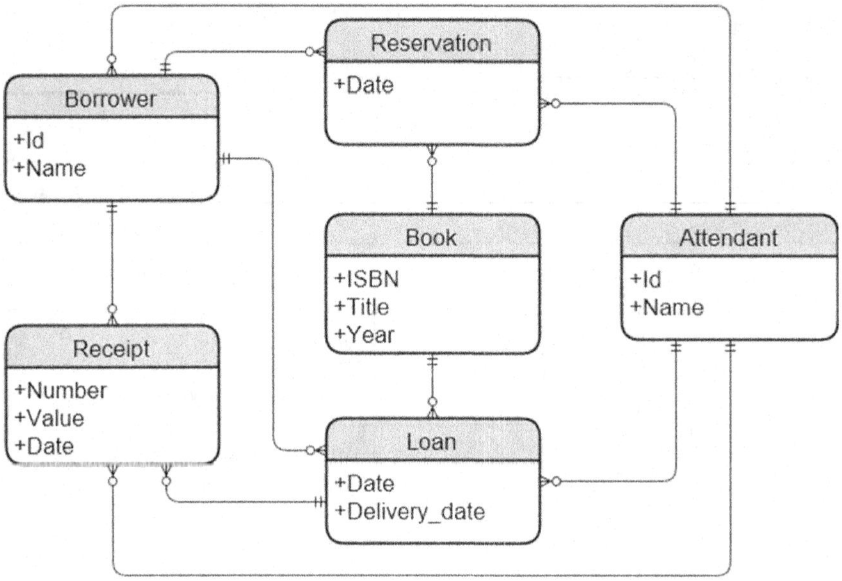

FROM BUSINESS PROCESS MODELS TO USE CASE MODELS

One of the most difficult, and crucial, activities in software development is the identification of system functional requirements. A popular way to capture and describe those requirements is through UML use case models. During system analysis, most of requirements information must be incorporated into use case descriptions.

This section proposes an approach to support the construction of use case models based on business process models emphasizing use cases descriptions, which are created using a set of predefined Natural Language (NL) sentences mapped from BPMN model elements.

The basic rules to obtain a use case diagram based in one business process model are:

- A BP activity gives rise to a use case (with the same name) in the use case diagram.
- A participant (represented by a pool) gives rise to an actor in the use case diagram, with the same name.
- The subdivision of a Pool (or Lane) into several lanes gives rise to a hierarchy of actors.

- The relationship between actors and use cases is derived from the participants (represented by the actor) responsible for the execution of the activity (represented by the use case) and from the exchange of information between an external participant and the activity.

Graphically a use case diagram is very simple, involving only actors and use cases (stickman's and ellipses with a brief description). A BPMN diagram is graphically more complex involving lots of graphical elements (activities, events, data stores, gateways, data objects, pools, messages, etc.). However, a use case model can represent as much information as a BPMN model, but most of the information must be embodied in use case descriptions. So, next subsection is specially focused on the generation of use case descriptions from the existent information in business process models.

Obtaining Use Case Descriptions

To describe a use case, a template, which is a simplification of the template presented by Cockburn in (Cockburn, 2001), has been defined. The proposed template is composed by six fields, which are named and described in Table 2.

Table 2. The template for describing use cases

Use case name	The use case name identifies the goal as a short active verb phrase.
Actors	List of actors involved in the use case.
Pre-Conditions	Conditions that must hold or represent things that happened before the use case starts.
Post-Conditions	Conditions that must hold at the conclusion of the use case.
Trigger	Event that starts the use case.
Scenario	Sequence of interactions describing what the system must do to move the process forward.

The main elements involved in a process are participants (pools and lanes), activities, gateways, events, messages, data objects, data stores and artifacts (OMG, 2011). These elements are connected by connecting objects (sequence flow, message flow, associations and data associations). The approach being presented intends to transform business process elements, and their associated information, in a controlled set of sentences in NL.

Based on the existing information in a business process model it is possible to identify the use case name, the related actors and, depending on the incoming and outgoing connections, it is also possible to identify use case's pre-conditions, post-conditions, trigger and the main scenario.

To obtain the descriptions of a use case one will focus on the activity that is represented by the use case, and all incoming and outgoing connections must be reflected in the descriptions of the use case by creating a sentence that describes the connection main purpose. In BPMN, there are different connecting objects (see Figure 12), each one connects different objects, so it will originate different sentences in the use case descriptions (Cruz et al., 2014a).

Very briefly, the use case name is the name of the activity represented by the use case. The actors related to the use case are obtained from the participants involved in the activity represented by the use case. Preconditions are obtained from incoming connections from activity flows and from gateways.

Post-conditions are obtained from the outgoing connections from the end or throwing events. Triggers are obtained from the connections coming from start and catching events. All other incoming connections give rise to a phrase that will be included in the use case scenario. As a consequence, several sentences may be included in the use case scenario. The sentences to be appended to the use case scenario must follow the next order: first, all incoming connections representing messages, associations, etc. received by the activity. Then all incoming data associations, representing data read by the activity. After that, all outgoing data associations, representing data written or sent by the activity. Finally, all outgoing connections representing messages, etc. sent by the activity.

Figure 13. Incoming and outgoing connections of an activity

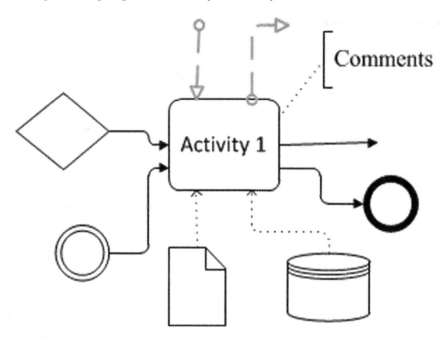

Gateways are used to control how the process flows, by diverging (splitting gateways) and converging (merging gateways) sequence flows (see Figure 13). Splitting gateways have one incoming sequence flow and two or more outgoing sequence flows. Merging gateways have two or more incoming sequence flows and one outgoing sequence flow (OMG, 2011).

The gateway's outgoing sequence flows may have a Condition that allows to select alternative paths. Each outgoing sequence flow originates a sentence represented as a pre-condition in the use case description of the sequence flow target activity. The generated sentences are represented in Table represented in Figure 15.

Data associations are used to move data between data objects (or data stores) and activities (OMG, 2011). The sentences generated by data associations and associated data objects, or data stores, are represented in Table represented in Figure 16. The sentences will be appended to the scenario of the use case description of the use case representing the activity.

Figure 14. Splitting and merging gateways

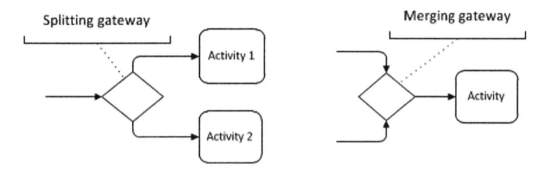

Figure 15. The use case pre-condition originated by gateways

Gateway	Graphical representation	Originated Pre-condition.
Exclusive Decision	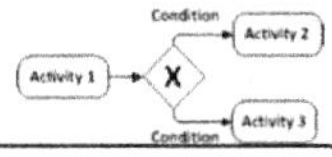	The \<gateway condition\> is \<sequence flow condition\>.
Parallel splitting	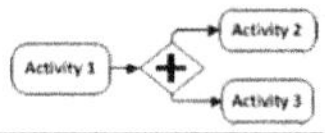	The \<source name\> has been completed.
Inclusive Splitting	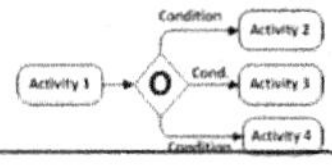	The \<sequence flow condition\> is true.
Complex Splitting	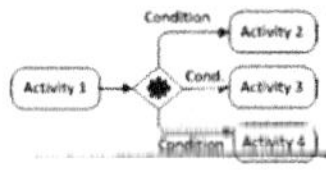	The \<sequence flow condition\> is true.
Exclusive merging	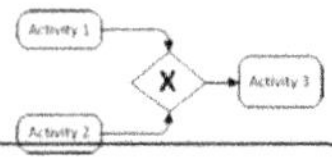	The \<source name\> [exclusive or \<source2 name\>] has been completed.
Parallel join	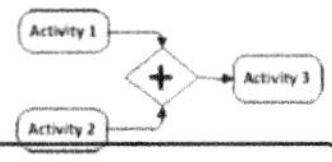	The \<source name\> [and \< source2 name\>] has been completed.
Inclusive merging	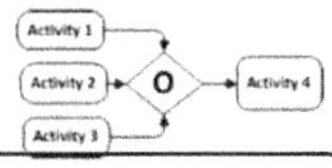	The \<source name\> [or \<source2 name\>] has been completed.
Complex merging	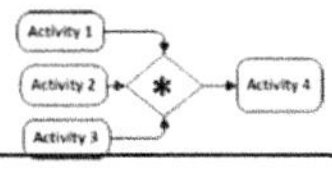	The \<source name\> [or \<source2 name\>] has been completed.

An event is something that happens during the course of a process and affects the process's flow (OMG, 2011). These events usually have a cause or produce an impact (OMG, 2011). In BPMN 2.0 there is a large number of event types, a general overview of the generic sentences originated in the use case template by the different events categories are presented in Table 3.

Figure 16. The use case sentences originated by Data Associations

Data	Graphical representation	Originated sentence in use case scenario.
Data Object as data association source	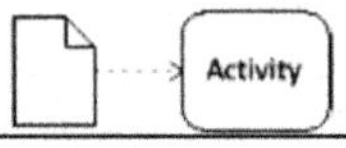	Receives <data object name>.
Data Object as data association target	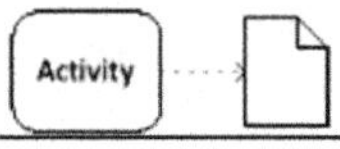	Sends <data object name>.
Data Input	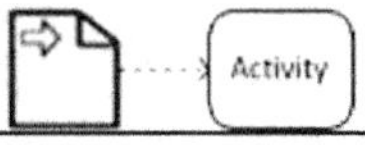	Receives <data object name>.
Data Input Collection (Input set)	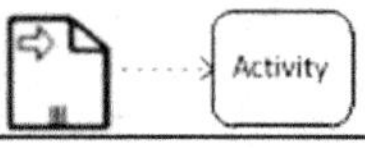	Receives a collection of <data object name>.
Data Output	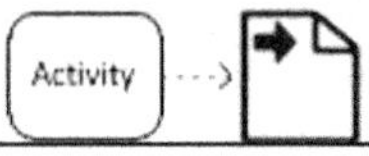	Sends <data object name>.
Data Output Collection (Output set)	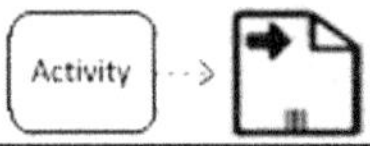	Sends a collection of <data object name>.
Data Store as data association source	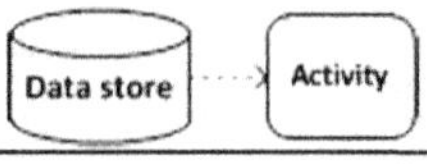	Reads information from <data store name>
Data Store as data association target	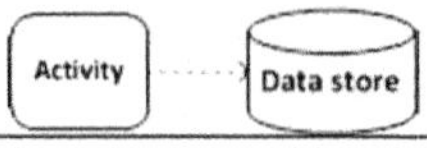	Writes information on <data store name>

Table 3. Generic sentences originated by events

Event type category	Generic sentence originated in use case template
Start	**Trigger:** The <event name - event definition > occurred.
Start (Sub-Process) Interrupting	**Trigger:** The event <event name – event definition > occurred.
Start (Sub-Process) Non-Interrupting	**Trigger:** The event <event name – event definition> occurred.
Intermediate Catching	**Trigger:** The <event name - event definition > is received.
Intermediate Boundary Interrupting	**Scenario:** If the <event name - event definition > occurs, the <activity name> is interrupted.
Intermediate Boundary Non-Interrupting	**Scenario:** The <event name - event definition > occurred.
Intermediate Throwing	**Post-condition:** The <event name – event definition > is created.
End	**Post-condition:** The <event name – event definition > is created. The process ends.

The events affect the sequence or the timing of the process's activities. There are three types of events: Start, Intermediate and End. Start events indicate where a process (or a sub-process) will start. End events indicate where a path of a process will end. Intermediate events indicate where something happens somewhere between the start and end of a process (OMG, 2011). Some events are prepared to catch triggers. These events are classified as catching events. Events that throw a result are classified as throwing *events* (OMG, 2011). All start events and some intermediate events are catching events (OMG, 2011). The sentence originated by a catching event is included as a trigger in the description of the use case that represents the activity that is started by the event. Catching events are represented as triggers because these events cause the start of the activity.

All End events and some Intermediate events are Throwing events (OMG, 2011). The sentences originated by the End and Throwing events are included as a post-condition in the description of the use case that represents the activity that throws the event. Throwing events are represented as a post-condition because the event is a consequence (or a result) of the activity execution.

Some events can also be classified as interrupting or non-interrupting events. Interrupting events stop its containing process whenever the event occurs. When Non-Interrupting events occur, its containing process is not interrupted (OMG, 2011). The sentences generated by Intermediate Interrupting events, are included in the use case scenario.

The identified categories are grouped in four tables to address differences that can exist between sentences generated by the events of these groups of categories. These tables, and others not presented in this document, can be found in (Cruz, 2016).

Next subsection presents an approach to aggregate in one use case model the information derived from a set of business process models.

Joining a Set of Business Process Models in One Use Case Model

The set of BPs, belonging to an organization, being supported by the software under development must be grouped in a single use case model because a software development team needs to understand the system context and scope before starting to plan and design a solution. For this reason, first it is needed to identify and specify which BPs are to be supported by the software under development.

A use case model can be created with a high abstraction level or low abstraction level (Cockburn, 2001). A use case model with a very detailed level can be much more useful to software development teams but, at the same time, it may become very complex and hard to understand.

The approach being presented in this section starts with high abstraction level use cases and ends with lower abstraction level use cases. To do that, the decomposition triangle approach, presented in (Cruz et al., 2014b), is being used. The decomposition triangle is an iterative and incremental approach that adopts a refinement mechanism to detail use cases, in a controlled way, to obtain a functional requirements model of the system to be designed. It is organized in several abstraction levels, starting with high abstraction level use cases and ending with lower abstraction level use cases (Cruz et al., 2014b).

When refining a use case, the use case is being decomposed in another use case model, decreasing the use cases abstraction level and, consequently, their ambiguity, by adding more details to them. The abstraction level decreases in every use case decomposition. When the abstraction level decreases, the use case description is enriched with details that may become useful for software development.

The approach starts by grouping all processes that will be supported by the software under development in one use case diagram, where each process is represented as a use case. Each use case is then refined and decomposed in a use case model (Cruz et al., 2015a). All identified use cases are numbered using the *tag=value* UML mechanism.

A generic scheme of applying the decomposition triangle is shown in Figure 14.

Figure 17. A generic decomposition scheme

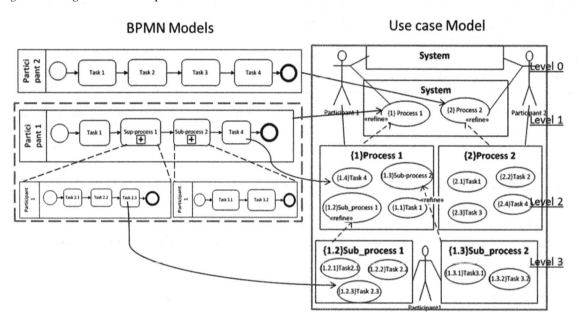

The approach organizes the use case models in different abstraction levels:

- **Level 0:** At this level, the system scope and frontier must be identified as well as all the actors involved, so the set of BPs that will be supported by the software under development must be identified. At this level all participants involved in the set of BPs are represented, as actors, in the actor's diagram (see Figure 17, level 0).
- **Level 1:** At this level, the first use case model is created with the highest abstraction level where each top level BP is transformed into a use case, in the use case model (a business use case) (see Figure 17, level 1). Each use case, representing a BP, is related with the corresponding actors representing the participants involved in the process. The use cases are numbered sequentially. The use case description is a general overview of the process it addresses.
- **Level 2:** At this level, each process (represented as a use case in level 1) is mapped to a use case model. Basically, one activity from a BP is transformed into a use case and each participant is transformed into an actor. All incoming and outgoing connection flows from the activity originate a NL sentence in the description of the use case that represents the activity. Each generated use case model in level 2 refines and decomposes a corresponding use case in level 1 (see Figure 17, level 2).

- **Level (i+1), (i>=2):** At this level, each use case that represents a sub process in *level i* is decomposed and refined in a use case model in *level (i+1)* (see Figure 17, level 3). BPMN has two types of activities: a task (atomic activity) and a sub-process (OMG, 2011). A sub-process is a process, consequently the use case that represents the activity can be decomposed and mapped to another use case model. The decomposition ends when all use cases representing processes or sub-processes are decomposed and refined. In the presented approach, refining a use case means detailing all activities involved in the corresponding BP, including all resources and/or data that are consumed and produced, messages exchanged, decisions that must be taken, events that can occur, etc.

The decomposition results in a tree structure where the leaf nodes represent the tasks and the non-leaf nodes represent the processes and sub-processes. The decomposition tree has high abstraction level use cases at level 1. The abstraction level decreases in every use case decomposition. The approach allows to relate use cases belonging to different abstraction levels allowing to drill down and roll up between different abstraction levels. This way, the approach allows tracing back from requirements to the BP and from the BPs to the corresponding requirements.

This approach helps to ensure the alignment between business and software, and enables traceability between BPs and the corresponding elements in software models.

Demonstration Case: Getting Use Case Model From a Set of BPs

As a demonstration case, the same set of five interrelated BP models presented previously, is being used. The final use case decomposition tree, derived from those five BP from the Library Demonstration Case, is represented in Figure 18.

Looking the selected BPs one may see that *Borrower* and *Attendant* participants are involved in all BPs, each one giving origin to an actor in the use case model. So, the use case diagram level 0 (actors diagram) only has two actors represented (*Borrower* and *Attendant*), each one representing a participant.

In the use case diagram level 1, each of the selected BPs is represented as a use case connected with the actors that represent the corresponding participants. A set of five BPs has been selected, thus, five use cases are presented in use case diagram level 1. Each of these use cases, is then detailed in a use case model at level 2.

Analyzing, for instance, the Return a Book business process model (refer to Figure 10), one can see that the BP comprises five activities: Receive returned book, Search for book's active loan, Check for delivery delay, Update Loan Info and Penalty treatment, each one giving origin to a use case in the use case model that refines the Return a Book use case (level 2). The Penalty Treatment use case represents a sub-process (Figure 11), so it can be represented as a use case model in the next level (level 3), more refined and with greater detail.

The descriptions of the use cases representing activities belonging to the *Register User* and *Lend a Book* BPs are presented in Table 4, as example. The descriptions of the other use cases may be consulted in (Cruz, 2016).

Figure 18. A use case diagram of the library demonstration case

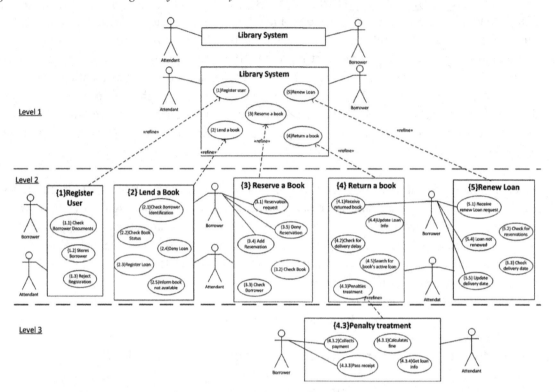

Table 4. Descriptions of the use cases

Use case name	Use case description
{U1.1} Check Borrower Documents	Actors: Borrower, Attendant Trigger: Borrower wants to register Scenario: Receives documents from <Borrower>.
{U1.2} Stores Borrower	Actors: Borrower, Attendant Pre-condition: Are Borrower documents OK? Is Yes. Scenario: Writes information on <Borrower>. Sends register confirmation to <Borrower>.
{U1.3} Reject Registration	Actors: Borrower, Attendant Pre-condition: Are documents OK? Is No. Scenario: Sends message documents not OK to <Borrower>.
{U2.1} Check Borrower Identification	Actors: Borrower, Attendant Trigger: The message <requests a book> arrives from <Borrower>. Scenario: Receives Borrower identification from <Borrower>. Reads information from <Borrower>.
{U2.2} Check Book status	Actors: Borrower, Attendant Pre-condition: Borrower is register as member? is yes. Scenario: Receives Book information from <Borrower>. Reads information from <Book>.
{U2.3} Register Loan	Actors: Borrower, Attendant Pre-condition: Is book available? is yes. Scenario: Writes information on <Loan>. Sends loan information to <Borrower>.
{U.2.4} Deny Loan	Actors: Borrower, Attendant Pre-condition: Borrower is register as member? is No. Scenario: Sends message you must be registered to <Borrower>.
{U2.5} Inform book not available	Actors: Borrower, Attendant Pre-condition: Is book available? is no. Scenario: Sends message book not available to <Borrower>.

DERIVING A DATA MODEL FROM LOGICAL SOFTWARE ARCHITECTURE

In the previous section, the decomposition triangle was used to aggregate in one use case model all the information that can be extracted from a set of business process models. The resulting use case model forms a functional requirements model, that is especially prepared to be used as input to the 4SRS approach. This resulting use case model may be represented as a tree structure. The 4SRS selects all leaves from the derived tree structure obtaining the most detailed and non-redundant information that is possible to obtain.

From the obtained use case model, the 4SRS will then generate the software logical architectural. To deal with the generated structured sentences the original 4SRS steps have been adapted as follows (Cruz, 2016):

- **Step 1:** Architectural elements identification - in this step, the original 4SRS method proposes the creation of three types of objects for each use case: interface, data and control (Machado et al., 2006). However, one can distinguish between persistent from non-persistent data, as it happens in the BPMN language (OMG, 2011). Following this idea, the 4SRS is adapted to distinguish persistent data from non-persistent data, by creating two different types of elements involving data: persistent data and volatile data. Each element is labeled with the name of the use case followed by the appropriate type: *i* (interface), *c* (control), *dp* (data persistent) and *dv* (data volatile).
- **Step 2:** Architectural elements elimination - based on the textual description of each use case, it is necessary to decide which ones of the four elements, created in step 1, must be maintained. This step allows detecting and eliminating redundancy in requirements.
- **Step 3:** Architectural elements aggregation and packaging - the architectural elements that remain after the elimination, and those in which it is possible and there is advantage in their unification, are aggregated.
- **Step 4:** Architectural elements association - associations must link the elements resulting from the aggregation based on use cases textual descriptions.

To define a persistent data model, one needs to identify the domain entities, their attributes, and the relationships between entities (Weske, 2012). Therefore, the 4SRS is extended with three additional steps, which are:

- **Step 5:** Entities creation - in this step, the entities involved in each use case are identified. Focusing on the *{-dp} architectural elements*, in the generated logical architecture, each read, written or updated element gives origin to an entity in the resulting data model.
- **Step 6:** Relationships identification - in this step, the relationship between the entities identified in step 5 are identified. When a *{-dp} – persistent data* element that stores information (write or update), is related with a *{-c} - control* element that verifies the information about another entity, one may conclude that the information stored is related with the information checked. Consequently, the entity that represents the written information is related with the entity that represents the checked (and read) information. The relationship is (1:n) from the entity that represents the information checked (previously written information) to the entity that represents the written information because the same information can be read several times and associated to different written information items. On the other hand, the information is stored only once.

- **Step 7:** Entity attributes identification - in this step, the attributes belonging to each entity are identified based on the attachments in BPMN data elements or messages or based on new information provided by stakeholders.

A Demonstration Case: Deriving a Data Model From Logical Software Architecture

Figure 16 illustrates the resulting logical software architecture from applying the 4SRS method to the use case model generated previously (Figure 15 and Table 4 - Descriptions of the use cases) based on the selected five business process models.

Figure 19. The resulting logical software architecture

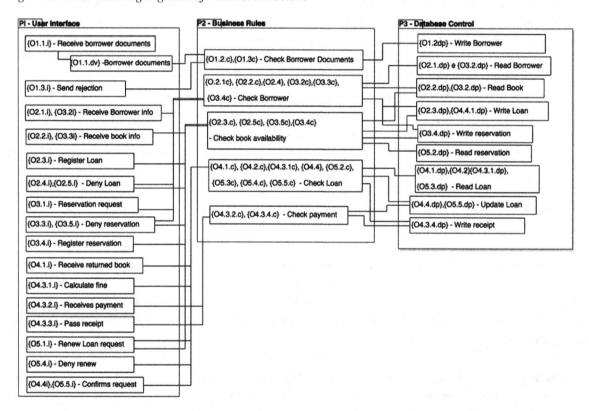

Analyzing the generated logical architecture, one may see that information about *Borrower, Book, Loan, Reservation* and *Receipt* is being written, so, by step 5, each one originates an entity in the data model.

Looking to the logical software architecture (Figure 19) one may see that the *Write Loan* is related with *Check Borrower* architectural element. Thus, by 6, *Loan* entity is related with the *Borrower* and the relationship is (1:n), mandatory on the Borrower side and not mandatory on the Loan side. The same happens with *Write reservation* element and *Check Borrower*, so *Reservation* entity is related with the *Borrower* and the relationship is (1:n), mandatory on the Borrower and not mandatory on the Reservation side.

The resulting data model is presented in Figure 20.

Figure 20. The resulting data model

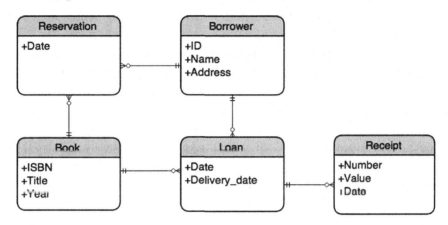

ANALYZING THE RESULTS

The BPMN most recent version has consolidated its importance as a business process modeling language and has become more complete allowing to distinguish persistent from non-persistent data (Aagesen & Krogstie, 2015). This enabled deriving the data model from business process models, which is the main goal of this research work. This has been achieved following two different approaches. A direct approach that derives a data model directly from the existing information in a set of interrelated business process models. And an indirect approach that uses the 4SRS method, which has been adapted to work with a use case model derived from a set of business process models and extended to derive a data model.

Comparing the data models obtained by applying the two presented approaches (Figure 12 and Figure 20), based on the same set of BPs (Figures from 6 to 11), one can see that they are very similar. Yet, the Attendant entity is only identified in the direct approach where it was identified as an entity because it represents a participant (rule R2). None of the BPs stores information about the Attendant, so it was not identified in the indirect approach (the 4SRS extended approach). It happens because the set of BPs selected to be used in the demonstrations cases is not complete. A BP representing the attendant registration is missing, similarly to what happens with borrower in BP *Register User*.

The two approaches can generate a complete data model including entities, entity attributes and the relationships between those entities, including cardinality and optionality. Still some differences may be pointed out between the two approaches.

Comparing the two presented approaches, one may say that the direct approach is automatable and easier to understand and apply, but it is totally dependent on the existing information in the BPMN models because the BPMN models are the only source of information. Consequently, the direct approach can generate correct and complete data models if the BPMN models are complete and correct. Otherwise, the correctness and completeness of the data model are not assured.

The indirect approach, which extends the 4SRS approach, is only partially automatable mostly because the derived software models need to be analyzed and validated by a software engineer, and the existing information on BPMN models may be complemented with information from other sources. The 4SRS extended approach generates not only the data model but also the use case model and the logical software architecture based on business process models, which can be used to the development of the software that will support the business. The generation of a use case model, including use cases descriptions, based on a set of business process models ensures the implementation of all requirements that come directly from the set of business process models.

Both approaches allow traceability from elements in software models to the BPs and from the BPs to the corresponding elements in software models. Nevertheless, using the 4SRS, the traceability between the software models and business process models may not be direct because of the information that can be provided by other sources.

For the reasons pointed before it may be concluded that the direct approach is suitable to deal with complete business process models, whereas the indirect approach is more suitable to deal with complex systems, being prepared to detect incomplete business process models and to complete the information derived from business process models with information from other sources.

RELATED WORK

It is recognized that the software that supports the business must be aligned with the BPs. Therefore, it is natural to try an approximation between business process modeling and software modeling. Following this idea, several authors proposed approaches to derive software models based in business process models.

The connection between use case models and BPs is studied in several ways. Some authors propose approaches to get use case models from business processes models, as is the case of (Rodríguez et al., 2007; Dijkman & Joosten, 2002). Others try to obtain a business process model from a use case model, as is the case of (Lubke et al., 2008).

Dijkman & Joosten (2002) propose an algorithm to derive a use case diagram from a business process model (using UML Activity Diagram).

Rodríguez et al. (2008) propose a systematic approach for obtaining the use case and class diagrams from the business process models using the UML activity diagram notation. The same authors also suggest an approach for the generation of a use case diagram based in one business process model using BPMN (Rodríguez et al., 2007).

Park et al. (2017) propose an approach to derive UCs representing the software requirements. The approach derives the functional and non-functional requirements (Park et al., 2017).

The importance of data in business process modeling is increasing, motivated by the need of controlling the BPs and the improvement of Business Analytics systems and technical BI (Business Intelligence), whose results are used by organizations to support and planning business (Meyer et al., 2011).

Data are not the focus of business process modelers. However, BPs involve lots of information that must be kept in a persistent manner. Thus, some authors try to obtain the data model based on one business process model. Almost all authors who worked with versions of BPMN prior to version 2.0 ended up proposing an extension to the BPMN to distinguish persistent data from non-persistent data, such as Brambilla et al. (2008) and Magnani & Montesi (2009).

Brdjanin et al. (2011) propose an approach to obtain a database design based on the information existing in a UML activity diagram. The authors propose a direct mapping of all business objects to the respective classes. Each participant is also mapped to a class. Associations between business objects and BP participants are based on the activities performed on those objects (Brdjanin et al., 2011). The same authors also propose an approach for the generation of a database model based on a collaborative BPMN diagram (Brdjanin et al., 2015). To do so, the authors defined a set of formal rules for the generation of the data model.

A. Leshob (2016) proposes an approach that generates a UML domain model from BP models written in BPMN. The approach is based on business patterns from REA (Resources, Events, Agents) ontology.

Most of the approaches cited before, generating software models from business process models, base their analysis in only one business process model. But, as said before, typically, in a real situation, a software product does not support only one process, but a reasonable set of processes. So, to generate useful software models, it is necessary to consider the complete set of business process that will be supported by the software product in development.

Regarding data, usually, interrelated BPs complement each other, meaning that the information written during the execution of one BP is, most of the times, used in another (or the same) BP. Therefore, working with a set of BPs, instead of one, allows to generate a much more complete data model and more resilient to error because if one miss the identification of an entity (or relationship) in one BP it may be identified in another BP.

The two approaches presented in this paper start by identifying the set of BPs that will be supported by the software under development, identifying the system scope. Based on those BPs, the approaches allow to generate the data model, a complete use case model (including use case descriptions) and the logical software architecture.

As mentioned previously, several approaches to obtain a use case diagram based on a business process model have been proposed, but, to our knowledge, there are no proposals to obtaining the use cases description. Nevertheless, the use cases descriptions are one of the most important components of the use case model (Cockburn, 2001). Moreover, without these descriptions most information present in a business process model would be lost when generating the use case diagram from business process models. Besides, none of the presented approaches aggregates in one use case model all information we have in a set of business process models defining this way the system scope and boundaries.

FUTURE RESEARCH DIRECTIONS

As future research, it is intended to create a model-driven approach to obtain a system's complete use case model including relations between use cases, and between these and the structural domain classes. The resulting integrated use case and domain models will then be transformed into the system's default abstract user interface model.

CONCLUSION

It is recognized that knowing business processes can help to ensure that the software under development will meet business needs.

By applying any of the approaches presented, one can collect all the information about persistent data involved in those BPs. The direct approach allows to obtain the data model solely based on existing information in a set of business process models.

Because some business process models have bad quality (incomplete, ambiguous, bad use of BPMN notation, etc.), and to deal with high complex systems, another approach to generate a data model from business process models has been proposed based on the 4SRS method. The 4SRS method has been adapted to deal with a use case model derived from a set of business process models. When necessary the generated use case model may be complemented with information from other sources allowing deriving a more complete data model. At this software development stage, the stakeholders are still involved in the process so they can provide useful information to complement the information provided by business process models.

To use the 4SRS, a use case model is needed. Thus, an approach to generate a use case model from a business process model is presented. The approach is focused on obtaining the descriptions of the use cases and uses a set of predefined sentences in NL.

The 4SRS method needs the intervention of an expert to analyze and validate the information provided by the set of BPMN models and the derived software models. If necessary, the information provided by the BPMN models may be complemented with information provided by other sources. Thus, the derived software models may be more complete and correct than the software models derived directly from a set of BPMN models, but, at the same time, it can involve much more work and it can be more time-consuming in implementing. Both approaches allow traceability from elements in software models to the business processes and from the business processes to the corresponding elements in software models.

The generation of a use case model, including use cases descriptions, based on a set of business process models ensures the implementation of all requirements that come directly from the process models.

The generated models are consistent with each other, meaning that the data entities referred to in the use case model are represented in the data model. This way, business and software modeling efforts can be joined together, reducing the analysis time and avoiding forgetting functional or data requirements.

REFERENCES

Aagesen, G., & Krogstie, J. (2015). BPMN 2.0 for modeling business processes. In Handbook on Business Process Management, International Handbooks on Information Systems (pp. 219-250). Springer Berlin Heidelberg.

Batoulis, K., Meyer, A., Bazhenova, E., Decker, G., & Weske, M. (2015). Extracting decision logic from process models. Advanced Information Systems Engineering, 9097, 349-366. doi:10.1007/978-3-319-19069-3_22

Brambilla, M., Preciado, J. C., Linaje, M., & Sanchez-Figueroa, F. (2008). Business process-based conceptual design of rich internet applications. *Web Engineering, International Conference on*, 155-161.

Brdjanin, D., Banjac, G., & Maric, S. (2015). Automated synthesis of initial conceptual database model based on collaborative business process model. In Bogdanova, A. M. and Gjorgjevikj, D. In I. C. T. Innovations (Ed.), *Advances in Intelligent Systems and Computing* (Vol. 311, pp. 145–156). Springer International Publishing.

Brdjanin, D., Maric, S., & Gunjic, D. (2011). Adbdesign: An approach to automated initial conceptual database design based on business activity diagrams. In Advances in Databases and Information Systems (pp. 117-131). Springer.

Chen, P. P.-S. (1976). The entity-relationship model toward a unified view of data. *ACM Transactions on Database Systems, 1*(1), 9–36. doi:10.1145/320434.320440

Cockburn, A. (2001). *Writing Effective Use Cases*. Addison Wesley.

Cruz, E. F. (2016). *Derivation of data-driven software models from business process representations* (PhD Thesis). Universidade do Minho, Portugal.

Cruz, E. F., Machado, R. J., & Santos, M. Y. (2014a). From business process models to use case models: A systematic approach. Advances in Enterprise Engineering VIII, 174, 167-181. doi:10.1007/978-3-319-06505-2_12

Cruz, E. F., Machado, R. J., & Santos, M. Y. (2014b). On the decomposition of use cases for the refinement of software requirements. In *Computational Science and Its Applications (ICCSA), 2014 14th International Conference on* (pp. 237-240). IEEE Computer Society. 10.1109/ICCSA.2014.54

Cruz, E. F., Machado, R. J., & Santos, M. Y. (2015a). Bridging the Gap between a Set of Interrelated Business Process Models and Software Models. *Proceedings of the 17th International Conference on Enterprise Information Systems,* 338-345. 10.5220/0005378103380345

Cruz, E. F., Machado, R. J., & Santos, M. Y. (2015b). Deriving a Data Model from a Set of Interrelated Business Process Models. *Proceedings of the 17th International Conference on Enterprise Information Systems,* 49-59. 10.5220/0005366100490059

Cruz, E. F., Machado, R. J., & Santos, M. Y. (2016). Deriving software design models from a set of business processes. *4th International Conference on Model-Driven Engineering and Software Development,* 489-496. 10.5220/0005657204890496

Dijkman, R. M., & Joosten, S. M. (2002). An algorithm to derive use cases from business processes. In 6th ICSEA (pp. 679–684). Academic Press.

Ferreira, N., Santos, N., Machado, R. J., & Gasevic, D. (2012). Derivation of process-oriented logical architectures: An elicitation approach for cloud design. In *PROFES'2012*. Berlin: Springer-Verlag. doi:10.1007/978-3-642-31063-8_5

Jalote, P. (2008). *A concise Introduction to Software Engineering*. Springer Science & Business Media. doi:10.1007/978-1-84800-302-6

Kocbek, M., Jost, G., Hericko, M., & Polancic, G. (2015). Business process model and notation: The current state of affairs. *Computer Science and Information Systems, 1*(00), 1–35.

Leshob, A. (2016). Towards a business-pattern approach for UML models derivation from business process models. *13th IEEE International Conference on e-Business Engineering,* 244-249. 10.1109/ICEBE.2016.049

Lubke, D., Schneider, K., & Weidlich, M. (2008). Visualizing use case sets as BPMN processes. In *Requirements Engineering Visualization* (pp. 21–25). IEEE. doi:10.1109/REV.2008.8

Machado, R., Fernandes, J. a., Monteiro, P., & Rodrigues, H. (2006). Refinement of software architectures by recursive model transformations. In Product-Focused Software Process Improvement (pp. 422-428). Springer Berlin Heidelberg. doi:10.1007/11767718_38

Magnani, M. & Montesi, D. (2009). *BPDMN: A conservative extension of BPMN with enhanced data representation capabilities*. arXiv preprintarXiv:0907.1978

Meyer, A., Smirnov, S., & Weske, M. (2011). *Data in business processes*. Universitatsverlag Potsdam.

OMG. (2011). *Business process model and notation (BPMN), version 2.0. Technical report*. Object Management Group.

Park, G., Fellir, F., Hong, J.-E., Garrido, J. L., Noguera, M., & Chung, L. (2017). Deriving use cases from business processes: A goal-oriented transformational approach. *Proceedings of the Symposium on Applied Computing, SAC '17*, 1288–1295. 10.1145/3019612.3019789

Rodríguez, A., Fernández-Medina, E., & Piattini, M. (2007). Towards CIM to PIM transformation: From secure business processes defined in BPMN to use-cases. Business Process Management, 408-415.

Rodríguez, A., Fernández-Medina, E., & Piattini, M. (2008). Towards obtaining analysis-level class and use case diagrams from business process models. In *Advances in Conceptual Modeling Challenges and Opportunities* (Vol. 5232, pp. 103–112). Springer Berlin Heidelberg.

Schmiedel, T., & vom Brocke, J. (2015). Business process management: Potentials and challenges of driving innovation. In BPM - Driving Innovation in a Digital World, Management for Professionals (pp. 3-15). Springer International Publishing.

van der Aalst, W. (2015). Business process simulation survival guide. In Handbook on Business Process Management 1, International Handbooks on Information Systems (pp. 337-370). Springer Berlin Heidelberg. doi:10.1007/978-3-642-45100-3_15

Weske, M. (2012). *Business Process Management Concepts, Languages, Architectures*. Springer Science & Business Media.

This research was previously published in New Perspectives on Information Systems Modeling and Design; pages 170-196, copyright year 2019 by Engineering Science Reference (an imprint of IGI Global).

Section 6
Managerial Impact

Chapter 88

Boosting the Competitiveness of Organizations With the Use of Software Engineering

Mirna Muñoz

https://orcid.org/0000-0001-8537-2695

CIMAT, A. C. Unidad Zacatecas, Mexico

ABSTRACT

Software has become the core of organizations in different domains because the capacity of their products, systems, and services have an increasing dependence on software. This fact highlights the research challenges to be covered by computer science, especially in the software engineering (SE) area. On the one way, SE is in charge of covering all the aspects related to the software development process from the early stages of software development until its maintenance and therefore is closely related to the software quality. On the other hand, SE is in charge of providing engineers able to provide technological-base solutions to solve industrial problems. This chapter provides a research work path focused on helping software development organizations to change to a continuous software improvement culture impacting both their software development process highlighting the human factor training needs. Results show that the implementation of best practices could be easily implemented if adequate support is provided.

INTRODUCTION

Nowadays in most organizations, the capacity of their products, systems, and services increasingly depends on software. The software allows them to compete, adapt and survive in a highly changing environment (Muñoz, Mejía & de León, 2020).

The importance acquired by the software industry becomes an opportunity for organizations of this domain, all of them (large, SMEs and SVEs), to have constant growth, and in most cases their survival. This opportunity brings a high demand for them to develop high-quality software. In this context, software development organizations have an increasing need to improve their software development process in an effort to meet the demand of the software industry (Muñoz et al., 2016).

DOI: 10.4018/978-1-6684-3702-5.ch088

Software Engineering is an area of Computer Science, which covers all the aspects related to the software development process from the early stages of software development until its maintenance (Pressman, 2002). The foundation of Software Engineering is the process because it defines a framework for a set of key areas that must be established for the effective delivery of software engineering technology (Pressman, 2002).

Due to the importance of the Process, the Software Process Improvement is a research field within the Software Engineering area that has emerged from the need to respond to the problems involved in software development offering to software development organizations the opportunity of increasing its efficiency, taking as base that the efficiency in software development depends largely on the quality of the processes used to create it (Williams, 2008).

In this context, Software Process Improvement (SPI) becomes an obvious and logical way to address the increasing need to be competitive in the software industry (Cuevas et al, 2002). However, although there are many organizations motivated to improve their software processes, very few know how best to do so. Therefore, introducing process improvement has been a path full of obstacles for most organizations, and always away from the original path (Potter & Sakry, 2006; Morgan, 2009). Moreover, most improvement efforts fail, stakeholders feel frustrated, and they are more convinced that they must continue doing their work as before and the resistance to change increases (Calvo-Manzano et al., 2010).

The goal of this chapter is to present a path of a research that has been developed since 2005, which aims to implement Software Process Improvement in a smooth and continuous way, depending on the improvement pace accepted by the organization, and addressing four aspects to be taken into account for a success SPI such as people, models and standards, methods and methodologies; and software tools (Cuevas et al, 2002). By this way, the rejection attitudes regarding the implementation of SPI are prevented; therefore, the resistance to change are reduced.

After the introduction, this chapter is structured as follows: Section 2 shows four aspects covered in this research; Section 3 presents the research path developed; Section provides 4 discussion, conclusions and future trends.

BACKGROUND

As exposed in the introduction section, according to Cuevas (Cuevas et al, 2002) four aspects should be taken into account to achieve a successful SPI: *people, models and standards, methods and methodologies; and software tools*. This way allows software development organizations to establish "how" to define and improve their software development process that will help them to provide high-quality software to meet the requirements of software market.

This section provides an overview of the four aspects this research took as base toward the reinforcement of the development processes of SDOs.

- *People.* It refers to the qualified professionals able to work with international models and standards to enhance the quality and effectiveness of software developed. Moreover, they are required to be able to work on teams. Then, this chapter covers the research done, on the one way, analyzing the training provided by professionals at universities (Muñoz et al., 2019b), and the research focused on motivate and organize talented people to integrate high effective teams (Muñoz et al., 2019c).

- *Models and standards.* It refers to the process improvement models and standards targeted for the software industry, to contribute to the development of quality products within budget and schedule, by optimizing efforts and resources. Then, this chapter focus not on the development of new models and standards, but in the correct implementation of them (Mejía, Muñoz & Muñoz, 2016; Muñoz, Mejía & Gasca-Hurtado, 2014), including the work done to help software development organizations, large (Calvo-Manzano et al., 2010), SMEs (Muñoz, Mejía & Gasca-Hurtado, 2014) and VSEs (Laporte et al., 2017; Muñoz, Mejía & Laporte, 2019) in the implementation of best practices provided by international models and standards to increase its competitiveness.
- *Methods and methodologies.* It refers to the set of defined steps that indicates how to build software in a systematic way (Pressman, 2002). However, these methods and models are not used by engineers due to they prefer craftsman software development. Then, this chapter focuses on supporting the reinforcement of software development methods and methodologies, and how to get users to accept it, according to the specific features of the software development organization (Cuevas et al., 2007; Muñoz et al., 2019).
- *Software tools.* It refers to the development of automatic or semi-automatic approaches to facilitate and support the implementation of processes or methods (Pressman, 2002). Then, this chapter focuses on those software tools both semi-automatic and automatic that have been developed to support people in tasks related to training (Muñoz Peña & Hernández, 2019), process definition and improvement (Duron & Muñoz, 2013; Muñoz-Mata et al., 2015), and to help teams in the use of engineering best practices (Muñoz et al, 2017; Ibarra & Muñoz, 2018).

RESEARCH PATH DEVELOPED TO BOOST THE COMPETITIVENESS OF SOFTWARE DEVELOPMENT ORGANIZATIONS USING SOFTWARE ENGINEERING

The research path to boost the competitiveness of software development organizations by using software engineering started in 2006, focusing on the implementation of SPI in a pace supported by software development organizations, and has been growing up highlighting the human factor as key element for the success in the implementation of improvements in software development process.

Then, this section will describe how has been addressing the research by providing a review of the focused problems, and the research achievements covering the four aspects mentioned in the previous section: people, models and standards, methods and methodologies, and software tools. All together build what in this chapter is called "the research path". It is important to highlight that throughout the development of this research the four aspect has been addressed due to its importance in the Software Engineering area.

Context, Problems and Research Achievements Related to the "Models and Standards" Aspect

This is considering the first step of the path because this research was performed during the PhD studies of the author. The research context was set on that even when a set of success stories related to software process improvements in organizations have been published (Software Engineering Institute, 2007; Gibson, Goldensen & Kost, 2006), the introduction of process improvements represented serious problems to most organizations becoming a path with a lot of obstacles (Potter & Sakry, 2006; Morgan, 2009), having none (Goldenson, 2007) or very limit success (Conradi & Fuggeta, 2002). The problem addressed are focused on helping software development organization to implement software process improvements with better results.

As result of performing this research, it was proposed a methodology that allows software development organizations to improve their development processes in a smooth and continuous way, depending on their business goals but in a pace supported by them. The methodology was named as *methodology for process improvement through basic components and focusing on the resistance to change* (MIGME-RRC) (Calvo-Manzano et al., 2010).

As Figure 1 shows, MIGME-RRC is composed of four phases: (1) identifying internal best practices; (2) assess the organizational performance; (3) analyze external best practices, and (4) implement improvements. All of them supported by activities that addressed the reduction of resistance to change (change management and knowledge management). Due to this methodology represents the foundation of the research path. Next each phase is briefly described.

Figure 1. MIGME-RRC methodology (Calvo-Manzano et al., 2010)

- **Identify Internal Best Practices:** This phase aims to start the implementation of the improvement but in a different way that assessments. It is focused on identifying the practices that are carry out within the organization. After the identification of the practices, it is possible to get an overview of the current organizational processes.

- **Assess the Organizational Performance:** This phase aims to evaluate the performance of the formalized practices regarding the coverage of the organizational business goals. This way allows identifying most and less covered business goals, and then, prioritizing the business goals needs.

- **Analyze External Best Practices:** This phase aims to build multi-model environments as reference to introduce the best practices within the organizational processes. Depending on the business goals the methodology allows provide a set of practices from different models and standards in such way that the organization has a candidate practices to be implemented focusing on their business goals needs and the way they work. A multi-model environment for this research work involves cultural aspects and the knowledge, which advises the use of the mix of best practices from more than one model or standard in a process, in order to achieve the organization's business goals (Muñoz, Mejía & Gasca, 2014).

- **Implement Improvements:** This phase aims to introduce best practices for improving the organizational processes. The way proposed by this methodology is integrating internal and external best practices, so that the organizational knowledge and experience is reinforced by external practices of a multi-model environment.

- **Activities to Reduce Change Resistance:** The methodology uses interviews and validations meeting to personnel selected by the organization. Besides, the activities related to knowledge management are focused on formalizing the current organizational practices.

Together with the MIGME-RRC methodology, the achievements of this research, regarding the models and standards were focused on implementing improvements by using multi-model environments, having as main results:

1. A mapping among the most used models, standards and methodologies for Project Management such as CMMI-DEV® v1.2, Project Management Book of knowledge (PMBOK), PRINCE2, Team Software Process® (TSP®), COBIT, ISO9001 and ISO/IEC 15504 (Calvo-Manzano et al., 2008). This mapping was the spearhead toward the understanding of process improvement models and standards.

2. A method to build multi-model environments. This method was result of a research who aims to incorporate elemental process improvement components in an organization. To achieve it, the method provides the minimum steps to find the similarities among the models and standards considered within a specific scope. By this way, it is possible to help an organization to choose those best practices compliant with the available models and standards in the market and that best meet their goals. The method was implemented in a case study for the project planning process obtained a multi-model environment for this process (more information of the case study is found in (Calvo-Manzano et al., 2008)).

3. A method to identify internal best practices. This method was the result of research focused on reducing the resistance to change starting the SPI analyzing the practices currently carried out in the organization so that if the practices are identified, it is possible to get an overview of the organizational current processes. Besides, the method allows involving relevant stakeholders since the beginning. The results of the case study executed to analyzed the viability of the method shown that using the method enable the extraction, collection, and formalization of the tacit knowledge of the organization in an organizational process (more information of the case study is found in (Calvo-Manzano et al., 2010)).

4. A case study performed in a multinational software development organization that allows confirming that people only accept assimilated changes with identified benefits, by this way the improvements are perceived as an evolution of their work (Calvo-Manzano et al., 2010).

5. The application of knowledge management to support the use of multi-model environments in software process improvements. This research aims to reinforce the use of multi-model environments by applying knowledge management technologies such is the case of ontologies. As result of this research a model process ontology was obtained. Besides, the ontology was proved encompassing a set of international models and standards such as CMMI®-v1.2, TSP®, PMBOK, ISO/IEC 15504 and ISO/IEC 12207 (more information of the case study is found in (Muñoz, Mejía & Muñoz, 2013)).

6. A methodology for establishing multi-model environments. This methodology is an evolution of the method published in (Calvo-Manzano et al., 2008). This research adds a new phase to the previous method base on an adaptation of the goal question metric (GQM) method to identify and formalize the business goals of an organization. This methodology focused on a gap that was detected in a set of SMEs on Mexico regarding the establishment of business goals. This methodology was validated by performing a case study in a SME, the results shown that the methodology allows providing a proposal of practices implementation sequence covering the need to provide a guide of how to implement the improvement (more information of the case study is found in (Muñoz, Mejía & Gasca-Hurtado, 2014)).

7. The participation as a member of the team in charge to translate the CMMI-Dev model v1.2 and 1.3 to the Spanish Language.

Recently, the author was expanded the work focusing on very small entities and the use of international standards getting as result:

1. An analysis of the weaknesses that VSEs present in the implementation of the international standard ISO/IEC 29110. Due to the importance of involving VSEs in a continuous improvement, this analysis is part of a project to support VSEs in the implementation of ISO/IEC 29110 to reinforce their software development process. The analysis provides a comparative between the state of art and the state of practices of VSEs toward the implementation of an international standard. The results show as main weakness in activities related to the execution of verification and validation to the project artifacts as well as the lack of definition of test cases and test procedures (Muñoz, Peralta & Laporte, 2019).

Context, Problems and Research Achievements Related to the "Software Tools" Aspect

The results of implementing the MIGME-RRC methodology highlighted the need to support the use and implementation of processes. Therefore, as part of a postdoctoral stay, a research focused on the development of software applications to be used by software development organizations, which facilitate the implementation and use of software process improvements, was performed.

The research context was set on that even when organizations were motivated to implement software process improvements, not all have the knowledge to do that. To achieve it, Small and Medium Enterprises (SMEs) were focused due to their importance in worldwide industry economy (Pino, García & Piattini,

2008), (Garcia, Pacheco & Cruz, 2010). SMEs cover two type of companies the small enterprises which are companies with between 25 and 50 employees, and medium enterprises which are companies that have between 50 and 249 employees (Muñoz et al., 2012). The problem addressed in this research are focused on facilitating the implementation of improvements taking into account that they do not invest much on software process improvements (Muñoz et al., 2012).

To perform this research, in-depth software process improvement analysis in SMEs were performed covering three steps: (1) to understand the SMEs work culture; (2) to understand the needs of SMEs to implement SPI initiatives, and (3) to analyze the existing support to allow SMEs implementing SPI (Muñoz et al., 2012).

As results of the first step were established a set of features classified in four categories, as next listed (Muñoz et al., 2012):

1. **Organization:** It refers to the SME environment, and it has 6 features (high innovation and adoption, agile for change, daily changes, limited customer with high dependency, focus on practices, and project with short delivery time).
2. **Staff:** It refers to the human resources working in a SME, and it has 3 features (limited staff, many activities, and lack of process culture).
3. **Software Process:** It refers to the importance of the processes for SME, and it has 2 features (minimum training related to process, and poorly formalization of process and procedures).
4. **Software Process Improvement:** It refers to how is performed activities related to the implementation of improvements, and it has 3 features (all staff involved, lack of resources and lack of support).

As result of the second step were identified a set of success factors toward the implementation of software process improvements in SPI (Muñoz et al., 2012):

1. *Regarding the organization*, there were highlighted the availability of resources as well as an efficient communication mechanism.
2. *Regarding the staff*, there were identified the commitment of stakeholders and senior management commitments; the involvement of stakeholder, and the training on process and on SPI.
3. *Regarding the software process*, an adequate assessment frequency was highlighted.
4. *Regarding the implementation of improvements*, there were highlighted the use of guides in order to base the improvement programs on real organizational needs, the uses of incremental approaches, to provide the support and infrastructure required, and the selection of adequate reference model and/or standard.

Finally, as result of the third step were identified that most of tools were focused on the first step of the SPI but not on the rest of the SPI cycle. Therefore, there were established a set of nine requirements that a support tool should meet to help SMEs in the implementation of SPI (Muñoz et al., 2012):

1. **Process Assessment:** It refers to provide a fast assessment to the organizational processes.
2. **Snapshot of Process:** It refers to get an overview of the organizational process at specific time.
3. **Guide the Process Selection:** It refers to support in the selection of the processes to be improved.

4. **Process Modeling:** It refers to provide the resources that allows SMEs the formalization, and storage of their organizational processes.
5. **Facilitate the Improvement Implementation:** It refers to provide information of roles, and activities to be performed during the implementation of an improvement.
6. **Low Cost:** It refers to not implying a great investment for the SME.
7. **Self- Training:** It refers to the training included as part of the tool.
8. Efficient communication: it refers to enable the communication channels and knowledge sharing among people involved in the SPI.
9. **Useful Information:** It refers to provide visible information regarding the achievements of goals related to the amount of work to do as part of the SPI.

The achievements of this research, regarding the software tools were focused on providing software tools as support for the implementation of process improvements, having as main results:

1. A tool for the selection of strategies for implementing software process improvements in VSEs. This tool is a result of a research that addressed the gap of the existence of software tools that support SMEs in the implementation of process improvement initiatives taking into account the way an organization develop software projects (Duron & Muñoz, 2013).
2. A tool for providing a starting point to help SMEs for implementing software process improvements. This tool is a result of a research that addressed the lack of knowledge on how to start a process improvement effort. Therefore, this tool allows addressing the improvements effort in a software development organization based on the identification of their main problems, to achieve it this tool used a set of patterns to provide a starting point regarding the model, standard or agile methodology to be used as reference and focusing on the organization current needs, features and work culture. The tool was implemented in four SMEs of Mexico providing them the information regarding the model, process and practices that should be implemented to reduce the problems (more information of the case study is found in (Muñoz-Mata, Mejía-Miranda & Valtierra-Alvarado, 2015), (Muñoz et al., 2015).
3. A tool for using a method for lightening software processes through optimizing the selection of software engineering best practices. This tool resulted from a research that focused on lightening software processes, especially SMEs, so that the processes are optimized based on practices that add more value to the SME. More information about the method and the tool resulted from this research, as well as the case study of its application is found in (Muñoz, Mejía & Miramontes, 2016).
4. A tool for reinforcing the implementation of multi-model environments in software process improvements using knowledge management. This tool is focused on the reinforcement of multi-model environments using ontologies, it allows performing an analysis of process improvement opportunities helping SMEs to know the level of coverage of its current project management process related to activities, tools, metrics and measures proposed by different models and standards. The tool and case study performed to validate this tool is found in management (Mejía, Muñoz & Muñoz, 2016).
5. A study of tools for assessing the implementation and use of agile methodologies. This study aims to identify a correct way to assess the implementation of an agile methodology. To achieve it, a set

of 41 diagnostic assessment tools found in literature were analyzed, to identify the agile elements covered by them (Muñoz et al, 2017b).

Context, Problems and Research Achievements
Related to the "Human Factor" Aspect

During the execution of the research from the models and standards and support tools aspects, there were detected the importance of the human factor as main actor to become reality the implementation, and use of Software Engineering. An important fact is that you can have the best models, standards, software tools, but if you have people who do not want to use it, those resources will not work.

Due to the importance of this factor, this research was starting since 2012 and has been reaching so that, this factor becomes a pivot of the other three factors. It is important to mention that this research has been done since the author started working in the Software Engineering unit at the Mathematic Research Center.

The research context was set on that the approaches created in software process improvement area are focused on providing formal process descriptions, where models and standards of best practices have been developed. However, the human factor has been forgotten. Therefore, even when organizations are motivated to implement improvements the lack of having a SPI culture becomes a really challenge to achieve it.

The problem addressed in this research are focused on analyzing the SPI needs from the human perspective, because most of times the failure in the implementation of SPI, and even in the development of software projects are not related to technical issues but on human issues.

It is important to highlight that this research covers as human factor: (1) people working in a SPI initiative; (2) people working on software development teams, (3) engineers related to software development, and (4) undergraduates related to software engineering. Then, the achievements on researching in the human factor will be listed according to the work developed for each of them.

1. **Research Work Related to People Working in a SPI Initiative:** The research developed in this topic is focused on providing triggers to involve people and get its commitment regarding the implementation of success SPI initiatives. The achievements of this research have been:
   a. A characterization of SPI from the human perspective. Performing this research work it was possible to characterized the SPI needs and related problems from SMEs focusing on aspects such as organization, people, processes, financial resources, projects and models and standards. Besides, as result a set of patters to address the identified problems were defined (Muñoz et al., 2014), (Muñoz et al., 2014b), (Muñoz-Mata, Mejía-Miranda & Valtierra-Alvarado, 2015).
   b. The creation of strategies to implement best practices according to the work culture of an organization. These strategies aim to provide a set of steps to implement an improvement initiative according to the way of work of a SME regarding the development of a software project (Duron & Munoz, 2013).
2. **Research Work Related to People Working of Software Development Teams:** The research developed in this topic is focused on developing a method to integrate high effective development teams. This research has been growing up becoming multidisciplinary, and adding other topics such as gamification, interactive styles, and virtual environments allowing to collaborate with other researchers. The achievements of this research have been:

    a.   An exploratory model to integrate high effective teams. This model aims to join topics such as software development methodology, interactive styles, virtual environments, and gamification to propose an innovative way to integrate effective teams. (Muñoz et al., 2016) (Muñoz et al., 2017). This method was developed in collaboration with the University of Guadalajara of Mexico.

    b.   A comparative analysis in which the implementation of an international standard is performed between team using adaptative and predictive software development methodologies. This analysis aims to identify the differences that VSEs using three development methodologies (traditional, agile and hybrid) to identify the differences regarding the implementation of an international standard (Muñoz et al., 2019d).

3.   **Research Work Related to Engineers Working with Software Development:** The research developed in this topic is to provide the resources to help software engineers to develop soft kills that will reinforce them to be able to work as a team member. The achievements have been:

    a.   The use of gamification to identify team members profiles, this research includes gamification, teams, and virtual environments to identify those gamification elements that can be useful for identifying team members that can be have a better performance in the integration of a team. Besides, virtual environments are used to provide an attractive way (Hernández et al., 2016; Hernández et al, 2017; Muñoz et al., 2018c; Muñoz, Peña & Hernández, 2019). This research was developed in collaboration with the University of Guadalajara of Mexico.

4.   **Research Work Related to Undergraduates Related to Software Engineering:** The research developed in this topic is related to analyze the gap among the software industry requirements, and the knowledge provided at universities. Then, the needs in the academic field, especially regarding the knowledge to be provided to students, are highlighted. The achievements of this research have been:

    a.   Analysis of the coverage among national and international standards, and a set of Mexican universities curricula, this research is focused on identify the gaps regarding the requested knowledge to work with quality standards and the knowledge provided at universities related with curricula related to Computer Science. Besides, this research covered an extension of the analysis in which it is analyzed the knowledge provided in Computer Science curricula at universities versus the knowledge requested in industry (Muñoz et al, 2015b; Muñoz et al, 2016b; Muñoz et al, 2016c; Muñoz et al, 2017c). This analysis was developed in collaboration with the University of Guadalajara of Mexico.

    b.   The implementation of the international standard ISO/IEC 29110 in Software Development Centers (SDCs). A SDC provides students the opportunity to get the experience of working under international standards to produce high-quality software products, as mentioned before one of the main problems SE has is the lack of knowledge transfer among software engineering researchers and the academy, then this research was focused on analyzing the implementation of a method to support a SDC in the implementation and use of an international standard. By this way, it is possible to reinforce the students' knowledge regarding the use of best practices to develop software for real customers. (Muñoz, Mejía & Laporte, 2018b; Muñoz et al., 2019b).

Context, Problems and Research Achievements Related to the "Methods and Methodologies" Aspect

Software engineering is relative a young area within Computer Science, therefore to provide the way "for doing something" has a high value. The context of this research was set on that most of software development organizations lack of experience and knowledge in the implementation of SPI, then it is necessary to provide a structured way to implement SPI, then it is necessary to provide "how" they can easily achieve it in an optimal way. The development of methods and methodologies has been mainly focused on SMEs and VSEs because they have limited resources (time, budget and human resources) to implement SPI, and therefore, to jump into a continuous software process improvement culture. The achievements of this research have been:

1. A method for establishing strategies to implement software process improvements. This method is the result of a research who is focused on providing strategies for the implementation of SPI based on the contextual aspects in which the software is developed, so that, the strategy is provided according to the organization needs and their work culture regarding project management (Muñoz et al., 2016).
2. A method that allows optimizing software process focusing on software engineering best practices. This method is the result of a research who aimed to addresses the optimization of an organizational software processes through optimizing the selection of software engineering practices while promoting a culture of continuous improvement (Muñoz, Mejía & Miramontes, 2016).
3. A method for developing catalogs to facilitate the implementation of software engineering practices. This method is the result of research who aimed to implement best practices tailored according to the size and type of the company and to get the tools and techniques that enable them to achieve it. Therefore, the method provides six steps to build catalogs of tools and techniques that can be easy adopted by the organization related to the targeted process (García et al, 2016). This method was developed in a collaboration with the Universidad de Medellín of Colombia.
4. A method to help VSEs to increment their competitiveness using the Basic profile of the international standard ISO/IEC 29110 This method is the result of a research who aimed to transfer the knowledge of SE researchers to industry, the method offers a set of steps that allows support the implementation of an international standard to VSEs. Besides, the method was proved in a set of VSEs of the Zacatecas Region, more information about the case study was published in (Muñoz, Mejía & Laporte, 2018; Muñoz, Mejía & Laporte, 2019). This method was built with in project to boost the VSEs that has been executed in collaboration with the secretary of economy of Zacatecas, Mexico, and another achievement of this research has been helping 19 VSEs to be certified in the basic profile of ISO/IEC 29110 (NYCE, 2020).

Another important result was to be invited to build the guide to help VSEs using agile environments to implement best practices of the basic profile of ISO/IEC 29110, as well as in the translation of the entry profile of the ISO/IEC 29110 to Spanish language.

5.   A Proposal to Avoid Issues in the DevOps Implementation: A Systematic Literature Review. This research aims to provides a guideline that allows establishing a generic DevOps process reinforced with the proven practices of the Basic profile of the ISO/IEC 29110 (Muñoz, Negrete & Mejía, 2019).

DISCUSSION, CONCLUSION AND FUTURE TRENDS

Discussion

Software Engineering (SE) pursue the establishment and use of software engineering practices, so that it boosting organizations (large, SMEs and VSEs), to obtain high-quality software products and services that are economical, reliable, and efficient to meet the needs of software market.

Even when Software Engineering is young area in Computer Sciences, it has becoming indispensable because the core of a great amount of organizations in different industrial domains is the software. The software allows software development organizations to generate software products, and services capable of providing high-performance solutions to problems of different domains (industrial, agricultural, aeronautics, Information and Communication Technologies, among others).

The above-mentioned highlights the opportunity for software development organizations to produce high-quality software products and services to satisfy market needs.

In this context, this chapter provides the results of a research performed since 2005, which is focused on software process improvement, covering the four aspects:

- **Models and Standards:** In this aspect, the main research results have been focused on the right implementation of models and standards for organizations (large, MSEs and VSEs).
- Support tools: in this aspect, the main results have been focused on providing support to facilitate the implementation of the SPI since the beginning and throughout all improvement implementation.
- **Human Factor:** In this aspect, the main results have been focused on the one hand to provide the resources to facilitate the implementation of SPI in organizations as well as the integration of effective teams using innovative way such as the use of gamification, interactive styles and virtual environments. On the other hand, to provide resources that serve as an input to reduce the gap between academic and industry knowledge requirements. Besides, to provide innovative ways to make the Software engineering topic training attractive for students and SE professionals.
- **Methods and Methodologies:** In this aspect, the main results have been focused on providing a guide to reduce the gap of "how" to implement and use best practices based on the organizational work culture and current needs.

All together has been integrating the research path toward boosting the competitiveness of software development organizations.

However, there is too much work to do, so this chapter aims to serve as base for the development future research in SE.

CONCLUSION

Software development organizations have increased their importance around the world because they create valuable products, and services to achieve the software market requirements. This fact provides an opportunity to them to a steady grow up, and its market survival. Besides, it brings the responsibility to researchers to provide the support to help them in the improvement of their development processes.

However, transferring the Software Engineering knowledge developed by researchers to the industry is a gap that should be reduced. In this context, this chapter provided a research path that has had an impact towards diminishing that gap, and providing the support that enables software development organizations to get advantage of the resources resulting of research works.

The author of this chapter hopes this could inspire young researchers to continue reducing the gap between industry and academic areas, because research can benefit industry but industry can benefit academic being the main source of challenges and problems to be solve. In this context, some finding that could be highlighted as challenges in SPI of the factors addressed in this chapter are next listed:

- **Models and Standards:** Regarding this factor, they should be broadened so that all type of software development organizations (large, SMEs, and VSEs) continue keeping the use of software engineering best practices no matter the domain they are providing software because no only the quality feature, but also security together are becoming very important and critical features that all software must achieve.
- **Software Tools:** One of the main findings regarding this factor is that they are an increasing demanding of tools that make it easy the implementation and use of software development processes, providing the required support that processes' users need to perform their daily tasks. One important aspect to highlight is that more than ever, these tools should allow knowledge sharing and resources among teams. Besides, software tools should take into account the type of new software services that software development organizations are demanding such as: infrastructure as a service, platform as a service, and software as a service.
- **People:** This factor is from the point of view of the author the one that could have most challenges because having the best models and standards, software tools and methods, and methodologies if people don't want to use it, nothing can be done. Therefore, it is important to change people's culture toward a continuous improvement culture in the early stages at universities, changing the view they perceived the usefulness of software engineering. Besides, for professionals working in teams and as part of software development organizations, keeping them in a continuous knowledge transfer from research results that can help them to get better results through the implementation of new resources to achieve both quality and security while perceiving them as an evolution of the way they work.
- **Methods and Methodologies:** Regarding this factor, they should be carefully analyzed and evolve according to the new needs of shape, design, develop, prove and deploy software, so that the use of them can help software development organizations to meet with time, budget and effort of software development projects while enabling the implementation of SPI in software development organizations.

FUTURE TRENDS

As mentioned in the Discussion section, in Software Engineering area there is too much to do. As Computer Science is progressing, new challenges in Software Engineering arise. Then, the research path provided in this chapter is growing up considering new topics with high impact in the four factors: (1) the reinforcement of DevOps development with engineering practices; (2) the use of Artificial Intelligence (AI) techniques applied to Software Engineering; (3) the reinforcement of AI with SE; (4) the reinforcement of software development organizations using agile methods for software development; (5) the reinforcement of resources to bring a practical Software Engineering to the academy using gamification and serious games; and (6) the development of soft skills to undergraduates, and engineers using Artificial Intelligence and gamification.

All above topics are the future trends that as researcher, the author of this chapter will work in next years.

ACKNOWLEDGMENT

The author would like to thanks all the coauthors of the papers included in this chapter and who has been shared this research path. The author would also like to thanks Gonzalo Cuevas, Jose A. Calvo Manzano, Tomas San Feliu, and Claude Y. Laporte for sharing their knowledge and experiences. Special thanks to Jezreel Mejía for his valuable time, effort, and support during this entire research period. Besides, I would like to thanks two strong women Adriana Peña and Gloria Gasca for keep with me throughout this path. Finally, I would like to thanks all my students Brenda Duron, Claudia Valtierra, Juan Jose Miramontes, Saul Hernández, Luis Ángel Hernández, Manuel Peralta, and Mario Rodriguez for their effort in the development of specific parts of this research path.

REFERENCES

Calvo-Manzano, J.A., Cuevas, G., Gómez, G., Mejia, J., Muñoz, M., & San Feliu, T. (2010). *Journal of Software Maintenance and Evolution: Research and Practice*. Doi:10.1002/smr.505

Calvo-Manzano, J. A., Cuevas, G., Muñoz, M., & San Feliu, T. (2008). Process similarity study: Case study on project planning practices based on CMMI-DEV v1.2. EuroSPI 2008 Industrial Proceedings.

Conradi, H., & Fuggetta, A. (2002). Improving software process improvement. *Software IEEE*, *19*(4), 92–99. doi:10.1109/MS.2002.1020295

Cuevas, G., Calvo Manzano, J., San Feliu, T., Mejia, J., Muñoz, M., & Bayona, S. (2007). Impact of TSPi on Software Projects. *Electronics, Robotics and Automotive Mechanics Conference (CERMA 2007)*, 706-711, 10.1109/CERMA.2007.4367770

Cuevas, G., De Amescua, A., San Feliu, T., Arcilla, M., Cerrada, J. A., Calvo-Manzano, J. A., & García, M. (2002). *Gestión del Proceso Software*. Universitaria Ramon Areces.

Durón, B., & Muñoz, M. (2013). Selección de estrategias para la implementación de mejoras. Revista electrónica de Computación, Informática, Biomédica y Electrónica (ReCIBE), 3, 1-15.

García, I., Pacheco, C., & Cruz, D. (2010). Adopting an RIA based tool for supporting assessment, implementation and learning in software in software process improvement under the NMX-I-059/02-NYCE-2005 standard in small software enterprises. *Eighth ACIS International Conference on Software Engineering Research. Management and Application.* 10.1109/SERA.2010.14

García, Y. M., Muñoz, M., Mejía, J., Martínez, J., Gasca-Hurtado, G. P., & Hincapié, J. A. (2016). Method for Developing Catalogs focused on Facilitating the implementation of Best Practices for Project Management of Software Development in SMEs, *Proceedings of the 5th International Conference in Software Process Improvement (CIMPS 2016),* 1-8. 10.1109/CIMPS.2016.7802805

Gibson, D., Goldenson, D., & Kost, K. (2006). *Performance results of CMMI-based process improvement.* Technical Report CMU/SEI-2006-TR-004 ESC-TR-2006-004, Software Engineering Institute (SEI), Carnegie Mellon University.

Goldenson D. (2007). Teach views, performance outcomes from process improvement. *Software Technology News, 10*(1).

Hernández, L., Muñoz, M., Mejia, J., & Peña, A. (2016). Gamification in software engineering team works: A systematic literature review, *Proceedings of the 5th International Conference in Software Process Improvement (CIMPS 2016),* 1-8.

Hernández, L., Muñoz, M., Mejia, J., Peña, A., Calvo-Manzano, J. A., & San Feliu, T. (2017). Proposal for identifying teamwork roles in software engineering through the construction of a virtual rube goldberg machine. *6th International Conference on Software Process Improvement (CIMPS),* 1-8. 10.1109/CIMPS.2017.8169953

Ibarra, S., & Muñoz, M. (2018). Support tool for software quality assurance in software development. *International Conference on Software Process Improvement CIMPS 2018,* 13-19. 10.1109/CIMPS.2018.8625617

Laporte, C. Y., Muñoz, M., Mejía, J., & O'Connor, R. (2017). Applying Software Engineering Standards in Very Small Entities. *IEEE Software,* 99-103.

Mejía J., Muñoz E., & Muñoz M. (2016). Reinforcing the applicability of Multi-model Environments for Software Process Improvement using Knowledge Management. Science of Computer Programming, Elsevier, Vol. SCICO, Pag.1-13. doi:10.1016/j.scico.2015.12.002

Morgan, P. (2009). Process improvement—Is it a lottery? *Software Development Magazine.* Available at: http://www.methodsandtools.com/archive/archive.php?id=52

Muñoz, M., Hernández, L., Mejía, M., Peña, A., Rangel, N., Torres, C., & Sauberer, G. (2017). A model to integrate highly effective teams for software development. In System, Software and services Process Improvement. Springer International Publishing AG. Doi:10.1007/978-3-319-64218-5_51

Muñoz, M., Mejía, J., Calvo-Manzano, J. A., Gonzalo, C., San Feliu, T., & De Amescua, A. (2012). Expected Requirements in Support Tools for Software Process Improvement in SMEs. *2012 IEEE Ninth Electronics, Robotics and Automotive Mechanics Conference*, 135-140. doi: 10.1109/CERMA.2012.29

Muñoz, M., Mejía, J., Calvo-Manzano, J. A., San Feliu, T., Corona, B., & Miramontes, J. (2017b). Diagnostic Assessment Tools for Assessing the Implementation and/or Use of Agile Methodologies in SMEs: An Analysis of Covered Aspects. *Software Quality Professional, 19*(2), 16-27.

Muñoz, M., Mejía, J., & de León, M. (2020). Investigación en el área de Mejora de Procesos de Software in Ingeniería de Software en México: Educación, Industria e Investigación. Academia Mexicana de Computación.

Muñoz, M., Mejía, J., Duron, B., & Valtierra, C. (2014). Software process improvement from a human perspective. In *New Perspectives in Information System and Technologies*. Springer International Publishing.

Muñoz, M., Mejia, J., & Gasca-Hurtado, G.P. (2014). A Methodology for Establishing Multi-Model Environments in Order to Improve Organizational Software Processes. *International Journal of Software Engineering and Knowledge Engineering, 24*, 909-933.

Muñoz, M., Mejía, J., Gasca-Hurtado, G. P., Gómez-Alvarez, M. C., & Duron, B. (2016). Method to Establish Strategies for Implementing Process Improvement According to the Organization's Context, System, Software and Services Process Improvement. Springer International Publishing.

Muñoz, M., Mejía, J., Gasca-Hurtado, G. P., Valtierra, C., & Duron, B. (2014b). Covering the human perspective in software process improvement. In *System, Software and Services Process Improvement*. Springer Berlin Heidelberg.

Muñoz, M., Mejía, J., Gasca-Hurtado, G. P., Vega-Zepeda, V., & Valtierra, C. (2015). Providing a Starting Point to Help SMEs in the Implementation of Software Process Improvements. In System, Software and Services Process Improvement. Springer.

Muñoz, M., Mejía, J., & Laporte, C. Y. (2018). *Reinforcing Very Small Entities Using Agile Methodologies with the ISO/IEC 29110. In Trends and Applications in Software Engineering. Springer*. https://doi-org.svproxy01.cimat.mx/10.1007/978-3-030-01171-0_8

Muñoz, M., Mejía, J., & Miramontes, J. (2016). Method for Lightening Software Processes through Optimizing the Selection of Software Engineering Best Practices. In Trends and Applications in Software Engineering. Springer International.

Muñoz, M., Mejía, J., & Muñoz, E. (2013). Knowledge management to support using muti-model environments in software process improvement. European System, Software & Service Process Improvement & Innovation EuroSPI 2013, 1-10.

Muñoz, M., Mejía, J., Peña, A., Lara, G., & Laporte, C. Y. (2019b, October). Transitioning international software engineering standards to academia: Analyzing the results of the adoption of ISO/IEC 29110 in four Mexican universities. *Computer Standards & Interfaces, 66*, 103340. doi:10.1016/j.csi.2019.03.008

Muñoz, M., Mejía, M., & Laporte, C. Y. (2018b). Implementación del Estándar ISO/IEC 29110 en Centros de Desarrollo de Software de Universidades Mexicanas: Experiencia del Estado de Zacatecas. *Revista Ibérica de Sistemas y Tecnologías de Informactión (RISTI), 29*(10).

Muñoz, M., Mejía, M., & Laporte, C. Y. (2019). Implementing ISO/IEC 29110 to Reinforce four Very Small Entities of Mexico under Agile Approach. *IET Software*, (March), 1–11. doi:10.1049/iet-sen.2019.0040

Muñoz, M., Mejía, M., Peña, A., & Rangel, N. (2016). Establishing Effective Software Development Teams: An Exploratory Model, System. In Software and Services Process Improvement. Springer International.

Muñoz, M., Negrete, M., & Mejía, J. (2019). Proposal to Avoid Issues in the DevOps Implementation: A Systematic Literature Review. In Á. Rocha, H. Adeli, L. Reis, & S. Costanzo (Eds.), *New Knowledge in Information Systems and Technologies. WorldCIST'19 2019. Advances in Intelligent Systems and Computing* (Vol. 930, pp. 666–677). Springer. https://doi-org.svproxy01.cimat.mx/10.1007/978-3-030-16181-1_63

Muñoz, M., Peña, A., & Hernández, L. (2019). Gamification in Virtual reality Environments for the integration of Highly Effective Teams. In Virtual Reality Designs. Science Publishers.

Muñoz, M., Peña, A., Mejía, J., Gasca-Hurtado, G. P., Gómez-Álvarez, M. C., & Hernández, L. (2018c). *Gamification to Identify Software Development Team Members' Profiles. In Systems, Software and Services Process Improvement. Springer.* https://doi-org.svproxy01.cimat.mx/10.1007/978-3-319-97925-0_18

Muñoz, M., Peña, A., Mejía, J., Gasca-Hurtado, G. P., Gómez-Alvarez, M. C., & Hernández, L. (2019c, April). Applying gamification elements to build teams for software development. *IET Software, 13*(2), 99–105. doi:10.1049/iet-sen.2018.5088

Muñoz, M., Peña, A., Mejía, J., Gasca-Hurtado, G. P., Gómez-Álvarez, M. C., & Laporte, C. Y. (2019d). A Comparative Analysis of the Implementation of the Software Basic Profile of ISO/IEC 29110 in Thirteen Teams That Used Predictive Versus Adaptive Life Cycles. In A. Walker, R. O'Connor, & R. Messnarz (Eds.), *Systems, Software and Services Process Improvement. EuroSPI 2019. Communications in Computer and Information Science* (Vol. 1060, pp. 179–191). Springer. doi:10.1007/978-3-030-28005-5_14

Muñoz, M., Peña, A., Mejía, J., & Lara, G. (2015b). *Analysis of Coverage of Moprosoft Practices in Curricula Programs Related to Computer Science and Informatics, Trends and Applications in Software Engineering Series: Advances in Intelligent Systems and Computing 405* (Vol. 405). Springer Berlin Heidelberg.

Muñoz, M., Peña, A., Mejía, J., & Lara, G. (2016b). Actual State of the Coverage of Mexican Software Industry Requested Knowledge Regarding the Project Management Best Practices. Computer Science and Information Systems (ComSIS), 13, 849-873.

Muñoz, M., Peña, A., Mejía, J., & Lara, G. (2016c). Coverage of the University Curricula for the Software Engineering Industry in Mexico. *IEEE Latin America Transactions, 14*, 2383-2389.

Muñoz, M., Peña, A., Mejía, J., & Lara, G. (2017c). ISO/IEC 29110 and Curricula Programs Related to Computer Science and Informatics in Mexico: Analysis of practices coverage. Springer International Publishing AG. doi:10.1007/978-3-319-69341-5_1

Muñoz, M., Peralta, M., & Laporte, C.Y. (2019). Análisis de las debilidades que presentan las Entidades Muy Pequeñas al implementar el estándar ISO/IEC 29110: Una comparativa entre estado del arte y el estado de la práctica. *RISTI, 34*(10).

Muñoz-Mata, M., Mejía-Miranda, J., & Valtierra-Alvarado, C. (2015). Helping Organizations to Address their Effort toward the Implementation of Improvements in their Software Process. *Revista Facultad de Ingeniería, 77*, 115-126.

NYCE. (2020). *Companies certified to ISO/IEC 29110-4-1:2011 standard.* Retrieved at https://www.nyce.org.mx/wp-content/uploads/2020/01/PADRON-DE-EMPRESAS-CERTIFICADAS-EN-LA-NORMA-ISO-IEC-29110-4-1-16-01-2020.pdf

Pino, J. F., García, F., & Piattini, M. (2008). Software process improvement in small and medium software enterprises: A systematic review. *SQJournal, 16*, 237–261.

Potter, N., & Sakry, M. (2006). *Making Process Improvement Work: A Concise Action Guide for Software Managers and Practitioners* (pp. 2–5). Addison-Wesley.

Pressman, R. S. (2002). *Ingeniería de Software: Un enfoque práctico. 5a edición.* McGraw-Hill.

Software Engineering Institute. (2007). *CMMI Performance Results. TATA Consultancy Services.* Software Engineering Institute (SEI), Carnegie Mellon University. Available at: http://www.sei.cmu.edu/cmmi/results/org29.html#BC2

Williams, T. (2008). How do organizations learn lessons from projects and do they? *IEEE Transactions on Engineering Management, 55*(2), 248–266. doi:10.1109/TEM.2007.912920

KEY TERMS AND DEFINITIONS

CMMI-DEV® v1.2: It is a capability and maturity model for software process improvement proposed by the Software Engineering Institute. This model aims to provide support to organizations for products and services development. It has a collection of best practices that address the development and maintenance of the activities that cover the product life cycle.

COBIT: Is an open standard, which structure provides best practices through a process domain and environment, and presents activities within a logical and manageable structure.

DevOps: It is a set of practices emerging to bridge the gaps between operation and developer teams to achieve a better collaboration.

ISO 9001-2000-Quality Management System: It is a standard focused on the efficiency of a quality management system to achieve customer requirements, covering the requirements for quality systems that support all product lifecycle, including initial agreements on deliverables, design, development and product support.

ISO/IEC 15504: Information Technology-Process Assessment: It is an international standard that provides a structured focus for the process assessment. It is five part "assessment model and indicators guide", it contains a set of software engineering best practices for each process: customers and suppliers, engineering, support, management, and organization.

Large Organizations: Is the term used to refer to an enterprise having from 51 to 250 people.

Multi-Model Environment: It involves all cultural aspects and the knowledge that makes advisable to use in each process a mix of best practices from more than one model or standard to achieve the organization's business goals.

PRINCE2: Methodology based on project management that present a ser of processes easy tailored and scalable for manage all type pf projects. It was designed to provide a common language through all stakeholders involved in the project. It describes how to divide a project in manage steps, enabling efficient control for resources, as well as a regular process through the project.

Project Management Book of Knowledge (PMBOK): Reference model that has project management process, tools, and techniques, and provides a set of high-level business process for all type of industry.

Small and Medium Enterprises: SMEs by its acronym is the term used to refer to an enterprise having from 25 to 50 people.

Software Engineering: It is the establishment and use of robust, targeted engineering principles to obtain economic, reliable, efficient software that satisfies the user needs.

Software Process Improvement: It is a field of research and practice, arising out of the need to solve software development issues. It covers the actions taken by organizations to change processes, according to the business needs and achieving their business goals more effectively.

Team Software Process® (TSP®): Methodology for developing software in teams, where they should plan and estimate their product, achieve their commitments, and improve their productivity and quality. TSP aims to provide a defined process, to recognize the process importance, and to know, base of available information, how to improve a process.

Very Small Entities: VSE by its acronym is the term used to refer to an enterprise, organization (e.g., public or non-profit organization), project or department having up to 25 people.

This research was previously published in Latin American Women and Research Contributions to the IT Field; pages 198-216, copyright year 2021 by Engineering Science Reference (an imprint of IGI Global).

Chapter 89

Evaluation of Determinants of Software Quality in Offshored Software Projects:
Empirical Evidences From India

Ganesan Kannabiran

National Institute of Technology, Tiruchirappalli, India

K. Sankaran

Independent Management Consultant, Chennai, India

ABSTRACT

Successful offshoring engagements of Indian software vendors is increasingly dependent upon the quality of the projects delivered rather than cost considerations. However, delivering quality software is reliant on effective management of various organizational, technological and people aspects. This research is to identify and evaluate the determinants of quality on software projects delivered by vendors through offshoring. Data related to recently completed projects were collected through a survey of 440 project managers from Indian vendors. Based on structural equation modeling, the authors analyze the influence determinants on specific product quality attributes. It is found that, out of six determinants, technical infrastructure and process maturity have significant influence on most of the attributes of quality in offshored IS projects from India. The authors provide a set of implications for practice and directions for further research.

1. INTRODUCTION

For many years, reaping benefits from substantially lower labor costs has been reported as one of the major reasons for offshoring (Khan et al., 2003; Rottman and Lacity, 2004, Conchuir et al., 2009; Deshpande et al., 2011). Both offshore vendors and customers have realized that improving software quality is crucial in order to derive maximum value out of IT investments. Researchers have also observed that

DOI: 10.4018/978-1-6684-3702-5.ch089

in view of the declining cost advantages, offshore vendors need to change focus from 'cost' to "quality" related measures of the software services provided (Carmel & Agarwal, 2002; Davis et al., 2006; Khan et al., 2009, Mukherjee, 2013, Kroll et al., 2014). The interest in the quality of software is receiving a great deal of attention as more system failures are attributable to issues in software quality (SQ) that may lead to higher maintenance cost, longer cycle time, customer dissatisfaction and loss of profits (Gopal et al., 2002; Nanda and Robinson, 2011). Researchers have also observed that SQ can determine the success in today's competitive market (Ethiraj et al., 2005; Luftman & Kempaiah, 2008; Karout and Awasthi, 2017). To effectively meet the challenges, both vendors and client organizations have to improve the quality of their development processes and techniques (Khan et al., 2017).

Many researchers have observed that software quality is one of the critical issues of the decade but there is inadequacy of empirical studies investigating the management and control of quality of software development (Jimenez et al., 2009; Gorla & Lin, 2010). They pointed out that theories and principles were being drawn from other areas; but empirical research have to be carried out. Past studies had also used a single quality construct that measured the quality of the final software product (Krishnan et al., 2000). Evaluating the software product alone seems insufficient since it is known its quality is largely dependent on the process that is used to create it (Trudel et al., 2006).

Therefore, many organizations were motivated to adopt maturity models (Pressman, 2001; Raman, 2000; Ashrafi, 2003). For example, capability maturity model (CMM) are being used by many software development organizations and by outsourcing contractors worldwide (Huang & Han, 2006, Palvia et al., 2010). According to Subramanian et al. (2007), CMM levels influence the choice of information system implementation factors such as training, executive commitment and simplicity which in turn influences software quality.

It is reported that there have been only few comprehensive studies on process characteristics that impact software quality and quantitative survey-based research is lacking on the subject (Verner & Evanco, 2005; Gorla and Lin, 2010). With the above background, objective of this research is to empirically evaluate the relationship between determinants and quality attributes in offshore software development, based on a survey of project managers and leads of software vendors in India. We have adopted the relationship between the independent variables (organizational, technological, and individual factors) and the dependent variables (characteristics of software quality), as proposed by Gorla and Lin (2010) and Curcio et al. (2016). The paper is organized as follows. The review of previous research is presented followed by research hypotheses and methodology. The next section covers the data analysis and interpretation, followed by a discussion on the impact of determinants on software quality attributes. The paper is concluded with implications for practice and directions for future research.

2. THEORETICAL BACKGROUND

Many researchers have addressed various aspects of product or service quality and identified the critical factors affecting quality management (Sureshchandar et al., 2002; Rajendran et al., 2006). Vitharana and Mone (1998) outlined efforts to identify critical factors, and proposed an instrument to measure critical factors of Software Quality Management (SQM). They proposed an instrument consisting of 57 items to measure the quality management levels in software firms which are based on six critical factors. Rajendran et al. (2006) developed a survey instrument to measure the critical factors of software quality management from customers' perspectives. Vitharana and Mone (2008) identified six critical factors of software quality management, viz., top IS management commitment, education and training, customer focus, process management, quality metrics, and employee responsibility.

Various models have been proposed to improve software quality. These include total quality management (TQM), ISO and CMM. Parzinger and Nath (2000) observed that many software development enterprises used the TQM philosophy to enhance the quality of software and achieve higher efficiencies in development. They empirically investigated the linkage between TQM implementation and software quality by identifying eight TQM factors with 43 items, and four software quality measures. Issac et al. (2004) proposed a framework on TQM in the software industry from customer perspective that addresses critical factors such as employee commitment and attitude, employee competence, benchmarking, technical infrastructure and facilities, and risk management, in addition to the critical factors that are considered in the ISO 9000 Quality System and CMM.

Gorla and Lin (2010) after surveying 112 IS project managers, collected data about their perceptions on the software quality attributes and their determinants to arrive at six factors through exploratory factor analysis. Their study detailed the individual factors that impacted the software quality attributes, namely, reliability, maintainability, usefulness, relevance and ease of use. They suggested that the study may be repeated with other quality attributes not considered in their research (Gorla & Lin, 2010). Further, they suggested that future research may consider a subset of software quality attributes that are important in environments such as in-house software development, outsourced software, etc., and thus determine the factors that influence those quality attributes. It was also reported that software quality should be defined based on the context and not all quality attributes are important in all contexts (Glass, 1998). To this end, this study aims to identify and evaluate factors that impact the quality of software in development projects and its use by the offshore vendors. The relevant previous research relating to software quality and its determinants are reviewed and presented in the following section.

2.1. Software Quality Attributes

Researchers have observed that development of high-quality software is an essential business activity and improving the quality requires the effective use of a software development process. The definition of software quality has evolved over time. Initially, it was defined as conformance to a standard or a specification. Traditionally, software quality has been defined to be composed of correctness, reliability, usability, and maintainability (Dromey, 1995). The definition was then changed to adapt to highly dynamic business environments leading to development of quality models. Of the Quality models which have been developed in the past, the ones most widely known are Dromey's, McCall's and Boehm's, and more recently, the ISO/IEC 9126. The International Organization for Standardization proposed ISO 9126 as the standard for evaluating software quality, which defines quality as "the totality of features and characteristics of a product or service that bears on its ability to satisfy given needs (Jung, 2007; Agrawal & Chari, 2007).

The ISO 9126 model for software quality and ISO/IEC 12207 on software life cycle processes may be analyzed to map the relationships between them for better measurement of software product quality Al-Qutaish (2009). Behkamal et al. (2009) customized the ISO 9126 model to desirable software quality attributes for web applications which are reliability, usability, security, availability, scalability, maintainability, and time to market. Boegh (2008) observed that software quality has also been defined in terms of two types of product characteristics: (i) external quality (how the product works in its environment), like usability and reliability; and (ii) internal quality (how the product was developed), such as, software structure and complexity. Authors have considered this perspective of quality (Kroeger et al., 2014). The present research focuses on the external quality, as perceived by the customer than internal quality.

According to Andreou & Tziakouris (2007), ISO 9126 model, having six major characteristics, namely, functionality, reliability, usability, efficiency, maintainability and portability, along with their associated sub-characteristics, can be suitably modified to a quality frame work for developing and evaluating original software components. However, this research study has not included 'portability' as the attribute portability is considered applicable only in software products that need to be implemented on multiple platforms (Glass, 1998). Similarly, 'efficiency' attribute is viewed as an internal quality attribute as it deals with time behavior and computing resources consumed (Gorla & Lin, 2010). Portability is regarded as an inherent characteristic of all components but it is also effectively superseded by the interoperability sub-characteristic of the functionality characteristic. Hence, based on suggestions from the practitioners, it has been modified in this study by using more suitable term 'performance' of the software to provide a comprehensive representation of the attribute in our chosen list of software quality attributes for the study. Therefore, the five main attributes, viz., functionality, reliability, maintainability, usability and performance are considered as measures of software quality in this study.

Functionality is the capability of the software product to provide functions which meet stated and implied needs when it is used under specified conditions. It includes the following sub-characteristics-suitability, accuracy, interoperability, compliance and security. Functionality expresses the ability of a system to provide the required services and functions, when used under specified conditions (Gorla & Lin, 2010, Mohagheghi & Conradi, 2004, Williams & Carver, 2010). Reliability is the ability of a software product to maintain its level of performance under stated conditions for a stated period of time. It includes the following sub-characteristics: maturity, fault tolerance and recoverability. Reliability is an indication of the confidence that the software will live up to the expectations (Catelani et al., 2010, Chinnaiyan & Somasundaram, 2010).

It is noted that software maintainability is not often a major consideration during software design and implementation. It includes the following sub-characteristics: analyzability, changeability, stability and testability. Chen and Huang (2009) and Malhotra and Chug (2016) have also advocated that a reduction in software maintenance costs could be achieved by a more controlled design and implementation process. Therefore, understanding of software development factors will help in ensuring the maintainability of delivered software systems (Behkamal et al., 2009, Chen & Huang, 2009). Usability is the capability of a software product to be understood, learned, used and liked by the user, when used under specified conditions. It includes the following sub-characteristics: understandability, learnability and operability. Usability indicates the understandability of software as well as the easiness to learn and operate it (Juristo et al., 2007).

Performance includes the set of attributes that bear on the relationship between the level of performance of the software product and the amount of resources used under stated conditions. It also relates to how quickly it responds to users (Kekre et al., 1995). It includes operational efficiency- the technical performance of the software; responsiveness-how well the software meets the needs of its users and flexibility- ability to support distinctly the new products or functions. In our research, the attribute efficiency is substituted by 'performance' of the software in our chosen list of software quality attributes (Andreou & Tziakouris, 2007; Khayami et al., 2008).

2.2. Determinants of Software Quality

Many previous researchers (Boehm, 2000; Dyba, 2005) have identified the factors influencing the success of software projects. While the perceptions of software practitioners vary considerably, Pereira et al. (2008) analyzed factors influencing success of software projects. Further, software quality has been considered as a surrogate measure of project success (Gorla & Lin, 2010). Kannabiran and Sankaran (2011) carried out a study in an Indian vendor through data of 70 projects, in which the impact of six factors, viz., requirements uncertainty, technical infrastructure, process maturity, knowledge transfer & integration, communication & control and trained manpower on the attributes of the software quality has been analyzed. Therefore, key determinants identified from the previous research that impact the software quality are presented in the following sections.

2.2.1. Requirements Uncertainty

A software project is conceptualized based on a set of requirements that are expected to satisfy some of the business objectives by creating value to its users (Gammelgard, 2007). Requirements uncertainty, the degree to which requirements changes during the project development process, which has a negative effect on final system quality (Zmud, 1980; Hsu et al., 2008). According to Pressman (2005), as requirements keep changing in the project life cycle, subsequent changes in the design and rework needs create disruptions in managing requirements and provide scope for defects. Requirements uncertainty has long been recognized as a major risk factor for IS development projects (Jiang and Klein, 2000; Jiang et al., 2002; Hickey and Davis, 2004). Davis (1982) is one of the earlier theorists to deal with the concept of requirements uncertainty. This concept is operationalized as the 'sum' of three variables viz., uncertainty deriving from the utilizing system, uncertainty deriving from the application and uncertainty deriving from the users and system analysts. A postmortem examination of failed IS projects reveals that interpersonal conflicts and uncertainty requirements are two significant symptoms (Kappelman et al., 2007).

Previous studies (Nidumolu, 1995; Harter et al. 2000; Wallace et al., 2004; Han & Huang, 2007) posit requirements uncertainty to be an important source of poor quality in software development in offshoring. Identifying all the requirements upfront and then developing the product is idealistic in today's software environment (Heberling, 1999). The managerial side of the software development project, meanwhile, is often conducted without adequate planning, with poor understanding of the overall development process, and a lack of a well-established management framework (Rai & Al-Hindi, 2000). Gopal and Koka (2009) observed while most studies have considered the effects of requirements uncertainty in in-house projects, its effects are magnified in the offshore domain due to barriers of geographical and organizational boundaries between the client and vendor. Further, when there is a user diversity in requirements, the vendor needs to address and reconcile the differences (Nidumolu, 1995). Therefore, it may be considered that requirements uncertainty will adversely affect the quality of software in offshored IS projects.

2.2.2. Technical Infrastructure

Technical Infrastructure (TI) is defined as the extent to which data and applications through communication networks can be shared and accessed for organizational use (Rajkumar & Mani, 2001; Guopeng & Bo, 2008). Jones (1998) identified that the improvement of infrastructure (support facilities) was one of the essential elements of successful development. Many researchers have found obsolescence of technologies as the major risk faced by software companies (Jalote, 2000, Ravichandran & Shareef, 2001). Therefore, the software quality paradigm had to incorporate a complete model of all aspects, including value, attitude and methodology (Fok et al., 2001). Therefore, it may be argued that a state-of-the-art TI enables software development process and helps to build quality software. Software Quality depends on availability of good tools, materials, methods and management techniques, and latest technological developments (Li et al., 2000). In the case of offshoring, several authors have expressed the need for telecommunication, software tools as part of the infrastructural facilities available for software development (Dedrick & Kramer, 2001; Sairamesh, 2002; Jennex et al., 2003). Thus, TI capability has been recognized as one of the key dimensions of IT capability of the vendor in existing information systems research for promoting software quality (Bharadwaj 2000; Santhanam & Hartono, 2003).

2.2.3. Knowledge Transfer and Integration

Software development is knowledge-intensive with high level of task interdependency, requiring the integration knowledge between client and service provider (Nicholson and Sahay, 2004). Knowledge transfer is an activity between individuals and organizations that allows the person or organization to absorb knowledge, apply it, and use it in project delivery (Wang et al., 2004; Teo & Bhattacherjee, 2013). Knowledge Transfer and Integration (KTI) is defined as the process of absorbing knowledge from the external sources and blending it with the technical and business skills, know-how, and expertise that reside in the business and IS units of a firm (Okhuysen and Eisenhardt, 2002; Tiwana et al., 2003). Knowledge Integration contains two parts, viz., Internal and external (Rus and Lindvall, 2002). Internal knowledge Integration refers to the extent to which the development team builds on the knowledge of the stakeholders during the development process. External integration refers to the knowledge relating to market needs, regulatory constraints, external environment and business and technical developments that may affect development project (Prahalad & Krishnan, 2002). Adopting the development project as the focal point, both external and internal integration are considered to be important in achieving quality (Lee 2001).

Based on field study of 82 firms in Korea, Kim et al (2010), found that potential knowledge complementarities are associated with IS offshoring effectiveness. In the case of offshoring, external integration would therefore measure the knowledge gained between the on shore and offshore unit as well as between the project teams, while internal integration would measure the knowledge gained within the teams. Based on a case study, Oshri et al. (2007) identified best practices for managing dispersed knowledge among onshore and offshore sites and acknowledged that knowledge transfer was a key part of successful offshoring. Finally, the adoption of a team-level perspective on IT knowledge integration involves individuals in an organization to perform in ways that allow it to exploit knowledge and to achieve desirable results (Klein & Kozlowski, 2000). Thus, such a perspective offers a finer level of granularity in understanding how employees integrate their knowledge to achieve higher performance in building software quality.

2.2.4. Process Maturity

Process maturity (PM) is defined as the indication of how close a developing process is being complete and capable of continuous improvement through quantitative measure and feedback (Jones, 2005). Many researchers have endorsed the view that process improvements are vital for improving software quality (Jalote, 2000; Li et al., 2000). Software development process is also viewed as vital for getting new products of good quality, quickly into the market (Rockart & Hoffman, 1992). Hevner (1997) observed that development of high-quality software is an essential business activity and improving the quality requires the effective use of a software development process. Therefore, to improve the product quality, the processes need to be improved continuously (Humphrey, 1989, Li, 2000). Maturity also implies a potential for growth in capability and indicates both the richness and consistency with which software processes are applied across the organization (Nidumolu 1995).

In the case of offshoring, the efficiency of the software development process is an important issue facing the researchers and practitioners (Wynekoop & Walz, 2000). Harter et al. (2000) observed that quality, cycle time and effort reduction can be simultaneously achieved by higher levels of CMM process maturity in software development. Researchers have shown that software process improvement activities could lead to less operating cost and better product reliability (Jiang et al., 2004). Subramanian et al., (2007) observed in their research study findings that higher CMM levels are associated with differing IS implementation strategies and improved software quality and project performance. The maturity of the vendor's communication processes can effectively handle degree of quality of information exchange (Blumenberg et al., 2008; Mao et al., 2008). Chen and Huang (2009) provided empirical evidence that process improvement can help in reducing the level of severity of the documentation quality and process management problems, thus help enhance software maintainability to a medium level. In light of the above background, it is proposed that process maturity has a positive association with software quality.

2.2.5. Trained Personnel

Trained Personnel (TP) relates to the competence and the level of skills of personnel in the software industry that are the main predictors of results. Software development is an intellectual activity that requires creative problem solving before and during the application of software processes, methodologies and tools (Osmundson et al., 2003). Trained personnel can easily adapt and perform in offshore projects without losing time. It is observed that trained programmers use better design techniques, are more aware of the link between requirements and systems parameters and are able to write better code (Pressman, 2005). Individual capability was found to be the most significant determinant of performance among the software developers. Studies have shown that a large number of software project failures are caused by personnel factors such as frequent turnover within the project team (Wallace et al., 2004), insufficient skills or experience (Jiang and Klein, 2000), lack of proper training (Han and Huang, 2007) and lack of commitment to the project (McDonough, 2000).

Many researchers have reported very significantly, the need of trained personnel and the effect of staff attrition in the offshore software development projects (Carmel & Agarwal 2001; Gopal et al. 2002; Mockus & Herbsleb 2003; Powell et al., 2004; Sahay et al., 2003; Khan et al., 2011). Further, the lack of trained personnel impacts quality of offshore projects in two ways: first, by the staffing of inexperienced and untrained personnel and second, by frequently shifting personnel between projects as managers seek to manage multiple projects with insufficient numbers of trained personnel (Gopal and Koka, 2009). Large variability in the quality of staff due to the frequent movement of developers also influences software quality (Nicholson & Sahay, 2004. The above observations from the past research strongly support the view that the availability of trained personnel for software development is of paramount importance.

2.2.6. Communication and Control

Proper communication and control (CC) among the developer teams is considered mandatory in order to achieve efficient software development process. CC is broadly defined as the proactive formal and informal sharing or exchange of meaningful and timely information between firms (Anderson & Narus, 1990). Particularly, this is viewed as more 'critical' in executing offshore development projects, as the communication between on-site and offshore teams is to be really effective and well-coordinated (Khan et al., 2011). Challenges in communication and coordination increases because of geographical distance and time-zone differences (Damian et al., 2007; Begal et al., 2008: Khan et al., 2011). Niazi et al. (2016) found communication is one of the top 3 factors which affects the success of the project. There will be much less contact and communication among employees who work in different time zones and the lack of face-to-face discussion can lead to a gradual loss of group cohesion (Rennecker, 2001; Guzdial et al., 2002).

According to Gopal et al (2002), communication and control mechanisms in offshore development reduce project uncertainty and thereby improve quality of software developed. Similarly, Grover et al (1996) and Han-Kuk Hong et al., (2008) found that good communication is the first important factor that helped the most successful companies achieves their project goals in offshoring. Communication was also found to be correlated positively with offshoring partnership quality (Lee and Kim, 1999). Knowledge of areas of potential misunderstandings enables the program manager to begin working on opening up the communication channels to better guide the development team's efforts and receive feedback on the processes and procedures which the program manager implements, enabling them to improve them (Osmundson et al., 2003), In light of the above findings reported by the previous research, it is understood that communication & control plays a key role in the in offshore development environment due to the challenges involved in achieving good communication between on-site and offshore teams.

3. RESEARCH MODEL AND HYPOTHESES

Researchers have identified specific quality factors namely, functionality, reliability, usability, maintainability and performance, along with their associated sub-characteristics for evaluating original software components (Rajendran et al., 2006; Andreou & Tziakouris, 2007; Williams & Carver, 2010; Chinnaiyan & Somasundaram, 2010). Previous researchers have also identified the key process characteristics that affect that affect software quality in general. It is also found clearly that despite few studies that focused on factors that impact software quality, quantitative survey-based research is lacking on studying the relationship between process characteristics (Gorla and Lin, 2010). Further, the projects carried out through offshoring are faced with many challenges due to the inherent complexities that need special attention to study the above relationship. Therefore, the objective this research is evaluate the impact of determinants on specific attribute of quality. The conceptual research model covering the dependent variables, software quality attributes and the independent variables, requirements uncertainty, process maturity, communication and control, knowledge transfer and integration, trained personnel and technical infrastructure is presented in Figure 1. The stated research objective along with its underlying conceptual research model is translated into sets of hypotheses and are presented below:

Set-1: Hypotheses related to Requirements Uncertainty:

$H_{1.1}$: Requirements uncertainty negatively influences the functionality of the software.

$H_{1.2}$: Requirements uncertainty negatively influences the reliability of the software.

$H_{1.3}$: Requirements uncertainty negatively influences the maintainability of the software.

$H_{1.4}$: Requirements uncertainty negatively influences the usability of the software.

$H_{1.5}$: Requirements uncertainty negatively influences the performance attribute of the software.

Set-2: Hypotheses related to Technical Infrastructure:

$H_{2.1}$: Technical Infrastructure facilities positively influence the functionality of the software.

$H_{2.2}$: Technical Infrastructure facilities positively influence the reliability of the software.

$H_{2.3}$: Technical Infrastructure facilities positively influence the maintainability of the software.

$H_{2.4}$: Technical Infrastructure facilities positively influence the usability of the software.

$H_{2.5}$: Technical Infrastructure facilities will positively influence the performance of the software.

Set-3: Hypotheses related to Trained Personnel:

$H_{3.1}$: Trained personnel available for the project positively influence the functionality of the software.

$H_{3.2}$: Trained personnel available for the project positively influence the reliability of the software.

$H_{3.3}$: Trained personnel available for the project positively influence the maintainability of the software.

$H_{3.4}$: Trained personnel available for the project positively influence the usability of the software.

$H_{3.5}$: Trained personnel available for the project positively influence the performance of the software.

Set-4: Hypotheses related to Knowledge Transfer and Integration:

$H_{4.1}$: Knowledge transfer and Integration positively influence the functionality of the software.

$H_{4.2}$: Knowledge transfer and Integration positively influence the reliability of the software.

$H_{4.3}$: Knowledge transfer and Integration positively influence the maintainability of the software.

$H_{4.4}$: Knowledge transfer and Integration positively influence the usability of the software.

$H_{4.5}$: Knowledge transfer and Integration positively influence the performance of the software.

Set-5: Hypotheses related to Communication & Control:

$H_{5.1}$: Communication & Control positively influence the functionality of the software.

$H_{5.2}$: Communication & Control positively influence the reliability of the software.

$H_{5.3}$: Communication & Control positively influence the maintainability of the software.

$H_{5.4}$: Communication & Control positively influence the usability of the software.

$H_{5.5}$: Communication & Control positively influence the performance of the software.

Set-6: Hypotheses related to Process Maturity:

$H_{6.1}$: Process maturity positively influence the functionality of the software.

$H_{6.2}$: Process maturity positively influence the reliability of the software.

$H_{6.3}$: Process maturity positively influence the maintainability of the software.

$H_{6.4}$: Process maturity positively influence the usability of the software.

$H_{6.5}$: Process maturity positively influence the performance of the software.

4. RESEARCH METHODOLOGY

The scale development has been based on an exhaustive survey of literature and discussions with senior executives and project managers in software companies. The scales of the constructs were developed in following three stages: (1) the scales were based on those used and reported in prior work (Nidumolu,

1995; Ravichandran and Rai, 2000; Rajendran et al., 2006; Gopal and Koka, 2009); (2) senior project managers of various software companies were consulted to verify the applicability of the various constructs used in our study. Thus, the content validity, and face validity of the instrument have been assured in the initial stages of questionnaire development; and (3) a pilot study was conducted involving senior managers, project managers and/or leads of software firms to further refine the scales and to develop a survey instrument. Based on inputs from the respondents of the pilot study, the modified final research questionnaire was designed.

Figure 1. Conceptual research model

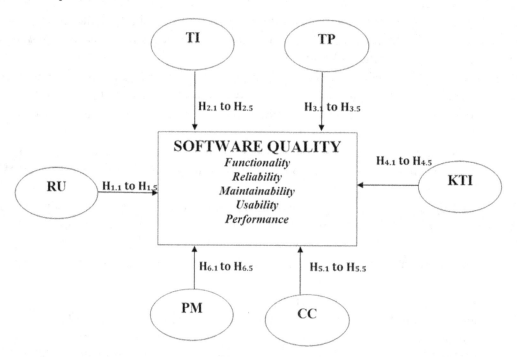

Items related to measure software quality attributes viz., functionality, reliability, maintainability, usability and performance were measured using a 5-point Likert Scale (strongly disagree, disagree, neutral, agree and strongly agree). Similarly, items related to measure the determinants, viz., requirements uncertainty, technical infrastructure, knowledge transfer and integration, process maturity, trained personnel and communication and control were also measured using a 5-point Likert scale. To ensure correct comprehension of the terminology used and also to level the participants' understanding of the concepts, a brief explanation of the research objectives was provided at the beginning of the survey instrument.

The final research questionnaire was divided into three sections. The first section was related to general details regarding the nature of software project like industry vertical, duration, project team size, technology platform, country of the client and process maturity level of the vendor. The second section covered the software quality which was further subdivided into 5 sub-sections namely, functionality, reliability, maintainability, usability and performance, each carrying questions anywhere between 4 and

6. The third section was pertaining to the independent variables with each variable contained questions in the range between 4 and 9.

The population of the study was project managers and leads were involved in managing software projects for clients through offshoring. Participants of the survey were requested to respond to the survey based on the most recently completed development project, which was managed by them. The sample size for the study was determined using the sample size determination for the fraction method and the organizations were chosen based on their size. However, the choice of respondents chosen from the vendor organizations was based on simple random sampling. Ten leading software firms were chosen and the HR-Heads of each firm was contacted and chosen 100 respondents for administering the survey. Out of a total of 1000 questionnaires distributed, 464 responses were received out of which 24 responses were rejected due to incomplete information and finally 440 responses were considered for data analysis. Thus, the response rate for the survey worked out to be 46.4% which is viewed to be quite good and acceptable.

5. DATA ANALYSIS AND INTERPRETATION

5.1. Validity and Reliability Analysis

The reliability is evaluated by assessing the internal consistency of the items representing each construct using Cronbach's alpha. The reliability of each construct is shown in Table 1 and all Cronbach's values are above 0.70 indicating that the scales have good reliability (Pedhazur and Schmelkin, 1991). After, verifying the scales using reliability analysis, confirmatory factor analysis (CFA) was performed using structural equation modeling to further test their convergent and discriminant validity.

Table 1. Reliability, unidimensionality and convergent validity results for constructs

Factor/Construct	No of Items	Cronbach's Alpha	CFI*	NFI**
Functionality	4	0.75	1.00	0.99
Reliability	4	0.79	0.98	0.98
Maintainability	6	0.85	0.98	0.98
Usability	4	0.81	0.78	0.78
Performance	5	0.80	1.00	1.00
Requirements Uncertainty	9	0.71	0.99	0.99
Technical Infrastructure	4	0.79	0.99	0.99
Knowledge Transfer and Integration	8	0.81	0.99	1.00
Process Maturity	6	0.88	0.99	0.99
Trained Personnel	4	0.70	0.95	0.94
Communication and Control	6	0.82	0.99	0.99
Cronbach's Alpha Value > 0.7 confirms reliability				
*CFI=Comparative Fit Index >0.90 indicates Unidimensionality				
** NFI=Normed Fit Index(Bentler-Bonnet Index) >0.90 indicates Convergent Validity				

5.2. Content Validity and Convergent Validity

To validate our measurement model, content validity, construct validity, convergent validity, and discriminant validity were assessed. Content validity was established by ensuring consistency between the measurement items and the extant literature. This was done by interviewing senior practitioners and pilot-testing the instrument. Convergent validity is shown by large significant correlations between each latent variable and its reflective indicators. The results of the CFA consisting of both Normed Fit Index (NFI) and Comparative Fit Index (CFI) are shown in Table 1, verifying the Convergent validity and Unidimensionality of the constructs under the study.

Convergent validity should be assured when multiple indicators are used to measure one construct. Convergent validity can be examined by the composite reliability of constructs which is recommended to be >0.7 (Fornell and Larcker, 1981; Kerlinger, 1986). The convergent validity was assessed by reviewing the t-tests for the factor loadings and by examining composite reliability (Hair et al., 1998). According to Chin (1998), many studies have used 0.5 as the threshold reliability of the measures against 0.7 which is a recommended value for a reliable construct. As shown in Table 2, composite reliability values range from 0.56 to 0.64, thus satisfying the acceptable values.

Table 2. Composite reliability and AVE results for constructs

Factor/Construct	No of Items	Composite Reliability
Functionality	4	0.56
Reliability	4	0.59
Maintainability	6	0.58
Usability	4	0.60
Performance	5	0.56
Requirements Uncertainty	6	0.58
Technical Infrastructure	4	0.58
Knowledge Transfer and Integration	8	0.60
Process Maturity	6	0.64
Trained Personnel	4	0.57
Communication and Control	6	0.56

If correlations between the latent variables themselves are significantly less than one, then that is an indication of Discriminant validity between the constructs (Kline, 1998). In order to ensure Discriminant validity of constructs of both dependent and independent variables, inter-correlations among the constructs are compared with square root of AVE and presented in Table 3 and Table 4 respectively. For the average variance extracted by a measure, a score of 0.5 indicates acceptability (Fornell & Larcker, 1981). In this study, the constructs have satisfied this criterion and thus supporting the Discriminant validity for the constructs as shown in Tables 3 and 7.

5.3. Structural Equation Modeling

The structural model tested in the present study is shown in Figure 2. This model was estimated using AMOS 16.0.

Table 3. Construct inter-correlations and evidence of discriminant validity of dependent variables

	Functionality[FUN]	Reliability [REL]	Maintainability [MAT]	Usability [USA]	Performance [PER]
FUN	0.692				
REL	0.530**	0.712			
MAT	0.602**	0.664**	0.703		
USA	0.510**	0.570**	0.663**	0.720	
PER	0.584**	0.601**	0.652**	0.646**	0.681

** Correlation is significant at the 0.01 level (2-tailed); shaded diagonal elements are the square root of shared variance between the constructs and their measures

Table 4. Construct inter-correlations and evidence of discriminant validity independent variables

	RU	TI	KTI	PM	TP	CC
RU	0.728					
TI	0.257**	0.699				
KTI	0.302**	0.568**	0.736			
PM	0.397**	0.640**	0.520**	0.762		
TP	0.369**	0.607**	0.480**	0.689**	0.691	
CC	0.362**	0.640**	0.473**	0.668**	0.610**	0.677

** Correlation is significant at the 0.01 level (2-tailed); shaded diagonal elements are the square root of shared variance between the constructs and their measures

Several goodness of fit indices of the measurement of the model that have been widely used in IS research are presented in Table 5.

The Goodness- of- fit index (GFI), Bentler-Bonett fit index, also known as the Normed Fit Index (NFI), and the Comparative Fit Index (CFI) are all above 0.90, suggesting a good fit between the structural model and the data. RMSEA is well below the suggested threshold value of 0.08 (Brwone & Cudeck, 1992). All of these fit indices are acceptable, suggesting that the overall structural model provides a good fit with the data.

5.4. Evaluation of the Structural Model

In the structural model, as many as 12 paths are significant and positive, supporting the corresponding hypotheses. A summary of the hypotheses test results is provided in Table 6.

Figure 2. Structural model for determinants of software quality

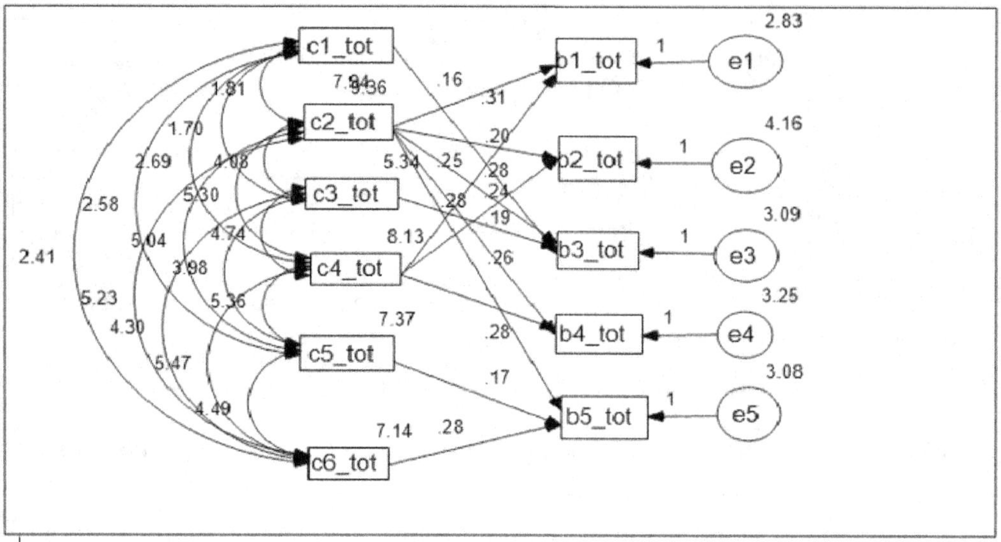

Legend:

INDEPENDENT VARIABLES	DEPENDENT VARIABLES
C1_tot ----> Requirements Uncertainty	b1_tot ---> Functionality
C2_tot ----> Technical Infrastructure	b2_tot ----> Reliability
C3_tot ----> Knowledge transfer and Integration	b3_tot -----> Maintainability
C4_tot ----> Process Maturity	b4_tot -----> Usability
C5_tot----> Trained Personnel	b5_tot -----> Performance
C6_tot----> Communication & Control	

Table 5. Model fit summary – SQ model

Chi-Square Value (p=0.058)	54.85
DF	38
Normed Fit Index (NFI)	0.968
Comparative Fit Index (CFI)	0.996
Goodness of Fit Index (GFI)	0.989
Root Mean Square Error of Approximation (RMSEA)	0.019
Root Mean Square Standardized Residual (RMSR)	0.025

5. RESULTS AND DISCUSSION

The main objective of the study is to investigate the relationship between the determinants and attributes of software quality in offshore projects. In the structural model, many of the paths are significant and positive, supporting the corresponding hypotheses. Our findings show to what extent the specific factors impact on attributes of software quality. Based on the results in Table 6, we present the findings in this section.

Table 6. Summary of the structural model fit for accepted hypotheses

Structural Path	Hypothesis	Beta Coefficient	t-value	Decision
Requirements Uncertainty→ Maintainability	$H_{1.3}$	0.196	4.872***	Supported
Technical Infrastructure->Functionality	$H_{2.1}$	0.161	3.751***	Supported
Technical Infrastructure -> Reliability	$H_{2.2}$	0.309	5.927***	Supported
Technical Infrastructure -> Maintainability	$H_{2.3}$	0.275	6.283***	Supported
Technical Infrastructure -> Usability	$H_{2.4}$	0.194	4.198***	Supported
Technical Infrastructure -> Performance	$H_{2.5}$	0.260	5.257***	Supported
Trained Personnel → Performance	$H_{3.5}$	0.167	3.065***	Supported
Knowledge Transfer and Integration→ Maintainability	$H_{4.3}$	0.242	1.117***	Supported
Communication & Control → Performance	$H_{5.5}$	0.281	4.905***	Supported
Process Maturity → Functionality	$H_{6.1}$	0.246	5.322***	Supported
Process Maturity ->Reliability	$H_{6.2}$	0.225	5.038***	Supported
Process Maturity ->Usability	$H_{6.4}$	0.277	5.586***	Supported
** $P < 0.01$ (Significant at 99% Confidence Level) *** $p < 0.001$ (significant at 99.9% Confidence Level)				
Beta => Structural Path Coefficient / Standardized Partial Regression Coefficient				

Out of the five hypotheses ($H_{1.1}$, $H_{1.2}$ $H_{1.3}$, $H_{1.4}$ and $H_{1.5}$) proposed to study the relationship between requirements uncertainty and the software quality attributes, except $H_{1.3}$, the rest of the hypotheses are not supported. Hence, requirements uncertainty affects the maintainability of the software. All the five hypotheses ($H_{2.1}$, $H_{2.2}$ $H_{2.3}$, $H_{2.4}$ and $H_{2.5}$) proposed for the relationship between Technical Infrastructure and software quality attributes, are supported as per the results of structural model. However, hypotheses $H_{2.2}$, $H_{2.3}$ and $H_{2.5}$ exhibit stronger impact of the Technical Infrastructure with the quality attributes, viz., reliability ($\beta = 0.309$), maintainability ($\beta = 0.275$) and performance ($\beta = 0.260$) with larger β values. In the case of Trained Personnel, out of the five hypotheses ($H_{3.1}$, $H_{3.2}$, $H_{3.3}$, $H_{3.4}$ and $H_{3.5}$), except $H_{3.5}$, the rest of the hypotheses are not supported. Hence, trained personnel positively affect the performance of the software.

In the case of Knowledge Transfer and Integration and quality attributes, out of the five hypotheses ($H_{4.1}$, $H_{4.2}$ $H_{4.3}$, $H_{4.4}$ and $H_{4.5}$) proposed, except $H_{4.3}$, the rest of the hypotheses are not supported. Hence, KTI positively affects the maintainability of the software. Out of the five hypotheses ($H_{5.1}$, $H_{5.2}$ $H_{5.3}$, $H_{5.4}$ and $H_{5.5}$) proposed for the relationship between communication & control and the software quality attributes, except $H_{5.5}$, the rest of the hypotheses are not supported. Hence, communication & control has strong impact on the performance of the software. Out of the five hypotheses ($H_{6.1}$, $H_{6.2}$ $H_{6.3}$, $H_{6.4}$ and $H_{6.5}$) proposed for the relationship between process maturity and the software quality attributes, hypotheses $H_{6.3}$ and $H_{6.5}$ are not supported. The results reveal that process maturity has significant positive impact on functionality ($\beta = 0.246$), reliability ($\beta = 0.225$) and relatively stronger impact on usability ($\beta = 0.277$) attributes of software quality.

Previous researchers have pointed out the inadequacy and insufficiency of empirical studies investigating factors that impact software quality, especially quantitative survey-based research (Verner & Evanco, 2005; Gorla and Lin, 2010). The present research has significant contributions based on the data from Indian vendors. It provides quantitative evidence of how the determinants affect the specific attributes of quality. Our analysis clearly indicates that Technical Infrastructure (TI) and Process maturity (PM) have significant impact on the attributes of software quality compared to other factors.

Requirements Uncertainty (RU) has been identified as a key factor which poses lot of challenges in the project execution, particularly in the case of offshore software projects (Gopal & Koka, 2009; Gorla & Lin, 2010; Rothenberger et al., 2010). As requirements keep changing throughout the life cycle of the project, subsequent changes to the design and the need for rework creates disruptions in the organization's processes for managing requirements resulting in significant scope for defects (Pressman, 2005). Thus, research findings are in line with the past research wherein RU has been a key factor affecting quality in software development (Nidumolu, 1995; Harter et al., 2000). Our research shows that RU has no significant impact on functionality, reliability, usability and performance. Normally in the case of offshoring, a team of members stay on-site with the clients and gather the requirements and then pass on to the off-shore team for further development in a coordinated approach. Over a period, vendors have improved their processes to precisely capture the requirements and thereby satisfy these quality requirements. However, our findings show that RU affects the maintainability attribute of software quality. This is likely because of dynamic changes in the business and therefore the solution needs to be maintained to meet the changing requirements. It may be understood that inherent offshoring approach does not provide the necessary opportunities to foresee the changes in the business requirements to develop a solution, which requires less maintenance.

The research shows that the technical infrastructure (TI) is the foremost determinant, as the quality of products also relies on good tools, good materials, good methods and management techniques, including the latest technological developments (Li et al., 2000). In this research, it is found that TI becomes very critical in the case of software quality, where the technological advancement is at a very rapid pace and the adaptation of technological advancement is compulsory for the very survival and sustained growth of software organizations (Jalote, 2000; Ravichandran & Shareef, 2001). It is also found that TI has strong impact on all quality attributes, viz. functionality, reliability, maintainability, and performance in the offshoring context. Technology-driven software development has been the hallmark of the offshoring vendors in India. To that extent, vendors extensively use automated tools such as CASE for the entire life-cycle, re-usable components, partnership with technology providers and high-end communication for remote testing and implementation. Use of technology helps the vendors to ensure error-free development thus leading to reliable and easily maintainable applications for the clients. TI also helps to optimize the components relating core functionalities and therefore offers better performance.

This research reinforces the previous research findings with regard to the role of process maturity in ensuring the SQ (Li et al., 2000; Jalote, 2000; Rajkumar & Mani, 2001; Subramanian et al., 2007). Researchers have shown that software process improvement activities could lead to less operating cost and better product reliability (Jiang et al., 2004). It is due to the fact that most of the vendors have achieved higher levels of process maturity and are certified at CMM level 5. The new contribution through this research is that PM has strong influence on the quality attributes, viz. functionality, reliability and usability in the offshoring context. PM provides the discipline for all the core activities of development and therefore contributes towards achieving these attributes. However, its non-impact on maintainability and performance shows that the present level of maturity focuses more on the core and immediate benefits and not necessarily on the long-term use and benefits to the clients.

The research outcomes support the importance of availability of trained personnel (TP) as one of the most perennial problems faced by offshore vendors is the increasing difficulty in attracting and retaining trained personnel (Gopal & Koka, 2009). Lack of proper training of developers was identified as a challenge affecting the development process (Wallace et al., 2004; Han and Huang, 2007). People are critical success factors for knowledge intensive software projects and people focus is crucial for success of offshore projects (Jensen and Menon, 2007). However, our research shows that TP has no significant impact on functionality, reliability, maintainability and usability. However, TP has impact on performance in the offshoring context. This may be explained as major parts of the projects are developed through automated methodologies and tools, the differential value, viz 'performance' is achieved through trained personnel. The availability of TP will enable vendors to move up the value chain through consulting engagements and package development and implementation.

The research results support that communication and control is a key organizational factor, found to have a significant positive influence on the software quality (Gopal et al., 2002; Han-Kuk Hong et al., 2008). It is observed that the communication among the team members is important in the software development, particularly, in the context of offshore outsourcing (Powell et al. 2004). The study reveals the importance assigned to the communication processes among various teams functioning at both on-site and offshore locations as observed and by many researchers (Herbsleb & Moitra, 2001; Osmundson et al., 2003) in the software development projects, particularly, in the context of offshore projects. Thus, this research subscribes to the view that communication and control, viewed as a key factor, found to have a significant positive influence on SQ. This research shows that CC has impact on specific quality attribute, namely performance in the offshoring context. It may be concluded that better CC enables teams in onsite and offshore to tightly synchronize the requirements and the able to develop and implement the systems, thus contributing towards high performance.

Previous research works showed the knowledge transfer & integration (KTI) as one of the main inputs for quality software development (Faraj and Sproull, 2000; Tiwana et al., 2003). Previous research also revealed that software development can be viewed as a process of integrating technical and business domain knowledge in developing a solution to a business problem (Rus and Lindvall, 2002; Patnayakuni et al., 2006). The research reveals that the KTI influences the maintainability of the systems and does not affect other factors. In the case of an offshore project, external integration gained between the onsite and offshore unit as well as between the project teams helps to improve the maintainability of the system. It is also due to the fact that the vendors have better knowledge levels of the clients' contexts based on continuous learning thus able to meet the quality requirements. However, KTI is likely to impact functionality, reliability, usability and performance as vendors move up the value chain through consulting and implementation of packaged solutions.

6. IMPLICATIONS FOR PRACTICE

This study has attempted to identify the key determinants which influence the SQ during the software development by the vendor. In the light of increasing pressures on managers to improve software quality and the growing importance of quality management systems in vendor organizations this study is both timely and significant. Our research has significant implications for practitioners in this field. Our findings show that technical infrastructure and process maturity have significant impact on achieving the overall quality. Therefore, organizations need to ensure that the above aspects are managed better to achieve consistent quality levels.

In the case of TI, although it impacts all quality attributes, it has more influence on the reliability, maintainability and usability of the software. Development projects, which are executed through high-end automated tools such as CASE, and use of reusable-code, would enable vendors to achieve higher levels of reliability and maintainability. Most of the large Indian vendors have achieved higher levels of process maturity and are certified at level 5 CMM. Such levels of process maturity are observed to impact functionality, reliability and usability attributes of software quality. However, the practitioners need to focus on maintainability, and performance, which result in long-term use and benefits to the clients. It shows that practitioners need to consider continuous improvement in their processes. Such process improvements would help the vendors to create mutual value as they move the value chain through consulting, package implementation and delivering value through software as service. Such engagements would need participation of more organizations like technology providers, beyond the clients and vendors.

Our research indicates that RU affecting maintainability shows the importance of gathering the requirements comprehensively in the case of offshoring. It is also to be noted that practitioners need to concentrate on capturing system requirements properly along with transfer of domain knowledge so that resulting systems are maintainable. Major parts of the projects are developed through automated methodologies and tools, the differential value, viz 'performance' is achieved through trained personnel. Similarly, communication and control were a key organizational factor, found to have a significant positive influence on the performance of the software. In the same line, KTI impacts maintainability and other factors are not affected probably due to the fact that the vendors have better knowledge levels of the clients' contexts. These factors are likely to have wider impact on as vendors move up the value chain through consulting and package development and implementation.

7. CONCLUSION

Considering the fact that in the software quality literature, there are very few empirical studies on offshore software development quality from the vendor's perspective, we hope our research, which explores and identifies the key factors that need to be addressed for ensuring high quality offshore software development, represents a significant attempt to fill this gap. This research study has evaluated and compared the impact of key process attributes on the attributes of software quality in offshore development projects delivered by Indian vendors. Two determinants namely, technical infrastructure and process maturity affect most of the quality attributes. The vendors have established very strong infrastructure and almost all the organizations that were considered for the study were certified for high level of maturity.

There are some limitations. This study has focused on external quality based on primary data collected from project managers and leads from vendors, but not from client organizations. Responses from clients on quality attributes are likely to be different from project managers' responses. In addition, the data is collected only from Indian vendors and therefore has limitations on generalizability. However, the results may be applicable to projects executed in similar geographies or environments. Future studies may explore the impact of project size and project type as variables affecting software quality. Comparative studies of software projects relating to different industry verticals such as banking, healthcare, retail, and others, will be useful to develop and deploy appropriate quality management approaches.

REFERENCES

Agarwal, M., & Chari, K. (2007). Software effort, quality, and cycle time: A study of CMM level 5 projects. *IEEE Transactions on Software Engineering*, *33*(3), 145–156. doi:10.1109/TSE.2007.29

Al-Qutaish, R. (2009). Measuring the Software Product Quality during the Software Development Life-Cycle: An International Organization for Standardization Standards Perspective. *Journal of Computational Science*, (5): 392–397.

Andreou, A. S., & Tziakouris, M. (2007). A quality framework for developing and evaluating original software components. *Information and Software Technology*, *49*(2), 122–141. doi:10.1016/j.infsof.2006.03.007

Anderson, J., & Narus, J. (1990). A model of distributor firm and manufacturer firm working partnerships. *Journal of Marketing*, *54*(1), 42–58. doi:10.1177/002224299005400103

Ashrafi, N. (2003). The impact of software process improvement on quality: In theory and practice. *Information & Management*, *40*(7), 677–690. doi:10.1016/S0378-7206(02)00096-4

Begel, A., & Nagappan, N. (2008, August). Global software development: Who does it? *Proceedings of the IEEE International Conference on Global Software Engineering ICGSE 2008* (pp. 195-199). IEEE.

Behkamal, B., Kahani, M., & Akbari, M. K. (2009). Customizing ISO 9126 quality model for evaluation of B2B applications. *Information and Software Technology*, *51*(3), 599–609. doi:10.1016/j.infsof.2008.08.001

Bharadwaj, A. S. (2000). A resource-based perspective on information technology capability and firm performance: An empirical investigation. *Management Information Systems Quarterly*, *24*(1), 169–196. doi:10.2307/3250983

Blumenberg, S., Beimborn, D., & Koenig, W. (2008, January). Determinants of IT outsourcing relationships: a conceptual model. *Proceedings of the 41st Annual Hawaii International Conference on System Sciences* (pp. 12-12). IEEE. 10.1109/HICSS.2008.119

Boegh, J. (2008). A new standard for quality requirement. *IEEE Software*, *25*(March/April), 57–62. doi:10.1109/MS.2008.30

Boehm, B. (2000) Project termination doesn't equal project failure. *IEEE Computer*, (September), 94-96.

Brwone, M. W., & Cudeck, R. (1992). Alternative ways of assessing model fit. *Sociological Methods & Research*, *21*(2), 230–258. doi:10.1177/0049124192021002005

Carmel, E., & Agarwal, R. (2001). Tactical Approaches for Alleviating Distance in Global Software Development. *IEEE Software*, *18*(March/April), 22–29. doi:10.1109/52.914734

Carmel, E., & Agarwal, R. (2002). The Maturation of Offshore Sourcing of Information Technology Work. *MIS Quarterly Executive*, *1*(2), 65–78.

Chin, W. (1998). Issues and Opinion on Structural Equation Modeling. *MIS Quarterly*, *22*(1), vii-xvi.

Chinnaiyan, R., & Somasundaram, S. (2010). Evaluating the reliability of component based software systems. *International Journal of Quality & Reliability Management*, *27*(1), 78–88. doi:10.1108/02656711011009326

Conchúir, E. Ó., Ågerfalk, P. J., Olsson, H. H., & Fitzgerald, B. (2009). Global software development: Where are the benefits? *Communications of the ACM*, *52*(8), 127–131. doi:10.1145/1536616.1536648

Damian, D., Izquierdo, L., Singer, J., & Kwan, I. (2007). Awareness in the wild: why communication breakdowns occur. *Presented at the Second IEEE International Conference on Global Software Engineering* (pp. 81-90). IEEE. 10.1109/ICGSE.2007.13

Davis, G. B. (1982). Strategies for information requirements determination. *IBM Systems Journal*, *21*(1), 3–30. doi:10.1147j.211.0004

Davis, G., Ein-Dor, P. R., King, W., & Torkzadeh, R. (2006). IT offshoring: History, prospects and challenges. *Journal of the Association for Information Systems*, *7*(1), 32.

Dedrick, J., & Kraemer, K. L. (2001). China IT Report. *The Electronic Journal on Information Systems in Developing Countries*, *6*(2), 1–10. doi:10.1002/j.1681-4835.2001.tb00007.x

Deshpande, S., Beecham, S., & Richardson, I. (2011). Global software development coordination strategies-a vendor perspective. In *New Studies in Global IT and Business Service Outsourcing* (pp. 153-174). Springer.

Dromey, R. C. (1995). A model of software product quality. *IEEE Transactions on Software Engineering*, *21*(February), 146–162. doi:10.1109/32.345830

Dyba, T. (2005). An empirical investigation of the key factors for success in software process improvement. *IEEE Transactions on Software Engineering*, *31*(5), 410–424. doi:10.1109/TSE.2005.53

Ethiraj, S. K., Kale, P., Krishnan, M. S., & Singh, J. V. (2005). Where Do Capabilities Come From and How Do They Matter? A Study in the Software Services Industry. *Strategic Management Journal*, *26*(1), 25–45. doi:10.1002mj.433

Faraj, S., & Sproull, L. (2000). Coordinating Expertise in Software Development Teams. *Management Science*, *46*(12), 1554–1568.

Fok, L. Y., Fok, W. M., & Hartman, S. J. (2001). Exploring the relationship between total quality management and information system development. *Information & Management*, *38*(6), 355–371. doi:10.1016/S0378-7206(00)00075-6

Fornell, C., & Larcker, D. F. (1981). Structural equation models with unobservable variables and measurement errors: Algebra and statistics. *JMR, Journal of Marketing Research*, *18*(2), 39–50. doi:10.1177/002224378101800104

Gammelgard, M. (2007). Business value assessment of IT investments – An evaluation method applied to the electrical power industry [PhD Thesis]. Royal Institute of Technology (KTH), Stockholm, Sweden.

Glass, R.L. (1998). Defining Quality Intuitively. *IEEE Software*, (May/June), 103-107

Gopal, A., Mukhapadhyay, T., & Krishnan, M. S. (2002). Role of software processes and communication in offshore software development. *Communications of the ACM*, *45*(4), 193–200. doi:10.1145/505248.506008

Gopal, A., & Koka, B. (2009). Determinants of Service Quality in Offshore Software Outsourcing. In Information Systems Outsourcing: Enduring Themes (3rd ed.). Springer.

Gorla, N., & Lin, S. C. (2010). Determinants of software quality: A survey of information systems project managers. *Information and Software Technology*, *52*(6), 602–610. doi:10.1016/j.infsof.2009.11.012

Grover, V., Cheon, M. J., & Teng, J. T. C. (1996). The effect of service quality and partnership on the Outsourcing functions. *Journal of Management Information Systems*, *12*(4), 89–116. doi:10.1080/07421222.1996.11518102

Yin, G., & Yang, B. (2008, October). Key capabilities for Chinese software services vendors in IT offshore outsourcing. *Proceedings of the 2008 4th International Conference on Wireless Communications, Networking and Mobile Computing* (pp. 1-4). IEEE.

Guzdial, M., Ludovice, P., Realff, M., Morley, T., & Carroll, K. (2002). When collaboration doesn't work. *Proc. Of international conference of the learning sciences* (pp. 125-130). Academic Press.

Han, W. M., & Huang, S. J. (2007). An empirical analysis of risk components and performance on software projects. *Journal of Systems and Software*, *80*(1), 42–50. doi:10.1016/j.jss.2006.04.030

Hong, H.-K., Kim, J.-S., Kim, T., & Leem, B.-H. (2008). The effect of knowledge on system integration project performance. *Industrial Management & Data Systems*, *108*(3), 385–404. doi:10.1108/02635570810858787

Hair, J. F., & Jr, R. E. (1998). *Anderson, R. L. Tatham, W. C. Black, Multivariate Data Analysis*. New Jersey: Prentice-Hall International.

Harter, D. E., Krishnan, M. S., & Slaughter, S. A. (2000). Effects of process maturity on quality, cycle time, and effort in software product development. *Management Science*, *46*(4), 461–475. doi:10.1287/mnsc.46.4.451.12056

Heberling, J. (1999). Software change management. *Software Development*, *7*(7), S7–S11.

Herbsleb, J. D., & Moitra, D. (2001). Global software development. *IEEE Software*, *18*(March/April), 16–20. doi:10.1109/52.914732

Hevner, A. R. (1997). Phase containment metrics for software quality improvement. *Information and Software Technology*, *39*(13), 867–877. doi:10.1016/S0950-5849(97)00050-5

Huang, S.-J., & Han, W.-M. (2006). Selection priority of process a areas based on CMMI continuous representation. *Information & Management*, *43*(3), 297–307. doi:10.1016/j.im.2005.08.003

Humphrey, W. S. (1989). *Managing the Software Process*. Reading, MA: Addison Wesley.

Issac, G., Rajendran, C., & Anantharaman, R. N. (2004). A Conceptual framework for Total Quality Management in Software Organizations. *Total Quality Management*, *15*(3), 307–344. doi:10.1080/1478336042000183398

Jalote, P. (2000). *CMM in Practice*. Massachusetts: Addison Wesley, Longman.

Jennex, M. E., Amroso, D., & Adelakun, O. (2003). E-Commerce Infrastructure Success factors for Small Companies in Developing economies. *Electronic Commerce Research*, *4*(3/4).

Jensen, M., & Menon, S. (2007) Managing Offshore Outsourcing of Knowledge-intensive Projects –A People Centric Approach. *Proceedings of the International Conference on Global Software Engineering (ICGSE 2007)*. IEEE Computer Society. 10.1109/ICGSE.2007.28

Jiang, J. J., & Klein, G. (2000). Software development risks to project effectiveness. *Journal of Systems and Software*, *52*(1), 3–10. doi:10.1016/S0164-1212(99)00128-4

Jiang, J. J., Klein, G., & Discenza, R. (2002). Perceptions of software success: Provider and user views of system metrics. *Journal of Systems and Software*, *63*(1), 17–27. doi:10.1016/S0164-1212(01)00135-2

Jiang, J. J., Klein, G., Hwang, H. G., Huang, J., & Hung, S.-Y. (2004). An exploration of the relationship between software development process maturity and project performance. *Information & Management*, *41*(3), 279–288. doi:10.1016/S0378-7206(03)00052-1

Chen, J.-C., & Huang, S.-J. (2009). Sun-Jen Huang, An empirical analysis of the impact of Software Development problem factors on software maintainability. *Journal of Systems and Software*, *82*(6), 981–992. doi:10.1016/j.jss.2008.12.036

Jimenez, M., Piattini, M., & Vizcaino, A. (2009). Challenges and improvements in distributed software development: A systematic review. Advances in Software Engineering.

Jones, C. R. (1998). Customer focused performance improvement: Developing a strategy for total quality. *International Journal of Technology Management*, *16*(4/5/6), 494–504. doi:10.1504/IJTM.1998.002675

Jung, H. W. (2007). Validating the external quality sub-characteristics of software products according to ISO/IEC 9126. *Computer Standards & Interfaces*, *29*(6), 653–661. doi:10.1016/j.csi.2007.03.004

Juristo, N., Moreno, A. M., & Sanchez-Segura, M. I. (2007). Analysing the impact of usability on software design. *Journal of Systems and Software*, *80*(9), 1506–1516. doi:10.1016/j.jss.2007.01.006

Kekre, S., Krishnan, M. S., & Srinivasan, K. (1995). Drivers of customer satisfaction for software products: Implication for design and service support. *Management Science*, *41*(9), 1456–1470. doi:10.1287/mnsc.41.9.1456

Kappelman, L. A., McKeeman, R., & Zhang, L. (2007). Early warning signs of IT project failure: The dominant dozen. *EDPACS*, *35*(1), 1–10. doi:10.1080/07366980701238939

Kerlinger, F.N. (1986). *Foundations of Behavioral Research*. New York: McGraw Hill.

Khan, N., Currie, W., Weerakkody, V., & Desai, B. (2003), Evaluating offshore IT outsourcing in India: supplier and customer scenarios. *Proceedings of the 36th Hawaii International Conference on Systems Sciences (HICSS'03)*. IEEE. 10.1109/HICSS.2003.1174617

Khan, S. U., Niazi, M., & Ahmad, R. (2009). Critical success factors for offshore software development outsourcing vendors: a systematic literature review. *Proceedings of the 2009 Fourth IEEE International Conference on Global Software Engineering*. IEEE. 10.1109/ICGSE.2009.28

Khan, S. U., Niazi, M., & Ahmad, R. (2011). Barriers in the selection of offshore software development outsourcing vendors: An exploratory study using a systematic literature review. *Information and Software Technology*, *53*(7), 693–706. doi:10.1016/j.infsof.2010.08.003

Khan, A. A., Keung, J., Niazi, M., Hussain, S., & Ahmad, A. (2017). Systematic literature review and empirical investigation of barriers to process improvement in global software development: Client–vendor perspective. *Information and Software Technology, 87*, 180–205. doi:10.1016/j.infsof.2017.03.006

Khayami, S. R., Towhidi, A., & Ziarati, R. (2008). Measurable characteristics of a software system on software architecture level. *International Review on Computers and Software, 3*(3), 234–239.

Kim, K. K., Shin, H. K., & Lee, M. H. (2010). The influence of partner knowledge complementarities on the effectiveness of IT outsourcing. *Journal of Organizational Computing and Electronic Commerce, 20*(3), 213–233. doi:10.1080/10919392.2010.494519

Kline, R. B. (1998). *Principles and Practice of Structural Equation Modeling*. New York: The Guilford Press.

Klein, K. J., & Kozlowski, S. W. (2000). From micro to meso: Critical steps in conceptualizing and conducting multilevel research. *Organizational Research Methods, 3*(3), 211–236. doi:10.1177/109442810033001

Krishnan, M. S., Kriebel, C. H., Kekre, S., & Mukhopadhyay, T. (2000). An empirical analysis of productivity and quality in software products. *Management Science, 46*(6), 745–759. doi:10.1287/mnsc.46.6.745.11941

Kroeger, T. A., Davidson, N. J., & Cook, S. C. (2014). Understanding the characteristics of quality for software engineering processes: A Grounded Theory investigation. *Information and Software Technology, 56*(2), 252–271. doi:10.1016/j.infsof.2013.10.003

Kroll, J., Richardson, I., Audy, J. L., & Fernandez, J. (2014, January). Handoffs management in follow-the-sun software projects: a case study. *Proceedings of the 2014 47th Hawaii International Conference on System Sciences (HICSS)* (pp. 331-339). IEEE. 10.1109/HICSS.2014.49

Lee, J.-N., & Kim, Y.-G. (1999). Effect of partnership quality on IS outsourcing success: Conceptual framework and empirical validation. *Journal of Management Information Systems, 15*(4), 29–62. doi:10.1080/07421222.1999.11518221

Li, E. Y., Chen, H. G., & Cheung, W. (2000). Total Quality Management in software development process. *The Journal of Quality Assurance Institute, 4*, 5–41.

Luftman, J., & Kempaiah, R. (2008). Key issues for IT executives 2007. *MIS Quarterly Executive, 7*, 99–112.

Malhotra, R., & Chug, A. (2016). Software Maintainability: Systematic Literature Review and Current Trends. *International Journal of Software Engineering and Knowledge Engineering, 26*(08), 1221–1253. doi:10.1142/S0218194016500431

Mao, J. Y., Lee, J. N., & Deng, C. P. (2008). Vendors' perspectives on trust and control in offshore information systems outsourcing. *Information & Management, 45*(7), 482–492. doi:10.1016/j.im.2008.07.003

Catelani, M., Ciani, L., Scarano, V. L., & Bacioccola, A. (2010) Software automated testing: A solution to maximize the test plan coverage and to increase software reliability and quality in use. In *Computer Standards & Interfaces*. Elsevier. Retrieved from http://www.elsevier.com/locate/csi

McDonough, E. F. (2000). Investigations of factors contributing to the success of cross functional teams. *Journal of Product Innovation Management, 17*(3), 221–235. doi:10.1111/1540-5885.1730221

Mockus, A., & Herbsleb, J. D. (2003). An empirical study of speed and communication in globally distributed software development. *IEEE Transactions on Software Engineering, 6*(29), 481–494.

Mohagheghi, P., & Conradi, R. (2004). An empirical study of software change: origin, acceptance rate and functionality vs quality attributes. *Proceedings of the 2004 International Symposium on empirical Software Engineering (ISESE'04)* (pp. 7–16). Academic Press. 10.1109/ISESE.2004.1334889

Nanda, V., & Robinson, J. A. (2011). *Six Sigma Software Quality Improvement: Success Stories from Leaders in the High Tech Industry*. New York, NY: McGraw-Hill.

Niazi, M., Mahmood, S., Alshayeb, M., Riaz, M. R., Faisal, K., Cerpa, N., ... Richardson, I. (2016). Challenges of project management in global software development: A client-vendor analysis. *Information and Software Technology, 80*, 1–19. doi:10.1016/j.infsof.2016.08.002

Nicholson, B., & Sahay, S. (2004). Embedded knowledge and offshore software development. *Information and Organization, 14*(4), 329–365. doi:10.1016/j.infoandorg.2004.05.001

Nidumolu, S. (1995). The Effect of Coordination and Uncertainty on Software Project Performance: Residual Performance Risk as an Intervening Variable. *Information Systems Research, 6*(3), 191–219. doi:10.1287/isre.6.3.191

Okhuysen, G., & Eisenhardt, K. (2002). Integrating knowledge in groups: How formal interventions enable flexibility. *Organization Science, 13*(4), 370–386. doi:10.1287/orsc.13.4.370.2947

Oshri, I., Kotlarsky, J., & Wilcocks, L. (2007). Managing distributed expertise in IT offshore outsourcing lessons from Tata Consultancy Services. *MIS Quarterly Executive, 6*(2), 53–65.

Osmundson, J. S., Michael, J. B., Machniak, M. J., & Grossman, M. A. (2003). Quality management metrics for software development. *Information & Management, 40*(8), 799–812. doi:10.1016/S0378-7206(02)00114-3

Palvia, P. C., King, R. C., Xia, W., & Palvia, S. C. J. (2010). Capability, quality, and performance of offshore is vendors: A theoretical framework and empirical investigation. *Decision Sciences, 41*(2), 231–270. doi:10.1111/j.1540-5915.2010.00268.x

Parzinger, M. J., & Nath, R. (2000). A study of the relationships between TQM implementation factors and software quality measures. *Total Quality Management, 11*, 353–371. doi:10.1080/0954412006874

Patnayakuni, F., Rai, A., & Seth, N. (2006). Relational Antecedents of Information Flow Integration for Supply Chain Coordination. *Journal of Management Information Systems, 23*(1), 13–49.

Pedhazur, E. J., & Schmelkin, L. P. (1991). *Measurement, Design, and Analysis: An Integrated Approach*. Hillsdale, NJ: Lawrence Erlbaum Associates.

Pereira, J., Cerpa, N., Verner, J., Rivas, M., & Procaccino, J. D. (2008). What do software practitioners really think about project success. *Journal of Systems and Software, 81*(6), 897–907. doi:10.1016/j.jss.2007.07.032

Powell, A., Piccoli, G., & Ives, B. (2004). Virtual teams: A review of current literature and directions for future research. *SIGMIS Database*, *35*(1), 6–36. doi:10.1145/968464.968467

Prahalad, C., & Krishnan, M. (2002). The dynamic synchronization of Strategy and Information Technology. *Sloan Management Review*, (Summer): 24–33.

Pressman, R. S. (2001). *Software Engineering: A Practitioner's Approach* (5th ed.). NY: McGraw-Hill.

Pressman, R. S. (2005). *Software Engineering: A Practitioner's Approach*. NY: McGraw-Hill.

Karout, R., & Awasthi, A. (2017). Improving software quality using Six Sigma DMAIC-based approach: A case study. *Business Process Management Journal*, *23*(4), 842–856. doi:10.1108/BPMJ-02-2017-0028

Rai, A., & Al-Hindi, H. (2000). The effects of development process modeling and task uncertainty on development quality performance. *Information & Management*, *37*(6), 335–346. doi:10.1016/S0378-7206(00)00047-1

Rajendran, C., Issac, G., & Anantharaman, R. N. (2006). An instrument for the measurement of customer perceptions of quality management in the software industry: An empirical study in India. *Software Quality Journal*, *14*(4), 291–308. doi:10.100711219-006-0037-2

Rajkumar, T. M., & Mani, R. V. S. (2001). Offshore Software Development: The view from Indian Suppliers. *Information Systems Management*, *18*(2), 63–73. doi:10.1201/1078/43195.18.2.20010301/31279.10

Raman, S. (2000). It is software process, stupid: Next millennium software quality key. *IEEE Aerospace and Electronic Systems Magazine*, *15*(6), 33–37. doi:10.1109/62.847929

Ravichandran, T., & Rai, A. (2000). Quality management in systems development: An organizational system perspective. *Management Information Systems Quarterly*, *24*(3), 381–415. doi:10.2307/3250967

Ravichandran, S., & Shareef, P. M. (2001). Managing risk in software projects. *Indian Management*, *40*, 56–62.

Patnayakuni, R., & Ruppel, C. (2006). Managing the Complementarity of Knowledge Integration and Process Formalization for Systems Development Performance. *Journal of the Association for Information Systems*, *7*(8), 545–567. doi:10.17705/1jais.00097

Rennecker, J. (2001). *The myth of spontaneous connection: An ethnographic study of the situated nature of virtual teamwork*. Unpublished doctoral dissertation, MIT Sloan School of Management, Cambridge, MA.

Rockart, J. F., & Hoffman, J. D. (1992). Systems delivery: Evolving new strategies. *Sloan Management Review*, (Summer), 21–31. PMID:10120624

Rothenberger, M. A., Kao, Y.-C., & Van Wassenhove, L. N. (2010). Total quality in software development: An empirical study of quality drivers and benefits in Indian software projects. *Information & Management*, *47*(7-8), 371–379. doi:10.1016/j.im.2010.10.001

Rottman, J. W., & Lacity, M. C. (2004). Twenty Practices for Offshore Outsourcing. *MIS Quarterly Executive*, *3*(3), 117–130.

Rus, I., Lindvall, M., & Sinha, S. (2002). Knowledge management in software engineering. *IEEE Software*, *19*(3), 26–38.

Sahay, S., Nicholson, B., & Krishna, S. (2003). *Global IT Outsourcing – Software Development across Borders* (1st ed.). United Kingdom: Cambridge University Press. doi:10.1017/CBO9780511615351

Sairamesh, J., Mohan, R., Kumar, M., Hassan, T., & Bender, C. (2002). A platform for business to business Sell-side: Private exchanges and Marketplaces. *IBM Systems Journal*, *41*(2), 242–252. doi:10.1147j.412.0242

Sankaran, K., & Kannabiran, G. (2011). Determinants of software quality in offshore development - an empirical study of an Indian vendor. *Information and Software Technology*, *53*(11), 1199–1208. doi:10.1016/j.infsof.2011.05.001

Mukherjee, S. (2017). Collaborative governance strategies for a strategic offshore IT outsourcing engagement. *Journal of Global Operations and Strategic Sourcing*, *10*(2), 255–278. doi:10.1108/JGOSS-11-2016-0037

Santhanam, R., & Hartono, E. (2003). Issues in linking information technology capability to firm performance. *Management Information Systems Quarterly*, *27*(1), 125–153. doi:10.2307/30036521

Subramanian, G. H., & James, J. J. (2007). Gary Klein, Software quality and IS project performance improvements from software development process maturity and IS implementation strategies. *Journal of Systems and Software*, *80*(4), 616–627. doi:10.1016/j.jss.2006.06.014

Sureshchandar, G. S., Rajendran, C., & Anantharaman, R. N. (2002). The relationship between management's perception of total quality service and customer perceptions of service quality. Total Quality Management, 13(1), 69-88.

Teo, T. S. H., & Bhattacherjee, A. (2013). Knowledge Transfer and Utilization in IT Outsourcing Partnerships: A Preliminary Model of Antecedents and Outcomes. *Information & Management*.

Tiwana, A., Bharadwaj, A., & Sambamurthy, V. (2003) The Antecedents 0f Information Systems Development Capability In Firms: A Knowledge Integration perspective. *Proceedings of the Twenty-Fourth International Conference on Information Systems* (pp. 246-258). Academic Press.

Trudel, S., Lavoie, J., Pare, M., & Suryn, W. (2006). PEM: The small company-dedicated software process quality evaluation method combining CMMI and ISO/IEC 14598. *Software Quality Journal*, *14*(1), 7–23. doi:10.100711219-006-5997-8

Verner, J. M., & Evanco, W. M. (2005). In-house software development: What project management practices lead to success? *IEEE Software*, *22*(January/February), 86–93. doi:10.1109/MS.2005.12

Vitharana, P., & Mone, M. A. (1998) Critical factors of software quality management. *Proceedings of the Association of Information Systems*, Baltimore, MD (pp. 906-908). Academic Press.

Vitharana, P., & Mone, M. A. (2008). Measuring critical factors of software quality management: Development and validation of an instrument. *Information Resources Management Journal*, *21*(2), 18–37. doi:10.4018/irmj.2008040102

Wallace, L., Keil, M., & Rai, A. (2004). Understanding software project risk: A cluster analysis. *Information & Management*, *42*(1), 115–125. doi:10.1016/j.im.2003.12.007

Wang, P., Tong, T. W., & Koh, C. P. (2004). An integrated model of knowledge transfer: From MNC parent to China subsidiary. *Journal of World Business*, *2*(39), 168–182. doi:10.1016/j.jwb.2003.08.009

Williams, B. J., & Carver, J. C. (2010). Characterizing software architecture changes: A systematic review. *Information and Software Technology*, *52*(1), 31–51. doi:10.1016/j.infsof.2009.07.002

Wynekoop, J. L., & Walz, D. B. (2000). Investigating traits of top performing software developers. *Information Technology & People*, *13*(3), 186–195. doi:10.1108/09593840010377626

This research was previously published in the International Journal of Information Technology Project Management (IJITPM), 11(1); pages 32-54, copyright year 2020 by IGI Publishing (an imprint of IGI Global).

Chapter 90
The ISO/IEC 29110 Software Lifecycle Standard for Very Small Companies

Rory V. O'Connor
https://orcid.org/0000-0001-9253-0313
Dublin City University, Ireland

ABSTRACT

For many small and start-up software companies, implementing controls and structures to properly manage their software development activity is a major challenge. It is commonly agreed that very small software companies, implementing management procedures, and controls to appropriately administer their software development activity is a significant challenge. To help meet the need for VSE-specific systems and software lifecycle profiles and guidelines, the ISO/IEC jointly published ISO/IEC 29110 "Lifecycle profiles for Very Small Entities" series of standards and guides, with the overall objective being to assist and encourage very small software organization in assessing and improving their software. The purpose of this chapter is to provide a primer on the ISO/IEC 29110 standard focusing on two main process areas of Project Management and Software Implementation.

INTRODUCTION

Software development is a complex socio-technical activity and in earlier work we have examined the complex interaction between a software development process and its situational context (Clarke et al, 2015) Part of the challenge of organising the software development process involves deciding upon the specific roles involved in the process and the responsibilities of individuals fulfilling these roles. Therefore, just as the process itself is subject to regular change (Clarke et al, 2017) so too are the roles subject to change. We have therefore examined the role of the software engineer and how this has changed over time, including how it might change into the future.

DOI: 10.4018/978-1-6684-3702-5.ch090

Quality orientated software process approaches and standards have gained mainstream acceptance in in the software development community over the year. There are many potential benefits of using standards due to the emphasizes on communication and having a shared common understanding of software lifecycle tasks.

For many small and start-up software companies, implementing controls and structures to properly manage their software development activity is a major challenge (Coleman & O'Connor, 2008c). It is commonly agreed that very small software companies, implementing management procedures, and controls to appropriately administer their software development activity is a significant challenge (Laporte et al, 2015). For example, a software company operating in Mexico may have a completely different set of operational problems when compared to a software company in the USA or Ireland. Even within a single geographical area such the range of operational issues faced by a small local firms can be radically different to those affecting a multinational subsidiary. The fact that all companies are not the same raises important questions for those who develop software process and process improvement models (Larrucea et al, 2016). To be widely adopted by the software industry, any process or process improvement model should be capable of handling the differences in the operational contexts of the companies making up that industry. But process improvement models, though highly publicized and marketed, are far from being extensively deployed and their influence in the software industry therefore remains more at a theoretical than practical level.

To help meet the need for VSE-specific systems and software lifecycle profiles and guidelines, the International Organization for Standardization and the International Electrotechnical Commission jointly published ISO/IEC 29110 "Lifecycle profiles for Very Small Entities" series of standards and guides, with the overall objective being to assist and encourage very small software organization in assessing and improving their software. These publications target VSEs, ranging from start-ups to grownups, with little or no experience or expertise in selecting the appropriate processes from systems or software engineering lifecycle standards (such as ISO/IEC/IEEE 12207) and tailoring them to a project's needs (Laporte et. al, 2017).

The purpose of this chapter is to provide a primer on the ISO/IEC 29110 standard focusing on two main process areas of Project Management and Software Implementation. This chapter will start with an explanation of the rationale and justification for the development of this new standard, followed by an overview of its structure and explain how to deploy ISO/IEC 29110 in a typical very small software company.

BACKGROUND

This section will introduce the problem with standards and explain the specific case of very small entities, before presenting the ISO/IEC 29110 standard as a solution specifically designed to address these problems for very small companies.

Very Small Companies (VSE)

Due to the rich variety of software development settings (for example: the nature of the application being developed, team size, requirements volatility), the implementation of a set of practices for software development may be quite different from one setting to another (Jeners et al., 2013a). Small and very small companies are the fundamental growth of many national economies. It is important to notice that the contribution from the small companies should be seen as important and significant as compare to the large one (Jeners et al., 2013b).

The context for the development of the ISO/IEC 29110 series of standard was specifically that of Very Small Companies and it is therefore necessary to examine such terms. The definition of "Small" and "Very Small" Entities is challengingly ambiguous, as there is no commonly accepted definition of the terms. The term "Very Small Entity" (VSE) had been defined by the ISO/IEC JTC1/SC7 Working Group 24 and subsequently adopted for use in the new ISO/IEC 29110 software process lifecycle standard as being "an entity (enterprise, organization, department or project) having up to 25 people" (Laporte et al, 2008).

A large majority of enterprises worldwide are VSEs. In Europe, for instance, as illustrated in Table 1, over 92% of enterprises are micro-enterprises. They have fewer than nine employees. Micro enterprises account for 70% to 90% of enterprises in OECD countries and about 57% in USA.

Table 1. Size of enterprises in Europe (Moll 2013).

Type	Number of Employees	Annual turnover	No. of enterprises (% of overall)
Micro	1-9	≤2M	92.2
Small	10-49	≤10M	6.5
Medium	50-249	≤50M	1.1

Typically, VSEs are economically vulnerable as they are driven by cash flow and depend on project profits, so they need to perform the projects within budget. They tend to have low budgets which have many impacts, such as: lack of funds to perform corrective post-delivery maintenance; few resources allocated for training; little or no budget to perform quality assurance activities; no budget for software reuse processes; low budget to respond to risks; and limited budget to perform Process Improvement and / or obtain a certification/assessment. Typically, the VSE's product has a single customer, where the customer is in charge of the management of the system and the software integration, installation and operation. It is normal practice for the customer not to define quantitative quality requirements and for customer satisfaction to depend on the fulfillment of specific requirements that may change during the project. A close relationship between all involved project members including the customer shows that software development in small and very small companies is strongly human-oriented and communication between them is important.

The internal business process of VSEs is usually focused on developing custom software systems, where the software product is elaborated progressively and which typically does not have strong relationship with other projects. Typically, most management processes (such as human resource and infrastructure management) are performed through informal mechanisms, with the majority of communication, decision-making and problem resolution being performed face-to-face.

Issues with Software Standards

Although commercial SPI models have been highly publicized, they are not being widely adopted and their influence in the software industry therefore remains more at a theoretical than practical level (O'Connor and Coleman, 2009). For example, in the case of Capability Maturity Model Integration (CMMI), an Australian study found that small organizations considered that adopting CMMI would be infeasible (Staples et al, 2007) and an Irish study found significant resistance due to negative perceptions surrounding levels of bureaucracy and required documentation (Coleman and O'Connor, 2006). Further investigation of the CMMI by Staples and Niazi (2006) discovered, after systematically reviewing 600 papers, that there has been little published evidence about those organizations who have decided not to adopt CMMI.

There is evidence that the majority of small and very small software organizations are not adopting existing standards / proven best practice models because they perceive the standards as being developed by large organizations and orientated towards large organizations, thus provoking the debate the in terms of number of employees, size does actually matter (O'Connor and Coleman, 2008a). Studies have shown that small firms' negative perceptions of process model standards are primarily driven by negative views of cost, documentation and bureaucracy. In addition, it has been reported that SMEs find it difficult to relate standards to their business needs and to justify the application of the international standards in their operations. Most SMEs cannot afford the resources for, or see a net benefit in, establishing software processes as defined by current standards and maturity models (O'Connor and Coleman, 2008b).

The ISO/IEC 29110 Standard as a Solution

Accordingly there is a need to help such organizations understand and use the concepts, processes and practices proposed in the ISO/IEC JTC1/SC7's international software engineering standards. The ISO/IEC 29110 standard "Lifecycle profiles for Very Small Entities" is aimed at addressing the issues identified above and addresses the specific needs of VSEs. The approach (Laporte et al, 2013a) used to develop ISO/IEC 29110 (2001) started with the pre-existing international standard ISO/IEC 12207 (2008) dedicated to software process lifecycles. The overall approach consisted of three steps: (1) Selecting ISO/IEC 12207 process subset applicable to VSEs of up to 25 employees; (2) Tailor the subset to fit VSE needs; and (3) Develop guidelines for VSEs.

Furthermore, in late 2009, the International Council on Systems Engineering (INCOSE) Very Small and Micro Entities Working Group (VSME) was established to evaluate the possibility of developing a standard, using the Generic profile group scheme of the ISO/IEC 29110 series, based on ISO/IEC 15288 (2008), for organizations developing systems. Late 2011 saw the launch of the official development of the systems engineering ISs and TRs for VSEs. In August 2014, ISO published the ISO/IEC 29110 systems engineering and management guide of the Basic profile ISO/IEC TR 29110-5-6-2:2014 (2014). The systems engineering and management guide of the Entry profile has been published in 2015 as ISO/IEC TR 29110-5-6-1:2015 (2015). Similar to the existing set of software ISO/IEC 29110 TRs, the Management and Engineering Guide for systems engineering should also be made available at no cost by ISO (Laporte et al, 2014).

For example a more recent study (Sánchez-Gordón and O'Connor, 2016). Understanding into software developers' use of software development processes in actual practice in the specific context of very small companies and highlighted three areas of concern: customer, software product and development tasks coordination and tracking, where small companies were lacking specific guidance (Sanchez-Gordon et al, 2017).

A full history of the evolution of the ISO/IEC 29110 series of software process lifecycle standards is given in O'Connor & Laporte (2017).

The Structure of ISO/IEC 29110

The basic requirements of a software development process are that it should fit the needs of the project and aid project success. And this need should be informed by the situational context (Marks et al, 2017) where in the project must operate and therefore, the most suitable software development process is contingent on the context. The core situational characteristic (Clarke and O'Connor, 2012) of the entities targeted by ISO/IEC 29110 is size, however there are other aspects and characteristics of VSEs that may affect profile preparation or selection. Creating one profile for each possible combination of values of the various dimensions introduced above would result in an unmanageable set of profiles. Accordingly, VSE's profiles are grouped in such a way as to be applicable to more than one category. Table 2 illustrates a Profile Group, which contains three profiles (labeled A, B and C) that are mapped to nine combinations of business models and situational factors (Giray et al, 2018).

Profile Groups are a collection of profiles, which are related either by composition of processes (i.e. activities, tasks), or by capability level, or both. The "Generic" profile group is applicable to a vast majority of VSEs that do not develop critical software and have typical situational factors (Clarke & O'Connor, 2015). This profile group does not imply any specific application domain, however, it is envisaged that in the future new domain-specific sub-profiles may be developed in the future. Table 3 illustrates this profile group as a collection of four profiles, providing a progressive approach to satisfying the requirements of profile group. To date the Basic Profile has been published, the purpose of which is to define a software development and project management guide for performing one project at a time.

Table 2. Allocating VSE characteristics to profile groups.

Business Models	Profile Situational Factors		
	Critical	User Uncertainty	Environment Change
Contract	*Profile A*	*Profile A*	*Profile A*
In-House	*Profile C*	*Profile B*	*Profile A*
Commercial	*Profile B*	*Profile A*	*Profile A*

Table 3. Graduated profile of the Generic profile group.

Entry	Generic Profile Group		
	Basic	Intermediate	Advanced

Engineering and Management Guide

At the core of this standard is a Management and Engineering Guide, officially known as ISO/IEC TR 29110-5-1-2 (2011), which focuses on *Project Management* and *Software Implementation* as illustrated in figure 1. The purpose of the Basic Profile is to define Software Implementation (SI) and Project Management (PM) processes from a subset of ISO/IEC 12207 (2008) and ISO/IEC 15289 (2011) appropriate for VSEs, as illustrated in figure 1.

Figure 1. ISO/IEC 29110 Project Management and Software Implementation Relationship.

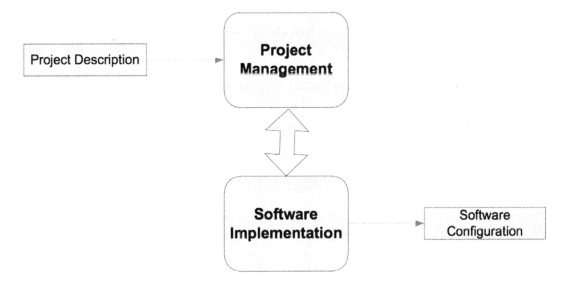

Table 4. Objectives of the Project Management process of the Basic Profile (ISO/IEC TR 29110-5-1-2 (2011).

Objective	Description
PM.O1	The Project Plan for the execution of the project is developed according to the Statement of Work and reviewed and accepted by the Customer. The tasks and resources necessary to complete the work are sized and estimated.
PM.O2	Progress of the project is monitored against the Project Plan and recorded in the Progress Status Record.
PM.O3	The Change Requests are addressed through their reception and analysis. Changes to software requirements are evaluated for cost, schedule and technical impact.
PM.O4	Review meetings with the Work Team and the Customer are held. Agreements are registered and tracked.
PM.O5	Risks are identified as they develop and during the conduct of the project.
PM.O6	A software Version Control Strategy is developed. Items of Software Configuration are identified, defined and baselined. Modifications and releases of the items are controlled and made available to the Customer and Work Team including the storage, handling and delivery of the items.
PM.O7	Software Quality Assurance is performed to provide assurance that work products and processes comply with the Project Plan and Requirements Specification.

Project Management Process

The purpose of the Project Management (PM) process is to establish and carry out the tasks of the software implementation project in a systematic way, which allows compliance with the project's objectives in terms of expected quality, time, and costs (O'Connor and Laporte, 2012). The seven objectives of the PM process are listed in table 4.

Figure 2 illustrates the 4 activities of the project management process as well as their input and output product. The four activities of the Project Management Process are:

- **Project Planning** - The primary objective of this process is to produce and communicate effective and workable project plans. This process determines the scope of the project management and technical activities, identifies process outputs, project tasks and deliverables, establishes schedules for project task conduct, including achievement criteria, and required resources to accomplish project tasks.
- **Project Plan Execution** - To implement the actual work tasks of the project in accordance with the project plan. Ideally when the project plan has been agreed and communicated to all teams members, work of the development of the product, which is the subject of the project, should commence.
- **Project Assessment and Control** - purpose is to determine the status of the project and ensure that the project performs according to plans and schedules, within projected budgets and it satisfies technical objectives.
- **Project Closure** - typically involves releasing the final deliverables to the customer, handing over project documentation to the business, terminating supplier contracts, releasing project resources and communicating project closure to all stakeholders.

For illustration purposes, two tasks of the Project Planning activity are listed in Table 5. The project manager (PM) and the customer (CUS) are involved in these 2 tasks. The customer is involved, during the execution of the project, when he submits change requests, during project review meetings, for the validation and approval of the requirements specifications and for the acceptance of the deliverables.

Software Implementation Process

The purpose of the Software Implementation (SI) process, illustrated in figure 3, is to achieve systematic performance of the analysis, design, construction, integration, and test activities for new or modified software products according to the specified requirements. The seven objectives of the SI process are listed in table 6.

The activities of the Software Implementation Process are:

- **Software Implementation Initiation** - ensures that the Project Plan established in Project Planning activity is committed to by the Work Team
- **Software Requirements Analysis** - analyzes the agreed Customer's requirements and establishes the validated project requirements. The activity provides:
- **Software Architectural and Detailed Design** - transforms the software requirements to the system software architecture and software detailed design

- **Software Construction** - develops the software code and data from the Software Design.
- **Software Integration and Tests** - ensures that the integrated Software Components satisfy the software requirements.
- **Product Delivery** - provides the integrated software product to the Customer.

Figure 2. ISO/IEC 29110 Project Management Process.

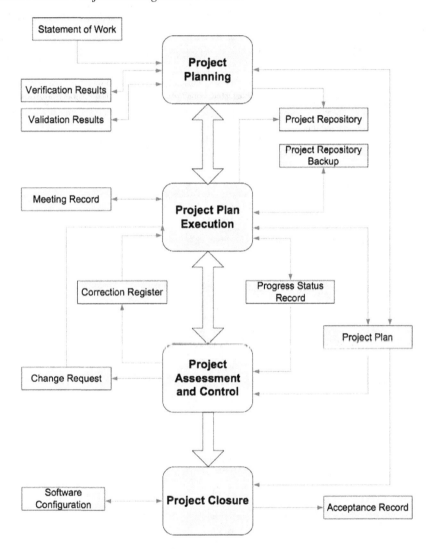

Table 5. Example of 2 tasks of the Project Planning Activity (ISO/IEC TR 29110-5-1-2 (2011).

Role	Task	Input	Output
PM CUS	PM.1.2 Define with the Customer the Delivery Instructions of each one of the Deliverables specified in the Statement of Work.	Statement of Work [reviewed	Project Plan Delivery Instructions
PM CUS	PM.1.14 Review and accept the Project Plan. Customer reviews and accepts the Project Plan, making sure that the Project Plan elements match with the Statement of Work.	Project Plan [verified]	Meeting Record Project Plan [accepted]

Table 6. Objectives of the Software Implementation process of the Basic Profile.

Objective	Description
SI.O21	Tasks of the activities are performed through the accomplishment of the current Project Plan.
SI.O2.	Software requirements are defined, analyzed for correctness and testability, approved by the Customer, baselined and communicated.
SI.O3.	Software architectural and detailed design is developed and baselined. It describes the Software Components and internal and external interfaces of them.
SI.O4.	Software Components defined by the design are produced. Unit test are defined and performed to verify the consistency with requirements and the design. T
SI.O5.	Software is produced performing integration of Software Components and verified using Test Cases and Test Procedures. Results are recorded at the Test Report.
SI.O6.	A Software Configuration, that meets the Requirements Specification as agreed to with the Customer, which includes user, operation and maintenance documentations, is integrated, baselined and stored at the Project Repository.
SI.O8.	Verification and Validation Tasks of all required work products are performed using the defined criteria to achieve consistency among output and input products in each activity.

Figure 3. ISO/IEC 29110 Software Implementation Process.

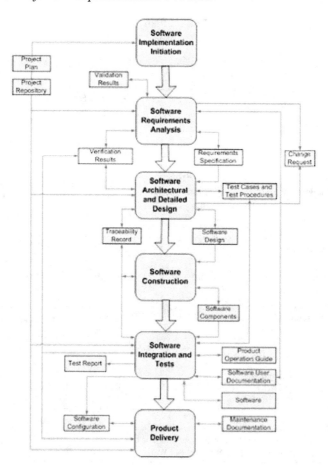

IMPLEMENTING THE ISO/IEC 29110 STANDARD

Guidance on Implementation

In order to facilitate the implementation, by VSEs, of a Profile, a set of Deployment Packages (2013) are available. A deployment package is a set of artifacts developed to facilitate the implementation of a set of practices, of the selected framework, in a VSE. A deployment package is not a process reference model (i.e. it is not prescriptive). The elements of a typical deployment package are: description of processes, activities, tasks, roles and products, template, checklist, example, reference and mapping to standards and models, and a list of tools. Deployment packages are not intended to preclude or discourage the use of additional guidelines that VSEs find useful.

The elements of a typical deployment package are: technical description, relationships with ISO/IEC 29110, key definitions, detailed description of processes, activities, tasks, roles and products, template, checklist, example, references and mapping to standards and models, and a list of tools. The mapping is only given as information to show that a Deployment Package has explicit links to Part 5, ISO standards, such as ISO/IEC 12207, or models such as the CMMI developed by the Software Engineering Institute. Hence by deploying and implementing a package (O'Connor and Sanders, 2013) a VSE can see its concrete step to achieve or demonstrate coverage to Part 5.

The working group (ISO/IEC JTC1/SC7 WG 24) behind the development of this standard is advocating the use of pilot projects as a mean to accelerate the adoption and utilization of ISO/IEC 29110. Pilot projects are an important means of reducing risks and learning more about the organizational and technical issues associated with the deployment of new software engineering practices. Pilot projects are based on the ISO/IEC 29110-5 Management and engineering guide and the deployment package(s).

Sample Implementations

Worldwide, hundreds of VSEs have implemented ISO/IEC 29110. For instance, in Thailand, an early adopter of ISO/IEC 29110, more than 350 public and private organizations have achieved the ISO/IEC 29110 Basic Profile certification. In addition, 33 other VSEs are certified in other states of Mexico in the state of Zacatecas in Mexico, industry, academia, and government came together in 2017 to promote ISO/IEC 29110 (Laporte et. al, 2016). In Zacatecas, approximately four Mexican VSEs and four software development centers of academic institutions are certified for the Basic Profile. In addition, 33 other VSEs are certified in other states of Mexico. Researchers in Canada have led numerous field trials with early-stage adopters of ISO/IEC 29110 (Laporte et. al, 2017).

For example, Ribaud et al. (2010) have documented the results of one pilot project that conducted with a 14-person VSE based in France, which successfully implemented ISO/IEC 29110 processes practices utilizing the available Deployment Packages. From which they have identified some potential additional infrastructure and support process activities and suggestions for future evolution of ISO/IEC 29110 Process Profiles. A further series of pilot projects are currently underway in research laboratories and enterprises in Canada, Ireland, Belgium and France, with further pilot projects planned in the near future.

The results from one pilot study in Canada concluded that the tools developed to support the project management processes proved very useful and helped the project managers rapidly integrate the knowledge required to execute the processes (Laporte et al, 2013b). In the case of this trial company, for the first time, the company has documented management processes for small-scale projects. Besides, some project managers have joined forces to promote project management practices within this engineering firm's division. The improvement programme was so successful that managers of the company's other divisions have shown an interest in learning this approach in order to implement it within their respective divisions.

Laporte et al (2015) report on two successful trials of ISO/IEC 29110, that demonstrate it was possible to properly plan the project and develop the software product using proven software practices documented in standards as well as not interfering with the creativity during the development of their web site. People who think that standards are a burden, an unnecessary overhead and a treat to creativity should look at this start-up project and revisit their results.

VSEs that have implemented ISO/IEC 29110 management and engineering guides have improved in one or more aspects of competitiveness including quality, cost, and schedule (Laporte & O'Connor, 2016). For example, projects using ISO/IEC 29110 for the first time had only 10 to 18 percent of rework as opposed to about 40 to 50 percent of rework typical of a majority of software developers (Laporte & O'Connor, 2017).

CONCLUSION

For most enterprises, but in particular for VSEs, international certifications can enhance credibility, competitiveness and access to national and international markets. Brazil has led the development of an ISO/IEC 29110 certification process. An ISO/IEC 29110 auditor should be competent in auditing techniques, have expertise in ISO/IEC 29110 and have experience in software development. For VSEs, such a certification should not be too expensive and short. The certification process has been successfully piloted in a few VSEs.

Finally, research studies have been undertaken to understanding the perception of VSEs towards the adoption of process standards (Basri et al, 2010) (O'Connor & Basri, 2018.) and also to evaluate management sentiment towards ISO/IEC 29110 (O'Connor, 2012) and management commitment to SPI and ISO/IEC 2910 in particular in Europe (O'Connor et al, 2010) and South America (Sanchez-Gordon et al, 2015). These revealed that the acceptance level of any type or model of software quality or lifecycle standard in VSEs is a very low priority item, but the level of awareness of standards and potential benefits was high. Furthermore, these studies showed the main reason for not adopting standards was a lack customer requirement, a lack of resources and the perceived difficulties in defining an organizational process. Furthermore, this analysis reveals a pattern that indicates that the acceptance level of quality standard such as ISO among VSEs are still low even though the staff and management are knowledgeable and aware the benefit of adopting such standards. The main reasons are more related to the lack of the customer requirement and the limited resources in the company. In addition, the perception a heavyweight process especially in terms of documentation, cost and non- alignment with current development process are among the reasons why the companies did not plan to adopt a lifecycle standard in the short to medium term. However from the analysis, VSEs may still be interested in lifecycle standards if certain important criteria are met and such standards are closely related to their needs. Therefore, it can be concluded that the market and demand for ISO/IEC 29110 in VSEs has a positive outlook.

Future Research

In terms of future work, as ISO/IEC 29110 is an emerging standard there is much work yet to be completed (O'Connor and Laporte, 2014). The main remaining work item is to finalize the development of the remaining three profiles: (a) Entry – a six person-months effort project or a start-up VSEs; (b) Intermediate - Management of more than one project and (c) Advanced - business management and portfolio management practices. In addition, the development of additional Profile Groups for other domains such as critical software, game industry, scientific software developments are being studied.

Whilst work is currently underway on an assessment mechanism for ISO/IEC 29110, a clear niche market need is emerging which may force the process assessment community to change their views on how process assessments are carried out for VSEs. In particular there is a strong need to ensure that VSEs are not required to invest the anything similar in terms of time, money and other resources on process assessments, as may be expected from their larger SMEs (small and medium enterprises), or even MNC (multinational corporations) counterparts. Indeed, some form of self-assessment, possibly supported by Internet based tools, along with periodic spot-checks may be suitable alternative to meet the unique needs of VSEs.

Furthermore, work is underway to integrate accessibility design patterns with the software implementation process of ISO/IEC 29110 (Sanchez-Gordon et al, 2019) and to examine the impact of cultural issues on the software process of very small entities (Nonoyama et al, 2018). Also, from an agile process perspective, research is being conducted into the compliance of the ISO/IEC 29110 Entry Profile with the Project Management process in the main agile methodologies (Galvan-Cruz et al, 2017a) and SCRUM in particular (Galvan-Cruz et a, 2017b). Finally, the area of serious games (Olgun et al, 2017) is being applied to the ISO/IEC 29110 and ISO/IEC 29110 project management process of basic profile (Calderón et al 2017).

REFERENCES

Basri, S., & O'Connor, R. (2010). Understanding the Perception of Very Small Software Companies towards the Adoption of Process Standards. In Proceedings of Riel et al (Eds), Systems, Software and Services Process Improvement (pp. 153 – 164). Springer-Verlag. doi:10.1007/978-3-642-15666-3_14

Calderón, A., Ruiz, M., & O'Connor, R. V. (2017, September). Coverage of ISO/IEC 29110 project management process of basic profile by a serious game. In *European Conference on Software Process Improvement* (pp. 111-122). Springer. 10.1007/978-3-319-64218-5_9

Clarke, P., & O'Connor, R. (2012). The situational factors that affect the software development process: Towards a comprehensive reference framework. *Information and Software Technology, 54*(5), 433–447. doi:10.1016/j.infsof.2011.12.003

Clarke, P., & O'Connor, R. V. (2015, September). Changing situational contexts present a constant challenge to software developers. In *European Conference on Software Process Improvement* (pp. 100-111). Springer. 10.1007/978-3-319-24647-5_9

Clarke, P., O'Connor, R. V., & Leavy, B. (2016, May). A complexity theory viewpoint on the software development process and situational context. In *Proceedings of the International Conference on Software and Systems Process* (pp. 86-90). ACM. 10.1145/2904354.2904369

Clarke, P., O'Connor, R. V., Leavy, B., & Yilmaz, M. (2015). Exploring the relationship between software process adaptive capability and organisational performance. *IEEE Transactions on Software Engineering, 41*(12), 1169–1183. doi:10.1109/TSE.2015.2467388

Clarke, P. M., O'Connor, R. V., Solan, D., Elger, P., Yilmaz, M., Ennis, A., Gerrity, M., McGrath, S., & Treanor, R. (2017, September). Exploring software process variation arising from differences in situational context. In *European Conference on Software Process Improvement* (pp. 29-42). Springer. 10.1007/978-3-319-64218-5_3

Coleman, G., & O'Connor, R. (2006, October). Software process in practice: A grounded theory of the Irish software industry. In *European Conference on Software Process Improvement* (pp. 28-39). Springer. 10.1007/11908562_4

Coleman, G., & O'Connor, R. (2008a). Investigating Software Process in Practice: A Grounded Theory Perspective. *Journal of Systems and Software, 81*(5), 772–784. doi:10.1016/j.jss.2007.07.027

Coleman, G., & O'Connor, R. (2008b). The Influence of Managerial Experience and Style on Software Development Projects. *International Journal of Technology, Policy and Management, 8*(1).

Coleman, G., & O'Connor, R. V. (2008c). An investigation into software development process formation in software start-ups. *Journal of Enterprise Information Management, 21*(6), 633–648. doi:10.1108/17410390810911221

Galván-Cruz, S., Mora, M., & O'Connor, R. (2017b, October). A Means-Ends Design of SCRUM+: an agile-disciplined balanced SCRUM enhanced with the ISO/IEC 29110 Standard. In *International Conference on Software Process Improvement* (pp. 13-23). Springer.

Galvan-Cruz, S., Mora, M., O'Connor, R. V., Acosta, F., & Álvarez, F. (2017a). An Objective Compliance Analysis of Project Management Process in Main Agile Methodologies with the ISO/IEC 29110 Entry Profile. *International Journal of Information Technologies and Systems Approach, 10*(1), 75–106. doi:10.4018/IJITSA.2017010105

Giray, G., Yilmaz, M., O'Connor, R. V., & Clarke, P. M. (2018, September). The Impact of Situational Context on Software Process: A Case Study of a Very Small-Sized Company in the Online Advertising Domain. In *European Conference on Software Process Improvement* (pp. 28-39). Springer. 10.1007/978-3-319-97925-0_3

ISO/IEC 12207 (2008). Information technology – Software lifecycle processes. Geneva, Switzerland: International Organization for Standardization/Inter- national Electrotechnical Commission.

ISO/IEC 15288 (2008). Systems and software engineering - System lifecycle processes, International Organization for Standardization/International Electrotechnical Commission: Geneva, Switzerland.

ISO/IEC 15289 (2011). Systems and software engineering – Content of lifecycle information products (documentation), International Organization for Standardization/International Electrotechnical Commission: Geneva, Switzerland.

ISO/IEC TR 29110-1 (2011). "Software Engineering - Lifecycle Profiles for Very Small Entities (VSEs) - Part 1: Overview". Geneva: International Organization for Standardization (ISO), 2011. Available at no cost from ISO at: http://standards.iso.org/ittf/PubliclyAvailableStandards/c051150_ISO_IEC_TR_29110-1_2011.zip

ISO/IEC TR 29110-5-1-2 (2011). Software Engineering - Lifecycle Profiles for Very Small Entities (VSEs) - Part 5-1-2: Management and engineering guide - Generic profile group: Basic profile, International Organization for Standardization/ International Electrotechnical Commission: Geneva, Switzerland. Available at no cost from ISO at: https://standards.iso.org/ittf/PubliclyAvailableStandards/c051153_ISO_IEC_TR_29110-5-1_2011.zip

ISO/IEC TR 29110-5-6-1:2015 - Systems Engineering – Lifecycle Profiles for Very Small Entities (VSEs) - Management and engineering guide: Generic profile group: Entry profile, International Organization for Standardization/International Electrotechnical Commission: Geneva, Switzerland. Available at no cost from ISO at: https://standards.iso.org/ittf/PubliclyAvailableStandards/index.html

ISO/IEC TR 29110-5-6-2:2014 - Systems Engineering – Lifecycle Profiles for Very Small Entities (VSEs) - Management and engineering guide: Generic profile group: Basic profile, International Organization for Standardization/International Electrotechnical Commission: Geneva, Switzerland. Available at no cost from ISO at: https://standards.iso.org/ittf/PubliclyAvailableStandards/index.html

Jeners, S., Clarke, P., O'Connor, R. V., Buglione, L., & Lepmets, M. (2013b). Harmonizing Software Development Processes with Software Development Settings – A Systematic Approach. In *20th European Conference on Systems, Software and Services Process Improvement (EuroSPI 2013), CCIS* (Vol. 364). Springer-Verlag.

Jeners, S., O'Connor, R.V., Clarke, P., Lichter, H., Lepmets, M., & Buglione, L. (2013a). Harnessing Software Development Contexts to inform Software Process Selection Decisions. *Software Quality Professional, 16*(1).

Laporte, C., & O'Connor, R. (2017). Software process improvement standards and guides for very small organization: An overview of eight implementations. *Crosstalk, 30*(3), 23–27.

Laporte, C., O'Connor, R., García Paucar, L. H., & Gerançon, B. (2014). An innovative approach in developing standard professionals by involving software engineering students in implementing and improving international standards. *International Cooperation for Education about Standardization Conference (ICES 2014).*

Laporte, C. Y., Alexandre, S., & O'Connor, R. V. (2008, September). A software engineering lifecycle standard for very small enterprises. In *European Conference on Software Process Improvement* (pp. 129-141). Springer. 10.1007/978-3-540-85936-9_12

Laporte, C. Y., Chevalier, F., & Maurice, J.-C. (2013b). *Improving Project Management for Small Projects, ISO Focus. Proceedings of International Organization for Standardization.*

Laporte, C. Y., Munoz, M., Miranda, J. M., & O'Connor, R. V. (2017). Applying software engineering standards in very small entities: From startups to grownups. *IEEE Software*, *35*(1), 99–103. doi:10.1109/MS.2017.4541041

Laporte, C. Y., O'Connor, R., & Fanmuy, G. (2013a). International Systems and Software Engineering Standards for Very Small Entities. *Crosstalk*, *26*(3), 28–33.

Laporte, C. Y., & O'Connor, R. V. (2014). A Systems Process Lifecycle Standard for Very Small Entities: Development and Pilot Trials. In *Proceedings of EuroSPI*. Springer-Verlag. doi:10.1007/978-3-662-43896-1_2

Laporte, C. Y., & O'Connor, R. V. (2016). Systems and software engineering standards for very small entities: Accomplishments and overview. *Computer*, *49*(8), 84–87. doi:10.1109/MC.2016.242

Laporte, C. Y., O'Connor, R. V., & Garcia Paucar, L. (2015). Software Engineering Standards and Guides for Very Small Entities: Implementation in two start-ups. *Proceedings of 10th International Conference on Evaluation of Novel Approaches to Software Engineering (ENASE 2015)*. 10.5220/0005368500050015

Laporte, C. Y., O'Connor, R. V., & Paucar, L. H. G. (2015, April). The implementation of ISO/IEC 29110 software engineering standards and guides in very small entities. In *International Conference on Evaluation of Novel Approaches to Software Engineering* (pp. 162-179). Springer.

Larrucea, X., O'Connor, R. V., Colomo-Palacios, R., & Laporte, C. Y. (2016). Software process improvement in very small organizations. *IEEE Software*, *33*(2), 85–89. doi:10.1109/MS.2016.42

Marks, G., O'Connor, R. V., & Clarke, P. M. (2017, October). The impact of situational context on the software development process–a case study of a highly innovative start-up organization. In *International Conference on Software Process Improvement and Capability Determination* (pp. 455-466). Springer. 10.1007/978-3-319-67383-7_33

Moll, R. (2013). *Being prepared – A bird's eye view of SMEs and risk management, ISO Focus+*. Geneva, Switzerland: International Organization for Standardization.

Nonoyama, T., Wen, L., Rout, T., Tuffley, D., & O'Connor, R. V. (2018). The Impact of cultural issues on the software process of very small entities. *Software Quality Professional*, *20*(2), 59–68.

O'Connor, R., Basri, S., & Coleman, G. (2010). Exploring Managerial Commitment towards SPI in Small and Very Small Enterprises. In Proceedings of Systems, Software and Services Process Improvement (pp. 268-278). Springer-Verlag. doi:10.1007/978-3-642-15666-3_24

O'Connor, R., & Coleman, G. (2009). Ignoring 'Best Practice': Why Irish Software SMEs are rejecting CMMI and ISO 9000. *AJIS. Australasian Journal of Information Systems*, *16*(1). Advance online publication. doi:10.3127/ajis.v16i1.557

O'Connor, R. V. (2012). Evaluating Management Sentiment towards ISO/IEC 29110 in Very Small Software Development Companies. In *SPICE 2012. CCIS* (Vol. 290, pp. 277–281). Springer. doi:10.1007/978-3-642-30439-2_31

O'Connor, R. V., & Basri, S. (2018). Understanding the Role of Knowledge Management in Software Development: A Case Study in Very Small Companies. In Computer Systems and Software Engineering: Concepts, Methodologies, Tools, and Applications (pp. 485-500). IGI Global. doi:10.4018/978-1-5225-3923-0.ch019

O'Connor, R. V., & Laporte, C. Y. (2012). Software Project Management with ISO/IEC 29110. In *19th European Conference on Systems, Software and Services Process Improvement (EuroSPI 2012), CCIS* (Vol. 301). Springer-Verlag.

O'Connor, R. V., & Laporte, C. Y. (2014). An Innova- tive Approach to the Development of an International Software Process Lifecycle Standard for Very Small Entities. *International Journal of Information Technologies and Systems Approach*, 7(1), 1–22. Advance online publication. doi:10.4018/ijitsa.2014010101

O'Connor, R. V., & Laporte, C. Y. (2017). The evolution of the ISO/IEC 29110 set of standards and guides. *International Journal of Information Technologies and Systems Approach*, 10(1), 1–21. doi:10.4018/IJITSA.2017010101

O'Connor, R. V., & Sanders, M. (2013). Lessons from a Pilot Implementation of ISO/IEC 29110 in a Group of Very Small Irish Companies. In *Proceedings 13th International Conference on Software Process Improvement and Capability Determination (SPICE 2013), CCIS* (Vol. 349). Springer-Verlag.

Olgun, S., Yilmaz, M., Clarke, P. M., & O'Connor, R. V. (2017, October). A systematic investigation into the use of game elements in the context of software business landscapes: a systematic literature review. In *International Conference on Software Process Improvement and Capability Determination* (pp. 384-398). Springer. 10.1007/978-3-319-67383-7_28

Package, D. (2013). *ISO/IEC JCT1/SC7 Working Group 24 Deployment Packages repository*. Retrieved November 10, 2013,from http://profs.logti.etsmtl.ca/claporte/English/VSE/index.html

Ribaud, V., Saliou, P., O'Connor, R., & Laporte, C. (2010). Software Engineering Support Activities for Very Small Entities. In Proceedings of Systems, Software and Services Process Improvement (pp. 165-176). Springer-Verlag. doi:10.1007/978-3-642-15666-3_15

Sanchez-Gordon, M. L., de Amescua, A., O'Connor, R. V., & Larrucea, X. (2017). A standard-based framework to integrate software work in small settings. *Computer Standards & Interfaces*, 54, 162–175. doi:10.1016/j.csi.2016.11.009

Sánchez-Gordón, M. L., & O'Connor, R. V. (2016). Understanding the gap between software process practices and actual practice in very small companies. *Software Quality Journal*, 24(3), 549–570. doi:10.100711219-015-9282-6

Sanchez-Gordon, M. L., O'Connor, R. V., & Colomo-Palacios, R. (2015). Evaluating VSEs Viewpoint and Sentiment Towards the ISO/IEC 29110 Standard: A Two Country Grounded Theory Study. *Proceedings 13th International Conference on Software Process Improvement and Capability dEtermination (SPICE 2015), CCIS* (Vol. 526). Springer-Verlag.

Sanchez-Gordon, S., Sánchez-Gordón, M., Yilmaz, M., & O'Connor, R. V. (2019). Integration of accessibility design patterns with the software implementation process of ISO/IEC 29110. *Journal of Software: Evolution and Process*, 31(1).

Staples, M., & Niazi, M. (2006). *Systematic Review of Organizational Motivations for Adopting CMM-based SPI*. Technical Report PA005957, National ICT Australia.

Staples, M., Niazi, M., Jeffery, R., Abrahams, A., Byatt, P., & Murphy, R. (2007). An exploratory study of why organizations do not adopt CMMI. *Journal of Systems and Software, 80*(6), 883–895. doi:. jss.2006.09.008 doi:10.1016/j

ADDITIONAL READING

Basri, S., & O'Connor, R. (2010). Organizational Commitment Towards Software Process Improvement An Irish Software VSEs Case Study, 4th International Symposium on Information Technology 2010 (ITSim 2010), Kuala Lumpur, Malaysia.

Basri, S., & O'Connor, R. (2011). Towards an Understanding of Software Development Process Knowledge in Very Small Companies, Proceedings International Conference on Informatics Engineering & Information Science (ICIEIS2011), CCIS, Vol. 253, Springer-Verlag. 10.1007/978-3-642-25462-8_6

Basri, S., & O'Connor, R. (2011). Knowledge Management in Software Process Improvement: A case study of very small entities. In M. Ramachandran (Ed.), *Knowledge Engineering for Software Development Life Cycles: Support Technologies and Applications* (pp. 273–288). IGI Global. doi:10.4018/978-1-60960-509-4.ch015

Basri, S., & O'Connor, R. (2011). The Impact of Software Development Team Dynamics on the Knowledge Management Process, *Proceedings of 23rd International Conference on Software Engineering and Knowledge Engineering (SEKE 2011)*, USA.

Basri, S., & O'Connor, R. V. (2012). A Study of Knowledge Management Process Practices in Very Small Software Companies. *American Journal of Economics and Business Administration, 3*(4), 636–644.

Clarke, P., & O'Connor, R. V. (2012). The influence of SPI on business success in software SMEs: An empirical study. *Journal of Systems and Software, 85*(10), 2356–2367. doi:10.1016/j.jss.2012.05.024

Clarke, P., & O'Connor, R. V. (2013). An empirical examination of the extent of software process improve- ment in software SMEs. *Journal of Software: Evolution and Process, 25*(9), 981–998.

Crowder, K., Systems Engineering for Very Small Enterprises, Insight, INCOSE, Vol. 10 No. 2 (April 2007).

Habra, N., Alexandre, S., Desharnais, J.-M., Laporte, C. Y., & Renault, A. (2008). Initiating Software Process Improvement in Very Small Enterprises Experience with a Light Assessment Tool. Information and Soft- ware Technology, 50(June), 763–771. doi:. infsof.2007.08.004 doi:10.1016/j

Laporte, C., Y, Fanmuy, Gauthier, Ptack, Ken, (2012). The Development of Systems Engineering International Standards and Support Tools for Very Small Enterprises, 22nd Annual International Symposium of the International Council on Systems Engineering, Rome (Italy). 10.1002/j.2334-5837.2012.tb01416.x

Laporte, C. Y., Fanmuy, G., Ptack, K., & Marvin, J. (2012). Systems and Software Engineering Standards for Very Small Entities. *Insight (American Society of Ophthalmic Registered Nurses)*, *15*(1), 32–33.

Laporte, C. Y., Séguin, N., & Villas Boas, G. (2013). *Seizing the benefits of software and systems engineering standards, ISO Focus*. International Organization for Standardization.

Mora, M., Gelman, O., O'Connor, R., Alvarez, F., & Macías-Luévano, J. (2009). An Overview of Models and Standards of Processes in the SE, SwE And IS Disciplines. In A. Cater-Steel (Ed.), *Information Technology Governance and Service Management: Frameworks and Adaptations* (pp. 371–387). IGI Publishing., doi:10.4018/978-1-60566-008-0.ch021

Mora, M., Gelman, O., O'Connor, R., Alvarez, F., & Macías-Luévano, J. (2009). An Overview of Models and Standards of Processes in the SE, SwE, and IS Disciplines. In Jakobs, K. Information Communication Technology Standardization for E-Business Sectors: Integrating Supply and Demand Factors (pp. 236–252). IGI Global. doi:10.4018/978-1-60566-320-3.ch016

Oktaba, H., Felix G., Mario P., Francisco R., Francisco P. and Claudia, A.; Software Process Improvement: The Competisoft Project, IEEE Computer, October 2007, Vol. 40, No 10

Ribaud, V., Saliou, P., & Laporte, C. Y. (2011). Towards Experience Management for Very Small Entities, International Journal On Advances in Software, vol. 4, no 1&2

Ribaud, V., & Salliou, P. (2010). Process Assessment Issues of the ISO/IEC 29110 Emerging Standard, 11th International Conference on Product Focused Software Development and Process Improvement (Profes2010), Hosted by LERO, Ireland.

KEY TERMS AND DEFINITIONS

Process Assessment: The disciplined examination of the processes by an organisation against a set of criteria to determine capability of those processes to perform within quality, cost and schedule goals.

Project Implementation: Is defined as a specified set of activities designed to put into practice an activity or program of known dimensions.

Project Management: This is the process and activity of planning, organizing, motivating, and controlling resources to achieve specific goals.

Software Process: A set of activities, methods, practices, and transformations that people use to develop and maintain software and the associated products.

Software Process Improvement (SPI): Aims to understand the software process as it is used within an organisation and thus drive the implementation of changes to that process to achieve specific goals such as increasing development speed, achieving higher product quality or reducing costs.

Very Small Entity: An enterprise, organization, department, or project having up to 25 people.

This research was previously published in the Encyclopedia of Organizational Knowledge, Administration, and Technology; pages 1498-1515, copyright year 2021 by Business Science Reference (an imprint of IGI Global).

Chapter 91
Agile Business Analysis for Digital Transformation

Busra Ozdenizci Kose
ⓘ https://orcid.org/0000-0002-8414-5252
Gebze Technical University, Turkey

ABSTRACT

The use of cutting-edge digital technologies and the realization of right project, program, and portfolio (3P) initiatives can trigger the intended company-wide change and the digital transformation. Today, organizations need to increase their agility for managing their information technology (IT) projects and transforming their business models. The integration of agile perspective and business analysis (BA) approach has a great potential to increase the success of digital transformation. This study aims to provide an overview of state-of-the-art in agile business analysis in scope of digital transformation. In accordance with the well-known frameworks, general principles and promising techniques of Agile BA are highlighted and discussed. The regarding agile practices provide valuable guidelines for research- ers and practitioners that how they can assist continuous feedback, continuous learning, continuous improvement, and continuous integration capabilities of organizations; and also how to maximize value to the stakeholders in agile project lifecycles and agile business transformations.

INTRODUCTION

In recent years, digital transformation paradigm has gained great importance by organizations in order to manage changing dynamics of globalization and remain competitive in digital world. In order to re- alize strategic Projects, Programs and Portfolios (3P) and operate efficient business models along with globalization, the integration of Information Systems (IS) with businesses; namely digital transformation of organizations became inevitable.

Understanding digital transformation phenomenon is essential; it is a journey of an organization start- ing from digitization, digitalization and finally the most pervasive phase digital transformation. Gartner Glossary (2020a) highlights the term digitization as "*the process of changing from analog to digital form*". The integration of Information Technologies (IT) with existing tasks allows to convert analog

DOI: 10.4018/978-1-6684-3702-5.ch091

information into digital information. As one further step, digitalization, aims to alter and optimize existing business processes by applying digital technologies; in other words, targets process improvements through new technologies or communication platforms and user experience (UX) enhancement (Verhoef et al., 2019). Accordingly, Gartner Glossary (2020b) defines digitalization as *"the process of moving to a digital business"* and *"the use of digital technologies to change a business model and provide new revenue and value-producing opportunities"*.

Beyond digitalization, digital transformation is the company-wide change that aims to lead the development of new business models or new business logic; namely to lead business model innovation with new value creation 3P in organizations. As stated by Verhoef et al. (2019), digital transformation is a company-wide phenomenon with broad organization implications; the core business model of the firm is subject to change using digital technology. Verhoef et al. (2019) highlights digital transformation as *"a change in how a firm employs digital technologies, to develop a new digital business model that helps to create and appropriate more value for the firm"*. In other words, companies focus on business model innovation affecting the whole company and the way of doing business as well as the way of creating business value.

It is obvious that digital transformation process is about *not only* utilizing digital technologies to facilitate changes in organizations or industry, *but also* creating new value networks, redesigning business models and developing right digital strategies in order to drive better operational performances. The use of cutting-edge digital technologies with a right strategy for digital business transformation can trigger the intended company-wide change and can facilitate right 3P initiatives and management practices. Organizations need to realize an effective 3P management using well-defined and adaptive methods in order to align their strategies with the global needs of competitive digital era.

Today, the competence and mindset of implementing adaptive approaches and agile practices for management of IT projects, programs or portfolios are becoming notable enablers of strategic digital transformation. Recently, various agile approaches are taking a considerable place in the agenda of companies. In order to realize agile 3P management lifecycles, pure agile approaches started to evolve into various forms such as hybrid agile approaches over time for utilizing benefits of different approaches concurrently. However, we need more to deliver successful IT projects. Identifying and articulating the need for change, seamless requirements elicitation and analysis, requirements traceability and monitoring processes with viable solution evaluation mechanisms are inevitable competence requirements for organizations. In other words, IT projects can succeed with the help of effective requirement engineering practices, in other words right mix of Business Analysis (BA) methodologies, tools and techniques.

The concept of BA is not novel; has a critical role in 3P management lifecycles. BA is *"the practice of enabling change in an organizational context, by defining needs and recommending solutions that deliver value to stakeholders"* (IIBA and Agile Alliance, 2015). There is a great effort of standardization bodies, researchers and practitioners over the world to introduce more effective and systematic implementation of BA for supporting project management capabilities of organizations. The notable issue is that today agile and adaptive methodologies are requiring efficient Agile Business Analysis (Agile BA) practices, instead of cumbersome, traditional BA work.

Researchers and practitioners are seeking for promising adaptive Agile BA practices in order to achieve successful project outcomes with high quality, speedy and flexible digital transformation; to maximize the value delivered by an organization to its stakeholders; and to support continuous improvement, namely continuous change. In this regard, the purpose of this chapter is to shed light on the importance of Agile BA in scope of digital transformation. As a building block in digital transformation, Agile BA principles and potential Agile BA techniques are investigated; trends and recommendations are presented with their benefits. As digital transformation requires an effective 3P management, Agile BA experience and competence of organizations can have a valuable potential for enabling digital transformation. Exploration of Agile BA methodologies will ensure new insights and opportunities for agile digital transformation.

RESEARCH BACKGROUND

Understanding Digital Transformation

The term digital transformation is not a new phenomenon. The roots of digital transformation as digital revolution can be traced back to late 1950s. With the third industrial revolution, adoption of digital technologies changed the way of doing business such as digital record keeping. Over time, the diffusion of IT into the all dimensions of organization required wide transformation of business processes and creation of new business models.

Venkatraman (1994) highlights the term "*IT-enabled business transformation*" with evolutionary and revolutionary levels of transformation. Organizations first perform localized improvements and internally integrate through IT functionalities. Later, in scope of revolutionary transformation, they redesign and redefine their business processes and business network for transforming IT into competitive advantage and financial performance.

In order to succeed digital transformation, the study of Berman (2012) explains two complementary approaches that can be followed by organizations: reshaping customer value propositions; and transforming the operations with the help of digital technologies. Organization can enhance, extend or redefine their existing customer value propositions with the help of accurate information and analytics. Delivery of new customer value propositions can be achieved with the remodeling and redesigning the business operations effectively and efficiently. Doing both approaches at the same time allows for broadest industry transformation.

The study of Vial (2019) reviews various definitions of digital transformation in order to put forward conceptual clarity challenges. In accordance with different views, Vial (2019) presents a brief conceptual definition for digital transformation as "*a process that aims to improve an entity by triggering significant changes to its properties through combinations of information, computing, communication, and connectivity technologies*".

In this regard, the enablers and building blocks of digital transformation are presented through an inductive framework by Vial (2019). These building blocks can be reviewed as follows: "use of digital technologies" such as Internet of Things (IoT), Industry 4.0, Blockchain, Artificial Intelligence, (AI) Mobile, Analytics and more; "disruptions" that are occurring in the society and industry; "strategic responses" triggering need for digital business strategy and digital transformation strategy in organizations; "changes in value creation paths" through use of promising digital technologies and in order to remain competitive which can generate not only "positive impacts" on organization performance, operational efficiency, industry improvements, but also "negative impacts" in terms of security and privacy. As last two blocks; "structural changes" such as organizational culture and structure and "organizational barriers" such as resistance to change, inertia can have effects on "changes in value creation". Changes in value creation paths can be achieved by rebuilding business models and redesigning of business processes (Berman 2012; Morakanyane et al., 2017); by reshaping value propositions, value networks, digital channels and agility (Vial, 2019).

One key driver towards digital transformation indicated by Li et al. (2019) is organizational mindfulness as a prerequisite of information processing capability which advances market agility of an organization. Another key driver of digital transformation is digital maturity of organization which is developed by organizational strategy, culture and talent (Ryan et al., 2019). Organizations need to adjust their digital technology portfolios and projects effectively. Realizing appropriate 3P and introducing of new digital platforms for their own business models is essential to reach desired IT capability and maturity. Such projects can strengthen firms' ability to collect, disseminate, store and analyze data; and can provide unique opportunities for firms to enhance their agility and also digital transformation (Roberts & Grover, 2012).

Lederer et al. (2017) also indicates that digital transformation is about optimization of processes with the aim of operational excellence; the process of value-adding business model creation. The role of Business Process Management (BPM) paradigm is emphasized in forming the basis of digitalization and driving the digital transformation efforts of organizations. BPM is a structured approach that supports business processes with the help of methods, techniques and software to design, enact, control and analyze operational processes (Zairi, 1997; Dumas et. al, 2013; Baiyere et al. 2020). Today, in context of digital transformation, traditional BPM paradigms -that follows a strict action sequence- do not provide quick response to business needs (Martins & Zacarias, 2017). Modern implementations are required for continuous process improvement (CPI) and business process redesign (Lederer et al, 2017, Ryan et al., 2019). Adoption of agile and lean approaches to process improvement and business model creation is a great concern of most organizations today (Martins & Zacarias, 2017; Xu and Koivumäki, 2019).

Implementing digital technologies is not enough to achieve digital transformation. As mentioned, digital transformation includes many components including effective portfolio or project management for integrating disruptive technologies or developing new digital platforms; business process improvements and redesign practices; introducing new business models and innovative value creation paths and more. The pervasiveness of digital technologies and the urgency to adapt new opportunities and business practices is a current concern. Organization need to increase their *agility* by adopting agile approaches to digital transformation. At this point, agile approaches have a great potential to assist the reconfiguration of business processes and models, governance and management of 3P.

Agility for Project Management and Business Transformation

As an important step in agile movement, the Agile Manifesto was published in 2001. Agile Alliance (2001) defines the term agile as "*the ability to create and respond to change*" and "*a way of dealing with, and ultimately succeeding in, an uncertain and turbulent environment*". It is the ability of organizations to take advantage of changes as opportunities (Sharifi & Zhang, 2000). Although some agile exercises were already used independently by practitioners before 2001 in response to the chaotic and unplanned conditions, the manifesto with its four core values and twelve principles created the foundation of agile as shown in Figure 1.

Agile approaches for adaptiveness and responsiveness to change were mostly used and adopted by *software development teams* in order to improve effectiveness of software development projects. Before 2001, traditional software development implementations are focusing on mostly plan driven practices that begin with heavyweight requirements elicitation and high-level design and development processes (Dora and Dubey, 2015). Traditional software development methodologies are based on a sequential series of steps like requirements definition, solution building, testing and deployment. They require defining and documenting a stable set of requirements at the beginning of a project; they are dependent on a set of processes and documentation. These documentations are developed as the work progresses and guide further development (Leau et al., 2012). Knowing and documenting all of the requirements before development phase provides valuable project outcomes; however, a change during the development lifecycle can create serious problems. Over time, implementations of heavyweight requirements engineering in projects become an obstacle for frequent changing requirements and achieving continuous improvement; digital transformation needs to be fast and adaptive (Dyba and Dingsoyr, 2009; Dingsøyr et al., 2010).

With Agile Manifesto in 2001, agile software development has rapidly become a mainstreams software development model in use today through industrial adoption of several its concrete manifestations such as Scrum and XP (Fowler and Highsmith, 2001; Loiro et al., 2019). Agile Alliance (2001) defines agile software development as *"an umbrella term for a set of frameworks and practices based on the core values and principles expressed in the Manifesto for Agile Software Development and the 12 Principles behind it"*. Agile mindset for software development addresses the collaborative development, reduction of unnecessary work, minimizing wasteful documentation and shorter development lifecycles in order to effectively guide and manage software development and control the variation of agile software development (Dingsøyr et. al, 2010; Dingsøyr and Moe, 2014; Conboy 2009). Agile methods allow to adopt changing business and user requirements, to deliver working software frequently and to achieve close collaboration of all stakeholders and project team.

Figure 1. Review of agile manifesto

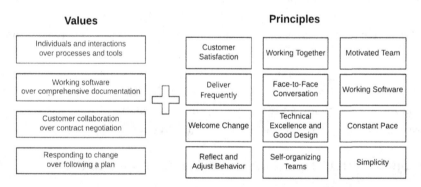

Agile software development is defined as adaptive, cooperative, incremental and straightforward by Suryaatmaja et al. (2019). Currently, diverse implementations of agile software development approaches are available over the world such as Scrum, Extreme Programming (XP), Feature Driven Development (FDD), Adaptive Software Development (ASD), Dynamic Software Development Method (DSDM), Crystal, Kanban and many other adaptive approaches (Awad, 2005; Phil, 2015; Flora et al., 2014; Collabnet Versione, 2019). Some of the popular ones are reviewed with their key practices and challenges in Table 1 in accordance with studies of Awad (2005), Phil (2015), Flora et al. (2014), Javanmard et al. (2015) and Ozdenizci Kose (2019).

According to the state of Agile Survey that VersionOne has been conducting annually since 2007, top three reasons for adopting agile methodologies are accelerating software delivery, enhancing ability to manage changing priorities and increasing productivity (Collabnet Versione, 2019). Therefore, adopting suitable agile software development process is considered as a strategic management decision with long term implications. In this regard, Scrum and XP approaches are highlighted as the most common agile methodologies used by today's organizations.

Table 1. Review of common agile methodologies

Methodology	Key Practices	Advantages	Challenges
Scrum	Iterative increments; 2 to 4 weeks iterations as sprints; product backlog; spring backlog; sprint planning; the daily scrum (or stand-up); sprint reviews, sprint retrospectives	High level communication; high involvement of user as Product Owner; self-organizing teams and feedback	Weak documentation; can easily get off track; changing requirements
XP (Extreme Programming)	Iterative increments; 1 to 6 weeks iterations; user stories; pair programming; test driven development; refactoring	Active end user involvement; frequent feedback opportunities; strong technical practice	Weak documentation; unclear needs of clients; lack of disciplines; small teams that are suitable only for smaller projects
DSDM (Dynamic Systems Development Method)	Iterative; detailed documentation; prototyping; feasibility and business study	Strong control on project lifecycle; user involvement through frequent releases; requirement priority approach	Complex and time-consuming documentation; expects continuous user involvement
FDD (Feature Driven Development)	Iterative; 2 days to 2 weeks iterations; suitable for complex projects; many members and multiple teams working in parallel; modeling with detailed documentation	Method simplicity; Easy to understand because of documentation; user involvement through frequent reports	Less communication within and out of team; individual code ownership; complex approach for small projects
ASD (Adaptive Software Development)	Incremental; 4 to 8 weeks iterations; basic documentation; learning cycle	User involvement through frequent releases	Weak documentation; small teams and suitable only for smaller projects
Crystal	Incremental, informal and face-to-face team communication	High risk and highly important component given first; efficient coordination and communication of bigger teams; user involvement through frequent releases	Planning and development are not depended on requirements

Another critical finding about the agile maturity in the agile survey report (Collabnet Versione, 2019) is underlined as "*vast majority of respondents (83%) said their organization were below a high level of competency with agile practices, further revealing opportunities for improvement through supporting training & coaching.*" Big majority of the organizations are using agile practices like daily stand ups, short iterations, sprint or iteration planning, retrospectives, sprint review, test-driven techniques, burn-down charts; however, the adoption of agile practices and agile approaches to market conditions is still evolving and maturing. It is important to highlight that agile software development is not only about practices and frameworks but also a "mindset" with its core values and principles.

The cooperation provided by agile mindset supports getting the potential of higher customer satisfaction and quicker adaptation to rapid changing business requirements (Cho, 2010; Miller and Larson, 2005). Agile approaches focus on context-specific development by achieving lower defect rates, performing faster development, and by being responsive to rapidly changing requirements (Boehm and Turner, 2003).

Beyond software development perspective, agile approaches started to be utilized in other areas of digital transformation such as business process redesign, process improvement, new value path creation, new opportunity discovery, new product development and more. Consideration of agile in business transformation allows organizations to discover changes or new opportunities, and to react quickly (Martins & Zacarias, 2017; Xu and Koivumäki, 2019).

Importance of Business Analysis

In order to realize efficient IT projects and digital business transformation; researchers and practitioners are taking advantage from BA which provides well-structured tools and techniques to identify needs; recommend solutions; elicit, document, and manage "requirements" to deliver expected benefits (PMI, 2017a).

The term BA provides a disciplined approach for introducing and managing the change to organizations whether they are non-profit or profit or government organizations. According to Project Management Institute (PMI) (2017a), BA allows to optimize the delivery of business value by providing the information needed to make wiser investment decisions on portfolios, programs, and projects once the decision to pursue an organizational change or transformation has been made.

Report of PMI (2017b) indicates the importance of BA as follows: "*Poor performance occurs when organizations lack maturity in significant BA processes and fail to recognize the value it provides. When BA is properly accounted for and executed on projects and programs, high-quality requirements are produced; stakeholders are more engaged; the solution delivers intended value; and projects are more likely to be delivered on time, within scope, and within budget. For many organizations, effective BA is not an integral part of their project work. That contributes to projects not delivering the intended value*".

BA can be defined as the work of "*requirements engineering*". As illustrated in Figure 2, PMI (2017a) defines knowledge areas of traditional BA as needs assessment, requirements elicitation, requirements analysis, requirements monitoring and controlling, solution evaluation and stakeholder engagement in all steps.

Currently, as a reaction to traditional software development methodologies, agile approaches have become popular that aims to expedite the software development lifecycle and to ensure that output satisfies "requirements". Integrating traditional requirements engineering perspective with agile software development processes generally does not work well; traditional BA techniques implementation on agile methodologies can seem overwhelming (Käpyaho & Kauppinen, 2015: 335-336; Parker, 2013).

Today, practitioners and researchers are seeking for lighter requirements engineering practices, in other words lightweight BA, that can handle the issues of abstract or unclear requirements and specifications, changing requirements, and at the same time that can satisfy the Agile Manifesto philosophy; fast delivery of software, high user involvement and executive support during software project implementation. More collaboration and less engineering practices are accepted as the key characteristics of agile methodologies.

Ambler (2018) emphasizes agile analysis as "*highly evolutionary and collaborative process where developers and project stakeholders actively work together on a just-in-time (JIT) basis to understand the domain, to identify what needs to be built, to estimate that functionality, to prioritize the functionality, and in the process optionally producing artifacts that are just barely good enough.*"

Figure 2. Knowledge areas of BA
Source: PMI, 2017a

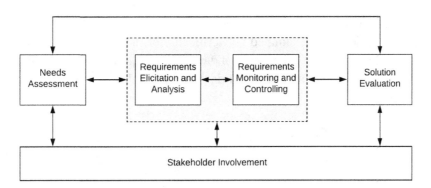

Today, enabling more Agile BA and agile requirements engineering practices is an interesting research field. Researchers are working on how requirements engineering approaches and techniques can be considered within context of agile business transformation and projects. Accordingly there are also some studies which provide useful information about implementation of agile requirements engineering practices, lighter requirement practices and its challenging issues (Ochodek, & Kopczyńska, 2018; Wagner et al., 2018; Kasauli et al., 2017; Schön et al., 2017; Musa et al., 2017; Käpyaho & Kauppinen, 2015; Leffingwell, 2010; Cao et al., 2008; Martins & Zacarias, 2017; Xu and Koivumäki, 2019).

The studies of Paetsch et al. (2003) and Schön et al. (2017) review the agile requirements engineering activities in five phases: discovery and elicitation of new requirements (through techniques such as interviews, use case, observation, focus groups, brainstorming, prototyping etc.); refinement and analysis of new ideas and requirements; prioritization of requirements through requirement value measurement; checking and review of requirements; and then documentation.

Fancott et al. (2012) puts forward that agile requirements engineering mainly relies on conversations with business and implicit knowledge of the stakeholder. Analysts needs to constantly ensure that the features demanded by the customers align with the business goals, and benefits from frequent feedbacks from customers. Results of successive iterations help analysts to refine requirements, mitigate risk early in the project and deliver right solution on time within budget.

As stated by the studies of Käpyaho et al. (2015) and Paetsch et al. (2003), the guidelines for requirements engineering provided by agile methods are ambiguous since the concepts related with agile requirements engineering are still being developed. Some common characteristics of agile requirements engineering are strong use of face-to-face communication, iterative requirements elicitation and design, continuous requirements prioritization, prototyping or other modeling activities to make sense of requirements, Test Driven Development (TDD) and acceptance testing to ensure the quality and right direction (De Lucia, & Qusef, 2010; Käpyaho et al., 2015).

Another study conducted by Cao & Ramesh (2008) in software development organizations indicates that face-to-face communication, prototyping and reviews and tests are common agile practices. However, it is seen that all of these practices bring some inherent challenges. The literature studies of Cao & Ramesh (2008), Bjarnason et al. (2011), Paetsch et al. (2003) show that projects that are realized by agile methodologies have requirements engineering challenges such as managing with very little documentation, not understanding the importance of writing tests first, not understanding the big picture, neglecting quality requirements, unrealistic expectations of customers due to early user interface (UI) prototypes, neglect of non-functional requirements, unavailability of customer during acceptance test writing.

The study of Wagner et al. (2018) provides a well-defined problem list that are commonly occurring in the context of agile projects and examined how criticality of those problems is judged by practitioners. According to research findings, incomplete and/or hidden requirements and communication flows between project team and customer are the top of the list of criticalities.

AGILE APPROACH FOR BUSINESS ANALYSIS

Today, BA is a critical competence requirement for organizations in order to deliver high quality project outcomes, transform business processes efficiently, and achieve maximum value. Agile BA is the integration of BA with agile mindset that can facilitate agile digital transformation within organizations. Since traditional BA practices in agile context have constraints for the practitioners and researchers, agile and adaptive mindset for performing BA is highly essential in today's digital era. For the effective management of 3P and improvement of business processes, high quality and agile *needs assessment* for the problem domain and *traceability the solution* is critical issue.

As one of the important bodies providing IIBA endorsed training programs, BAE (Business Analysis Excellence Pty Ltd) highlights that *"Agile BA can provide a competitive advantage in fast-paced and complex environments and has moved beyond software development initiatives to any business domain. Organizations have adopted agile practices at all levels of planning and in many diverse business areas."* (BAE, 2018a)

Agile BA focuses on continuous feedback and continuous learning in order to *prioritize delivery, reduce waste* and *raise customer value* (BAE, 2018b). Continuous feedback can be encouraged by engagement of internal or external stakeholders such as customers, team members, experts, investors and other partners in BA. Feedback mechanism allows organizations to comprehend if they are delivering right value for customer; which will trigger continuous learning in organizations. The collected feedback helps to prioritize the work items in product backlogs and focuses on the most valuable story for the customer. In this regard, feedback mechanism forms the basis of Agile BA.

As mentioned in Figure 1, Agile Manifesto highlights four core value: individuals and interactions, customer collaboration, working software and respond to change. The core values of Agile software development emphasize *being people centric* and *results driven*. In this regard, Agile Extension to the BABOK® Guide by IIBA and Agile Alliance (2017) states seven key principles for realizing Agile approach in BA for practitioners: *see the whole, think as a customer, analyze to determine what is valuable, get real using examples, understand what is doable, stimulate collaboration and continuous improvement*, and *avoid waste*.

See the whole, think as a customer and *analyze to determine what is valuable* principles address elicitation and analysis of requirements in context of BA. Understanding the big picture and focusing on needs of customers allow to discover the most valuable requirements as user stories and perform necessary analysis on them instead of non-value adding user stories. *Get real using examples, understand what is doable, stimulate collaboration and continuous improvement* and *avoid waste* principles address delivery of requirements, monitoring and controlling of requirements in context of BA. Depending on these seven principles, two main frameworks are presented for Agile BA: *the discovery framework* and *the delivery framework*, which corroborate somewhat with the traditional BA knowledge areas (PMI, 2017a) as reviewed in Figure 3.

So, *what do we know about recent Agile BA techniques?* In accordance with the seven principles of Agile BA, techniques required for Agile BA need to mainly focus on prioritization of work in an agile manner, extracting most valuable work, and responding to change. Regarding the seven principles and knowledge areas, promising techniques for realizing Agile BA are described and reviewed comprehensively in two phases: Agile Requirements Elicitation and Analysis, and Agile Requirements Monitoring and Controlling.

Figure 3. Knowledge areas of BA

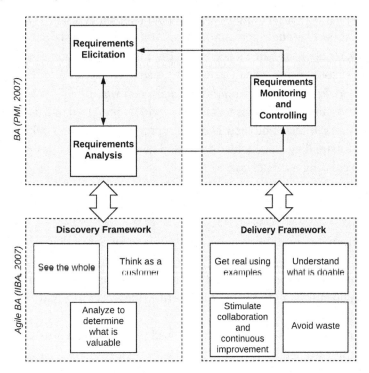

Agile Requirements Elicitation and Analysis

This section presents state-of-the-art techniques for requirements elicitation and analysis in accordance with the guidelines of PMI (2017a), and IIBA and Agile Alliance (2017). Recent promising requirements discovery techniques are reviewed; future trends and directions are presented for advancing requirements discovery in various agile projects of software development, process improvement and business transformation.

Personas

Persona is a very popular "user centric" practice for enhancing elicitation of requirements in agile software development. When system as project outcome has a large number of users or customers, developing persona -as a class of users- with enough characteristics is a good choice for understanding the big picture as whole system. A persona was first introduced by Alan Cooper which is virtual person or archetypical user or customer of the system (Pruitt & Grudin, 2003). PMI (2017a) defines Persona as *"a fictional character created to represent an individual or group of stakeholders, termed a user class."* This fictional character has descriptive features like a name, demographics, skills, goals, behaviors, motivations, hobbies and more.

Robertson & Robertson (2012) states that *"Personas are useful when real users are not available or are too numerous for you to interview all of them. The persona is a virtual character that substitutes for the human users. We strongly suggest using a persona when you do not have access to the real users or customers. Almost always, the persona is a better representation of the user than a human proxy."*

Persona analysis allows to design user experiences by extracting the big picture. In order to draw out the stakeholder -actual person- requirements, fictional characters are used to determine how a user interacts with the solution. Through persona analysis, business analysts can easily put forward the whole picture by thinking about persona's needs. By thinking like persona as someone real or treating the persona as a real person, business analysts can ask questions like *"What does Alice want now?"* or *"How does Alice want to do?"* or *"What would Alice do in this situation?"*. When developing personas, narratives, namely stories are created. This technique is widely preferred and used by agile practitioners to analyze a group of users, understand their needs and product design and behavior requirements. It is a powerful tool for understanding stakeholder needs and targeting product design and behavior for each class of user, and also creating user stories.

User Stories

In order to think as a customer, in addition to personas, user stories are valuable assets in Agile BA. PMI (2017a) describes the term user story as *"a one or two sentence description written from the viewpoint of the actor that describes a function that is needed."* User stories are generated to document stakeholder or user requirements depending on the value of benefit achieved by users with the completion of the corresponding story.

Personas -virtual characters with the problem- are used for developing user stories; broad features are decomposed into user stories, and then elaborated to acceptance criteria. The boundaries of each user story should be defined by acceptance criteria which describes conditions that the solution must provide in order to be accepted by user or stakeholder. A user story can be written in the following format: *as an <actor>, I need to <function>, so that I can <benefit>*. Who, What and Why questions should be summarized in a user story; for example, *As a student, I want to generate a transcript report, so that I can evaluate my overall performance*. User stories should meet some criteria, generally identified as INVEST criteria which stands for Independent, Negotiable, Valuable, Estimable, Sized to fit, Testable (Wake, 2003). Identified user stories in a product backlog should be simple and powerful statements describing the functionality, need or goal from the perspective or the user (IIBA and Agile Alliance, 2017).

It is essential to highlight that the primary technique for representing requirements is to work with user stories in most agile environments. Development of user stories allows to understand the requirements of the solution effectively and efficiently. They are the fundamental constructs of Product Backlog which presents all the work that needs to get done in an agile system development project.

Backlog Grooming

Backlog Grooming, in other words Backlog Refinement is a must practice within context of Agile BA work. Product Backlog including list of requirements as user stories for an iteration prioritized by highest customer value (IIBA and Agile Alliance, 2017). Agile software development projects cannot succeed without continuous prioritization work. The backlog and user stories should periodically revised and updated by the Product Owner and agile team members as the acceptance criteria is developed.

Collaboration of all team members, stakeholders and customers is essential for refinement and management of Product Backlog. Backlog Grooming ensures sufficiently detailed and clearly defined user stories with the implementation of story decomposition, story elaboration, prioritization of stories and sequencing.

Value Stream Mapping for Lean Mindset

Another considerable agile practice is to perform Value Stream Mapping (VSM) for presenting the big picture of as-is and to-be environments. As a variation of process flows, VSM is firstly originated in Lean Manufacturing methodologies, but now it has gained high popularity in agile project management frameworks. Scaled Agile (2020) highlights value streams as *"the series of steps that an organization uses to implement solutions that provide a continuous flow of value to a customer"*. Scaled Agile Framework (SaFE) also encourages the development of value streams for set of solutions in its portfolio.

As a lean methodology, VSM is a powerful tool in order to *"identify process steps that add value (value stream) and those that do not add value (waste)"* as indicated by PMI (2017a). The flow of information, people and materials is required to provide solution (e.g., system, product, or service) to a customer is analyzed by VSM technique; in other words, the "value" created by solution is identified and optimized through process maps.

The main focus behind VSM technique is to achieve shortest lead time and highest quality, and to deliver maximum value for customer. The value stream process maps are visualized by flowcharts for effective problem detection and problem solving. In Agile BA context, the developed maps enable to explore process value adding and non-value adding steps in existing business process and also in future state of business process. Moreover, it can help to quickly discover non-value adding steps, separate waste/constraints/delays from value added steps, eliminate waste, discover opportunities for improvement, optimize a process and create a future state process in an agile manner. The technique is especially valuable within scope of agile business process improvement and reengineering projects.

Story Mapping with Minimum Viable Product

Story mapping is a visual view of the sequence of activities or user stories to be supported by a solution. As a promising Agile BA practice, Story Mapping is *"used to sequence user stories, based upon their business value and the order in which their users typically perform them, so that teams can arrive at a shared understanding of what will be built"* (PMI, 2017a).

A story map includes two main components: the backbone and the walking skeleton. The backbone part includes the Minimum Viable Product (MVP) which aims to present the smallest set of core capabilities, user stories as requirements that should be in the first release product for the solution to provide its purpose PMI (2017a). At this point, business analysts should clearly identify the target market involving early adapters of the solution. Story mapping allows to build the MVP line on the board and facilitates team to develop the release that includes MVP features. In adaptive and agile approaches, MVP has a notable importance since it allows to reduce cost and risk by gaining customer feedback before releasing the full solution and tests actual usage scenario instead of relying on market research (IIBA and Agile Alliance, 2017). By this way, customers do not face with a product that they don't want, which reduces the risk.

The walking skeleton presents the full set of functionality and requirements that the stakeholders require for the solution to be accepted as functional (PMI, 2017a). The stories are ranked in order of highest business value at the top to lowest business value at the bottom as shown in Figure 4. Story maps help to communicate the features, stories and requirements effectively and quickly through collaboration with stakeholders. Story mapping can be generated by using sticky notes on white-boards or using software tools during workshops or brainstorming sessions. Since it describes the customer's journey in a flow, this visual technique has also a considerable support for developing user stories, managing product backlog and refining backlog.

Storyboarding

Another valuable agile practice is storyboarding which can be defined as a kind of prototyping. Unlike story mapping, storyboarding presents sequence of illustrations or images that explains the big picture. It is also known as navigation flow, dialogue map, or dialog hierarchy. Storyboarding is generally used with user stories in order to detail the sequence of activities visually and to show the interactions of user with the system through workshops or brainstorming sessions. Storyboarding mainly contributes and support UI and UX design as a popular agile analysis technique today. Storyboarding allows to elaborate and validate requirements visually and effectively with the stakeholders since it easily communicates to team what needs to be develop (PMI, 2017a).

User Experience Design

Beyond UI design, today UX design is most concerned with how systems or application will look and feel and how customer will interact. It enables to focus on consumer's journey: *How does the user feel and think about their experience?* UX designers are mainly responsible from building wireframes and high-fidelity prototypes, creating interaction design, developing content structure and information architecture, and performing usability testing tasks.

Currently, UX design has gained a great attention in adaptive and agile environments. Agile approaches started to place more UX studies to get in touch with customers and understand their overall look and feel for each release. Business analysts should collaborate with UX designers in order to integrate personas, user stories and customer's journey with visual screens and prototyping. Understanding the user flow and experience and getting continuous feedback from customers have a critical role in streamlining the agile development process. Currently, various UX design software and tools are available in software industry for expanding the Agile UX design studies.

Figure 4. Story mapping

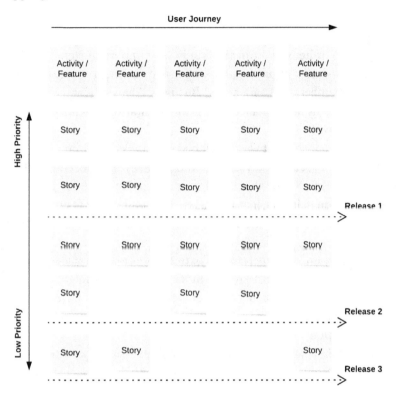

Impact Mapping

Impact Mapping is a lightweight, fast and collaborative planning technique through face-to-face brain-storming and workshop sessions to present the big picture of a software development project. Agile teams and stakeholders discover the information from different perspectives; visualizes the organizational goals and deliverables; answers how these deliverables connect to use needs and how user outcomes relate higher level organizational goals. During impact mapping technique, a visual tree map is developed and continuous refined with the continuous feedback mechanism.

An impact map includes organizational goals, actors contributing to achieve these goals, impacts as actions that actors can take to realize these goals and deliverables helping to achieve these goals. The technique allows to connect goals and actors with impacts and deliverables. The information is structured as a mind map; importance and priority are described with symbols or colors. Instead of feature development (what) perspective, the value creation (why) perspective is the main focus of impact mapping. This practice, but not limited, easily engages stakeholders together, exposes deliverables with their impacts, and facilitates effective planning and prioritization of deliverables and impacts (Neuri Consulting, 2020; IIBA and Agile Alliance, 2017).

Kano Analysis

As mentioned, agile approaches and also Agile BA give high importance for determining and developing the most valuable feature(s) or item(s). Prioritization is very important step of agile software development. Prioritization of user stories in product backlog and refinement of backlog iteratively should be performed by agile team members, customers and Business Analyst. Kano analysis is a powerful tool for analyzing the valuable items and enhances the prioritization work with stakeholders and customer in agile environments effectively.

Kano analysis is not a new concept; it was developed by Professor Noriaki Kano in 1980s for product development and customer satisfaction analysis. According to PMI (2017a), five product categories shown in Figure 5 are generally used in Kano model to understand and analyze the product features and characteristics. This categorization helps the team members to capture each feature's expected contribution for customer's satisfaction level (Sauerwein et al., 1996). The categories can be summarized as follows:

- Basic are must features; their absence causes extreme dissatisfaction;
- Performance represents features that provide more satisfied customers;
- Delighters (also known as Excitement) represents the features that have "great" effect on customers; when they are available, they provide extreme satisfaction; but absence of those features do not create a dissatisfaction;
- Indifferent represents the features that neither satisfy not dissatisfy customers;
- Reverse represents the features that customers do not want; decrease customer satisfaction directly.

The practice has a great potential in Agile BA for understanding and analyzing product features and quality from customer perspective, and prioritizing and sequencing user stories. It helps to determine which user stories or requirements are significant to develop before releasing the full solution.

Purpose Alignment Model

Another valuable technique for supporting the most valuable analysis and prioritization is Purpose Alignment Model. This model aims to evaluate the ideas in terms of customer and business value and categorizing options in accordance with the business purpose. Similar to Kano model, this model also provides a strong mechanism for making prioritization in agile environments and performing strategic decisions. The greatest value providing features, requirements and capabilities are explored with this model; by the way it enhances the prioritization work with stakeholders and customer effectively.

Purpose alignment model evaluates the characteristics, features or user stories in two perspectives: market differentiation and criticality (PMI, 2017a). The market differentiation dimension focuses on whether the feature creates a differentiation; on the other side the mission critical dimension focuses on whether the feature is critical for the company and its mission. In this regard, four categories are identified where a feature or story can be categorized as shown in Figure 6:

- Differentiating features are mission critical and present high differentiation in the market;
- Parity features are mission critical, but present low differentiation in the market;
- Partner features present high market differentiation, but are not considered as critical;
- Who cares features are neither differentiating nor critical for the organization.

Figure 5. Kano model
Source: PMI, 2017a

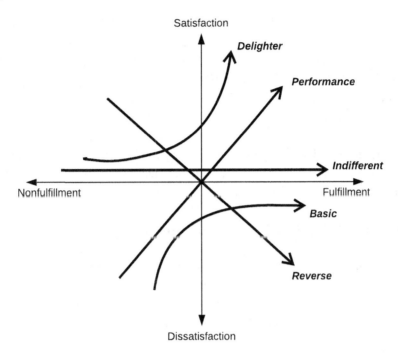

Figure 6. Purpose alignment model
Source: PMI, 2017a

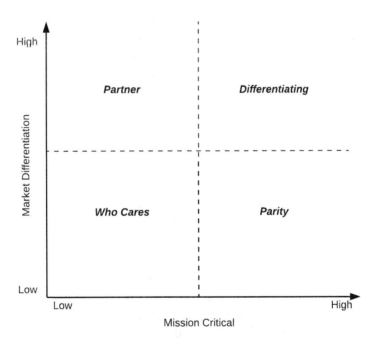

MoSCoW Model

MoSCoW stands for *Must have, Should have, Could have,* and *Won't have* classification of priority. This practice is very easy and effective for agile teams in order prioritize of stories and features during Product Backlog management. With MoSCoW model, most critical set of stories can be explored, sequenced, prioritized and managed in backlog by agile team members.

The agile approaches focus on continuous feedback and continuous assessment of business value to enhance the prioritization and determination of most valuable work at that time. Agile BA practice is the art of maximizing and delivering the value continuously. Drawing the big picture; thinking as a customer; being customer or centric; and identifying most valuable requirements, features or user stories are primary purposes of most agile approaches. Hence, the techniques regarding Agile Requirements Elicitation and Analysis phase should be enriched with valuable techniques by researchers and practitioners over time.

Agile Requirements Monitoring and Controlling

This section presents state-of-the-art practices for agile requirements delivery, monitoring and controlling phase in accordance with the guidelines of PMI (2017a) and IIBA and Agile Alliance (2017). Similarly, recent techniques are reviewed; and future directions are suggested for advancing release and monitoring of requirements in various agile projects of software development, process improvement and business transformation.

Behavior Driven Development (BDD) for More Automated Testing

As a software development methodology, Behavior Driven Development (BDD) is an extension, branch of TDD. The technique focuses on *"customer behavior"* in order to meet customer needs. The technique mainly allows to get real using examples. The aim is to increase value, eliminate waste and advance communication between stakeholders and agile team members.

As highlighted by IIBA and Agile Alliance (2017), BDD expresses customer needs in natural language which allows all team members to understand easily. Beyond user story format, BDD uses Gherkin format that allows to express product needs as concrete scenarios or real examples: *GIVEN <a context> WHEN <an event> THEN <expected outcome>*. Given conditions and expected outcomes are triggered only one When event. The format aims to put forward multiple dimensions of the corresponding system or product solution: user role, user actions, data rules and business rules.

The scenarios written in BDD format describe events, conditions and actions which can serve as acceptance criteria for user stories and also as tests. Real scenarios of BDD enhance the development of test cases; scenarios can be effectively converted into automated tests. Executable form of behavior codes is compiled and executed to verify that code matches the behavior and validate functionality. Easy and quick automation of customer behavior scenarios speeds up agile analysis verification and validation of requirements. BDD is also a continuous practice; enables not only agile delivery of requirements, but also agile delivery customer value incrementally. As studied by Egbreghts (2017), Table 2 provides a brief description of execution steps performed by TDD and BDD.

Lean Traceability and Kanban Boards

Remember that, lean is the process philosophy that aims to eliminate and avoid waste. Waste can be defined as something that negatively affects the process quality and productivity. In order to avoid waste in agile software project management, lightweight BA practices should be explored and implemented for requirements delivery, traceability and even for documentation of Agile BA practices. In this regard, a promising approach is incorporating Kanban principles as a lean methodology into agile software development methodology.

Table 2. Comparison of TDD and BDD execution

	TDD	BDD
1	Write a test	Write a test scenario
2	Run the test and check if it fails	Execute the scenario and check if it fails
3	Write a code sufficient for the test to pass	Write a code sufficient to implement the expected behavior
4	Run the test and check if it passes	Execute the scenario check if it passes
5	Refactor the code	Refactor the code

Source: Egbreghts, 2017

PMI (2007a) defines Kanban as *"an adaptive life cycle in which items are pulled from a backlog and started when other product backlog items are completed"* and also it *"establishes work-in-progress limits to constrain the number of product backlog items that can be in progress at any point in time"*.

Currently, Kanban boards are used in adaptive environments within continuous improvement scope of Kanban, to monitor and track work in-progress (WIP) by agile team members. It is a variation of the original Kanban cards. Kanban boards allow to visually plan the work and depict the workflow and capacity, support agile team members. The visual representation enhances planning, monitoring and controlling of the user stories and work; shows clearly planned, in-progress, completed and incomplete user stories; and avoids bottlenecks in item development and release management. Various software tools for Kanban board are introducing today for agile projects in scope of digital transformation; as an example, Figure 7 shows a view from one of the popular Kanban boards; Trello (2020) by Atlassian.

Reviews and Retrospectives

In order to monitor and control the requirements, retrospectives and review meetings should be encouraged in adaptive and agile digital transformation. Especially in Scrum framework, retrospectives and reviews are highly used by stakeholders with the purpose of continuous improvement of agile environment.

Retrospectives are used to benefit from the past experience and plan the future. Meetings should be scheduled and conducted on a regular basis such as after each iteration of agile environment. As stated by PMI (2017a), the following questions are discussed in these meetings: *What worked well? What is not working or is unclear? What will we commit to doing in next iteration? What could be improved? What changes can we make now?*

Figure 7. An example for Kanban board
Source: Trello (2020)

With the collaboration -of all team members, stakeholders, product owners and business analysts- and communication approach, team members can make actionable commitments. By the way, continuous feedback and continuous improvement can be ensured effectively by retrospectives and reviews.

DISCUSSION AND RECOMMENDATIONS

Traditional BA knowledge areas indicate three requirements engineering phases which are triggered with needs assessment, supported throughout the lifecycle with stakeholder engagement and ends up with solution evaluation. Requirements elicitation, analysis and requirements monitoring and controlling are the building blocks of BA. General knowledge of BA states various techniques; however, it is clear that incorporating all these techniques into agile approaches is impossible due to the nature of agile approaches; some of these techniques can work well in agile environments.

Requirements elicitation and analysis focuses on discovering and examining product information in sufficient detail depending on customer needs, organizational goals and business objectives. There are various techniques from interviews, document analysis, observation, focus groups to collaborative games, wireframing, timeboxing, affinity diagrams, context diagrams and more. In terms of agile perspective, high potential and promising techniques are highlighted for realizing value adding requirements elicitation and analysis. Using personas, developing user stories and story boards, creating value steam maps, building story maps, focusing on MVPs, working with UX designs enable to explore the requirements in an agile manner effectively. These techniques can be easily integrated to agile digital transformation. They allow to extract the big picture of system solution with its features from the eye and mindset of customer. Describing features and user stories helps to explain the customer's journey in an agile manner. Especially, visual representation of customer's journey through UX designs as high-fidelity prototypes including interactions without coding enables to purely develop the navigation flows, and even value stream process flows. Today, UX designers with appropriate UX design platforms should be considered by organizations to react quickly to changes.

Besides requirements discovery, continuous requirements prioritization is another significant part of release planning and backlog management. In order to enhance prioritization of requirements, three popular known models are suggested and explained which can be effectively integrated to agile approaches. These models provide assessment of requirements in different valuable perspectives. Kano Model allows to analyze features and user stories in terms of customer satisfaction level; on the other side Purpose Alignment Model enables to assess features in terms of market differentiation and business criticality; and another model, MoSCoW provides an easy evaluation of requirements based on the need for customers and stakeholders. Continuous requirements prioritization can be enhanced by continuous feedback mechanism. In this regard, workshops, face-to-face brainstorming sessions, review meetings after each iteration and retrospectives are inevitable supporting mechanisms for continuous feedback environment and prioritization of requirements. These agile mechanisms should be encouraged and used by members of any type project in terms of digital transformation.

The next phase, requirements monitoring and controlling focuses on ensuring that requirements are approved, managed and tracked. Today, implementing BDD methodology which originally emerged from TDD methodology is a powerful delivery tool for many agile software development projects. It enhances the automated testing practices which means high quality acceptability and traceability of user stories as product releases. BDD is also stated by IIBA and Agile Alliance (2017) as an enabler of getting real using examples principle. In addition to BDD, lean mindset should be also incorporated to agile software development processes. Lean methodology feeds continuous feedback, continuous improvement and waste elimination which are current needs of agile environments.

Instead of manual testing, implementation of BDD advances automated testing processes and continuous integration in agile organizations. Continuous integration practice under lean methodology is becoming very popular which aims to reduce the lack of automation in processes and avoid transportation and waiting waste. For improving productivity and increasing automation in testing practices of agile environments, it should be considered that BDD and lean principles should work together.

Use of Kanban board technique as one of the popular ways of implementing lean mindset have the capability for improving traceability and monitoring of requirements. Similarly, review meetings after each iteration and retrospectives support continuous feedback and improvement; in turn traceability of requirements. In this regard, a useless meeting means a kind of waiting waste for the attendee; notable and valuable actions should be taken after each meeting. As a principle of Agile BA, agile team members, stakeholders and business analysts must avoid waste; value adding review meetings, workshops, brainstorming sessions and also high-quality retrospectives should be conducted for continuous integration and continuous feedback. Another important lean need for Agile BA is producing lightweight documents. Working with visual representations -like UX designs, interaction diagrams, process flows, and story maps- is a good way for documenting Agile BA in scope of agile digital transformation.

CONCLUSION

The pervasiveness of digital technologies and the urgency to adapt new opportunities and business practices are significant subjects in the age of digital transformation. Organizations need to increase their agility and realize agile digital transformation. At this point, agile approaches have a great potential to assist the reconfiguration of business processes and models, governance and management of 3P. Agile and adaptive methodologies are requiring powerful Agile BA practices, instead of heavyweight requirements engineering. Need for change identification, clear problem definition, seamless requirements elicitation and analysis, lean requirements traceability and monitoring processes are inevitable competence needs for organizations.

This chapter reviews recent issues and directions on Agile BA; and presents state-of-the-art techniques of BA for adaptive and agile lifecycles that can be used for software project management, process improvement, business transformation and more. In context of the frameworks of IIBA and Agile Alliance (2017) and knowledge areas of PMI (2017a), promising agile techniques are examined in order to ensure new insights and opportunities. The regarding best agile practices present valuable guidelines for researchers and practitioners that how they can advance continuous feedback, continuous learning, continuous improvement and continuous integration capabilities of organizations, and also how to maximize value to the stakeholders in agile project lifecycles and agile business transformations.

REFERENCES

Agile Alliance. (2001). *Agile manifesto*. http://agilemanifesto.org/

Ambler, S. W. (2018). *Agile Analysis. Agile Modeling*. Available at: http://www.agilemodeling.com/essays/agileAnalysis.htm#AgileAnalysis

Awad, M. A. (2005). A comparison between agile and traditional software development methodologies. University of Western Australia.

BAE. (2018a). *Agile Business Analysis: Why you should start taking note of the Agile Extension to the BABOK Guide*. Available at: https://business-analysis-excellence.com/agile-business-analysis-start-taking-note-agile-extension-babok-guide/

BAE. (2018b). *Agile Business Analysis – The role of agile analysis, key principles and the planning horizons*. Available at: https://business-analysis-excellence.com/agile-business-analysis-the-role-of-agile-analysis-key-principles-and-the-planning-horizons/

Baiyere, A., Salmela, H., & Tapanainen, T. (2020). Digital transformation and the new logics of business process management. *European Journal of Information Systems*, 1–22. doi:10.1080/0960085X.2020.1718007

Berman, S. J. (2012). Digital transformation: Opportunities to create new business models. *Strategy and Leadership*, *40*(2), 16–24. doi:10.1108/10878571211209314

Bjarnason, E., Wnuk, K., & Regnell, B. (2011, July). A case study on benefits and side-effects of agile practices in large-scale requirements engineering. In *Proceedings of the 1st Workshop on Agile Requirements Engineering* (p. 3). ACM. 10.1145/2068783.2068786

Cao, L., & Ramesh, B. (2008). Agile requirements engineering practices: An empirical study. *IEEE Software*, *25*(1), 60–67. doi:10.1109/MS.2008.1

Cho, J. J. (2010). An exploratory study on issues and challenges of agile software development with scrum. *All Graduate theses and dissertations, 599.*

Cockburn, A. (2004). *Crystal clear: a human-powered methodology for small teams.* Pearson Education.

Collabnet Versione. (2019). *StateofAgile Report: 13th Annual State Of Agile Report.* Available at: https://www.stateofagile.com/#ufh-i-521251909-13th-annual-state-of-agile-report/473508

Conboy, K. (2009). Agility from first principles: Reconstructing the concept of agility in information systems development. *Information Systems Research, 20*(3), 329–354. doi:10.1287/isre.1090.0236

De Lucia, A., & Qusef, A. (2010). Requirements engineering in agile software development. *Journal of Emerging Technologies in Web Intelligence, 2*(3), 212–220. doi:10.4304/jetwi.2.3.212-220

Dingsøyr, T., Dybå, T., & Moe, N. B. (2010). *Agile software development: current research and future directions.* Springer Science & Business Media. doi:10.1007/978-3-642-12575-1

Dingsøyr, T., & Moe, N. B. (2014). Towards principles of large-scale agile development. *International Conference on Agile Software Development*, 1-8.

Dora, S. K., & Dubey, P. (2015). Software Development Life Cycle (SDLC) Analytical Comparison and Survey on Traditional and Agile Methodology. *National Monthly Referred Journal of Research Science and Technology, 2*(8).

Dumas, M., La Rosa, M., Mendling, J., & Reijers, H. A. (2013). Introduction to business process management. In *Fundamentals of business process management* (pp. 1–31). Springer. doi:10.1007/978-3-642-33143-5_1

Dyba, T., & Dingsoyr, T. (2009). What do we know about agile software development? *IEEE Software, 26*(5), 6–9. doi:10.1109/MS.2009.145

Egbreghts, A. (2017). A Literature Review of Behavior Driven Development using Grounded Theory. *27th Twente Student Conference on IT.*

Fancott, T., Kamthan, P., & Shahmir, N. (2012). Towards next generation requirements engineering. *2012 IEEE International Conference on Social Informatics*, 328-33. 10.1109/SocialInformatics.2012.11

Flora, H. K., & Chande, S. V. (2014). A systematic study on agile software development methodologies and practices. *International Journal of Computer Science and Information Technologies, 5*(3), 3626–3637.

Fowler, M., & Highsmith, J. (2001). The agile manifesto. *Software Development, 9*(8), 28–35.

Gartner Glossary. (2020a). Available at: https://www.gartner.com/en/information-technology/glossary/digitization

Gartner Glossary. (2020b). *Digitalization.* Available at: https://www.gartner.com/en/information-technology/glossary/digitalization

IIBA and Agile Alliance. (2015). *A Guide to Business Analysis Body of Knowledge.* Author.

IIBA and Agile Alliance. (2017). *Agile Extension to the BABOK®Guide.* Author.

Javanmard, M., & Alian, M. (2015). Comparison between Agile and Traditional software development methodologies. *Cumhuriyet Science Journal*, *36*(3), 1386–1394.

Käpyaho, M., & Kauppinen, M. (2015, August). Agile requirements engineering with prototyping: A case study. In *2015 IEEE 23rd International requirements engineering conference (RE)* (pp. 334-343). IEEE. 10.1109/RE.2015.7320450

Leau, Y. B., Loo, W. K., Tham, W. Y., & Tan, S. F. (2012). Software development life cycle AGILE vs traditional approaches. In *International Conference on Information and Network Technology* (*Vol. 37*, No. 1, pp. 162-167). Academic Press.

Lederer, M., Knapp, J., & Schott, P. (2017, March). The digital future has many names—How business process management drives the digital transformation. In *2017 6th International Conference on Industrial Technology and Management (ICITM)* (pp. 22-26). IEEE.

Leffingwell, D. (2010). *Agile software requirements: lean requirements practices for teams, programs, and the enterprise*. Addison-Wesley Professional.

Li, H., Wu, Y., Cao, D., & Wang, Y. (2019). Organizational mindfulness towards digital transformation as a prerequisite of information processing capability to achieve market agility. *Journal of Business Research*. Advance online publication. doi:10.1016/j.jbusres.2019.10.036

Loiro, C., Castro, H., Ávila, P., Cruz-Cunha, M. M., Putnik, G. D., & Ferreira, L. (2019). Agile Project Management: A Communicational Workflow Proposal. *Procedia Computer Science*, *164*, 485–490. doi:10.1016/j.procs.2019.12.210

Martins, P. V., & Zacarias, M. (2017). An agile business process improvement methodology. *Procedia Computer Science*, *121*, 129–136. doi:10.1016/j.procs.2017.11.018

Miller, K. W., & Larson, D. K. (2005). Agile software development: Human values and culture. *IEEE Technology and Society Magazine*, *24*(4), 36–42. doi:10.1109/MTAS.2005.1563500

Morakanyane, R., Grace, A. A., & O'Reilly, P. (2017). Conceptualizing Digital Transformation in Business Organizations: A Systematic Review of Literature. In Bled eConference (p. 21). doi:10.18690/978-961-286-043-1.30

Neuri ConsultingL. L. P. (n.d.). Available at: https://www.impactmapping.org

Ozdenizci Kose, B. (2019). Recent Agile Requirement Engineering Practices In It Projects: A Case Analysis. *Business & Management Studies: An International Journal*, *7*(4), 1776–1805.

Paetsch, F., Eberlein, A., & Maurer, F. (2003, June). Requirements engineering and agile software development. In WET ICE 2003. Proceedings. Twelfth IEEE International Workshops on Enabling Technologies: Infrastructure for Collaborative Enterprises, 2003 (pp. 308-313). IEEE. doi:10.1109/ENABL.2003.1231428

Parker, J. (2013). *Requirements Engineering vs. Business Analysis*. Enfocus Solutions. Available at: https://enfocussolutions.com/requirements-engineering-vs-business-analysis/

Phil, M. (2015). Comparative analysis of different agile methodologies. *International Journal of Computer Science and Information Technology Research*, *3*(1).

PMI, Project Management Institute (2017a). *The PMI Guide to Business Analysis*. PMI.

PMI, Project Management Institute. (2017b). *Business Analysis: Leading Organizations to Better Outcomes*. Available at: https://www.pmi.org/business-solutions/white-papers/-/media/pmi/documents/public/pdf/white-papers/business-analysis-outcomes.pdf?v=702d20b8-6248-4f6b-b49e-bfc3ec82f560

Pruitt, J., & Grudin, J. (2003). Personas: practice and theory. *Proceedings of the 2003 conference on Designing for user experiences*, 1-15.

Roberts, N., & Grover, V. (2012). Leveraging information technology infrastructure to facilitate a firm's customer agility and competitive activity: An empirical investigation. *Journal of Management Information Systems*, *28*(4), 231–270. doi:10.2753/MIS0742-1222280409

Robertson, S., & Robertson, J. (2012). *Mastering the requirements process: Getting requirements right*. Addison-Wesley.

Ryan, J., Doster, B., Daily, S., & Lewis, C. (2019). *Business Process Redesign in the Perioperative Process: A Case Perspective for Digital Transformation*. Academic Press.

Sauerwein, E., Bailom, F., Matzler, K., & Hinterhuber, H. H. (1996). The Kano model: How to delight your customers. *International Working Seminar on Production Economics, 1*(4), 313-327.

Scaled Agile. (2020). *Value Streams*. Available at: https://www.scaledagileframework.com/value-streams/

Schön, E. M., Thomaschewski, J., & Escalona, M. J. (2017). Agile Requirements Engineering: A systematic literature review. *Computer Standards & Interfaces*, *49*, 79–91. doi:10.1016/j.csi.2016.08.011

Suryaatmaja, K., Wibisono, D., & Ghazali, A. (2019). The Missing Framework for Adaptation of Agile Software Development Projects. In *Eurasian Business Perspectives* (pp. 113–127). Springer. doi:10.1007/978-3-030-18652-4_9

Trello by Atlassian. (2020). Available at: https://trello.com/en

Venkatraman, N. (1994). IT-enabled business transformation: From automation to business scope redefinition. *Sloan Management Review*, *35*, 73–73.

Verhoef, P. C., Broekhuizen, T., Bart, Y., Bhattacharya, A., Dong, J. Q., Fabian, N., & Haenlein, M. (2019). Digital transformation: A multidisciplinary reflection and research agenda. *Journal of Business Research*. Advance online publication. doi:10.1016/j.jbusres.2019.09.022

Vial, G. (2019). Understanding digital transformation: A review and a research agenda. *The Journal of Strategic Information Systems*, *28*(2), 118–144. doi:10.1016/j.jsis.2019.01.003

Wagner, S., Méndez-Fernández, D., Kalinowski, M., & Felderer, M. (2018). Agile requirements engineering in practice: Status quo and critical problems. *CLEI Electronic Journal, 21*(1), 15. doi:10.19153/cleiej.21.1.6

Wake, B. (2003). *INVEST in Good Stories, and SMART Tasks*. Available at: https://xp123.com/articles/invest-in-good-stories-and-smart-tasks

Xu, Y., & Koivumäki, T. (2019). Digital business model effectuation: An agile approach. *Computers in Human Behavior*, *95*, 307–314. doi:10.1016/j.chb.2018.10.021

Zairi, M. (1997). Business process management: A boundaryless approach to modern competitiveness. *Business Process Management Journal*, *3*(1), 64–80. doi:10.1108/14637159710161585

Zhang, Z., & Sharifi, H. (2000). A methodology for achieving agility in manufacturing organisations. *International Journal of Operations & Production Management*, *20*(4), 496–513. doi:10.1108/01443570010314818

KEY TERMS AND DEFINITIONS

Agile: The ability to create and respond to change; a way of dealing with, and ultimately succeeding in, an uncertain and turbulent environment (Agile Alliance, 2001).

Business Analysis: A disciplined approach including set of activities performed to support delivery of solutions that align to business objectives and provide continuous value to the organization (PMI, 2017a).

Business Process Management: A structured approach including methods, techniques, and software to analyze and improve business processes of a company (Zairi, 1997; Dumas et al., 2013).

Digital Transformation: A change in how a firm employs digital technologies, to develop a new digital business model that helps to create and appropriate more value for the firm (Verhoef et al., 2019).

Project: A temporary endeavor undertaken to create a unique product, service, or result (PMI, 2017a).

Project Management: The application of knowledge, skills, tools and techniques to project activities to meet the project requirements (PMI, 2017a).

Requirement: A condition or capability that is necessary to be present in a product, service, or result to satisfy a business need (PMI, 2017a).

This research was previously published in the Handbook of Research on Multidisciplinary Approaches to Entrepreneurship, Innovation, and ICTs; pages 98-123, copyright year 2021 by Business Science Reference (an imprint of IGI Global).

Chapter 92

A Contingent Approach to Facilitating Conflict Resolution in Software Development Outsourcing Projects

Donghwan Cho

Gyeongnam National University of Science and Technology, Gyeongnam, South Korea

ABSTRACT

With the wide spread of IT outsourcing, internal IT personnel have been required to change their roles from system development to organizational change agents such as securing software development outsourcing (SDO) success. Conflict resolution is critical to secure the SDO success, but the understanding of how IT personnel facilitate conflict resolution as change agents is limited. The purpose of this study is to understand the negative impact of conflicts on SDO outcomes and to investigate the moderating effect of IT personnel's conflict resolution facilitation (process facilitation, content facilitation) between conflicts and two SDO outcome dimensions (project efficiency and system effectiveness). In order to test the model, data was collected through a cross-sectional field survey using questionnaires, and a total of 144 SDO projects were used in the final analysis. Research results show that conflicts have a negative impact on both of the SDO outcome dimensions, and the effect of conflict resolution facilitation by IT personnel is contingent on the dimensions of SDO outcomes.

1. INTRODUCTION

"Even operational conflicts (in outsourcing arrangements) that seem quite small—typically over contracts and service—can lead to underperformance, damage relationships, and in a highly connected business eco-system, disable strategy." (Lacity and Willcocks, 2017, p. 81)

DOI: 10.4018/978-1-6684-3702-5.ch092

Nowadays IT (Information Technology) outsourcing is an important alternative for modern enterprises. The scope and impact of IT outsourcing has been expanded increasingly. Modern IT outsourcing includes software development, IT function outsourcing, data center, cloud service, and offshore outsourcing (Bapna et al., 2010; Gregory et al., 2009). This widespread of IT outsourcing has been making internal IT functions change their roles. Their roles have been changing mostly from delivering information systems for their organizations to system analysis, network management and especially strong change agents in their organizations (Laudon & Laudon, 2016). They play a vital role in aligning technological developments with organizational planned changes. This paper focuses on their new emerging roles of change agents in acquiring organizational IT outsourcing success.

Despite the various types of IT outsourcing have been emerging and IT outsourcing has become a viable alternative, the effective management of IT outsourcing is still a challenge for many internal IT functions (Lacity & Willcocks, 2017). This challenge has been widely documented in prior studies. Some sources estimate that more than 50% of IT outsourcing fail or perform very poorly (Ditmore, 2012; Keiser, 2014). In the context of SDO (software development outsourcing) relationships which this study focuses on among the various types of IT outsourcing, only 29% are successful, and 71% are considered failures or challenged (Wojewoda & Hastie, 2015). Many SDO projects have failed to meet customer expectations as well as been reported to result in delayed schedule, budget overrun, and failure to business needs (Wojewoda & Hastie, 2015; Gefen et al., 2008; Tiwana and Keil, 2004).

This high failure rate of SDO originates from the highly complex risks of SDO tasks (Choudhury & Sabherwal, 2003; Wallace & Keil, 2004). SDO tasks wherein external service providers (or vendors) technically implement the information requirements of their client companies generally involve two types of distinct risks. The first is performance risk, that is difficult to achieve performance goals such as project schedule and budget, caused by very high complexities of software development task; the other is relational risk, wherein the parties involved in outsourcing relationships seek to achieve its own interests and exhibit opportunistic behaviors (Gefen et al., 2008; Choudhury and Sabherwal, 2003). This complex inherent risks of SDO make internal IT difficult to handle the inter-organizational development issues and prone to conflict. If the SDO risks are not effectively managed, conflicts generally arise. Therefore, the inability to resolve conflicts that arise in SDO relationships is a major cause of poor outcomes (Goo et al., 2009; Lacity and Willcocks, 2017; Rai et al., 2012).

Defined as a serious dispute between client and external service provider (e.g., Lee and Kim, 1999), the subject of SDO conflict remains an important issue in IS research. While prior research has examined the types of inter-organizational conflicts and conflict resolution styles in joint ventures, networks, consortia, alliances, and trade associations (Barringer & Harrison, 2000; Cropper, Huxham, Ebers, & Ring, 2008) and in various inter-organizational contexts such as natural resource rights, labor relations, international relations, volunteering, and manufacturing alliance networks (e.g., Dyer and Nobeoka, 2000; Mandell and Keast, 2009; Molnar and Rogers, 1979; Renner et al., 2007), relatively little research has examined inter-organizational conflicts in the SDO context (Lacity and Willcocks, 2017).

Prior studies on conflict in IT outsourcing mostly discovered that the capability to resolve conflicts in outsourcing relationships was significantly correlated with outsourcing outcomes (e.g., Goo et al., 2009; Lacity and Willcocks 2017; Ndubisi, 2011, 2013; Swar et al., 2012; Winkler et al., 2008; Rai et al., 2012). In these previous studies, notably some studies examined the impact of conflict resolution styles between the two outsourcing parties (e.g., integrating, accommodating, and compromising) on outsourcing outcomes (Lacity and Willcocks 2017; Ndubisi, 2011, 2013). These studies provide valuable insights into approaches to handling conflicts and managing outsourcing relationships, but they fail to consider the inherent triangular relationship comprised of vendor, client users and client IT group.

They regarded outsourcing relationship as a dyadic one comprised of client and vendor rather than a triangular one. However, if you look at the outsourcing relationships more deeply, you notice that there are three typical stakeholders comprised of vendor, client users and client IT group. On client side, user group and IT group have their own unique positions and interests that are not easy to negotiate. In the software development outsourcing, client user group has their own unique system requirements and client IT group has the intermediary and managing roles for SDO projects (Gregory et al., 2009; Choudhury and Sabherwal 2003). It is often the case that client IT personnel interact with vendors, and client users do not have many chances to directly interact with them. Therefore, system developmental issues and concerns that client users have tend to be communicated and handled through internal IT personnel, and the conflict between client users and vendors may be resolved by the intervention of internal IT rather than the direct conflict resolution between them (Goo et al., 2009). This type of conflict resolution facilitation by IT personnel has been scarce in previous studies although it is a very vital method for SDO success in practice.

Focusing on conflict resolution facilitation by IT personnel, this study also seeks to examine the relationship between the conflict resolution facilitation types and the outsourcing outcomes. SDO outcomes are multi-faceted, mainly comprised of two very distinctive dimensions of project efficiency and system effectiveness (Gopal and Gosain 2010; Choudhury and Sabherwal 2003). Prior studies on outsourcing conflict addressed this relationship, but their findings are rather limited in terms that the outsourcing outcomes did not cover the project efficiency and system effectiveness together. Among the previous studies, Lacity and Willcocks (2017) explored how the conflict resolution styles affect client/vendor satisfaction, and Ndubisi (2011, 2013) examined the relationship between the conflict resolution styles and trust and commitment in outsourcing relationships. In these studies, the measure for outsourcing success was client/vendor satisfaction and trust and commitment; however, these variables can represent only a part of outsourcing success. To measure the whole picture of SDO success, both project efficiency and system effectiveness should be considered simultaneously (Gregory et al., 2009; Choudhury and Sabherwal, 2003).

This research addresses this gap found in previous studies. Therefore, the research question of this study is as follows: How do IT personnel's conflict resolution behaviors affect the SDO outcome dimensions, namely project efficiency and system effectiveness? To determine an answer, we conducted a study of 144 SDO projects performed in various South Korean companies. We focused on conflict resolution facilitating behavior by IT personnel aimed at resolving conflict between the parties involved. We differentiate between project efficiency which assesses the degree to which the software development process is adequately managed, and system effectiveness, which captures the quality-attributes of the developed software. Our study contributes to theory by examining the impact of the conflict resolution facilitation by IT personnel on SDO outcomes, which has received little attention.

2. PRIOR WORKS AND HYPOTHESIS DEVELOPMENT

2.1. Conflicts in SDO

SDO is a multifaceted and complex activity involving high level of project risks. Clients and vendors interact in many different ways to achieve their own project goals. Most SDOs are complex activities involving significant technical tasks combined with a social interaction process of various stakeholders such as users, project managers, developers, and clients (Gopal & Gosain, 2010). In such a context, appropriate conflict resolution is vital in reconciling the diverse interests of the stakeholders and improving project performance (Lacity and Willcocks, 2017).

Table 1 summarizes the previous research on conflicts in SDO related studies. All these works provide general insights into SDO conflicts. The research shows that conflicts directly have a negative effect on SDO outcomes or moderated SDO outcomes (e.g., Kudaravalli et al., 2017; Lacity and Willcocks, 2017; Goo et al., 2009; Winkler et al., 2008; Yeh and Tsai, 2001). The research also demonstrates that at a general level, resolving conflicts have a positive impact on SDO outcomes (e.g., Kern and Willcocks, 2002; Cohen et al., 2004; Ndubisi, 2011; Rai et al., 2012; Lacity and Willcocks, 2017). Although these studies are valuable, most did not aim to assess specific SDO conflict resolution facilitation by third parties or to comprehensively consider the dimensions of SDO outcomes with the following exceptions:

Lacity and Willcocks (2017) and Ndubisi (2011) investigated how conflicts are resolved between the client and service provider in outsourcing relationships. In Ndubisi (2011), three types of conflict handling styles—integrating, accommodating, and compromising—are found to have direct and positive effect on trust and commitment in HRO (Human Resources Outsourcing) relationship. Lacity and Willcocks (2017) added three conflict resolution styles (avoiding, competing, and switch to collaborative style) to Ndubisi (2011) and specified conflict types as three: commercial, service, and relationship conflict. They found that only the collaborative and switched to collaborative styles resolved conflicts to the satisfaction of both partners in business services outsourcing relationships. Cohen et al. (2004) provides a different perspective from those of the above two studies, focusing on IT manager's conflict resolution facilitation role. Their focus was on conflict resolution achieved by the IT manager who is in charge of the project, rather than conflict resolution by the parties involved, namely, software testers and developers. Gopal and Gosain (2010) argues that there can be trade-off between project efficiency (adherence to schedule, budget, and user requirements) and system effectiveness (information quality, system quality, and maintainability) in SDO, and these two dimensions of SDO outcomes should be considered simultaneously for a comprehensive understanding of SDO success. Yeh and Tsai (2001) also assessed project success as including project efficiency and system effectiveness and investigated conflict potentials during software development.

2.2. Conflict Resolution Facilitation

There are three types of conflict management systems or dispute resolution systems in an organization, and these three types are complementary (Bendersky, 2003). These include conflicts directly between the parties in conflict, facilitating or mediating conflict resolution by third parties (those other than the parties involved), and arbitration by referring to the intervention of third parties with authority. In prior studies pertaining to conflict in SDO related research, Lacity and Willcocks (2017) and Ndubisi (2011) employed the first type of conflict resolution, i.e., resolving conflicts directly between the parties involved.

Table 1. Previous research on conflict in SDO related studies

Authors	Study method	SDO conflict resolution styles	Two dimensions of SDO outcomes	Study results
Cohen et al. (2004)	Case study	Conflict resolution facilitation	Not investigated	Authors investigated the antecedents of conflicts in software test processes and how to manage conflicts. In order to resolve conflicts between software testers and developers, project managers intervene. The process described in this paper does not cover the entire process of software development, but only the testing process.
Goo et al. (2009)	Survey	Not investigated	Not investigated	Authors argued that ITO relationships are "rife with potential disputes and opportunism" because of uncertainty and information asymmetry in ITO relationships (p. 126). The authors found that "Harmonious Conflict Resolution" positively and directly affects "Trust"
Gopal and Gosain (2010)	Survey	Not investigated	Project efficiency System quality	Authors examined the consequences of control mode choices on project performance and also the moderating role of boundary spanning behavior in SDO. Through boundary spanning between client and vendor, mutual understanding and conflict arise.
Gregory et al. (2009)	Case study	Not investigated	Not investigated	Authors focused on the interpersonal relationships between client team members and supplier team members in IT offshore outsourcing. "Cultural intelligence" results in a "negotiated culture" characterized by trust, shared understanding, and conflict resolution.
Kern and Willcocks (2002)	Case studies	Not investigated	Not investigated	Authors conducted 12 IT outsourcing cases to investigate relational governance. Conflicts were resolved by managers or escalated to top management.
Kudaravalli et al. (2017)	Survey	Not investigated	Not investigated	Team conflict mediates the relationship between design collaboration centralization (also technical collaboration centralization) and coordination outcomes in SDO.
Lacity and Willcocks (2017)	Case studies	Conflict resolution by the parties involved	Not investigated	Authors investigated how conflicts in BSO relationships are resolved through 13 case studies. They classified the conflict types into three (commercial, relationship, and service) and examined how conflict resolution styles affect the client/ provider satisfaction.
Ndubisi (2011)	Survey	Conflict resolution by the parties involved	Not investigated	The author explored the effects of three types of conflict handling styles (integrating, accommodating, and compromising) on outsourcing success (measured by trust and commitment). All the three styles (integrating, accommodating, and compromising) positively and directly affected "Trust" and "Commitment."
Rai et al. (2012)	Survey	Not investigated	Not investigated	Authors investigated if conflict resolution as a factor of relational governance would substitute for goal expectations in positively influencing BPO satisfaction. The study results show that "Conflict Resolution" (and other relational governance factors) substitutes for contractually specified goal expectations
Winkler et al. (2008)	Case studies	Not investigated	Not investigated	Authors viewed "conflict" as an aspect of relationship quality that affects outsourcing success. Through five case studies of IT offshore outsourcing, they found that power distance can result in conflicts, which adversely affect outsourcing success.
Yeh and Tsai (2001)	Survey	Not investigated	Perceived project success	Authors examined the potential causes of conflicts and reinvestigated the role of user participation in software development.

Apart from this type of conflict resolution, the focus of this research is directed toward conflict resolution facilitation by IT personnel. Facilitating conflict resolution is similar to mediation as a means of intervention by a third party to encourage voluntary consultation between the parties through various methods (Thomas, 1992). Conflict resolution facilitation implies that a person who is accepted by all the team members, neutral to the topic covered by the team, and is not accorded the official authority to make decisions performs the process of diagnosing and intervening to help improve problem recognition, problem solving, and decision making for the purpose of promoting the effectiveness of the team (Schwarz, 2002).

The main role of the conflict resolution facilitator is to help the team improve its own conflict resolution process and structure, including content facilitation and process facilitation, to increase its effectiveness (Miranda & Bostrom, 1999). This classification is consistent with Schwarz (2002)'s basic facilitation and developmental facilitation. Content facilitation involves directly addressing a problem or issue, for example, a facilitator providing an interpretation of his or her opinions, insights, and events in a case or of facts. Process facilitation, on the other hand, provides structural procedures and general support during a meeting, encouraging team members to adhere to the agenda, encouraging them to refrain from criticizing the other party, and promoting uniform participation by all the team members.

IT personnel in a client firm typically intervene and facilitate conflict resolution between client users and external vendors because, in general, they are responsible for project success, and they understand each party's needs and situations. As part of their control over the project's success, they coordinate the differences of opinion and disagreements between users and vendors and improve project performance (Kern and Willcocks, 2002; Choudhury and Sabherwal 2003). Project planning meetings and status review meetings are the typical mechanisms for them to facilitate conflict resolution as a boundary spanning behavior (Gopal and Gosain, 2010). Code inspections and software design reviews are also employed for them to facilitate conflict resolution.

2.3. SDO Performance

Software development project performance has been established to be largely composed of effectiveness and efficiency dimensions (Gopal and Gosain, 2010; Wallace et al., 2004; Nidumolu, 1995). The effectiveness dimension captures the quality attributes of the developed software. This construct evaluates the degree to which the developed software meets the customer requirements and is also known as product performance (Henderson and Lee, 1992; Nidumolu, 1995). Wallace et al. (2004) captures this attribute by focusing on the reliability, maintainability, meeting requirements, and response time of applications, developed using five items of the Likert-scale. Nidumolu (1995) and Barki and Hartwick(2001) measure this attribute by focusing on system operational efficiency, system flexibility, and information quality.

On the contrary, the efficiency dimension assesses the degree to which the software development process is adequately managed and is also referred to as project efficiency (Gopal and Gosain, 2010; Wallace et al., 2004). This construct measures whether the software project was completed on time and within the budget. Budget overruns and schedule overruns characterize the efficiency dimensions of software development (Tiwana, 2004; Barki and Hatwick, 2001) and allowed more effective comparisons across diverse projects. Prior research has studied efficiency by focusing on project effort and cycle time (Harter & Slaughter, 2003), project cost (Krishnan, Mukhopadhyay, & Kriebel, 2004), process satisfaction (Barki and Hatwick, 2001), interaction quality (Guinan, Cooprider, & Faraj, 1998), and quality of work (Aladwani, 2002).

As can be seen in the literature, it is possible to focus on only one aspect of the two software development project performance dimensions. However, it is critical to study both the dimensions together to completely understand the project performance. It is often easy to lower costs (and increase efficiency) by negotiating the quality aspect of the software (Pressman, 2010). Similarly, the practitioner journal discussed the widespread practice of releasing software products with known quality problems to shorten cycle times and improve efficiency (Thibodeau & Rosencrance, 2002). Thus, in this study, we investigate the effect of conflict resolution facilitation on both the performance dimensions simultaneously. Figure 1 summarizes our proposed theoretical model.

Figure 1. Theoretical model

2.4. Hypothesis Development

2.4.1. Conflicts in SDO and Project Performance

The high failure rate and high levels of conflict in SDO projects are due to the inherent complex risks of SDO projects (Choudhury and Sabherwal, 2003; Wallace et al., 2004). These risks are mainly categorized into two: the first is performance risk, which represents the challenge in achieving the goals owing to the complexity of the software development tasks, and the second is relational risk, which is exposed to the other party's opportunistic behavior as a result of collaboration between different organizations. Conflict is observed to be a major factor affecting project performance, in studies to reduce performance risks, whose subjects are predominantly internal system development (Barki & Hartwick, 1994; Robey, Smith, & Vijayasarathy, 1993). In these studies, conflicts appear in a variety of forms in the interaction process between users with system requirements and developers, to develop information systems; moreover, it makes a negative effect on project performance (Robey et al., 1993; Barki and Hartwick, 2001; Cohen et al., 2004).

In prior studies to reduce relational risk mostly situated in the outsourcing context, the conflict between the vendor and client is a major factor influencing outsourcing success (Winkler et al., 2008; Goo et al., 2009; Ndubisi, 2011; Rai et al., 2012; Lacity and Willcocks, 2017). In the outsourcing context, the relational risk is increased owing to the opportunistic behavior of the other party, which is derived from the different positions and interests of customers and vendors (Lee and Kim, 1999; Goo et al., 2009). In the case of internal development, the parties involved in conflict belong to the same organization, and they are likely to have known each other before, and the relationship among them is likely to last longer than the end of the project. On the contrary, in the case of development through outsourcing, it is highly likely that the parties involved in the conflict are not members of the same organization, such as the vendor and client. Moreover, they are not familiar with each other in advance, and most importantly, that they are susceptible to opportunistic behavior of the other party (Choudhury and Sabherwal, 2003; Goo et al., 2009). Thus, there are high possibilities of conflict between client users, who have system requirements, and vendor developers, whose tasks are developing software, and the impact of the conflict becomes even more serious.

Similar to the previous study results on conflicts in outsourcing (e.g., Goo et al., 2009; Winkler et al., 2008; Kudaravalli et al., 2017; Lacity and Willcocks, 2017), conflict will have a direct negative impact on SDO project performance in this study. However, to consider the impact of conflict on project performance comprehensively, we examine two aspects of project performance together: project efficiency and system effectiveness (Nidumolu, 1995; Barki and Hartwick, 2001). This is because the development schedule is likely to be delayed or the budget likely to be exceeded in order to improve the performance of the developed system. In addition, even if the project deadline is met and budget is not exceeded, the final system quality is likely to be low. In this study, the following hypotheses are set up pertaining to the conflict in SDO and the project performance:

Hypothesis 1a (H1a): Higher level of conflict is associated with lower level of project efficiency in SDO.
Hypothesis 1b (H1b): Higher level of conflict is associated with lower level of system effectiveness in SDO.

2.4.2. Conflict Resolution Facilitation and Project Performance

The role of third parties for conflict resolution in the software development process has been discussed in some previous studies. Sonnenwald(1995) observed that in the internal software development process, an agent facilitates interaction between users and developers and mediates conflict. In Linux projects, it was important to effectively coordinate conflicts among diverse participants with different perspectives (De Joode, 2004). In the SDO project, IT personnel are generally responsible for promoting interactions between vendor and client users and facilitate conflict resolution between parties with different perspectives and interests (Kern and Willcocks, 2002; Choudhury and Sabherwal, 2003). It is because they link the user departments and vendors from the outset of outsourcing agreement, communicate or broker knowledge between user departments and vendors, and have a diverse range of knowledge required to develop software (Choudhury and Sabherwal, 2003).

As the outsourcing project progresses, there will be a variety of problems and disagreements regarding the software to be developed, between the client user and the vendor. To solve such a problem and reconcile the differences, IT personnel engage in the process of resolving conflicts or occasionally intervene directly in problems or issues that cause conflicts (Miranda and Bostrom, 1999). It is challenging to achieve all specified goals of SDO projects because these goals are highly diverse and occasionally conflicting, such as process and system effectiveness. Therefore, according to project priorities or situations, it is necessary to select either process facilitation or content facilitation for conflict resolution.

Through process facilitation by IT personnel for conflict resolution, the negative impact of conflict on project efficiency can be decreased. Project planning meetings and status review meetings are effective mechanisms for this purpose (Gopal and Gosain, 2010). If the conflicts are managed and resolved effectively, the perceived quality of interactions for development can be improved, and team members or stakeholders can be more satisfied with the development process (Guinan et al., 1998; Barki and Hartwick, 2001). In addition, the development team can perform their job more efficiently and effectively (Aladwani, 2002).

Through process facilitation by IT personnel for conflict resolution, the negative impact of conflict on system effectiveness can also be decreased. For this purpose, code inspections and software design reviews can be employed (Gopal and Gosain, 2010). The intervention of IT personnel provides customers and vendors an opportunity to understand what the other party needs and wants and can help develop the high-quality system desired by the users. The operational efficiency and maintenance of the software can be improved, resulting in higher system effectiveness. These arguments lead to the following hypotheses:

Hypothesis 2a (H2a): Process facilitation by IT personnel for conflict resolution will positively moderate the relationship between conflicts and project efficiency in SDO.

Hypothesis 2b (H2b): Process facilitation by IT personnel for conflict resolution will positively moderate the relationship between conflicts and system effectiveness in SDO.

Apart from process facilitation, IT personnel conduct content facilitation for conflict resolution in SDO. Thereby, the negative impact of conflict on project efficiency can be decreased. Content facilitation is the intervention that directly addresses the problem or issue being discussed. Specifically, it is the intervention where in the facilitator provides his or her opinion or insight into the problem and an interpretation of facts or events (Miranda and Bostrom, 1999). During the project planning meetings and status review meetings, IT personnel can undertake content facilitation activities (Gopal and Gosain, 2010). The problem or issue causing the conflicts can be solved in a relatively shorter time with his/her interventions. Thus, the project schedule and budget can be met, resulting in project efficiency enhancement (Nidumolu, 1995; Barki and Hartwick, 2001).

Through content facilitation by IT personnel for conflict resolution, the negative impact of conflict on system effectiveness can be decreased. During software design reviews or code inspections, IT personnel can provide his or her opinion or insight that is likely to help to improve system effectiveness (Gopal and Gosain, 2010). This results in system quality improvements that include information accuracy, completeness, system utility, and reliability (Rivard, Poirier, Raymond, & Bergeron, 1997). These arguments lead to the following hypotheses:

Hypothesis 3a (H3a): Content facilitation by IT personnel for conflict resolution will positively moderate the relationship between conflicts and project efficiency in SDO.

Hypothesis 3b (H3b): Content facilitation by IT personnel for conflict resolution will positively moderate the relationship between conflicts and system effectiveness in SDO.

3. RESEARCH METHODS

3.1. Sample

In this study, data were collected through cross-sectional field survey using questionnaires. Data were collected through mail questionnaires, e-mail questionnaires, faxes, and direct visits, in order to ensure effective data-collection. A sampling frame for extracting samples was selected from 200 companies participating in the CEO courses of a Korean university and approximately 200 companies participating in the PMP (Project Management Professional) courses held in Korea. The reason for selecting these sampling frames is that it is suitably located for us to obtain these firms' management support for survey administration. The survey was anonymous to ensure strict confidentiality: No identifying information of any kind was gathered from the participants in order to ensure that they could not be identified.

The unit of analysis was software development outsourcing project, and the population were comprised of all types of software development outsourcing projects conducted by Korean IT service firms. The questionnaires used in this study were divided into sections A and B to be responded to by the IT personnel and users of the client company, who participated in the project, respectively. This separation of questionnaire items through matched-pair surveys prevents single respondent bias or the common method bias. From the IT personnel, we received responses to the questionnaire items on conflicts and some of project performance (adherence to project schedule, budget, and initial specifications); from the users, we received responses on conflicts, conflict resolution, and all other project performance variables.

A total of 144 projects were used in the final analysis. We excluded the cases where the response was inconsistent, inaccurate, or had only one-side responses (not matched-pair). The project dimension characteristics of the collected samples are as follows: Of the software types developed through outsourcing, ERP accounted for 52, comprising 36% of the total, followed by CRM (16), MIS (13), and SCM (10). From the project duration aspect, projects that lasted one year was 20, accounting for 13.9% of the total, followed by 7 month projects (17). In terms of team size, there are 40 projects with 6 to 10 teams, accounting for 27.9% of the total, followed by 11 to 15 teams (25).

Differences between the respondents and non-respondents for the final sample were tested for non-response bias. The test results did not show any significant differences in the number of employees or sales revenue between these groups, indicating that non-response bias was not a problem in the studied sample.

3.2. Measures

All the survey items were rated on a seven-point Likert-type scale, anchored by 1 = to a very small extent, 7 = to a very large extent. As our model and analysis are focused on the project team level, one response such as team leader representing the project team was gathered and used for analysis.

3.2.1 Conflict

In this study, conflict implies the degree of conflict between client users and vendors in the development process of SDO project. To capture this unique context of conflicts in software development outsourcing, conflicts were measured using the metrics used in the previous studies on conflicts in the information systems field (Barki and Hartwick, 2001). We used the five items that measure disagreement, intervention, and negative emotions (Cronbach's alpha = .875). These items are presented in Appendix A.

3.2.2. Conflict Resolution Facilitation

In this study, conflict resolution facilitation distinguishes between process facilitation and content facilitation. Process facilitation is the intervention that provides a procedural structure and general support for resolving conflicts between the parties, and content facilitation is the intervention that directly addresses problems or issues discussed between the parties. In this study, measures from Miranda and Bostrom (1999) were applied to this research context of SDO. We used four items (Cronbach's alpha = .882) as process facilitation and three items (Cronbach's alpha = .859) as content facilitation.

3.2.3. Project Performance

SDO project performances were measured in terms of project efficiency and system effectiveness, as proposed by Nidumolu (1995). Project efficiency represents the degree to which the development process through outsourcing has progressed adequately, and was based on Barki and Hartwick (2001) and Nidumolu (1995). The first objective of every IT project is to complete the project within time and budget goals. Thus, for the project efficiency measure, three items were used to measure the time, budget, and goal achievement during the outsourcing development project (Cronbach's alpha = .781).

System effectiveness represents the actual performance of software implemented for users, through outsourcing (Barki and Hartwick, 2001; Nidumolu, 1995). It is highly critical to capture the highly distinct features such as system operational efficiency from the various aspects of the system effectiveness. For this purpose, three items measure the reliability, response time, and how easy to use (Cronbach's alpha = .909).

3.2.4. Control Variables

We control for other factors that could be confounding our examination of conflict resolution facilitation. For this purpose, we control for project duration and team size. First, generally, short-term contracts tend to have a lower uncertainty than long-term contracts and a higher success rate. Secondly, larger teams have access to more resources to develop and manage the outsourced project and exhibit a higher success rate (Koh et al., 2004; Kudaravalli et al., 2017). Thus, these two variables were controlled.

4. RESULTS

In order to test the construct validity of the reflective latent constructs in our variables, we conducted principal component factor analysis with varimax rotation (Table 2). We excluded the measurement items which were not suitable for this study, through validity tests. Accordingly, the criterion for removing the measurement items is the one with factor loadings less than 0.5, and the higher the factor loadings in the other constructs after the exploratory factor analysis using SPSS. Through this process, one item each from process facilitation (PF4) and content facilitation (CF1) were removed. The communalities for the items were above .6, and none of the cross-loadings were above .4, thus showing good construct validity. In addition, as shown in Table 3, the Cronbach alpha levels for all the relevant variables are higher than .7 and therefore demonstrate good internal consistency of measurement.

Table 3 presents the descriptive statistics including the means, standard deviations, reliability, and correlations of the variables employed in this study. The correlations are considerably lower than the levels that are likely to indicate multicollinearity. To ensure that multi-collinearity does not pose a potential problem to our study, we examined the variance inflation factor (VIF) for all the independent variables and found them to be well below the acceptable level of 5 (the highest VIF statistic was 1.168) (Belsley, Kuh, & Welsch, 1980).

Table 2. Factor analysis results

Item	Factor 1	Factor 2	Factor 3	Factor 4	Factor 5
Conflict1	0.746				
Conflict2	0.778				
Conflict3	0.785				
Conflict4	0.861				
Conflict5	0.837				
Process Facilitation1		0.607			
Process Facilitation2		0.888			
Process Facilitation3		0.884			
Process Facilitation5		0.763			
System Effectiveness1			0.850		
System Effectiveness2			0.889		
System Effectiveness3			0.900		
Content Facilitation2				0.610	
Content Facilitation3				0.883	
Content Facilitation4				0.855	
Project Efficiency1					0.830
Project Efficiency2					0.827
Project Efficiency3					0.757
Eigen Values	3.424	2.978	2.602	2.456	2.247
% of Variance explained	19.0	16.5	14.5	13.6	12.5

Note: All loadings smaller than .40 are not shown.

To ensure that our sample size was adequate to test the research hypotheses, we conducted statistical power analysis. Following standard conventions, we assumed a power level of .8, which is considered reasonable for the social sciences (Cohen, 1988), resulting in a sample size of 68 for the number of variables used in this study. Since our sample size is 144, it exceeds the sample size requirement.

As the data for all the constructs are gathered from survey respondents comprised of IT personnel and users, our study was designed to minimize the common method bias (Podsakoff & Organ, 1986). Apart from this separation of questionnaire items, our study conforms to a number of procedural and statistical remedies to alleviate the potential threats that have been outlined (Podsakoff, MacKenzie, Lee, & Podsakoff, 2003). First, as the questions concerning SDO outcomes were mixed with other questions and the survey was not described as focusing on SDO outcomes, the respondents could not be expected to make the connection between the predictors and outcomes. Secondly, the conflict and facilitation items appeared substantially before the SDO outcome items. Finally, we used Harman's single factor test to test for the bias by entering the independent and dependent variables in one factor analysis (Lindell & Whitney, 2001). If a single factor is obtained, it could be evidence of common method bias; however, the factors obtained equaled the number of constructs entered.

Table 3. Descriptive statistics

	Variable	Mean	S.D.	Cronbach Alpha	1	2	3	4	5	6
1	Project Duration	11.70	9.74	NA	1					
2	Team Size	28.85	41.40	NA	0.097	1				
3	Conflict	3.71	1.18	0.875	-0.046	-0.014	1			
4	Process Facilitation	5.03	1.15	0.882	-0.13	.187*	-0.094	1		
5	Content Facilitation	5.17	1.01	0.859	-0.085	0.027	-.256**	.641**	1	
6	Project Efficiency	5.33	1.20	0.781	-.230**	.222**	-.273**	.292**	.337**	1
7	System Effectiveness	4.63	1.20	0.909	-0.104	0.083	-.301**	.342**	.304**	.337**

*p < 0.05, **p < 0.01

4.1. Hypothesis Testing Results

In this study, we argue that the impact of conflict on SDO outcomes is dependent on the level of conflict resolution facilitation. In addition, we hypothesize both the direct effects of conflict on SDO outcomes as well as the moderating effects of conflict resolution facilitation. Since our research model has control variables, independent variables and moderation effects, hierarchical regression analysis is chosen to test the hypotheses using the two dependent variables of project efficiency and system effectiveness. Hierarchical regression is a framework for model comparison rather than a statistical method, and a way to show if variables of interest explain a statistically significant amount of variance in dependent variable after accounting for all other variables (Babbie, 2013). Table 4 presents the facilitation model of conflict and SDO outcomes. We entered the variables in the regression analyses in a stepwise fashion starting with the control variables (project duration, team size), followed by the conflict variable as well as the moderator variable of process facilitation and content facilitation variables. As the final step, we entered the interaction terms for the interaction between conflict and the two types of facilitation.

4.1.1. Project Efficiency

Model 1 in Table 4 shows the relationship between the control variables and project efficiency. The model statistics show that project duration and team size are associated with project efficiency (the R-square is 10.5% and statistically significant). Model 2 exhibits the effect of adding the independent variables of conflict and process and content facilitation, the moderator. The model statistics indicate significant improvement over the control variables model ($\Delta R^2 = 16.3\%$, F for $\Delta R^2 = 3.176$). Hypothesis 1a proposed a negative association between conflict and project efficiency and is supported. The next step tested the interaction between conflict and conflict resolution facilitation variables. As the model statistics show (Model 3), there is a marked improvement over the previous model, and it is significant ($\Delta R^2 = 20.7\%$, F for $\Delta R^2 = 3.78$). However, only content facilitation out of the two conflict resolution facilitation variables moderates the effect of conflict on project efficiency. As Model 3 shows, the main effect of conflict is still significant in the presence of the interaction terms. Despite some debate, research indicates that the interaction terms can be interpreted on their own without considering the main effects in the model (Cohen et al., 2003; Jaccard et al., 1990). While hypothesis 2a regarding the interaction of conflict and process facilitation is not supported, hypothesis 3a regarding the interaction of conflict and content facilitation is supported. This indicates that conflict is associated with increased project efficiency only when content facilitation is high.

Table 4. Regression results

	Project Efficiency			System Effectiveness		
	Model 1	Model 2	Model 3	Model 4	Model 5	Model 6
Controls						
Project Duration	-0.242**	-0.256**	-0.226**	-0.076	-0.092	-0.047
Team Size	0.239**	0.24**	0.219**	0.056	0.058	0.000
Main Effects						
Conflict		-0.237**	-0.184*		-0.272**	-0.244**
Process Facilitation		0.009	0.002		-0.048	-0.082
Content Facilitation		0.044	-0.005		0.127	0.101
Moderation						
Conflict x Process Facilitation			0.109			0.242**
Conflict x Content Facilitation			0.197*			0.113
Model Statistics						
R^2	0.105	0.163	0.207	0.008	0.097	0.161
Adjusted R^2	0.092	0.132	0.166	-0.006	0.064	0.118
Model F	8.188***	5.333***	5.044***	0.570	2.953*	3.713**
Change in R^2		0.058	0.044		0.089	0.064
F for Change in R^2		3.176*	3.780*		4.512**	5.164**

*p < 0.05, **p < 0.01, ***p < 0.001, N = 144

To further investigate the nature of the interaction, we plotted the interaction effects for the dependent variables of project efficiency (Toothaker, Aiken, & West, 1991). It is shown graphically in Figure 2, which exhibits the interaction between content facilitation and conflict for the model of project efficiency. Figure 2 indicates that when content facilitation is high, the negative effect of conflict is reduced and project efficiency is improved. However, when content facilitation is low, conflict has a full negative effect on performance, lowering project efficiency. Therefore, IT personnel in charge of SDO project should undertake more content facilitation in project situations marked by elevated levels of conflict in order to improve project efficiency; however, more content facilitation is not needed in project situation marked by lower level of conflict.

Figure 2. Interaction effect between conflict and content facilitation on project efficiency

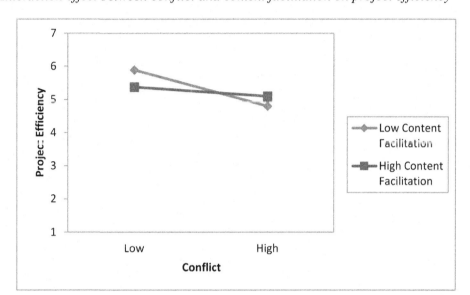

4.1.2. System Effectiveness

The same steps were followed for the hierarchical regression model of system effectiveness. Model 4 shows that the model with the control variables is not significant. The model statistics show that project duration and team size are not associated with system effectiveness (the R-square is 0.8% and statistically not significant). With the addition of the independent variables, the model statistics indicate significant improvement over the control variables model ($\Delta R^2 = 9.7\%$, F for $\Delta R^2 = 4.512$, $p < .01$). Therefore, hypothesis 1b is supported. Just as with project efficiency, Model 6, which includes the interaction terms, exhibits marked improvement over the previous model and is significant ($\Delta R^2 = 16.1\%$, F for $\Delta R^2 = 5.164$, $p < .001$). However, only process facilitation, out of the two conflict resolution facilitation variables, moderates the effect of conflict on system effectiveness. As Model 6 shows, the main effect of conflict is still significant in the presence of the interaction terms. While hypothesis 2b regarding the interaction of conflict and process facilitation is supported, hypothesis 3b regarding the interaction of conflict and content facilitation is not supported. This indicates that while conflict has a negative association with system effectiveness, the effect is reduced with increased process facilitation.

Figure 3 shows the interaction between process facilitation and conflict for the model of system effectiveness. It indicates that when process facilitation is high, the negative effect of conflict is reduced and system effectiveness is improved. However, when process facilitation is low, conflict has a full negative effect on performance, lowering system effectiveness. Therefore, IT personnel in charge of SDO project should undertake more process facilitation when the conflict level of a project is high in order to improve system effectiveness. However, when the conflict level is low, undertaking more process facilitation could be a waste of resources.

Figure 3. Interaction effect between conflict and process facilitation on system effectiveness

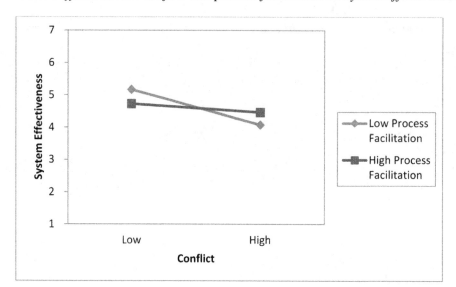

5. DISCUSSION

This study offers three major findings. First, conflict in SDO has a detrimental effect on SDO outcomes comprised of process efficiency and system effectiveness. It has the same negative effect on both dimensions of SDO outcomes. Therefore, IT managers need to make efforts to manage conflict in the beginning of a SDO project and to decrease the conflict in order to achieve the SDO success. Second, conflict resolution facilitation weakens the negative relationship between conflict and SDO project performance. IT managers can take process and/or content facilitation to lower the negative impact of conflict on SDO outcomes. Third, in order to mitigate the negative impact of conflict on SDO outcome dimensions, different facilitation approaches by IT personnel aimed at each project's own priorities should be exercised. This type of IT role as organizational change agents has been emerging and more significant required by changing IT trends these days (Laudon and Laudon 2016).

The negative impact of conflict on SDO performance dimensions weakens depending on the types of conflict resolution facilitation exercised. More specifically, in order to enhance project efficiency and reduce the detrimental effect of conflict on project efficiency, content facilitation should be exercised. Conversely, in order to increase system effectiveness and reduce the negative effect of conflict on system effectiveness, process facilitation is necessary. These findings highlight the practical and theoretical value of focusing on the conflict resolution facilitation efforts as team members collaborate and dispute to achieve the diverse goals of an SDO project.

5.1. Theoretical Contributions

Our findings contribute to the evolving research on the literature of IT outsourcing management. Previous research on outsourcing conflict (e.g. Lacity and Willcocks, 2017; Lee and Kim, 1999; Goo et al., 2009) mostly focused on conflict resolution between parties involved rather than the role of third parties such as IT personnel. Conflicts in the outsourcing context are occasionally resolved by the parties involved as well as by third parties. This research differentiates itself by focusing on the triangular relationship among client user group, IT personnel, and vendor. The conflicts between client users and vendor developers are occasionally resolved between themselves and in some cases resolved by IT personnel who are responsible for the SDO project success. This research investigated the IT personnel's role in facilitating conflict resolution between them. With this behavior, conflicts can be resolved and project performance can be improved in terms of process efficiency and system effectiveness.

The conflict in this study is highly unique in terms of the following aspects, which provide unique contributions for the conflict literature. The conflict characteristics in SDO are mixed and they comprise different types of conflicts such as task, process, and value conflict (Jehn, 1997). All these conflicts occur while the SDO project proceeds, because there are three main groups who have different view and opinions on SDO project goals and processes. These differences and conflicts tend to be rooted from intragroup conflict (project team conflict), intergroup conflict (user and developer groups), and even organizational conflict (client and vendor organization) (Robbins & Judge, 2011). Therefore, this type of complicated conflict in SDO is very unique in nature and needs to be highlighted. Through empirical method, this research revealed the negative impact of conflict on SDO outcomes.

Another contribution of this study is to investigate the relationship between conflict and the two facets of SDO outcomes simultaneously. This contributes to the software development performance improvement literature. Prior research mostly focused on a single aspect of software project performance rather than considering both the aspects, namely, project efficiency and system effectiveness simultaneously, except a few studies (e.g., Gopal and Gosain, 2010; Choudhury and Sabherwal, 2003). Even if the project efficiency aspect of SDO project is met and achieved, the quality of the delivered software is not guaranteed. Following a similar argument, the final software quality can be improved considerably if the project is provided access to enough additional resources and time by delaying project schedule and budget. With this consideration, this study includes both aspects of software project performance and examined the possible relationships between conflict and SDO performance.

5.2. Practical Implications

The first imperative for IT managers is likely to be the achievement of each project goal and improvement of project performance; this influences organizational performance considering that an organization is a myriad of various project outputs. Nevertheless, it is a significantly challenging task for them to achieve all of the multi-faceted goals of software development project. This is because software development project has many diverse goals—from project adherence to schedule and budget to delivered software quality. In many cases, there are trade-offs between these process and system goals; moreover, constraints on organizational time and resources are always present (Gopal and Gosain, 2010; Pressman, 2001; Thibodeau and Rosencrance, 2002). It is critical for him or her to focus on the top priorities of the SDO project in a real world environment. The priorities tend to depend on each project's specific characteristics. Therefore, it is occasionally crucial to meet the project schedule and budget by negotiating the quality aspect of the software, and vice versa.

IT managers can employ this study's findings on conflict resolution facilitation in a manner suited to each SDO project situation. If the priority is on project efficiency, they can produce better results through content facilitation rather than process facilitation. For example, during the project planning meetings and status review meetings, IT personnel can provide his or her opinion or insight into the problem and an interpretation of facts or events. With this type of content facilitation activities, the problem or issue causing the conflicts can be solved in a relatively shorter time. Thus the project schedule and budget can be met, resulting in project efficiency enhancement (Nidumolu, 1995; Barki and Hartwick, 2001).

If the priority is on system effectiveness, they can produce better outcomes through process facilitation rather than content facilitation. Through code inspections and software design reviews intervened by them, customers and vendors can have an opportunity to understand what the other party actually needs and wants, and to develop the high-quality system that client users actually desire(Gopal and Gosain, 2010). Thus the information quality and system quality can be improved, resulting in higher system effectiveness.

5.3. Limitations and Future Research

The study has limitations that point to opportunities for future research. First, the study is based on a cross-sectional data collection, and therefore, we cannot draw any inferences about how the changes in conflict affect performance or how conflict or conflict resolution is related to the different phases of the software development outsourcing life cycle. Secondly, contrary to the findings of project efficiency, the (control) relationship between the two control variables (project duration and team size) and system effectiveness was not significant. This is likely to be owing to the unique characteristics of the sample. Thirdly, instead of gathering multiple responses from a team, the study used one representative response for a team. There could be a marginally different opinion on conflict level, conflict resolution facilitation, and project performance among the members of a team.

Future research can deepen our understanding of conflict and conflict resolution by employing different research methods. For example, in contrast to cross-sectional studies, case studies deeply explore the whole SDO processes. In these processes, you can observe how the conflict occurs and IT personnel facilitate conflict resolution using various mechanisms and tools. These findings based on this type of closer observation can help for IT managers to employ intervention mechanisms and tactics necessary for SDO project success.

6. CONCLUSION

The changing nature of IT outsourcing has been widely documented in different streams of literature. As the outsourcing market grows rapidly and new types of outsourcing such as BSO (Business Services Outsourcing; including HR, accounting, finance, procurement, or legal service) have consistently emerged, the opportunity for collaboration with other parties has increased dramatically. Concurrently, the possibility of conflict with the other parties can also be increased drastically. Therefore, the way how to manage conflicts effectively becomes more critical and calls for further research. Scholars have only recently begun to empirically examine conflict resolution in emerging diverse outsourcing context such as BPO (Business Process Outsourcing) and BSO (Ndubisi, 2011; Rai et al., 2012; Lacity and Willcocks, 2017).

In conclusion, our study investigated the impact of conflict and conflict resolution facilitation by IT personnel on SDO outcomes, a topic that has received little attention in the literature so far. Our key finding is that the choice between process facilitation and content facilitation is contingent on the type of project outcomes quested in the project. As a result, our study underlines the need to differentiate between process and content facilitation and points to the importance of certain exercise of conflict resolution facilitation for improving project performance in software development outsourcing teams. This study questions the conventional wisdom that all types of conflict resolution facilitation are necessary for improving the SDO project performance dimensions. Instead, we suggest that optimal conflict resolution facilitation type may be associated with SDO project performance dimensions. Thus, this study opens up new research avenues to explore the conflict resolution mechanisms underlying various outsourcing team performance.

REFERENCES

Aladwani, A. M. (2002). An integrated performance model of information systems projects. *Journal of Management Information Systems*, *19*(1), 185–210. doi:10.1080/07421222.2002.11045709

Babbie, E. R. (2013). *The practice of social research*. Wadsworth Cengage Learning.

Bapna, R., Barua, A., Mani, D., & Mehra, A. (2010). Cooperation, coordination, and governance in multisourcing: An agenda for analytical and empirical research. *Information Systems Research*, *21*(4), 785–795. doi:10.1287/isre.1100.0328

Barki, H., & Hartwick, J. (1994). User participation, conflict, and conflict resolution: The mediating roles of influence. *Information Systems Research*, *5*(4), 422–438. doi:10.1287/isre.5.4.422

Barki, H., & Hartwick, J. (2001). Interpersonal conflict and its management in information system development. *Management Information Systems Quarterly*, *25*(2), 195–228. doi:10.2307/3250929

Barringer, B. R., & Harrison, J. S. (2000). Walking a tightrope: Creating value through interorganizational relationships. *Journal of Management*, *26*(3), 367–403. doi:10.1177/014920630002600302

Belsley, D., Kuh, E., & Welsch, R. (1980). Detecting and assessing collinearity. In *Regression Diagnostics* (pp. 85–91). doi:10.1002/0471725153

Bendersky, C. (2003). Organizational dispute resolution systems: A complementarities model. *Academy of Management Review, 28*(4), 643–656. doi:.10899444 doi:10.5465/AMR.2003

Choudhury, V., & Sabherwal, R. (2003). Portfolio of control in outsourced software development projects. *Information Systems Research*, *14*(3), 291–314. doi:10.1287/isre.14.3.291.16563

Cohen, C. F., Birkin, S. J., Garfield, M. J., & Webb, H. (2004). Managing conflict in software testing. *Communications of the ACM*, *47*(1), 76–81. doi:10.1145/962081.962083

Cohen, J. (1988). *Statistical power analysis for the behavioral sciences*. Routledge. doi:10.1234/12345678

Cropper, S., Huxham, C., Ebers, M., & Ring, P. S. (2008). The oxford handbook of inter-organizational relations. Oxford. doi:10.1093/oxfordhb/9780199282944.001.0001

Ditmore, J. (2012). Why IT Outsourcing Often Fails. *Information Week*. Retrieved from https://www.informationweek.com/it-leadership/why-it-outsourcing-often-fails/d/d-id/1105317

Dyer, J. H., & Nobeoka, K. (2000). Creating and Managing a High-Performance Knowledge-Sharing Network: The Toyota Case. *Strategic Management Journal*, *21*(21), 345–367. doi:10.1002/(SICI)1097-0266(200003)21:3<345::AID-SMJ96>3.0.CO;2-N

Gefen, D., Wyss, S., & Lichtenstein, Y. (2008). Business familiarity as risk mitigation in software development outsourcing contracts. *Management Information Systems Quarterly*, *32*(3), 531–551. doi:10.2307/25148855

Gopal, A., & Gosain, S. (2010). The role of organizational controls and boundary spanning in software development outsourcing: Implications for project performance. *Information Systems Research*, *21*(4), 960–982. doi:10.1287/isre.1080.0205

Gregory, R., Beck, R., & Keil, M. (2013). Control Balancing in Information Systems Development Offshoring Projects. *Management Information Systems Quarterly*, *37*(4), 1211–1232. doi:10.25300/MISQ/2013/37.4.10

Gregory, R., Prifling, M., & Beck, R. (2009). The role of cultural intelligence for the emergence of negotiated culture in IT offshore outsourcing projects. *Information Technology & People*, *22*(3), 223–241. doi:10.1108/09593840910981428

Guinan, P. J., Cooprider, J. G., & Faraj, S. (1998). Enabling Software Development Team Performance during Requirements Definition: A Behavioral Versus Technical Approach. *Information Systems Research*, *9*(2), 101–125. doi:10.1287/isre.9.2.101

Harter, D. E., & Slaughter, S. A. (2003). Quality Improvement and Infrastructure Activity Costs in Software Development: A Longitudinal Analysis. *Management Science*, *49*(6), 784–800. doi:10.1287/mnsc.49.6.784.16023

Henderson, J. C., & Lee, S. (1992). Managing I/S Design Teams: A Control Theories Perspective. *Management Science*, *38*(6), 757–777. doi:10.1287/mnsc.38.6.757

Jaccard, J., Wan, C. K., & Turrisi, R. (1990). The Detection and Interpretation of Interaction Effects Between Continuous Variables in Multiple Regression. *Multivariate Behavioral Research*, *25*(October), 467–478. doi:10.120715327906mbr2504_4 PMID:26820822

Jehn, K. A. (1997). A Qualitative Analysis of Conflict Types and Dimensions in Groups Organizational. *Administrative Science Quarterly*, *42*(3), 530–557. doi:10.2307/2393737

Keiser, G. (2014). Gartner Says Half of Outsourcing Projects Doomed to Failure. CRN. Retrieved from https://www.crn.com/news/channel-programs/18822227/gartner-says-half-of-outsourcing-projects-doomed-to-failure.htm?itc=refresh

Kern, T., & Willcocks, L. (2002). Exploring relationships in information technology outsourcing: The interaction approach. *European Journal of Information Systems*, *11*(1), 3–19. doi:10.1057/palgrave. ejis.3000415

Koh, C., Ang, S., & Straub, D. W. (2004). IT outsourcing success: A psychological contract perspective. *Information Systems Research*, *15*(4), 356–373. doi:10.1287/isre.1040.0035

Krishnan, M. S., Mukhopadhyay, T., & Kriebel, C. H. (2004). A decision model for software mainte-nance. *Information Systems Research*, *15*(4), 396–412. doi:10.1287/isre.1040.0037

Kudaravalli, S., Faraj, S., & Johnson, S. L. (2017). A Configurational Approach to Coordinating Ex-pertise in Software Development Teams. *Management Information Systems Quarterly*, *41*(1), 43–64. doi:10.25300/MISQ/2017/41.1.03

Lacity, M., & Willcocks, L. (2017). Conflict resolution in business services outsourcing relationships. *The Journal of Strategic Information Systems*, *26*(2), 80–100. doi:10.1016/j.jsis.2017.02.003

Laudon, K. C., & Laudon, J. P. (2016). *Management Information Systems: Managing the Digital Firm* (Vol. 14). Pearson. doi:10.1590/S1415-65552003000100014

Lee, J.-N., & Kim, Y.-G. (1999). Effect of Partnership Quality on IS Outsourcing Success: Conceptual Framework and Empirical Validation. *Journal of Management Information Systems*, *15*(4), 29–61. doi :10.1080/07421222.1999.11518221

Lindell, M. K., & Whitney, D. J. (2001). Accounting for Common Method Variance in Cross-Selectional Research Designs. *The Journal of Applied Psychology*, *86*(1), 114–121. doi:10.1037/0021-9010.86.1.114 PMID:11302223

Mandell, M. P., & Keast, R. (2009). Voluntary and Community Sector Partnerships: Current Inter-orga-nizational Relations and Future Challenges. In The Oxford Handbook of Inter-Organizational Relations. Oxford. doi:10.1093/oxfordhb/9780199282944.003.0007

Miranda, S. M., & Bostrom, R. P. (1999). Meeting Facilitation: Process Versus Content Interventions. *Journal of Management Information Systems*, *15*(4), 89–114. doi:10.1080/07421222.1999.11518223

Molnar, J. J., & Rogers, D. L. (1979). A Comparative Model of Interorganizational Conflict. *Administra-tive Science Quarterly*, *24*(3), 405–425. doi:10.2307/2989920

Ndubisi, N. O. (2011). Conflict handling, trust and commitment in outsourcing relationship: A Chinese and Indian study. *Industrial Marketing Management*, *40*(1), 109–117. doi:10.1016/j.indmarman.2010.09.015

Ndubisi, N. O. (2013). Role of Gender in Conflict Handling in the Context of Outsourcing Service Marketing. *Psychology and Marketing*, *30*(1), 26–35. doi:10.1002/mar.20586

Nidumolu, S. (1995). The effect of coordination and uncertainty on software project performance: Residual performance risk as an intervening variable. *Information Systems Research*, *6*(3), 191–219. doi:10.1287/isre.6.3.191

Podsakoff, P. M., MacKenzie, S. B., Lee, J. Y., & Podsakoff, N. P. (2003). Common method biases in behavioral research: A critical review of the literature and recommended remedies. *The Journal of Applied Psychology*, *88*(5), 879–903. doi:10.1037/0021-9010.88.5.879 PMID:14516251

Podsakoff, P. M., & Organ, D. W. (1986). Self-Reports in Organizational Research: Problems and Prospects. *Journal of Management*, *12*(4), 531–544. doi:10.1177/014920638601200408

Pressman, R. S. (2010). *Software Engineering: A Practitioner's Approach* (7th ed.). Mc Graw Hill India. doi:10.1017/CBO9781107415324.004

Rai, A., Keil, M., Hornyak, R., & Wüllenweber, K. (2012). Hybrid Relational-Contractual Governance for Business Process Outsourcing. *Journal of Management Information Systems*, *29*(2), 213–256. doi:10.2753/MIS0742-1222290208

Renner, S. S., Beenken, L., Grimm, G. W., Kocyan, A., & Ricklefs, R. E. (2007). The evolution of dioecy, heterodichogamy, and labile sex expression in Acer. *Evolution; International Journal of Organic Evolution*, *61*(11), 2701–2719. doi:10.1111/j.1558-5646.2007.00221.x PMID:17894810

Rivard, S., Poirier, G., Raymond, L., & Bergeron, F. (1997). Development of a measure to assess the quality of user-developed applications. *ACM SIGMIS Database*, *28*(3), 44–58. doi:10.1145/272657.272690

Robbins, S., & Judge, T. (2011). *Conflict and Negotiation*. Organizational Behavior.

Robey, D., Smith, L. A., & Vijayasarathy, L. R. (1993). Perceptions of Conflict and Success in Information Systems Development Projects. *Journal of Management Information Systems*, *10*(1), 123–139. doi:10.1080/07421222.1993.11517993

Sabherwal, R. (2003). The evolution of coordination in outsourced software development projects: A comparison of client and vendor perspectives. *Information and Organization*, *13*(3), 153–202. doi:10.1016/S1471-7727(02)00026-X

Schwarz, R. (2002). *The Skilled Facilitator: A Comprehensive Resource for Consultants, Facilitators, Managers, Trainers and Coaches*. Jossey-Bass. Retrieved from http://library.capella.edu/login?url=http://search.proquest.com/docview/215898898?accountid=27965

Sonnenwald, D. H. (1995). Contested collaboration: A descriptive model of intergroup communication in information system design. *Information Processing & Management*, *31*(6), 859–877. doi:10.1016/0306-4573(95)00002-X

Swar, B., Moon, J., Oh, J., & Rhee, C. (2012). Determinants of relationship quality for IS/IT outsourcing success in public sector. *Information Systems Frontiers*, *14*(2), 457–475. doi:10.100710796-010-9292-7

Thibodeau, P., & Rosencrance, L. (2002). Users losing billions due to bugs. *Computerworld*.

Thomas, K. W. (1992). Conflict and conflict management: Reflections and update. *Journal of Organizational Behavior*, *13*(3), 265–274. doi:10.1002/job.4030130307

Tiwana, A., & Keil, M. (2004). The one-minute risk assessment tool. *Communications of the ACM*, *47*(11), 73–77. doi:10.1145/1029496.1029497

Toothaker, L. E., Aiken, L. S., & West, S. G. (1991). Multiple regression: Testing and interpreting interactions. *The Journal of the Operational Research Society*, *45*(1), 119. doi:10.2307/2583960

van Wendel de Joode, R. (2004). Managing Conflicts in Open Source Communities. *Electronic Markets*, *14*(2), 104–113. doi:10.1080/10196780410001675059

Wallace, L., & Keil, M. (2004). Software project risks and their effect on outcomes. *Communications of the ACM*, *47*(4), 68–73. doi:10.1145/975817.975819

Wallace, L., Keil, M., & Rai, A. (2004). How Software Project Risk Affects Project Performance: An Investigation of the Dimensions of Risk and an Exploratory Model. *Decision Sciences*, *35*(2), 289–321. doi:10.1111/j.00117315.2004.02059.x

Winkler, J. K., Dibbern, J., & Heinzl, A. (2008). The impact of cultural differences in offshore outsourcing-Case study results from German-Indian application development projects. *Information Systems Frontiers*, *10*(2), 243–258. doi:10.100710796-008-9068-5

Wojewoda, S., & Hastie, S. (2015). Standish Group 2015 Chaos Report - Q&A with Jennifer Lynch. *INFOQ*. Retrieved from https://www.infoq.com/articles/standish-chaos-2015

Wuellenweber, K., Koenig, W., Beimborn, D., & Weitzel, T. (2009). The impact of process standardization on business process outsourcing success. In Information Systems Outsourcing (3rd ed., pp. 527–548). Springer. doi:10.1007/978-3-540-88851-2_23

Yeh, Q. J., & Tsai, C. L. (2001). Two conflict potentials during IS development. *Information & Management*, *39*(2), 135–149. doi:10.1016/S0378-7206(01)00088-X

This research was previously published in the Journal of Organizational and End User Computing (JOEUC), 32(2); pages 20-41, copyright year 2020 by IGI Publishing (an imprint of IGI Global).

APPENDIX: SURVEY ITEMS

(1 = to a very small extent, 7 = to a very large extent)

Conflict (Adapted from Barki and Hartwick, 2001)
1.   Were there important opinion differences between your user group and outside vendors concerning system goals and objectives, design and implementation?
2.   Did the vendor interfere with your system goals and objectives?
3.   Did the vendor interfere with the physical design that you desired?
4.   During the project, did the vendor do things which made the users feel frustrated?
5.   During the project, did the vendor do things which made the users feel angry?

Process facilitation (Adapted from Miranda and Bostrom, 1999)
1.   Our company's IT personnel helped us to reconcile our differences with outside vendors.
2.   If it were not for the internal IT personnel, the outcome of the disagreement with the outside vendor would have been worse.
3.   Without internal IT personnel, the process of coordinating disagreements with vendors would have been more confusing.
4.   We might have taken a longer time to reach a consensus if the internal IT personnel had not been present.

Content facilitation (Adapted from Miranda and Bostrom, 1999)
1.   Internal IT personnel helped us better understand the unclear part of the problem with external vendors.
2.   If the problem or issue with an external vendor is unclear, the internal IT personnel provide additional information (e.g. best practices or business cases) to solve the problem.
3.   The internal IT personnel presented the decision criteria or alternative.

Project efficiency (Adapted from Nidumolu, 1995; Barki and Hartwick, 2001)
1.   Compared to its estimated schedule, the project was completed (much earlier than scheduled – much later than scheduled).
2.   Compared to its estimated cost, the project was completed (way under budget – way over budget).
3.   Compared to its original specifications, the scope of the completed project is (much smaller than promised – much larger than promised).

System effectiveness (Adapted from Nidumolu, 1995; Barki and Hartwick, 2001)
1.   The system is reliable (it is always up and running, runs without errors, and does what it is supposed to do).
2.   The system is easy to use.
3.   The system performs its functions quickly.

Chapter 93
New Factors Affecting Productivity of the Software Factory

Pedro Castañeda

https://orcid.org/0000-0003-1865-1293

Universidad Peruana de Ciencias Aplicadas (UPC), National University of San Marcos (UNMSM), Lima, Peru

David Mauricio

https://orcid.org/0000-0001-9262-626X

National University of San Marcos, Lima, Peru

ABSTRACT

Productivity is very important because it allows organizations to achieve greater efficiency and effectiveness in their activities; however, it is affected by numerous factors. While these factors have been identified for over two decades, all of the previous works limited the software factory to the programming work unit and did not analyze other work units that are also relevant. 90% of a software factory's effort is absorbed by the software production component, 85% of which is concentrated in the efforts of the analysis and design, programming, and testing work units. The present work identifies three new factors that influence the software factory, demonstrating that the use of rules and events influences analysis & design, team heterogeneity negatively affects analysis and design and positively affects programming; and the osmotic communication affects programming. An empirical study on software factories in Peru, determined that 95% of the influence came from these factors, which corroborated as well that team size and trust within the team influences in software production.

DOI: 10.4018/978-1-6684-3702-5.ch093

INTRODUCTION

Cusumano (1989) defines a software factory as a company whose characteristics include large-scale software production, task standardization, control standardization, labor division, mechanization, automation, and the systematic application of the good practices of software engineering. The software factory offers great advantages, such as the ability to decrease production costs per product up to 60%, the time savings of putting a product on the market up to 98%, labor requirement reductions by up to 60%, the improvement of productivity by approximately 10 times, and the quality of each product with 10 times fewer of the errors. This increases the portfolio of products and services offered and the possibility of winning new markets (Clements & Northrop, 2001).

When measuring productivity, a software factory has indicators that allow for it to be compared in the market in a way that helps with the consideration of actions to increase the overall efficiency, which will allow for the use of all resources in an effective and efficient way in order to obtain the best possible results. A business needs to know how the organization is performing in relation to previous periods and its competitors and must ask questions such as the following. Is it increasing, decreasing, advancing, or receding? What is the magnitude of this progress or setback? Are the implemented strategies effective?

All models that measure productivity in a software factory consider various elements such as the processes, resources, units of measurement, etc., but often do not consider what affects people and how it impacts on the results of the productivity measurement. For example, the motivation and confidence in the team are factors that could have positive impacts on productivity, while in a demotivated team it could have the opposite effect (Yilmaz & O'Connor, 2011). This is the reason why studies are being conducted to identify the factors that affect productivity. However, the following is evident. (i) The factors identified are oriented to the Programming work unit, which could not be generalized to the software factory, given that it contemplates other work units and each unit has its own particularities. (ii) There are factors that influence productivity in other knowledge domains, but they have not been analyzed in the software factory.

In addition, previous studies have not considered that productivity is dependent upon various factors beyond inputs and outputs that influence the processes and context, among others (Arcudia-Abad, Solís-Carcaño & Cuesta-Santos, 2007; Nomura, Spinola, Hikage & Tonini, 2006).

In this article, the authors introduce new factors that affect productivity in software factories that are supported by theories including language action perspective, transactive memory theory, and good agile practices, such as time-boxing. In addition, we study how these factors affect the work units: Analysis & Design, Programming and Testing. To validate the influence of the introduced factors, 150 responses were collected and assessed of one survey published. The present work is part of a research study on productivity models for software factories.

This article is divided into seven sections. Section 2 presents the literature review about the software factory, productivity, and the factors that affect it. Section 3 details the proposed conceptual model and the elements that comprise it. Section 4 describes the research methodology and includes the strategy applied to obtain the information and analyze the results. Section 5 presents the results of the study. In Section 6, a discussion is established about the findings found in the validation. Finally, the conclusions are presented in Section 7.

LITERATURE REVIEW

Software Factory

Although the term "software factory" began to be used in the 60s and 70s in the United States and Japan, only in the 90s did the specialized literature contain works about its organization. It started with the work of Basili, Caldiera and Cantone (1992), which was the first work that proposed the organization of the software factory that was focused on software development. Li C., Li H. and Li M. (2001) extended the approach of Basili et al. (1992) by considering Capability Maturity Model Integration (CMMI) and International Standarization Organization 9001 (ISO 9001). Kruchten (2004) described the process of software development in terms of disciplines of the Unified Rational Process (RUP). Fernandes and Teixeira (2004) proposed a model that classified the factory according to the scope or phases of development defined in the process, thus offering an idea of what the life cycle of a project should be.

Nomura et al. (2006) proposed a software factory structure based on the reuse concepts of Basili et al. (1992), operational management, organizational division (Fernandes & Teixeira, 2004), the application of software engineering activities cited by Swanson, McComb, Smith and McCubbrey (1991), the improvement of work methods (Cusumano, 1989), and engineering practices cited in the Project Management Body of Knowledge (PMBOK) and RUP. Some authors limit the organization of the software factory to the development of the product, as seen in the works of Basili et al. (1992), who proposed dividing the software factory into two areas. One is the software production area whose purpose is to conduct the analysis and design to establish the products' requirements, data, and architecture. The other is the component production area whose objective is to develop the components and meet the requirements requested by the software production area.

Rockwell and Gera (1993) adapted the Eureka model (distributed software development process) for the components' development into two layers (services and interface).

Yanosky (2005) proposed three work units: production organization model, component production unit, and software production unit. Fabri, Trindade, Begosso, Lerario, Silveira and Pessoa (2004); Fabri, Trindade, L'erário, Pessoa and Spinola (2004a); Fabri, Trindade, Durscki, Spinola and Pessoa (2005); Fabri, Trindade, Begosso, Lerario and Pessoa (2007); Fabri, Trindade, Silveira and Pessoa (2007a); Fabri, Scheible, Moreira, Trindade, Begosso, Braun and Pessoa (2007b); Fabri, Trindade, Begosso, Pessoa and L'erário (2007c) and Pessoa, Fabri, L'erário, Spinola and Begosso (2004) proposed an organization based on software production and component production. Trujillo (2007) discussed how an organization must adapt to a methodology of software development, which must be commensurate with the project's magnitude and the number of people. Table 1 summarizes the studies on the organizational structure of the software factory.

As shown in Table 1, there is an overlap in the work units (as verified in Kruchten (2004)) where it identifies the implementation work unit. However, for Nomura et al. (2006), this work unit is part of Coding and Testing. Furthermore, authors have used different terms to identify the same work unit, as seen in Kruchten (2004) where it identifies the work unit of Analysis & Design, while in Fernandes and Teixeira (2004), it is called the Detailed Project. Therefore, some authors consider the Project Management unit (Nomura et al., 2006; Kruchten, 2004) and others call it the Organization of Production (Yanosky, 2005) or Management of the Factory and Process Assets (Li et al., 2001).

Table 1. Organizational structure software factories

Author	Work Unit						
Basili et al., 1992	Software Production						Components Production
Li et al., 2001	Management Factory & Process Assets	Process & Workers					Techniques, Tools, Components
Rockwell & Gera, 2003	Services & Interface						
Kruchten, 2004	Project Management	Business Model	Requirements	Analysis & Design	Implementation	Testing	Configuration & Change Management, Deployment, Environment
Fernandes & Teixeira, 2004		Solution Architecture / Conceptual Project	Logical Specification	Detailed Project	Construction & Testing	Integration Testing / Testing	
Yanosky, 2005	Organization Production	Software Production					Component Production
Nomura et al., 2006	Project Management	Software Production / Business	Architecture & Engineering		Coding & Testing		Support
Trujillo, 2007	Software Development Methodology						
Fabri et al., 2004; Fabri et al., 2004a; Fabri et al., 2005; Fabri et al., 2007; Fabri et al., 2007a; Fabri et al., 2007b; Fabri et al., 2007c; Pessôa et al., 2004	Software Production						Component Production

Source: Castañeda & Mauricio, 2018, P.51

Additionally, very generic work units that have grouped all of the disciplines of software development together can be identified (Basili et al., 1992; Li et al., 2001; Rockwell & Gera, 2003; Yanosky, 2005; Fabri et al., 2004; Fabri et al., 2007c; Pessoa et al., 2004) that could hinder the internal analysis of the software factory. Some authors do not consider the Project Management Office component in the structure of the software factory (Basili et al., 1992; Fernandes & Teixeira, 2004; Rockwell & Gera, 2003; Fabri et al., 2004; Fabri et al., 2007c; Pessoa et al., 2004).

From what is observed, there is no standard on how a software factory should be organized, which makes analysis work difficult for measuring productivity.

Productivity

Productivity in the software factory is a very important aspect to consider since it allows for organizations to be more efficient in achieving their objectives. Table 2 presents the definitions of software productivity.

Table 2. Definition software productivity

Definition	Reference
Productivity = (Size Application Developed) / (Labor consumed in development)	Banker & Kauffman, 1991
The ratio of work product to work effort. Productivity = (Work Product) / (Work Effort)	IEEE, 1992
The ratio size product to work effort. Productivity=Size/Effort	Fenton & Pfleeger, 1997
Productivity= Output/Input Where: Output: function points (FP), source lines code (SLOC) Input: person-hours (PH), person-months (PM)	Scacchi, 1995; Basili, Briand & Melo, 1996; Blackburn, Scudder & Van Wassenhove, 1996; Briand, El-Emam & Bomarius, 1998; Card, 2006; Jeffery, Ruhe & Wieczorek, 2001; Maxwell, 2001; Wagner & Ruhe, 2008; Nwellh & Amadin, 2008

There is no standard definition of productivity. However, the authors have a common aspect since they consider that productivity is the ratio of the product obtained with the efforts. The studies about the productivity of a software factory are reduced to the measurement of productivity in the software programming work unit, as seen in the inputs and outputs that have been evaluated (SLOC, FP, PH and PM by the developer), which has led to the development of many performance measurement models that have become imprecise, because the studies have not comprehensively reviewed the software factory and have precluded other important work units such as Analysis & Design and Testing.

In the previous studies, there is very little discussion about software factories despite the fact that a working model has been used in the industry for many years. In this context, the authors define the productivity of the software factories as "an indicator of efficiency of used resources over different work units of a software factory for the achievement of the final product" (Castañeda & Mauricio, 2018, P.62). This definition has been raised because it considers that all the work units participate in software development, and in addition, it allows for the evaluation of the different factors that influence the entire software production cycle.

Factors in Software Production

Based in Cheikhi, Al-Qutaish and Idri (2012) and Trendowicz (2007), a factor can be defined as "an element or conditioner that is directly or indirectly involved in the different activities of the work units of a software factory that impacts, positively or negatively, in the achievement of objectives" and, consequently, productivity. This is why factors that impact the results of the software factory are being studied. An inventory of the factors can be seen in Table 13 of the Appendix.

CONCEPTUAL MODEL

Work Units

In Table 1, three major components can be identified in the organization of the software factory: Project Management Office, Software Production, and Support (see Table 3). Furthermore, each component can be divided into work units, as shown in Table 4. These were obtained from the analysis and pairing of the work done on the structure of the software factory since; in many cases, the authors overlap the units or a defect has provided another denomination.

Table 3. Software factory components

Component	Description	Reference
Project Management Office	Responsible for the relationship with the customer, negotiation, planning, preparation and management of contracts in accordance with the company strategic planning, as well as the management, preparation, programming and distribution of service orders and allocation of resources needed to the execution of service, structured in the following work units: Service, Project Management, Production Planning and Control.	Li et al., 2001; Kruchten, 2004; Yanosky, 2005; Nomura et al., 2006
Software Production	Responsible for activities specific to the development process. This component includes the work units of: Business Modeling, Solution Architecture, Conceptual Project, Requirements, Analysis & Design, Implementation and Testing.	Basili et al., 1992; Li et al., 2001; Rockwell & Gera, 1993; Kruchten, 2004; Fernandes & Teixeira, 2004; Yanosky, 2005; Nomura, et al., 2006; Trujillo, 2007; Fabri et al., 2004; Fabri et al., 2004a; Fabri et al., 2005; Fabri et al., 2007; Fabri et al., 2007a; Fabri et al., 2007b; Fabri et al., 2007c; Pessôa et al., 2004
Support	It provides support for the integration and development of activities of the development process, including in others: process management, infrastructure and support, interface design, security, documentation, and others.	Basili et al., 1992; Li, et al., 2001; Kruchten, 2004; Yanosky, 2005; Nomura et al., 2006; Fabri et al., 2004; Fabri et al., 2004a; Fabri et al., 2005; Fabri et al., 2007; Fabri et al., 2007a; Fabri et al., 2007b; Fabri et al., 2007c; Pessôa et al., 2004

Additionally, in Table 4, the work units that make up the different components of the software factory are displayed.

Table 4. Work units of software factory components

Component	Work Unit	Description	Reference
Project Management Office	Service	Definition of the type of service will be provided to the client.	Nomura et al., 2006
	Project Management	Assignment of the management layer will be in charge of the execution of the project.	
	Production Planning and Control	Definition of the team will meet the requirements, as well as the information needed for the Production Plan.	
Software Production	Business Project	Definition and elaboration of the business modeling of product to be developed.	Li et al., 2001; Kruchten, 2004; Yanosky, 2005; Nomura et al., 2006
	Analysis & Design	Definition of the base architecture and the functional specification of the requirement.	Kruchten, 2004, Fernandes & Teixeira, 2004; Nomura et al., 2006
	Programming	Implementation of the solution required by the customer.	
	Testing	Definition and execution of test cases, which are corroborated with the acceptance criteria defined by the client.	
Support	Process	Establishment of the key processes for the attention of the requirements according to the type of service to be provided to the client.	Li et al., 2001
	KPI Management	Definition and measurement of the KPIs that will be used in the project.	CMMI, 2016
	Knowledge Management	Definition of policies and organizational assets.	
	Software Architecture	Support of programming assets and software components.	Basili et al., 1992; Li et al., 2001; Yanosky, 2005
	Methodologies, Techniques, Tools	Taking the defined process as a reference, the methodologies, techniques and tools that will support the project are defined.	Li et al., 2001; Kruchten, 2004

Figure 1 illustrates the software factory's operations, in which it can be seen that customers request different types of requirements, which are served by the Project Management Office (PMO) component. In this component, considering the capacity of the factory and the agreed upon requirements to be served, the service is estimated and planned in periods agreed upon by the PMO and client, thus generating the Production Plan.

Then, the requirements accepted in PMO are transferred to the Software Production component, where the key activities for the development of the final product are performed, such as the analysis, design, programming, and testing. The Support component is responsible for facilitating the operation of the work units of the Software Production Component, focusing its attention on providing tools that facilitate the implementation of the services provided to customers.

Ninety percent of the effort of the software factory is absorbed by the Software Production component. Of this, the Analysis & Design, Programming, and Testing work units consume 85% of the efforts of this component (Jacobson, Booch & Rumbaugh, 2000). This is why the present work is oriented to the search for factors that affect productivity in this component and the work units of Analysis & Design, Programming, and Testing.

Figure 1. Structure software factories (Source: Adapted from Nomura et al. (2006))

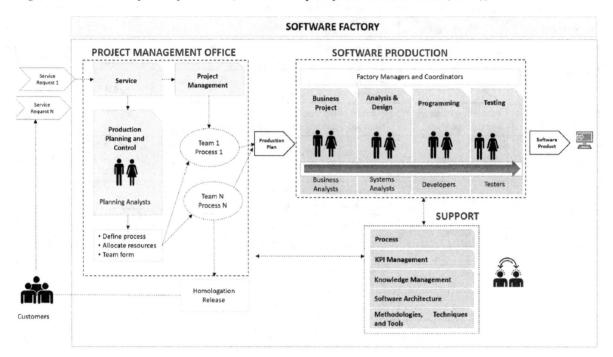

Factors Proposed

The authors reviewed 40 theories that have been applied in the formation of teams, team behaviors, organizational behaviors, and effective communication to discover their relationships to productivity, subsequently discarding those that did not have a relationship. Then, the factors that affect productivity were identified based on these theories and other sources. Several were already identified in the literature. Thus, we obtained four new factors and two existing factors, which were applied to the Programming work unit, which are described in the following paragraphs.

The Use of Rules and Events (RULE) factor refers to compliance with the standards and rules of behavior that are defined by the same team, which allows for the team to clearly and specifically meet the goals and objectives that can be measured. One of the best practices to implement these standards is time-boxing, which "ensures that Team members do not use up too much or too little work for a particular period of time, and do not expend their time and energy on work for which they have little clarity" (SBOK, 2016). Some advantages include a more efficient development process, less overhead and high-speed equipment, which lead to improvements in productivity. For example, the team should be required to participate in an event named the daily meeting, which allows for them to review the product progress. This meeting is set in a time-box of 15 minutes in order to be an effective meeting.

The Heterogeneity of the Team (HETE) factor refers to the improvement of team performance through the formation of multifunctional teams in a way that facilitates the use of the knowledge of all the participating roles. In Ancona and Caldwell (1992), it was demonstrated that functional diversity in teams can influence performance through internal processes and external communication. The authors mentioned that "while diversity produces processes that facilitate performance, it also directly affects performance."

In Cohen and Bailey (1997), the view was that team diversity results in a better use of knowledge, better communications, and better cooperation in teams, thus leading to better team productivity.

The Face-to-Face Communication in the Team (FACE) factor refers to the way in which people interact to improve the understanding of the requirements, thereby facilitating the learning process and collaboration in the team. Simmons (1991) stated that communication has a great influence on productivity according to the theory "Language Action Perspective," (Flores & Ludlow, 1980), which considers language as the main dimension of human cooperation activity. For example, the importance that has been given to this factor in agile could be considered one of the fundamental principles of the Agile Manifesto in that "the most efficient and effective method of communicating information to the development team and among its members is the face-to-face conversation" (SBOK, 2016).

The Osmotic Communication in the Team (OSMO) factor refers to the information that flows in the auditory background of the team members in such a way that they capture the relevant information as if by osmosis, which usually is produced by being in the same work environment. Thus, when a person asks a question, others in the environment can synchronize or disconnect, contribute to the discussion, or continue with their work. In "Transactive Memory Theory," Wegner (1987) stated that members are able to benefit from the knowledge and experience of others by developing a good understanding through group sharing.

The Team Size (SIZE) factor refers to the number of participants in the work team. It is necessary to ensure the skills and abilities that are required and facilitate collaboration between team members. This is because the larger the communication channels, the more complex the transfer of information to different levels becomes. According to Rodríguez, Sicilia, García & Harrison (2011), the software team size was viewed as one of the drivers of project productivity. In addition, many authors have conducted studies on this factor and have determined the impact on software productivity, but this has only been applied to the Programming work unit (Verner, Evanco & Cerpa, 2007; Brooks, 1995; Abdel-Hamid, 1989; Abdel-Hamid & Madnick, 1991; Montgomery, 1981; Smith, Hale & Parish, 2001; Trendowicz & Munch, 2009; Norden, 1958; Norden, 1977; Pillai & Sukumaran Nair, 1997; Harman & Jones, 2001; Di Penta, Harman, Antoniol & Qureshi, 2007; Alba & Chicano, 2005; Alba & Chicano, 2007; Gueorguiev, Harman & Antoniol, 2009; Chicano, Luna, Nebro & Alba, 2011; Kremmel, Kubalik & Biffl, 2010; Kremmel, Kubalik & Biffl, 2011; Pendharkar & Rodger, 2007).

The Trust within the Team (TRUS) factor refers to the ability of team members to trust one another, which contributes to greater cohesion and consequently ensures better productivity. Sridhar, Paul, Nath and Kapur (2007) found that trust between team members and their effective communications have a positive correlation with the success of the project, which affects the performance of the developmental team. Additionally, several authors have demonstrated the importance of confidence in productivity (Yilmaz & O'Connor, 2011; Sudhakar, Farooq & Patnaik, 2011). A synthesis of the introduced factors is presented in Table 5.

Table 5 considers six factors that affect the productivity of the software factory, being four new factors: RULE, HETE, FACE, OSMO, and two existing factors in the literature: SIZE and TRUS. The existing factors have been considered as new, since the studies conducted have only been applied in the Programming work unit, however in the present study they will be applied to the Analysis & Design and Testing work units.

Table 5. New factors affecting productivity

Id	Factor	Description	Support
RULE	Use of Rules and Events	Compliance with rules and behavior rules that are defined by the same team.	Agile Methodologies (SBOK, 2016)
HETE	Heterogeneity of the Team	Formation of multifunctional work teams.	Ancona & Caldwell, 1992; Cohen & Bailey, 1997
FACE	Face to Face Communication in the Team	Communication method that allows people to interact to improve understanding of the requirements.	Agile Methodologies (SBOK, 2016); Language Action Perspective (Flores & Ludlow, 1980; Simmons, 1991)
OSMO	Osmotic Communication in the Team	Learning through information that flows in the auditory background of the members of the team, in such a way that they capture the relevant information.	Transactive Memory Theory (Wegner, 1987)
SIZE (*)	Team Size	Number of participants in the work team	Rodríguez et al., 2011; Verner et al., 2007; Brooks, 1995; Abdel-Hamid & Madnick, 1991; Abdel-Hamid, 1989; Montgomery, 1981; Smith et al., 2001; Trendowicz & Munch, 2009; Norden, 1958; Norden, 1977; Pillai & Sukumaran Nair, 1997; Harman & Jones, 2001; Di Penta et al., 2007; Alba & Chicano, 2005; Alba & Chicano, 2007, Gueorguiev et al., 2009; Chicano et al., 2011; Kremmel et al., 2010; Kremmel et al., 2011; Pendharkar & Rodger, 2007
TRUS (*)	Trust in the Team	Capacity of team members to trust each other.	Yilmaz & O'Connor, 2011; Sridhar et al., 2007; Sudhakar, 2011

(*) Existing factors in the literature

Hypotheses

Next, we propose hypotheses to determine the influence of the factors introduced in Table 5: *1. RULE, 2. HETE, 3. FACE, 4. OSMO, 5. SIZE and 6. TRUS*, on the work units: *1. Analysis & Design, 2. Programming, and 3. Testing*. The hypotheses were obtained based on theories described in previous paragraphs. We use the notation HX.Y to denote a hypothesis that relates X factor to Y work unit, for example H3.1 refers to the FACE factor with the Analysis & Design work unit.

Influence of the Use of Rules and Events (RULE) Factor

Analysis activities involve adequate planning and constant interactions with the client and the team in such a way that a good understanding of the requirements is acquired and conducted to produce the desired product. As such, it is necessary that the analysts concentrate on defining the scope of the analysis in order to establish and prioritize activities to achieve the objectives and minimize distractions that may cause delays. Thus, it is necessary and beneficial to establish rules and events that support the fulfillment of these activities.

Hypothesis H1.1: The Use of Rules and Events factor influences the Analysis & Design work unit.

Influence of the Heterogeneity of the Team (HETE) Factor

Diversity in the team is a good way to incorporate new perspectives that can help members overcome problems from different angles. That is, why if the Analysis & Design team members have different profiles, the result will lead to a better understanding of the requirements and a different way of proposing alternative solutions. Likewise, since programming is an activity that incorporates various disciplines, it is necessary that the team is multifunctional and that it has skills and capabilities that allow for it to be more efficient in the development of the product.

Hypothesis H2.1: The Heterogeneity of the Team factor influences the Analysis & Design work unit.
Hypothesis H2.2: The Heterogeneity of the Team factor influences the Programming work unit.

Influence of the Face-to-Face Communication in the Team (FACE) Factor

"Face-to-face" communications are essential to create a bond between the participants of the project. It is the most efficient and effective method of communication within a development team since it produces an energy exchange that concurrently energizes the human experience and facilitates interactions between many people, thereby fostering greater fluidity, effectiveness, and speed in terms of dialogue, discussion, and decision-making.

Hypothesis H3.1: The Face-to-Face Communications in the Team factor influences the Analysis & Design work unit.

Influence of the Osmotic Communication in the Team (OSMO) Factor

The development teams usually work in co-located places. Therefore, this type of communication is necessary in the team. It requires that everyone know the activities in order to avoid dependence and so that the team can move forward.

Hypothesis H4.2: The Osmotic Communication in the Team factor influences the Programming work unit.

Influence of the Team Size (SIZE) Factor

The team size is a critical factor in software development since more team members leads to more communication channels that are generated. Therefore, it is necessary that the team is large enough to ensure adequate skills but small enough to facilitate communication. Various studies have shown the influence of this factor in the Programming work unit. That is, why we pose a question about the influence in the Analysis & Design work unit.

Hypothesis H5.1: The Team Size factor influences the Analysis & Design work unit.
Hypothesis H5.2: The Team Size factor influences the Programming work unit.

Influence of the Trust in the Team (TRUS) Factor

A successful team is built on trust. Each team member must establish trust and cultivate it through their actions, their words, and their work to maintain it. Each member also needs to be able to trust the members of their team to make a commitment to them and their goals.

Hypothesis H6.1: The Trust in the Team factor influences the Analysis & Design work unit.
Hypothesis H6.2: The Trust in the Team factor influences the Programming work unit.
Hypothesis H6.3: The Trust in the Team factor influences the Testing work unit.

Table 6 summarizes the hypotheses that were presented.

Table 6. Summary of hypotheses

Factor	Work Unit		
	Analysis and Design (ADI)	**Programming (PRO)**	**Testing (TES)**
RULE	H1.1		
HETE	H2.1	H2.2	
FACE	H3.1		
OSMO		H4.2	
SIZE	H5.1	H5.2	
TRUS	H6.1	H6.2	H6.3

Model

After reviewing different factors and based on established hypotheses, Figure 2 shows the conceptual model of the proposed factors and the impact on the productivity of the different work units of the software factory.

To validate the hypotheses proposed in the conceptual model described in Figure 2, an empirical study was carried out that required data collection for the evaluation of the results obtained.

METHODOLOGY

Data Collection

In the present investigation, a questionnaire was used as the instrument of study, and an online survey with Google Forms was prepared. The survey was taken during the period from June to October 2017, and the participants were professionals and experts who participated in the supervision and monitoring of the software factory. This study has been developed in organizations that have implemented models of software factories in Peru, with operations in South America, and that play a very important role in the

Figure 2. Initial conceptual model

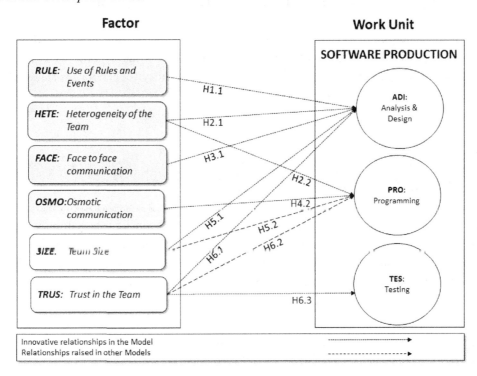

software industry. The objective of the survey was to determine the perceptions of different professionals and experts that interact in the software factory in relation to the factors that influence productivity.

The survey was structured in three sections. i) Section 1 - General Information consisted of five questions related to the company's characterization and the people who filled out the questionnaire. ii) Section 2 - Productivity Factors of the Software Factory corresponding to questions to determine the influence of factors that were affecting productivity in the different work units of the Software Factory. It was measured based on a Likert scale of five response levels (1: No Influence; 2: Low Influence; 3: Medium Influence; 4: High Influence, and 5: Total Influence). iii) Section 3 - Other Aspects. This section provides a better understanding of the factors that impact the productivity of the work units of the software factory. The survey is available at https://tinyurl.com/y7m7ltxl.

After preparing the survey, a pilot test was conducted to validate the questions. It involved managers and senior project managers. It checked to see if the questions were related to the hypotheses and then corrected the structure of the questions and the language used.

Letters and emails were sent to solicit participation in the surveys to public and private institutions that have an IT department. In total, 160 surveys were obtained, and 10 of those were discarded due to inconsistencies in the answers.

Analysis of Results

The instrument used in analyzing the data was the questionnaire, and statistical analyses were performed on the data obtained. This included the following. i) A descriptive analysis of the sample. This included the analysis of the demographic aspects of the survey, including the size of the company, the business sector, and the respondent's years of experience. The mean, variance, mode, and the distribution of respondents' answers were measured. ii) The reliability of data was assessed using Cronbach's alpha whose value reflects the internal consistency and shows the correlation between each of the questions. iii) A multiple linear regression was conducted for the verification of the hypotheses and to explain the level of significance between the work units of the software factory (dependent variable) and the six proposed factors (independent variables).

RESULTS

Determination of the Sample

Having obtained the participation of 150 people, it is necessary to consider the sample percent error in order to establish the validity of the present study. By not having historical information from similar studies, the sample error was based on the maximum possible variance, which ensured the validity (representativeness) of the sample. To calculate the error level, the following sample size formula was applied:

$$n = \frac{z^2 pq}{\varepsilon^2} \tag{1}$$

where:

n = 150 (sample size)

z = 1.96 (95% trust level)

and:

p = 0.5 (maximum variance)

From this:

$$\varepsilon^2 = \frac{z^2 pq}{n} = \frac{1.96^2 \times 0.5 \times 0.5}{150} = 0.0064$$

which means that $\varepsilon = 0.08$ (8% sample error).

Therefore, we can be assured of a confidence level of 95%, a p of the maximum variance that is equal to 0.5, a q = 1-p = 0.5, and a sampling error of 8% from a sample of 150 people was taken (n = 150).

The surveys were disseminated to different organizations that provided software factory services in Peru. They are characterized as follows:

- A total of 88.7% of the participants work in software factories whose size varied from 10 to 500 people, with only 11.3% of the participants working in companies with more than 500 people, as shown in Figure 3;
- A total of 60% of the study's participants work in software factories that provide services to the Government sector. This was followed by 11.3% who worked in the Transportation and Services sectors, and 17.4% was divided among the other sectors, as shown in Figure 3. Additionally, 65.3% of the participants have one to five years of experience in software factories, and 34.7% of the participants have more than five years of experience.

Figure 3. Characterization of data of the sample

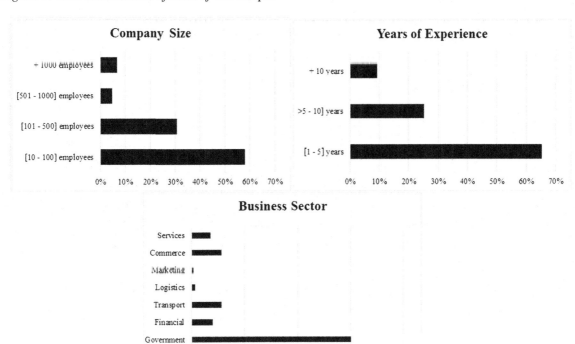

Data Reliability

According to Celina and Campo (2005), the acceptable value for Cronbach's alpha is 0.7. A value higher than this reveals a strong relationship between the questions and the validity of the instrument is acceptable. According to the results obtained with the IBM SPSS Statistics tool, for the 10 elements considered in the evaluation, a value of Cronbach's alpha equal to 0.783 was obtained, which verifies that the validity of the instrument is acceptable.

Hypothesis Testing

For the analysis of the results, it was considered that if the t-test was less than 0.05, it implied that the independent variable was significantly related with the dependent variable. Therefore, it would be influential and explanatory (Ramanathan, 2002).

Work Unit: ADI - Software Analysis and Design

Using the multiple linear regression technique, we will explain the levels of significance between the dependent variable (ADI) and the six independent variables (RULE, HETE, FACE, OSMO, SIZE, and TRUS) in order to determine which variables have the greatest impacts on the productivity of this work unit.

As shown in Table 7, the most significant variables are RULE, HETE, and TRUS.

Table 7. Regression of dependent variable (ADI) with all independent variables

Factor	B	Standard Error	t	Sig.
RULE	0.154	0.069	2.240	0.027
HETE	-0.141	0.061	-2.312	0.022
FACE	0.068	0.087	0.781	0.436
OSMO	-0.005	0.059	-0.087	0.931
SIZE	-0.056	0.072	-0.778	0.438
TRUS	0.235	0.078	3.009	0.003

To have a predictive model, and considering these significant variables, a linear regression was performed that obtained the results shown in Table 8.

Table 8. Regression of dependent variable (ADI) with significant independent variables

Factor	B	Standard Error	t	Sig.
RULE	0.163	0.054	2.991	0.003
HETE	-0.129	0.053	-2.436	0.016
TRUS	0.243	0.049	5.002	0.000

The predictive model is shown below:

$$ADI = 0.163\ RULE - 0.129\ HETE + 0.243\ TRUS$$

Model interpretation:

- Each time the RULE factor is increased by one point (intensity), the ADI will increase by 0.163. This means that the greater Use of Rules and Events will lead to a better performance of the team's activities;
- When the level of influence is increased by one unit due to the effect of the Heterogeneity of the Team (HETE), then the impact on the Analysis & Design work unit is -0.129 units. This, means that less Heterogeneity of the Team generates more efficiency in the results;
- Each time the TRUS factor increases by one point (intensity), the ADI will increase by 0.243. This means that greater Trust within the Team will lead to a better performance in the results achieved.

Work Unit: PRO - Software Programming

Through the multiple linear regression technique, we will explain the levels of significance between the dependent variable (PRO) and the six independent variables (RULE, HETE, FACE, OSMO, SIZE, TRUS) in order to determine which variables have the greatest impact on productivity in the Programming work unit.

As shown in Table 9, the most significant variables are HETE, OSMO, SIZE, and TRUS.

Table 9. Regression of dependent variable (PRO) with all independent variables

Factor	B	Standard Error	t	Sig.
RULE	-0.048	0.052	-0.923	0.357
HETE	0.100	0.048	2.062	0.041
FACE	0.061	0.047	1.301	0.195
OSMO	0.120	0.051	2.182	0.032
SIZE	0.125	0.056	2.225	0.028
TRUS	0.170	0.058	2.932	0.004

To establish a predictive model that considers these significant variables, a linear regression was performed, thus obtaining the results shown in Table 10.

Table 10. Regression of dependent variable (PRO) with significant independent variables

Factor	B	Standard Error	t	Sig.
HETE	0.076	0.040	1.894	0.060
OSMO	0.115	0.042	2.282	0.001
SIZE	0.147	0.045	3.282	0.001
TRUS	0.157	0.046	3.418	0.001

The predictive model is shown below:

PRO = 0.076 HETE + 0.115 OSMO + 0.147 SIZE + 0.157 TRUS

As seen, the four variables positively influence the productivity of the Programming work unit.

Component: TES - Software Testing

Using the multiple linear regression technique, we will explain the levels of significance between the dependent variable (TES) and the six independent variables (RULE, HETE, FACE, OSMO, SIZE, and TRUS) to determine which variables have more impact on the productivity in the Testing work unit.

As shown in Table 11, the most significant variable is TRUS. To establish a predictive model that considered these significant variables, a linear regression was performed, thereby obtaining the results shown in Table 12.

Table 11. Regression of dependent variable (TES) with all independent variables

Factor	B	Standard Error	t	Sig.
RULE	0.039	0.034	1.151	0.252
HETE	0.040	0.035	1.159	0.248
FACE	-0.006	0.034	-0.174	0.862
OSMO	-0.022	0.033	-0.678	0.499
SIZE	-0.004	0.034	-0.125	0.901
TRUS	-0.085	0.037	-2.271	0.025

Table 12. Regression of dependent variable (TES) with significant independent variables

Factor	B	Standard Error	t	Sig.
TRUS	0.044	0.007	6.071	0.000

The predictive model is shown below:

TES = 0.044 TRUS

As observed, each time the TRUS factor increases in one point (intensity), TES will increase by 0.044. This means that more Trust within the Team will lead to a better performance in the results achieved.

Finally, in Figure 4, the final conceptual model can be visualized with the factors that have a greater impact in each of the work units of the software factory.

Figure 4. Final model of factors affecting productivity

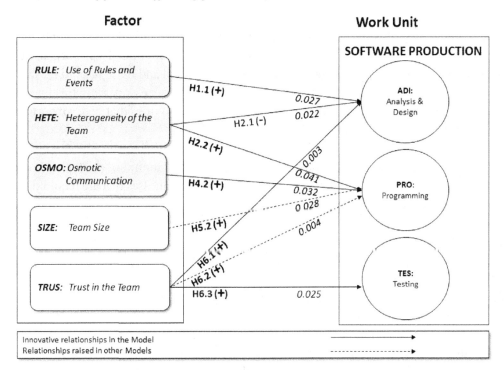

DISCUSSION

Work Units

As has been observed in previous studies (Basili et al., 1992; Li et al., 2001; Kruchten, 2004; Fernandes & Teixeira, 2004; Nomura et al., 2006; Rockwell & Gera, 1993; Yanosky, 2005; Fabri et al., 2004; Fabri et al., 2004a; Fabri et al., 2005; Fabri et al., 2007; Fabri et al., 2007a; Fabri et al., 2007b; Fabri et al., 2007c; Pessoa et al., 2004; Trujillo, 2007) there is no standard about how a software factory should be organized, which makes it difficult to analyze work to measure productivity. Normally, the studies simplify the software factory only to the software production component, which has several disadvantages. Since the management of the project and other units that interact within it would not be considered, it could skew the interpretation of the productivity.

It has been possible to identify that a software factory is organized into three main components: Project Management Office, Software Production, and Support. Furthermore, it can be divided into different work units, such as Service, Project Management, Production Planning and Control, Business Project, Analysis & Design, Programming, Testing, Process, KPI Management, Knowledge Management, Software Architecture, Methodologies, Techniques and Tools. This means that the areas in which the necessary activities are conducted comply with the component's objective.

In addition, it has been determined that in Peru, software factories have been implemented primarily in public entities (60%). Additionally, it can be seen that the software factory approach in Peru is very recent, as corroborated by 65.3% of the study's participants who had an average of five years of experience.

Factors

From the data obtained in this study, it has been shown that the Use of Rules and Events (RULE) factor has a significant positive influence on the Analysis & Design work unit. This is because the analyst needs to establish an adequate plan of the activities to be conducted and these have to be aligned to the scope of the requirements. The analyst should not be distracted by accessory activities that impede the fulfillment of the objective, which is why it is important to establish rules that give support and specify these activities.

The Heterogeneity of the Team (HETE) factor has a negative influence on the Analysis & Design work unit. However, it has a significant positive influence on Programming, which could be explained by the analysis tasks in general and the specialists in the types of businesses that are required. The reason to involve more specialists would be to reduce productivity. Nevertheless, programming tasks require different abilities and capacities for product development.

The Face-to-Face Communication (FACE) factor has no significant impact on the Analysis & Design work unit, ruling out the initial hypothesis that had been supported based on the language action perspective theory (Flores & Ludlow, 1980), which could be explained by the increased use of technology for interactions. The interaction between the participants in software development is very important for the achievement of the objectives. However, the face-to-face version is being overcome by the virtual media.

The Osmotic Communication in the Team (OSMO) factor has a significant positive influence on the Programming because programming activities require different skills and abilities. This means that more people have knowledge of what the other members of the team are doing. Therefore, there is an easier integration of the product, and there will be greater contingency in the case of the absence of any member of the team, which will lead to greater productivity.

The impact of the Team Size (SIZE) factor in Programming is corroborated (Verner et al., 2007; Brooks, 1995; Abdel-Hamid & Madnick, 1991; Abdel-Hamid, 1989; Montgomery, 1981; Smith et al., 2001; Trendowicz & Munch, 2009; Norden, 1958; Norden, 1977; Pillai & Sukumaran Nair, 1997; Harman & Jones, 2001; Di Penta et al., 2007; Alba & Chicano, 2005; Alba & Chicano, 2007; Gueorguiev et al., 2009; Chicano et al., 2011; Kremmel et al., 2010; Kremmel et al., 2011; Pendharkar & Rodger, 2007). However, there is no significant impact of this factor on the Analysis & Design work unit.

The Trust in the Team (TRUS) factor has a significant positive influence on the three work units. This reinforces the need to design strategies to improve the confidence between team members, which allows for the achievement of the goal through the integrated work between all the work units of the software factory.

While the other factors that were analyzed also have a level of positive or negative influence on the productivity of the software factory, the values obtained are not significant enough to be considered. This implies that although these factors are managed correctly or incorrectly, their influence on productivity will not generate a high impact. For example, the use of the osmotic communication in the team (OSMO) generates an improvement in productivity in the Analysis & Design work unit, but this influence will not be very significant.

Study Limitations

This study has used the technique of the survey to obtain the results shown. Therefore, it is subject to some limitations such as the following. a) The experimental study has used the survey technique with those involved in the software development process in Peru, and b) the study has been applied only to the Software Production component.

Future Works

Future studies could consider analyzing the factors that affect the Business Project work unit of the Software Production, component and the Project Management Office and Support components in such a way that an integral study of the software factory can be obtained. Additionally, an aspect to be taken into account in future work would be to perform an analysis of the "Face-to-Face" Communications in teams (FACE) to determine their impact on virtual and face-to-face work environments. Additionally, it is advisable to have a database of information generated in software factory projects in such a way that it facilitates research studies in this area. This will establish strategies that allow for the enhancement of positive factors and the reduction of negative factors in order to mitigate their impacts on productivity.

CONCLUSION

The authors have introduced six factors that influence software productivity, four of them are supported by theories: Use of Rules and Events (RULE), Heterogeneity of the Team (HETE), Face-to-Face Communication (FACE) and Osmotic Communication in the Team (OSMO). And the other two, which have their origin in studies of the Programming work unit, have also been extended to the Analysis & Design and Testing work units, which are: Team Size (SIZE) and Trust in the Team (TRUS).

The results obtained from a survey administered to 150 professionals involved in software development activities in the factory environment in Peru corroborated the influence of the proposed factors. For instance, in the Analysis & Design work unit, Use of Rules and Events (RULE) and Trust in the Team (TRUS) have a significant positive influence, and the Heterogeneity of the Team (HETE) has a negative influence.

Conversely, in the Programming work unit, the Heterogeneity of the Team (HETE), Osmotic Communication in Team (OSMO), Team Size (SIZE), and Trust within the Team (TRUS) have significant positive influences. Additionally, in the Testing work unit, it has been demonstrated that Trust within the Team (TRUS) has a significant positive influence.

Likewise, it can be seen that the Trust within the Team (TRUS) factor affects the three work units. Additionally, it is reaffirmed that the Team Size (SIZE) factor has a significant positive influence on the Programming work unit. However, it does not have this same effect in the other work units.

ACKNOWLEDGMENT

The authors thank dedicated senior reviewers who helped us with their professional feedback, exhaustive review, experience and extensive knowledge in the area of study, to improve the clarity of the article. This research was supported by the Universidad Peruana de Ciencias Aplicadas (UPC); and the Universidad Nacional Mayor de San Marcos (UNMSM).

REFERENCES

Abdel-Hamid, T. K. (1989). The dynamics of software project staffing: A system dynamics based simulation approach. *IEEE Transactions on Software Engineering, 15*(2), 109–119. doi:10.1109/32.21738

Abdel-Hamid, T. K., & Madnick, S. E. (1991). *Software project dynamics: an integrated approach.* Upper Saddle River, NJ, USA: Prentice-Hall, Inc.

Alba, E., & Chicano, J. (2005). Management of software projects with GAs. In *Proceedings of the 6th Metaheuristics International Conference (MIC'05)*, Vienna, Austria (pp. 13–18). Elsevier Science Inc.

Alba, E., & Chicano, J. (2007). Software project management with GAs. *Information Sciences, 177*(11), 2380–2401. doi:10.1016/j.ins.2006.12.020

Ancona, D. G., & Caldwell, D. F. (1992). Demography and design: Predictors of new product team performance. *Organization Science, 3*(3), 321–341. doi:10.1287/orsc.3.3.321

Arcudia-Abad, E., Solís-Carcaño, R. G., & Cuesta-Santos, A. R. (2007). Propuesta tecnológica para incrementar la productividad en la construcción masiva de vivienda. *Ingeniería, Investigación y Tecnología, 8*(2), 11. doi:10.22201/fi.25940732e.2007.08n2.006

Banker, R. D., & Kauffman, R. J. (1991). Reuse and productivity in integrated computer-aided software engineering: An empirical study. *Management Information Systems Quarterly, 14*(3), 374–401.

Basili, V. R., Briand, L. C., & Melo, W. L. (1996). How reuse influences productivity in object-oriented systems. *Communications of the ACM, 39*(10), 104–116. doi:10.1145/236156.236184

Basili, V. R., Caldiera, G., & Cantone, G. (1992). A reference architecture for the component factory. *ACM Transactions on Software Engineering and Methodology, 1*(1), 53–80. doi:10.1145/125489.122823

Blackburn, J. D., Scudder, G. D., & Van Wassenhove, L. N. (1996). Improving speed and productivity of software development: A global survey of software developers. *IEEE Transactions on Software Engineering, 22*(12), 875–885. doi:10.1109/32.553636

Briand, L. C., El-Emam, K., & Bomarius, F. (1998). COBRA: A hybrid method for software cost estimation, benchmarking, and risk assessment. In *Proceedings of the 20th International Conference on Software Engineering*, Kyoto, Japan, April 19-25 (pp. 390-399). Academic Press. 10.1109/ICSE.1998.671392

Brooks, F. P. (1995). The mythical man-month (Anniversary ed.). Boston, MA: Addison-Wesley Longman Publishing Co. Inc.

Cao, Q., Gu, V. C., & Thompson, M. A. (2012). Using complexity measures to evaluate software development projects: A nonparametric approach. *The Engineering Economist: A Journal Devoted to the Problems of Capital Investment, 57*(4), 274-283.

Card, D. N. (2006). The challenge of productivity measurement. In *Proceedings of Pacific Northwest Software Quality Conference*, Portland, OR. Academic Press.

Castañeda, P., & Mauricio, D. (2018). A review of literature about models and factors of productivity in the software factory. *International Journal of Information Technologies and Systems Approach, 11*(1), 48–71. doi:10.4018/IJITSA.2018010103

Celina, H., & Campo, A. (2005). Aproximación al uso del coeficiente alfa de Cronbach. *Revista colombiana de psiquiatría, 34*(4), 572 – 580. Retrieved from http://redalyc.uaemex.mx/pdf/806/80634409.pdf

Çetin, F., & Alabaş-Uslu, Ç. (2015). Performance evaluation of projects in software development. *Journal of Aeronautics and Space Technologies, 8*(2), 1–6.

Cheikhi, L., Al-Qutaish, R. E., & Idri, A. (2012). Software productivity: Harmonization in ISO/IEEE software engineering standards. *Journal of Software, 7*(2), 462–470. doi:10.4304/jsw.7.2.462-470

Chicano, I., Luna, F., Nebro, A. J., & Alba, E. (2011). Using multi-objective metaheuristics to solve the software project scheduling problem. In *Proceedings of the 13th Annual Conference on Genetic and evolutionary computation (GECCO'11), GECCO'11* (pp. 1915–1922). New York, NY: ACM. 10.1145/2001576.2001833

Clements, P. C., & Northrop, L. M. (2001). *Software Product Lines: Practices and Patterns.* Addison-Wesley Professional.

CMMI. (2016). Capability maturity model integration. *CMMI Institute.* Retrieved from http://cmmiinstitute.com/

Cohen, S. G., & Bailey, D. E. (1997). What makes teams work: Group effectiveness research from the shop floor to the executive suite. *Journal of Management, 23*(3), 239–290. doi:10.1177/014920639702300303

Cusumano, M. A. (1989). The software factory: A historical interpretation. *IEEE Software, 6*(2), 23–30. doi:10.1109/MS.1989.1430446

Di Penta, M., Harman, M., Antoniol, G., & Qureshi, F. (2007). The effect of communication overhead on software maintenance project staffing: a search-based approach. In *Proceedings of the IEEE International Conference on Software Maintenance (ICSM 2007)* (pp. 315–324). IEEE. 10.1109/ICSM.2007.4362644

Fabri, J. A., Scheible, A. C. F., Moreira, P. M. L., Trindade, A. L. P., Begosso, L. R., Braun, A. P., & Pessoa, M. S. P. (2007b). Meta-process used for production process modeling of a software factory: The Unitech case. In *Managing Worldwide Operations and Communications with Information Technology.* Vancouver, Canada: IRMA.

Fabri, J. A., Trindade, A. L. P., Begosso, L. R., Lerario, I., & Pessoa, M. S. P. (2007). A Organização de uma Máquina de Processo e a Melhoria do Processo de Produção de Software em um Ambiente de Fábrica. In VI Jornadas Iberoamericana de Ingeniería del Software e Ingeniería del Conocimiento, Lima, Perú. Academic Press.

Fabri, J. A., Trindade, A. L. P., Begosso, L. R., Lerario, I., Silveira, F. L. F., & Pessoa, M. S. P. (2004). Techniques for the development of a software factory: Case CEPEIN-FEMA. In *Proceedings of the 17th International Conference Software & Systems Engineering and their Applications,* Paris. Academic Press.

Fabri, J. A., Trindade, A. L. P., Begosso, L. R., Pessoa, M. S. P., & L'erário, A. (2007c). The use of the idef-0 to model the process in a software factory. In Proceedings of the Managing Worldwide Operations and Communications with Information Technology–IRMA 2007, Vancouver, Canada. Academic Press.

Fabri, J. A., Trindade, A. L. P., Durscki, R., Spinola, M. M., & Pessoa, M. S. P. (2005). Proposta de um Mecanismo de Desenvolvimento e Customização de uma Fábrica de Software Orientada a Dominios. In *Proceedings of the XXXI Latin American Computing Conference*. Academic Press.

Fabri, J. A., Trindade, A. L. P., L'erário, A., Pessoa, M. S. P., & Spinola, M. (2004a). Desenvolvimento e Replicação de uma Fábrica de uma Software. In *VI Simpósio Internacional de Melhoria de Processo de Software*. São Paulo: SIMPROS.

Fabri, J. A., Trindade, A. L. P., Silveira, M., & Pessoa, M. S. P. (2007a). O Papel do CMMI na Configuração de um Meta-Processo de Produção de Software com Características Fabris: Um Estudo de Caso. In VI Jornadas Iberoamericanas de Ingeniería del Software e Ingeniería del Conocimiento, Lima, Perú (pp. 375-383). Academic Press.

Fenton, N. E., & Pfleeger, S. L. (1997). Measuring productivity. In Software metrics: A Rigorous Practical Approach (pp. 412–425). CRC Press.

Fernandes, A. A., & Teixeira, D. S. (2004). *Fábrica de software: Implantação e gestão de operações*. São Paulo: Editora Atlas.

Flores, F., & Ludlow, J. (1980). Doing and speaking in the office. In G. Fick & R. H. Sprague (Eds.), *Decision Support Systems: Issues and Challenges* (pp. 95–118). New York: Pergamon Press. doi:10.1016/B978-0-08-027321-1.50011-0

Gueorguiev, S., Harman, M., & Antoniol, G. (2009). Software project planning for robustness and completion time in the presence of uncertainty using multi objective search based software engineering. In *Proceedings of the 11th Annual Conference on Genetic and Evolutionary Computation (GECCO'09)*, Montreal, Canada (pp. 1673–1680). ACM. 10.1145/1569901.1570125

Harman, M., & Jones, B. F. (2001). Search-based software engineering. *Information and Software Technology*, *43*(14), 833–839. doi:10.1016/S0950-5849(01)00189-6

IEEE. (1992). IEEE Std 1045-1992 - Standard for Software Productivity Metrics.

Jacobson, I., Booch, G., & Rumbaugh, J. (2000). *El proceso unificado de desarrollo de software* (pp. 321–322). Madrid: Pearson Educación S.A.

Jeffery, R., Ruhe, M., & Wieczorek, I. (2001). Using public domain metrics to estimate software development effort. *Proceedings of METRICS*, *01*, 16–27.

Khan, R., Ahmed, I., & Faisal, M. (2014). An industrial investigation of human factors effect on software productivity: Analyzed by SEM model. *International Journal of Computer Science and Mobile Computing*, *3*(5), 16–24.

Kremmel, T., Kubalik, J., & Biffl, S. (2010). Multiobjective evolutionary algorithm for software project portfolio optimization. In *Proceedings of the 12th Annual Conference on Genetic and Evolutionary Computation (GECCO'10)*, Portland, OR (pp. 1389–1390). ACM. 10.1145/1830483.1830738

Kremmel, T., Kubalik, J., & Biffl, S. (2011). Software project portfolio optimization with advanced multiobjective evolutionary algorithms. *Applied Soft Computing*, *11*(1), 1416–1426. doi:10.1016/j.asoc.2010.04.013

Kruchten, P. (2004). *The rational unified process: An introduction* (3rd ed.). Boston: Addison-Wesley.

Li, C., Li, H., & Li, M. (2001). A software factory model based on ISO 9000 and CMM for Chinese small organizations. In *Proceeding of the Second Asia-Pacific Conference on Quality Software (APAQS'01)*, Hong Kong, China. Academic Press.

López, C., Kalichanin, I., Meda, M. E., & Chavoya, A. (2010) Software development productivity prediction of small programs using fuzzy logic. In *Proceedings of the Seventh International Conference on Information Technology*, Las Vegas, Nevada, April 12-14. Academic Press.

Machek, O., Hnilica, J., & Hejda, J. (2012). Estimating productivity of software development using the total factor productivity approach. *International Journal of Engineering Business Management*, *4*, 4–34.

Maxwell, K. D. (2001). Collecting data for comparability: Benchmarking software development productivity. *IEEE Software*, *18*(5), 22–25. doi:10.1109/52.951490

Montgomery, P. Jr. (1981). A model of the software development process. *Journal of Systems and Software*, *2*(3), 237–255. doi:10.1016/0164-1212(81)90022-4

Moreira, C. I., Carneiro, C., Pires, C. S., & Bessa, A. (2010). A practical application of performance models to predict the productivity of projects. In T. Sobh (Ed.), Innovations and Advances In Computer Sciences And Engineering (pp. 273-277). Springer Science & Business Media.

Nomura, L., Spinola, M., Hikage, O., & Tonini, A. C. (2006). FS-MDP: Um Modelo de Definição de Processos de Fábrica de Software. In *XXVI Encontro Nacional de Engenharia de Producão*, Fortaleza, Brazil, October 9-11. Academic Press.

Norden, P. (1977). *Project life cycle modeling: background and application of the life cycle curves*. U.S. Army Computer Systems Command.

Norden, P. V. (1958). Curve fitting for a model of applied research and development scheduling. *IBM Journal of Research and Development*, *2*(3), 232–248. doi:10.1147/rd.23.0232

Nwelih, E., & Amadin, I. F. (2008). Modeling software reuse in traditional productivity model. *Asian Journal of Information Technology*, *7*(8), 484–488.

Pai, D. R., Subramanian, G. H., & Pendharkar, P. C. (2015). Benchmarking software development productivity of CMMI level 5 projects. *Information Technology Management*, *16*(3), 235–251. doi:10.100710799-015-0234-4

Pendharkar, P. C., & Rodger, J. A. (2007). An empirical study of the impact of team size on software development effort. *Information Technology Management*, *8*(4), 253–262. doi:10.100710799-006-0005-3

Pessoa, M. S., Fabri, J. A., L'erário, A., Spinola, M., & Begosso, A. (2004). Desenvolvimento e Replicação de uma Fábrica de uma Software. In *Proceedings of the IV Jornadas Iberoamericanas de Ingeniería del Software e Ingeniería del Conocimiento*, Madrid, España. Academic Press.

Pillai, K., & Sukumaran Nair, V. S. (1997). A model for software development effort and cost estimation. *IEEE Transactions on Software Engineering, 23*(8), 485–497. doi:10.1109/32.624305

Premraj, R., Shepperd, M., Kitchenham, B., & Forselius, P. (2005). An empirical analysis of software productivity over time. *Presented at 11th IEEE International Software. Metrics Symposium (Metrics05),* Como, Italy, September 19-22. Academic Press. 10.1109/METRICS.2005.8

Ramanathan, R. (2002). *Introductory Econometrics with Applications, 5a edn.* South-Western.

Rockwell, R., & Gera, M. H. (1993). The Eureka Software Factory CoRe: A conceptual reference model for software factories. In *Proceedings of the Software Engineering Environments Conference,* UK, United Kingdom, July 7-9. Academic Press. 10.1109/SEE.1993.388419

Rodger, J. A., Pankaj, P., & Nahouraii, A. (2011). Knowledge management of software productivity and development time. *Journal of Software Engineering and Applications, 4*(11), 609–618. doi:10.4236/jsea.2011.411072

Rodríguez, D., Sicilia, M. A., García, E., & Harrison, R. (2011). Empirical findings on team size and productivity in software development. *Journal of Systems and Software, 85*(3), 562–570. doi:10.1016/j.jss.2011.09.009

SBOK. (2016). *A guide to the Scrum body of knowledge.* USA: SCRUMStudy. Retrieved from https://www.scrumstudy.com/

Scacchi, W. (1995). Understanding software productivity. In D. Hurley (Ed.), Software Engineering and Knowledge Engineering: Trends for the next decade (Vol. 4, pp. 37–70). Los Angeles, CA: World Scientific Press. doi:10.1142/9789812798022_0010

Simmons, D. (1991). Communications: A software group productivity dominator. *Software Engineering Journal, 6*(6), 454–462. doi:10.1049ej.1991.0044

Smith, R. K., Hale, J. E., & Parish, A. S. (2001). An empirical study using task assignment patterns to improve the accuracy of software effort estimation. *IEEE Transactions on Software Engineering, 27*(3), 264–271. doi:10.1109/32.910861

Sridhar, V., Paul, R., Nath, D., & Kapur, K. (2007). Analyzing factors that affect performance of global virtual teams. In *Proceedings of the 2nd International Conference on Management of Soft factors affecting performance 203 Globally Distributed Work 2007,* Indian Institute of Management (IIM), Bangalore, India, July 25-27 (pp. 159-69). Academic Press.

Sudhakar, G., Farooq, A., & Patnaik, S. (2011). Soft factors affecting the performance of software development teams. *Team Performance Management, 17*(3/4), 187–205. doi:10.1108/13527591111143718

Swanson, K., McComb, D., Smith, J., & McCubbrey, D. (1991). The application software factory: Applying total quality techniques to systems development. *Management Information Systems Quarterly, 15*(4), 567–579. doi:10.2307/249460

Trendowicz, A. (2007). Factors influencing software development productivity—state of the art and industrial experiences. Kaiserslautern, Germany: Fraunhofer IESE.

Trendowicz, A., & Munch, J. (2009). Factors influencing software development productivity - state of the art and industrial experiences, Advances in Computers, 77, 185-241.

Trujillo, Y. T. (2007). Modelo de factoría de software aplicando inteligencia. *Serie Científica de la Universidad de las Ciencias Informáticas, 1*(1).

Unluturk, M. S., & Kurtel, K. (2015). Quantifying productivity of individual software programmers: Practical approach. *Computer Information, 34*(4), 959–972.

Verner, J., Evanco, W., & Cerpa, N. (2007). State of the practice: An exploratory analysis of schedule estimation and software project success prediction. *Information and Software Technology, 49*(2), 181–193. doi:10.1016/j.infsof.2006.05.001

Wagner, S., & Ruhe, M. (2008). A systematic review of productivity factors in software development. In *Proceedings of 2nd International Workshop on Software Productivity Analysis and Cost Estimation*, State Key Laboratory of Computer Science, Institute of Software. Academic Press.

Wegner, D. M. (1987). Transactive memory: a contemporary analysis of the group mind. In B. Mullen & G.R. Goethals (Eds.), Theories of Group Behavior (pp. 185–208). New York, NY: Springer-Verlag. doi:10.1007/978-1-4612-4634-3_9

Yanosky, M. M. (2005). Modelo funcional de la Factoría de Software de la UCI para la línea Carrefour.

Yilmaz, M., & O'Connor, R. V. (2011). An empirical investigation into social productivity of a software process: An approach by using the structural equation modeling. In *Proceedings of the European Conference on Software Process Improvement 2011* (pp. 155-166). Academic Press. 10.1007/978-3-642-22206-1_14

This research was previously published in the International Journal of Information Technologies and Systems Approach (IJITSA), 13(1); pages 1-26, copyright year 2020 by IGI Publishing (an imprint of IGI Global).

APPENDIX

Table 13. Factors affecting productivity

Factor	Reference
Average number properties given object type	Cao, Ching Gu & Thompson, 2012
Average number properties relationship type	
Average number relationship types	
Number properties given object type	
Number properties relationship type	
Number relationship types	
Object types technique	
Property types technique	
Relationship types per technique	
Documentation	Cheikhi et al., 2012
Staff-Cost	
Function Points	Cheikhi et al., 2012; Pai, Subramanian & Pendharkar, 2015; López, Kalichanin, Meda & Chavoya, 2010
Source Statements	Cheikhi et al., 2012; Unluturk & Kurtel, 2015
Baselines	Çetin & Alabaş-Uslu, 2015
Change Request	
Actual -planned baseline dates	
Duration analysis	
Duration development	
Duration project	
Duration stand by	
Duration test	
Issues	
Launches	
Methodology	
Occurrence stand by	
Project	
Reason stand by	
Risks	
Severity	
Interest Individual Job	Khan, Ahmed & Faisal, 2014
Manager Skills	
Technology	
Working Culture	
Count type	López et al., 2010
Statement	

continues on following page

Table 13. Continued

Factor	Reference
Continuous Integration Utilization	Moreira, Carneiro, Pires & Bessa, 2010
Development Environment	
Experience	Moreira et al., 2010
Requirements Unstableness	
Unit Test Coverage	
Defect Density Systemic Tests	Moreira et al., 2010; Pai et al., 2015; Unluturk & Kurtel, 2015
Defects Technical Revisions	
Data	Machek, Hnilica & Hejda, 2012
Documentation	
Engineering labour	
Intangible capital stock	
Materials and services	
Other capital	
Support labour	
Tangible capital stock	
Testing labour	
Training	
Management labour	Machek et al., 2012; Cheikhi et al., 2012
Functionality	Machek et al., 2012; Nwelih & Amadin, 2008
Length	
Complexity	Machek et al., 2012; Yilmaz & O'Connor, 2011; Khan et al., 2014; Çetin & Alabaş-Uslu, 2015; Nwelih & Amadin, 2008
Reuse	Machek et al., 2012; Yilmaz & O'Connor, 2011; Nwelih & Amadin, 2008
Business Sector	Premraj, Shepperd, Kitchenham & Forselius, 2005
Volatility	Rodger, Pankaj & Nahouraii, 2011
Development Platform	
Programming Language	
Team Size	Rodger et al., 2011; Yilmaz & O'Connor, 2011; Khan et al., 2014; Çetin & Alabaş-Uslu, 2015
Cohesion	Yilmaz & O'Connor, 2011; Khan et al., 2014
Meetings	
Social Relations, Social Life	
Collective Outcomes	Yilmaz & O'Connor, 2011
Communication	
Information Awareness	
Leadership	
Motivation	
Process	
Team Leadership	
Transparency	
Trust	

Source: Castañeda & Mauricio, 2018, P.70

Chapter 94

Disciplined or Agile?
Two Approaches for Handling Requirement Change Management

Danyllo Wagner Albuquerque
Federal University of Campina Grande, Brazil

Everton Tavares Guimarães
Pennsylvania State University, USA

Felipe Barbosa Araújo Ramos
 https://orcid.org/0000-0002-0937-811X
Federal University of Campina Grande, Brazil

Antonio Alexandre Moura Costa
Federal Institute of Paraiba, Brazil

Alexandre Gomes
Federal University of Campina Grande, Brazil

Emanuel Dantas
Federal University of Campina Grande, Brazil

Mirko Perkusich
VIRTUS, Brazil

Hyggo Almeida
Federal University of Campina Grande, Brazil

ABSTRACT

Software requirements changes become necessary due to changes in customer requirements and changes in business rules and operating environments; hence, requirements development, which includes requirements changes, is a part of a software process. Previous studies have shown that failing to manage software requirements changes well is a main contributor to project failure. Given the importance of the subject, there is a plethora of efforts in academia and industry that discuss the management of requirements change in various directions, ways, and means. This chapter provided information about the current state-of-the-art approaches (i.e., Disciplined or Agile) for RCM and the research gaps in existing work. Benefits, risks, and difficulties associated with RCM are also made available to software practitioners who will be in a position of making better decisions on activities related to RCM. Better decisions can lead to better planning, which will increase the chance of project success.

DOI: 10.4018/978-1-6684-3702-5.ch094

INTRODUCTION

The acceptance of changes is low in disciplined software development due to detailed planning, extensive design, and documentation (Awad, 2005). In contrast, as stated in the Agile Manifesto, agile software development continually "welcomes changing requirements, even late in development" due to its characteristic of incrementally elaborating the product as a means to assure customer satisfaction (Stålhane et al., 2014)(Cao & Ramesh, 2008). Therefore, it promotes constant feedback and communication between stakeholders.

In agile software development, changes in requirement are frequent, occurring due to several causes such as organizational, market demand, customer need, or increase in the knowledge of the software engineers. As a result, it can be a challenge to identify, analyze and evaluate the consequences and impacts of these changes (Eberlein & Leite, 2002). Therefore, Requirements Change Management (RCM) is a challenging task, and neglecting it might lead a project failure (Cohn, 2004).

More recently, there is an increasing number of reported studies on research topics such as identifying change causes (Bano et al., 2012), change taxonomies (Saher et al., 2017)(McGee & Greer, 2012) and requirements change process models (Bano et al., 2012). From a researcher's perspective, the diversity of requirements change management makes it hard to develop general theories. Empirical research in RCM thereby becomes a crucial and challenging task (Wagner et al., 2019). Empirical studies of all kinds, ranging from classical action research through observational studies to broad exploratory surveys, are necessary to understand the practical needs and improvement goals in RCM to guide problem-driven research and to empirically validate new research proposals (Wagner et al., 2019).

To the extent of our knowledge, there is no precise definition of an RCM in agile context or even a catalog of agile practices to support the various steps that comprise the ARCM process. In order to address this research gap, the present chapter book focuses on (i) defining a process to agile requirement change management and (ii) identifying the agile practices used to support the steps that comprise the ARCM process.

The authors conducted an exploratory study where 21 research papers have been analyzed. As result, we identified and classified 11 distinct agile practices that provide support for RCM in the context of agile development. For doing so, the present chapter book study followed the guidelines described by (Kitchenham & Charters, 2007)(Petersen et al.., 2015). For the sake of simplicity, to identify the primary studies, we performed a hybrid search strategy procedure (Mourão et al., 2017). Although agile practices seem to have a very efficient way of managing change, we were able to identify practical challenges in some of the practices described in this study. This study provided information related to many aspects of ARCM, giving a holistic view to handle this process. Additionally, we described the key features, as well as some research gaps in existing work for ARCM. Benefits, risks, and difficulties associated with ARCM are also made available to software researchers and practitioners making better decisions on processes and practices to support ARCM.

The remainder of this chapter is structured as follows. Section 2 presents the main related studies. Section 3 presents the main causes of requirement changes pointed out in the literature. Section 4 describes in details the disciplined requirement change management. Section 5 point out the definition of agile requirement change whereas Section 6 describes the proposed agile requirement change management process. Section 7 outlines the main research gaps in RCM. Finally, Section 8 presents the final remarks and future work.

RELATED WORK

More recently, there is an increasing number of reported work on research topics such as identifying change causes (Bano et al., 2012), change taxonomies (Saher et al., 2017)(McGee & Greer, 2012) and requirement change process models (Bano et al., 2012). In what follows, the authors will describe some these works.

Identifying Causes of Requirement Change: The study of Bano *et al.*. (2012) identifies the causes of requirement change and groups these causes into two main categories: (i) essential and (ii) accidental. Similarly, the study of McGee *et al.*. (2012) identifies various causes of requirement change and uses taxonomy to group these causes for better understanding and future identification. In regards to identifying change causes, we mention the study of Saher *et al.*. (2017) identifies the requirement change and further categorizes the requirement change element based on reason and origin of change, for a better understanding of change request. Finally, the study of Spichkova and Schimidt (2019) investigated how to manage the diversity of cultural and technical aspects to optimize the process of requirements specification and the corresponding change management.

Requirement Change Process Models: The study of Ramzan *et al.*. (2006) brings together various requirement management models, identifying their key features and challenges. Similarly, the study of Inayat *et al.*. (2015) mapped the evidence about requirements engineering practices adopted and challenges faced by agile teams to understand how traditional requirements engineering issues are resolved using agile requirements engineering. Finally, the study of Melegati *et al.* (2019) showed how requirements engineering practices are performed in the context of startups context. They constructed a model to show that software startups do not follow a single set of practices. Although requirements engineering activities in software startups are similar to those in agile context, some steps vary as a consequence of the lack of an accessible customer.

Requirements Change Management: First, Schon *et al.* (2017) concluded a study aims to capture the current state of art of the literature related to Agile RE with focus on stakeholder and user involvement. In particular, the authors investigated what existing approaches involve stakeholder in the process, which methodologies are commonly used to present the user perspective and how requirements management is been carried out. Second, Jayatilleke and Lai (2018) presented a systematic review of research in Requirements Change Management (RCM) as reported in the literature. They used a systematic review method aims to answer four key research questions related to causes of requirements changes, as well as process and techniques providing support to requirements change management. They have also investigated how organizations make decisions regarding requirements changes. These questions are aimed at studying the various directions in the field of requirements change management and at providing suggestions for future research work. Finally, Curcio *et al.* (2018) conducted a systematic mapping study resulting 2171 papers. These papers were initially identified and further narrowed to 104 by applying exclusion criteria and analysis. The authors identified 15 areas of research of which 13 are document in the SWEBOK). Five of such areas points to the need of future researches, among them are requirement elicitation, change management, measuring requirements, software requirements tools and comparative studies between traditional and agile requirements.

In contrast to the studies above, the present chapter book investigates the process as well as the agile practices to support ARCM. It explores in-depth the techniques used in ARCM and provides a critical analysis of the agile practices extracted by identifying the key features, significant challenges, and research gaps. In summary, this chapter book provides information related to many aspects of ARCM in more detail, giving a holistic view for researchers and practitioners.

WHAT ARE THE CAUSES OF REQUIREMENTS CHANGE?

Requirements can change during a project life cycle. Whilst this fact is a constant, delayed discovery of such changes poses a risk to the cost, schedule and quality of the software (McGee & Greer, 2012) and such volatility constitutes one of the top ten risks to successful project development McGee and Greer (McGee & Greer, 2012). Pfleeger (2008) recommends that a method needs to be developed to understand and anticipate some of the inevitable changes during the development process in order to reduce these risks.

The identification of factors that cause requirements uncertainty is a necessity. The recognition of such factors will support requirements change risk visibility and also facilitate better recording of change data. Change cause factors were collected from Jayatilleke and Lai (2017) exploratory study. Most literature extracted mentioned/indicated the reasons for requirement changes. Of the literature extracted, there were three studies that formally classify the causes of RCs.

Weiss and Basili (1985) divide changes into two categories: *error correction and modifications*. This classification appears to be simplistic and categorizing all the identified change causes may not create an in-depth understanding.

Bano et al.. (2012) classifies change causes also under two categories; *essential and accidental*. They further classify the change causes based on their origin: within the project, from the client organization and from the business environment.

McGee and Greer (2012) use five areas/domains to classify change causes. The five change areas are: external market, customer organization, project vision, requirement specification and solution.

For this chapter book, we use the classification presented by McGee and Greer (2012) as it has a more comprehensive categorization. Within the five change areas, they distinguish between two causes of change: trigger and uncertainty. The difference between these two categories is that an event can cause a change without pre- or post-uncertainty. However, uncertainty cannot cause a change to occur without an event that is triggered to manage the risk of the uncertainty. The factors that were identified as causes of requirements change were sorted into five areas as follows:

External Market: In this category, the changes to the requirements are triggered by the events and uncertainties that occur in the external market which also include stakeholders. These stakeholders include parties such as customers, government bodies and competitors. Therefore, events such as changes in government policy regulations (Van Lamsweerde, 2009), fluctuations in market demands and response to competitors can be considered (Wiegers & Beatty, 2013). Also, uncertainties such as the stability of the market and the changing needs of the customers (Daneva et al., 2013) are also part of this category.

Customer Organization: In this category, changes to the requirements are triggered by the events and the uncertainties that arise from a single customer and their organizational changes. Although the changes occur within the customer's organization, such changes have a tendency to impact the needs of the customer and as a result, impact the design and requirements of the software project. Therefore, events such as strategic changes within the organization (Bano et al., 2012), restructuring of the organization, changes in organizational hierarchy and changes in software/hardware in the organization should be considered (Wiegers & Beatty, 2013). The stability of the customer's business environment can create uncertainties that may lead to changes and these are also part of this category.

Project Vision: In this category, the changes to the requirements are triggered by changes in the vision of the project. These changes are in response to a better understanding of the problem space from a customer point-of-view and the emergence of new opportunities and challenges. Events such as improvements to business processes (Sommerville, 2011), changes to business cases due to return on investment (Bano et al., 2012), overrun in cost/schedule of the project (Van Lamsweerde, 2009), identification of new opportunities (Saher et al., 2017) and more participation from the stakeholder (Stålhane et al., 2014) should be considered (Wiegers & Beatty, 2013). Uncertainties, such as the involvement of all stakeholders, novelty of application, clarity in product vision, improved knowledge development team in the business area, identification of all stakeholders, experience and skill of analyst, size of the project can also cause changes under this category (Christel & Kang, 1992).

Requirement Specification: In this category, changes in the requirements are triggered by events and uncertainties related to requirements specification. These trigger events are based on a developer's point-of-view and their improved understanding of the problem space and resolution of ambiguities related to requirements. Events such as increased understanding of the customer (Wiegers & Beatty, 2013), resolution of misunderstandings and miscommunication (Curtis et al., 1988) and resolution of incorrect identification of requirements (Nurmuliani et al., 2004) can be considered as change triggers. Uncertainties, such as the quality of communication within the development team (Bano et al., 2012), insufficient sample of user representatives (Bano et al., 2012), low staff morale, quality of communication between analyst/customer (Christel & Kang, 1992), logical complexity of problem (Boehm, 2000, techniques used for analysis (Van Lamsweerde, 2009), development teams' knowledge of the business area (Boehm, 2000), involved customers' experience of IT, quality of requirement specification (Bano et al., 2012), and the stability of the development team (Bano et al., 2012) can contribute towards change under this category.

Solution: In this category, changes in the requirements are triggered by events and uncertainties related to the solution of the customer's requirements and the techniques used to resolve this. Events such as increased understanding of the technical solution (Bano et al., 2012), introduction of new tools/technology (Curtis et al., 1988) and design improvement (Van Lamsweerde, 2009) should be are considered as change triggers. Technical uncertainty and complexity can also be considered under this category as a cause of change (Bano et al., 2012).

Table 1. Comparison between classifications.

Bano et al.'s Classification	Mc Gee and Greer's Classification		
Essential	External Market	Customer Organization	
Accidental	Porject Vision	Requirement Specification	Solution

The five change areas listed above can be mapped to the classification proposed by Bano et al.. (2012). According to this study, change causes under the essential category are those that are inherent in nature and cannot be controlled i.e. "fluctuating market demand" cannot be controlled or avoided by the development team or the organization. In comparison, accidental causes can be controlled and avoided i.e. "overrun in cost/schedule of the project" can be avoided or at least controlled by putting better techniques and mechanisms in place. Being able to categorize change causes under these two categories has added benefits in managing RCs. With essential causes, the focus should be to deal with their impact and therefore use techniques that will reduce time and effort for their management. With the accidental causes, the focus should be to use techniques that avoid such occurrences. Table 1 show how these five categories in McGee and Greer's classification (2012) can be mapped to Bano et al..'s classification (Bano et al., 2012) of essential and accidental categories.

DISICIPLINED REQUIREMENT CHANGE MANAGEMENT

Change is an intrinsic characteristic of the software engineering discipline compared to other engineering disciplines. In real-world scenarios, it is difficult to specify all the requirements for software as the need and the circumstance of the scenario is subject to change. According to described in previous section, factors such as customer needs, market change among others contribute profoundly to the changing nature of requirements. The need for increasingly complex software is in high demand as organizations struggle to survive in a highly competitive market. Therefore, managing change in software development is not just important but crucial for the success of the final product.

Nurmuliani (2004) defines requirements volatility as "the tendency of requirements to change over time in response to the evolving needs of customers, stakeholders, the organization and the work environment". Requirements, in principle, are the needs and wants of the users and stakeholders of the system captured by an analyst through an elicitation process. These requirements change throughout the system development and maintenance process, which includes the whole lifecycle of a system: requirement formation, analysis, design, evaluation and learning (Curtis et al., 1988). Therefore, requirements change management (RCM) can be defined as the management of such changing requirements during the requirements engineering process, system development and the maintenance process (Sommerville, 2011). This definition of RCM is an adaptation of the definition provided by Sommerville (2011) who states RCM is a process of "managing changing requirements during the requirements engineering process and system development".

According to Jayatilleke and Lai (2017), there are three key areas of a practical approach to managing change (i.e. change identification, change analysis and change cost estimation). It is important to understand how these areas can be practically implemented and what best practices are available in an organizational setting. As shown in Fig. 1, none of these areas are standalone. They need to communicate with each other in terms of updates and verifications. The reason for this is that each area has the ability to feed information to another area. For example, although change analysis can be undertaken once the change has been identified, the cost estimation may provide additional information for the analysis step that may not have been identified previously. A good RCM process does not have steps that are stand alone, rather they are interconnected with information following to and fro from the steps.

Change Identification: This step is important for the rest of the management process as the steps to follow will be based on the correct identification of the problem space as well as the change requirement. According to Fig. 1, the change management process starts with change identification. Within this identification, there are two major activities, i.e. change elicitation and change representation. In order to ensure the correct elicitation of changes, the change requirements need to be identified. The correct elicitation should then lead to identifying further details of the change and if possible, where in the system the change has to be made. This signifies the representation part of the identification step. In most situations, the personnel involved in this step will need to have continuous communication with the stakeholders in order to verify that identification is done correctly, as illustrated in Fig. 1. Through the literature, we identified two methods of change identification: taxonomies and classification. The following sections describe these two methods and several other methods that do not fall under these categories.

Figure 1. Change management process based on Jayatilleke and Lai (2017).

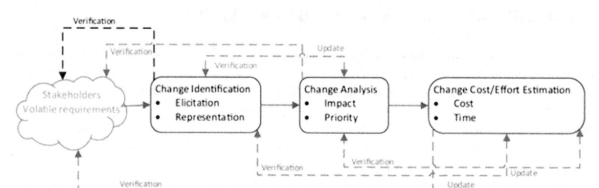

Change Analysis: Once a change has been identified, it needs to be further analyzed to understand its impact on the software system so that informed decisions can be made. One of the key issues is that seemingly small changes can ripple throughout the system and cause substantial impact elsewhere (Ibrahim et al., 2005). As stated in the literature, the reason for such a significant impact is that the requirements of a system have very complex relationships. Therefore, the way to realize this is to undertake change impact analysis, which according to Bohner (1998) is defined as "the activity of identifying the potential consequences, including side effects and ripple effects, of a change, or estimating what needs to be modified to accomplish a change before it has been made". Change impact analysis provides visibility into the potential effects of the proposed changes before the actual changes are implemented (Ibrahim et al., 2005). The ability to identify the change impact or potential effect will help decision makers to determine the appropriate actions to take with respect to change decisions, schedule plans, cost and resource estimates.

Software cost/effort estimation is referred to as the process of predicting the effort required to develop a software system. It is noteworthy that although effort and cost are closely related, they are not a simple transformation of each other (Leung & Fan, 2002). Effort is often measured in person-months of the development team whilst cost (dollars) can be estimated by calculating payment per unit time for the required staff and then multiplying this by the estimated effort (Leung & Fan, 2002). Cost estimation is usually carried out at the beginning of a project but as we have demonstrated, changes to the system can occur at any stage of the project. Therefore, there is a need to estimate the additional cost for implementation of the change. There are some basic factors to be considered when estimating, regardless as to whether it is for the entire project or just for a change. The first step in cost/effort calculation is the calculation of the size of the software, which is considered to be the most important factor affecting estimation (Leung & Fan, 2002). Therefore, it is essential to understand the popular software sizing methods used and their suitability for estimating the cost/effort of implementing requirements changes.

DEFINING AGILE REQUIREMENT CHANGE MANAGEMENT

Aims to properly defining the notion of Agile Requirement Change Management (ARCM), the authors conducted an exploratory study. This research method allows categorizing relevant solutions and concepts in a specific field, as well as visualizing the coverage and maturity of an entire research field. For doing so, the authors followed the guidelines proposed by Kitchenham and Charters (2007) and specific guidelines proposed by Petersen et al.. (2015).

The authors seek identify the practices that have been proposed in the scientific literature to handle Agile Requirements Change Management (ARCM). To achieve this goal, the following steps were derived from the objective to characterize the identified agile practices further.

What are the key steps that make up the requirements change management process in the agile context? This step aims at getting a holistic view of the ARCM and understanding how to handle this process.

What are the agile practices that support the various steps of the ARCM process? This step aims to identify the specific agile practices that address the steps of ARCM process. While it is not our intention to analyze particular requirements engineering practices, this categorization helps in understanding the purpose of the agile practices.

In fewer words, whereas the first one shall structure the process and steps of the ARCM, the last one shall provide a catalog of agile practices to support ARCM. From the conclusion of these research steps, the authors can provide a foundation to discuss the current state of evidence and implications for future research in ARCM.

Search Strategy - The exploratory study employed a hybrid search strategy (Mourão et al., 2017) that involves conducting a string-based search on the Scopus digital library. Next, the authors complemented the set of papers with backward and forward snowballing using Google Scholar. This strategy allows us to identify studies indexed in other digital libraries. As shown in (Mourão et al., 2017), the employed strategy generally tends to provide similar results as when conducting searches on several digital libraries. The hybrid search strategy allows a simplified string supporting reproducibility and replicability.

Study Selection - The primary inclusion criterion was on papers that describe how to handle Requirements Change Management in the context of agile development. When several papers reported the same agile practice (e.g., in the case of journal extensions), only the most recent one was included. When multiple studies were reported in the same paper, each relevant study was considered separately. The exclusion criteria applied for filtering the papers are: (i) Papers that do not have information about agile practices or how they handle the ARCM process, (ii) Papers not written in English, (iii) Grey literature, including white papers, theses, and papers that were not peer-reviewed and (iv) Papers only available in the form of abstracts/posters and presentations.

Fig. 2 presents the search procedure steps and results. The first step (Search) consisted of searching for papers using the search string in the digital library selected for this study. For this purpose, we used the string "Requirement change management AND agile". This search returned 359. In the second step

(Filter 1), the first filtering took place by applying the exclusion criteria. As a result, we reduced the set of candidate papers to 11. All exclusions were peer-reviewed and agreed by an independent researcher. In the third step (Snowballing), we applied backward and forward snowballing iteratively following the snowballing guidelines in (Wohlinl, 2014). For the sake of work simplification, only one backward snowballing and forward snowballing iterations were applied. The backward snowballing involved analyzing 124 papers (including duplicates) and allowed included six papers. The forward snowballing iterations involved analyzing 89 papers (including duplicates) and allowed identifying included four papers. The StArt tool (Fabri et al.., 2016) aided the execution of this study. It is worthy to mention the snowballing process was peer-reviewed.

Figure 2. Search Strategy conducted to identify the primary papers.

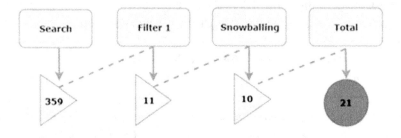

PROPOSED AGILE REQUIREMENT CHANGE MANAGEMENT

The agile manifesto suggests to value working software over comprehensive documentation as well as individuals and interactions over processes and tools. To extend of our knowledge, the documentations and formalization of Agile Requirement Change Management remains unclear (Kleebaum et al., 2019). It occurs due to the requirement documentation in agile context is non-intrusive in comparison to disciplined context. The challenges are that the documented requirement might be hard to access and exploit for developers since it can be distributed and might be not fully formalized. Further, decisions related to requirement changes can rapidly be changed which might lead to inconsistent and outdated requirement documentation (Kleebaum et al., 2019). Therefore, Agile Requirements Change Management (ARCM) is a challenging task, and neglecting it might lead a project failure

In what follows, this section outlines the results of the exploratory study regarding the Agile Requirement Change Management (ARCM). First, the authors provided an overview of the ARCM process in Section 6.1. Similarly, the authors addressing pointed out the practices which provide support to some step of the ARCM process in Sections 6.2, 6.3, and 6.4.

THE PROCESS OF ARCM

Examining the processes introduced in Section 3, the authors have identified three key steps of a practical approach for managing requirements change. Fig. 3 illustrates these steps (i.e., change identification, change analysis, and cost/effort estimation) which will be described as follows.

Figure 3. ARCM process

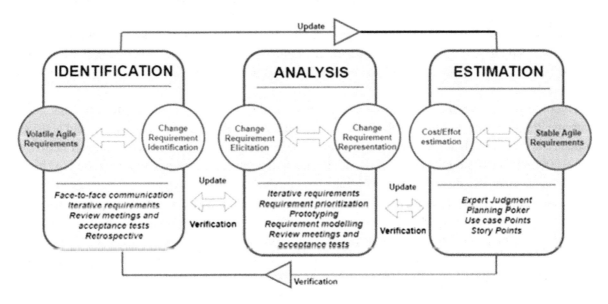

Change Identification: As depicted in Fig. 3, the ARCM process starts with the "*Change identification*" step. Within this step, there are two major activities: change elicitation and change representation. The changing must be identified to ensure its correct elicitation, leading to the identification of more details about the change and its impact on the system. In most situations, the personnel involved in this step needs to have continuous communication with the stakeholders aims to verify that identification is made correctly, as illustrated in Fig. 3.

Change Analysis: Once a change has been identified, it needs to be further analyzed to understand its impact on the software system. One of the critical issues is that seemingly small changes can ripple throughout the system and cause a substantial impact elsewhere (Ibrahim et al., 2005). As stated in the literature, the reason for such a significant impact relies on the complex relationships between system requirements (Dahlstedt & Persson, 2005). This step provides visibility into the potential effects of the proposed changes before the actual changes are implemented (Ibrahim et al., 2005). The ability to identify the change impact or potential effect assists the decision-making process, determining the appropriate actions to take concerning schedule plans, change decisions, cost, and resource estimates.

Cost/effort Estimation: The "Software cost/effort estimation" step includes the set of activities aiming at predicting the cost/effort required to implement the change (Leung & Fan, 2002). Effort is often estimated in person-months of the development team whereas cost can be measured by calculating payment per unit time for the required staff and then multiplying this by the estimated effort (Leung & Fan, 2002). Cost/effort estimation is usually carried out at the beginning of a software project, but in the context of agile projects, it is common, and expected, that they occur at any stage of the project, including late stages. Therefore, due to the constraints of the project, such as time, cost, and scope, there is a need to estimate the additional cost/effort for the implementation of the change.

It is important to understand how these steps can be practically implemented and what practices are available to address them. In the agile development context, none of these steps are standalone, given that each one can feed another with information (e.g. update and verification). For example, although analysis step (step 2) can be undertaken once the change has been identified (step 1), the cost/estimation step may provide additional information for the analysis that may not have been identified previously. In summary, although the process presents an order to carry out the steps, this does not imply that they must be carried out in this order (i.e. dentification -> analysis -> Estimation). Therefore, the Agile Requirement Change Management (ARCM) process has interconnected steps with information following to and from the steps.

Over the years, several agile software development models have been used, the most popular being Extreme Programming, Scrum, and RUP (Bilgaiyan et al., 2016). Regardless of the agile model of development used, the underlying practices have an inbuilt capacity to manage requirement change (Eberlein & Leite, 2002). Since development is done in small and continuous releases, agile practices tend to absorb requirements changes into these small iterations. The main reported changes in requirements are to add or to drop features due to the frequent face-to-face communication between the development team and the client (Cao & Ramesh, 2008). The plainness gained by clients helps development teams to refine their requirements, which results in less rework and fewer changes in subsequent iterations (Inayat et al., 2015). Given this scenario in which agile practices are prone to change requirements, we identified 11 distinct ones that deal with the 3 steps of ARCM process as follows.

PRACTICES FOR CHANGE IDENTIFICATION IN ARCM

In contrast to traditional requirement engineering methods, agile development welcomes changes in various stages (Inayat et al., 2015). As discussed, changes can be identified in several different phases of the development process. In what follows, the authors present the different characteristics of agile development that contribute to the identification of requirements changes, the challenges faced, and solutions, as suggested by the scientific literature.

Face-to-Face Communication: In agile development, this is a frequent activity between the client and the development team (Cao & Ramesh, 2008)(Wagner et al., 2017). The frequency of this activity helps clients to steer the project in their direction as the understanding of needs tends to develop and evolve the requirements (Inayat et al., 2015)(Jun et al., 2010). The success rate of the change identification at this stage is dependent on customer availability. However, this dependency is often unrealistic and a challenge, as confirmed by studies (Ramesh et al., 2010). The major challenge from this practice is that the frequency of the communication depends on the availability and willingness of the team members. Customers may not be familiar with this agile technique, or available to apply it (Daneva et al., 2013).

Iterative Requirements: In contrast to traditional software development, in agile development, the requirements are identified throughout the entire project lifecycle through the feedback of stakeholders (Ramesh et al., 2010). The feedback loops make this an iterative process, allowing the requirements to evolve with less volatility (Cao & Ramesh, 2008). This practice can create budget and schedule overruns as initial estimations might be affected by the requirement changes (Ramesh et al., 2010). Inayat et al.. (2015) suggest frequent communication to identify as many requirements as possible at early iterations to keep these overruns to a minimum.

Prototyping: Prototype is a model of the software application that supports the evaluation of design alternatives and communication. This is a simple technique to review the specification of the requirements with clients to obtain timely feedback before moving to subsequent iterations (De Lucia & Qusef, 2010). This assists in the ARCM process by identifying (i) what new additions are required and (ii) what current requirements are to be changed or removed. Since this is a review phase of the development, the client may have a large number of changes to be included based on the prototype; consequently, schedule overruns can be created (Inayat et al., 2015). Some actions, like frequent communication, high customer involvement, and interaction in stages before prototyping, can mitigate the problem, as mentioned earlier (Inayat et al., 2015).

Review Meetings and Acceptance Tests: During review meetings, which occur at the end of every iteration on Scrum, the stakeholders inspect the delivered product increment to ensure that it satisfies their expectations. During this meeting, the stakeholders might also adapt the requirements to address their updated needs, causing an influx of changes (Carlson & Matuzic, 2010), as with prototyping. Also, if the product backlog is not maintained in detail, finding information related to changes made during the iterations is challenging. Daneva et al.. (2013) suggest maintaining a detailed artifact called delivery stories aims to cope with the previously mentioned challenge. This artifact provide additional information to user stories, helping developers to make the right implementation choices in the coding stage of a sprint. On the other hand, acceptance tests are similar to a unit test, resulting in a pass or a fail for a user story (Ramesh et al., 2010)

Retrospective: In the context of agile development, this practice comprises meetings that are held after the completion of an iteration (Carlson & Matuzic, 2012). These meetings inspects and adapt the team process. In terms of ARCM, this meeting can trigger changes such as refactoring in the product (Carlson & Matuzic, 2012) (Ramesh et al., 2010). If there are many changes identified Agile Requirements Change Management: A Systematic Mapping Study in the completed user story at this stage, there might be a considerable amount of rework to be done, causing budget and schedule overruns (Inayat et al., 2015). Increase customer involvement and interaction in the stages before the completion of user stories is essential to mitigate previously mentioned challenges (Inayat et al., 2015).

PRACTICES FOR CHANGE ANALYSIS IN ARCM

In agile development, requirement engineering activities are less explicit compared to traditional software development. Partially, this is due to lack of documentation that could assist in the traceability of activities and serve as a milestone for marking its beginning and end (Abdullah et al., 2011). As minimal documentation is a characteristic, there are only two main documents: user stories (US) and product backlog (Cohn, 2012). This characteristic becomes a problem when there is a communication lapse or project representatives are unavailable (Daneva et al., 2013). It is also problematic when requirements must be communicated to stakeholders in distributed geographical locations (Ramesh et al., 2010).

Similar to change identification, the change analysis in agile development is not restricted to a particular phase of the development, being addressed by a mixture of techniques used interactively. Following, we point out agile practices identified in this exploratory study that can be applied to the "Change analysis" step.

Iterative Requirements: As previously depicted, not all the requirements related to a user story are properly detailed (or identified) at the beginning of a project. Requirements are built on iterations which allow stakeholders to gain a better understanding of what is required and therefore analyze and understand the need for changes (Jun et al., 2010).

Requirement Prioritization: This is a part of each iteration in the context of agile development (Inayat et al., 2015). In each iteration, requirements are prioritized by customers who focus on some factors such as risk or business value, technical dependency and effort (Ramesh et al., 2010). Iterative requirement prioritization helps in ARCM by comparing the need for the change with the current requirements and then placing it an appropriate priority location for implementation (Daneva et al., 2013). In each iteration, the identified requirements are prioritized. This means that any changes that occur during the iterations are compared to current requirements and are assigned a place in the hierarchy of implementation. The iterative nature of this activity ensures that the priority of requirements remains current.

Prototyping: As previously mentioned, this is a simple way to review the specification of the requirements with clients (De Lucia & Qusef, 2010). This technique allows the agile team to review the requirement specifications with clients to obtain feedback. However, prototyping problems may occur if there a high influx in client requirements at a particular iteration. It highlights issues with the changes identified so far and prompts the development team to find better solutions (Cao & Ramesh, 2008).

Requirement Modeling: This practice identifies the requirements that a software application must meet to solve the business problem. The goal-sketching is a technique used in requirement modeling in the agile development context. This technique provides goal graphs that are easy to understand and evolve (Boness & Harrison, 2007). The outcome is an easy-to-read goal graph that allows stakeholders to refine the goals, making them well defined. Changes that are introduced in the iterations can be mapped to goals, and this can help with decision making in the implementation of changes (Ernst et al., 2014).

Review Meetings and Acceptance Tests: As previously depicted, the developed requirements and product backlogs are reviewed to identify if user stories have been completed. In terms of change analysis, this evaluates if changes have been implemented correctly and satisfy the end goal.

PRACTICES FOR COST/EFFORT ESTIMATION IN ARCM

There are many popular practices for estimating cost/effort in agile development. Regardless of the used practice, none of them discussed in this section can be used off-the-shelf. One of the key findings in this section is to identify the appropriateness of these practices for estimating the cost/effort of implementing ARCM. Following, we describe several popular Cost/Effort estimation practices associated with agile development:

Expert Judgment: The developers look to past of the iterations or projects and use their own experiences to produce estimates for the user stories (Abrahamsson et al., 2011). The primary challenge associated with this practice is the dependence on experts, in which human error is a significant risk, and there can be bias. This practice can be suitable since it is fast and can be quickly adapt to various circumstances. However, the limitation carries a lot of risk (Ceschi et al., 2005).

Planning Poker: This practice is a variation of the Wideband Delphi, in which all the team members of the agile team use cards to estimate effort and reveal their estimates simultaneously (Haugen, 2006). The highest and lowest estimates need to be justified by their estimator. The group continues the discussion until they agree with the estimation value. The primary challenge from this practice in the case the estimation process is unstructured, factors such as group pressure, company politics, anchoring, and dominant personalities, may reduce estimation performance. This practice has similar suitability as expert judgment but is still dependent on the skill and experience of the team members (Mahnič & Hovelja, 2012).

Use Case Points (UCP): Once the use cases are identified from the user stories, UCPs are calculated based on (i) the number and complexity of use cases, (ii) actors of the system, (iii) non-functional requirements and (iv) characteristics of the development environment (Khatri et al., 2016). The UCP can then be used to calculate the estimated effort for a particular project. The primary challenge from this practice is that UCP can be used only when the design is done using RUP or UML. Finally, this technique can be suitable for changes during the early stages of the development process. Changes in the latter phases require more effort due to size of the backlog. Therefore, this practice may not be suitable (Nunes et al., 2010) in this particular case.

Story Points: Story point is a measure for expressing the overall size of a user story. The value of the story point is dependent on (i) development complexity, (ii) the effort involved, (iii) the inherent risk, among other factors (Cohn, 2004). The major challenge from this practice is story points create lots of vagueness to the agile development. For every team, depending on what baseline they chose, story size could mean different things. Story points do not relate to hours. Accordingly, this practice may only be suitable for teams that are collocated, based on the challenges of the practice. Also, it may not be suitable for effort calculation in hours as it will take additional calculations to convert story points to hours (Panda et al., 2015).

RESEARCH GAPS IN RCM

Research Gaps in Change Identification: Accurate change identification not only leads to a better understanding of the required change but also the impact it can cause on the entire system and project. The techniques discussed in change identification can be divided into two categories: change taxonomies and change classification as discussed in previous section. Given the existence of these methods, their still remains several major gaps that need to be addressed:

1. The parties involved in the elicitation and identification process of changes are from a variety of backgrounds and experience levels. Common knowledge for one group may be completely foreign for another. This is especially true in the case of communication between the analyst and the stakeholder(s).
2. The language and terminology used to communicate the changes to and from the stakeholder to the analyst and then to software practitioners (designers, developers, testers, etc.) may be either too formal or informal to meet the needs of each party involved.
3. There will be a large amount of information gathered that is part of one single change. Not having a common structure to categorize this information may lead to misinterpretation of the need for the change and the change itself.
4. Information gathered at one level of the organization could be biased based on the parties involved if one form of structure is not used to capture the changes at all levels.
5. The methods already in existence provide minimal guidance in terms of applying them to identify changes.

Research gaps in Change Analysis:As seen in the previous section on change analysis, it is clear that traceability is one of the most popular techniques to analyses the impact of changes on a system, either in existence or in the design phase. Several other non-conventional methods were also identified that contribute to change analysis. Through these methods and the existing knowledge on the volatility of requirements, several gaps in the research are identified:

1.   Although traceability is a common method of identifying impact, it can be costly and time consuming, and in most cases, the benefits (of traceability) are realized immediately. This gives rise to a need for another method that addresses these limitations.
2.   In most existing methods of change impact analysis, the priority of changes is not established. Understanding priority benefits the decision-making process by allowing software practitioners to establish which change to implement first and also how critical the change is to the existing system and hence, resources can be allocated accordingly.
3.   The existing literature is unclear on ways to identify the difficulty of implementing a change in an early phase of the change request process. Understanding the difficulty associated with a change leads to better decision making in two ways: firstly, if the difficulty of implementing the change is too high and the delivery of the product is time sensitive, the change could be held back for a consecutive version; secondly, the difficulty can be used as a gauge of the effort required to implement the change.

Research Gaps in Change Cost Estimation: The cost estimation methods discussed in the previous section were not explicit for the estimation of implementing changes. In practice, these methods can still be applied for this purpose yet there is still much room for improvement. Based on the information discussed earlier and in the other related literature, several gaps in the research were identified:

1.   No significant work in the existing literature caters explicitly for estimating the cost of implementing RCs. As demonstrated in the previous sections, changes occur for a plethora of reasons and can occur during any phase of the software development life cycle. Therefore, it would be beneficial if there was a dedicated method by which to estimate the cost of such changes as the implication of these changes based on the project's timeline results in different outcomes.
2.   Estimation done at an early stage of the development process is usually based on expert judgement with less precise input and less detailed design specification. In some cases, this may result in effort estimation which is too low which leads to issues such as delayed delivery, budget overrun and poor quality while high estimates may lead to loss of business opportunities and the inefficient use of resources.
3.   Estimating the cost in the early stages of development depends on expert judgment and historical data which can be biased and inconsistent. There needs to be ways to eliminate these ambiguities in change cost estimation.

The research gaps identified indicate the importance of having a full-scale model that increases the efficiency of managing change with better accuracy. The review highlights that although the concept of change management has been in existence for many years, the applicability of the available methods has many limitations and has room for improvement. With challenges such as poor communication, impact identification issues and no dedicated method for change cost calculation, the avenues for future research is promising.

Finally, we highlight the use of ML-based approaches to support the aforementioned RCM activities. For instance, The study of Binkhonain et al. (2019) showed ML-based approaches have generally performed well, achieving an accuracy of more than 70% in detecting and classifying NFRs. Therefore, hopefully these results can be achieved in RCM activities.

FINAL REMARKS

It is evident that changes in requirements can be caused by multiple stakeholders or may occur for many reasons. Regardless of who or what cause these changes, the need for appropriate management is great due to the undesirable consequences if left unattended. However, through this chapter book, it was discovered change management is an elusive target to achieve and that there are two main ways to tackle it. The main objective of this chapter book was to collate information and techniques related to RCM and critically analyze the functionality of such techniques in managing change. This also led to identifying strengths and limitations of these techniques, which signifies the need to enhance the existing change management approaches.

This chapter book is also a guide for future researchers on change management in terms of what major work has been undertaken thus far. In this study, the section on factors that cause change in requirements provides an understanding on how vast and constant these changes can be. There is no one root cause for changes which makes change management a challenging task. Therefore, even with an abundance of research on change management, there is still room for improvement. Given the complexity of changes, it is important to identify the processes in place to manage them. It is clear from the available literature that there is no consensus on how to manage change. In some instances, it is based on the type of organization and the environment and in many cases, it is based on the type of changes. Through the available process steps, three common processes were identified; identification, analysis and cost estimation of change.

Significant work has been done in each of these areas and disciplined and agile models that encompass these steps have been developed in an effort to provide a full-scale solution for change management. It is also important to understand that the approaches vary depending on the level of the organization managing the change. When identifying future work in RCM, we deemed it useful to focus on the three areas of RQ3 where the majority of the techniques have been discussed. We do not directly suggest future work but identify the research gaps in the areas of change identification, analysis and cost estimation where the possibility for new research lies.

Although agile development seems to have a very efficient way of managing change requirements, we were able to identify practical challenges in some of the agile practices. This paper provided information about the key features, challenges, and some research gaps in existing work related to ARCM. The results described on this study can benefit: (i) Researchers who are interested in knowing the state of the art of ARCM and (ii) Practitioners who may be interested in understanding the reported solutions in terms of practices for support the ARCM process.

REFERENCES

Abdullah, N. N. B., Honiden, S., Sharp, H., Nuseibeh, B., & Notkin, D. (2011). Communication patterns of agile requirements engineering. In *Proceedings of the 1st workshop on agile requirements engineering*. ACM.

Abrahamsson, P., Fronza, I., Moser, R., Vlasenko, J., & Pedrycz, W. (2011). Predicting development effort from user stories. In *2011 International Symposium on Empirical Software Engineering and Measurement*, (pp. 400–403). IEEE. 10.1109/ESEM.2011.58

Awad, M. (2005). *A comparison between agile and traditional software development methodologies*. University of Western Australia.

Bano, M., Imtiaz, S., Ikram, N., Niazi, M., & Usman, M. (2012). *Causes of requirement change - A systematic literature review*. Academic Press.

Bilgaiyan, S., Mishra, S., & Das, M. (2016). A review of software cost estimation in agile software development using soft computing techniques. In *2016 2nd international conference on computational intelligence and networks (CINE)*, (pp. 112–117). IEEE. 10.1109/CINE.2016.27

Binkhonain, M., & Zhao, L. (2019). A review of machine learning algorithms for identification and classification of non-functional requirements. *Expert Systems with Applications*, *10*. doi:10.1016/j.eswax.2019.100001

Boehm, B. (2000). Requirements that handle IKIWISI, COTS, and rapid change. *Computer*, *33*(7), 99–102. doi:10.1109/2.869384

Bohner, S. A., & Arnold, R. S. (1996). *Software change impact analysis* (Vol. 6). IEEE Computer Society Press.

Boness, K., & Harrison, R. (2007). Goal sketching: Towards agile requirements engineering. In *International Conference on Software Engineering Advances (ICSEA 2007)*, (pp. 71–71). IEEE. 10.1109/ICSEA.2007.36

Cao, L., & Ramesh, B. (2008). Agile requirements engineering practices: An empirical study. *IEEE Software*, *25*(1), 60–67. doi:10.1109/MS.2008.1

Carlson, D., & Matuzic, P. (2010). Practical agile requirements engineering. *Proceedings of the 13th Annual Systems Engineering Conference*.

Carlson, R., Matuzic, P., & Simons, R. (2012). Applying scrum to stabilize systems engineering execution. *Crosstalk*, 1–6.

Ceschi, M., Sillitti, A., Succi, G., & De Panfilis, S. (2005). Project management in plan-based and agile companies. *IEEE Software*, *22*(3), 21–27. doi:10.1109/MS.2005.75

Christel, M. G., & Kang, K. C. (1992). *Issues in requirements elicitation (No. CMU/SEI-92-TR-12)*. Carnegie-Mellon Univ Pittsburgh Pa Software Engineering Inst.

Coelho, E., & Basu, A. (2012). Effort estimation in agile software development using story points. *International Journal of Applied Information Systems*, *3*(7), 7–10. doi:10.5120/ijais12-450574

Cohn, M. (2004). *User stories applied: For agile software development*. Addison Wesley Professional.

Curcio, K., Navarro, T., Malucelli, A., & Reinehr, S. (2018). Requirements engineering: A systematic mapping study in agile software development. *Journal of Systems and Software*, *139*, 32–50. doi:10.1016/j.jss.2018.01.036

Curtis, B., Krasner, H., & Iscoe, N. (1988). A field study of the software design process for large systems. *Communications of the ACM*, *31*(11), 1268–1287. doi:10.1145/50087.50089

Dahlstedt, Å. G., & Persson, A. (2005). Requirements interdependencies: state of the art and future challenges. In *Engineering and managing software requirements* (pp. 95–116). Springer. doi:10.1007/3-540-28244-0_5

Daneva, M., Van Der Veen, E., Amrit, C., Ghaisas, S., Sikkel, K., Kumar, R., Ajmeri, N., Ramteerthkar, U., & Wieringa, R. (2013). Agile requirements prioritization in large-scale outsourced system projects: An empirical study. *Journal of Systems and Software*, *86*(5), 1333–1353. doi:10.1016/j.jss.2012.12.046

De Lucia, A., & Qusef, A. (2010). Requirements engineering in agile software development. *Journal of Emerging Technologies in Web Intelligence*, *2*(3), 212–220. doi:10.4304/jetwi.2.3.212-220

Eberlein, A., & Leite, J. (2002). Agile requirements definition: A view from requirements engineering. *Proceedings of the International Workshop on Time Constrained Requirements Engineering (TCRE ' 2002)*, 4–8.

Ernst, N. A., Borgida, A., Jureta, I. J., & Mylopoulos, J. (2014). Agile requirements engineering via paraconsistent reasoning. *Information Systems*, *43*, 100–116. doi:10.1016/j.is.2013.05.008

Fabbri, S., Silva, C., Hernandes, E., Octaviano, F., Di Thommazo, A., & Belgamo, A. (2016). Improvements in the StArt tool to better support the systematic review process. In *Proceedings of the 20th International Conference on Evaluation and Assessment in Software Engineering* (pp. 1-5). 10.1145/2915970.2916013

Haugen, N. C. (2006). An empirical study of using planning poker for user story estimation. In AGILE 2006 (AGILE'06). IEEE. doi:10.1109/AGILE.2006.16

Ibrahim, S., Idris, N. B., Munro, M., & Deraman, A. (2005). A requirements traceability to support change impact analysis. *Asian Journal of Information Tech*, *4*(4), 345–355.

Inayat, I., Salim, S. S., Marczak, S., Daneva, M., & Shamshirband, S. (2015). A systematic literature review on agile requirements engineering practices and challenges. *Computers in Human Behavior*, *51*, 915–929. doi:10.1016/j.chb.2014.10.046

Jayatilleke, S., & Lai, R. (2018). A systematic review of requirements change management. *Information and Software Technology*, *93*, 163–185. doi:10.1016/j.infsof.2017.09.004

Jun, L., Qiuzhen, W., & Lin, G. (2010). Application of agile requirement engineering in modest-sized information systems development. In *2010 Second world congress on software engineering*, (vol. 2, pp. 207–210). IEEE.

Khatri, S. K., Malhotra, S., & Johri, P. (2016). Use case point estimation technique in software development. In *2016 5th international conference on reliability, infocom technologies and optimization (trends and future directions) (ICRITO)*, (pp. 123–128). IEEE. 10.1109/ICRITO.2016.7784938

Kitchenham, B., & Charters, S. (2007). Guidelines for performing systematic literature reviews in software engineering version 2.3. *Engineering*, *45*(4ve), 1051.

Kleebaum, A., Johanssen, J. O., Paech, B., & Bruegge, B. (2019). How do Practitioners Manage Decision Knowledge during Continuous Software Engineering? In *31st International Conference on Software Engineering and Knowledge Engineering, SEKE* (pp. 735-740). Academic Press.

Kotonya, G., & Sommerville, I. (1998). *Requirements engineering: processes and techniques*. Wiley Publishing.

Leung, H., & Fan, Z. (2002). Software cost estimation. In Handbook of Software Engineering and Knowledge Engineering: Volume II: Emerging Technologies, (pp. 307–324). World Scientific. doi:10.1142/9789812389701_0014

Mahnič, V., & Hovelja, T. (2012). On using planning poker for estimating user stories. *Journal of Systems and Software*, *85*(9), 2086–2095. doi:10.1016/j.jss.2012.04.005

McGee, S., & Greer, D. (2012). Towards an understanding of the causes and effects of software requirements change: Two case studies. *Requirements Engineering*, *17*(2), 133–155. doi:10.100700766-012-0149-0

Melegati, J., Goldman, A., Kon, F., & Wang, X. (2019). A model of requirements engineering in software startups. *Information and Software Technology*, *109*, 92–107. doi:10.1016/j.infsof.2019.02.001

Mourão, E., Kalinowski, M., Murta, L., Mendes, E., & Wohlin, C. (2017). Investigating the use of a hybrid search strategy for systematic reviews. In *2017 ACM/IEEE International Symposium on Empirical Software Engineering and Measurement (ESEM)*, (pp. 193–198). IEEE. 10.1109/ESEM.2017.30

Nunes, N. J., Constantine, L., & Kazman, R. (2010). Iucp: Estimating interactivesoftware project size with enhanced use-case points. *IEEE Software*, *28*(4), 64–73. doi:10.1109/MS.2010.111

Nurmuliani, N., Zowghi, D., & Powell, S. (2004, April). Analysis of requirements volatility during software development life cycle. In *2004 Australian Software Engineering Conference. Proceedings* (pp. 28-37). IEEE. 10.1109/ASWEC.2004.1290455

Panda, A., Satapathy, S. M., & Rath, S. K. (2015). Empirical validation of neural network models for agile software effort estimation based on story points. *Procedia Computer Science*, *57*, 772–781. doi:10.1016/j.procs.2015.07.474

Petersen, K., Vakkalanka, S., & Kuzniarz, L. (2015). Guidelines for conducting systematic mapping studies in software engineering: An update. *Information and Software Technology*, *64*, 1–18. doi:10.1016/j.infsof.2015.03.007

Pfleeger, S. L. (2008). Software metrics: Progress after 25 years? *IEEE Software*, *25*(6), 32–34. doi:10.1109/MS.2008.160

Ramesh, B., Cao, L., & Baskerville, R. (2010). Agile requirements engineering practices and challenges: An empirical study. *Information Systems Journal*, *20*(5), 449–480. doi:10.1111/j.1365-2575.2007.00259.x

Ramzan, S., & Ikram, N. (2006). Requirement change management process models: Activities, artifacts and roles. In *2006 IEEE International Multitopic Conference*, (pp. 219–223). IEEE. 10.1109/INMIC.2006.358167

Saher, N., Baharom, F., & Ghazali, O. (2017). Requirement change taxonomy and categorization in agile software development. In *2017 6th International Conference on Electrical Engineering and Informatics (ICEEI)*, (pp. 1–6). IEEE. 10.1109/ICEEI.2017.8312441

Schön, E.-M., Thomaschewski, J., & Escalona, M. J. (2017). Agile requirements engineering: A systematic literature review. *Computer Standards & Interfaces*, *49*, 79–91. doi:10.1016/j.csi.2016.08.011

Sommerville, I. (2011). Software engineering (9th ed.). Addison-Wesley/Pearson.

Spichkova, M., & Schmidt, H. (2019). *Requirements engineering for global systems: cultural, regulatory and technical aspects*. arXiv preprint arXiv:1910.05008

Stålhane, T., Katta, V., & Myklebust, T. (2014). *Change impact analysis in agile development*. EHPG Røros.

Van Lamsweerde, A. (2009). *Requirements engineering: From system goals to UML models to software* (Vol. 10). John Wiley & Sons.

Wagner, S., Fernández, D. M., Felderer, M., & Kalinowski, M. (2017). Requirements engineering practice and problems in agile projects: Results from an international survey. CIbSE 2017, 85–98.

Wagner, S., Fernández, D. M., Felderer, M., Vetrò, A., Kalinowski, M., Wieringa, R., Pfahl, D., Conte, T., Christiansson, M.-T., Greer, D., Lassenius, C., Männistö, T., Nayebi, M., Oivo, M., Penzenstadler, B., Prikladnicki, R., Ruhe, G., Schekelmann, A., Sen, S., ... Winkler, D. (2019). Status quo in requirements engineering: A theory and a global family of surveys. *ACM Transactions on Software Engineering and Methodology*, *28*(2), 1–48. doi:10.1145/3306607

Weiss, D. M., & Basili, V. R. (1985). Evaluating software development by analysis of changes: Some data from the software engineering laboratory. *IEEE Transactions on Software Engineering*, *SE-11*(2), 157–168. doi:10.1109/TSE.1985.232190

Wiegers, K., & Beatty, J. (2013). *Software requirements*. Pearson Education.

Wohlin, C. (2014). Guidelines for snowballing in systematic literature studies and a replication in software engineering. *Proceedings of the 18th international conference on evaluation and assessment in software engineering*, 38. 10.1145/2601248.2601268

KEY TERMS AND DEFINITIONS

Agile Software Development: Agile Software Development or Agile Method is a discipline that studies a set of behaviors, processes, practices, and tools used to create products and their subsequent availability to end users.

Disciplined Software Development: Disciplined (or Traditional) software development methodologies are based on pre-organized phases/stages of the software development lifecycle. Here the flow of development is unidirectional, from requirements to design and then to development, then to testing and maintenance.

Planning Poker: Planning poker, also called Scrum poker, is a consensus-based, gamified technique for estimating, mostly used to estimate effort or relative size of development goals in software development.

Requirement: The software requirements are description of features and functionalities of the target system. Requirements convey the expectations of users from the software product. The requirements can be obvious or hidden, known or unknown, expected or unexpected from client's point of view.

Requirement Change Management: Requirement change management is defined as a process of managing changing requirements during the requirements engineering process and system development. A requirement change management process in the organization not only improves the organizational processes but success and predictability of projects as well.

Requirement Management: Requirements management is a systematic approach to finding, documenting, organizing, and tracking the changing requirements of a system.

Use Case: A use case is a methodology used in system analysis to identify, clarify and organize system requirements. The use case is made up of a set of possible sequences of interactions between systems and users in a particular environment and related to a particular goal. The method creates a document that describes all the steps taken by a user to complete an activity.

User Story: User Story is a concise description of a user's need for the product (that is, a "requirement") from that user's point of view. User Story seeks to describe this need in a simple and light way.

This research was previously published in Balancing Agile and Disciplined Engineering and Management Approaches for IT Services and Software Products; pages 130-150, copyright year 2021 by Engineering Science Reference (an imprint of IGI Global).

Chapter 95
Dilbert Moments:
Exploring the Factors Impacting Upon the Accuracy of Project Managers' Baseline Schedules

James Prater

School of Natural and Built Environments, University of South Australia, Adelaide, Australia

Konstantinos Kirytopoulos

School of Natural Built Environments, University of South Australia, Adelaide, Australia

Tony Ma

School of Natural and Built Environments, University of South Australia, Adelaide, Australia

ABSTRACT

Developing and delivering a project to an agreed schedule is fundamentally what project managers do. There is still an ongoing debate about schedule delays. This research investigates the development of schedules through semi-structured in-depth interviews. The findings reveal that half of the respondents believe that delays reported in the media are not real and should be attributed to scope changes. IT project managers estimating techniques include bottom-up estimates, analogy, and expert judgement. Impeding factors reported for the development of realistic schedules were technical (e.g. honest mistakes) and political (e.g. completion dates imposed by the sponsor). Respondents did not mention any psychological factors, although most were aware of optimism bias. However, they were not familiar with approaches to mitigate its impacts. Yet, when these techniques were mentioned, the overwhelming majority agreed that these mitigation approaches would change their schedule estimate.

DOI: 10.4018/978-1-6684-3702-5.ch095

INTRODUCTION

Software development projects are a key enabler for any organisation (De Reyck et al., 2005) but when reviewing the literature as to whether these projects are successful, there is an abundance of literature highlighting issues with their performance when compared to initial estimates (Frese & Sauter, 2014).

The impacts of a project exceeding its original schedule or cost estimate include the inability to fully deliver the identified business benefits, potential loss of market share and company reputation (Pinto 2013, p. 644). There is also a loss of trust from the project stakeholders to the project management team (Baccarini, 1999, p. 26; Davis, 2014) and in some cases, significant financial impact to the company that is providing the project management services, due to contractual conditions. Specifically, if the project was undertaken under a fixed price agreement (a valid risk reduction strategy) the inability of the contractor to complete the project within the agreed timeframe would cause significant issues for the contractor.

One of the key tools to manage a project is the initial schedule. This tool is used extensively by the project manager to motivate the project team as well as to communicate the aims and approach of the project. Psychological factors (Flyvbjerg, 2008), such as optimism bias can and do impact on the development of schedules and research has recommended a number of mitigation approaches.

One specific area that there is limited research into is what tools and techniques have been developed by project management practioners to mitigate these psychological factors as several of their projects that they have managed would have been impacted by optimism bias. Thus, over time, whether at a conscious or subconscious level, they would have developed to tools or techniques to mitigate or minimize the impacts.

As a result, to the ongoing debate about schedule delays, this research, aims to investigate and evaluate the implementation of software development project schedules. Specifically, the investigation focuses on whether project managers are aware of psychological factors, such as optimism bias and its impact on initial schedules. Respondents were also asked to comment on the frequent media reporting about poor initial schedule development and how this related to their own personal experiences whilst managing software development projects.

In order to achieve the aim of this research, the researchers explored whether project management practitioners' experience reflects the schedule overruns reported in the media, what, if any, specific approaches are used to develop and check initial schedules, what do project management practitioners believe is the main barrier to creating an accurate initial schedule and finally whether project management practitioners understand the terms and approaches identified in research, to mitigate psychological factors affecting schedule development.

DEVELOPING REALISTIC SCHEDULES: IMPEDING FACTORS AND MITIGATION TECHNIQUES

Software Development Project Scheduling

This research was initiated to explore what project managers perceive crucial, among several issues relating to managing projects and initial schedule estimates. Issues with initial schedules, can and do receive significant media attention, particularly with the reporting of software development projects when they run over time or budget (Eveleens & Verhoef, 2010). These issues include insights into how project managers develop and validate schedules in practice, when compared to what is recommended within the literature (Jorgensen, 2014).

One significant challenge that any project faces is to develop a realistic, achievable schedule that is accepted by both the project team and key stakeholders. This has been highlighted by Eizakshiri, Chan and Emsley (2015) who reiterated that the problem was not the execution of the project, but the flawed plans developed at the initiation of a project. Software development projects are no different to other projects and suffer from poor plan development. This was highlighted by Budzier and Flyvbjerg (2011, pp. 11-12) who extensively reviewed previous literature and proposed a concept of "Black Swan Blindness" which is where decision makers overemphasise common events and underestimate uncommon events. They then developed a model, via statistical distributions, to understand which projects may be impacted by these Black swan events. Finally, project stakeholders, sometimes, can go as far as asking the project manager to manipulate the initial baseline estimate for political reasons, such as an upcoming election or to gain business (Pinto, 2013).

Inherently, the schedule is an attempt by the project manager and team to predict the future which by its very nature is uncertain. The schedule must also provide a clear direction and plan for the team to achieve in this uncertain environment. Several research papers (Meyer, 2014; Smith, Bruyns & Evans, 2011) have shown that one of the characteristics of successful project managers and teams is that they are optimistic, even in this uncertain environment. Meyer's research showed that the impacts of optimism bias allowed a project to continue, even when it was clearly failing. Another finding from this research showed that once a decision was made to terminate the project, optimism bias then seemed to dissipate. Optimism bias has also been investigated as to whether it can be learnt (Dolfi & Andrews, 2007), given its strong correlation to successful projects. All in all, one of the significant challenges to developing realistic schedules, is that it is highly likely that they will be developed by a team with a pre-disposition to optimism. Therefore, several tools and techniques have been developed to help provide a more realistic and less optimistic schedule.

Schedule Techniques

In reviewing tools and techniques used to create the initial baseline, Jørgensen (2004a) researched the use of expert estimation to develop schedules for software-based projects and found that the use of expert estimation was the most common. In a more recent paper, Jorgensen (2014) found that there is no one "Best Effort Estimation Model," but recommended the use of historical data to set minimum and maximum values, whilst still allowing expert estimation to develop the P50 case. A P50 case is where there is a 50% chance that the estimate will be met, inherently that also means that there is a 50% chance that it won't be met. One of the other findings from this research by Jorgenson was that using relevant historical data and checklists does improve forecast accuracy as does the use of multiple estimation methods.

Chowdary and Reddy (2016) broadly categorised estimation methods into Expert Judgement; where either an expert or a group of experts' give the estimation. Analogy; where similar projects or tasks are used for the estimation. Top-Down; where large attributes of the project dividing into smaller pieces are used for the estimation. Bottom-Up; where one breaks down the components to the lowest level possible and then estimates upwards. Algorithmic; where mathematical equations are used for the estimation.

Factors Impacting Schedule Development

Factors that have been shown to have a detrimental impact on the development of a schedule have been categorised by Flyvbjerg (2009), who identified three distinct themes or causes for issues in the estimation of projects, as below:

1. **Technical:** "In terms of imperfect forecasting techniques, inadequate data, honest mistakes, inherent problems in predicting the future, lack of experience on the part of the forecasters, etc." (p. 150);
2. **Psychological explanations:** In terms of what psychologist's call "the planning fallacy and optimism bias" (p. 150) overestimating benefits and underestimating costs. This can be traced back to a cognitive bias;
3. **Political-economic explanations:** See planners and promoters as deliberately and strategically overestimating benefits and underestimating costs when forecasting the outcomes of projects.

This research was primarily into psychological factors, specifically the concept of planning fallacy, which was discovered and defined as "a consequence of the tendency to neglect distributional data, and to adopt what may be termed an 'internal approach' to prediction, where one focuses on the constituents of the specific problem rather than on the distribution of outcomes in similar cases. The internal approach to the evaluation of plans is likely to produce underestimation" (Kahneman & Tversky, 1977, p.12).

Meyer (2014) & Batselier and Vanhoucke (2016) have re-iterated the importance of managing this psychological factor, Meyer's research highlighted that project team members will remain optimistic, even when there is overwhelming evidence to the contrary. Whist Vanhoucke demonstrated the value of Reference Class Forecasting, a technique developed by Flyvbjerg (2008) to mitigate against optimism bias, showing that this technique, via an experiment was the most effective method of improving forecasting. This technique, which is similar to the conclusion that Jorgensen (2014) research came to, is based upon using historical data to provide a correction factor to the initial estimate. Pinto (2013) also suggests that this technique can be used to improve initial estimates against what he calls the seven deadly sins of the planning process, one of which is optimism bias. Prater, Kirytopoulos and Ma (2017) highlighted that within the project management literature, the reference class approach is the dominant recommended approach to mitigate optimism bias, however they were unable to find validated research into its use within software development projects. Of interest is that Dawson and Dawson (1998) research highlighted the requirement for some type of statistical model to improve estimates nearly 30 years ago, so the concept is not new. Using statistical techniques and analysis has also been recommended by Hadad, Keren and Laslo (2013) to select project managers.

RESEARCH METHOD

To ensure that the project management community could respond to the research questions raised, the research method chosen was to use semi-structured in-depth interviews. This allows time to discuss and probe the interviewee to ensure that key concepts and knowledge are discovered. Veal (2005, p. 127) suggests that this is the appropriate choice when subjects are relatively few, information obtained from each varies, that each subject may have an important story to share and the research is in the "preliminary stage in planning of a larger study".

Based on these criteria, this approach was suitable for this research and was thus applied. This research method allows the respondent to voice their opinion on the questions, with responses frank and open. Respondents were also allowed to make as many comments as they wished. It also allowed the research to fill the gap in the academic literature as to what approach to create initial schedules was used in practise. A relatively small sample size was selected as suggested by Fellows and Liu (2008) which is based on the understanding that a small number of respondents with a strong understanding of the topic are more suitable to than larger samples with limited knowledge. Based on the concept of data saturation (Francis et al., 2010), initially eight interviews were completed and the findings from these interviews were summarised, a further three interviews were then undertaken with no additional findings found. Thus, in total 11 Experienced Project Managers were interviewed in the period between May – July 2016. A purposive sampling technique was used with candidates selected, with assistance from the local Project Management Institute Chapter. Selection was based upon an understanding of their experience and length of time within the profession. Respondents were primarily South Australian based, but two interstate respondents were also interviewed. Based upon a deliberate choice no demographic information was captured, such as Age, Sex, and the type of organisation that the respondent had either worked in or was currently employed in. Interview times ranged from 15 to 50 minutes and were conducted at mutually agreed locations. Questions were arranged to encourage engagement between the interviewer and respondents, with early questions that were relatively straight forward, such as years in the industry, with later questions which were more open and allowed the respondents to elaborate upon their answers. The interview questions were developed based upon an extensive literature review, the researchers' relevant project management experience and informal discussions with other researchers. The aim of the interview questions was to understand, from a project management practitioner's point of view, what methods were used to create and validate initial baseline schedules and whether the practitioners were aware of any cognitive biases that could impact their schedules.

To ensure accuracy interviews were recorded, then transcribed and issued for corrections and comments to the respondent. Respondent then emailed their changes and the final interview document was then approved. All information was captured and managed within a database with version control. Answers for individual questions were coded by the lead researcher and were tabulated and summarised per question (i.e. all the answers for question one from the eleven respondents were reviewed at the same time). These codes were developed by labelling phrases, words and sentences from the interviews and comparing them to both other responses and codes developed from the literature review. These codes were then used to categorise the responses and form the basis for the analysis of findings.

Using the Project Management Institutes PMI (2015) definition of roles, respondents self-selected as to their category, five of the respondents self-selected themselves as a project manager (level 3) which was defined as "Under general direction of either a Portfolio Manager or in some cases a Program Manager, oversees high-priority projects, which often require considerable resources and high levels of functional integration." Four of the respondents self-selected themselves as a Program Manager which was defined as "Responsible for the coordinated management of multiple related projects, and in many (most) cases, ongoing operations which are directed toward a common objective." The remaining two respondents self-selected themselves as Portfolio Manager which is defined as "Responsible for the management of the entire set of projects undertaken by an organization or division in a manner that optimizes the ROI from these projects and ensures their alignment with the organizations strategic objectives."

Based upon the self-selection of roles, all respondents were operating at a very senior level. This is also reflected in the length of time that the respondents had worked within this profession.

It is very clear from the respondents' answers to the previous questions that the group had significant expertise in managing many projects, several of which had significant budgets.

RESEARCH FINDINGS

In this section, we present the results of the interviews. The results are accompanied with representative quotes from the respondents to detail the narratives. This section is organised into four sub-sections, namely, media reports of project disasters, theoretical and empirical evidence aligned on approaches to create and validate schedules, main barriers against preparing a realistic schedule and the missing links: optimism and reference class.

Media Reports of Project Disasters

One important issue that this research explored was whether the project management community thought that there was a problem with initial estimates, as, often, the media report schedule delays of projects. Six of the respondents agreed that there was a problem, four did not agree and one response was not clear enough to assess. In reviewing the responses from all respondents, three themes (or causes) were identified. The first theme was understated requirements, which was mentioned by four respondents. Understated requirements translates to requirements that have not either been fully understood or have changed along the course of the project. Specific areas impacted by this included schedule and budget estimates. Other comments from the respondents included issues with the quality of requirements definition or development of software code.

The second theme identified was misreporting and it was mentioned four times. Misreporting is where stakeholders do not understand that the original schedule or scope of the project is subject to change. In these respondents' view the media tended to misreport problems with IT projects, with several respondents commenting that the media did not understand the complexities of software development project management and that there is a common misconception that you can reliably estimate scope, time and schedule, to forecast an accurate finish line. In the view of these respondents the media then magnified the reporting of issues with original schedules as demonstrated by the following quotes:

The other comment is that IT projects that are failing are over amplified, painting a very bad picture. So, in my view the statistics seem very high. [Respondent 3]

I believe this has to be with the media or external customers fixated on the initial schedule / target dates published by the project team, which are always a projection and caveated by many assumptions. [Respondent 10]

The third theme identified was project change management, which was mentioned by four respondents. This is where stakeholders do not understand or will not accept that projects are subject to the change management process. The key issue here for the respondents was to control and articulate the change management process. A lack of understanding as to how projects following the appropriate change management process will follow a formal process to accept scope changes, which may result in both an increase of budget and schedule. Respondent [11] summarised this perfectly by "Projects must be reported with context and facts."

The theme of Politics which is often noted in the literature was mentioned directly only once. This is where "planners and promoters act deliberately and strategically overestimating benefits and underestimating costs when forecasting the outcomes of projects" (Flyvbjerg 2009, p. 152).. This particular response related to the approval of the business case.

Further analysing these themes using the categories developed by Flyvbjerg (2008) arguably Understated Requirements and Misreporting fall under the Psychological explanations, Project Change Management under Technical and the Politics, under Political-economics.

Theoretical and Empirical Evidence Aligned on Approaches to Create and Validate Schedules

Respondents were asked a series of questions about how they went about preparing, checking and validating both internally and vendor-developed schedules. Like the approach in the previous section, representative quotations have been used to demonstrate the results.

The opening question about baseline schedules was designed to understand what methods and techniques were used to create the initial baseline schedule. Based upon the respondents' answers, the Bottom Up approach was used by all respondents to prepare baseline schedules. Several respondents specifically mentioned the breakdown of deliverables into components which were then used to develop the schedule. The use of the team to assist with this process was also mentioned extensively. Using a team approach was also mentioned by Respondent [1] in relation to ensuring commitment to the agreed target. Respondent [3] had a company approach which used two teams, one nominated as the red team the other as the blue team and both were asked to breakdown the estimate and then the results were compared. Eight of the eleven respondents used two or more methods, where four respondents used three different types of estimation; best demonstrated by the quote below:

There are different schedules at different stages, I use both bottom up and top down, bottom up to the extent that you can, for software projects I undertake a functional decomposition and then use metrics from previous functional point analysis work and go on to calculate the theoretical effort from this breakdown. Post this estimate I then add proportional/fixed overheads such as project management. Separate estimates are prepared by different team members for change/training and other resourcing overheads. I then apply the top down customer constraints, letting the associated resourcing plan derive price (or cost). [Respondent 2]

These additional methods included Top Down which was used three times, Milestones used twice and four estimation approaches that were used by only one respondent. These were the red/blue team approach, which asks one team to develop an alternative schedule which is then compared to the one developed by the project team. Delphi, which is an information gathering technique used to reach consensus on a subject, where experts participate anonymously, via a few rounds to reach consensus Nasir (2006, p.4). Independent Review, which is where an external party is asked to develop or review the schedule and finally PERT which estimates project duration through a weighted average of optimistic, pessimistic and most likely activities.

Seven of the respondents mentioned the use of a team to prepare the initial schedule, five included subject matter experts within the estimation and one respondent used the schedule as a tool to motivate the project team.

The key finding from this question was that all respondents used the Bottom Up approach and eight of the eleven respondents then used another method to validate the schedule.

The next question was designed to understand what approaches were used by the project manager to validate the project team's estimates and it was found that the most popular response to this question was analogy, which is an approach based on using previous projects and was used by six respondents. Whilst Bottom Up and the project managers experience were used by four of the respondents respectively. Whilst the red/blue team, questioning, which was defined as asking the estimator to justify their estimate, and external expert, were each used by one respondent respectively.

Project managers also used techniques that tried to ascertain from past performances as to which of the team members were optimistic or pessimistic. The project managers could then use this understanding to apply a correction factor to the raw estimates from these team members. Respondent [5] also mentioned a reasonability test, which was based upon their previous experience. The use of analogy as the basis for checking estimates raises an interesting dilemma, as one of the key impacts of optimism bias is the brain's tendency to only remember positive experiences, thus using memories of past project performance may be misleading.

In summary eight of the eleven respondents used either previous projects or experience to validate their estimates. Of note was the use of the red/blue team and external expert to validate the estimates. This reflects the classic "Outside view approach" which was discussed within the literature review and is the basis for the development of the reference class approach.

One of the other sources for estimates for the initial baseline schedule were vendors, and what approach was used to validate vendor estimates. Three of the respondents did not use vendors, only internal resources thus the question was not relevant to them. Four of the respondents used three different methods to validate vendor estimates, two respondents used two methods, whilst one method was used by two respondents.

Analogy was used by the five of the respondents, other competitive vendors by four respondents, contractual, bottom up and expert judgement by three respondents whilst using the project team was mentioned by two of the respondents and one project manager used himself as an "Outside View". The use of multiple techniques when estimating is best represented by the following quote from Respondent [4]:

Ask for a vendor breakdown including what skill set and number of resources have been allocated to the tasks and then compare to what effort would be involved if using internal resourcing, to get a sense of whether it is fair and reasonable. I also consider the type of contractual relationship with the vendor, fixed price or time and materials, understanding and accepting that there is a reasonable margin required. Also compare against other vendors, market assessment of services offered to ensure that they are comparable / within market. [Respondent 4]

Respondent [11] applied an approach that combined both the vendor and the project team to validate and then challenged both the vendor and project team by continually asking "why?" to prompt them to justify their estimates.

Like the answers to the previous question, each respondent used a multitude of methods to validate vendors' estimates. Of note was the use of historical and/or other vendors which was mentioned by seven of the eight project managers that did respond to this question.

In relation to schedule achievability, the two most popular ways to check it were the project manager's Expert Judgement used by five of the respondents. This was closely followed by Analogy and Technical, used by four of the respondents. Technical was defined as "using a scheduling tool to validate the estimate". The use of the Project Team and the "Outside View" was mentioned respectively by one respondent.

One could argue that experience and previous projects are very similar methods to validate baseline as both rely on historical data which is by its very nature, analogous, thus the main method to check whether the baseline is achievable is by analogy. Whilst the technical approach was of interest as it applied specific tools to validate the schedule, these tools included resource levelling, ensuring commitment from key staff to agreed dates, checking of the impacts of public holidays on the schedule:

... ask the vendor for a breakdown of tasks, what dependencies they have on business resources. Also apply gut feel based upon experience, review estimates for any padding, activities breakdown, pay for Time and Materials work to come up with detailed schedule and fixed price. [Respondent 4]

The following response highlights the use of the project manager's intuition when checking whether the schedule is achievable:

Good question, gut feel and past project experience. [Respondent 8]

Main Barriers Against Preparing a Realistic Schedule

From the respondents two of these categories previously discussed and identified by Flyvbjerg (2009) emerged as themes, these were Technical mentioned by six respondents and Political mentioned by five. From the respondents interviewed, none mentioned any impact to preparing a realistic schedule from Psychological factors, such as optimism bias. This was best enforced by respondent [6] who stated:

That the sponsor or project client, doesn't like the number or they don't understand it, I refer to this as the Dilbert moment, where the pointy headed guy upsets everyone. This could be because they have pre-committed to a number or target already and you now have to explain why this is not possible. Once you put a date out there, you are also locked down, and people will forget everything else about what the number was based upon but hold you accountable to that number. Just to reiterate this is the biggest problem with estimates.

The Missing Links: Optimism and Reference Class

Potential psychological impacts to the development of the initial schedule were also explored. The familiarity of the respondents to the term "optimism bias" was investigated. Nine of the eleven respondents could define the term, two were not able to do so, thus within the respondents the term was relatively well understood by the majority. All users were unanimous that optimism bias had impacted their baseline schedule, yet when reviewed in conjunction with a previous question about barriers to realistic scheduling none of the respondents had mentioned optimism bias as one of the main barriers to preparing their original baseline schedule. This is best demonstrated by the following quote:

Oh Yeah! Yes, all the time, but not just in projects, in other aspects of life where people make commitments, duration estimate and effort estimates, where a task will take 5 consecutive days to complete but end up taking 3 weeks as these days are not available, found this especially within a Matrix environment. [Respondent 1]

Respondent [6] highlighted that in his view optimism bias was one of the major reasons behind having an appropriate contingency. The lack of the mention of optimism bias as one of main barriers to schedule preparation is very interesting and raises two separate hypotheticals, these are:

1.   That the impacts of optimism bias are not the main barrier to the preparation of a baseline schedule; or
2.   Having mentioned the term "optimism bias" to the respondents, this had then prompted the immediate response and thus provided a positive answer.

Unfortunately, the information gathered during the interviews was unable to clarify, which, if any, of these hypotheticals could apply.

The final questions asked were whether the respondents had heard of the techniques of "Outside View" and "Reference Class Forecasting" to mitigate the impacts of optimism bias and whether applying these techniques would change their forecasts.

Three of the respondents had heard of the term "Outside View' and one of these respondents had also heard of the term Reference Class Forecasting, thus, these terms are not widely used nor understood by the project managers interviewed.

Nine of the eleven respondents agreed that using these approaches would significantly change their baseline. One respondent was not sure and one did not think that it would change the baseline. Thus, most respondents believed that there is significant merit in applying these techniques to a new baseline. One respondent mentioned that their organisation used a risk checklist, which had been developed over several years. This checklist helped project managers evaluate risks and then recommended a financial contingency level. Another respondent mentioned the pressure from stakeholders to develop an optimistic schedule, but at the same time to ensure that they applied lessons learned from previous projects.

This reiterates the point made by Flyvbjerg (2008) who strongly recommends the use of reference class forecasting where there are political-economic pressures on the baseline. Politics was also one of the themes that emerged from the answer to one of the previous questions "What do you see as the main barrier or issue to prepare a realistic schedule" and was mentioned by five of the respondents.

CONCLUSION AND FURTHER RESEARCH

This research has provided a valuable insight into what project managers perceptions are in relation to realistic project scheduling. These areas included the media view of success, creation and validation of schedules, main barriers to realistic schedule development, the impacts of optimism bias and reference class forecasting. The three themes developed by the research undertaken by Flyvbjerg of political, technical and psychological, provided an insightful framework which was then applied to the question-naires responses.

Considering that the number of interviews undertaken was relatively small and Australia-based, there were several distinct conclusions from this research. Reviewing the initial questions, the following conclusions are drawn.

In response to the first research question as to whether media reporting and how the project management community viewed whether this was an accurate portrayal of the area, the results from this research are interesting. Approximately half of respondents, believed that the results were reflective of their experiences, whilst the other half did not. Comments, also reflected a degree of frustration that the wider audience did not understand the complexity involved in managing a large software development project and that the original estimate, is that, an estimate and is not likely to be what happens in practice. Research in this area is inconsistent as an often-cited report from the Standish group called the Chaos report has proposed back in 1994 that software development projects had only a 16% success rate. This result improved over the subsequent years to 29%. However, this result has been questioned by Eveleens and Verhoef (2010, p.30) who argue that the Standish report is "misleading, one-sided, perverts the estimation process and results in meaningless figures". Thus, this area still requires further research and a wider survey of project managers would provide more insight into this area.

The second research question was developed to help understand approaches used to develop schedules. Arguably, this is one of the key elements in setting a project up for success, this paper, based upon interviews from within the project management community, in the main, reinforces current research. That is, adopting approaches such as building a schedule based upon using the bottom up approach (Jørgensen 2004b) applying a variety of estimating methods (Jorgensen 2014) and utilising Expert Judgement (Jorgensen 2005) will improve the likelihood of an achievable schedule. Within the respondents' answers, there was also a degree of applying intuition to the schedule. This was backed up by comments such as:

I used heuristics and rule of thumb, does this pass the sniff test, challenge and look for any areas of schedule compression which as mentioned previously has an inverse impact when adding more resources. [Respondent 6]

This demonstrated that these experienced project managers, were continuously reviewing and challenging their estimates.

Kahneman and Klein (2009) highlighted that intuitive judgements can be trusted within environments of high-validity, where there are clearly identifiable cue's which then cause subsequent events. Even though there is an argument that all projects are distinct, there are in fact, several common causes for problems. For example, if the chosen vendor is not able to meet their first deliverable time, this is a lead indicator that they may have issues in meeting their timelines. Thus, project managers with significant experience, such as the ones interviewed, would be looking for these types of patterns for early warning on schedule issues. Extending this concept, the project managers interviewed, could have been potentially automatically adding some type of extension of time, a de-facto contingency to all estimates provided to them by either their team or the vendor.

When reviewing the responses to what the main barriers to initial schedules are (third research question), two out of the three themes which had been identified in previous research emerged. These were Technical and Political. The impact of Psychological explanations to initial schedule creation, was not mentioned by any respondent as the main barrier, yet when asked directly whether optimism bias had impacted their initial schedule, there was unanimous agreement by the respondents that it had impacted their schedules.

There was little awareness within the respondents related to the fourth research question on approaches to mitigate the impacts of psychological factors, cited by Flyvbjerg (2009) such as outside view and reference class forecasting. Which given the level of support within the research literature for these approaches was a very significant finding of this research. In the sample interviewed, there was little, if any, knowledge, of either psychological factors and their impact on estimates, nor of the tools and techniques developed to mitigate them. This then also raises several other questions as to why the project managers were not aware of these tools and techniques to mitigate not only the psychological factors, but also political influence. Whether this is a training, communication or credibility issue with encouraging the use of these techniques is worthy of further research. Thus, it appears that we all accept that we have internal perceptions which cannot be quantified or actualised in real term. But because we are talking about professional expertise, you can't simply explain to your clients that my schedules are affected by psychological factors. This then leads to several further research questions into this area as to why project managers are not aware of these psychological factors, nor of approaches to mitigate them.

REFERENCES

Baccarini, D. (1999). The logical framework method for defining project success. *Project Management Journal, 30*(4), 25–32. doi:10.1177/875697289903000405

Batselier, J., & Vanhoucke, M. (2016). Practical application and empirical evaluation of reference class forecasting for project management. *Project Management Journal, 47*(5), 36–51. doi:10.1177/875697281604700504

Budzier, A., & Flyvbjerg, B. (2011). Double whammy–How ICT projects are fooled by randomness and screwed by political intent.

Chowdary, V., & Reddy, V. K. (2016). Software Effort Estimation: A Comparative Analysis. *International Journal of Progressive Sciences and Technologies, 2*(2), 48-60.

Davis, K. (2014). Different stakeholder groups and their perceptions of project success. *International Journal of Project Management, 32*(2), 189–201. doi:10.1016/j.ijproman.2013.02.006

Dawson, R. J., & Dawson, C. W. (1998). Practical proposals for managing uncertainty and risk in project planning. *International Journal of Project Management, 16*(5), 299–310. doi:10.1016/S0263-7863(97)00059-8

De Reyck, B., Grushka-Cockayne, Y., Lockett, M., Calderini, S. R., Moura, M., & Sloper, A. (2005). The impact of project portfolio management on information technology projects. *International Journal of Project Management, 23*(7), 524–537. doi:10.1016/j.ijproman.2005.02.003

Dolfi, J., & Andrews, E. J. (2007). 'The subliminal characteristics of project managers: An exploratory study of optimism overcoming challenge in the project management work environment. *International Journal of Project Management, 25*(7), 674–682. doi:10.1016/j.ijproman.2007.02.002

Eizakshiri, F., Chan, P. W., & Emsley, M. W. (2015). Where is intentionality in studying project delays? *International Journal of Managing Projects in Business, 8*(2), 349–367. doi:10.1108/IJMPB-05-2014-0048

Eveleens, J. L., & Verhoef, C. (2010). The rise and fall of the chaos report figures. *IEEE Software, 27*(1), 30–36. doi:10.1109/MS.2009.154

Fellows, R., & Liu, A. (2008). *Research Methods for Construction*. Chichester, UK: Wiley-Blackwell.

Flyvbjerg, B. (2008). Curbing optimism bias and strategic misrepresentation in planning: Reference class forecasting in practice. *European Planning Studies, 16*(1), 3–21. doi:10.1080/09654310701747936

Flyvbjerg, B. (2009). Optimism and misrepresentation in early project development. Making essential choices with scant information (pp. 147-168). Springer.

Francis, J. J., Johnston, M., Robertson, C., Glidewell, L., Entwistle, V., Eccles, M. P., & Grimshaw, J. M. (2010). What is an adequate sample size?: Operationalising data saturation for theory-based interview studies. *Psychology & Health, 25*(10), 1229–1245. doi:10.1080/08870440903194015 PMID:20204937

Frese, R., & Sauter, V. (2014). Improving your odds for software project success. *Engineering Management Review, IEEE., 42*(4), 125–131. doi:10.1109/EMR.2014.6966952

Hadad, Y., Keren, B., & Laslo, Z. (2013). A decision-making support system module for project manager selection according to past performance. *International Journal of Project Management, 31*(4), 532–541. doi:10.1016/j.ijproman.2012.10.004

Jørgensen, M. (2004a). A review of studies on expert estimation of software development effort. *Journal of Systems and Software, 70*(1), 37–60. doi:10.1016/S0164-1212(02)00156-5

Jørgensen, M. (2004b). Top-down and bottom-up expert estimation of software development effort. *Information and Software Technology, 46*(1), 3–16. doi:10.1016/S0950-5849(03)00093-4

Jorgensen, M. (2005). Practical guidelines for expert-judgment-based software effort estimation. *Software, 22*(3), 57–63. doi:10.1109/MS.2005.73

Jorgensen, M. (2014). What we do and don't know about software development effort estimation. *Software, 31*(2), 37–40. doi:10.1109/MS.2014.49

Kahneman, D., & Klein, G. (2009). Conditions for intuitive expertise: A failure to disagree. *The American Psychologist, 64*(6), 515–526. doi:10.1037/a0016755 PMID:19739881

Kahneman, D., & Tversky, A. (1977). *Intuitive prediction: Biases and corrective procedures*. DTIC Document.

Meyer, W. G. (2014). The effect of optimism bias on the decision to terminate failing projects. *Project Management Journal, 45*(4), 7–20. doi:10.1002/pmj.21435

Nasir, M. (2006). A survey of software estimation techniques and project planning practices. In *Seventh ACIS International Conference on Software Engineering, Artificial Intelligence, Networking, and Parallel/Distributed Computing (SNPD'06)*. 10.1109/SNPD-SAWN.2006.11

Pinto, J. K. (2013). Lies, damned lies, and project plans: Recurring human errors that can ruin the project planning process. *Business Horizons*, *56*(5), 643–653. doi:10.1016/j.bushor.2013.05.006

PMI. (2015). *Earning Power: Project Management Salary Survey*. Project Management Institute.

Prater, J., Kirytopoulos, K., & Ma, T. (2017). Optimism bias within the project management context: A systematic quantitative literature review. *International Journal of Managing Projects in Business*, *10*(2), 370–385. doi:10.1108/IJMPB-07-2016-0063

Smith, D. C., Bruyns, M., & Evans, S. (2011). A project manager's optimism and stress management and IT project success. *International Journal of Managing Projects in Business*, *4*(1), 10–27. doi:10.1108/17538371111096863

Veal, A. J. (2005). *Business research methods: A managerial approach*. Pearson Education Australia.

This research was previously published in the International Journal of Information Technology Project Management (IJITPM), 10(2); pages 29-40, copyright year 2019 by IGI Publishing (an imprint of IGI Global).

Chapter 96
Agile Team Measurement to Review the Performance in Global Software Development

Chamundeswari Arumugam

Sri Sivasubramaniya Nadar College of Engineering, India

Srinivasan Vaidyanathan

Cognizant Technology Solutions, India

ABSTRACT

This chapter is aimed at studying the key performance indicators of team members working in an agile project environment and in an extreme programming software development. Practitioners from six different XP projects were selected to respond to the survey measuring the performance indicators, namely, escaped defects, team member's velocity, deliverables, and extra efforts. The chapter presents a comparative view of Scrum and XP, the two renowned agile methods with their processes, methodologies, development cycles, and artifacts, while assessing the base performance indicators in XP setup. These indicators are key to any agile project in a global software development environment. The observed performance indicators were compared against the gold standard industry benchmarks along with best, average, and worst-case scenarios. Practitioners from six agile XP projects were asked to participate in the survey. Observed results best serve the practitioners to take necessary course corrections to stay in the best-case scenarios of their respective projects.

INTRODUCTION

The software organization has completely moved on to Global Software Development(GSD) (Chamundeswari, Srinivasan & Harini, 2018) as its tends to improve the productivity, in spite of the risk they undergo in terms of the practitioners, environment, culture, etc. Organization gives more priorities to these mainly for cost reduction. Practitioners also on their part has many risk to undergo to take up assignment in this GSD, but in spite of it they take up the assignment because of the money, relocation,

DOI: 10.4018/978-1-6684-3702-5.ch096

etc. This software development practice undergo four stages (Pressman, 2005), such as forming, stroming, norming and performing. Stage by stage the project progresses as a team for the product delivery. Due to agile approach the project team members can also progress in their skills to produce the best in them.

Though agile practices are many, taking the widely used aspect into concern, scrum and extreme programming is concentrated in this work. Agile, a Scrum process model (Bertrand, 2018) follow sprints or iteration to deliver a product. As the iteration flows it enables the customer to update their feedback and gets linked to next iteration delivery. Thus the incremental delivery for each iteration or sprint is achieved by this model. The team members co-operate to deliver the product in sprint as the project progress. Scrum has many key role members to execute a project development. It includes product owner, scrum master and team members. Each member has a role and task to be get committed on based on onsite or offshore project.

Extreme Programming (XP) is another agile framework that is widely used to produce high quality software by ensuring ease of development and quality of life for the team. XP is suitable when software requirements change dynamically, new technology is involved in a definitive timeline projects, team needs to be collocated for extended development, the selected technology lends itself for automated tests. It revolves around simplicity, communication, respect, courage and feedback. From a communication perspective, XP stresses on face to face communication through collocated teams. Simplicity involves keeping the design, coding simple so as to maintain easier support and revisions. Courage denotes bold decisions to doing what is right in the face of fear. Respect means demanding respect among the team members to freely give and accept feedback. In the feedback principle, teams identify areas of improvements and implement best practices.

The focus of the proposed work is inclined to analyze the key performance measure team members working in an Agile project environment in a Global Software Development(GSD)environment. Vital parameters that are important for the practitioners in various projects were chosen to survey the analyzes. Software production divisions follow many methodologies for GSD. Some organization follow scrum 100% while other follow extreme programming. Still it is open to follow any approach as far as the organization has the culture and practices deployed for ease of the productivity. Now, in this chapter, the two popular agile approaches scrum and extreme programming is taken up for discussion in the context of GSD practitioners. In this work, influencing parameters taken up to measure team member performance in XP is discussed.

BACKGROUND

Diane et al. (2012) proved agile model increases co-ordination effectiveness. Meghann et al. (2012) worked on decision making principles in agile software development. Emily et al. (2013) investigated the team performance using the team factors. Fabian et al. (2014) suggested few factors to improve the developer's performance. Mikko et al. (2014) identified five communication wastes in global agile projects and how to mitigate them to increase development. Srikrishnan et al. (2014) highlighted the risk culture and practice in agile software development. Ashay et al. (2014) worked on the virtual team member contribution towards global projects. Georgieos et al. (2015) observation states agile improves employee and customer satisfaction.

Paul et al. (2015) concentrated on various aspects beyond technical skill sets for the project team members and listed 53 attributes to assess their performance. Rafael et al. (2016) proposed guidelines to improve development strategy for developing quality product using virtual team members. Serhat et al (2016) proposed eleven influencing factors and dependency among the factors with respect to global project team members. Ricardo et al. (2016) used stochastic automata networks (SAN) to study the coordination in distributed project for a specific project configuration. Rafael (2016) analysed the agile software development practices and observed that it makes a positive effect. Torgeir et al. (2014) assessed the co-located team performance that follows agile practices for development.

David et al. (2016) assessed the traditional and targeted scrum and confirmed that targeted scrum has no remarkable change in top and worst performing teams. Yngve et al. (2016) assessed and observed that agile development has only minimal variation with respect to traditional software team. Daniel et al. (2017) performed a survey and analyzed the unhappiness of the software developer. Suggested and recommended the means to improve the fall condition. Itanaua et al. (2017) identified psychological factors with team members in agile method and concluded that trust has more significant impact among team members. Lucas et al. (2017) proved the fact that group maturity in team agility has influence towards the contribution of product. Leo at al. (2016) remarked industry has high use of agile methodologies and also its factors has influence in software development.

Christof et. al. (2017) discusses the five agile framework and its adaption in industry for delivery. Dinesh (2018) explored the agile values and mentioned that the productivity increases by adapting this practice. Sadath et al. (2018) applied extreme programming in student projects to improve the learning capability, knowledge and skill of the students. Ramlall et al. (2018) studied the influence of personality traits of programmers when working from same and remote locations in Extreme programming. The literature survey reveals that many researchers have done performance measures on agile practices. But in this research work, the performance measures of two agile practices that is followed in the industry is explored and one of the measures is discussed in detail.

Table 1. Literature survey comparison

Year	References	Comparison parameter	Number of authors (referred)
2012	[17]	Agile practices	6
2016	[22][15][9]		
2017	[6]		
2018	[10]		
2014	[18][28]	Risk	2
2000	[3]	Team Performance	18
2012	[17][7]		
2013	[11]		
2014	[1][12]		
2015	[13][19]		
2016	[21][27][25][29][9][30]		
2017	[8][14][16]		
2018	[23]		
2015	[13]	Customer satisfaction	1

OVERVIEW

Agile methodology (2016) has many methods to adapt for software development. Notably Scrum, Extreme programming are the two different types of methods taken up in this work for performance measurement. Agile methodology, scrum in GSD projects has scrum master, product owner, and team members to play a vital role in development (2018). Product owner may be a business analyst or customer who is responsible for product backlog, while scrum master organizes sprint meeting and responsible for sprint backlog. Product backlog has all feature information and sprint backlog has details about user stories and the delivery plan of various units in sprint. Team members split the tasks, in various sprint or iteration. Scrum block diagram is represented in Fig 1. It is expected that all team members complete the task without affecting business. But in normal scenario things may change.

Extreme programming (XP) is a well-known agile software development methodology created by Kent Beck (2000). XP is used for software development in various organization to produce high quality software with quality life for development team. XP is practiced because it follows five values, such as communication, simplicity, feedback, courage, and respect. Coding, testing, listening and designing are the four basic activities (SelectBS, n.d.) in this agile method. Customer or business analyst, who is a part of the team will jointly work with the developers. User stories of the customer requirements are delivered in short cycles of iteration and the stakeholder communicate their feedback to the developer for changes. To improve quality code, refactoring feature is enabled in testing. Extreme programming block diagram is represented in Fig 2.

Figure 1. Scrum process

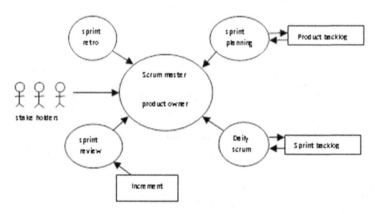

Figure 2. XP process - collocated environment

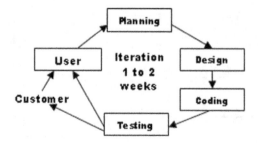

Scrum and XP are quite aligned but there are some delicate differences between them (Differences, n.d.). Scrum work is in sprints, that last for 2 to 4 weeks. Whereas XP work in iterations that last for 1 to weeks. While Scrum product backlog items are packaged and committed into a Sprint, changes are not entertained throughout the sprint cycle, XP allows for changes in its iterations. If the work on a specific features hasn't started, a new feature can be substituted into its iteration in swap of the other feature. In XP, customer determines the order of the work to be executed, whereas SCRUM product owner determines order of priority in SCRUM and the team gets the flexibility of working in a sequence according to the project resources and code constraints. XP advocates engineering practices while SCRUM doesn't prescribe any. Simple design, Pair programming, test-driven development, refactoring and automated testing are some of the practices XP mandates. SCRUM doesn't mandate such practices rather let the team figure them out on their own. Figure 3. represents the differences between scrum and XP.

Figure 3. Difference between Scrum and XP

Agile Metrics

The success factor in GSD projects depends on the productive team members. Adapting XP practice and measuring the team members to study the progress of success rate in the organization is really challengeable. Already the KPI for agile scrum practice to measure the team member performance was defined (Chamundeswari, Sriraghav, & Baskaran, 2017) and here this measurement is compared with XP practice to study the resultant outcome of the two agile practices. The productive team members are the building blocks of the organization and the Key Performance Indicator (KPI) to measure them is discussed in Equation 1 to 4.

Escaped defects, a metrics to track the defects in the delivered product. It is essential to measure this metrics to apply the corrective steps at the early stage. The metric function F1, is stated in Equation 1.

Equation 1: Escaped defects$_{\text{iteration\#i}}(F1) =$

$$\frac{\text{No. of escaped defects in an iteration by a team member}}{\text{Total no. of escaped defects in an iteration}}$$

An iteration has many user stories, and each user stories has many tasks to which team members get committed in an iteration. Generally, each iteration may span to 1 to 2 weeks. The metric function F2, is stated in Equation 2.

Equation 2: Team member velocity$_{\text{iteration\#i}}$(F2) =

$$\frac{\text{No. of task completed by a team member in an iteration}}{\text{Total no. of committed tasks in an iteration}}$$

Deliverables metrics, measures actual hours taken by a team member in an iteration to complete a task from the total planned hours. The metric function F3, is stated is Equation 3.

Equation 3: Deliverables$_{\text{iteration\#i}}$(F3) =

$$\frac{\text{Actual hrs spent to complete committed task in an iteration}}{\text{Total planned hrs to complete committed task in an iteration}}$$

Extra effort spent by a member to develop defect free complete his task is an important metrics to measure the total effort spent to deliver a defect free product. The metrics function F4, is given in Equation 4.

Equation 4: Extra Effort$_{\text{sprint\#i}}$ (F4) =

$$\frac{\text{Extra hrs worked to fix bugs in an iteration by a team member}}{\text{Actual hrs spent to complete committed task in an iteration} + \text{Extra hours}}$$

RESULTS AND DISCUSSION

Four defined metrics in Section 4 are assessed by framing seven questions to extract the response from practitioners, following the context given in this work. Table 2. represents the questions framed to extract the answers for the metrics defined in Section "Agile Metrics". Judgmental or purposive sampling was done in identifying the projects for participation in the survey. The practitioners were chosen from 6 different IT companies who executed Agile XP projects. Anonymity of data was ensured prior to analyzing and interpreting the results.

Table 2. Survey questions for defined metrics.

Metrics	Survey questions
F1	• How many defects likely occur in your task per iteration ? • How many defects likely occur by all team members in a project per iteration ?
F2	• Quantify the tasks committed in a project per iteration. • Quantify the tasks you complete in an iteration.
F3	• What is the actual hours taken to complete your committed task in an iteration? • What is the planned hours to complete committed task in an iteration?
F4	• Did you took extra hours to fix bugs in your committed task in an iteration ?
-	• Feedback about the survey.

Seven survey questions were framed for the four metrics defined. Survey questionnaire was circulated to the identified practitioners, practicing the agile extreme programming for their projects in their respective organizations. Metrics data along with industry bench mark (Chamundswari et al., 2018), best, average, and worst case is represented in Table 3.

Table 3. Metrics data

Metrics	Project 1 (P1)	Project 2 (P2)	Project 3 (P3)	Project 4 (P4)	Project 5 (P5)	Project 6 (P6)
F1	0.1(best case)	0.2(avg case)	0.3(avg case)	0(best case)	0.3(avg case)	0.25(best case)
F2	0.1(worst case)	0.375(worst case)	0.3(worst case)	1 (best case)	1 (best case)	1(best case)
F3	1(best case)	1.2(best case)	10	0.8(avg case)	1(best case)	1(best case)
F4	0.16(best case)	0.05(best case)	0.25(avg case)	0(best case)	0(best case)	0(best case)

It is identified that the 5 project metrics out of 6 projects is measurable and only one project data, project 3 is not correct. Project 1, 2, 4, 5 and 6 were measurable. The graph was plotted with collected data and represented in Fig. 4. From the graph, it is observed that the P1 and P2 has some worst case scenario and need focus on the software practitioners who are involved in development.

FUTURE RESEARCH DIRECTIONS

As a future extension, with a larger sample base, AI based clustering and prediction algorithms can be leveraged in grouping the inputs and predicting the output respectively based on historical data patterns. Future researchers can assume and study the effect of additional performance indicators for empirical analysis from both Scrum and XP perspectives to verify the consistency of results. Also, the study can be repeated with projects of varying degrees of complexity and observe results. Finally the study can also be repeated for varying scopes of the projects and technological implementations, may it be legacy, new or digital technologies.

Figure 4. Metrics data representation

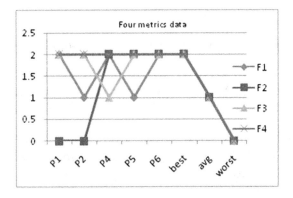

CONCLUSION

This chapter has taken a plunge into the set of base performance indicators to measure the team performance and act upon the right signals on a XP project. Practitioners from six Agile XP projects in IT industry participated in the survey. From the preliminary data analysis, Project 3's data weren't measurable and hence was discarded. Other set of projects' data were subjected to detailed analysis and it was concluded that:

- The performance metric "Team Member Velocity" needed focus for the practitioners of Projects 1 and 2. They need to implement substantial changes to the committed total number of tasks in an iteration and the number of tasks completed by the team members in that iteration. That will help them to improve from worst case to the best case scenario to stay aligned with industry benchmarks.
- The performance metric "Escaped Defects" needed focus for the practitioners of Projects 2 and 5. They need to implement moderate changes to the escaped total number of defects in an iteration and the number of escaped defects by the team members in that iteration. That will help them to improve from average case to the best case scenario to stay aligned with industry benchmarks.
- The performance meric "Deliverables" needed focus for the practitioner of Project 4. The practitioner needs to implement moderate changes to the planned total number of hours to complete committed tasks in an iteration and the actual number of hours spent by the team members in that iteration. That will help to improve from average case to the best case scenario to stay aligned with industry benchmarks.

Observed results best serve the practitioners to take necessary course corrections to stay in the best case scenarios of their respective projects. The study also proves the point that while Scrum and XP are two different agile methodologies, the base performance indicators to measure the project and team members productivity are applicable to both.

REFERENCES

Ashay, S., & Johanna, B. (2014). Factors affecting team performance in globally distributed setting. *Proceedings of the 52nd ACM conference on Computers and people research*, 25-33.

Beck, K. (2000). *Extreme Programming Explained: Embrace Change*. Reading, MA: Addison Wesley Longman, Inc.

Bertrand, M. (2018). Making Sense of Agile Methods. *IEEE Software*, 91–94.

Chamundeswari, A., Srinivasan, V., & Harini, K. (2018). Global Software Development: Key Performance Measures of Team in a SCRUM based Agile Environment. In *19th International Conference on Computational Science and Applications, Proceedings published in Springer LNCS*. Monash University.

Chamundeswari, A., Sriraghav, K., & Baskaran, K. (2017). Global Software Development: A design framework to measure the risk of the global practitioners. In *ACM International Conference on Computer and Communication Technology*. Motilal Nehru National Institute of Technology.

Christof, E., & Maria, P. (2017). Scaling Agile. *IEEE Software*, 98–103.

Daniel, G., Fabian, F., Xiaofeng, W., & Pekka, A. (2017). Consequences of unhappiness while developing software. *Proceedings of the 2nd International Workshop on Emotion Awareness in Software Engineering*, 42-47.

David, P. H., & Arvin, A. (2016). Targeted Scrum: Applying Mission Command to Agile Software Development. *IEEE Transactions on Software Engineering*, *42*(5), 476–489. doi:10.1109/TSE.2015.2489654

Diane, E. S., Sid, L. H., Beverley, H., & Sebastian, L. (2012). Coordination in co-located agile software development projects. *Journal of Systems and Software*, *85*(6), 1222–1238. doi:10.1016/j.jss.2012.02.017

Differences Between Scrum And Extreme Programming. (n.d.). Retrieved from https://www.mountaingoatsoftware.com/blog/differences-between-scrum-and-extreme-programming

Dinesh, B. (2018). Agile values or plan-driven aspects: Which factor contributes more toward the success of data warehousing, business intelligence, and analytics project development? *Journal of Systems and Software*, *146*, 249–262. doi:10.1016/j.jss.2018.09.081

Emily, W., Ariadi, N., Joost, V., & Aske, P. (2013). Towards high performance software teamwork. *Proceedings of the 17th International Conference on Evaluation and Assessment in Software Engineering*, 212-215.

Fabian, F., Marko, I., Petri, K., Jürgen, M., Virpi, R., & Pekka, A. (2014). How do software developers experience team performance in lean and agile environments? *Proceedings of the 18th International Conference on Evaluation and Assessment in Software Engineering*.

Georgios, P. (2015). Moving from traditional to agile software development methodologies also on large, distributed projects. *Procedia: Social and Behavioral Sciences*, *175*, 455–463. doi:10.1016/j.sbspro.2015.01.1223

Itanauã, F. B., Marcela, P. O., Priscila, B. S. R., Tancicleide, C. S. G., & Fabio, Q. B. D. S. (2017). Towards understanding the relationships between interdependence and trust in software development: a qualitative research. *10th International Workshop on Cooperative and Human Aspects of Software Engineering*, 66-69.

Leo, R. V., & Charles, W. B. (2016). Choice of Software Development Methodologies Do Organizational, Project, and Team Characteristics Matter? *IEEE Software*, 86–94.

Lucas, G., Richard, T., & Robert, F. (2017). Group development and group maturity when building agile teams: A qualitative and quantitative investigation at eight large companies. *Journal of Systems and Software*, *124*, 104–119. doi:10.1016/j.jss.2016.11.024

Meghann, D., Kieran, C., & Ken, P. (2012). Obstacles to decision making in Agile software development teams. *Journal of Systems and Software*, *85*(6), 1239–1254. doi:10.1016/j.jss.2012.01.058

Mikko, K., & Frank, M. (2014). Waste identification as the means for improving communication in globally distributed agile software development. *Journal of Systems and Software*, *95*, 122–140. doi:10.1016/j.jss.2014.03.080

Paul, L., Andrew, J. K., & Jiamin, Z. (2015). What makes a great software engineer? *37th International Conference on Software Engineering*, 700-710.

Pressman, R. (2005). *Software Engineering: A Practitioner's Approach*. McGraw-Hill.

Rafael, P., Casper, L., Evelyn, T., & Jeffrey, C. C. (2016). Trends in Agile Perspectives from the Practitioners. *IEEE Software*, 20–22.

Rafael, P., Marcelo, P., & Sabrina, M. (2016). Virtual Team Configurations that Promote Better Product Quality. *Proceedings of the 10th ACM/IEEE International Symposium on Empirical Software Engineering and Measurement*.

Ramlall, P., & Chuttur, M. Y. (2018). An Experimental Study to Investigate Personality Traits on Pair Programming Efficiency in Extreme Programming. *5th International Conference on Industrial Engineering and Applications*, 95 - 99.

Ricardo, B., Darja, Š., & Lars-Ola, D. (2016). Experiences from Measuring Learning and Performance in Large-Scale Distributed Software Development. *Proceedings of the 10th ACM/IEEE International Symposium on Empirical Software Engineering and Measurement*.

Ricardo, M.C., Paulo, F., Lucelene, L., Afonso, S., Alan R. S., & Thais, W. (2016). Stochastic Performance Analysis of Global Software Development Teams. *ACM Transactions on Software Engineering and Methodology*, 25(3), 26:1-26:32.

Sadath, L., Karim, K., & Gill, S. (2018). Extreme programming implementation in academia for software engineering sustainability. *International Conference on Advances in Science and Engineering Technology*, 1-6. 10.1109/ICASET.2018.8376925

Serhat, S., Ramazan, K., & Bulent, S. (2016). Factors Affecting Multinational Team Performance. *Procedia: Social and Behavioral Sciences*, 25(3), 60–69.

Srikrishnan, S., Marath, B., & Pramod, K. V. (2014). Case study on risk management practice in large offshore-outsourced Agile software projects. *IET Software*, 8(6), 245–257. doi:10.1049/iet-sen.2013.0190

Torgeir, D., Tor, E. F., Tore, D., Børge, H., & Yngve, L. (2016). Team Performance in Software Development Research Results versus Agile Principles. *IEEE Software*, 106–110.

What Is Extreme Programming? (XP). (n.d.). Retrieved from http://www.selectbs.com/process-maturity/what-is-extreme-programming

Yngve, L., Dag, I. K. S., Torgeir, D., Gunnar, R. B., & Tore, D. (2016). Teamwork quality and project success in software development: A survey of agile development teams. *Journal of Systems and Software*, 122, 274–286. doi:10.1016/j.jss.2016.09.028

ADDITIONAL READING

Saru, D., Deepak, K., & Singh, V. B. (2018). Success and Failure Factors that Impact on Project Implementation Using Agile Software Development Methodology. *Software Engineering. Springer AISC.*, *731*, 647–654.

This research was previously published in Crowdsourcing and Probabilistic Decision-Making in Software Engineering; pages 81-93, copyright year 2020 by Engineering Science Reference (an imprint of IGI Global).

Chapter 97
Measuring Developers' Software Security Skills, Usage, and Training Needs

Tosin Daniel Oyetoyan
Western Norway University of Applied Sciences, Norway

Martin Gilje Gilje Jaatun
https://orcid.org/0000-0001-7127-6694
SINTEF Digital, Norway

Daniela Soares Cruzes
SINTEF Digital, Norway

ABSTRACT

Software security does not emerge fully formed by divine intervention in deserving software development organizations; it requires that developers have the required theoretical background and practical skills to enable them to write secure software, and that the software security activities are actually performed, not just documented procedures that sit gathering dust on a shelf. In this chapter, the authors present a survey instrument that can be used to investigate software security usage, competence, and training needs in agile organizations. They present results of using this instrument in two organizations. They find that regardless of cost or benefit, skill drives the kind of activities that are performed, and secure design may be the most important training need.

INTRODUCTION

Traditional security engineering processes are often associated with additional development efforts and are likely to be unpopular among agile development teams (ben Othmane et al., 2014; Beznosov & Kruchten, 2004). A software security approach tailored to the agile mind-set thus seems necessary.

DOI: 10.4018/978-1-6684-3702-5.ch097

Some approaches have been proposed to integrate security activities into agile development, e.g., the Microsoft SDL for Agile (Microsoft, 2012). However, these approaches have been criticised for looking too similar to the traditional versions in terms of workload (e.g., performing a long list of security verification and validation tasks) (ben Othmane et al., 2014). As a result, "agile" organizations have approached software security in a way that better fits their process and practices. Thus, regardless of whether agile is perceived to be incompatible with any particular secure software development lifecycle, the major discussion we should have is how to improve security within the agile context (Bartsch, 2011). Previous studies (Ayalew et al., 2013; Baca & Carlsson, 2011) have investigated which security activities are practiced in different organizations, and which are compatible with agile practices from cost and benefit perspectives. Using a survey of software security activities among software practitioners, they identify and recommend certain security activities that are compatible with agile practices.

While these activities could be argued to be beneficial and cost effective to integrate, there are still gaps between what is "adequate" security (Allen, 2005), and what is currently practiced within several organizations. According to Allen (2005), adequate security is defined as *"The condition where the protection and sustainability strategies for an organization's critical assets and business processes are commensurate with the organization's tolerance for risk"*.

BACKGROUND

Software security has existed as a distinct field of research for over a decade, and reached prominence with the publication of the book "Software Security" (Gary McGraw, 2006).

The studies by Ayalew et al. (2013), Baca and Carlsson (2011), and Morrison et al. (2017) have investigated security activities from cost and benefit dimensions to advise on frameworks and selection of security activities that can be integrated to agile software development. Jaatun et al. (2015) have used BSIMM to measure security practices but with focus on security maturity at an organisational level. Other studies not directly related to our work have looked into market skills relevant for cybersecurity jobs. For example, Potter and Vickers (2015) used a questionnaire to answer and address the question of what skills does a security professional need in the current information technology environment, and they explored this question by looking at the current state of the Australian industry. Fontenele (Fontenele, 2017) developed a conceptual model and an ontological methodology to aid a robust discovery of the fittest expertise driven by the specific needs of cyber security projects, as well as benchmarking expertise shortages.

Our work differs from these studies as we have measured developers' skills and training needs along software security activities.

Secure Software Development Lifecycles

A number of Secure Software Development Lifecycles (SSDLs) have been proposed, in the following we briefly introduce to most important ones as they relate to this paper.

OWASP CLASP

The Comprehensive, Lightweight Application Security Process (CLASP) (OWASP, 2006) was a project under the Open Web Application Security Project (OWASP). A high-level overview of CLASP is given in Figure 1. CLASP was based on seven best practices:

1. Institute awareness programs
2. Perform application assessments
3. Capture security requirements
4. Implement secure development practices
5. Build vulnerability remediation procedures
6. Define and monitor metrics
7. Publish operational security guidelines

CLASP has not been updated since 2006, and is currently considered abandoned. However, some of the CLASP activities can still be considered useful by themselves.

Figure 1. CLASP Overview

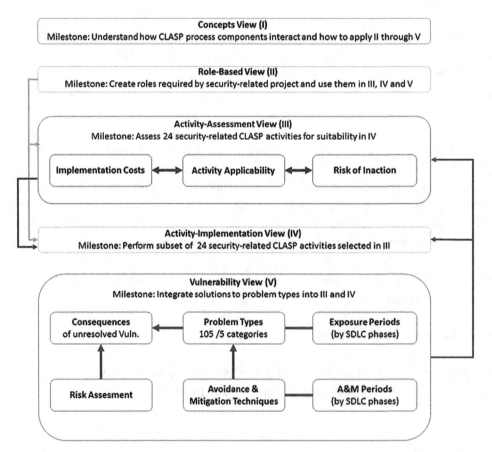

Microsoft SDL for Agile

The Microsoft Security Development Lifecycle for Agile Development (SDL-Agile) (Microsoft, 2012) is the agile version of the traditional Microsoft SDL (Howard & Lipner, 2006). SDL-Agile is split into three types of activities (see Table 1);

- **"Every-Sprint Requirements" (S):** These activities should be performed in every iteration
- **"Bucket Requirements" (B):** These activities must be performed on a regular basis during the development lifecycle; there are three types of such requirements defined (each type referred to as a bucket) and typically one is picked from each bucket in each sprint
- **"One-Time Requirements" (O):** These activities typically only need to be performed once at the beginning of the project.

Figure 2. The SDL-agile one-time and bucket requirements illustrated

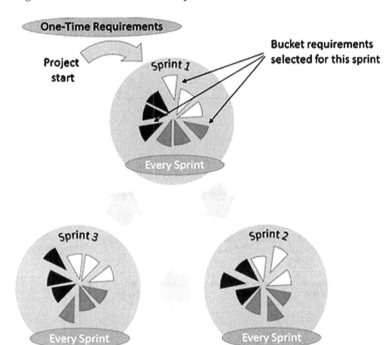

Cigital Touchpoints

The Cigital Touchpoints (Gary McGraw, 2004; Gary McGraw, 2005) (de Win et al., 2009) were introduced as a lightweight way of distilling the essence of practical software security. They have been presented slightly different over the years, but the essence is as illustrated in Figure 3.

In order of effectiveness, the 7 touchpoints are:

1. Code review

2.   Architectural risk analysis
3.   Penetration testing
4.   Risk-based security tests
5.   Abuse cases
6.   Security requirements
7.   Security operations

Table 1. MS SDL-agile activities – (o)ne-time, (s)print, and (b)ucket

1. Training	2. Requirement	3. Design	4. Implementation	5. Verification	6. Release	7. Response
1. Core Security Training	2. Establish Security Requirements (O)	5. Establish Design Requirements (O)	8. Use Approved Tools (S)	11. Perform Dynamic Analysis (B)	14. Create an Incident Response Plan (O)	17. Execute Incident Response Plan
	3. Create Quality Bug Bars (B)	6. Perform Attack Surface Analysis/ Reduction (O)	9. Deprecate Unsafe Functions (S)	12. Perform Fuzz Testing (B)	15. Conduct Final Security Review (S)	
	4. Perform Security and Privacy Risk Assessments (O)	7. Use Threat Modeling (S)	10. Perform Static Analysis (S)	13. Conduct Attack Surface Review (B)	16. Certify Release and Archive (S)	

Figure 3. The cigital touchpoints

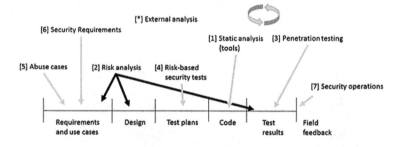

ISO/IEC Application Security Standard

In 2011, the International Standards Organization published an application security standard as part of its 27000-series (ISO/IEC, 2011). We have not seen this standard in use in any of the organizations we have worked with, but it may prove relevant in the future.

Measuring Software Security Activities

Measuring software security is difficult (Jaatun, 2012), and therefore second-order metrics are often employed, i.e., measuring what kind of software security activities are performed when developing the software.

OpenSAMM

The OWASP Software Assurance Maturity Model (SAMM or OpenSAMM) (OWASP, 2016) is an open software security framework divided into four business functions: Governance, Construction, Verification and Deployment. Each business function is composed of three security practices, as shown in Table 2.

Table 2. The OpenSAMM software security framework

Governance	Construction	Verification	Deployment
Strategy and Metrics	Threat Assessment	Design Review	Vulnerability Management
Policy & Compliance	Security Requirements	Code Review	Environment Hardening
Education & Guidance	Secure Architecture	Security Testing	Operational Enablement

Each practice is assessed at a maturity level from 1 to 3 (plus 0 for "no maturity"), and for each maturity level there is an objective and two activities that have to be fulfilled to achieve that level. OpenSAMM is "prescriptive", in the sense that it advocates that all the specified activities must be performed in order to be a high-maturity organisation.

BSIMM

The Building Security In Maturity Model (BSIMM) first saw the light of day in 2009, based on a study of 9 software development organizations. BSIMM is structured around a Software Security Framework of four domains, each divided into three practices, as illustrated in Table 3. As is evident from the table, BSIMM shares origins with the OpenSAMM framework described above. The latest version of the BSIMM report (Gary McGraw et al., 2018) features results from 120 companies, measuring 116 different software security activities.

Although BSIMM also ranks software security activities in three maturity levels, it purports to be descriptive rather than prescriptive, and there is no implicit expectation that all organizations should do all 116 activities. Due to the large number of software security activities, BSIMM can said to be more specific than OpenSAMM. New BSIMM activities are added as they are observed in the field, and activities that fall out of use are removed. The maturity level of a given activity can also be changed from one version of the study to the next.

Table 3. The BSIMM software security framework

Governance	Intelligence	SSDL Touchpoints	Deployment
Strategy and Metrics	Attack Models	Architecture Analysis	Penetration Testing
Compliance and Policy	Security Features and Design	Code Review	Software Environment
Training	Standards and Requirements	Security Testing	Configuration Management and Vulnerability Management)

BSIMM has also been used to measure security practices in different organizations. Jaatun et al. (2015) used a questionnaire based on the BSIMM activities to measure the security maturity of Norwegian public organizations. They found that there is a need for improvements in metrics, penetration testing and training developers in secure development. BSIMM is useful for measuring the software security maturity of an organization and helping them formulate overall security strategy (Gary McGraw et al., 2018). However, it is not perceived as a lightweight measurement tool to directly measure developers' skill or usage of software security activities within a development team.

Common Criteria

The Common Criteria (ISO/IEC, 2009) (CC) emerged toward the end of the previous century as an amalgamation of the US DoD Trusted Computer Systems Evaluation Criteria (TCSEC, a.k.a. "the Orange Book"), the European ITSEC and the Canadian CTCPEC. CC is used in the security evaluation of computer-based systems, typically for military or critical infrastructure use. A fundamental concept of CC is that a Protection Profile containing functional security requirements and security assurance requirements is established. A security assurance requirement is intended to help achieve a certain level of confidence that the claimed (functional) security requirements are fulfilled, and typically relate to *how* the system is developed. There are sets of predefined security assurance requirements which are referred to as Evaluation Assurance Levels (EAL1-7). The manufacturer will create a Security Target document which elaborates how the requirements of the Protection Profile are met, and finally an external evaluator will perform an evaluation to confirm or reject the claims.

CC is essentially a long list of requirements, and it is totally up to the Protection Profile which requirements are considered for a given product. Some of the assurance requirements are effectively software security activities.

The Top 10 Software Security Design Flaws

The IEEE Center for Secure Design has published a document (Arce et al., 2014) explaining how to avoid the ten most common software security design flaws. The recommendations are as follows:

1. Earn or Give, but Never Assume, Trust
2. Use an Authentication Mechanism that Cannot be Bypassed or Tampered With
3. Authorize after You Authenticate
4. Strictly Separate Data and Control Instructions, and Never Process Control Instructions Received from Untrusted Sources
5. Define an Approach that Ensures all Data are Explicitly Validated
6. Use Cryptography Correctly
7. Identify Sensitive Data and How They Should Be Handled
8. Always Consider the Users
9. Understand How Integrating External Components Changes Your Attack Surface
10. Be Flexible When Considering Future Changes to Objects and Actors

RESEARCH METHODOLOGY AND STUDY DESIGN

The research presented here is motivated based on the perceived knowledge gaps in software security in agile software development organizations in Norway (Jaatun et al., 2015). In order to address these gaps, management must first understand the current status of software security practices and capability within their organization. We used our survey instrument in a study carried out in 2 organizations (in the following referred to as "Org-1" and "Org-2"), that develop software in telecommunication and transportation, respectively. The case study is described in more detail in our previous work (Oyetoyan et al., 2016; Oyetoyan et al., 2017) investigating existing practice, skills, and training needs within agile teams. The survey instrument is intended to shed light on the training needs and understand the relationships between skills and usage of security activities among teams and across roles. The findings are important to guide management decisions towards improving security within their organization.

The sections below describe the research questions, hypotheses, data collection procedure that we used in our case studies, the instruments used, and the type of data analysis performed.

Research Questions

We make the following assumptions that:

- Developers have relatively different skills in software security, regardless of the organization where they currently work.
- Agile organizations have different usage patterns with software security activities. An agile team is mostly autonomous and self-confident (Robinson & Sharp, 2004), and thus makes decisions that the team members think best contribute to customer satisfaction and product quality. Since activities are chosen in a voluntary manner in agile settings, we believe that organizations would use activities that best fit their process and business needs.
- Based on conventional wisdom, using an activity requires certain level of know-how. Hence, teams would use activities where they have competence.
- Experienced developers would most probably have taken security related decisions during their development career, and thus have knowledge and experience in software security.

Our instrument is suitable for investigating whether the skills, usage and training needs in software security activities in several organizations are similar or different. Understanding the similarities and differences between organizations also help during replications and adoptions of software security activities and programs across different organizations.

The research questions that could be addressed include:

- Which software security activities are most used within the organization?
- Which training needs are important to the organization?
- How are security experience and the perceived need for software security training influenced by years of developer of experience?
- What is the relationship between usage of, and skill in software security activities?

Data Collection

The method of choice for the project is Action Research (Greenwood & Levin, 2006). Action research is an appropriate research methodology for this investigation for several reasons. First, the study's combination of scientific and practical objectives is a good match with the basic tenet of action research, which is to merge theory and practice in a way that real-world problems are solved by theoretically informed actions in collaboration between researchers and practitioners (Greenwood & Levin, 2006). Therefore, the design of the instruments had to take in consideration the usefulness of the results for the companies and for research.

In addition, for the interpretation and discussion of the results, answers from the survey should be complemented by document analysis of project artifacts, observations of meetings, and discussions with different stakeholders in the companies. Other focused interviews on specific topics, and the feedback from the survey results, should be compared with the collected information about the organizational contexts and documents.

Survey Questionnaire

The questionnaire was designed in phases, getting feedback from the companies and experts for getting to the final version. The first version of the questionnaire contained questions on different software security activities from OWASP CLASP, Microsoft SDL for Agile, Common Criteria, and Cigital Touchpoints that have been used in previous studies (Ayalew et al., 2013; Baca & Carlsson, 2011). The table also includes additional practices such as "pair programming" and "drawing a countermeasure graph" considered in these studies; both are common security activities used in agile settings, e.g., when security experts rotate through programming pairs (Bartsch, 2011; Wäyrynen et al., 2004).

The instrument has been jointly reviewed by the authors, a security professional, a security champion and a project manager. The activities are classified differently than in the traditional software development lifecycle (SDLC), but they do, however, fit into each development lifecycle. The rationale is to invoke a different way of perceiving these activities than from a traditional viewpoint. This could make it possible to spot some assumptions such as for instance, whereas secure design involves many activities from "Threat modelling and risk management", we can argue that software designers could make assumptions about secure design when they include, e.g., authentication mechanisms (Arce et al., 2014). However, performing a comprehensive threat analysis could reveal an insecure design, e.g., a possibility to bypass an authentication or authorization mechanism by directly navigating to an obscure webpage or resource.

Similarly, we have considered software security tools separately in order to identify strong and weak areas of usage and skills. Findings from the survey can trigger further questions, e.g., why certain implemented tools are not used within the organization, and this could lead to useful actions. These activities are divided into: Inception, threat modelling and risk management, secure design and coding, security tools, security testing, and release. Table 5 shows the software security activities. In addition, we provided a short explanation of each term we have used in the survey for the respondents. We have used a scale for the skill level as shown in Table 4; the respondents were instructed to use this scale when assessing their own skill level.

For the software activities listed in Table 5, we asked the following 3 questions:

Q1: What is your skill level in this activity or tool?
Q2: Do you currently use this activity or tool? (Check box for yes)
Q3: Do you want to have training in this activity or tool? (Check box for yes)

In addition, we asked 2 questions about security and development experience:

Q4: Do you have security experience? (Yes or no)
Q5: Number of years with software development.

We have designed both an online questionnaire and a paper-based version. We further refined the instrument by running a test on our industrial contacts, an independent architect and a post-doctoral fellow in software engineering. The target response time was 10-12 minutes. In our experience, administering the questionnaire manually to the development teams on site will increase the response rate, and provide the opportunity to clarify questions that respondents might have.

The final questionnaire can be found in the original paper (Oyetoyan et al., 2017), and is also provided in Appendix A in this chapter. The skills are listed in Table 5, and additional explanations are further provided in Appendix A.

Table 4. Scale for skill level

Novice [1]	Basic [2]	Moderate [3]	High [4]	Expert [5]
Have no experience working in this area	You have the level of experience gained in a classroom and/or experimental scenarios or as a trainee on-the-job. You are expected to need help when performing in this area	You are able to successfully complete tasks in this area as requested. Help from an expert may be required from time to time, but you can usually perform the skill independently	You can perform the actions associated in this area without assistance. You are certainly recognized within your immediate organization as "a person to ask" when difficult questions arise regarding this area	You are known as an expert in this area. You can provide guidance, troubleshoot and answer questions related to this area of expertise and the field where the skill is used

Comparing with the software security activities defined in BSIMM (Gary McGraw et al., 2018), we find that most of the activities in Table 5 are fully or partly covered by BSIMM, except "Countermeasure techniques", "Pair programming", and "Use of threat modelling tool". Threat modelling is equivalent to what BSIMM calls "Architecture Analysis", but this practice does not mention using a tool.

RESULTS

We used our survey instrument on two local companies (Oyetoyan et al., 2017), and in the following we briefly present some results of the survey and analysis conducted among the two organizations, discussing each research question in turn.

Table 5. Mapping of software security activities

	CLASP	MS-SDL	CT	CC	Others	BSIMM Activities
Inception						
Functioning as project security officer/ champion	*	*				SM1.2, SM2.3, T2.5, T2.7, T3.1, T3.5
Gathering security requirements	*	*	*	*		Partly covered by SR1.3 (Maybe whole practice SR)
Writing abuse stories/cases	*		*			AM2.1, ST3.5
Threat Modeling and Risk Management						
Threat modeling	*	*				Practice AM
Attack surface analysis	*	*				Partly covered by Practice AM
Countermeasure techniques	*	*				-
Asset analysis				*		Partly covered by AM1.2, CP2.1
Risk analysis	*		*	*		AA2.1
Role matrix identification	*					SM1.1
Secure Design and Coding						
Secure design	*	*	*			SFD1.2, SFD2.1, SFD2.2, SFD3.3
Secure coding	*	*	*			SR2.6, CR3.5
Pair programming				*		-
Static code analysis	*	*	*			Practice CR
Use of Security Tools						
Use of threat modeling tool				*		-
Use of dynamic code analysis tool				*		Partly covered by practice PT
Use of static code analysis tool				*		Partly covered by CR1.4
Use of code review tool				*		CR1.4, CR2.5, CR2.6, CR3.4
Security Testing						
Vulnerability assessment						Partly covered by practice AM
Penetration testing			*			Practice PT
Red team testing						PT1.1, PT1.3, PT3.1
Fuzz testing		*				ST2.6
Dynamic testing	*					Partly covered by Practice CR and ST
Risk-based testing			*			Practice ST
Security code review	*		*			Practice CR
Release						
Incident response management	*	*				CMVM1.1, CMVM2.1, CMVM3.3

Which Activities Are Most Used Within the Organizations?

Research performed by Microsoft (Adams, 2012) indicates that only 36% of developers are confident to write secure software. Our small sample indicates that this situation still persists. Our results show that the three most commonly used activities were:

- Use of code review tool
- Static code analysis
- Pair programming.

Note that none of these are necessarily pure software security activities, and may indeed be used without improving software security at all.

Which Training Needs Are Important to the Organizations?

In our study, secure design was indicated as the single most important training need expressed by teams in both organizations. There is thus a need to focus on how to address and assist agile teams in the area of secure design. Architectural-related challenges such as lack of time, motivation to consider design choices, and unknown domain and untried solutions have been shown to affect agile development teams (Babar, 2009).

Figure 4. % of Training Needs across all roles compared between the 2 organizations

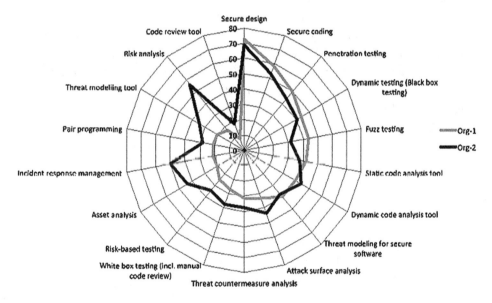

How Are Security Experience and the Perceived Need for Software Security Training Influenced by Years of Developer Experience?

We can infer that training needs may or may not be influenced by years of development experience. Factors such as an organization's working culture, teams' distribution, teams' interactions, security experience, and how new employees are integrated could be responsible for training needs perceptions across different years of experience.

Zhu et al. (2013) argued that only a small fraction of developers are well trained in secure software development. This is because most Computer Science (CS) and Software Engineering (SE) curricula train students in programming and application development, but not secure software development. As a result, CS and SE graduates are not trained in programming techniques to reduce security bugs and vulnerabilities and would unintentionally introduce avoidable security bugs in the application. While this result is not surprising, we believe it should be a call to integrate software security education in the curriculum for the next generation of CS and SE graduates.

What Is the Relationship Between Usage of, and Skill in Software Security Activities?

Correlation analysis between indicated skill levels and usage of activities shows that skill drives usage of activities. In both organizations, the correlation result is very high at more than 0.9 and statistically significant at 95% confidence interval. Regardless of the cost of activity, we found that teams do well in activities where they indicate high level of skills. The studies by Baca & Carlsson (2011) and Ayaew et al. (2013) report code review to be detrimental in cost and benefit and pair programming to have marginal benefit and detrimental in cost to agile. However, our findings reveal that code review and pair programming are well practiced in both organizations and are areas where respondents indicate high skill levels.

Pair programming is an important practice in eXtreme Programming (XP) and by itself includes the art of code review (Beck, 1999). In addition, peer code review is claimed to catch about 60% of the defects (Boehm & Basili, 2005). These could explain the reasons both organizations have adopted these practices. The work of Dybå et al. (2004) that investigated the factors affecting software developer acceptance and utilization of Electronic Process Guides (EPG) corroborates this finding. Their results suggest that software developers are mainly concerned about the usefulness of the EPG regardless of whether it is easy to use, how much support they receive, or how much they are influenced by others.

On the other hand, we could hypothesize that management can increase usage in certain software security activity if they invest into increasing the team's skill in this area.

DISCUSSION

A brief summary of our research questions and results (Oyetoyan et al., 2017) is presented in Table 6. Note that despite the interpretation by Rindell et al. (Rindell et al., 2017), our contribution is not intended as another secure software development lifecycle.

Through interviews we discovered that certain security relevant tools (e.g. static analysis tools) are not used for finding security defects. This implies that simply making tools available will not improve security, unless the tools are actually used with security in mind.

Although both organizations deliver solutions for critical infrastructures, Org-1 has a higher level of security awareness, which is driven by the security expert group. This context is important in order to understand why this organization's usage is higher than the other. We need to further investigate the drivers for increase in software security adoption in an organization, such as research efforts, government funding and policies, education, and commitments by management to security.

Furthermore, the results from our survey show gaps in secure software development and opportunity for improvement. Among the development team, secure coding is practiced by less than half of the developers in both organizations. Invariably, over 50% of the developers are not paying attention to secure coding. The main question is whether this number is an acceptable risk for the management.

Similarly, secure design is practiced by less than 40% of architects in both organizations. The high level of individual and team autonomy in agile settings requires a careful balance with respect to software security integration. While different approaches to integrate software security into agile teams have been proposed (Baca et al., 2015; Bartsch, 2011; ben Othmane et al., 2014), there are still many challenges about how to achieve it. The cost and benefit in terms of additional activity such as in ben Othmane et al. (2014) and additional security personnel, as in Baca et al. (2015) need to be acceptable to the agile team and management.

Table 6. Summary of results per research question

RQs	Conclusion
1. Which software security activities are most used within the organizations?	Use of code review tool, static code analysis, and pair programming
2. Which training needs are important to the organizations?	The organizations agree on secure design and secure coding, and additionally they identify training need in penetration testing and risk analysis
3. How are security experience and the perceived need for software security training influenced by years of developer of experience?	Security experience increases with development experience, but perceived need for software security varies between organizations
4. What is the relationship between usage of, and skill in software security activities?	Usage increases for activities where teams have a high level of skill

An important result from our survey is that secure design is the highest training need expressed by all roles in both organizations. We believe that this is not accidental. The need for secure design is corroborated in Arce et al. (2014). Critics of agile software development have argued that the lack of attention to design and architectural issues is a serious limitation of the agile approach (Dybå & Dingsøyr, 2008; Rosenberg & Stephens, 2003). About 60% of defects in a system is introduced during design (Bernstein & Yuhas, 2005), and fixing defects after release is a hundred times costlier than fixing it during requirement or design (Boehm & Basili, 2005). In terms of security defects in design, the strongest statement comes from a group of software security professionals (Arce et al., 2014): *While a system may always have implementation defects, we have found that the security of many systems is breached due to design flaws*. In agile development, the lack of a complete overview of the system leaves room for unidentified risks during design.

Our impression is that none of the top 10 security design flaws (Arce et al., 2014) are particularly well known among developers, but many fall into the trap of equating authentication mechanisms with software security. Thus, this aspect is often implicitly covered, when good-practice standard authentication solutions are employed.

Clearly, there is a need for more practice-oriented research efforts to find an acceptable approach that can help agile organization move towards their "adequate" level of security. We argue that security loopholes could be created by any team or individual within the organization with weak approaches to security. There are two major points to ponder in this result regarding software security adoption: 1) How can skill be increased in specific software security areas relevant to the development team and the goal of the organization? and 2) How can we create an environment that make replication of software security successes possible among teams? Creating a learning environment is central to point 1. Although agile development and learning are highly related (Aniche & de Azevedo Silveira, 2011), building a learning environment for security is not that easy. Differences in technologies and team autonomy are just two of the challenges to consider.

CONCLUSION

We have presented an instrument for measuring the current usage, team competencies and training needs in software security activities in agile organizations. Our survey instrument complements maturity models such as BSIMM and OpenSAMM by focusing on the individuals rather than on organizations.

We have found that the individuals in our small sample of organizations were similar in terms of employing certain activities such as use of code review tool, pair programming, and use of static code analysis/tool, but since these activities may or may not be used specifically for security, particular focus on software security is necessary for these to have an impact on software security. Furthermore, skill drives the usage of activities, and we found that secure design may be the topmost area where there is a need for training.

We have identified learning and knowledge transfer as important to increase software security usage among teams.

ACKNOWLEDGMENT

The work in this chapter was supported by the Research Council of Norway through the project SoS-Agile: Science of Security in Agile Software Development (grant number 247678). We are grateful to our industrial partners and the survey respondents.

REFERENCES

Adams, E. (2012). *The Biggest Information Security Mistakes that Organizations Make and How to Avoid Making Them*. Retrieved from https://web.securityinnovation.com/the-biggest-information-security-mistakes-that-organizations-make

Allen, J. (2005). *Governing for enterprise security* (CMU/SEI-2005-TN-023). Retrieved from http://resources.sei.cmu.edu/library/asset-view.cfm?assetid=7453

Aniche, M. F., & de Azevedo Silveira, G. (2011). *Increasing learning in an agile environment: Lessons learned in an agile team*. Paper presented at the Agile Conference (AGILE), 2011. 10.1109/AGILE.2011.13

Arce, I., Clark-Fisher, K., Daswani, N., DelGrosso, J., Dhillon, D., Kern, C., . . . West, J. (2014). *Avoiding The Top 10 Software Security Design Flaws*. Retrieved from https://www.computer.org/cms/CYBSI/docs/Top-10-Flaws.pdf

Ayalew, T., Kidane, T., & Carlsson, B. (2013). *Identification and Evaluation of Security Activities in Agile Projects. In Secure IT Systems* (pp. 139–153). Springer.

Babar, M. A. (2009). *An exploratory study of architectural practices and challenges in using agile software development approaches.* Paper presented at the 2009 Joint Working IEEE/IFIP Conference on Software Architecture & European Conference on Software Architecture. 10.1109/WICSA.2009.5290794

Baca, D., Boldt, M., Carlsson, B., & Jacobsson, A. (2015). *A Novel Security-Enhanced Agile Software Development Process Applied in an Industrial Setting.* Paper presented at the Availability, Reliability and Security (ARES), 2015 10th International Conference on. 10.1109/ARES.2015.45

Baca, D., & Carlsson, B. (2011). Agile development with security engineering activities. *Proceedings of the 2011 International Conference on Software and Systems Process.*

Bartsch, S. (2011). *Practitioners' perspectives on security in agile development.* Paper presented at the Availability, Reliability and Security (ARES), 2011 Sixth International Conference on. 10.1109/ARES.2011.82

Beck, K. (1999). Embracing change with extreme programming. *Computer, 32*(10), 70–77. doi:10.1109/2.796139

ben Othmane, L., Angin, P., Weffers, H., & Bhargava, B. (2014). Extending the agile development process to develop acceptably secure software. *IEEE Transactions on Dependable and Secure Computing, 11*(6), 497-509.

Bernstein, L., & Yuhas, C. M. (2005). *Trustworthy systems through quantitative software engineering* (Vol. 1). John Wiley & Sons. doi:10.1002/0471750336

Beznosov, K., & Kruchten, P. (2004). Towards agile security assurance. *Proceedings of the 2004 workshop on New security paradigms.*

Boehm, B., & Basili, V. R. (2005). *Software defect reduction top 10 list. In Foundations of empirical software engineering: the legacy of Victor R* (Vol. 426). Basili. doi:10.1007/3-540-27662-9

de Win, B., Scandariato, R., Buyens, K., Grégoire, J., & Joosen, W. (2009). On the secure software development process: CLASP, SDL and Touchpoints compared. *Information and Software Technology, 51*(7), 1152–1171. doi:10.1016/j.infsof.2008.01.010

Dybå, T., & Dingsøyr, T. (2008). Empirical studies of agile software development: A systematic review. *Information and Software Technology, 50*(9), 833–859. doi:10.1016/j.infsof.2008.01.006

Dybå, T., Moe, N. B., & Mikkelsen, E. M. (2004). An empirical investigation on factors affecting software developer acceptance and utilization of electronic process guides. *Software Metrics, 2004. Proceedings. 10th International Symposium on.* 10.1109/METRIC.2004.1357905

Fontenele, M. P. (2017). *Designing a method for discovering expertise in cyber security communities: an ontological approach.* University of Reading.

Greenwood, D. J., & Levin, M. (2006). *Introduction to action research: Social research for social change.* SAGE Publications.

Howard, M., & Lipner, S. (2006). *The Security Development Lifecycle.* Microsoft Press.

ISO/IEC. (2009). Information technology -- Security techniques -- Evaluation criteria for IT security -- Part 1: Introduction and general model: ISO/IEC 15408-1:2009.

ISO/IEC. (2011). Information technology -- Security techniques -- Application security -- Part 1: Overview and concepts: ISO/IEC 27034-1:2011.

Jaatun, M. G. (2012). Hunting for Aardvarks: Can Software Security be Measured? In G. Quirchmayr, J. Basl, I. You, L. Xu, & E. Weippl (Eds.), *Multidisciplinary Research and Practice for Information Systems* (pp. 85–92). Springer Berlin Heidelberg. doi:10.1007/978-3-642-32498-7_7

Jaatun, M. G., Cruzes, D. S., Bernsmed, K., Tøndel, I. A., & Røstad, L. (2015). *Software Security Maturity in Public Organisations*. Paper presented at the Information Security: 18th International Conference, ISC 2015, Trondheim, Norway. 10.1007/978-3-319-23318-5_7

McGraw, G. (2004). Software Security. *IEEE Security and Privacy*, 2(2), 80–83. doi:10.1109/MSECP.2004.1281254

McGraw, G. (2005). The 7 Touchpoints of Secure Software. *Dr. Dobb's Journal*.

McGraw, G. (2006). Software Security: Building Security In. Addison-Wesley Professional.

McGraw, G., Migues, S., & West, J. (2018). *Building Security In Maturity Model (BSIMM 9)*. Academic Press.

Microsoft. (2012). *Security Development Lifecycle for Agile Development*. Retrieved from https://msdn.microsoft.com/en-us/library/windows/desktop/ee790621.aspx

Morrison, P., Smith, B. H., & Williams, L. (2017). *Surveying security practice adherence in software development*. Paper presented at the Hot Topics in Science of Security: Symposium and Bootcamp. 10.1145/3055305.3055312

OWASP. (2006). *CLASP concepts*. Retrieved from https://www.owasp.org/index.php/CLASP_Concepts

OWASP. (2016). *Software Assurance Maturity Model*. Retrieved from http://www.opensamm.org/

Oyetoyan, T. D., Cruzes, D. S., & Jaatun, M. G. (2016). *An Empirical Study on the Relationship between Software Security Skills, Usage and Training Needs in Agile Settings*. Paper presented at the Availability, Reliability and Security (ARES), 2016 11th International Conference on. 10.1109/ARES.2016.103

Oyetoyan, T. D., Jaatun, M. G., & Cruzes, D. S. (2017). A Lightweight Measurement of Software Security Skills, Usage and Training Needs in Agile Teams. *International Journal of Secure Software Engineering*, 8(1), 27. doi:10.4018/IJSSE.2017010101

Potter, L. E., & Vickers, G. (2015). What skills do you need to work in cyber security?: A look at the Australian market. *Proceedings of the 2015 ACM SIGMIS Conference on Computers and People Research*. 10.1145/2751957.2751967

Rindell, K., Hyrynsalmi, S., & Leppänen, V. (2017). Busting a Myth: Review of Agile Security Engineering Methods. *Proceedings of the 12th International Conference on Availability, Reliability and Security*. 10.1145/3098954.3103170

Robinson, H., & Sharp, H. (2004). Extreme Programming and Agile Processes in Software Engineering. *5th International Conference, XP 2004 Proceedings.* 10.1007/978-3-540-24853-8_16

Rosenberg, D., & Stephens, M. (2003). *Extreme programming refactored: the case against XP.* Apress.

Wäyrynen, J., Bodén, M., & Boström, G. (2004). *Security engineering and eXtreme programming: An impossible marriage? In Extreme programming and agile methods-XP/Agile Universe 2004* (pp. 117–128). Springer. doi:10.1007/978-3-540-27777-4_12

Zhu, J., Lipford, H. R., & Chu, B. (2013). Interactive support for secure programming education. *Proceeding of the 44th ACM technical symposium on Computer science education.* 10.1145/2445196.2445396

This research was previously published in Exploring Security in Software Architecture and Design; pages 260-286, copyright year 2019 by Information Science Reference (an imprint of IGI Global).

APPENDIX

SURVEY INSTRUMENT AND EXPLANATION OF TERMS

Software Security Activities in Agile Software Development Team

Instructions: Please mark the options that best fit your responses to these questions.

Section A: General Information

(Multiple answers are possible, see Table 7)

Table 7.

	Developer	Tester	Architect	Project Manager	Product Owner	Others (Please indicate)		
What is your role(s) in the agile team?								
	Scrum	Extreme Programming (XP)	Feature Driven Development (FDD)	Lean Software Development	Crystal Methods	Kanban	Agile Unified Process (AUP)	Dynamic Systems Development Method (DSDM)	Others
Which Agile Method-ologies do you use?								
	Yes	No						
Do you have software security experience?								
No of years with software development:								
Name of product:								
Type of product (e.g. web, mobile, network, control system, e-commerce, etc.):								

Section B: Capability and Interest

See Tables 8 and 9.

Table 8.

Novice [1]	Basic [2]	Moderate [3]	High [4]	Expert [5]
Have no experience working in this area	You have the level of experience gained in a classroom and/or experimental scenarios or as a trainee on-the-job. You are expected to need help when performing in this area	You are able to successfully complete tasks in this area as requested. Help from an expert may be required from time to time, but you can usually perform the skill independently	You can perform the actions associated in this area without assistance. You are certainly recognized within your immediate organization as "a person to ask" when difficult questions arise regarding this area.	You are known as an expert in this area. You can provide guidance, troubleshoot and answer questions related to this area of expertise and the field where the skill is used.

Table 9.

	Currently Do/Use It	What Is Your Skill Level in This Activity?						What Is Your Level Of Interest in This Activity?				
		Novice 1	2	3	4	Expert 5	Don't know	Not Interested	Slightly Interested	Moderately Interested	Very Interested	Don't Know
Security code review												
Secure design												
Secure coding												
Static code analysis tool												
Dynamic code analysis tool												
Code review tool												
Threat modeling tool												
Static code analysis												
Dynamic code analysis												
Vulnerability assessment												
Penetration testing												
Red team testing												
Fuzz testing												
Dynamic testing												
Risk-based testing												
Threat modelling												
Attack surface analysis												
Risk analysis												
Role matrix identification												
Asset analysis												
Countermeasure techniques												
Pair programming												

continues on following page

Table 9. Continued

	Currently Do/Use It	What Is Your Skill Level in This Activity?						What Is Your Level Of Interest in This Activity?				
		Novice 1	2	3	4	Expert 5	Don't know	Not Interested	Slightly Interested	Moderately Interested	Very Interested	Don't Know
Functioning as project security officer/Champion												
Writing abuse stories/cases												
Gathering security requirements												
Incident Response Management												

Section C: Training

Instruction: Please tick the activities you would like to receive training on (see Table 10).

Table 10.

	I want to have training in this activity/tool
Threat and Risk Management	
Threat modeling for secure software	
Attack surface analysis	
Threat countermeasure analysis	
Asset analysis	
Risk analysis	
Secure design & coding activities	
Secure coding	
Pair programming	
Secure design (e.g. attack surface reduction, secure defaults)	
Security tools	
Static code analysis tool	
Dynamic code analysis tool	
Code review tool	
Threat modeling tool	
Security Testing (Note that several techniques exist for security testing and some of these techniques may be overlapping)	
Penetration testing	
Dynamic testing (Black box testing)	
Fuzz testing	
White box testing (Including manual code review)	
Risk-based testing	
Release Activity	
Incident Response Management	

Comment/Feedback

Please provide any comment or feedback in the space below.

Explanation of Terms in Questionnaire

See Table 11.

Table 11.

I	Term	Definition	Examples
A	Abuse stories	Brief and informal stories that identify how attackers may abuse the system and jeopardize stakeholders' assets	
	Attack surface	All different points where an attacker could get into a system and get data out of the system	• user interface forms & fields • HTTP headers and cookies • APIs • Files • Databases • etc.
	Asset analysis	Identifying both physical and abstract assets of the organization. Assets are threat target. For example, an asset of an application might be a list of clients and their personal information; this is a physical asset. An abstract asset might be the reputation of an organization. Analysis may include identifying the trust levels (i.e. The level of access required to access the entry point is documented here)	
C	Code signing	Providing the stakeholder with a way to validate the origin and integrity of the system	
	Countermeasure	Action taken in order to protect an asset against threats	• Threat – Tampering with data • Countermeasures – appropriate authorization, hashes, digital signatures, etc.
D	Dynamic analysis tools	Automated runtime testing tools	• Penetration testing tools (e.g. ZAP, IBM AppScan, etc)
	Dynamic testing	Run-time verification of software programs	• memory corruption • user privilege issues • etc.
F	Final security review	A deliberate examination of all the security activities performed on a software application prior to release	
	Fuzz testing	Dynamic testing used to induce system failure by deliberately introducing malformed or random data to an application	
I	Incident response plan	A set of written instructions for detecting, responding to and limiting the effects of an information security event	
P	Pair programming	Two people create code where one writes the code while the other reviews each line of code as it is typed.	
	Penetration testing	Proactive and authorized attempt to evaluate the security of a system, by finding and exploiting vulnerabilities, technical flaws, or weaknesses to compromise the system	
Q	Quality gates/bug bars	Minimum acceptable levels of security and privacy quality before the code goes into production	• All SQL statements must be parameterized before deployment • All API classes must be reviewed before deployment • Mandatory check for known vulnerabilities of all 3rd party libraries • All critical security bugs must be resolved

continues on following page

Table 11. Continued

I	Term	Definition	Examples
R	Red team testing	Simulate real-world attacks against an organization, challenging its defenses against electronic, physical and social exploits	Red team – an external[1] team with the goal to hack the system
	Risk analysis	An approach of gathering requisite data to make informed decision based on knowledge about asset, vulnerability, threat, impact, countermeasures and probability	
	Risk-based testing	Test approach that takes a risk into account by identifying and analyzing the risks related to the system	
	Role matrix	Identifying all possible user roles and their access levels to the system	
S	Secure coding	Development practices that assure secure software	• Input validation • parameterized SQL • etc.
	Secure design	Design practices that assure secure software	• reducing attack surface during design • placement of security checks before input processing • etc.
	Security code review	Manual review of source code for finding security bugs	
	Security metrics	Metrics that measure organization's defense against attacks	• Defect density • Windows of exposure (how long a security defect is open) • #Vulnerability • etc.
	Security patterns	A well understood solution to security problems	
	Security testing	An activity to assess a system for security bugs (technical flaws, vulnerabilities or weaknesses)	• Vulnerability assessment • Penetration testing • Dynamic testing (black box testing) • Code review (white box testing) • Automated analysis (dynamic and static)
	Static code analysis	Verification of source code	
	Static code analysis tools	Automated code review tools	• IDE vulnerability rule checker • Anti-XSS library • etc.
T	Threat modeling	An approach to identify, quantify, and address the security risks associated with a system	• identifying external dependencies • entry points • assets • trust levels • data flow diagrams • Categorize threats (attacker goals) e.g. Spoofing • Determine countermeasures (e.g. security controls) • etc.
U	UMLSec	Extension of Unified Modeling Language that allows to express security-relevant information within the diagrams in a system specification	
V	Vulnerability assessment	Scanning for security issues using a combination of automated tools and manual assessment techniques. The goal is to confirm the presence of a vulnerability without actually exploiting it	

Section 7
Critical Issues and Challenges

Chapter 98
Towards a Security Competence of Software Developers:
A Literature Review

Nana Assyne
ⓘD https://orcid.org/0000-0003-0469-6642
University of Jyväskylä, Finland

ABSTRACT

Software growth has been explosive as people depend heavily on software on daily basis. Software development is a human-intensive effort, and developers' competence in software security is essential for secure software development. In addition, ubiquitous computing provides an added complexity to software security. Studies have treated security competences of software developers as a subsidiary of security engineers' competence instead of software engineers' competence, limiting the full knowledge of the security competences of software developers. This presents a crucial challenge for developers, educators, and users to maintain developers' competences in security. As a first step in pushing for the developers' security competence studies, this chapter utilises a literature review to identify the security competences of software developers. Thirteen security competences of software developers were identified and mapped to the common body of knowledge for information security professional framework. Lastly, the implications for, with, and without the competences are analysed and presented.

INTRODUCTION

The current explosive growth being observed in the software industry requires high-level corresponding software security. This is because "software vulnerabilities or flaws are often key entrance door for attackers" (Sametinger, 2013). They include buffer overflows, SQL injection, cross-site scripting, stack overflow, inconsistent error handling, and so on (McGraw, 2004). Previously, software security used to be an afterthought, but recently it is being addressed actively from the planning stage of software development. Additionally, in today's software development process, software testing includes security testing instead of only functional testing (Mano, Duhadway, & Striegel, 2006), thus making the security

DOI: 10.4018/978-1-6684-3702-5.ch098

competences of the developers more eminent in software development. Coupled with the fact that research work on software developers' competence is not lacking (Lenberg, Feldt, & Wallgren, 2015), the security competences of software developers should be well recorded in literature. But on the contrary, that is not the case. However, when they are recorded, they are recorded as a subsidiary of security engineers' competence instead of software engineers' competence, thus making it counterproductive to develop and maintain the security competences of software developers to the benefit of the possessors (developers), those who train the possessors of the competences (educators), and users of the competences (industry).

McGraw (2004) defines software security as "the idea of engineering software so that it continues to function correctly under malicious attack". And, Hazeyama & Shimizu (2012), goes further with the definition by stating that "software security deals with security during the whole software development process". On the other hand, software engineering competence is defined by the Institute of Electrical and Electronics Engineers (IEEE) as knowledge, skills, and attitudes of software developers to fulfil a given task in a software development project (IEEE, 2014). Thus, the author of this chapter defines security competence of software developers as those specific security competences required by a developer to deal with security during the whole software development process. An example is an SQL injection skills and security pattern skills.

As mentioned above, one cannot afford to leave software security as an afterthought; developers must strive to improve software security issues from the planning stage to the maintenance stage. The works of Cheng et al. (2008), Hilburn and Mead (2013), and Riehle and Nürnberg (2015) are studies that investigated methods to handle software security using the lifecycle of software development. It is also well established that vulnerabilities and flaws are the doors attackers exploit. Works such as Kaur and Kaur (2016), McGraw (2004), Park et al. (2010), and Wegerer and Tjoa (2016) confirm this assertion in literature. In addition, assailants of software systems are persons or entities, who are active and keep on improving their skills in attacking software systems to satisfy their desire (Cheng et al., 2008). However, the security competences of the developers of the software are not well established in literature.

Whilst introducing security engineering environment studies for software developers, Cheng et al. (2008) point out that there is urgent need to create an environment that integrates various tools and provides comprehensive facilities to the designers, developers, users, and maintainers of a software system (Cheng et al., 2008). The development and maintenance of such an environment requires knowledge of security competences of the developers to prepare and develop them to withstand the intrinsic difficulty of assailants of a software system (Cheng et al., 2008). This implies that security know-how of the developer is very crucial. Hazeyama and Shimizu (2012) and Hilburn and Mead (2013) reiterate the need for awareness to be channelled towards developers' skills regarding security. However, previous studies provide less concise and coordinated information on security competences of developers.

Summarily, these competences are scattered in several different studies. Thus, the following questions arise: *what are the security competences of software developers? How can they be improved?* As part of broader research on software developers' competences, we set our research question as *what are the security competences of a software developer that are available in literature?* The remainder of this work includes: Section 2 presents previous studies and background. Section 3 looks at the methodology used in this study. Section 4 looks at the results. Section 5 and 6 presents the discussion and conclusion.

PREVIOUS STUDIES AND BACKGROUND

In this section of the study, three literature review studies on software developers' competences are iden-tified. These literature reviews are Cruz et al. (2015); Moustroufas et al. (2015) and Vishnubhotla et al. (2018). Two of the studies utilized systematic literature review methods and the last study employed a traditional literature review method. Cruz et al. (2015) and Vishnubhotla et al. (2018) that used system-atic literature review, focused on specific areas of software developers' competence. Cruz et al. (2015) investigated the personality of software engineers and their roles in software development. Vishnubhotla et al. (2018) also presented the capability and competence measurement of software engineers, including team working in agile software development. Moustroufas et al. (2015) utilized a traditional literature review to evaluate the adequacy of software engineer competences and created a software competence profiling model for recruiting software engineers. Moustroufas et al. (2015) investigated and reviewed software developers' competence in general contrary to the first two that focused on specific areas. The software security competence of developers did not appear in any of the three studies, thus the need for this paper.

It is also worth mentioning that there are several efforts being made to improve security matters in the development of software. They include the development processes and the methods to reduce vul-nerabilities and flaws in software. Hazeyama & Shimizu (2012) proposed a software security learning process using the traditional software development cycle. Cheng et al. (2008) reiterated for security engineering environment for software development since security requires continuous support. Thus, they make use of the lifecycle of software engineering for their solution which is based on International Organization for Standardization (ISO) and the International Electrotechnical Commission (IEC) stan-dards. The work of Verdon (2006) and McGraw (2004) examined the security policies and best practices that are essential for software developers.

The Open Web Application Security Project (OWASP) that is OWASP top 10 -2017 that focused on software developers and designers stated that "insecure software is undermining our financial, healthcare, defense, energy, and other critical infrastructure." The increasing complexity and the connectedness of software, is making it more difficult in attaining an increase in application security. Additionally, we face the rapid process of developing software which increases our common security risks. This makes it impossible to accept simple security problems as listed in the OWASP top 10 – 2017. The top five on the list are (i) Injection, (ii) Broken Authentication, (iii) Sensitive Data Exposure, (iv) XML External Entities (XXE), and (v) Broken Access Control. The rest of the OWASP top 10 – 2017 are (vi) Security Misconfiguration, (vii) Cross-Site Scripting (XSS), (viii) -Insecure Deserialization, (ix) Using Components with Known Vulnerabilities, and (x) Insufficient Logging & Monitoring (OWASP, 2017). Such security problems require corresponding skills to handle them. Given this, software developers' need to develop their security competences. For them to be able to develop and maintain such competences, it requires that such competences are identified and placed in the appropriate domain. Thus, the need for this study.

A survey to identify the guidance available on the web to help software developers' to fix security matters was conducted by Acar et al. (2017). They concluded that not all the information on the web is readily made for fixing security issues (Acar et al., 2017). Therefore, it may require security competences of the developers' to adjust the available code to meet the security demand. Hilburn & Mead (2013), developed a software security assurance model by providing capabilities. The capability of the assurance model was addressed by utilizing the knowledge areas. The main knowledge areas of assurance model that were identified were: assurance across lifecycles, risk management, assurance assessment, assurance management, system security assurance, system functionality assurance and system operational assurance (Hilburn & Mead, 2013). Even though, this work focused on assurance in software security, it also provided some capabilities or knowledge areas that are useful for this paper. Work such as Meng et al. (2018); Miller and Heymann (2018) and Qian et al. (2018) provide some information on the security competences of software developers. Therefore, we employ these studies stated above and other existing studies to set the agenda for identifying the security competences of software developers and highlight the importance of software developers' security competences for further studies. Thus, this study seeks to employ traditional literature reviews to identify the security competences of software developers as the first step in broader research.

In presenting Common Body of Knowledge (CBK) for Information security professionals, Theoharidou & Gritzalis (2007) made a case for technical and behavioural skills for information security professionals. The framework was achieved using 135 academic intuitions from Africa, Asia, Australia, Europe, and South and North America to provide a skill set for information security professionals. The framework can be utilized in identifying and assessing the skills of information security professionals. The framework has three major areas: information communications technology skills area, security skills area and behavioural skills area. This study aimed at identifying the security competences of software developers from literature using traditional literature review and maps the result to the Common Body of Knowledge for information security professional skills framework (CBK). As a result, the CBK framework will be employed as a theoretical lens for this study.

METHODOLOGY

Primarily a literature review will be mainly employed in this study. Fink defines a research literature review as "a systematic, explicit and reproducible method for identifying, evaluating and synthesizing the existing body of completed and recorded work produced by researchers, scholars, and practitioners" (Fink, 2010, p. 3). In this section, an attempt is also made to distinguish between a traditional literature review and a systematic literature review. Systematic literature review is defined by Kitchenham and Charters as "a form of secondary study that uses a well-defined methodology to identify, analyse and interpret all available evidence related to a specific research question in a way that is unbiased and (to a degree) repeatable" (Kitchenham & Charters, 2007, p. vi, pp. 8). A traditional literature review is used to demonstrate a gap or a problem in an area one seeks to research without an explicit method for reviewing the literature (Moustroufas et al., 2015). Since this is the first step towards broader research, a traditional literature review will be utilized.

Given this, the IEEE database was used as the database to find studies that investigated software security. The identified competences were grouped into two areas: programming related competences and non-programming related competences. The detail of the classification is explained in the result section. The identified competences were then mapped to technical and behavioural skills of information security professionals' skill set framework. With regard to data collection, data was collected from the IEEE database. The search strings that were utilized for the search were: software engineers/developers' skills, competence, and security knowledge. This was done without any strict protocol. Only peer-review papers were employed for the study. The names of the competences were extracted, descriptions of the competences were recorded into an excel sheet for the next stage of the research. On data analysis, competences with the same meaning were group together. Different implications of the competences were analysed and recorded against the individual competences identified. Using conventional content analysis guideline of Hsieh & Shannon (2005), competences were classified into two areas. They are programming related competences and non-programming related competences. Lastly, the identified competences were mapped to the information security professional skills set framework.

RESULTS

The identified competences were categorized into two. They are programming related competences and non-programming related competences. Programming related competences are those that involve coding. Non-programming related competences are those that do not directly deal with coding. The competences were mapped to the common body of knowledge information security professional skills framework. Table 1 depicts the competence area, the competence name, the citation of the papers that the competences were extracted from and the CBK of information security professional's framework.

Table 1. Security competences of software developers

Competence area	Competence name	Reference	CBK of information security professionals framework (Theoharidou & Gritzalis, 2007)
Programming related skills	Secure programming or coding skills	(Acar et al., 2017; Mano et al., 2006; Miller & Heymann, 2018; Qian, Lo, et al., 2018; Zainuddin & Normaziah, 2011)	Information communications technology/ security
	Secure mobile software development skills	(Meng et al., 2018; Qian, Parizi, & Lo, 2018)	Information communications technology/ security
	Secure socket layer/transport layer security (SSL/TLS) skills	(Verdon, 2006)	Information communications technology/ security
	Web Application security development skills	(Qian, Lo, et al., 2018)	Information communications technology/ security
	Integrated development environment (IDE) security skill	(Meng et al., 2018)	Information communications technology
	Code Analysis tools skills	(Meng et al., 2018)	Information communications technology
	Modelling SQL injection skills	(Kaur & Kaur, 2016; Wegerer & Tjoa, 2016)	Information communications technology/ security
	Handling buffer overflow skills	(Park et al., 2010)	Information communications technology/ security
	Security patterns skills	(Hazeyama & Shimizu, 2012)	Information communications technology/ security
Non-Programming related skills	Software security policy skills	(Verdon, 2006)	Information communications technology
	Software security best practice and standard skills	(McGraw, 2004)(Hazeyama & Shimizu, 2012)(Cheng et al., 2008)	Information communications technology
	System Security assurance skills	(Hilburn & Mead, 2013)(Miller & Heymann, 2018)	Information communications technology
	Vulnerability assessment tool skills	(Miller & Heymann, 2018)	Information communications technology

Table 1 shows the competences identified, their classifications, the literature from which the competence is extracted from and their relationship to CBK of information security professionals' framework. In all 13 competences were identified, nine competences were programming related and 4 competences were non-programming related. Seven of the competence maps to both information communication technology and security criterial and 6 maps to information communication technology. The next section provides the definition/descriptions of the competences and implications.

PROGRAMMING RELATED COMPETENCES

Secure Programming/Coding Skills

Description

The art of adopting a secure practice in the development of software. This includes the skill of being able to guide against vulnerabilities and flaws in software development. The majority of vulnerabilities and flaws in software appear when developers ignore secure practices in programming. More details of secure programming/coding competences can be found in the works of Mano et al. (2006); Miller & Heymann (2018) and Zainuddin & Normaziah (2011).

Implication

Without the adoption of secure coding, developers may create software with flaws and vulnerabilities. As pointed out by Sametinger (2013), vulnerabilities and flaws are the key entrants for attackers. Improving secure coding or programming will reduce security flaws. Secure coding must be part of a software development curriculum. There is a need to include fundamental security principles programming courses. Organizations must continue to introduce fresh courses on secure coding. In today's software development, secure coding must be started from the planning stage of the development to the end of the software development lifecycle. This implies that developers' competence in secure coding is essential. As suggested by Mano et al. (2006), secured programming must be taught in the early part of a software program. It must also be recognized as important skill for software developers.

Secure Mobile Software Development Skills

Description

Mobile devices may have software applications that we utilize frequently or perhaps even daily. The process of developing apps for these devices differ from the main devices. Furthermore, the database and the storage for these devices also differ. Thus, requiring different programming and security competences for the development of mobile apps. More about secure mobile software development skills can be found in the works of Meng et al. (2018); Qian, Lo, et al. (2018); Qian, Parizi, et al. (2018).

Implication

Most of the developers of these apps lack the necessary skill for developing mobile apps, thereby creating vulnerabilities for attackers to exploit those devices. The common nature (maybe you could be more specific here?) of the devices makes them more vulnerable. Thus, delays in providing bug fixings for new versions of applications can provide a door for attackers. Un-updated operating systems (OS) on mobile devices can allow attackers to exploit the vulnerabilities on the OS to attack the software application. Developers must pay attention to secure mobile development skills since techniques used for developing mobiles are different from that of normal devices. Fundamentally the increased usage of mobile technology is putting pressure on mobile developers. Both the trainers and users of the security competence of developers must adopt modern techniques to upgrade the developers to withstand the modern attackers.

Secure Socket Layer Skills

Description

Communication – data transmission between devices - is important in the applications function. This requires developers' skills in standard cryptographic protocol and technology for communicating on the internet. More importantly the use of transport layer security (TLS). Developers need to have skills in socket programming to enable them to develop this type of communication. More details of secure socket layer skills can be found in the work of Verdon (2006)

Implications

Most attackers take advantage of eavesdropping on transmission and launch their attack. This happens when strong encryptions are not used. Developers are to have skills in SSL or TLS encryptions technology. This is because most devices use the internet as a means to transmit data. Without such skills will mean that most attackers can eavesdrop on the communication and launch attacks. Developers should understand and have skills in symmetric encryption.

Web Application Security Skills

Description

Skills to protect devices or applications against web attacks such as cross-site scripting, SQL injection, denial-of-service, etc. Most attackers use vulnerabilities of web applications to attack. It is important to know that web application security directly relates to websites, web applications and web services such as APIs. Again, one needs to distinguish between network security and web application security. Therefore, the competences may defer. More details of secure socket layer skills can be found in the works Anand & Ryoo (2017); Uskov (2013) and Uskov & Avenue (2013).

Implication

In today's world, most of our business is done using the internet. Thus, not having the skills of developing software that can reduce web vulnerability will mean that most businesses could face catastrophes in their dealings. There is the need to have developers who understand using up-to-date skills in proper authentication methods, encryptions and development of patching for discovered vulnerabilities.

Integrated Development Environment (IDE) Security Skills

Description

Most developers of software make use of IDE for the development of software. They are software applications that provide the environments for software development. Thus, they are attitude, skills, and knowledge for using IDE securities in developing software. More details of IDE security skills can be found in the work of Meng et al. (2018).

Implication

Such environments sometimes if not well protected, can leave vulnerabilities in the software being developed and can be exploited by attackers. Having the skills related to the security of the use of the said IDE provides the developer with an environment free of vulnerabilities and flaws. Security updates are important and other security in the transmission of data. Developers must understand such security environments and use them appropriately to avoid leaving vulnerabilities that can be taken advantage of attackers.

Code Analysis Tools Skills

Description

Code analysis tools are used during coding to aid in analysing the code of the developer. Such tools help in identifying bugs and guide the developer to fix them before deploying the applications. They are attitude, skills, and knowledge for performing code analytics in software development. More details of code analysis tools skills can be found in the work of Meng et al. (2018)

Implication

If developers do not have the skill of using code analysis tools it may mean that time to identify bugs during coding may be long. It can result in leaving bugs to be exploited by attackers. It is also important to note that most of these bugs are difficult to be identified by the human eye. Examples of such tools are PMD java and SonarQube.

Modelling SQL Injection Skills

Description

It is a code injection technique that attackers take advantage of data-driven applications using SQL statements. It mostly happens when user inputs are not well-typed. They are attitude, skills, and knowledge for developing software free of SQL injection. More detail of SQL injection skills can be found in the works of Kaur & Kaur (2016) and Wegerer & Tjoa (2016).

Implication

It allows attackers to use malicious SQL statements to attack. This can be used on websites and databases. This is done by using spoof identity to temper with existing data. Such attacks are known as vector. Without skills in SQL injection handling in web applications and applications using databases, it will give attackers the chance to attack just systems since such vulnerability is commonly committed by developers.

Handling Buffer Overflow Skills

Description

It happens when a program writing to the buffer, which is a memory area set aside to hold data overflow. Mostly, when malformed inputs are used. they are attitude, skills, and knowledge needed to avoid buffer overflows. More details of handling buffer overflow skills can be found in the work of Park et al. (2010).

Implication

This happens when programmers or developers assume that all inputs may be smaller, but this may not always be the case. In case there is an overflow, the system may write beyond the allocated size causing erratic in execution leading to access error or crashing of the system. There is the need to write code that has built-in protections in the programming codes. The possession of such skills may reduce buffer overflows in memory, since not all input size can be predicted well by the developer.

Security Patterns Skills

Description

Security patterns are applied during software development by developers to achieve security goals. Such security patterns are pre-defined to guide developers. Having such skills will enable developers to know what security pattern can be used to achieve a particular security goal. That is the protected system patterns for confidentiality and integrity of information and error detection/correction pattern for deducing errors for corrections. More detail of security patterns skills can be found in the work of Hazeyama & Shimizu (2012).

Implication

Without such patterns, developers are to start from scratch to develop such protections. Understanding or having such skills, they can also develop security patterns to meet a specific goal that is not available.

NON-PROGRAMMING RELATED SKILLS

Software Security Policy Skills

Description

A software security policy defines the specific rules of security that software to be developed must have. That means that developers must frequently reference to make sure that the software obeys such policy. Understanding software security policy as a skill will enable the developer to develop software that will meet the security policy of the organization, the state and the world in general. Thus, they are attitude, skills, and knowledge needed to develop software to meet software security policies of the organization, the state, and the international community. More details of software security policy skills can be found in the work of Verdon (2006).

Implication

If developers do not have the skill to understand security policies and cannot develop software to meet what the organization, the state, and the international community have set as their policy for software security, consumers may not trust those software products. Furthermore, software security policies are standards, established to help reduce security threats. This means that, without them, developers may develop software according to their skills. This can lead to a lower security standard for the software they develop.

Security Best Practice and Standard Skills

Description

Best practice and standard are what has been used, tested and agreed as the best way of handling security in software development. Security best practices and standards can guide developers in secure software development. Thus, they are the attitude, skills, and knowledge needed to develop software security best practices and standards. More details of software security policy skills can be found in the works Cheng et al. (2008); Hazeyama & Shimizu (2012) and McGraw (2004).

Implication

If developers do not have such skills, it will mean they may not follow the best way of developing secure software. Mostly, security best practices and standards serve as a guide, but also provide a means to develop to meet certain accepted way that leads to trust.

This will mean that software developed by such developers with security best practices and standards skills will develop secured software, thereby, reducing the vulnerabilities that an attacker can exploit.

System Security Assurance Tools Skills

Description

These are tools that help developers of software from protecting the data and resources controlled by the software. They are the first line in for defending the attackers and also assessing the software security. Thus, they are the attitudes, skills, and knowledge needed to use system security assurance tools when developing software. More details of system security assurance tools skills can be found in the works of Hilburn & Mead (2013) and Miller & Heymann (2018).

Implication

Mostly, the human resources of the developer alone may not be enough for handling the development of software. Therefore, tools are needed to support the development of secured software. System security assurance tools support developers in such a situation. Not having the skill of using such tools will require more human hand in the development process. Alternatively, they will develop software that does not provide the required assurance for the people.

Vulnerability Assessment Tool Skills

Description

Tools are needed to identify the threats and risks that may be in software during development. In using such tools developers will need some special skills. Thus, they are attitude, skills, and knowledge needed by developers to use vulnerability assessment tools during software development. More detail of vulnerability assessment tool skills can be found in the work of (Miller & Heymann, 2018)

Implication

Without such tools, the human factor is to be used for such identification of vulnerability and threats thus, making such skills important for developers. It is important to note that most of such vulnerabilities are difficult to be identified by the human eye, thus if developers have no skills in using these tools, it may mean suck vulnerabilities and threats may be left in the software for attackers to exploit.

DISCUSSIONS

As stated in the related works, there were three review papers on software developers' competences. Two made use of a systematic review and one used a traditional review. None of these reviews mentioned the security competences of software developers. Nevertheless, there are some similarities. The work of Moustroufas et al. (2015) also used a traditional review, which was the same method used by this paper.

The difference between this paper and Moustroufas et al. (2015) is that they looked at software developers competence in general, whereas this paper looked at is security competence of the developers which is a specific area in software developers' competence. On the other hand, the other two reviews also looked at specific areas of developers' competence similar to this paper but used a systematic literature review as a method. This paper agrees with these authors that competences of software developers are essential for software development and effort must be made to maintain them especially in academia.

In proposing a security engineering environment for software developers, Cheng et al. (2008) claimed that the tools and the developers must integrate for a secure engineering environment. We support their assertion, but their work falls short of the implication of not having such an environment. To add to their work, this paper has provided the security competences of the developers which are essential for the security engineering environment they proposed. Furthermore, this paper has responded to the call by Hazeyama and Shimizu (2012) and Hilburn and Mead (2013), that there is the need to pay attention to security competences of the developers'. This paper has provides some of the competences, therefore agreeing with Hazeyama and Shimizu (2012) and Hilburn and Mead (2013) that the security competences of the developers are an essential parts of software developers' competences. For that reason, we support their call for more research on security competences of software developers'.

Researchers such as Cheng et al. (2008); Hilburn & Mead (2013) and Riehle & Nürnberg (2015) have called for security competence development through the lifecycle of developers. We concede, we could not do that, but we have identified some security competences of the developer that can be used as a starting stage for security competences of the developers' studies. Acar et al. (2017)stated that not all web security resources can be used fully to solve security problems by developers. Therefore, with the identification of the security competences of software developers, industry players can add to such work (web resources) by using the competences they have. Thus, this chapter supports the work of Hilburn & Mead (2013) that, knowing those security competences of software developers will help the users, possessors, and educators. Meng et al. (2018); Miller and Heymann (2018) and Qian et al. (2018) provided individual security competences of software developers, though this paper could not provide a full list, the paper has provided the basis for more work to be done. Theoharidou & Gritzalis (2007) work identified the technical and behavioural competences of information security professionals. This assertion has been established in the literature. We did not identify any behavioural security competences of software developers. Nevertheless, we hold the belief that there are behavioural security competences of developers and that empirical work must be conducted to identify them.

CONCLUSION

This chapter proposes a security competence for software developers. It uses a literature review to identify and classify security competence of software developers. Thirteen security competences of software developers were identified. They were classified as programming related competence and non-programming related competence. The author agrees that the methodology used has some limitations. Nevertheless, the competence identified and the linkage provided between the security competence of software developers and the information security professional framework will serve as a base for the development of the security competence of software developers. Furthermore, this chapter also makes a call for empirical research to identify the security competence of software developers. By that, the author calls for a systematic literature review on the security competence of software developers. Again, there is the need also to identify those security competences using the lifecycle of the software development process.

REFERENCES

Acar, Y., Stransky, C., Wermke, D., Weir, C., Mazurek, M. L., & Fahl, S. (2017). *Developers Need Support, Too : A Survey of Security Advice for Software Developers. In 2017 IEEE Cybersecurity Development IEEE Secure Development Conference Developers* (pp. 22–26)., doi:10.1109/SecDev.2017.17

Anand, P., & Ryoo, J. (2017). Security Patterns As Architectural Solution - Mitigating Cross-Site Scripting Attacks in Web Applications. In *2017 International Conference on Software Security and Assurance (ICSSA)* (pp. 25–31). IEEE. 10.1109/ICSSA.2017.30

Cheng, J., Goto, Y., Morimoto, S., & Horie, D. (2008). A Security Engineering Environment Based on ISO / IEC Standards : Providing Standard, Formal, and Consistent Supports for Design, Development, Operation, and Maintenance of Secure Information Systems. In *2008 International Conference on Information Security and Assurance* (pp. 350–354). 10.1109/ISA.2008.106

Cruz, S., Fabio, Q. B., & Fernando, L. (2015). Forty years of research on personality in software engineering : A mapping study. *Computers in Human Behavior, 46,* 94–113. doi:10.1016/j.chb.2014.12.008

Fink, A. (2010). Conducting Research Literature Reviews: From the Internet to Paper (3rd ed.). SAGE.

Hazeyama, A., & Shimizu, H. (2012). Development of a Software Security Learning Environment. In *2012 13th ACIS International Conference on Software Engineering, Artificial Intelligence, Networking and Parallel/Distributed Computing* (pp. 518–523). IEEE. 10.1109/SNPD.2012.65

Hilburn, T. B., & Mead, N. R. (2013). Building Security In. *IEEE Security and Privacy, 11*(October), 89–92. doi:10.1109/MSP.2013.109

Hsieh, H.-F., & Shannon, S. E. (2005). Three Approaches to Qualitative Content Analysis. *Qualitative Health Research, 15*(9), 1277–1288. doi:10.1177/1049732305276687 PMID:16204405

IEEE. (2014). *Software Engineering Competency Model (SWECOM).* IEEE. Retrieved from http://www.dahlan.web.id/files/ebooks/SWECOM.pdf

Kaur, N., & Kaur, P. (2016). Modeling a SQL Injection Attack. In *2016 3rd International Conference on Computing for Sustainable Global Development (INDIACom)* (pp. 77–82). Bharati Vidyapeeth.

Kitchenham, B., & Charters, S. (2007). Guidelines for performing Systematic Literature reviews in Software Engineering Version 2.3. Engineering (Vol. 45). doi:10.1145/1134285.1134500

Lenberg, P., Feldt, R., & Wallgren, L. G. (2015). Behavioral software engineering: A definition and systematic literature review. *Journal of Systems and Software, 107,* 15–37. doi:10.1016/j.jss.2015.04.084

Mano, C. D., Duhadway, L., & Striegel, A. (2006). A Case for Instilling Security as a Core Programming Skill. In *Proceedings. Frontiers in Education. 36th Annual Conference* (pp. 13–18). IEEE. 10.1109/FIE.2006.322347

McGraw, G. (2004). *Software Security*. IEEE Security & Privacy. doi:10.1109/MSECP.2004.1281254

Meng, X., Qian, K., Lo, D., & Wu, F. (2018). Secure Mobile Software Development with Vulnerability Detectors in Static Code Analysis. *2018 International Symposium on Networks, Computers and Communications (ISNCC)*, 1–4. 10.1109/ISNCC.2018.8531071

Miller, B. P., & Heymann, E. (2018). *Tutorial: Secure Coding Practices, Automated Assessment Tools and the SWAMP. In 2018 IEEE Cybersecurity Development (SecDev)* (pp. 124–125). IEEE; doi:10.1109/SecDev.2018.00025

Moustroufas, E., Stamelos, I., & Angelis, L. (2015). Competency profiling for software engineers: Literature review and a new model. In *Proceedings of the 19th Panhellenic Conference on Informatics* (pp. 235–240). Athens, Greece: ACM. 10.1145/2801948.2801960

OWASP. (2017). *OWASP Top 10 - 2017 The Ten Most Critical Web Application Security Risks*. OWASP.

Park, C. S., Lee, J. H., Seo, S. C., & Kim, B. K. (2010). Assuring software security against buffer overflow attacks in embedded software development life cycle. In *2010 The 12th International Conference on Advanced Communication Technology (ICACT)* (Vol. 1, pp. 787–790). IEEE.

Qian, K., Lo, D., Parizi, R., & Wu, F. (2018). Authentic Learning Secure Software Development (SSD) in Computing Education. *2018 IEEE Frontiers in Education Conference (FIE)*, 1–9.

Qian, K., Parizi, R. M., & Lo, D. (2018). OWASP Risk Analysis Driven Security Requirements Specification for Secure Android Mobile Software Development. In *2018 IEEE Conference on Dependable and Secure Computing (DSC)* (pp. 1–2). IEEE. 10.1109/DESEC.2018.8625114

Riehle, D., & Nürnberg, F.-A.-U. E. (2015). How Open Source Is Changing the Software Developer's Career. *Computer Practice*, *48*(5), 51–57. doi:10.1109/MC.2015.132

Sametinger, J. (2013). Software Security. In *2013 20th IEEE International Conference and Workshops on Engineering of Computer Based Systems (ECBS)* (p. 216). IEEE. 10.1109/ECBS.2013.24

Theoharidou, M., & Gritzalis, D. (2007). Common Body of Knowledge for Information Security. *IEEE Security & Privacy*, 64–67.

Uskov, A. V. (2013). Software and Web Application Security: State-of-the-Art courseware and Learning Paradigm. In *IEEE Global Engineering Education Conference (EDUCON)* (Vol. 0, pp. 608–611). 10.1109/EduCon.2013.6530168

Uskov, A. V., & Avenue, W. B. (2013). Hands-On Teaching of Software and Web Applications Security. 2013 3rd Interdisciplinary Engineering Design Education Conference, 71–78. 10.1109/IEDEC.2013.6526763

Verdon, D. (2006). *Security Policies and the Software Developer*. IEEE Security & Privacy. doi:10.1109/MSP.2006.103

Vishnubhotla, S. D., Mendes, E., & Lundberg, L. (2018). An Insight into the Capabilities of Professionals and Teams in Agile Software Development A Systematic Literature Review. In *ICSCA 2018* (pp. 10–19). Kuantan, Malaysia: ACM. doi:10.1145/3185089.3185096

Wegerer, M., & Tjoa, S. (2016). Defeating the Database Adversary Using Deception - A MySQL Database Honeypot. In *2016 International Conference on Software Security and Assurance (ICSSA)* (pp. 6–10). IEEE. 10.1109/ICSSA.2016.8

Zainuddin, H. N., & Normaziah, A. A. (2011). Secure Coding in Software Development. In *2011 Malaysian Conference in Software Engineering* (pp. 458–464). IEEE. 10.1109/MySEC.2011.6140716

KEY TERMS AND DEFINITIONS

Competence: A set of knowledge, skills, and attitudes for performing a task.

Non-Programming-Related Competences: Software security skills that do not directly deal with coding. For example, software security policy skills and system security assurance tools skills.

Programming Related Competences: Software security skills needed for coding. For example, secure programming/coding skills and secure mobile software development skills.

Security Competence of Developers: A set of specific security competencies required by a developer to deal with security during the whole software development process; For example, SQL injection skills, and security pattern skills.

Software Developer: Individuals who employ software development skills to design, construct, test, and maintain computer software.

Software Engineering Competence: A set of knowledge, skills, and attitudes of software developers to fulfill a given task in a software development project.

Software Security: An art of providing protection to software against hackers and attackers during the life cycle of the software.

Traditional Literature Review: A method used to demonstrate a gap or a problem in an area one seeks to research without an explicit method for reviewing the literature.

This research was previously published in Modern Theories and Practices for Cyber Ethics and Security Compliance; pages 73-87, copyright year 2020 by Information Science Reference (an imprint of IGI Global).

Chapter 99
Knowledge Management Initiatives in Agile Software Development:
A Literature Review

Shanmuganathan Vasanthapriyan
https://orcid.org/0000-0002-0597-0263
Sabaragamuwa University of Sri Lanka, Sri Lanka

ABSTRACT

Agile software development (ASD) is a knowledge-intensive and collaborative activity and thus Knowledge Management (KM) principals should be applied to improve the productivity of the whole ASD process from the beginning to the end of the phase. The goal is to map the evidence available on existing researches on KM initiatives in ASD in order to identify the state of the art in the area as well as the future research. Therefore, investigation of various aspects such as purposes, types of knowledge, technologies and research type are essential. The authors conducted a systematic review of literature published between 2010 and December 2017 and identified 12 studies that discuss agile requirements engineering. They formulated and applied specific inclusion and exclusion criteria in two distinct rounds to determine the most relevant studies for their research goal. Reuse of knowledge of the team is the perspective that has received more attention.

INTRODUCTION

Software development is a process which is a collection of steps like analyzing, designing, programming, documenting, testing, maintaining and bug fixing (Vasanthapriyan, Tian, & Xiang, 2015). It is clear that software development has organized to deliver final better-quality solutions to the end users or customers. When the term "software development" converts to the term "agile software development", ASD has become a new turning point in the world. Although development teams have habituated traditional

DOI: 10.4018/978-1-6684-3702-5.ch099

software methods like waterfall and prototyping, it is a good forethought to use agile for the development teams worldwide (Dybå & Dingsøyr, 2008).

There's a big focus in the ASD community on collaboration and the self-organizing team. That doesn't mean that there aren't managers. It means that teams have the ability to figure out how they're going to approach things on their own. It means that those teams are cross-functional. Those teams don't have to have specific roles involved so much as that when you get the team together, you make sure that you have all the right skill sets on the team.

Software development is a knowledge intensive and collaborative process which mainly depends on knowledge and experience of software engineers (Bjørnson & Dingsøyr, 2008; Vasanthapriyan et al., 2015). Therefore, the knowledge of the members of a team and the outside team within the organization should be properly managed by capturing, storing and reusing when needed. Even though traditional software methods use detailed specifications and design upfront and rigorous documentations (Abrahamsson, Salo, Ronkainen, & Warsta, 2017) to manage the knowledge, agile methods and principals (Petersen, Feldt, Mujtaba, & Mattsson, 2008) emerge to the software development which brings collaboration and interaction within the team and the outside of the team. It helps to manage the knowledge more efficiently and effectively by presenting the right knowledge in the right form to the right person at the right time.'

KM is about making the right knowledge available to the right people. It is about making sure that an organization can learn, and that it will be able to retrieve and use its knowledge assets in current applications as they are needed. In the words of Peter Drucker it is "the coordination and exploitation of organizational knowledge resources, in order to create benefit and competitive advantage" (Drucker, 1999). Where the disagreement sometimes occurs is in conjunction with the creation of new knowledge. Wellman (2009) limits the scope of KM to lessons learned and the techniques employed for the management of what is already known. He argues that knowledge creation is often perceived as a separate discipline and generally falls under innovation management. Williams and Bukowitz (1999) link KM directly to tactical and strategic requirements. Its focus is on the use and enhancement of knowledge-based assets to enable the firm to respond to these issues. According to this view, the answer to the question "what is knowledge management" would be significantly broader.

A similarly broad definition is presented by Davenport and Prusak (1970), which states that KM "is managing the corporation's knowledge through a systematically and organizationally specified process for acquiring, organizing, sustaining, applying, sharing and renewing both the tacit and explicit knowledge of employees to enhance organizational performance and create value". The knowledge must be constructed in a social and evolutionary process involving all stakeholders during the software development. Nakamori introduced a generic knowledge construction framework "Theory of knowledge construction systems" which is a systems approach to synthesize a variety of knowledge and to justify new knowledge (Nakamori, 2013).

Alahyari reported that only a substantial amount of papers has been published in recent years topics related to agile software development. Most of them were related to particular agile methods or comparing agile and other development processes (Alahyari, Svensson, & Gorschek, 2017). However, no recent study was found to have a dedicated focus on the concept of knowledge management. Previous reviews and investigations have been conducted for KM in ASD in different perspectives such as principals, methods, pros and cons, opportunities (Neves, Rosa, Correia, & de Castro Neto, 2011) and supporting agile practices (Fowler & Highsmith, 2001). However, what are the influences of KM in ASD and what kind of tools help to proceed with KM in ASD is not well understood. To identify and address this gap, mapping study has been performed to determine that there is research evidence on a relevant topic. Results of the mapping study help to recognize the gaps in order to suggest of future research and give the direction to a suitable position new research activity (Boden & Avram, 2009; Dorairaj, Noble, & Malik, 2012; Razzak & Ahmed, 2014). Further, in the context of ASD, KM can be used to capture knowledge and experience generated during the development process. Knowledge sharing is viewed as an important set of processes that can contribute to effective agile software development projects (Razzak, 2015).

The rest of this paper presents as below. Section 2 presents a background of KM and ASD and also related research. Section 3 discusses the research method applied to perform the mapping study. Results and discussions are presented in Section 4. Section 5 presents the conclusion and possibilities and directions for future works.

BACKGROUND

In this section, the main concepts related to the topic addressed namely: KM and ASD. Moreover, we briefly discuss related research, i.e. secondary studies that are related to these topics.

Knowledge Management

Knowledge is the possession of the information within its context. Knowledge is one of the most valuable assets for most organizations. That is, organizational knowledge is considering as the most valuable and the important asset the organization has. They are tacit and explicit. Tacit knowledge is derived from the experience which can be difficult to define and also to write down. For example, tacit knowledge covers knowledge that is unarticulated and associated to the senses, movement skills, physical experiences, intuition, or implicit rules of thumb. Explicit knowledge, in turn, represents the objective and rational knowledge that can be documented, and, thus can be accessed by multiple individuals. Explicit knowledge is very formal and can be documented (Begoña Lloria, 2008). Therefore, explicit knowledge can be shared and communicated easily (Dingsoyr & Smite, 2014). When approaching the KM, simply we can describe this as making the availability of the right knowledge to the right people in an organization. But in broadly KM can be identified as systematic management of the most valuable and important assets of the organization on behalf of creating value and meeting strategic requirements (Kavitha & Ahmed, 2011). KM can be viewed as the development and leveraging of organizational knowledge to increase organization's value (Begoña Lloria, 2008). KM is a method that simplifies the process of sharing, distributing, creating, capturing, and understanding of an organization's knowledge that should be employed (Davenport and Prusak (1970). ''The Knowledge-Creating Company'' by Nonaka and Takeuchi seeks in explaining the success of Japanese companies by their skills in ''organizational knowledge creation'' (Nonaka, Toyama, & Konno, 2000). According to Alavi and Leidner, the basic generic KM activities are known as "knowledge creation", "knowledge transfer" and "knowledge application" (Alavi & Leidner, 2001). Bhatt stated that KM process can be categorized into knowledge creation, knowledge validation, knowledge presentation, knowledge distribution, and knowledge application (Vasanthapriyan, Xiang, Tian, & Xiong, 2017). KM can be a formal process of determining what internally held information could be used to benefit an organization and ensuring that this information is easily made available to those who need it. Vasanthapriyan considered knowledge identification, knowledge acquisition, knowledge creation, knowledge sharing, knowledge storage, and knowledge application as KM activities to use in their study context (Vasanthapriyan et al., 2017). The importance of such KM becomes critical for some key positions, who manage daily activities, especially when it requires critical decision makings with their know-how experiences. Further, models like SECI process which stands for Socialization, Externalization, Combination, and Internalization, can be used for knowledge transfer and creation within the organizations.

Agile Software Development

In 2001, failures of the waterfall model were identified and the Agile methodology was introduced (Schwaber & Beedle, 2002). The term agile has been presented in 2001 when seventeen software developers met to explore and share new and improved ways of software development (Fowler & Highsmith, 2001). Agile development methodologies consist with a set of software development practices that are defined by well experienced practitioners (Schwaber & Beedle, 2002). ASD has become an efficient and effective way of software development which is used to build software or the final output iteratively and incrementally. ASD is used to build software in multiple iterations and increments (Abrahamsson et al., 2017). Each iteration is ending up with a workable product which is getting early feedback of the customer or the end user. As well this helps in delivering the product more reliably and timely.

These agile development practices reacts to traditional or plan driven methods which emphasize ''an engineering based, rationalized approach'' (Dorairaj et al., 2012). Agile software development is more than frameworks such as Scrum, Extreme Programming or Feature-Driven Development (FDD) (Schwaber & Beedle, 2002). Agile methods share few common characteristics which include iterative development process, adaptive which means accept changes, less documentation, interact with customer, focus on delivery, frequent testing, communication and collaboration among team members, improve motivation, high quality codes, knowledge transfer through openness and high-quality products with customer satisfaction (Schwaber & Beedle, 2002). Agile practices involved in software engineering field are simple design, small releases, pair programming, test driven development, daily stand-up meetings, task boards, product backlog, user stories, and on-site customer. Agile practitioners have perceived benefits which include cost reduction, quality improvements, improve flexibility among development teams, improve productivity, and improve customer satisfaction and reduction of time to market. Those benefits are achieved in software development phase and it is needed to investigate that these benefits are addressed in software maintenance phase (Vasanthapriyan, 2017).

Agile is the ability to create and respond to change. It is a way of dealing with, and ultimately succeeding in, an uncertain and turbulent environment. ASD is more than practices such as pair programming, test-driven development, stand-ups, planning sessions and sprints. ASD is an umbrella term for a set of frameworks and practices based on the values and principles expressed in the Manifesto for ASD and the 12 Principles behind it. When you approach software development in a particular manner, it's generally good to live by these values and principles and use them to help figure out the right things to do given your particular context (Vasanthapriyan et al., 2017). On the other hand, activities such as informal communication, face-to-face meetings, and knowledge sharing through social practices can create a more flexible and unstructured environment (Vasanthapriyan, 2017).

Knowledge Management in Organizations

Knowledge in organizations takes many forms such as the competencies and capabilities of employees, the knowledge about its customers and suppliers, know-how of conducting certain processes, the systems used in the company for leveraging performance and intellectual properties owned by the company such as; copyrights, licenses, patents and so on (North & Kumta, 2018). All the knowledge intensive organizations rely on making the most effective use of the available knowledge within the organization in order to compete and survive. If there is not available a proper knowledge sharing process within the organization, software practitioners would proceed with the knowledge that they already have or with the knowledge that is most easily available. Even that knowledge is accurate and of good quality, sometimes it may not be good enough to achieve the success of the projects or the sustainability of today's market (Zammit, Gao, & Evans, 2016). Omotayo states the important factors that drives KM requirement for an organization, as; organizational survival, competitive differentiation, globalization effects and aging of workforce. As his explanation, it is an undisputed fact that organizations have to compete on the basis of knowledge, since products and services are becoming increasingly complex and competitive (Omotayo, 2015).

Focusing on the question 'Is knowledge management important for an organization?', Omotayo (2015) suggests, 'when you know better, you do better'. Therefore, in order to succeed in the corporate world and put your business on top, the company needs to possess the best management of knowledge (Omotayo, 2015).

Common KM practices of the organizations are as follows (Murali & Kumar, 2014)

1. Knowledge repositories: Store and manage the various knowledge artefacts like white papers, articles, videos and other knowledge materials created by the employees.
2. Communities of knowledge: Especially through cross functional teams containing experts from different departments.
3. Knowledge sharing sessions: Share the knowledge gained in training sessions or by other knowledge sources such as courses offered by the company. They are recorded and made available through knowledge repositories.
4. Mentoring: Share the skills or knowledge of an expert in a certain domain to others who don't possess that knowledge.

As a result of the above definitions, it can thus be concluded that management of knowledge is promoted as an important and necessity factor for organizational survival (Omotayo, 2015). Further, Teamwork and collaboration among software developers produce significant amount of knowledge, which makes the sense of effective knowledge sharing among individuals (Vasanthapriyan et al., 2017). In addition, the knowledge management processes that transitioned to agile (requirements and domain knowledge, continuous learning, knowledge repositories) concentrate on tacit knowledge (Cram & Marabelli, 2018). Knowledge sharing could be identified as a process between units, teams and organizations where people exchange their knowledge with others ((Andreasian & Andreasian, 2013). Knowledge sharing starts at the individual level, since every person has tacit and explicit knowledge to share with others. Sharing tacit knowledge is more challenging as it cannot be easily expressed (Vasanthapriyan et al., 2015).

Related Works

This paper presents a secondary study which is based on analyzing primary studies (Kitchenham, Budgen, & Brereton, 2011). Mapping studies are intended to provide an overview of a topic area and identify whether there are sub-topics where more primary studies are needed (Kitchenham et al., 2011). At the beginning of this study, a tertiary study has been performed to look for secondary studies investigating the state of art in KM in ASD. Because of having a research gap in research studies related to the software development in Sri Lanka, this study has been conducted on all the research studies related to the field of KM and ASD regardless of the country to get the clear and wide view of KM in ASD. Consequently, the country has not been considered in the search string and other used search string is shown in Table 1 which has been applied in three metadata fields (title, abstract and keywords). The search string has been applied in the following electronic databases: IEEE Xplore, ACM Digital Library, Springer Link, Science Direct, Emerald Insight, and Research Gate. Since some of the electronic databases don't have any secondary study which is addressed KM in ASD, another investigation has been done to search KM and ASD separately. For that tertiary study, used search strings are shown in Table 2 and Table 3. After searching the six databases, returning 404 results. After eliminating duplications and applying the selection criteria, 147 studies are presenting secondary studies which are related to the KM and ASD both. Regarding the study which has been conducted on searching for the secondary studies, at last, 12 studies have been selected.

Table 1. Search terms of the study on KM in ASD

Areas	Search terms
ASD	"ASD ", "agile and software development"
Review	"systematic literature review", "systematic review", "systematic mapping", "mapping study", "systematic literature mapping"
Search string	("Agile software development) AND ("systematic literature review" OR "systematic review" OR "systematic mapping" OR "mapping study" OR' 'systematic literature mapping")

Table 2. Search terms of the study on ASD

Areas	Search terms
ASD	"ASD ", "agile and software development"
KM	"Knowledge Management"
Review	"systematic literature review", "systematic review", "systematic mapping", "mapping study", "systematic literature mapping"
Search string	("Agile software development" OR "Agile and software development") AND ("knowledge management") AND ("systematic literature review" OR "systematic review" OR "systematic mapping' 'OR "mapping study" OR "systematic literature mapping")

Table 3. Search terms of the study on KM

Areas	Search terms
KM	"Knowledge Management"
Review	"systematic literature review", "systematic review", "systematic mapping", "mapping study", "systematic literature mapping"
Search string	("Agile software development") AND ("systematic literature review" OR "systematic review" OR "systematic mapping" OR "mapping study" OR "systematic literature mapping")

Table 4. Inclusion and exclusion criteria

No.	Inclusion criterion (IC)
IC1	The study EKR use and project success in software companies
No.	Exclusion criteria (EC)
EC1	The study does not contain an abstract
EC2	The study is published just as an abstract
EC3	The language used in writing the study is not English
EC4	The study is an older version of a study already selected previously
EC5	The study is not a primary study. The study is either an editorial or a summary

RESEARCH METHOD

Research method of this mapping study is defined according to the guidelines described by Brereton, Kitchenham, Budgen, Turner, and Khalil (2007). Under the research method section, this paper discusses the main steps followed in the mapping study including research questions, study selection, data extraction and synthesis, classification schema that have been used in mapping and eventually, limitations of the mapping study. In the first selection stage, we looked for the current status of the research studies regarding in KM applied to ASD in organizations. In the second selection stage, a selection process has been performed to retrieve the studies. Here, following selection criteria were addressed:

1. Definition of the search string and terms
2. Sources for searching
3. Definition for inclusion and exclusion criteria (shown in Table 4) and
4. Way of storing data.

In the third selection stage, publications until December 2017 were considered. In the search process, as the searching result, a total of 404 publications were returned. Out of the total search result, 43 from IEEE Xplore, 107 from ACM Digital Library, 73 from Springer Link, 63 from Science Direct, 51 from Emerald Insight and 67 from Research Gate were found. To extract the most relevant studies, the selection process was performed on the selected publications. In the first stage, we eliminated duplications (publications that appear in more than one source), achieving 257 publications (reduction of approximately 63%). In the second stage, we applied the selection criteria (inclusion and exclusion criteria) over the title, abstract and keywords, resulting in 17 papers (reduction of 93%). 5 papers were eliminated by EC5 (The study is not a primary study) and 235 for not satisfying IC1 (The study discusses a KM initiative in ASD). In the third stage, the selection criteria were applied considering the full text, resulting in a set of 10 studies (reduction of approximately 41%). 1 paper was eliminated by EC4 (The study is an older version of another study already considered), and 6 papers were eliminated for not satisfying IC1 (The study discusses KM initiatives in ASD). Over these 10 studies considered relevant, the 4th stage, snowballing was performed which resulted in 6 papers. After applying the selection criteria over title, abstract and keywords, 3 papers remained (reduction of 50% over the 6 papers selected by snowballing). For the remaining, the selection criteria were applied considering the full text and only one paper remained (reduction of approximately 67% over the 3 previously selected papers).

Finally, we have selected 11 papers and in the 5th stage, we have looked for publications authored by the researchers and research groups involved in these studies. As a result of this searching, 2 papers identified and after analyzing the full text 1 paper was identified as more appropriate to the subject were selected as a direct search. Total of 12 papers was retrieved as the final result of this searching process, including, 10 from the sources, 1 from snowballing and 1 from direct searching researchers and research groups. Summary of each selection stage and their results are shown in Table 5. Table 5 clearly emphasizes the progressive elimination of the studies during the selection process. Table 6 provides the bibliographic references of the studies selected. Each study has been provided with a unique identifier (#id) and these identifiers are used in the rest of this paper to represent each study. When systematic mapping is conducting, a classification scheme is necessary to be defined (Petersen et al., 2008). The main finding of the selected research is; Factors affect KM using in ASD reported by the selected studies.

Table 5. Results of the selection stages

Stage	Applied criteria	Analyzed content	Initial number of studies	Final number of studies	Reduction
1st	Duplicate removal	Title, abstract and keywords	404	257	36.0
2nd	IC1 and EC3	Title, abstract and keywords	257	17	93.0
3rd	IC1, EC1, EC2, EC4 and EC5	Full text	17	10	41.0
4th (a)	Snowballing	Title, abstract and keywords	6 (added by snowballing)	3 (added by snowballing)	50.0
4th (b)	Snowballing and IC1	Full text	3 (added by snowballing)	1 (added by snowballing)	67.0
5th	Research groups	Full text	2 (added by research groups)	1 (added by research groups)	-
Final Result			404 (sources) + 6 (snowballing) + 2 (research groups) = 412	10 (sources) + 1 (snowballing) + 1	97.0

In this section, different kinds of limitation of this mapping study are discussed.

This study may have some embedded subjectivity regarding selected studies and extracted data since major steps of this mapping study like selecting studies and extracting data is performed by one author.

1. This study is performed by just one author and major steps of this study; selecting studies and extracting data; are also performed by a single author. Therefore, this study may have some embedded subjectivity regarding selected studies and extracted data.

2. Also search string may include problems in the terminology. In such situations, it may have caused missing of certain primary studies. In the search string, term "Knowledge management" was included in order to investigate the research area more widely.

3. Only specific numbers of databases were selected for retrieving data. Snowballing technique is used to the references of studies selected from sources in order to reduce this limitation. Direct

search of researchers and research groups were performed for selected studies but there may have the considerable possibility of missing some valuable studies from the analysis performed.

4. For some databases limitations on publication, the year was applied in order to select most updated research studies. Most of the times publications during 2010-2017 were searched so some important studies which were published before 2010 may have missed.

5. Hence, it may not fit with the context used in this study. Also, due to classification's dependency over background and expertise of researcher, there may have classification bias.

6. This study is used classification scheme proposed by Wieringa, Maiden, Mead, and Rolland (2006). But some researchers suggest that this method is inappropriate scheme to classify research types in secondary studies. So, there can be classification bias due to the expertise of the researchers and classification dependency over the background.

Table 6. Selected studies

ID	Bibliographic reference
#1	G. Borrego, A. L. Morán, R. R. P. Cinco, O. M. Rodríguez-Elias, and E. García-Canseco, "Review of approaches to manage architectural knowledge in Agile Global Software Development," IET Software, vol. 11, no. 3, pp. 77–88, Jan. 2017.
#2	J. Paredes, C. Anslow, and F. Maurer, "Information Visualization for Agile Software Development," 2014 Second IEEEWorking Conference on Software Visualization, 2014.
#3	M. A. Razzak and D. Mite, "Knowledge Management in Globally Distributed Agile Projects -- Lesson Learned," 2015IEEE 10th International Conference on Global Software Engineering, 2015
#4	Y. Andriyani, R. Hoda, and R. Amor, "Understanding Knowledge Management in Agile Software DevelopmentPractice," Knowledge Science, Engineering and Management Lecture Notes in Computer Science, pp. 195–207, 2017.
#5	M. Alawairdhi, "Agile development as a change management approach in software projects: Applied case study," 20162nd International Conference on Information Management (ICIM), 2016.
#6	Y. Andriyani, "Knowledge Management and Reflective Practice in Daily Stand-Up and Retrospective Meetings," LectureNotes in Business Information Processing Agile Processes in Software Engineering and Extreme Programming, pp. 285–291, 2017.
#7	F. O. Bjørnson and T. Dingsøyr, "A Survey of Perceptions on Knowledge Management Schools in Agile and TraditionalSoftware Development Environments," Lecture Notes in Business Information Processing Agile Processes in SoftwareEngineering and Extreme Programming, pp. 94–103, 2009.
#8	S. Dorairaj, J. Noble, and P. Malik, "Knowledge Management in Distributed Agile Software Development," 2012 AgileConference, 2012.
#9	A. R. Y. Cabral, M. B. Ribeiro, and R. P. Noll, "Knowledge Management in Agile Software Projects: A SystematicReview," Journal of Information & Knowledge Management, vol. 13, no. 01, p. 1450010, 2014.
#10	R. Vallon, B. J. D. S. Estácio, R. Prikladnicki, and T. Grechenig, "Systematic literature review on agile practices in globalsoftware development," Information and Software Technology, vol. 96, pp. 161–180, 2017.
#11	S. Ghobadi and L. Mathiassen, "Perceived barriers to effective knowledge sharing in agile software teams," InformationSystems Journal, vol. 26, no. 2, pp. 95–125, 2014.
#12	A. C. A. Menolli, M. A. Cunha, S. Reinehr, and A. Malucelli, "Old theories, New technologies: Understanding knowledge sharing and learning in Brazilian software development companies," Information and Software Technology, vol. 58, pp. 289–303, 2015.

RESULTS AND DISCUSSION

In this section, findings and results derived through the mapping study are discussed. All the results were summarized in a table with the identifier of the paper, its bibliographic reference and that table were used as the source of extracting information to answer each research question. Figure 1 is represented to elaborate the distribution of selected papers over the year of publication. Only the papers published from 2009 to December 2017 were taken into account in order to get an updated view of the study area. According to Figure 1, researchers have focused on KM in ASD in recent years, since, there have been published 10 papers out of 12 selected papers in a 2014-2017 period of time.

Figure 1. Distribution of the selected studies over the years

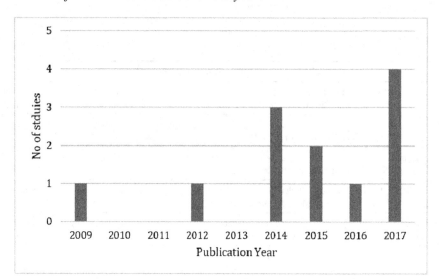

That is 83% of the total selected studies. The selected studies were published in Journals and conferences. Most of the papers have been published in journals which is approximately 67% of publications. Other 33% of the papers are conference papers. As an overall view, it seems these publications covered the area of KM, ASD. According to the data shown in Table 7, distribution of the studies which are relevant to the research focuses from the ASD perspective. Most of the papers are addressing KM in ASD without focusing on any aspects of ASD (7 out of 12). As well the papers which are addressing KM in ASD process are also showing high value (5 out of 12). Table 8 shows, most of the studies are discussing the aspects which are related to the KM process as a whole or focusing on one of its activities. Most of the papers (83.33%) discuss knowledge representation to provide KM support in ASD. Table 9 shows the distribution of research types. All the selected 12 studies propose some solution for KM in ASD.

Evaluation research and Solution proposal were the two types of research types. 8 papers out of 12 were classified into evaluation research (66.67%) and four papers present solution proposals (approximately 33.33%). Considering the distribution over the years, Table 10 shows the problems reported by software organizations related to knowledge in ASD. As well as we think these problems as a motivation for performing a research in KM to ASD. When we consider the results in Table 10, "Barriers in transferring ASD knowledge" and "ASD knowledge is not properly shared" are showing similar and the largest percentages (6 out of 12, corresponding to 50%). Table 11 shows the distribution of the purposes of the organization in managing ASD knowledge. When we consider the results, we can notice that "Organizational Learning" (8 studies-66.67%) has the largest value. "Process of knowledge in ASD" (6 studies-50%) and "Competitive advantages" (5 studies-41.67%) are showing next large percentages. Although "Reuse of knowledge related to ASD" (3 studies-25%) and "Cost reduction" (1 study) are showing some less percentage, all the purposes help to manage the knowledge in ASD.

Table 7. Research focus from the ASD perspective along the years

Research Focus	2009	2010	2011	2012	2013	2014	2015	2016	2017	Total
KM in ASD Process				#8		#11	#3	#1, #4		5 (41.67%)
KM in various kind of ASD phases							#3			1 (8.33%)
KM in ASD in general without focusing on any aspects of ASD	#7					#2, #9	#12	#5	#6, #10	7 (58.33%)

Table 8. Distribution over research focus regarding the KM perspective

Research Focus	2009	2010	2011	2012	2013	2014	2015	2016	2017	Total
KM Model						#9			#1	2 (16.67%)
Knowledge Representation	#7			#8		#9, #11	#3, #12	#5	#1, #4, #6	10 (83.33%)
Knowledge Elicitation				#8			#3		#1	3 (25%)
Knowledge Evolution				#8			#3			2 (16.67%)
Knowledge Management Systems (KMS)				#8		#2			#10	3 (25%)

Table 9. Distribution over research type

Research Focus	2009	2010	2011	2012	2013	2014	2015	2016	2017	Total
Evaluation Research	#7			#8		#9, #11	#3		#1, #4, #10	8 (66.67%)
Proposal Solution						#2	#12	#5	#6	4 (33.33%)

Table 10. Distribution of related problems (Motivation)

Research Focus	2009	2010	2011	2012	2013	2014	2015	2016	2017	Total
Barriers to transferring ASD knowledge				#8		#9, #11	#3		#1, #4	6 (50%)
Loss of ASD Knowledge	#7							#5	#10	3 (25%)
ASD knowledge is not properly shared	#7					#2, #9, #11	#12		#6	6 (50%)

Table 11. Distribution of purposes

Research Focus	2009	2010	2011	2012	2013	2014	2015	2016	2017	Total
Reuse of knowledge related to ASD						#2			#1, #10	3 (25%)
Knowledge Representation				#8		#9, #11			#1, #4, #10	6 (50%)
Knowledge Elicitation						#11				1 (8.33%)
Knowledge Evolution				#8		#9, #11	#3		#6	5 (41.67%)
Knowledge Management Systems (KMS)	#7			#8		#9	#12, #3	#5	#6, #4	8 (66.67%)

Table 12 shows the distribution of the knowledge types in ASD over the years. Here the research focus fact "General" (3 studies- 25%) has got the largest percentage from the selected studies. "Product knowledge" (2 studies -16.7%), "Project knowledge" (3 studies-25%) and "Process knowledge" (1 studies-8.33%) are having the percentages among the selected studies as given. The distributions of the technologies which are used to implement KM in ASD are shown in Table 13. Here, we have presented three different technologies in the research. It should be noticed that 2 studies do not address this question (#2, #5), representing 16.67%. The majority of the below studies uses conventional technologies (5 in 12 studies, corresponding to 41.67%). This category concerns IT conventional technologies such as databases, intranets, and internet.

Table 12. Distribution of knowledge

Research Focus	2009	2010	2011	2012	2013	2014	2015	2016	2017	Total
Product knowledge						#2			#4	2 (16.67%)
Project knowledge							#3		#1, #4, #10	3 (25%)
Process knowledge									#4	1 (8.33%)
General	#7			#8		#9, #11	#12	#5	#6, #10	8 (66.67%)

Table 13. Distribution of technologies used

Research Focus	2009	2010	2011	2012	2013	2014	2015	2016	2017	Total
Ontology	#7					#11			#1	3 (25%)
Recommendation Systems				#8			#3		#4	3 (25%)
Process knowledge						#9, #11	#12		#6, #10	5 (41.67%)

According to the results of this mapping, there are many benefits to implementing KM in organizations for managing ASD knowledge.

Increasing the Effectiveness

It is necessary to increase the effectiveness of the ASD since knowledge and experience about the domain and the system which is going to develop are directly affecting to the effectiveness.

Selection and Application of Suited Techniques and Methods

It is not a doubt that experience plays a key role in ASD and managing the past experience of the whole team members helps to effectively tailor the techniques and methods to the on-going project.

Competitive Advantages

KM is now seen as a strategic factor and knowledge is also identified as a factor of cost savings and competitive advantage. The ability to transfer best practices in the organization helps to bring a competitive advantage to the organization.

Cost Reduction

In ASD, the cost is strongly related with the time. Here the experience of all the team members helps to develop the product according to the timeline. As well development team decreases the risk of cost overruns and avoids costly activities that do not provide value by focusing on business value with every activity.

Increase the Productivity

It can be considered that there will be a new understanding of KM in ASD that it involves managing three different types of knowledge which are identified as process, project, and product. These three are helping to implement KM strategies like discussions, artifacts and visualizations during every day agile process in a business organization. Therefore, these strategies will help agile practitioners to become aware of and enable those to manage the knowledge in every agile practice productively.

Table 14 shows how the benefits are accommodating by the selected studies. Two of these benefits which are mentioned above are cited by over half of the studies. Although there are many benefits in KM in ASD, there are problems also. Those problems are,

KM Systems Are Not Appropriated

There are many difficulties in implementing the KM strategies such as knowledge acquisition, coding, storage, and searching functionalities effectively in KM systems because it involves all the problems mentioned above such as how to represent knowledge and time and interest of the employees.

Increased Workload

Since there are short timelines, it is a potential risk to incorporate the principles of KM in ASD because knowledge sharing can imply in increasing the team members' workload and costs. Table 15 shows how the problems are distributed in the selected studies.

Table 14. Distribution of the identified benefits

Research Focus	2009	2010	2011	2012	2013	2014	2015	2016	2017	Total
A				#8		#9	#3	#5	#1, #4, #10	7 (58.33%)
B							#3		#1, #4	3 (25%)
C				#8		#2	#12		#1, #4	5 (41.67%)
D	#7			#8		#9, #11	#3, #12	#5	#4, #6, #10	10 (83.33%)

Table 15. Distribution of problems

Research Focus	2009	2010	2011	2012	2013	2014	2015	2016	2017	Total
A	#7			#8		#9, #11	#3, #12	#5	#1, #4, #10	10 (83.33%)
B						#2, #11			#6	3 (25%)

CONCLUSION

As a summary of results, knowledge is treated as a cornerstone for software companies to achieve sustainable competitive advantage. However, knowledge management in ASD generate both positive and negative effects.

The study describes the results of ten research questions which have done investigations of the following points:

1. Distribution of the selected studies over the years;
2. Research focus from the software testing perspective;
3. Research focus from the KM perspective;
4. Research type;
5. Reported problems;
6. Purposes of employing in ASD;
7. Purposes to employ KM in ASD;
8. Types of knowledge typically managed in ASD;
9. Technologies used in KM in ASD;
10. Main conclusions (benefits and problems) reported on the KM in ASD.

The major problem in organizations are low reuse rate of knowledge and barriers in knowledge transfer in ASD is a recent research;

1. Knowledge types which are used in ASD are not identified correctly in the organizations;
2. Reuse of development knowledge is the main purpose of applying KM in ASD;
3. There is a great concern with explicit knowledge using in ASD, although tacit knowledge has been also recognized as a very useful knowledge item;
4. Advanced technologies used to provide KM in ASD.

Hence, future software engineering-based researchers could be able to conduct their research focusing on tacit and explicit knowledge management. In the context of results and findings of this mapping, following future research topics are highlighted:

1. Tacit Knowledge Management in globally distributed agile software development.
2. Investigating the scope of agile project management to be adapted by software companies.
3. Analysis of KM involvement in Kanban and Scrum for software development projects.
4. Understanding architectural knowledge sharing in agile software development.

According to these specific dimensions of knowledge will help agile practitioners have become aware of and enable them to manage, the knowledge in everyday agile practices effectively.

ACKNOWLEDGMENT

We thank some of the key officials from the Sri Lankan software companies to motivate us for this kind of study. We also thank the Sabaragamuwa University of Sri Lanka to encourage this research.

REFERENCES

Abrahamsson, P., Salo, O., Ronkainen, J., & Warsta, J. (2017). *Agile software development methods: Review and analysis.* arXiv preprint arXiv:1709.08439

Alahyari, H., Svensson, R. B., & Gorschek, T. (2017). A study of value in agile software development organizations. *Journal of Systems and Software*, *125*, 271–288. doi:10.1016/j.jss.2016.12.007

Alavi, M., & Leidner, D. E. (2001). Review: Knowledge management and knowledge management systems: Conceptual foundations and research issues. *Management Information Systems Quarterly*, *25*(1), 107–136. doi:10.2307/3250961

Andreasian, G., & Andreasian, M. (2013). *Knowledge Sharing and Knowledge Transfer Barriers. A Case Study.* Academic Press.

Begoña Lloria, M. (2008). A review of the main approaches to knowledge management. *Knowledge Management Research and Practice*, *6*(1), 77–89. doi:10.1057/palgrave.kmrp.8500164

Bjørnson, F. O., & Dingsøyr, T. (2008). Knowledge management in software engineering: A systematic review of studied concepts, findings and research methods used. *Information and Software Technology*, *50*(11), 1055–1068. doi:10.1016/j.infsof.2008.03.006

Boden, A., & Avram, G. (2009). *Bridging knowledge distribution-The role of knowledge brokers in distributed software development teams.* Paper presented at the Cooperative and Human Aspects on Software Engineering, 2009. CHASE'09. ICSE Workshop on. 10.1109/CHASE.2009.5071402

Brereton, P., Kitchenham, B. A., Budgen, D., & et al, . (2007). Lessons from applying the systematic literature review process within the software engineering domain. *Journal of Systems and Software, 80*(4), 571–583. doi:10.1016/j.jss.2006.07.009

Cram, W. A., & Marabelli, M. (2018). Have your cake and eat it too? Simultaneously pursuing the knowledge-sharing benefits of agile and traditional development approaches. *Information & Management, 55*(3), 322–339. doi:10.1016/j.im.2017.08.005

Davenport, T., & Prusak, L. (2000). *Working knowledge: How organizations manage what they know.* Brighton, MA: Harvard Business Press.

Dingsoyr, T., & Smite, D. (2014). Managing knowledge in global software development projects. *IT Professional, 16*(1), 22–29. doi:10.1109/MITP.2013.19

Dorairaj, S., Noble, J., & Malik, P. (2012). *Knowledge management in distributed agile software development.* Paper presented at the Agile Conference (AGILE), 2012. 10.1109/Agile.2012.17

Drucker, P. F. (1999). Knowledge-worker productivity: The biggest challenge. *California Management Review, 41*(2), 79–94. doi:10.2307/41165987

Dybå, T., & Dingsøyr, T. (2008). Empirical studies of agile software development: A systematic review. *Information and Software Technology, 50*(9), 833–859. doi:10.1016/j.infsof.2008.01.006

Fowler, M., & Highsmith, J. (2001). The agile manifesto. *Software Development, 9*(8), 28–35.

Kavitha, R., & Ahmed, M. I. (2011). *A knowledge management framework for agile software development teams.* Paper presented at the Process Automation, Control and Computing (PACC), 2011 International Conference on. 10.1109/PACC.2011.5978877

Kitchenham, B. A., Budgen, D., & Brereton, O. P. (2011). Using mapping studies as the basis for further research–a participant-observer case study. *Information and Software Technology, 53*(6), 638–651. doi:10.1016/j.infsof.2010.12.011

Murali, A., & Kumar, S. K. (2014). Knowledge Management and Human Resource Management (HRM): Importance of Integration. *FIIB Business Review, 3*(1), 3–10.

Nakamori, Y. (2013). Knowledge and systems science: enabling systemic knowledge synthesis. Boca Raton, FL: CRC Press. doi:10.1201/b15155

Neves, F. T., Rosa, V. N., Correia, A. M. R., & de Castro Neto, M. (2011). *Knowledge creation and sharing in software development teams using Agile methodologies: Key insights affecting their adoption.* Paper presented at the Information Systems and Technologies (CISTI), 2011 6th Iberian Conference on.

Nonaka, I., Toyama, R., & Konno, N. (2000). SECI, Ba and leadership: A unified model of dynamic knowledge creation. *Long Range Planning, 33*(1), 5–34. doi:10.1016/S0024-6301(99)00115-6

North, K., & Kumta, G. (2018). *Knowledge management: Value creation through organizational learning*. Springer. doi:10.1007/978-3-319-59978-6

Omotayo, F. O. (2015). Knowledge Management as an important tool in Organisational Management: A Review of Literature. University of Nebraska-Lincoln.

Petersen, K., Feldt, R., Mujtaba, S., & Mattsson, M. (2008). *Systematic Mapping Studies in Software Engineering*. Paper presented at the EASE.

Razzak, M. A. (2015). *Knowledge Management in Globally Distributed Agile Projects--Lesson Learned*. Paper presented at the Global Software Engineering (ICGSE), 2015 IEEE 10th International Conference on, Sri Lanka.

Razzak, M. A., & Ahmed, R. (2014). *Knowledge sharing in distributed agile projects: Techniques, strategies and challenges*. Paper presented at the Computer Science and Information Systems (FedCSIS), 2014 Federated Conference on. 10.15439/2014F280

Schwaber, K., & Beedle, M. (2002). Agile software development with Scrum (Vol. 1). Upper Saddle River, NJ: Prentice Hall.

Vasanthapriyan, S. (2017). Agile and scrum in a small software development project: a case study. In *Proceedings of 7th International Symposium*. South Eastern University of Sri Lanka.

Vasanthapriyan, S., Tian, J., & Xiang, J. (2015). *A survey on knowledge management in software engineering*. Paper presented at the Software Quality, Reliability and Security-Companion (QRS-C), 2015 IEEE International Conference on, Vancouver, Canada. 10.1109/QRS-C.2015.48

Vasanthapriyan, S., Xiang, J., Tian, J., & Xiong, S. (2017). Knowledge synthesis in software industries: a survey in Sri Lanka. Knowledge Management Research & Practice, 15(3), 413-430. doi:10.105741275-017-0057-7

Wellman, J. (2009). *Organizational learning: How companies and institutions manage and apply knowledge*. Springer. doi:10.1057/9780230621541

Wieringa, R., Maiden, N., Mead, N., & Rolland, C. (2006). Requirements engineering paper classification and evaluation criteria: A proposal and a discussion. *Requirements Engineering*, *11*(1), 102–107. doi:10.100700766-005-0021-6

Williams, R. L., & Bukowitz, W. R. (1999). *The knowledge management field book*. London, UK: FT Management.

Zammit, J., Gao, J., & Evans, R. (2016). Capturing and sharing product development knowledge using storytelling and video sharing. *Procedia CIRP*, *56*, 440–445. doi:10.1016/j.procir.2016.10.081

This research was previously published in Human Factors in Global Software Engineering; pages 109-130, copyright year 2019 by Engineering Science Reference (an imprint of IGI Global).

Chapter 100

A Systematic Literature Review on Risk Assessment and Mitigation Approaches in Requirement Engineering

Priyanka Chandani

Jaypee Institute of Information Technology, Noida, India

Chetna Gupta

Jaypee Institute of Information Technology, Noida, India

ABSTRACT

Risk assessment and management practice is an organized way to identify, analyze, and assess the impacts of risks and mitigate them when they arise. Risk can occur in any phase of software development and is a significant step for better supervision of threats. The purpose of this study is to identify and analyze existing risk assessment and management techniques from a historical perspective that address and study risk management and perception of risk. The chapter presents extensive summary of existing literature on various techniques and approaches related to requirements defects, defect taxonomy, its classification, and its potential impact on software development as the main contributions of this research work. The primary objective of this study was to present a systematic literature review of techniques/methods/ tools for risk assessment and management. This research successfully identifies and discovers existing risk assessment and management techniques, their limitations, taxonomies, processes, and identifies possible improvements for better defect identification and prevention.

BACKGROUND, MOTIVATION AND INTRODUCTION

The software industry is going through a revolution at a rapid pace where both business and technology domains are evolving very fast. This time-to-deliver market puts pressure on software development teams to deliver quality software well in time which establishes the need for performing rigorous risk analysis

DOI: 10.4018/978-1-6684-3702-5.ch100

(Arshad, 2007). Studies have shown that inappropriate and misleading requirement gathering is the most expensive and are one of the fundamental drivers of project failures (Glass, 1998). As reported by (Pohl & Rupp, 2010), 60% of project venture disappointments fall into requirements engineering phase and generally aren't found until late in development life cycle or when the project has gone live (Boehm, 1981). The same facts are supported by (Lindquist, 2005) which conclude that *"poor requirements management can be attributed to 71% of software projects that fail; greater than bad technology missed deadlines, and change management issues"*. Therefore, one of the significant challenges in requirements engineering is to have legible requirements, which are free from unknowns and failures. Any failures during RE phase have an adverse impact on the overall development process (Hall, Beecham & Rainer, 2002) as it acts as a roadmap for calculating schedule and cost of the system under development.

Risk assessment and management is a sub disciple of software engineering which in an organized way identifies, analyze and assess the impacts of risks and mitigate them when they arise. Risk can occur in any phase of software lifecycle due to the scope of an assortment of potential problems that can emerge in different levels of software development. To have confidence in fulfilling product roadmap and complete release based on their timeline, the risk has to be eliminated as early as possible (Rabia & Muhammad, 2013). It is one of the overlooked aspects in requirements engineering (Stern & Arias, 2011) and is generally considered as a potential problem that can negatively affect the projects. However, risk can also have a positive effect in terms of opportunities. As per guide to the Project Management Body of Knowledge (PMBOK), *"project risk is an uncertain event or condition, that, if occurs, has a positive or a negative effect on a project objective"* (2017). Conventional risk management process as exercised by a larger part of project managers tend to focus on risk by spending considerable effort on identifying and managing threats, ignoring positive side of risk (Hillson, 2002). According to (McConnell, 1997), risk management requires 5% of the aggregate project budget to get a 50–70% possibility of staying away from time to avoid overrun. Researchers in the past have proposed a considerable amount of risk identification, analysis, and management models, for better supervision of threats (Guiling & Xiaojuan, 2011).

This chapter aims to provide a critical review of the studies conducted by researchers in the past focusing mainly in the area of software risk assessment at requirement engineering phase of SDLC. The scope of the survey is to find out assessment tools and methods there are available, what results they produce and risk management process as a whole. The research community will be able to use this literature study as a starting point for further research.

The chapter is structured as follows: first, the details about the systematic review process are given and discussed. The studies related to risk management models are briefly discussed along with the current practices of risk assessment and mapping of the models on different life cycle stages to give a complete view on risk management. Finally, the current state of the art is summarized followed by the conclusion.

RESEARCH METHOD

This study has been undertaken as a complete literature review based on the work done by various researchers in the risk assessment and management field. In this case, the goal of the review is to assess the literature available on the subject of discussion. Steps in this complete literature review method involve the selection of sources and search process as depicted below in Figure 1:

Figure 1. Complete Literature Review Process

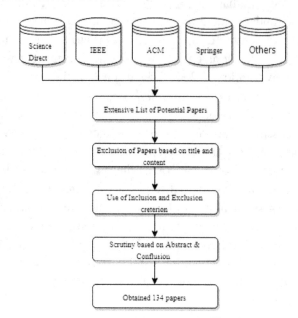

Source Selection

The following resources were explored to mine relevant data resources to conduct this review work: IEEE Xplore, ACM Digital Library, ScienceDirect, Web of Science, Springer, Google Scholar, and other databases. In addition to search results returned by popular databases, an intensive manual search on title, abstract and index term was conducted to accumulate research work of different dimensions for analysis. For in-depth analysis, reference lists of shortlisted papers were inspected for additional relevant papers.

Search Process

More analysis was necessary to streamline these studies to relevant ones. First, the title of each study and their contents were briefly studied. Hence, all the papers that do not address the topic of discussion were excluded from the relevant studies list. Also, only studies are written and published in the english language from journals, conference proceedings, workshops, symposiums, book chapters, and relevant technical articles were considered for inclusion in the list of relevant studies. The duplicate and ambiguous papers are removed from the list. Specifically, we performed a complete literature review for risk assessment and management on articles published since 1986. Table 1 shows the inclusion and exclusion criteria for selecting primary studies and filtering out the publications that match the exclusion criteria:

Final scrutiny of the papers was done based on the abstract and conclusion of the papers. A total of 134 studies were selected for this research. Among them, 61 papers were published in journals, 39 papers appeared in conference proceedings, 3 papers came from workshops, 2 papers were extracted from symposiums, 10 papers were from book chapters, and 9 papers were technical reports and 8 papers in others category. The respective percentages of the selected studies are represented in Figure 2 while the number of papers by year of publication is shown in Figure 3.

Table 1. Inclusion and exclusion criteria

Inclusion Criteria	Exclusion Criteria
All the papers published in the English language	Language is other than English
Papers that focus on risk assessment for improving requirements in particular	Studies whose findings are unclear and ambiguous
Paper having different types of proposals: Models, framework, techniques, tools, etc	Papers that are duplicate
Papers published from the year 1986	Paper focusing on risk assessment but not software engineering oriented.

Figure 2. Paper Distribution

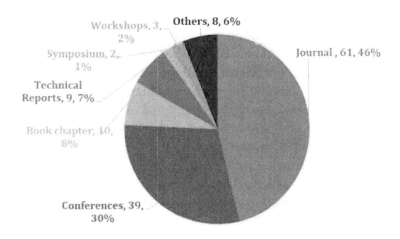

Figure 3. Number of papers by year of publication

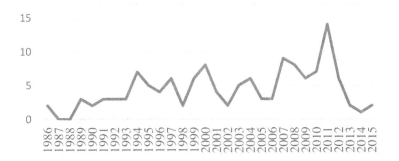

Research Questions

Following research questions are addressed in this study:

RQ1: What are the existing approaches used for risk assessment and management?
RQ2: What are the descriptions and limitations of existing risk assessment and management techniques?

RQ3: What are various dimensional scales of risk assessment factors each technique exhibit?

RQ4: What are different risk factors and perspectives adopted by stakeholders and developer for risk assessment and mitigation?

RQ5: What are various risk factors related to requirement schedule for risk assessment and management?

RQ6: Which risk management model fits the best for which phase of software lifecycle?

STUDIES RELATED TO RISK ASSESSMENT AND MANAGEMENT (RQ1 AND RQ2)

The demand for software solutions and high customer requirements creates stiff competition in the software development market. It would propel software companies to manage risks effectively and efficiently helping to improve the success-to-failure ratio (Wanderley et al., 2015). Analysis on the research in the last three decades shows that an attempt has been made to manage risk factors by using various methods, approaches, process and models for incrementing the success rate and decrementing failure in software development activities (Janjua, Jaafar & Lai, 2016). Risk assessment and management practices provide a structured and coherent way to assess and manage risk (Noraini & Bokolo, 2015). Various approaches in the past have focused on assessing risks in all phases of software life cycle, by integrating risk management practices at every juncture. However, several attempts have been made where risk assessment is integrated in the initial phase of the software development, which benefits the software project by handling risk at the early stage (Bhukya, Pabboju, 2018; Cornford et al., 2006). A set of studies have used structured and methodical models for risk assessment in which analytical hierarchy process, UML, decision trees, goal-oriented techniques, fuzzy entropy, risk metrics, machine learning and bayesian belief network were used (Hsieh, Hsu & Lin, 2016; Ghane, 2017; Meng, 2017; Zhi et al., 2017; Kamila & Sutikno, 2016; Cailliau & Lamsweerde, 2015; Anthony, 2015; Amber, Shawoo & Begum, 2012; Li & Liu, 2009; Kumar & Yadav, 2015). They culminate that the reduction in software risk is primarily due to effective risk management practices. Most of the risk management practices divide risk management into basic processes which start with identification of risk, further on to analysis, followed by mitigation and monitoring of risk (Guiling & Xiaojuan, 2011; Kumar, Sagar & Sudheer, 2010). Major studies perform risk analysis both qualitative and quantitatively which assesses risk based on probability and impact. Contrary, some models analyze risk related to software projects only. Some studies also work on project time delays which too is an indirect impact from software risk (Genuchten, 1991; Swede & Vliet, 1994). However, risk management is also dealt through research work in special cases like requirement engineering, risk-based QA and project risk dependencies (Amber, Shawoo & Begum, 2012; Lobato, Neto & Machado, 2012; Gallardo, 2012; Veenendaal, 2011). This section answers RQ1 and RQ2 and presents descriptions of existing risk assessment practices proposed till date in Table 2 followed by the limitations.

RESULTS AND DISCUSSION

This section presents and discusses the findings of this study. The detailed description of the finding is presented by answering selected research questions.

Table 2. Risk Assessment Methods

S. No	Method	Description
1	BOEHM (Boehm, 1991)	• It highlights the concept of "risk exposure" which is a relationship between the chances of occurrence of an unexpected event and the loss as a result. • Top ten risk identification checklist is identified and the decision tree method used to ascertain risk items. • The risk management approach has two steps, each subdivided into three steps. Risk assessment, the premier step involves risk identification, analysis, and prioritization. The second step is risk control which involves management planning, resolution, and monitoring of the risk. This model is applicable in all phases of software development.
2	SEI-SRE (Carr et al., 1993)	• SEI-SRE (Software Engineering Institute -Software Risk Evaluation) was developed by the Software Engineering Institute. This method is very efficient and is mainly used in defense IT projects. • Project manager expectations are managed by preparing high-level strategic plans for mitigating risk as a template. This paradigm shows a set of functions: identify, analyze, plan, track, control, and communicate. This is a continuous activity, which goes throughout the lifecycle of a project.
3	RISKIT (Kontio & Basili, 1997)	• This method defines risks more precisely and formally and provides support for multiple stakeholders by considering the definition of items which influence the project like goals, objectives, and drivers all of which are explicitly mentioned. • It models different aspects of risks qualitatively and prioritizes risk using ratio and ordinal scales. • This model is flexible and can be applied to many domains apart from of software development.
4	SERUM (Greer, 1997)	• Software Engineering Risk: Understanding and Management (SERUM) looks at both explicit and implicit risk making the risk management easier and handling them more adequately. • It is used in software released in versions and considers the risk in the current system as well as in proposed system. • Feedback of similar kind of projects does not account for in SERUM.
5	SERIM (Karolak, 1995)	• Software Engineering Risk Index Management model follows "Just in Time" strategy, it helps to assess risk factors from various analytical perspectives and develops action plans to risk management before they come live. • This method defines prior and urgent risk areas, develops proactive plans for risk mitigation • Ten risk factors are identified which are assessed quantitatively, by the project manager as lower the score the riskier projects.
6	SRAM (Foo & Muruganantham, 2000)	• This model considers the nine risk elements that are the complexity of software, project staff, targeted reliability, product requirement, a method of estimation, Monitoring practice, the process of development, usability of software/tools. • This model is questionnaire based and provides a quantitative assessment of risk with good accuracy.
7	PRORISK (Suebkuna & Ramingwong, 2011)	• Project Oriented Risk Management Model is a decision support tool that works on linking project management and risk management in a software project. • It is a practical approach, which can be easily understood and efficiently applied in any software projects. Three important elements are risk management, project management, and risk database which is used to manage risk control information.
8	SRAEM (Gupta & Sadiq, 2008)	• In SRAEM (Software risk assessment and estimation model) estimation of risk is done using software metric and risk exposure based on Mission Critical Requirements Stability Risk Metrics (MCRSRM) • This model shows cumulative and phase-wise risk and handles the issues related to requirement analysis.
9	SRAEP (Sadiq et al., 2010)	• SRAEP (Software Risk Assessment and Evaluation Process) is a model-based approach which uses Software Fault Tree (SFT) for identifying a risk • Issues at the requirements phase are handled in this model
10	SPRMQ (Mofleh & Zahary, 2011)	• SPRMQ (Software Product Risk Management based on Quality attributes and operational lifecycle) manages software product risk. • It has four processes. Identification of risk factors using brainstorming technique, analyze risk probabilities using probability/impact approach; risk mitigation using avoidance, minimization, and contingency strategy, and risk monitoring.
11	Soft Risk (Keshlaf & Hashim, 2000)	• Keshlaf and Hashim developed a prototyping tool called Soft Risk for managing software risks. • This model focuses on risk documentation and concentrates on top risks, it saves developers time and effort by reducing software risks to a great extent.
12	Agle et al. (2003)	• Agle et al. proposes effective handling of risk and handling team structure by knowledge building and effective communication. • This approach can only be used in a multi-team environment.
13	Hoodat and Rashidi (2009)	• This paper presents relations between classified risk using risk tree structure. • Risk analysis and assessment is done by Probabilistic calculations and helps in the qualitative and quantitative estimation of risk.
14	RIMAM (Shahzad & Al-Mudimigh, 2010)	• Risk Identification, Mitigation and Avoidance Model (RIMAM) highlight the strategies for risk identification, management, and avoidance of risk factors. • This model is used to check various risk factors due to an immature requirement, delivery deadline, etc. It is easily implemented with minimum cost and can be customized w.r.t the environment
15	TRM (Higuera et al., 1994)	• Team Risk Management focuses on customer-supplier risk management activities. • TRM establishes a set of processes including methods and tools that enable a relationship between the customer and supplier to work seamlessly.
16	ARMOR (Lu et al., 1995)	• Analyzer for Reducing Module Operational Risk (ARMOR) is a tool for software risk analysis. It identifies the operational risks of all the software program modules. • It can measure software programs risks, identify the origin of risks and evaluate how to reduce their risk levels
17	RAT (Sharif & Rozan, 2010)	• RAT (Risk Analysis Tool) is used to do a hybrid assessment of risks • It is an expert system where the project manager can assess, monitors, and gives preliminary solutions automatically based on the project plan.
18	ERM (Snekir & Walker, 2007)	• Enterprise Risk Management (ERM) helps in identifying and minimize the risk that could cause an organization to fail to meet its strategies and objectives. • It includes risk associated with accidental losses and also financial, strategic, operational, and other risks
19	RMM (Hillson, 1997)	• RMM (Risk Maturity Model) provides the benchmark for an organization to check its maturity of handling risks in projects • Naïve, Novice, Normalized, and Natural are the four levels of maturity which are mapped to attributes culture, process, experience and application

continues on following page

Table 2. Continued

S. No	Method	Description
20	Amber et al. (2012)	• A model is proposed for modeling and reasoning the risk at the requirements analysis phase and is based on UML oriented approach • The use case scenarios are handled using McCabe's cyclomatic complexity process. It helps in finding high-risk functional requirements.
21	Pandey et.al (2011)	• A framework is proposed that incorporate security requirement and risk management technique. It helps in improving the iterative security engineering activity at the initial phase of software development
22	Van Veenendaal (2011)	• PRISMA (Product Risk Management) is an approach for highlighting the parts having the maximum business and technical risk and support risk-based testing. • This approach can be used at each level of testing, and valid across organization and project level. It improves the effectiveness and efficiency of the defect detection process and is easy to use.
23	Nancy R. Mead (2012)	• Helps in determining security requirements engineering process using Security Quality Requirements Engineering (SQUARE) method • The SQUARE method has nine steps to categorizes and prioritizes security requirements • It can be used for any large-scale design project.
24	GSRM (Islam & Houmb, 2010)	• Islam and Houmb proposed a goal-driven software development risk management model (GSRM). Technical as well as non-technical development components are taken into consideration. • It effectively identifies and showcases the project goals, risk factors and control actions for mitigating risks and is advantageous at the initial phases of the development.
25	Kwan and Leung (2011)	• This work handles risk dependency issues by introducing a management methodology • It details two sets of risk response strategies for posterior risks and other for risk dependencies. The communication between projects can be improved with this approach.
26	Nolan et al.(2011)	• This paper shows the use of requirement uncertainty analysis technique. This technique was used for Rolls-Royce traditional software development and explains how it operates regarding a software product line • The analysis technique reduces Scrap & Rework on a traditional project from an average of 50% to below 5%.
27	Lobato et al.(2012)	• The purpose is to identify SPL (Software Product Lines) risks while project scoping and requirement disciplines are in progress for a better understanding of risk management. • Benefits of applying SPL are generally related to business objectives and various organizational issues.
28	IRMAS (Khoo et al., 2007)	• This effort shows a quick risk mapping and assessment system (IRMAS) to support risk management for multi-site projects. The system follows the standard risk management framework (AS/NZS 4360, 1999). • It is extended to support risk tracking, reporting and risk management in other applications also.
29	RISICARE (Costa et al., 2007)	• RISICARE tool was planned and implemented to calculate project risk • Five modules are: Project characteristics, questionnaire, project portfolio, risk level, and simulation
30	Ropponen (2000)	• This paper presents a survey covering more than 80 project managers (1,100 projects), it shows how detailed know-how of environmental context and current managerial practices can be integrated with risk management considerations for managing software risks in an optimum manner.
31	Dey and Ogunlana (2007)	• A risk management framework is proposed from a developer perspective for software development projects and is user-friendly and simple • It uses a qualitative/quantitative technique with the stakeholder's involvement in the identification, analysis, and response to risk

Limitations of Existing Approaches (RQ2)

Many existing approaches have various limitations that are generally not addressed by practitioners. Here some of the main limitations of existing approaches are highlighted.

Many approaches address a limited number of goals, such as schedule and cost. There can be other important goals that can affect the success of the project and should be taken care of such as compatibility with other domain/systems, the reputation of the company, etc. Very few approaches support communication among stakeholders. It is known that risk perceptions can be influenced by various external factors, as the subjective element cannot be eliminated from the analysis of risk. Hence, it is essential to include a decision-making element in the risk assessment, to ensure its effectiveness it is essential to involve stakeholders in the decision-making.

Most risk frameworks only consider risk, which has a negative impact on the system. However, there are risks, which can have a positive impact on the system as opportunities, which are generally ignored by these approaches. Hence, it is required to cater to negative risk while enhancing the opportunities. The traditional risk-assessment techniques do not necessarily provide an easy guide of all potential risk to consider at a component/environment level. That is why systematic literature review is required on risk assessment tailored to the situations faced.

Dimensional Scales of Risk Assessment Techniques (RQ3)

Seven major dimensional scales of risk assessment practices have been identified as shown in Figure 4.

Figure 4. Risk assessment dimensional scales

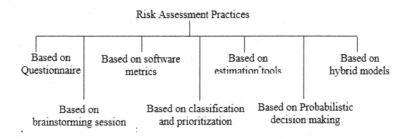

Williams et al. (1999), Foo and Murganantham (2000), Mc- Connell (1996) and Carr et al. (1993) proposed questionnaire-based risk assessment methods. Mc- Connell (1996) approach also covered coding issues and a list of schedule risk factors in their approach. Carr et al. (1993) introduced SEI risk taxonomy having three major groups: development environment, program constraints, and product engineering. This taxonomy has a hierarchical structure with 194 open questions from the software development risk perspective. Konito (2001) monitored brainstorming sessions and considered them useful for risk identification. Brainstorming session requires interaction among several project stakeholders to identify the risk in the project, it involves extensive human involvement. This technique has certain advantages like improving the interaction, getting the response and concerned actions fast, etc. However, there are few limitations like non-availability of stakeholders when required, dependency on participant's expertise. Hyatt and Rosenberg (1996) used software metrics for risk assessment in the project where specific quality attributes and goals were defined. As an output metrics were defined which relates to software development practices. Gupta and Sadiq (2008) also used software metrics which identifies set of risk from each phase of software development and finds total cumulative risk. Sadiq et al. (2010) used SRAEP (Software Risk Assessment and Evaluation Process) which is based on fault tree method. Boehm (1991) used quantitative/qualitative assessment of risk in software projects. This model uses a decision tree for risk event classification based on their dependence. Uzzafer (2011) proposed a risk assessment model for generating cost estimates when integrated with models for cost estimation. This model focuses on the classification of risk events of software projects qualitatively. Fairley (1994) used attributes where congenial risk events like size, time, etc. to recognize the statistical dependence of the risk events. Keshlaf and Hashim (2000) worked on a generic tool for software risk management named SoftRisk. This model focuses on technical, cost, and schedule risks and is based on SERIM (Software Engineering risk model). However, they fail to deal with issues of requirement complexity. Sadiq et al. (2010) introduced a tool esrc Tool based on SRAEM model. It uses the function point approach and helps in estimating the risk and cost of the software.

Probabilistic decision-making techniques like Artificial Neural Networks (ANN) are also used to identify risk in software development. It is a machine learning technique which is helpful in solving problems which has unclear definition and not understood. Kutlubayet al. (2006) introduced a method using machine-learning methods for identifying software defects. Salvatore et al. (2007) did substantial work by improving the existing risk management models through equating the historical risk data of similar projects risks that were found with every framework through direct integration with stakeholders. Another study by Goonawardeneet al. (2010) where the use of neural and fuzzy systems is examined over various disparate areas like forecasting of project success, the decision on year-end appraisal or flavor on job recruiting. Fenton and Neil (1999) have proposed a model using Bayesian Belief Networks and shown that models using Bayesian Belief Networks are advantageous over the classical approaches. Fuzzy logic technique from many other forms is used to assess risks in new software projects. Li et al. (2009), proposed a model for expert assessment based on the fuzzy linguistic multiple attribute decision making. In this model risk assessment is done by prioritizing the risk based on a set of linguistic terms and on criteria which have been predefined for risk assessment. An approach using Fuzzy Inference system (Iranmanesh et al., 2009) uses Schmidt risk factors. Ekananta et al. (2013), introduced a Fuzzy expert-COCOMO model which integrates risk assessment with effort estimation. There are several researches where combinations of approaches are used like Deursen, and Kuipers (2003) introduced a method that has questionnaires integrated with software metrics. Hu et al. (2007) proposed a model using techniques like support vector machine (SVM), Neural Network (NN), and genetic algorithm approaches which are used for project risk assessment. The model is tested on data from questions answered, and SVM is seen to be better than NN. Then NN model is improved with a genetic algorithm to show better results.

Risk Factors and Perspectives Adopted by Developer and Stakeholders for Risk Assessment and Mitigation (RQ4)

Software Engineering Institute (SEI) (Stern & Arias, 2011; Carr et al., 1993; Tianyin, 2011) lists following risk factors listed in Table 3, which are associated with every software development because software development project holds unique and surprising elements of uncertainty.

Table 3. Potential SEI Risk factors (Developers perspective)

1	**Incorrect Resources estimation:** In case resourcing is not done correctly, the correct skills do not exist for finishing the work, the work items are assigned but do not get completed, it can get the managers jittery and completing the project shall be risky.
2	**User/Customer uncertainty:** The stakeholder consensus and presence is required for fetching details on the project work, the requirements are fetched, understanding validated, application output validated through users and customers without which objective cannot be met.
3	**Ambiguous requirements:** Unclear requirements, which either mean something else or are wrong, can cause loss of functionality to the application. The development team is not implementing against the correct objective and risky for delivery.
4	**Improper design risk:** If a design decision that is hard to change later gets put in the project, it shall be risky on delivery the product. The improper design can happen due to any reason associated with the project.
5	**Development system and risk with development system:** The tools used for development if not available or wrongly assigned can work towards the development team not starting to fulfill the correct objective, the risk is enormous on the completion.
6	**Inadequate management process:** The top management or project managers must support the execution of the project, disinterest in proceedings, manual processes, etc. can be significant risks due to which project completion can be an issue.
7	**Improper work environment:** The corporate culture or environments the team uses to implement should be proper and mimic environments which users want to visualize, an improper environment can cause a risk.

In addition to the above factors, some commonly encountered factors are in direct control of project managers and have a substantial impact on the success of the project. This chapter provides a broad classification and discussion of these factors as discussed by various researchers in their work, as stakeholder perspective risk which is presented and discussed in Table 4.

Table 4. Stakeholder Perspective Risk

S. No	Stakeholder Risk Perspective	Description
1	Lack of top management support	• Keil et al. (1998) found that if senior management lacks the commitment, it can end up being a disruptive risk • The top management attention and support is required throughout the project implementation. The management team has to prioritize the responsibilities and identify software projects as a top priority (Leitheiser, 1986; Barki & Hartwick, 1989; Gioia, 1996; Nah et al., 2001).
2	Corporate culture not supportive	• Corporate culture should be correctly placed, any unknown agenda can hamper delivery progress when ideas change based on will and not policy • This results in collaterally damaging the management support, as the objectives are not met (Baccarini et al., 2004; Leitheiser, 1986; Engming &Hsieh, 1994; Irani & Love, 2001).
3	Inadequate user involvement	• As per many researchers, it is one of the top ten causes of software failure • Client involvement and management is required in managing scope and objective, lack of which causes issues in budget and schedule (Keil et al.,1998; Zhou et al., 2008; Addison & Vallabh, 2002; Smith et al., 2006)
4	Lack of client responsibility and ownership	• Keil et al. (1998) identified this as a fundamental risk • User or client involvement in the software project helps in making a better product. When things go wrong, and the users are not involved, the project managers of the software project are generally blamed for the lack of client responsibility (Mursu et al., 1999).
5	Friction between clients and contractors	• Opposing ideas between vendors and software contractors cause operational problems and can have an adverse effect on the work which is another reason for the cause of friction (Jones, 1993).

Risk Factors Related to Requirement Schedule (RQ5)

In continuation of the discussion above there are risk factors related to requirement schedule, which have a severe impact. Table 5 presents and discusses all these factors.

Mapping of Various Risk Assessment and Management Models with Software Lifecycle Phases (RQ6)

It can be observed that risk(s) in software projects can happen in any of phase of SDLC. Therefore, it is essential to map models/strategies with different phases of SLDC, in order to analyze which risk management model fits the best for which phase of the software lifecycle. Table 6 outlines this mapping.

Table 5. Requirement and Schedule Risk

S. No	Requirement and Schedule Risk	Description
1	Miscommunication of requirements	• Missing clarity or miscommunication is one of the causes due to which requirements are not understood correctly. It causes an original set of requirements and other information being wrong or wrongly understood (Iacovou & Nakatsu, 2008)
2	Unclear scope/objectives	• Different stakeholders have different objectives as explained by Boehm (1989) • These differences drive a clash in the understanding of the scope resulting in unclear and hazy requirements understanding. Ambiguous requirement specifications are more likely to create problems related to project budget and schedule (Boehm, 1989; Shull, 2000)
3	Changing requirements	• The stakeholders often modify the requirements based on business values and user's need. However, frozen requirements do enable the completion of the project on time, but they would not be able to accommodate changes. • It has been shown that continuous changes in the requirements enviably lead to affect the schedule (Keil, 1998; Mursu et al., 2009; Jones,1993; King, 1994)
4	Improper change management	• Improper change management often hurts the stability of the application and increases cost in operations/support, which becomes a significant cause for software failure (Smith, 2006; Rasmussen et al., 2006; Han & Huang, 2007; Keil et al., 2002).
5	Unrealistic schedule and budget	• Sometimes the planning for the project is not done diligently, and the project does not reach completion due to either a very rigorous schedule or lower budget. • A fixed schedule might lead to work completion pressures which can have risk on the timely schedule or project results output (Boehm, 1989; King, 1994; Turner, 1999; Hamid et al., 1999).
6	Misunderstanding of requirements	• If the requirement is not understood clearly, it can take multiple cycles of clarification from stakeholders resulting in a delay of the software project. It is one of the significant risks in software projects which affects the project (Keil, 1998; Field, 1997; Schmidt et al., 2001; Addison & Vallabh, 2002; Mursu et al., 2009).
7	Unrealistic expectations	• Keil et al. (1998) pointed out that if the user expectations are incorrect or unrealistic, the project cannot be planned and completed. • Sometimes, internally wrong expectations are set through top management that causes even further issues in the team.
8	Gold plating	• The developers can add features to make system attractive and application sustainable but sometimes increases the cost and make users unhappy (Boehm, 1989; Cunningham, 1999).
9	Inaccurate estimation of schedule or cost	• A wrong estimate can be detrimental for the project. If the estimate were wrong, it would follow with the wrong budget and resulting delay in release. Both under-estimating and overestimating leads to multiple issues with the projects (Galorath, 2006; Masticola, 2007).

Table 6. Risk models mapping with phases of SDLC (Roy, Dasgupta & Chaki, 2016)

S. No	Methods/ Models	Purpose	Risk considered	SDLC Phases
1	BOEHM (1991)	Risk Identification, analysis, Prioritization, control	Generic risks (a risk that is a potential threat to every software project) and project-specific risks	Requirement analysis and planning
2	SoftRisk (Keshlaf & Hashim, 2000)	Risk identification, assessment, monitoring		Requirement and planning phase, maintenance phase
3	ARMOR (Lu et al., 1995)	Risk Identification, analysis	All program module risks	
4	PRORISK (Suebkuna & Ramingwong, 2011)	Risk assessment, risk control	Software related Generic risks	Requirement phase, coding phase, maintenance phase

continues on following page

Table 6. Continued

S. No	Methods/ Models	Purpose	Risk considered	SDLC Phases
5	RMM (Hillson, 1997)	Risk assessment	Organizational risks	Not followed
6	ERM (Snekir & Walker, 2007)	Risk identification, assessment	Generic risks and project-specific risks	
7	RAT (Sharif & Rozan, 2010)	Risk assessment, treatment and monitoring	Projects risks of Small and medium software	
8	TRM (Higuera et al., 1994)	Risk analysis, mitigation	Team risks	
9	Agle et al. (2003)	Risk handling	Risk related to team structure	
10	SEI-SRE (Carr et al., 1993)	Risk Evaluation: Detection, specification, assessment, consolidation, mitigation	Product risks, Process risks	Requirement phase, coding phase, testing phase, maintenance phase
11	SRAM (Foo & Muruganantham, 2000)	Risk assessment, prioritization	Development risk	Requirement analysis
12	Armestrong (2008)	Risk identification	Economic risk, business risk	
13	RISKIT (Kontio & Basili, 1997)	Risk identification, analysis, monitoring, prioritize as per probability and impact	Generic risk, project risk, technical risk, schedule risk, business risk	Requirement phase, application, and maintenance phase
14	Hoodat and Rashidi (2009)	Risk measurement	Project risk, product risk, schedule risk, cost risk, quality risk, business risk	Planning phase, testing and debugging phase, application phase.
15	SERIM (Karolak, 1995)	Risk assessment, risk ranking	Technical risk, cost risk, schedule risk, organizational risk, application risk	Requirement analysis and planning phase
16	RIMAM (Shahzad & Al-Mudimigh, 2010)	Risk identification, management, avoidance	schedule risk and cost risk	
17	SRAEM (Gupta & Sadiq, 2008)	Risk estimation	technical risk, organization risk, environmental risk	
18	SRAEP (Sadiq et al., 2010)	Risk assessment, prioritization		
19	SERUM (Greer, 1997)	Implicit and explicit risk management	Generic risk, risk related to planning, development risk	
20	SPRMQ (Mofleh & Zahary, 2011)	risk factor identification, risk probability computation, effects on product quality, risk mitigation and monitoring	Product risks	
21	Danny (2013)	Risk mitigation	Operational risk	Application phase

SUMMARY OF CURRENT STATE OF ART

This section summarizes the current state of the art in practice for risk management:

- A few frameworks are available which follow similar kind of process to manage the risks in the software projects. Many researchers have emphasized to initiate risk management early in the software project lifecycle but how to integrate still has credible questions. Some work considering risk management has been done in software design (Verdon & McGraw, 2004) though on analysis a change of design or re-elicitation of requirements can have an adverse effect on the project and other work is done in requirement engineering (Borland, 2005; Boness et al., 2008). The real risk management tasks happen at the forefront of the project helping to curtail problems.

- The most prevalent practice in software risk management has significant impetus on schedule and budget. Nowadays, new goals have gained importance such as stakeholder consensus, market de-lighter, integration, etc. The new goals need to be focused on for viewing the risks in requirements from a holistic software development perspective.

- Risk Management in the software industry is still naive; many frameworks have been developed for performing software risk management activities (Karolak, 1995; Boehm, 1991; Karolak, 1995; Kontio, 2001). The implementation of the risk management activities is still not applied and practiced (Ropponen, 1999; Pfleeger, 2000) The project managers know about the risks and its effects but the effort concentrates on minimizing the cost and time in the project, and that is why risk management does not hold a high priority.

- Several taxonomies are available for categorizing requirement defects, they help in effectively managing defect detection and prevention (Alshazly et al., 2014; Beizer, 1990; Chillarege et al., 1992; Grady, 1992; Margarido, Faria, Vidal & Vieira, 2011; Walia & Carver, 2009; Hayes, 2003). In the past, there have been few methods and defect taxonomies used on validation of requirements (Ackerman, Buchwald & Lewski,1989; Sommerville, 2004; Laitenberger, Atkinson, Schlich & Emam, 2000; Felderer & Beer, 2013, 2015). However, they are used in the later part of the software lifecycle and not really on requirement validation (Felderer & Beer, 2013, 2015) and only little has been done in that direction. Hence, there is a need to focus and put more onus on relating requirements to defect taxonomy to find the risk in them.

- The traditional/old risk management practice is followed by a majority of project managers that tends to concentrate really on the potential negative risk or issues by spending considerable effort on identifying and managing threats, ignoring the positive side of risk (Hillson, 2002). More focus is needed on enhancing and exploring the opportunities in the project as well.

CONCLUSION

The primary objective of this study was to present a systematic literature review of techniques/methods/ tools for risk assessment and management. This research identifies and discovers existing risk assessment and management techniques, their limitations, taxonomies, and processes. The goal of this study was to discover potential problems and identify possible improvements for better defect identification and prevention. It can be concluded that there is a need to focus on the effect of executing every single requirement from the viewpoint of risk it can pose to the system under development. It is essential to identify and analyze various requirement defects before a decision of inclusion of a requirement is taken. These defect prevention techniques or models are necessary and essential in order to be sure that all business requirements are captured correctly (with clear vision and scope), and only the correct requirements which focus on delivering value to the customer are selected by taking a right decision using risk estimation. This research will help the research community to improve software quality by developing more effective tools and methods.

REFERENCES

Ackerman, A. F., Buchwald, L. S., & Lewski, F. H. (1989). Software Inspections: An Effective Verification Process. *IEEE Software*, 6(3), 31–36. doi:10.1109/52.28121

Addison, T., & Vallabh, S. (2002). Controlling software project risks: An empirical study of methods used by experienced project managers. In *Proceedings of SAICSIT*. Port Elizabeth, South Africa: ACM.

Alge, B. J., Witheoff, C., & Klein, H. J. (2003). When does the Medium matter? Knowledge building experiences and opportunities in decision-making teams. *Organizational Behavior and Human Decision Processes*, 91(1), 26–37. doi:10.1016/S0749-5978(02)00524-1

Alshazly, A. A., Elfatatry, A. M., & Abougabal, M. S. (2014). Detecting defects in software requirements specification. *Alexandria Engineering Journal*, 53(3), 513–527. doi:10.1016/j.aej.2014.06.001

Amber, S., Shawoo, N., & Begum, S. (2012). Determination of Risk During Requirement Engineering Process. *International Journal of Emerging Trends in Computing and Information Sciences*, 3(3), 358–364.

Anthony, B., Noraini, C. P., Nor, R. N. H., & Jusoh, Y. Y. (2015). A risk assessment model for collaborative support in software management. *9th Malaysian Software Engineering Conference (MySEC)*, 217-223. 10.1109/MySEC.2015.7475224

Armestrong, R., & Adens, G. (2008). Managing Software Project Risks. TASSC Technical Paper.

Arshad, N. R., Mohamed, A., & Matnor, Z. (2007). Risk factors in software development projects. In *Proceedings of the 6th WSEAS international conference on software engineering, parallel and distributed systems*. Corfu Island, Greece: ACM.

Avdoshin, S. M., & Pesotskaya, E. Y. (2011). Software risk management. *Proceedings of 7th Central and Eastern European Software Engineering Conference*, 1-6.

Baccarini, D., Salm, G., & Love, P. E. D. (2004). Management of risks in information technology projects. *Industrial Management & Data Systems*, 10(4), 286–295. doi:10.1108/02635570410530702

Barki, H., & Hartwick, J. (1989). Rethinking the concept of user involvement. *Management Information Systems Quarterly*, 13(1), 53–63. doi:10.2307/248700

Beizer, B. (1990). *Software testing techniques (2nded.)*. New York, NY: Van Nostrand Reinhold.

Bhukya, S. N., & Pabboju, S. (2018). Software engineering: Risk features in requirement engineering. *Cluster Computing*, 1–13.

Boehm, B. (1981). *Software Engineering Economics*. Prentice- Hall.

Boehm, B. W. (1989). Organizational Climate and Culture. Jossey-Bass.

Boehm, B. W. (1991). Software Risk Management: Principles and Practices. *IEEE Software, 8*(1), 32–41. doi:10.1109/52.62930

Boness, K., Finkelstein, A., & Harrison, R. (2008). A lightweight technique for assessing risks in requirements analysis. *IET Software, 2*(1), 46–57. doi:10.1049/iet-sen:20070068

Borland. (2005). *Mitigating risk with effective requirements engineering*. Technical report, White paper.

Cailliau, A., & Lamsweerde, A. (2015). Handling knowledge uncertainty in risk-based requirements engineering. *IEEE 23rd International Requirements Engineering Conference (RE)*, 106-115.

Carr, M., Konda, S., Monarch, I., Ulrich, C., & Walker, C. (1993). *Taxonomy based risk identification. Technical report*. Pittsburgh, PA: Software Engineering Institute, Carnegie Mellon University. doi:10.21236/ADA266992

Chillarege, R., Bhandari, I. S., Chaar, J. K., Halliday, M. J., Moebus, D. S., Ray, B. K., & Wong, M. Y. (1992). Orthogonal Defect Classification-A Concept for In-Process Measurements. *IEEE Transactions on Software Engineering, 18*(11), 943–956. doi:10.1109/32.177364

Cornford, S. L., Feather, M. S., Heron, V. A., & Jenkins, J. S. (2006). Fusing quantitative requirements analysis with model-based systems engineering. *Proceedings of the 14th IEEE international requirements engineering conference*, 279–284. 10.1109/RE.2006.24

Costa, H. R., Barros, M. D. O., & Travassos, G. H. (2007). Evaluating software project portfolio risks. *Journal of Systems and Software, 80*(1), 16–31. doi:10.1016/j.jss.2006.03.038

Cunningham, M. (1999). It's all about the business. *Inform (Silver Spring, Md.), 13*(3), 83.

Danny, L. (2013). Reducing Operational Risk by improving production software quality. *Software Risk Reduction Rev, 13*, 1–15.

Deursen, T., & Kuipers, A. V. (2003). Source-Based Software Risk Assessment. In *Proceedings of the International Conference on Software Maintenance*. Los Alamitos, CA: IEEE Computer Society.

Dey, P. K., Kinch, J., & Ogunlana, S. O. (2007). Managing risk in software development projects: A case study. *Industrial Management & Data Systems, 107*(2), 284–303. doi:10.1108/02635570710723859

Ekananta, M., Capretz, L. F., & Ho, D. (2013). Software Project Risk Assessment and Effort Contingency Model based on COCOMO Cost Factors. *Journal of Computations and Modeling, 3*(1), 113–132.

Engming, L., & Hsieh, C. T. (1994). Seven deadly risk factors of software development projects. *Journal of Systems Management, 36*(6), 38–42.

Fairley, R. (1994). Risk Management for Software Projects. *IEEE Software, 11*(3), 57–67. doi:10.1109/52.281716

Felderer, M., & Beer, A. (2013). Using Defect Taxonomies for Requirements Validation in Industrial Projects. In *Proceedings of the 21st IEEE International Requirements Engineering Conference(RE)*. Rio de Janeiro, Brasil: IEEE. 10.1109/RE.2013.6636733

Felderer, M., & Beer, A. (2015). Using Defect Taxonomies for Testing Requirements. *IEEE Software*, *32*(3), 94–101. doi:10.1109/MS.2014.56

Fenton, N., & Neil, M. (1999). A Critique of Software Defect Prediction Models. *IEEE Transactions on Software Engineering*, *25*(5), 675–689. doi:10.1109/32.815326

Field, T. (1997). When BAD things Happen to GOOD projects. *CIO (Framingham, Mass.)*, 55–62.

Foo, S. W., & Muruganantham, A. (2000). Software risk assessment model. *Proceedings of the 2000 IEEE International Conference on Management of Innovation and Technology, 2*, 536-544.

Gallardo, E. (2012). Using Configuration Management and Product Line Software Paradigms to Support the Experimentation Process in Software Engineering. *Proceedings of International Conference on Research Challenges in Information Science RCIS-2012*, 1-6. 10.1109/RCIS.2012.6240454

Galorath, D. D., & Evans, M. W. (2006). *Software Sizing Estimation and Risk Management*. Auerbach Publications. doi:10.1201/9781420013122.ch10

Genuchten, M. V. (1991). Why is software late? An empirical study of reasons for delay in software development. *IEEE Transactions on Software Engineering*, *17*(6), 582–590. doi:10.1109/32.87283

Ghane, K. (2017). *Quantitative planning and risk management of Agile Software Development. In IEEE Technology & Engineering Management Conference* (pp. 109–112). Santa Clara, CA: TEMSCON.

Gioia, J. (1996). Twelve Reasons Why Programs Fail. *PM Network*, *10*(11), 16–19.

Glass, R. L. (1998). *Software Runaways: Monumental Software Disasters*. Upper Saddle River, NJ: Prentice-Hall, Inc.

Goonawardene, N., Subashini, S., Boralessa, N., & Premaratne, L. (2010). A Neural Network Based Model for Project Risk and Talent Management. In *International Symposium on Neural Networks* (vol. 6064, pp. 532-539). Springer. 10.1007/978-3-642-13318-3_66

Grady, R. B. (1992). *Practical Software Metrics for Project Management and Process Improvement*. Upper Saddle River, NJ: Prentice-Hall.

Greer, D. (1997). SERUM - Software Engineering Risk: Understanding and Management. *Journal of Project and Business Risk Management*, *1*(4), 373–388.

Guiling, L., & Xiaojuan, Z. (2011). Research on the risk management of IT project. *Proceedings of International conf. on E-Business and E -Government (ICEE)*, 1-4.

Gupta, D., & Sadiq, M. (2008). Software Risk Assessment and Estimation Model. In *International Conference on Computer Science and International Technology*. IEEE Computer Society.

Hall, T., Beecham, S., & Rainer, A. (2002). Requirements problems in twelve software companies: An empirical analysis. *IEEE Software*, *149*(5), 153–160. doi:10.1049/ip-sen:20020694

Hamid, A., Sengupta, T. K., & Swett, C. (1999). The Impact of Goals on Software Project Management: An Experimental Investigation. *Management Information Systems Quarterly*, *23*(4), 531–555. doi:10.2307/249488

Han, W. M., & Huang, S. J. (2007). An empirical analysis of risk components and performance on software projects. *Journal of Systems and Software*, *80*(1), 42–50. doi:10.1016/j.jss.2006.04.030

Hayes, J. H. (2003). Building a Requirement Fault Taxonomy: Experiences from a NASA Verification and Validation Research Project. In *Proceedings of the 14thInternational Symposium on Software Reliability Engineering (ISSRE'03)*. Denver, CO: IEEE Computer Society.

Higuera, R. P., Gluch, D. P., Dorofee, A. J., & Murphy, R. L. (1994). An introduction to team risk management. Software Engineering Institute. CMU/SEI-94-SR-001.

Hillson, D. A. (1997). Towards Risk Maturity Model. *International Journal of Project and Business Risk Management*, *1*(1), 35–45.

Hillson, D. A. (2002). Extending the risk process to manage opportunities. *International Journal of Project Management*, *20*(3), 235–240. doi:10.1016/S0263-7863(01)00074-6

Hoodat, H., & Rashidi, H. (2009). Classification and Analysis of Risks in Software Engineering. *World Academy of Science. Engineering and Technology WASET*, *3*(8), 446–452.

Hsieh, M. Y., Hsu, Y. C., & Lin, C. T. (2016). Risk assessment in new software development projects at the front end: A fuzzy logic approach. *Journal of Ambient Intelligence and Humanized Computing*. doi:0.100712652-016-0372-5

Hu, Y., Huang, J., Chen, J., Liu, M., & Xie, K. (2007). Software project risk management modelling with neural network and support vector machine approaches. In *Third International Conference on Natural Computation*. Washington, DC: IEEE Computer Society.

Hyatt, L., & Rosenberg, L. (1996). A Software Quality Model Metrics for Risk Assessment. *European Space Agency Software Assurance Symposium*.

Iacovou, C. L., & Nakatsu, R. (2008). A risk profile of offshore-outsourced development projects. *Communications of the ACM*, *51*(6), 89–94. doi:10.1145/1349026.1349044

IEEE. (1998). IEEE Standard for Software Reviews, IEEE Std 1028– 1997. IEEE.

Irani, Z., & Love, P. E. D. (2001). The propagation of technology management taxonomies for evaluating information systems. *Journal of Management Information Systems*, *17*(3), 161–177.

Iranmanesh, S. H., Khodadadi, B., & Taheri, S. (2009). Risk Assessment of Software Projects Using Fuzzy Inference System. *International Conference on Computers and Industrial Engineering*, 1149-1154. 10.1109/ICCIE.2009.5223859

Islam, S., & Houmb, S. H. (2010). Integrating Risk Management Activities into Requirements Engineering. *Fourth IEEE International Conference on Research Challenges in Information Science RCIS-2010*, 299-310. 10.1109/RCIS.2010.5507389

Janjua, U., Jaafar, J., & Lai, F. (2016). Expert's opinions on software project effective risk management. *Proceedings of 3rd International Conference on Computer and Information Sciences (ICCOINS)*, 471-476. 10.1109/ICCOINS.2016.7783261

Jones, C. (1993). *Assessment and Control of Software Risks*. Englewood Cliffs, NJ: Prentice-Hall.

Kamila, A. R., & Sutikno, S. (2016). Analysis of cause and effect relationship risk using fishbone diagram in SDLC SPASI v. 4.0 business process. In *International Conference on Information Technology Systems and Innovation (ICITSI)*. Bandung: IEEE.

Karolak, D. W. (1995). *Software Engineering Risk Management. IEEE Computer Society*. Los Alamitos, CA: Wiley.

Keil, M., Cule, P., Lyytinen, K., & Schmidt, R. (1998). A framework for identifying software project risks. *Communications of the ACM, 41*(11), 76–83. doi:10.1145/287831.287843

Keil, M., Tiwana, A., & Bush, A. (2002). Reconciling user and project manager perceptions of IT project risk: A Delphi study. *Information Systems Journal, 12*(2), 103–119. doi:10.1046/j.1365-2575.2002.00121.x

Keshlaf, A. A., & Hashim, K. (2000). A Model and Prototype Tool to Manage Software Risks. In *Proceedings of the 1st Asia-Pacific Conference on Quality Software (AP AQS'00)*. Washington, DC: IEEE.

Khoo, Y. B., Zhou, M., Kayis, B., Savci, S., Ahmed, A., Kusumo, R., & Rispler, A. (2007). IRMAS-development of a risk management tool for collaborative multi-site, multi-partner new product development projects. *Journal of Manufacturing Technology Management, 18*(4), 387–414. doi:10.1108/17410380710743770

King, J. (1994). Sketchy plans, politics stall software development. *Computerworld, 29*(24), 81.

Kontio, J. (2001). *Software Engineering Risk Management: A Method, Improvement Framework and Empirical Evaluation* (Ph.D. thesis). Helsinki University of Technology.

Kontio, J., & Basili, V. R. (1997). Empirical Evaluation of a Risk Management Method. *SEI Conference on Risk Management*, Atlantic City, NJ.

Krasner, H. (1998). Looking over the legal edge of unsuccessful software projects. *Cutter IT Journal, 11*(3), 11–22.

Kumar, C., & Yadav, D. (2015). A Probabilistic Software Risk Assessment and Estimation Model for Software Projects. *Procedia Computer Science, 54*, 353–361. doi:10.1016/j.procs.2015.06.041

Kumar, N. S., Vinay, S. A., & Sudheer, Y. (2010). Software Risk Management- An Integrated Approach. *Global Journal of Computer Science and Technology, 10*(15), 53–57.

Kutlubay, O., Bener, A., & Ceylan, E. (2006). Software Defect Identification Using Machine Learning Techniques. *Proceedings of Conference on Software Engineering and Advanced Applications (EURO-MICRO-SEAA 2006)*.

Kwan, T. W., & Leung, H. K. N. (2011). A Risk Management Methodology for Project Risk Dependencies. *IEEE Transactions on Software Engineering, 37*(5), 635–648. doi:10.1109/TSE.2010.108

Laitenberger, O., Atkinson, C., Schlich, M., & El Emam, K. (2000). An experimental comparison of reading techniques for defect detection in UML design documents. *Journal of Systems and Software, 53*(2), 183–204. doi:10.1016/S0164-1212(00)00052-2

Leitheiser, R. L., & Wetherbe, J. C. (1986). Service Support Levels: An Organized Approach to End-User Computing. *Management Information Systems Quarterly, 10*(4), 336–350.

Li, X., & Liu, Q. (2009). Requirement Risk Assessment Focused-on Stakeholder Risk Analysis. *Proceedings of 33rd Annual IEEE International Computer Software and Applications Conference, COMPSAC '09, 1,* 640-641. 10.1109/COMPSAC.2009.199

Li, Y., & Li, N. (2009). Software project risk assessment based on fuzzy linguistic multiple attribute decision making. *IEEE International Conference on Grey Systems and Intelligent Services,* 1163-1166. 10.1109/GSIS.2009.5408087

Lindquist, C. (2005). Required: Fixing the requirements mess; The requirements process, literally, deciding what should be included in the software, is destroying projects in ways that aren't evident until its too late. Some CIOs are stepping in to rewrite the rules. *CIO (Framingham, Mass.), 19*(4), 53–60.

Lobato, L. L. (2012). Risk Management in Software Product Lines: An Industrial Case Study. *Proceedings of International Conference on Software and System Process ICSSP,* 180-189. 10.1109/ICSSP.2012.6225963

Lobato, L. L., Neto, P. A., & Machado, I. (2012). A Study on Risk Management for Software Engineering. *Proceedings of 16th International Conference on Evaluation and Assessment in Software Engineering,* 47-51. 10.1049/ic.2012.0006

Lu, M. R., Yu, J. S., Keramidas, E., & Dalal, S. R. (1995). ARMOR: analyzer for reducing module operational risk. *Twenty-Fifth International Symposium on Fault-Tolerant Computing. Digest of Papers,* 137-142. 10.1109/FTCS.1995.466989

Margarido, I. L., Faria, J. P., Vidal, R. M., & Vieira, M. (2011). Classification of defect types in requirements specifications: Literature review, proposal, and assessment. Paper Presented at *6th Iberian Conference on Information Systems and Technologies (CISTI),* Chaves, Portugal.

Masticola, S. P. (2007). A simple estimate of the cost of software project failures and the breakeven effectiveness of project risk management. In *Proceedings of the First International Workshop on the Economics of Software and Computation.* IEEE. 10.1109/ESC.2007.1

McConnell, S. (1996). *Rapid Development, Taming wild software schedules.* Microsoft Press.

McConnell, S. (1997). *Software Project Survival Guide: How to Be Sure Your First Important Project Isn't Your Last.* Redmond, WA: Microsoft Press.

Mead, N. R. (2012). Measuring The Software Security Requirements Engineering Process. *Proceedings of 36th International Conference on Computer Software and Application Workshops,* 583-588. 10.1109/COMPSACW.2012.107

Meng, Y. (2017). Study on software project risk assessment based on fuzzy analytic hierarchy process. *IEEE 3rd Information Technology and Mechatronics Engineering Conference (ITOEC),* 853-857.

Mofleh, H. M., & Zahary, A. (2011). A Framework for Software Product Risk Management Based on Quality Attributes and Operational Life Cycle (SPRMQ). *12th International Arab Conference on Information Technology ACIT'2011*, Riyadh, Saudi Arabia.

Mursu, A., Soriyan, H. A., Korpela, M., & Olufokunbi, K. C. (1999). Toward Successful ISD in Developing Countries: First Results from a Nigerian Risk Study Using the Delphi Method. *Proceedings of the 22nd Information Systems Research Seminar in Scandinavia*.

Nah, F., Lau, J., & Kuang, J. (2001). Critical factors for successful implementation of enterprise systems. *Business Process Management Journal*, *7*(3), 285–296. doi:10.1108/14637150110392782

Nolan, A. J., Abrahão, S., Clements, P. C., & Pickard, A. (2011). Requirements Uncertainty in a Software Product Line. In *Proceedings of 15th International Software Product Line Conference*. Munich, Germany: IEEE. 10.1109/SPLC.2011.13

Noraini, C. P., & Bokolo, A. J. (2015). A Review on Decision Making of Risk Mitigation for Software Management. *Journal of Theoretical and Applied Information Technology*, *76*, 333–341.

Pandey, D., Suman, U., & Ramani, A. K. (2011). Security Requirement Engineering Issues in Risk Management. *International Journal of Computers and Applications*, *17*(5), 11–14. doi:10.5120/2218-2827

Pfleeger, S. L. (2000). Risky business: What we have yet to learn about risk management. *Journal of Systems and Software*, *53*(3), 265–273. doi:10.1016/S0164-1212(00)00017-0

Pohl, K., & Rupp, C. (2010). *Basiswissen Requirements Engineering* (2nd ed.). Heidelberg, Germany: Dpunkt Verlag. doi:10.1007/978-3-642-12578-2

Project Management Institute. (2017). A guide to the project management body of knowledge (PMBOK ® guide) (6th ed.). Author.

Rabia, H., & Muhammad, A. (2013). Critical success factors assessment in Software Projects. *Science and Information Conference*, London, UK.

Rasmussen, M., Orlov, L. M., & Bright, S. (2006). *Taking Control Of IT Risk Defining A Comprehensive IT Risk Management Strategy*. Forrester Research.

Ropponen, J. (1999). Risk assessment and management practices in software development. In L. P. Willcocks & S. Lester (Eds.), *Beyond the IT Productivity Paradox* (pp. 247–266). Chichester, UK: John Wiley & Sons.

Ropponen, J., & Lyytinen, K. (2000). Component of Software Development Risk: How to address them? A project manager survey. *IEEE Transactions on Software Engineering*, *26*(2), 98–112. doi:10.1109/32.841112

Roy, B., Dasgupta, R., & Chaki, N. (2016). A Study on Software Risk Management Strategies and Mapping with SDLC. In R. Chaki, A. Cortesi, K. Saeed, & N. Chaki (Eds.), *Advanced Computing and Systems for Security. Advances in Intelligent Systems and Computing, 396*. New Delhi: Springer. doi:10.1007/978-81-322-2653-6_9

Sadiq, M., Rahman, A., Ahmad, S., Asim, M., & Ahmad, J. (2010). esrcTool: A Tool to Estimate the Software Risk and Cost. *IEEE second International Conference on Computer Research and development*, 886-890.

Sadiq, M., Rahmani, M. K. I., Ahmad, M. W., & Jung, S. (2010). Software risk assessment and evaluation process (SRAEP) using model-based approach. In *International Conference on Networking and Information Technology (ICNIT)*. Manila: IEEE. 10.1109/ICNIT.2010.5508535

Sarci, S. A., Cantone, G., & Basili, V. R. (2007). A Statistical Neural Network Framework for Risk Management Process - From the Proposal to its Preliminary Validation for Efficiency. *Proceedings of the Second International Conference on Software and Data Technologies*.

Schmidt, R., Lyytinen, K., Keil, M., & Cule, P. (2001). Identifying software project risks: An international Delphi study. *Journal of Management Information Systems*, *17*(4), 5–36. doi:10.1080/07421222 .2001.11045662

Shahzad, B., & Al-Mudimigh, A. S. (2010). Risk Identification, Mitigation and Avoidance Model for Handling Software Risk. In *Proceedings of the 2010 2nd International Conference on Computational Intelligence, Communication Systems and Networks*. Liverpool, UK: ACM.

Sharif, A. M., & Rozan, M. Z. A. (2010). Design and Implementation of Project Time Management Risk Assessment Tool for SME Projects using Oracle Application Express. *World Academy of Science, Engineering and Technology*, *65*, 1221–1226.

Shull, F., Rus, I., & Basili, V. (2000). How perspective-based reading can improve requirements inspections. *Computer*, *33*(7), 73–79. doi:10.1109/2.869376

Smith, D., Eastcroft, M., Mahmood, N., & Rode, H. (2006). Risk factors affecting software projects in South Africa. *South African Journal of Business Management*, *37*(2), 55–65.

Snekir, W. G., & Walker, P. L. (2007). Enterprise Risk Management: Tools and Techniques for effective implementation. Institute of Management Accounts, 1-31.

Sommerville, I. (2004). *Software Engineering* (7th ed.). Pearson Addison Wesley.

Stern, R., & Arias, J. C. (2011). Review of Risk Management Methods. *Business Intelligence Journal*, *4*(1), 59–78.

Suebkuna, B., & Ramingwong, S. (2011). Towards a complete project-oriented risk management model: A refinement of PRORISK. In *Eighth International Joint Conference on Computer Science and Software engineering (JCSSE)*. IEEE. 10.1109/JCSSE.2011.5930146

Swede, V. V., & Vliet, J. V. (1994). Consistent development: results of a first empirical study on the relation between project scenario and success. In G. Wijers, S. Brinkkemper, & T. Wasserman (Eds.), Lecture Notes in Computer Science: Vol. 811. *Advanced Information Systems Engineering, CAiSE 1994*. Berlin: Springer.

Tianyin, P. (2011). Development of software project risk management model review. *Proceedings of International conference on Artificial Intelligence, Management Science and Electronic Commerce*, 2979-2982. 10.1109/AIMSEC.2011.6011139

Turner, J. R. (1999). Project Management: A profession based on knowledge or faith. *International Journal of Project Management, 17*(6), 329–342.

Uzzafer, M. (2011). A Novel Risk Assessment Model for Software Projects. *International Conference on Computer and Management (CAMAN)*, 1-5. 10.1109/CAMAN.2011.5778729

Veenendaal, E. V. (2011). Practical Risk-Based Testing - Product Risk Management: The PRISMA Method. EuroSTAR-2011, 1-24.

Verdon, D., & McGraw, G. (2004). Risk analysis in software design. *IEEE Security and Privacy, 2*(4), 79–84. doi:10.1109/MSP.2004.55

Walia, G. S., & Carver, J. C. (2009). A systematic literature review to identify and classify software requirement errors. *Information and Software Technology, 51*(7), 1087–1109. doi:10.1016/j.infsof.2009.01.004

Wanderley, M. Jr, Menezes, J. Jr, Gusmão, C., & Lima, F. (2015). Proposal of Risk Management Metrics for Multiple Project Software Development. *Procedia Computer Science, 64*, 1001–1009. doi:10.1016/j.procs.2015.08.619

Williams, R. C., Pandelios, G. J., & Behrens, S. G. (1999). *Software Risk Evaluation (SRE) Method description (Version-2.0).* Technical report CMU/SEI-99-TR-029.

Zhi, H., Zhang, G., Liu, Y., & Shen, Y. (2017). A novel risk assessment model on software system combining modified fuzzy entropy-weight and AHP. *IEEE 8th Conference on Software Engineering and Service Science*, 451-454.

Zhou, L., Vasconcelos, A., & Nunes, M. (2008). Supporting decision making in risk management through an evidence-based information systems project risk checklist. *Information Management & Computer Security, 16*(2), 166–186. doi:10.1108/09685220810879636

ADDITIONAL READING

Bannerman, P. (2008). Risk and risk management in software projects: A reassessment. *Journal of Systems and Software, 81*(12), 2118–2133. doi:10.1016/j.jss.2008.03.059

Boehm, B., & Basili, V. (2001). Software Defect Reduction Top 10 List. *IEEE Computer, 34*(1), 135–137. doi:10.1109/2.962984

CHAOS Report 2015. 2015.

Hamill, M., & Katerina, G. P. (2009). Common Trends in Software Fault and Failure Data. *IEEE Transactions on Software Engineering, 35*(4), 484–496. doi:10.1109/TSE.2009.3

IEEE Computer Society Professional Practices Committee. (2014). *Guide to the Software Engineering Body of Knowledge (SWEBOK® Guide). Version 3.0.* IEEE.

Marasco, J. (2007). *"What Is the Cost of a Requirement Error?* Stickyminds. Available at: https://www.stickyminds.com/article/what-cost-requirement-error

Pressman, R. S. (2014). *Software Engineering: A Practitioner's Approach* (8th ed.).

Spacey, J. (2016). *9 Examples of Positive Risk, 2016.* Available at: https://business.simplicable.com/business/new/9-examples-of-positive-risk

This research was previously published in Crowdsourcing and Probabilistic Decision-Making in Software Engineering; pages 51-80, copyright year 2020 by Engineering Science Reference (an imprint of IGI Global).

Chapter 101
The Dynamics of Product Development in Software Startups:
The Case for System Dynamics

Narendranath Shanbhag

La Trobe University, Melbourne, Australia

Eric Pardede

La Trobe University, Melbourne, Australia

ABSTRACT

Software startups are increasingly under high pressure to deliver successful products to survive and thrive in the modern highly competitive technology market. Larger organizations with deep pockets can replicate the same business ideas used by startups with relative ease. So how does the average startup stand a chance at succeeding at this seemingly David vs. Goliath contest? This article looks at the available literature and identifies such factors that can affect the success of software development startups. Using causal loop constructs from the field of system dynamics, the interactions among the various identified factors are visualised to reveal the dynamics of the system. The result is as a three-dimensional view of success factors in form of time, capital and (product) differentiation. The modelled system is then simulated, and the resultant trend is reviewed and interpreted. This research acts as ground work for analysing the workings of software development startups and sets the stage for a more holistic study of the area, upon which further research can be carried out.

1. INTRODUCTION

In recent times, startups have disrupted the status quo and taken the market by storm with new, innovative products and services, which attempt to simplify everyday tasks in both business and personal spaces. From a product or service perspective, most software startups face stringent resource constraints (Fayad

DOI: 10.4018/978-1-6684-3702-5.ch101

et al., 2000) such as time (Paternoster et al., 2014), human resources and finances (Song et al., 2010). Additionally, startups need to be flexible and steadily evolve to stay relevant in the modern rapidly changing technology landscape (Duchesneau and Gartner, 1990). To this end, there is evidence to support the adoption of adaptable process frameworks like lean startup methodology among newer startups (Ries, 2011). There is also a good amount of interest in research directed towards startups, particularly in software development sectors. However, the software industry has some of the highest failure rates when compared to most industries. Therefore, an in-depth study of the factors that can lead to better insight on factors that influence success of a product development undertaking in an aspiring software startup and would merit further study (Davis and Zweig, 2005).

Startups and the processes such as product development within it, can be considered as an example of a Socio-Economic or Socio-Technical system (Groen et al., 2008) and the complexities involved in such systems cannot be studied easily by most tools and techniques which view the problem at hand from a linear or deterministic viewpoint. According to reviewed literature, such Socio-Economic or Socio-Technical systems fall under the category of multi-loop non-linear feedback systems (Forrester, 1971). Forrester goes on to state that, as a consequence of the human evolutionary process, humans have not evolved to be good at understanding the dynamic behaviour of such complex systems. To add to this, a study found that policies and solution which have their base in linear viewpoints tend to produce solutions of a temporary nature and a higher amount of escalating problems (Holling, 2001).

However, simply studying the various factors by isolating each one from the entire system might not be sufficient to provide enough insight. As an example, with a Socio-Technical system, one case can be considered (Tvedt and Gollofello, 1995), where system dynamics has been used to evaluate software development cycle time for effectiveness. In this study, in place of studying each factor for effectiveness in isolation, the study considered the various factors that would collectively affect the entire system. For instance, if a new software tool was introduced to a company with the intention of reducing cycle time of software development, this might reduce the amount of time the professional (using the software) needs to be involved with that task. However, the time gained by quickly accomplishing this task using the software tool might be spent as slack time by that professional. Therefore, there might be no real benefit or change to the cycle time, which was the original intention of introducing the software tool in the first place. This illustrates that a coordinated study of the various factors should be done in unison and in advance, rather than in isolation done later. By introducing an intervention such as a new software into a system and then modelling how the various elements of the system will be affected can help understand the positive and negative implications better. This is especially relevant in the case of software startups since failing to understand such implications can lead to an increase in cost, effort needed in product development and subsequently, time to market.

The aim of this research work is twofold. The first is to propose a framework for grouping success factors, which are determined after exploring the literature and deducing various elements which affect success in software product development from the perspective of a software startup. This is done while keeping in mind aspects of dynamic behaviour which effects such Socio-Economic/Socio-Technical systems. While there are a variety of factors that lead to the success of a startup, this would be too broad an area to study considering startups can offer a wide range of services, products, support for products/ services as part of their venture. For the purposes of this study, most aspects of startup success will be considered from a software products development startup's perspective. Therefore, the factors studied in this work have been primarily shortlisted from the viewpoint of success from a software product development perspective.

Cornerstones and goals for each cornerstone are defined from each grouping, which will be used in later on during systems modelling. The second is to explore the interaction among the various identified factors and define the trends within the system, so as to gain an understanding of how these factors and cornerstones influence one another and the system as a whole. As a part of this work, a review of literature is done by studying over 50 articles and a total of 14 factors are investigated. However as previously stated, to truly understand the impact these factors have on any system, they cannot be studied in isolation from one another. Optimal understanding can only be achieved when an attempt is made to study these factors with the effect they have on each other and the system as an entirety. To achieve this, this paper uses *Causal Loop* and *Stock & Flow Diagrams* from the System Dynamics methodology to highlight the factors and depict the interactions among them. The system's working is then simulated to show the state of the stocks over time. The use of trend graphs to reveals how each cornerstone has changed over time and these trends can be compared with the respective goals of each cornerstone, providing useful insight into the direction the system is headed towards.

2. RELATED WORK

Startups, being more resource constrained (Davis and Zweig, 2005), need to be concerned with optimal use of their resources. Towards this end, the adoption of lean and agile based methodologies have been picking up pace in recent years. Klein introduces the idea of using a design driven framework for lean startups, which focuses on usage of agile thinking (Klein, 2013). The traditional process of product development in agile development usually involves the user requirements being gathered, the product is then developed and then user feedback is considered. Products are subsequently modified based on the feedback, shown to the end user and once again user feedback is taken. Klein introduces a simpler but more efficient technique based on agile principles. She points out that by creating a minimum viable product and collecting relevant metrics early on during idea validation, a good product can be built while keeping the cost low. Klein also emphasises the importance of user research, mentioning the high likelihood of heavy rework on the product after it is designed & developed, if the user research is not done previously. Although Klein's approach is geared towards efficiency, the focus is the design driven development along with lowering the overall cost of development and not specifically on the time to market. In such a case, the benefit of faster development time appears to be a by-product.

Hokkanen et al. (2016) delve deeper into the concept of devising a framework to assist designing of products in startups, while keeping in mind the various factors and constraints faced by startups. The framework, which is referred to as MVUX, talks about four main elements which include Approachability, Attractiveness, Selling the idea and Professionalism (Hokkanen et al., 2016). The strength of the MVUX framework lies in its base of centring the framework on "Selling the idea", since it is one of the primary end goals of any startup to get feedback from the end user, who is in a position to appreciate the idea of the product. The remaining elements of attractiveness, approachability and professionalism then contribute by working to pique the user's interest in the product and initiate usage of the product. Furthermore, thinking in factors rather than relying on the expertise of evaluator(s) has been considered more prudent, as seen in instances of usability evaluation (Lin et al., 1997). Although the MVUX approach considers the usage of lightweight tools to assist design decisions for startups, it does not take into account the capital spent on various tasks involved or the game changing benefits enjoyed by a startup with early time to market. Keeping in mind these are constraints which startups are faced with are non-trivial, it is important to take these into consideration.

Even though various frameworks, processes and methods have been proposed to deal with the aspect of design and development, the impact of the adoption of the method is not always studied. For instance, according to Eason, the process of designing the product is still largely techno-centric (Eason, 2001). This implies that the development teams run the show and drive the product design process. The consequences could be that the process results in unforeseen outcomes. Eason goes on to state that the trending predictions over these results are over simplified. This leaves room for systems-based methodologies like system dynamics to fill the gap and provide a wider and well-rounded perspective on this subject.

3. RESEARCH METHODOLOGY

As a tool to understand systems from the perspective of synthesis rather than analysis, System Dynamics serves as an excellent modelling technique to study the non-linearity in complex systems.

To gather the variables for the systems model, over 50 articles are studies and 4 factors are shortlisted and investigated using causal loop diagrams. Soft variables such as user experience and quality will be included as a part of the study. The study focuses on noting down a list of important factors that play a role in the success of a startup and then categorises them based on the nature of their influence. For instance, decision time and development time would come under the category of Time. The Cornerstones are then defined for each of the categories, since System Dynamics models are created to solve a problem and not just to model a system's working (Sterman and Sterman, 2000). This is done based on the defined objective or goal (defined in Figure 4). For instance, for the time dimension the objective would be to reduce the time to market. The outline of the research methodology used is show in Figure 1.

Along with the categorization and the subsequent development of cornerstones, a causal loop diagram is drawn out to visualize the interactions of the different factors identified. The intention behind using the causal loop construct is to visualize the categorization or grouping of the factors and observe the nature of the influence (positive or negative). Using the causal loop structure to visualize the relationships will result in a much clearer understanding of the dynamics within the different elements of the system and of the system as a whole.

One caveat of Systems Dynamics is that there is no standard way or set rules to utilise qualitative or quantitative data as a part of the modelling process (Sterman and Sterman, 2000). In the case of this research work, qualitative data, in the form of observations are taken from literature and are used to simulate the working of the system via the stock and flow diagrams. The identified success factors are used as variables in building the stock and flow model. Sterman highlights that it is not possible to prove that model developed in System Dynamics is completely accurate (Sterman and Sterman, 2000). However, it must be noted that the idea of System Dynamics models is not to provide accurate predictive outcomes which are precise in nature, but rather to provide an analysis of the trend, which can then lead to recommendations based on the insight gained from these trends. In keeping with this line of thinking, the stock & flow diagrams are created, and the results of the subsequent simulations are then discussed.

To demonstrate the full potential of this tool, two different instances within the same system were chosen to show that System Dynamics can be used in a variety of cases, depending on the purpose of usage.

Figure 1. Overview of the research methodology

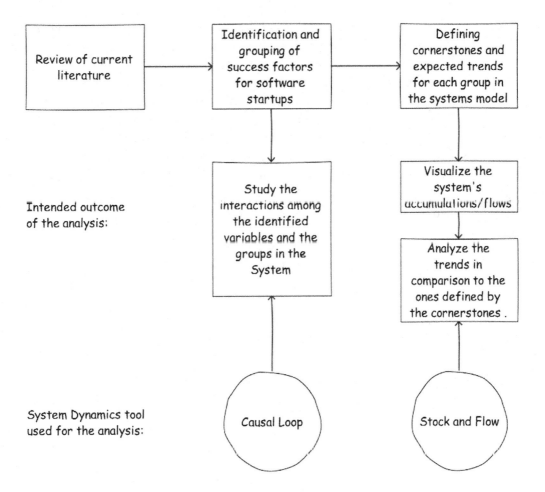

The intended purpose of this paper is to show that System Dynamics can be used as a technique to model complex systems such as startups. The objective of using system dynamics in this case would be two-fold. The first is to gain a better understanding of how the system works (using causal loop diagrams), which in turn will contribute to better decision making on part of the modeler. The second is to view the system's trends under the current configuration of the system (using stock and flow diagrams). This will provide the modeler with a general idea of the direction in which is system is headed towards, so that the modeler can change the system's configuration to check how aspects of the system can be changed to lead the system towards more desirable results. However, to limit the scope of the work, the model does not explicitly attempt to determine feedback loops. Although this might make it hard to control the complexity of the model, it makes for a more realistic representation of the model. Additionally, when using software applications such as Vensim, it provides options to check for scenario-based evaluation (via a feature called SyntheSim), wherein the value of one variable can be increased with the others being kept constant and the influence on the system can be subsequently studied.

4. THE TRIPLE CORNERSTONE FRAMEWORK: A PROPOSAL

Based on the available literature, three factors have been chosen to represent dimensional viewpoints. Time dimension represents the types of product development time and related factors, Capital represents the business and related factors for the startup and Product represents the product related factors such as quality and user experience of the offering. The viewpoints help group the factors from the respective perspectives (such as time and capital). The literature points to various variables which affect one another but can ultimately be categorized under one or more of the three dimensions. Therefore, to simplify details of the knowledge gained from this literature review and the process of the creation of the systems model in the latter portion of this work, this study is divided into the respective key areas or dimensions. Furthermore, the grouping takes into account the complexity of the interconnecting factors. Each area covers those factors and provides a basis for the causal connection. The overview of the framework is pictorially represented in Figure 2.

Figure 2. The triangle framework with the various factors illustrated

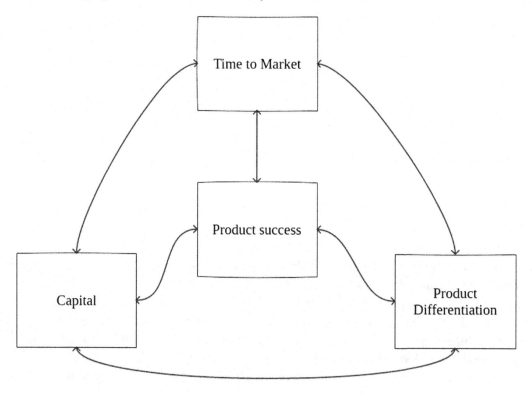

It is worth noting that certain factors might overlap across dimensions, but this demonstrates the complexity of the influence the various factors have and the interconnections in the role they play in the outcome of the product's future. This overlap of the various factors within the dimensions is depicted using a Venn diagram in Figure 3.

As mentioned as part of the research methodology earlier, the cornerstones and their objectives are defined after the grouping of the factors.

Figure 3. A Venn diagram depicting the overlap of the various success factors

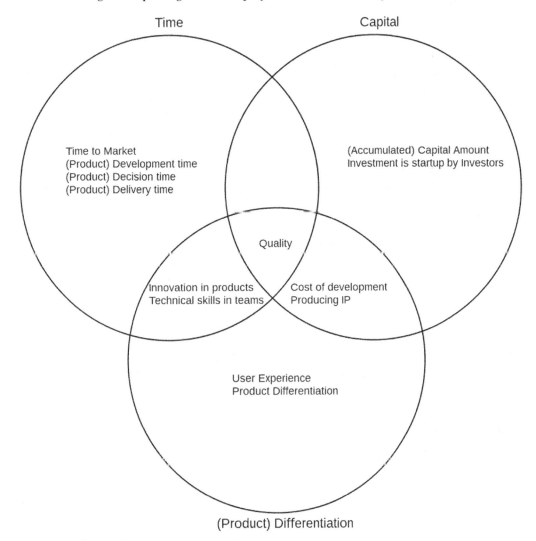

4.1. Cornerstone Grouping #1: Capital and Related Factors

4.1.1. Cost of Development

Conventional thinking might lead one to believe that without a large amount of capital, it is not possible to form a startup. However, Gelderen et al. (2005) provide evidence that in the case of startups in general, getting started with a small amount of capital is easier than a larger amount, since acquiring a smaller amount of capital is easier than a larger amount. Reducing cost for the product development in a startup was identified as a critical factor for success (Schwaber and Beedle, 2001). Lowering cost increases the chances of a product's success since more capital is left over to spend on other aspects of a product success like testing for higher quality or marketing.

4.1.2. Patents and IP

Software startups holding patents and other intellectual property in general are found to have an edge when receiving investments from potential investors (Bessen, 2011; de Wilton, 2011; Dove and Sethumadhavan, 2012) and strategically patenting software can prove to be valuable (Noel and Schankerman, 2013). Additionally, software patents are also found to create incentives to invest in product innovation (Mann and Sager, 2007; Noel and Schankerman, 2013). Although there are growing concerns that patenting might result in a drag on innovation, Noel et al. (2013) argues that investing in Research and Development to procure patents will have a positive spill over towards the technology side.

However, the costs involved with filing for a patent are usually quite high (de Wilton, 2011; Graham and Sichelman, 2008). This can have a substantial impact on the amount of capital a startup can invest in to invest in protecting its intellectual property.

4.2. Cornerstone Grouping #2: Time and Related Factors

4.2.1. Time to Market

From the perspective of managing any software product development process as a project, aspects of quality, time (along with the previously noted aspect of cost) can be identified as key factors for success (Schwaber and Beedle, 2001). The idea is to reduce time and cost needed to develop the product and increase the quality. Even in the early days of software, when software was considered as 'software package', the benefits of faster time to market was acknowledged as it could reveal product-market fit early on in the development phase, significantly increase market share, increase customer loyalty and reduce overall cost (Carmel, 1994; Erran Carmel and Steve Sawyer, 1998; Giardino et al., 2014). Time to market can be defined as the time measured from the conception of the startup to the time when the first product is sold to customers (Hellmann and Puri, 2000).

Another advantage of considering timing in general, is that the organization could control the choices (both tactical and strategic) during the time of launch of the product, although Song et al. (2010) emphasize the need for the timing to be right rather than having a faster time to market. This perspective however, may not be applicable to the case of a startup since Song et al. (2010) mention that the luxury of checking for the right timing is one that mostly larger organizations can afford, rather than most startups.

Various elements can affect timing and the time to market in organizations. Hellman and Puri (2000) state that although not necessarily causal in nature, the presence of venture capital correlates to quicker time to market, and this correlation is particularly evident in companies which innovate. This is understandable since such organization would invest the gained capital to create innovative products and get it to the market sooner to capitalize on the relatively lesser competition during those stages.

4.2.2. Product Decision, Development and Delivery Time

Another such success criteria identified when considering the aspect of time, was quicker delivery times for the software product (Fayad et al., 2000; Misra et al., 2009) and shorter decision time with regard to product development (Misra et al., 2009). Although decision time is considered in an organizational context in the stated study, it can be argued that shorter decision times has a direct impact on the outcome of the product development process, since lesser time spent on making product related decisions will lead to more time available to complete other product related tasks. In cases when the product is developed using the agile methodology, the decision, development and delivery time is relatively shorter and iterative and found to deliver a product with good performance (Poppendieck and Cusumano, 2012).

4.3. Cornerstone Grouping #3: Product Differentiation and Related Factors

4.3.1. Product Differentiation and Innovation

Product differentiation has been found to positively impact the success of a new product (Song et al., 2010) and is consistently seen as a factor for success for most software products. Cozzie et al. (2006) argue that a guarantee of IP protection will lead to a greater focus on quality, but this will negatively impact product differentiation and variety/diversity of product offerings in the market. Hence a balance between differentiating the product and seeking IP protection will need to be struck. In addition to this, attempting to differentiate products from the competition might also lead to additional usage of capital amount. The capital used in this case will be to educate the customer about the product and in advertising to increase awareness of the products differentiating characteristics (Boadway and Tremblay, 2003). As a differentiating trait, Innovation has also been known to have a strong impact on the product's success and subsequently the startup's success (Cooper and Kleinschmidt, 1987a; Parry and Song, 1994).

4.3.2. User Experience Design

Terms like User Experience (UX) are often considered elusive and vague (Hassenzahl and Tractinsky, 2006). However, even though leaders in areas such as marketing, acknowledge that for any organization, a powerful differentiator which offers a competitive edge over the competition is the factor of design (Kotler et al., 2015). In many cases, UX is acknowledged as a key product differentiator (Chapman and Plewes, 2014; May, 2012). This is particularly evident when viewing the landscape of the modern day competitive technology market. In cases where the experience (UX) in using an application is poor and dissatisfying, it is often found difficult to learn as well. This is especially seen to be the case in enterprise software (Finstad et al., 2009).

4.3.3. Quality

Earlier quality was identified as one of the key factors for product success (Schwaber and Beedle, 2001). Carmel (1994) however, mentions in the context of time-to-completion in startups that it is usually a matter of balancing the desired level of quality with the amount of time and cost available to spend on it. In case of products developed using the agile methodology, quality is baked in as one of the seven principles of the methodology (Poppendieck and Cusumano, 2012). Despite this there is still needs to further investigate the role of quality in the context of software product development in startups (Klotins et al., 2015).

4.3.4. Technical Skills

Appropriate technical skills among team members are needed to innovate and differentiate the product in the market (Song et al., 2010), although it is important that the members of the development team are experienced and work well together (Crowne, 2002).

4.4. The Cornerstones and the Goals Guiding the Systems Model

Each factor identified in the previous section has been grouped into one of three areas based on the nature of its influence on the system. However, as mentioned earlier, modelling of systems can be achieved if goals are defined for the modelling process. To this end, cornerstones were identified for each of the groupings. The criteria for defining a cornerstone was twofold. Firstly, it had to have a direct influence on the success of a software startup. Secondly, the other identified factors in the grouping had to have a significant influence on the cornerstone. Studying all the factors in the three groupings, the following were determined to be the ideal candidates for the cornerstones.

The first cornerstone defined is to increase the amount of capital that the startup has. The reason for this is for the startup to be able to invest in resources as and when required throughout the product development process. As startups are typically resource constrained (Fayad et al., 2000), access to greater accumulated capital can help provide better access to resources. The intended trend for this cornerstone is to increase the accumulations in capital amount over time.

Time to market is the second cornerstone for the next grouping. The idea is to get the product in the hands of the customers as quickly as possible, with the end goal of achieving the several benefits associated with getting the product out to the market sooner than the competition (Carmel, 1994; Giardino et al., 2014). The intended trend for this cornerstone is for time to market to decrease over time.

The final cornerstone deals with the aspect of product differentiation. The benefits of product differentiation are well documented (Song et al., 2010). Given the limited initial resources affecting most startups, the best chance a startup has of succeeding when competing with established market players is if they have a differentiating factor which makes their product offering standout from that of the competition. The intended trend for this cornerstone is for product differentiation to increase over time, so that the product offering remains unique when compared with the competition. A summarised view of all the cornerstones along with the goals and intended trends can be seen in Figure 4.

5. SYSTEM DYNAMICS: AN INTRODUCTION

To understand most complex scenarios, which are observable in socio-economic and socio-technical systems, there is a need to use better and more efficient tools which enable the observer to understand the underlying dynamics at work. These tools must also help associate the potential effect of each action on the system and lead us in the direction of possible causes of observed phenomenon within the bounds of that system. System Dynamics provides us such tools to achieve this kind of understanding (Sánchez, 2014). Two of the more prominent ones being the causal loop diagrams and simulation models (Ford and Sterman, 1998; Sterman, 2001). Work on using System Dynamics techniques like causal loop diagrams or simulation modelling in software development and related fields has been done before (Hilmola et al., 2003; Rahmandad and Weiss, 2009). Other areas in Information Technology where system dynamics

Figure 4. A summarized view of the cornerstones for the systems model

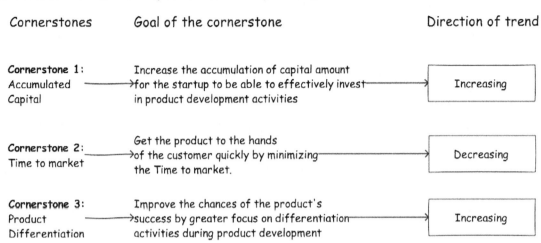

have been applied includes Data Sciences (Casado, 2005; Pruyt, 2017), Information Systems research (Georgantzas and Katsamakas, 2008), Decision support systems (Kljajic et al., 2012; Qudrat-Ullah, 2009), software project staffing (Abdel-Hamid, 1989), market dynamics in the technological sector (Morecroft, 1986).

However, an important question many are faced with when considering the usage of a tool like System Dynamics is what complexities and challenges are faced by startups to warrant the usage of system tools for a detailed study? Apart from having almost no operating history and limited resources to work with, software startups face the challenges of having multiple influences such as pressures from various entities within the system. These can include investors, partners, customers and competitors (Sutton, 2000), depending on the circumstance. Sutton (2000) also states the challenge of the dynamic nature of technologies and markets, citing the need to work with newer technologies to enter unexplored markets. In addition, there is also a growing need to understand the relationship between product differentiators such as quality, user experience and the challenges in integrating it with the software development process (Kashfi et al., 2016). The field of user experience is itself considered to be complex and subjective, with interrelated elements which are hard to separate (Kashfi et al., 2016). It has been acknowledged that one of the factors affecting usability is the dynamics based on user and system interaction (Goodwin, 1987).

Working with such a varied network of influences can potentially introduce unforeseen complexities and when combined with the ever-changing nature of the technology market, it is safe to state that a tool like Systems Dynamics is appropriate to visualize and model this problem space, to achieve a more comprehensive understanding of the underlying structure.

5.1. Causal Loop Diagrams

The nature of feedback and time delays in Socio-Economic and Socio-Technical systems can be realized using Causal loop diagrams (CLD). CLDs are System Dynamics constructs which represent the structure of systems and provide a visual depiction of the nature of relations within that system. As an example, in a linear or event driven view of a system, an issue is encountered in the current circumstance, which leads to the need to take a purpose driven action. On completion of this action an outcome is achieved, which might meet the goal or purpose of action (the overview of this view is depicted in Figure 5).

Figure 5. Example of an event driven view of a system

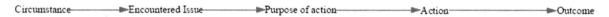

Figure 6. Example of a causal view of a system

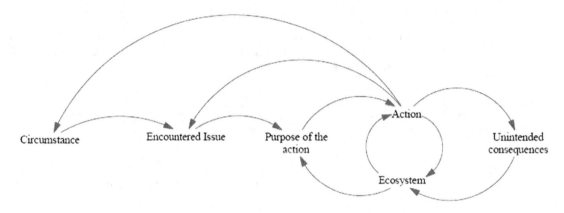

However, in reality, most systems are a lot more complex than this event driven view. The causal view comes closer to representing this complexity. If the same system is observed from a causal viewpoint, an issue which is encountered in the current circumstance leads to the need to take a purpose driven action. However, the action will affect the ecosystem or the environment in which the issue is taking place. This in turn will guide the subsequent action (also known as feedback) and the original purpose of the action. The action can also have unintended consequences which will also affect the ecosystem or the environment in which the issue is taking place. The action will also affect both the encountered issue and the circumstance leading to that issue as well. Therefore, the causal view sees the system as an interconnected confluence of events which affect each other and the system as whole. A depiction of this is shown in Figure 6.

The feedback occurring in complex systems, as seen in Figure 6 can be represented in CLDs using feedback loops and these loops can be either positive or negative. A feedback loop can depict reinforcing or balancing patterns. Reinforcing loops represent a compounding pattern, which reinforces itself in a single direction. As an example, employee rewards and recognition can result in better employee performance. In turn, better employee performance can result in more rewards, thereby the cycle of events reinforcing itself. A balancing loop on the other hand represents a goal seeking behaviour. As an example, a thermostat detects the temperature of the area to check if it is at the desired level. If the temperature is lesser, the heat is turned on and a check is performed again. This kind of a loop/system balances itself. Irrespective of, if these loops can be found within the system or not, it is useful to list and map out the nature of influence (positive or negative) which each identified factor have on other factors within the system. This aids in verifying the causal loop diagram which will be explained as part of the later section of this work.

5.2. Stock and Flow Diagrams

CLDs can model the influence of the various factors of a system on one another and the system as an entirety. The idea of applying CLDs to a system is to gain a high-level understanding of the system's structure, rather than to simulate the system's working and study the trends. The kind of understanding gained from CLDs is therefore purely qualitative in nature. However, the creation of stock and flow diagrams to such systems considers the accumulation and release of resources within the system as well. This would provide additional quantitative insight and enables the understanding of the trends in relation to the system. As an example, consider tracking the accumulation and depletions taking place within a repository. If a stock and flow diagram were to be created then Repository would be the stock (represented by rectangular boxes). Considering filling the repository would add to the accumulations and draining would cause depletion of the stock, Fill and Drain would become the flow for this model (represented by directed arrows as shown in Figure 7). The flows can be regulated to increase or decrease the rate of the flow and is represented by an hour glass symbol in the arrow. The Fill rate and Drain rate regulate the flows in and out of the repository respectively. The cloud like symbols on both ends of Figure 7 indicate portions of the system which are not within the scope of the current model. By observation, it is noted that the fill rate is twice of that of the drain rate. This observation is coded into the Fill rate and Drain rate variables respectively. Figure 7 represents a stock and flow model of this system, which is created using the information discussed in this section.

Figure 7. Example of a Stock and Flow representation of a system

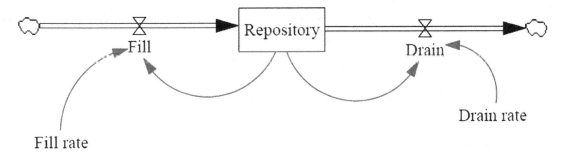

Although the stock and flow diagram help us visualize the accumulations and flows occurring in a system, another helpful aspect of System Dynamics is to simulate the behavior of a system over time. In the current configuration of the system (let's call it configuration 1), if it is already known that the flow rate is twice that of the drain rate. Given an initial accumulation of 100 units, the growth trend can be visualized in the graph in Figure 8a. Since the systems structure has already been established, the configuration settings for the model can then be modified depending on the circumstance, should they change. For instance, if the drain rate were to change and become twice that of the flow rate, the graph resulting from a subsequent simulation (let's call it configuration 2) would look very different from the original configuration (Figure 8b).

It is worth noting that the aim of this model is not to get exact values of the repository over time, as values can vary depending on the point in time that the system is viewed and the sources. The idea here is to study the trend of the system over time, given the current structure or model of the system. This

Figure 8. Behaviour over time graph for repository

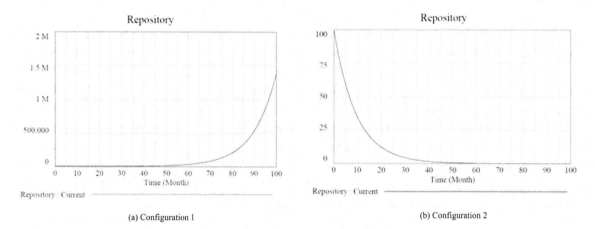

(a) Configuration 1   (b) Configuration 2

is because even though the initial value of the system might be different, the trend represented by the graph will not vary by much as the system's structure remains constant.

Another point to note is that there might be variables that have been left out of the system modeling process for various reasons. For example, additional factors affecting the drain rate or fill rate. Taking this into account in the model can alter the system's structure and provide a different value of repository over time, possible changing the trend line. How many variables to consider for creation of the model will depend on the scope of the analysis and the objectives of the modeling process as well. The time steps used in the model can also be customized.

In most cases, developing a stock and flow model of a system would involve the identification of both hard and soft variables within the system. A hard variable is any factor that is tangible or easy to perceive in amounts or numbers. As an example, lines of code or the number of sales of a certain unit per day. Soft units on the other hand are qualitative in nature and much harder to quantify. For example, customer satisfaction or student's motivation towards studies.

6. THE SYSTEMS MODEL: A CAUSAL VIEW OF THE TRIANGLE FRAMEWORK USING SYSTEM DYNAMICS

The goal of the systems model is to use the previously discussed concepts of System Dynamics to highlight the factors affecting success in software product development in startups. After a detailed literature study and subsequently identifying these factors, the next step would be to model the influence each of the factors might have on one another and ultimately the influence they collectively have on the system as whole (As shown in Figure 9).

6.1. A Causal Analysis View of the System

The CLDs is created using the causal loop constructs discussed in the previous sections. In the current scenario, the process begins by outlining the time dimension of the model. Time to market is critical to ensure the success of any software product development undertaking and quicker time to market has a positive influence on chances of success (Erran Carmel and Steve Sawyer, 1998; Giardino et al., 2014). Decision time is another important factor which impacts the product development time, delivery time and the time to market. Faster decision times can result in reduced product development time (Misra et al., 2009), faster delivery time and quicker time to market (Fayad et al., 2000; Misra et al., 2009). Considering another perspective of the time dimension is that markets tend to value early innovation (Hilmola et al., 2003). To achieve the realisation of planned innovations, Giardino et al. (2014) talks about the idea of releasing prototypes quickly with incremental and iterative development updates. The idea is that faster releases of the product will validate innovative product ideas, which in turn can positively impact the time to market and innovation at the same time.

Figure 9. The causal loop diagram representing the systems model

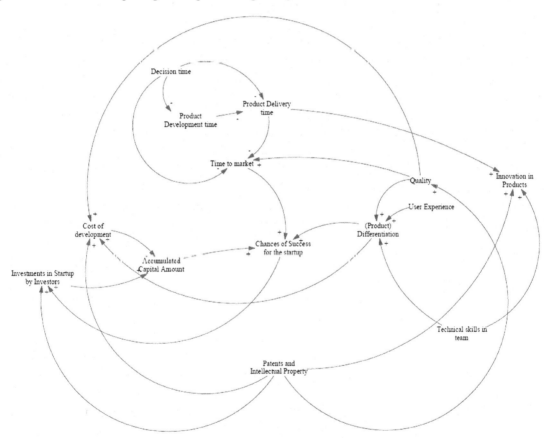

The next consideration is the aspect of startup capital. At some stage, most startups depend on capital to build the product, so as to give the startup an opportunity at being successful (Mann and Sager, 2007). Startup capital amount can be provided by investors including but not limited to angel investors, venture capitalists and other sources like personal financing or crowd sourcing. The cost of development could be covered by the accumulated capital (Mann and Sager, 2007), thereby reducing the startup capital amount. Additional measures to improve quality will further add to the cost of development (Carmel, 1994).

Investors are encouraged to invest in startups which secure intellectual property like patents (Bessen, 2011; Cockburn and MacGarvie, 2009; Mann, 2006), since intellectual properties like patents are typically considered as assets. However, the process of procuring intellectual property is expensive which might deplete some of the capital from the startup (de Wilton, 2011; Graham and Sichelman, 2008), thereby adding to the overall cost of (product) development. Patents are also found to increase the incentives for innovation among startups (Mann and Sager, 2007; Noel and Schankerman, 2013), since patents provide a degree of assurance that the investment on innovation will not be infringed upon by competitors. Furthermore, innovation is another aspect that is found to be critical to a product's success (Cooper and Kleinschmidt, 1987a; Parry and Song, 1994).

The final aspect of product success discussed in this model is the need for differentiation in the product, given the competitive landscape of today's market. Product differentiation improves the chances of success in any product development undertaking (Song et al., 2010). This is especially true in case of startups since most startups do not have the capital or resources to compete with already established organizations. Established contenders in the market have both an established product in the market and in most cases, a loyal customer base as well. However, in order to foster innovation and create differentiation, greater technical skills are necessary (Song et al., 2010). In the modern technology driven landscape, some of the most common differentiators are considered to be quality (Cooper and Kleinschmidt, 1987b; Gatignon and Xuereb, 1997) and user experience (Beauregard and Corriveau, 2007; Pandey and Srivastava, 2014). Gatignon et al. (1997) mentions quality as an enabler of competitive advantage and a means of separating one's own offering from that of other organizations with a competing offering. To add to this, Cooper and Kleinschmidt (1987b) go on to highlight the importance for organizations to look for a competitive advantage via product differentiation to achieve success with their products. They go on to mention that product differentiation can be achieved by creating higher quality products (Cooper and Kleinschmidt, 1987a). As demonstrated by companies like Apple and Google, a positive user experience can radically differentiate a product offering from that of a competitor's product.

The main loops for this model can be seen as in the dynamics between Time-to-market, Accumulated Capital amount and (Product) differentiation. The objective is to emphasise the factors that contribute the most to the chances of success for the startup. The other factors eventually contribute to one or more of these three factors. The study of this loop and the causal loop diagram as a whole is just to better understand the system (in this case, the startup) as a whole and it's functioning.

6.2. The System Dynamics Model: A Representation in Stocks and Flows

When attempting to analyse any system, a better understanding of that system can be achieved by quantifying the variables in the diagram and assigning values to them. The elements of the CLD can be mapped to create stocks and flows (as shown in Figure 10). In this representation, the models are created not just to map out the system's structure of the system but rather to simulate the system's working by creating a more elaborate version of the mental model. In the case of this research work, the goals of the stock and flow models are centred around the goals of the cornerstones i.e., Time to market, Capital and Product differentiation. Therefore, the creation of the stock and flow diagram is to visualize the trends based on the goals of the cornerstones rather than predict the chances of success. The equations for the models have been created based on literature and is meant to be indicative of the general direction of trends of each section of the system. The goal is to demonstrate that a startup when considered as a system can be modelled using System Dynamics methodology. The model does not include aspects of system dynamics such as delays or balancing loops or limiting of growth mechanisms since this is not covered in the scope of the model. Although this can lead to behaviours such as exponential trends in certain cases or demonstrate a degree of linear behaviour, the goal of the model is to demonstrate the ability to use the systems modelling technique in the specific context rather than demonstrate all aspects of systems dynamics. These aspects can be considered as future scope for a upcoming study on the same subject.

The outcome of the trend analysis (in section 7.1) is also compared with commonly occurring trends observed in literature. The idea is to see if using the systems dynamics approach will replicate the same trends as observed in similar cases observed in literature.

In the interest of demonstrating the working of the system efficiently, just the core elements of the system are going to be included in the model. Many of these elements are what are termed as 'soft' variables. For example, Investor interest and product development effort among others. This practice is justified since the aim of any System Dynamics model is to show the general trend of the system rather than providing accurate predictions in the form of numbers (Coyle, 2009).

The assumption for the model is that a software development startup starts its journey from scratch. There is no incoming revenue at this point and the capital accumulated up until this point is used to finance all operations. To acquire any further capital from investors, the startup will need to influence investor interest via investment in intellectual property. The startup can also attract new investments if they have strong resources in the form of technical skills in team members and have an innovative solution concept. In order for the startup be able to start generating revenue they will need to have a working product in the hands of the customers as early as possible. The time-to-market is calculated to demonstrate this trend and is an accumulation of the time taken in decision making for product design and development activities, the time taken for product development and the time taken to deliver the product to the hands of the customers. These factors also tend to influence each other in turn. For instance, the product development time will be affected by the time taken to make design and development related decisions. Of course, the technical skills of the startup team also factor into the time consumed in development of the product. The product development, on the other hand, is influenced by (User experience) design, the disruptiveness of the solution idea and the development effort needed to realise the solution concept. The startup aims to have a good amount of differentiation for their product so that the offering has a better chance of standing up to the existing competition when competing in the market.

Equation (1): Investment in Startups = Accumulated Capital Amount*Investment in Startups by Investors*Technical skills Multiplier*Innovation Multiplier

Equation (2): Development of the Solution idea = (Innovation Multiplier*Quality Multiplier*Technical skills Multiplier*Product Differentiation quotient) *Disruptiveness Multiplier*Product development effort

Equation (3): Time consumed = (Decision time (For development activities) +Delivery time +Product Development time)/(Investment in IP*Technical skills Multiplier*(Time to market))

Figure 10. The stock and flow diagram for the systems model

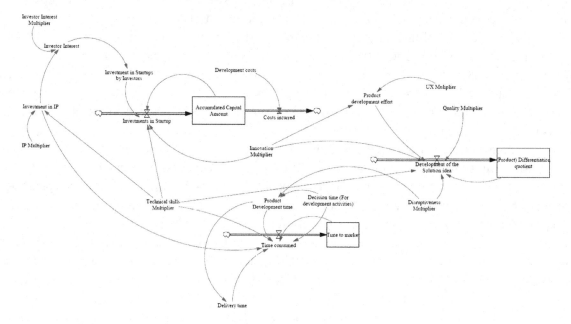

7. DISCUSSION AND CONTRIBUTIONS

7.1. Simulation of the Model and Interpretation of the Results

One of the major benefits of using System Dynamics is the ability to simulate the working of a system using modelling software. As part of the analysis of the model, the system as depicted in Figure 10 is simulated using the Vensim software package. As mentioned earlier, the system is modelled based on the use of an agile approach to systems development. As previously noted, soft variables have been considered when creating the systems model. The model is simulated to show the trends of the system over time. As a part of the system's simulation, each of the three stocks or accumulations are analysed for their trends, along with comparing each trend with the results of a corresponding similar study. These are the accumulated capital amount, the time to market and the differentiation quotient.

The first stock observed as a part of the systems model is the one that deals with Accumulated capital (Figure 11). When the system is initially being developed, there is very little investor interest since there is no product/prototype available for the investors to examine, nor is there any intellectual property available in the initial time frame. An initial product offering which serves as a proof of concept is only developed after a considerable understanding of the customer problem is gained. Even after the initial product is developed, it takes time for the Intellectual property to be registered and the mainstream customer base to take notice of the product, based on the reviews of the early adopters. Then eventually the potential investors will take notice. From the graph it can be seen that it takes up to 3 years for the investments to slowly pour in. Until this time, the potential investors tend to wait till the discovery and validation stages of the business idea are complete. In keeping with the goals of the first cornerstone, the trend presented in the graph is increasing over time, from the third year onwards. Consistently successful startups tend to follow this pattern (Marmer et al., 2011), although the length of time for discovery and validation stages might vary between different startups.

Figure 11. A graph of 'accumulated capital amount' over time (Config. AC)

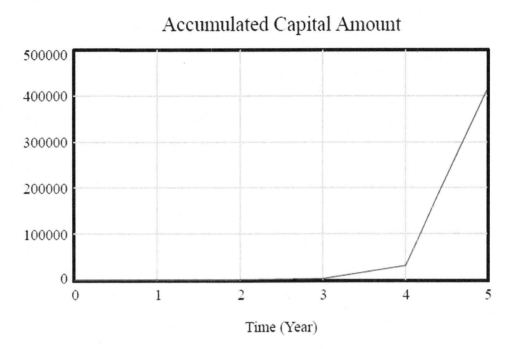

Figure 12. Config AC with technical skills improved

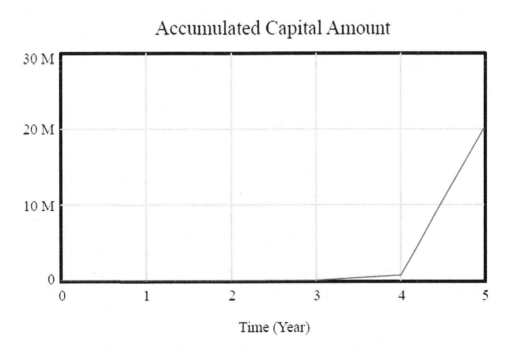

Figure 13. Config AC with Innovation improved

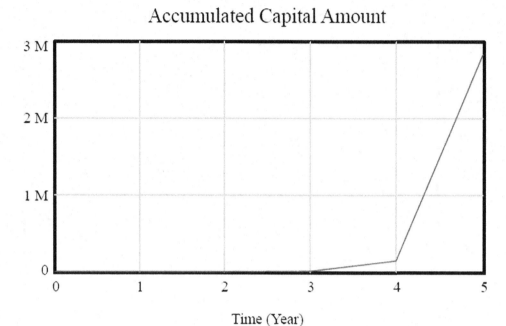

In the interest of exploring variations in the system, if the Technical skills in the startup team were to be improved while keeping the other factors constant, it might incur more expenses in the form of higher salaries or provision of training. In which case, the number of years it can take for the investments to pour in, will increase. However, the higher talent can attract more investor interest since it positively impacts investments in intellectual property, and therefore more investments by investors, as can be seen in Figure 12.

Conversely, an increase in the innovation factor in the model, when other aspects kept constant might result in a similar increase in accumulated amount after year, owing to the potential created by the improved innovation (as seen in Figure 13).

Figure 14 shows the time to market for the product increases sharply over an initial time period. This is attributed to time consumed in during various product activities such as developing an initial product prototype based on customer requirements, delivering the developed product or prototype for customer usage and review and then taking product related decisions involved in the overall process. The sharp increase in time to market at this stage is due to the fact that a good understanding of the customer problem is steadily being gained and product is iteratively changed/developed based on this. At one stage, the understanding of the customer problem is good enough that the changes made to the product/prototype decreases. It can be seen that this point reached when year 1 is completed in the graph. From this point onward, there is only very steady increases since any change made to the product is only iterative improvements to the existing system, owing to business process changes or user interface improvements. When comparing the goals of the second cornerstone, it can be observed that the graph represents a goal seeking behaviour. This indicates that although the trend is increasing over time, the rate of increase is decreasing over time. A very similar pattern can be observed in most systems which adopt agile methodologies for their development efforts (Pressman, 2014).

Figure 14. A graph of 'Time to market' over time (Config CB)

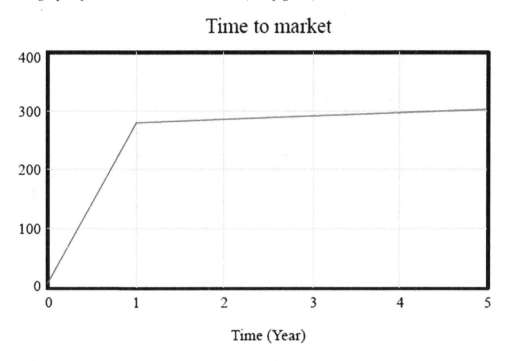

Figure 15. Config CB with decision time increased

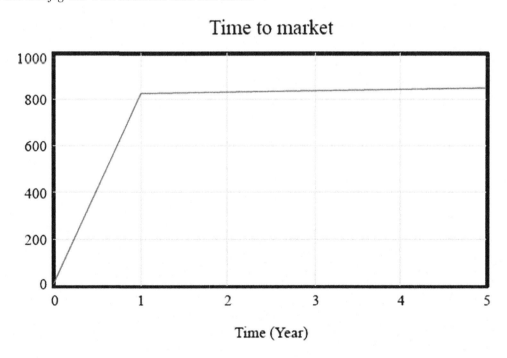

When exploring them model further from the context of time-to-market, if decision time were to increase during the product development process, the initial time to market period would increase significantly (As seen in Figure 15). The model therefore encourages keeping the decision time as low as possible for decreasing the time to market.

Figure 16. A graph of 'product differentiation' over time (Config CC)

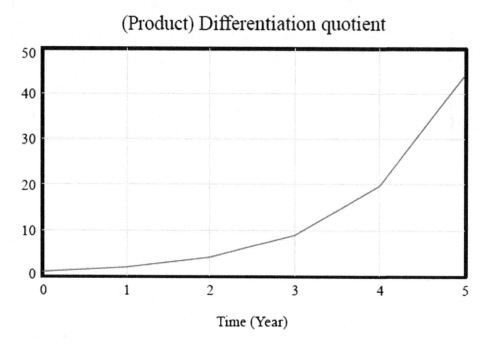

Figure 17. Config CC with disruptiveness increased

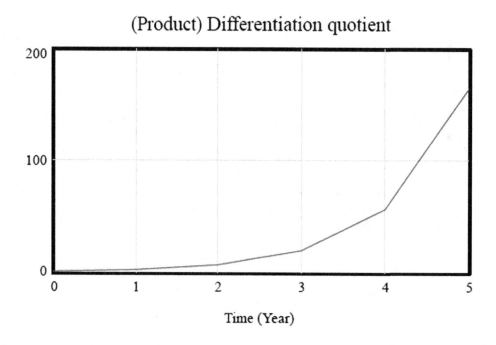

The product differentiation factor (Figure 16) is far less complex to interpret. The factor is an amalgamation of the design and development of the product effort which involves attributes such as quality, disruptiveness, innovation and user experience (UX). In the initial phases, although the efforts towards improving these attributes goes hand in hand with development efforts, the differentiation observed as part of the output is very moderate. Once the customer problem is well understood and a product is developed to cater to the customer problems, then a steady year over year progress in product differentiation can be observed, as per the goals of the third cornerstone. In year 1, the efforts are focused towards resolution of the customer problems rather than the emphasis on differentiation.

As previously mentioned, product differentiation can be seen as a union of aspects such as design and quality, among other aspects. When comparing this graph with the ones representing general quality or design related aspects from real world instances, certain variations can be noticed (Dubberly, 2008). In this instance, the graph takes a S-shaped curve, which is explained by a slow initial growth till it reaches an inflection point after which it rapidly increases. At one point of time, saturation is reached, and growth slows down owing to market saturation or the stabilization of the system at some stage. However, the variation of the S-shaped curve from the current graph can be explained by the fact that aspects such as market saturation are out of the scope of the current model and hence have not been factored into the stock and flow diagram.

When varying parts of this section of the model, the disruptiveness can be increased to reveal that it would take longer for the product differentiation aspects of the product to be identified. But when it does get identified, the increase is steeper (As shown in Figure 17).

7.2. Comparison with Existing Work

Table 1 presents a comparison of the current work's contribution with some of the notable works studied as part of the literature study for this body of work. In the first comparison, the authors use the Gartner's framework to structure their work (Gelderen et al., 2005). If compared with the context of the current study, the area of research focus is the capital amount. Other aspects such as time to market, product differentiation have not been a focus of this study. Carmel (1994), on the other hand, highlights the importance of setting up a core team in order to deliver faster and better differentiated products. This can serve as an indicator for potential investors when considering investments in software product startups. Meanwhile the central theme of the study by Song et al. (2010) involves product differentiation, with the aim of developing a model to gain competitive advantage for the initial product offering of a startup. The study although does not place emphasis on the other cornerstones noted as part of this work. A more holistic approach is taken in the study by Hellman and Puri (2000), as various aspects of the capital amount and time to market have been discussed in the context of studying product differentiation though the comparative study between Innovator and Imitator firms. The current study attempts to integrate the various considered aspects discussed by the considered literature. It also attempts to extend the study by using a framework based on establishing a set of cornerstones, defining goals for each cornerstone and then study the trends of the overall system using system dynamics. The outcome is a synthesis oriented study which views the working of the complex system of the typical software development startup from a causal interconnected viewpoint and defines the trends of the critical cornerstones of the system.

Table 1. Comparative analysis of similar attacks

	Identification of Cornerstones and subsequent goals	[Cornerstone 1] Accumulated capital amount	[Cornerstone 2] Time to market	[Cornerstone 3] Product Differentiation	Trend Analysis
(Gelderen et al., 2005)	Use the Gartner's Framework	✓	-	-	-
(Carmel, 1994)	-	✓	✓	✓	-
(Song et al., 2010)	-	-	-	✓	-
(Hellmann & Puri, 2000)	-	✓	✓	✓	-
Current work	✓	✓	✓	✓	✓

7.3. Research Contributions

Most research uncovered so far in the domain of software product development, as with many other spheres, has been done so by understanding the area in viewpoints which do not take causal thinking into account (Davis and Zweig, 2005; Ries, 2011; Song et al., 2010). One of the major drawbacks of such perspectives is that it assumes that actions performed when interacting with the system do not create side effects or delays in th system, which cannot be anticipated (Sterman, 1994). Most research work in disciplines like product design or development rarely work in such deterministic patterns. Instead, one can observe causal patterns of behaviour when observing these disciplines (Sterman, 1994). This study includes aims to avoid the trap of linear thinking and instead focus on causal thinking by leveraging the potential of Systems Thinking and Systems Dynamics. This is done by building mental models that are likely to be a more accurate representation of the workings of real world systems and subsequently gaining a better understanding of the working of the said system. In the current case of software development in software startups, this is accomplished by identifying success factors for development and visualizing the interactions within the system using CLDs.

Another aspect of this study is the focus on Synthesis based collective assessment rather than Analysis based deconstructive assessment of the entire system. Since it has been observed that most systems work as a collective whole rather than a mere sum of its parts, it should be noted that the method of studying such systems must also take this nature into account. Understanding of the system could therefore be better achieved by understanding each part in its working with the entirety of the system. Perceiving systems in this pattern is known as Synthesis (Barton and Haslett, 2007). Most research techniques instead apply the underlying principle of analysis, which separates each individual aspect of the system from the collective whole and aims to study these aspects in isolation. Using the principle of Synthesis, via System Dynamics can provide the advantage of observing the systems functioning and understanding the underlying complexity of system as a single functioning unit (Ackoff, 1994). In the current case, the System Dynamics model is depicted using Stocks and Flows, based on the identified success factors and using the Vensim software package. The system is then simulated, and the trends are identified. These trends collectively represent the holistic functioning of the system and individually represent the manifestation of the system's working through the viewpoint of each cornerstone.

A lesser emphasised advantage of using a systems-based approach would be that it provides superior explanatory abilities and handles deeper contexts, along with being able to better represent newer emerging patterns in the system (Barton and Haslett, 2007). As evidence of this, one can observe the employment of constructs such as Feedback, Time delays and Attribution errors within the sphere of system dynamics (Sterman, 2001).

8. CONCLUSION AND FUTURE WORK

The research findings discussed in this work is exploratory in nature and delves into success factors for software product development in a startup environment. This research provides not only the various factors which could determine the success of a product development undertaking in a startup but also defines the potential causal effects, the various factors might have on one another. Using the system dynamics methodology, the variables can be understood, which both directly and indirectly impact the chances of success in a new venture. The findings in the study show that although there are several factors which directly impact the chances of success of a startup venture, the cornerstones such as time to market and accumulated capital are complex factors which is in turn influenced by many variables and merits further investigation. The reviewed literature also indicates that product differentiation has a significant role to play in the success of a product and hence the startup.

The viewpoint considered here is from a software product development perspective and does not go in-depth on aspects of strategy, finance, team dynamics, traits of founders or founding members etc. This can be the scope for a future study. Another direction for future work could be understanding if the discussed factors can be integrated with the product development process, considering the pivotal role factors such as time to market and product differentiators play in the products success. Startups will benefit from such an integrated approach, particularly considering the constraints that startups need to work with.

REFERENCES

Abdel-Hamid, T. K. (1989). The dynamics of software project staffing: A system dynamics based simulation approach. *IEEE Transactions on Software Engineering*, *15*(2), 109–119. doi:10.1109/32.21738

Ackoff, R. L. (1994). Systems thinking and thinking systems. *System Dynamics Review*, *10*(2-3), 175–188. doi:10.1002dr.4260100206

Barton, J., & Haslett, T. (2007). Analysis, synthesis, systems thinking and the scientific method: Rediscovering the importance of open systems. *Systems Research and Behavioral Science*, *24*(2), 143–155. doi:10.1002res.816

Beauregard, R., & Corriveau, P. (2007). User Experience Quality: A Conceptual Framework for Goal Setting and Measurement. In V. G. Duffy (Ed.), *Digital Human Modeling* (pp. 325–332). Springer Berlin Heidelberg; Retrieved from http://link.springer.com/chapter/10.1007/978-3-540-73321-8_38 doi:10.1007/978-3-540-73321-8_38

Bessen, J. E. (2011). *A Generation of Software Patents (SSRN Scholarly Paper No. ID 1868979)*. Rochester, NY: Social Science Research Network. Retrieved from http://papers.ssrn.com/abstract=1868979

Boadway, R., & Tremblay, J.-F. (2003). *Public Economics and Startup Entrepreneurs (SSRN Scholarly Paper No. ID 385781)*. Rochester, NY: Social Science Research Network. Retrieved from http://papers.ssrn.com/abstract=385781

Carmel, E. (1994). Time-to-completion in software package startups. In *Proceedings of the Twenty-Seventh Hawaii International Conference on System Sciences* (Vol. 4, pp. 498–507). 10.1109/HICSS.1994.323468

Carmel, E., & Sawyer, S. (1998). Packaged software development teams: What makes them different? *Information Technology & People*, *11*(1), 7–19. doi:10.1108/09593849810204503

Chapman, L., & Plewes, S. (2014). A UX Maturity Model: Effective Introduction of UX into Organizations. In A. Marcus (Ed.), *Design, User Experience, and Usability. User Experience Design Practice* (pp. 12–22). Springer International Publishing. Retrieved from http://link.springer.com/chapter/10.1007/978-3-319-07638-6_2 doi:10.1007/978-3-319-07638-6_2

Cockburn, I. M., & MacGarvie, M. J. (2009). Patents, Thickets and the Financing of Early-Stage Firms: Evidence from the Software Industry. *Journal of Economics & Management Strategy*, *18*(3), 729–773. doi:10.1111/j.1530-9134.2009.00228.x

Cooper, R. G., & Kleinschmidt, E. J. (1987a). New products: What separates winners from losers? *Journal of Product Innovation Management*, *4*(3), 169–184. doi:10.1016/0737-6782(87)90002-6

Cooper, R. G., & Kleinschmidt, E. J. (1987b). Success factors in product innovation. *Industrial Marketing Management*, *16*(3), 215–223. doi:10.1016/0019-8501(87)90029-0

Coyle, G. (2009). Qualitative and quantitative modelling in system dynamics. *System Dynamics*, *2*, 33.

Crowne, M. (2002). Why software product startups fail and what to do about it. Evolution of software product development in startup companies. In *2002 IEEE International Engineering Management Conference IEMC '02* (Vol. 1, pp. 338–343). IEEE. doi:10.1109/IEMC.2002.1038454

Davis, A. M., & Zweig, A. S. (2005). The Rise and Fall of a Software Startup. *Journal of Information Technology Case and Application Research*, *7*(2), 31–48. doi:10.1080/15228053.2005.10856064

de Wilton, A. (2011). Patent Value: A Business Perspective for Technology Startups. *Technology Innovation Management Review*, *1*(3), 5–11. doi:10.22215/timreview/501

Dove, L., & Sethumadhavan, A. (2012). Breaking down barriers: the interdependence of research and design. *Interaction*, *19*(6), 76–80. doi:10.1145/2377783.2377799

Dubberly, H. (2008). On modeling learning curves for design. *Interaction*, *15*(4), 13–16. doi:10.1145/1374489.1374492

Duchesneau, D. A., & Gartner, W. B. (1990). A profile of new venture success and failure in an emerging industry. *Journal of Business Venturing*, *5*(5), 297–312. doi:10.1016/0883-9026(90)90007-G

Eason, K. (2001). Changing perspectives on the organizational consequences of information technology. *Behaviour & Information Technology*, *20*(5), 323–328. doi:10.1080/01449290110083585

Fayad, M. E., Laitinen, M., & Ward, R. P. (2000). Thinking Objectively: Software Engineering in the Small. *Communications of the ACM*, *43*(3), 115–118. doi:10.1145/330534.330555

Finstad, K., Xu, W., Kapoor, S., Canakapalli, S., & Gladding, J. (2009). FEATURE: Bridging the Gaps Between Enterprise Software and End Users. *Interaction, 16*(2), 10–14. doi:10.1145/1487632.1487635

Ford, D. N., & Sterman, J. D. (1998). Dynamic modeling of product development processes. *System Dynamics Review, 14*(1), 31–68. doi:10.1002/(SICI)1099-1727(199821)14:1<31::AID-SDR141>3.0.CO;2-5

Forrester, J. W. (1971). Counterintuitive behavior of social systems. *Technological Forecasting and Social Change, 3*, 1–22. doi:10.1016/S0040-1625(71)80001-X

Gatignon, H., & Xuereb, J.-M. (1997). Strategic Orientation of the Firm and New Product Performance. *JMR, Journal of Marketing Research, 34*(1), 77–90. doi:10.2307/3152066

Georgantzas, N. C., & Katsamakas, E. G. (2008). Information systems research with system dynamics. *System Dynamics Review, 24*(3), 247–264. doi:10.1002dr.420

Giardino, C., Wang, X., & Abrahamsson, P. (2014). Why Early-Stage Software Startups Fail: A Behavioral Framework. In C. Lassenius & K. Smolander (Eds.), *Software Business. Towards Continuous Value Delivery* (pp. 27–41). Springer International Publishing. Retrieved from http://link.springer.com/chapter/10.1007/978-3-319-08738-2_3 doi:10.1007/978-3-319-08738-2_3

Goodwin, N. C. (1987). Functionality and Usability. *Communications of the ACM, 30*(3), 229–233. doi:10.1145/214748.214758

Graham, S. J. H., & Sichelman, T. (2008). Why Do Start-Ups Patent? *Berkeley Technology Law Journal, 23*(3), 1063–1097.

Groen, A. J., Wakkee, I. A. M., & De Weerd-Nederhof, P. C. (2008). Managing Tensions in a High-tech Start-up: An Innovation Journey in Social System Perspective. *International Small Business Journal, 26*(1), 57–81. doi:10.1177/0266242607084659

Hassenzahl, M., & Tractinsky, N. (2006). User experience - a research agenda. *Behaviour & Information Technology, 25*(2), 91–97. doi:10.1080/01449290500330331

Hellmann, T., & Puri, M. (2000). The Interaction between Product Market and Financing Strategy: The Role of Venture Capital. *Review of Financial Studies, 13*(4), 959–984. doi:10.1093/rfs/13.4.959

Hilmola, O.-P., Helo, P., & Ojala, L. (2003). The value of product development lead time in software startup. *System Dynamics Review, 19*(1), 75–82. doi:10.1002dr.255

Hokkanen, L., Kuusinen, K., & Väänänen, K. (2016). Minimum Viable User EXperience: A Framework for Supporting Product Design in Startups. In *Agile Processes, in Software Engineering, and Extreme Programming* (pp. 66–78). Cham: Springer; doi:10.1007/978-3-319-33515-5_6

Holling, C. S. (2001). Understanding the Complexity of Economic, Ecological, and Social Systems. *Ecosystems (New York, N.Y.), 4*(5), 390–405. doi:10.100710021-001-0101-5

Kashfi, P., Nilsson, A., & Feldt, R. (2016). Integrating User eXperience Practices into Software Development Processes: Implications of Subjectivity and Emergent Nature of UX. arXiv:1605.03783

Klein, L. (2013). *UX for Lean Startups: Faster, Smarter User Experience Research and Design.* O'Reilly Media, Inc.

Klotins, E., Unterkalmsteiner, M., & Gorschek, T. (2015). Software Engineering Knowledge Areas in Startup Companies: A Mapping Study. In J. M. Fernandes, R. J. Machado, & K. Wnuk (Eds.), *Software Business* (pp. 245–257). Springer International Publishing. Retrieved from http://link.springer.com/chapter/10.1007/978-3-319-19593-3_22 doi:10.1007/978-3-319-19593-3_22

Kotler, P., Keller, K. L., Manceau, D., & Hémonnet-Goujot, A. (2015). *Marketing management* (Vol. 14). NJ: Prentice Hall Englewood Cliffs.

Lin, H. X., Choong, Y.-Y., & Salvendy, G. (1997). A proposed index of usability: A method for comparing the relative usability of different software systems. *Behaviour & Information Technology*, *16*(4-5), 267–277. doi:10.1080/014492997119833

Mann, R. J. (2006). *Do Patents Facilitate Financing in the Software Industry? (SSRN Scholarly Paper)*. Rochester, NY: Social Science Research Network. Retrieved from http://papers.ssrn.com/abstract=510103

Mann, R. J., & Sager, T. W. (2007). Patents, venture capital, and software start-ups. *Research Policy*, *36*(2), 193–208. doi:10.1016/j.respol.2006.10.002

Marmer, M., Herrmann, B. L., Dogrultan, E., Berman, R., Eesley, C., & Blank, S. (2011). Startup genome report extra: Premature scaling. *Startup Genome*, *10*, 1–56.

May, B. (2012). Applying Lean Startup: An Experience Report – Lean amp;amp; Lean UX by a UX Veteran: Lessons Learned in Creating amp;amp; Launching a Complex Consumer App. In 2012 *Agile Conference (AGILE)* (pp. 141–147). 10.1109/Agile.2012.18

Misra, S. C., Kumar, V., & Kumar, U. (2009). Identifying some important success factors in adopting agile software development practices. *Journal of Systems and Software*, *82*(11), 1869–1890. doi:10.1016/j.jss.2009.05.052

Morecroft, J. D. W. (1986). The dynamics of a fledgling high-technology growth market: Understanding and managing growth cycles. *System Dynamics Review*, *2*(1), 36–61. doi:10.1002dr.4260020104

Noel, M., & Schankerman, M. (2013). Strategic Patenting and Software Innovation. *The Journal of Industrial Economics*, *61*(3), 481–520. doi:10.1111/joie.12024

Pandey, S., & Srivastava, S. (2014). Data Driven Enterprise UX: A Case Study of Enterprise Management Systems. In S. Yamamoto (Ed.), *Human Interface and the Management of Information. Information and Knowledge in Applications and Services* (pp. 205–216). Springer International Publishing. Retrieved from http://link.springer.com/chapter/10.1007/978-3-319-07863-2_21 doi:10.1007/978-3-319-07863-2_21

Parry, M. E., & Song, X. M. (1994). Identifying new product successes in China. *Journal of Product Innovation Management*, *11*(1), 15–30. doi:10.1016/0737-6782(94)90116-3

Paternoster, N., Giardino, C., Unterkalmsteiner, M., Gorschek, T., & Abrahamsson, P. (2014). Software development in startup companies: A systematic mapping study. *Information and Software Technology*, *56*(10), 1200–1218. doi:10.1016/j.infsof.2014.04.014

Poppendieck, M., & Cusumano, M. A. (2012). Lean Software Development: A Tutorial. *IEEE Software*, *29*(5), 26–32. doi:10.1109/MS.2012.107

Pressman, R. (2014). *Software Engineering: A Practitioner's Approach: Software Engineering: A Practitioner's Approach* (8th ed.). McGraw-Hill Higher Education.

Rahmandad, H., & Weiss, D. M. (2009). Dynamics of concurrent software development. *System Dynamics Review*, *25*(3), 224–249. doi:10.1002dr.425

Ries, E. (2011). *The Lean Startup: How Today's Entrepreneurs Use Continuous Innovation to Create Radically Successful Businesses*. Crown Publishing Group. Retrieved from https://books.google.com.au/books?id=tvfyz-4JILwC

Schwaber, K., & Beedle, M. (2001). *Agile Software Development with Scrum* (1st ed.). Upper Saddle River, NJ: Prentice Hall PTR.

Song, L. Z., Benedetto, C. D., & Song, M. (2010). Competitive Advantages in the First Product of New Ventures. *IEEE Transactions on Engineering Management*, *57*(1), 88–102. doi:10.1109/TEM.2009.2013836

Sterman, J., & Sterman, J. D. (2000). *Business Dynamics: Systems Thinking and Modeling for a Complex World with CD-ROM (HAR/CDR edition)*. Boston, MA: McGraw-Hill Education.

Sterman, J. D. (1994). Learning in and about complex systems. *System Dynamics Review*, *10*(2-3), 291–330. doi:10.1002dr.4260100214

Sterman, J. D. (2001). System Dynamics Modeling: Tools for Learning in a Complex World. *California Management Review*, *43*(4), 8–25. doi:10.2307/41166098

Sutton, S. M. (2000). The role of process in software start-up. *IEEE Software*, *17*(4), 33–39. doi:10.1109/52.854066

Tvedt, J. D., & Gollofello, J. S. (1995). Evaluating the effectiveness of process improvements on software development cycle time via system dynamics modelling. In *Computer Software and Applications Conference, 1995. COMPSAC 95. Proceedings., Nineteenth Annual International* (pp. 318–325). 10.1109/CMPSAC.1995.524796

van Gelderen, M., Thurik, R., & Bosma, N. (2005). Success and Risk Factors in the Pre-Startup Phase. *Small Business Economics*, *24*(4), 365–380. doi:10.100711187-004-6994-6

This research was previously published in the International Journal of System Dynamics Applications (IJSDA), 8(2); pages 51-77, copyright year 2019 by IGI Publishing (an imprint of IGI Global).

Chapter 102
Open Source Software Development Challenges:
A Systematic Literature Review on GitHub

Abdulkadir Seker
Sivas Cumhuriyet University, Turkey

Banu Diri
Yıldız Technical University, Turkey

Halil Arslan
Sivas Cumhuriyet University, Turkey

Mehmet Fatih Amasyalı
Yıldız Technical University, Turkey

ABSTRACT

GitHub is the most common code hosting and repository service for open-source software (OSS) projects. Thanks to the great variety of features, researchers benefit from GitHub to solve a wide range of OSS development challenges. In this context, the authors thought that was important to conduct a literature review on studies that used GitHub data. To reach these studies, they conducted this literature review based on a GitHub dataset source study instead of a keyword-based search in digital libraries. Since GHTorrent is the most widely known GitHub dataset according to the literature, they considered the studies that cite this dataset for the systematic literature review. In this study, they reviewed the selected 172 studies according to some criteria that used the dataset as a data source. They classified them within the scope of OSS development challenges thanks to the information they extract from the metadata of studies. They put forward some issues about the dataset and they offered the focused and attention-grabbing fields and open challenges that we encourage the researchers to study on them.

DOI: 10.4018/978-1-6684-3702-5.ch102

INTRODUCTION

Thanks to distributed version control systems such as Git, Mercurial, etc., open-source development platforms have reached a considerable number of users. The most common of these platforms is GitHub (based on git). GitHub has become the world's largest code server with more than 40 million developers hosting and collaborating over 100 million repositories.

On platforms such as GitHub, the development process is distributed. Developers can participate in a project, contribute, discuss bugs with each other, and write comments about code from various locations. In this way, a considerable amount of textual, numerical and network or collaboration-based features about the projects and developers are extracted from the platform. Besides, GitHub includes many social relations among users or projects. GitHub is the most common code hosting and repository service for open-source software projects. For the researchers that focus on software engineering, the content of this platform provides many valuable sources. Most of the studies about this domain use GitHub as a data source because of easy to access, amount of data, and diversity of features. In this context, we think that is important to conduct a literature review on studies that used GitHub data.

There are several options to reach GitHub data. In a survey study which is given the usage rates of GitHub dataset, they addressed that the most used dataset is GHTorrent (34%) in the articles that are reviewed according to the certain criteria (Cosentino, Luis, & Cabot, 2016). In Cosentino's systematic mapping study, the GHTorrent dataset is in the lead with a 41\% use rate (Badashian, Shah, & Stroulia, 2015; Cosentino, Canovas Izquierdo, & Cabot, 2017). In the another study, GHTorrent is the most cited dataset (Kotti & Spinellis, 2019). The GHTorrent dataset was developed by Georgios Gousios in the software engineering department at Delft University of Technology(Gousios, 2013). The dataset is generated by systematically crawling with the GitHub API and includes information about all public projects and users on the platform. GHTorrent stores some information about repositories, projects, issue descriptions, comments, and pull request (PR) conversations in 26 relational tables totally.

We saw from other systematic literature review (SLR) papers that some studies can be missed when reviewing with a text-based (keyword) search from search engines or digital libraries. Because of that, to reach the studies, we conducted this literature review based on a GitHub dataset source study instead of a keyword-based search in digital libraries. Due to GHTorrent is the most widely known and used GitHub dataset according to the literature, we considered the studies which cite this dataset for the systematic literature review.

In this study, we offered to find out the topics of all studies and classified them. We focused on the studies with the context of open-source software development. We divided the studies into some categories and challenges. Besides, some distributions (type, venue, year, method, data, topic) have been obtained from the studies that used the dataset. We show which challenges are mentioned in the studies and how each study is using the dataset. Thus, we hope the study guided the researchers who interest in software engineering challenges with open-source systems. We formed this review following these research questions:

RQ1: What are the trends of open-source software development challenges?
RQ2: What are the handicaps/cons of GHTorrent?
RQ3: What are the open challenges that have not yet been studied with this dataset?

In this context, we reviewed the articles which use GHTorrent and offered a systematic mapping study. We applied 3 phased systematic literature review protocol as suggested by Kitchenham (Brereton, Kitchenham, Budgen, Turner, & Khalil, 2007). Firstly, we developed a review method using citations of the main paper of the dataset. Then, we conducted a review as extract trend topics from metadata of studies and made assessments. Finally, we revealed some discussions and open challenges. The protocol and details are given Figure 1. We used a cross-checked mechanism (two of the authors) while finding studies and classifying them.

Figure 1. Systematic literature review protocol

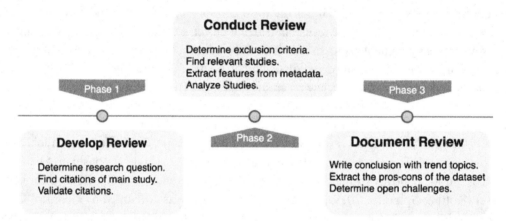

METHODOLOGY

Developing Review

In these other SLR studies, they noticed that some studies can be missed when reviewing with a keyword based search from digital libraries (Khan & Keung, 2016; Schreiber & Zylka, 2020). Because of that, we followed the citation of the main study of the dataset. We used an application[1] to extract all citations of the GHtorrent's study. All 332[2] studies which cited the main study of GHTorrent (Gousios, 2013) were reviewed. We applied exclusion criteria similar to the recently published an SLR study (Schreiber & Zylka, 2020). We exclude the studies that were written in any language other than English, paid studies, and reports/books/theses (Table 1). In addition, the articles refer GHTorrent only as related works or similar dataset were also eliminated.

After we applied the exclusion protocol, we reviewed 172 studies. 49 of the studies were published in journals, and the remaining 123 were published in conferences.

Firstly, we started to review as extracting some features from the metadata of studies.

- Title, authors, keywords, and abstract.
- The aim, methods, and research questions
- The datasets that were used alongside GHTorrent
- The date of used dataset dump

- Publishing venue information
- Citation counts

Table 1. Selecting studies with some criteria

Exclusion Criteria	Amount	Total
Language problem	25	
Paid/non-accessible article	18	
Book/thesis	49	160
Refers it as related work	47	
Refers as similar dataset	16	
Report/speech etc.	5	

Overview of Reviewed Studies

The distribution by years of studies is given in Table 2. The increase over the years is an indication that the data set is used effectively. In 2012, Gousios published a paper about dataset but the source paper is published in 2013. We reviewed studies that cite only the citation article on GHTorrent website.

Table 2. Number of studies in years

Year	2012	2013	2014	2015	2016	2017	2018	2019
Amount	1	1	22	26	28	36	41	17

The source journal distribution of the studies is given in Table 3. The highest number of publications (8 papers) were in "Empirical Software Engineering" (Excluding ArXiv papers). Only 1 study was published in the journals labeled "Others".

Apart from journals, most of the articles were published in various conferences (Table 4). The foremost among them were the MSR and ICSE. Conferences with 1–2 publications are labeled "Others".

Apart from using the dataset, some extended datasets were generated by adding various features to GHTorrent. Furthermore, some studies produced sub/derivative datasets from GHTorrent by filtering some features. In this context, the most common derivative dataset is TravisTorrent. The dataset that was used for the continuous integration challenge was produced with some features from GHTorrent and information extracted from Travis CI. Moreover, information obtained from various platforms, such as Stackoverflow and Twitter, were used in some studies. While 133 (77\%) of papers used only GHTorrent, the remaining 39 were used other datasets with GHTorrent. Table 5 shows the usage rates of datasets with GHTorrent. Most of the studies that used extra dataset addressed the GitHub users' activities in other social networks.

Table 3. Number of studies in journals

Journal Name	Amount
Empirical Software Engineering	8
Information and Software Technology	6
IEEE Transactions of Software Engineering	4
Journal of System and Software	2
Physica A	2
IEEE Access	2
PeerJ	2
ArXiv	10
Others	13

Table 5. Number of studies according to usage dataset

Dataset	Amount
GHTorrent	133
GHTorrent + Stackoverflow	15
GHTorrent + TravisTorrent	13
GHTorrent + Twitter	2
GHTorrent + Others	9

Table 4. Number of studies in conferences

Conference Name	Amount
Int. Conf. on Mining Soft. Repository (MSR)	40
Int. Conf. on Soft. Eng. (ICSE)	9
Int. Conf. on Soft. Eng. Knowledge Eng. (SEKE)	5
Int. Conf. on Soft. Analysis, Evolution and Reengineering (SANER)	5
Int. Conf. on Soft. Maintenance and Evolution (ICSME)	3
Asia-Pacific Soft. Eng. Conference (APSEC)	3
Symposium on the Foundations of Soft. Eng. (FSE)	3
Int. Conf. on Connected Health: App., Systems and Eng. (CHASE)	3
Int. Workshop on Emotion Awareness in Soft. Eng. (SEmotion)	3
Others	49

The methods used in all studies were also extracted (Table 6). The category labeled "statistics" is the most used method group. This group includes statistical, mathematical, and probabilistic methods, etc. Text mining studies are relatively less than other methods despite the dataset includes rich textual features. In this regard, we thought using text mining methods based on deep learning with the dataset will be worthwhile and distinctive. The studies that contain topics such as data visualization, use of the dataset, or creating a new dataset are in the "Others" category.

The words in the abstracts of an article roughly give information about its topic. Starting from this point of view, another important feature extracted from these studies was relation of words in the abstracts. The cluster density graph[3] was created by use frequency of these words (Figure 2). The clusters and underlined words were played crucial roles on separating studies into categories.

Table 6. Number of studies according to usage methods

Dataset	Amount
Statistic	68
Machine Learning	41
Survey	25
Text Mining	25
Others	34

Figure 2. The cluster density graph of words in abstracts

RESULTS

RQ1: What are the trends of open-source software development challenges?

Firstly, to group studies on domains, we used the nature of GitHub itself. "User" (developer) and "project" are the backbones of open-source software platforms. Secondly, in considerations of the density graph (Figure 2), apart from these it is seen that the "development" topic is also at the center. Besides, the "dataset" topic is added because some of the studies are related to the dataset directly. Thus, the studies have been separated into 4 domains. In order to determine challenges under these domains, we appealed to Cosentino's GitHub review article (Cosentino et al., 2017) and the cluster density graph. We chose the most inclusive ones while determining the challenges. After all processes, the software engineering challenges were separated into 16 challenges under four domains.

The studies were split into four domains, User (USR), Development (DEV), Project (PRO), and Dataset (DAT). The challenges of these domains and related studies are given in Table 7. The reason the total numbers in the table are greater than the total number of studies is that some of them focus on more than one challenge. The abbreviations of these challenges that are going to use following tables are given in this table. We used the cluster density graph and chose the most inclusive ones while determining the challenges.

Table 7. Number of studies in domains and challenges

Domains	Amount	Challenges	Amount	Alias
USER	69	Activity	39	ACTV
		Interaction	39	INTR
		Revision-Assignment	9	REVI
		Characterization	35	CHAR
DEVELOPMENT	59	Pull Request	18	PREQ
		Source Code	35	CODE
		Continuous Integrations	17	CONT
		Quality	12	QUAL
PROJECT	63	Issue/bug	24	ISSU
		Team-Member	11	TEAM
		Dependency	9	DEPE
		Characterization	36	CHAR
DATASET	28	Definition-Usage	4	DEFI
		Subsets	4	SUBS
		Augments-Derivatives	7	AUGM
		Helper	13	HELP

In addition to these numbers, the detailed information about each domain is given in Tables 8–11 below. The given tables for each domain contain the reference id of studies and related challenges ("x" in a cell indicates that the study focuses on a challenge in this column).

User

GitHub users are the main roles in software projects positioned as contributors (with codes or comments), developers, project managers, etc. to perform all activities in the software life cycle. In this context, a lot of studies have been published about user's domain. The user domain challenges were divided into four topics, activity, interaction, revision/assignee, and characterization (Table 8).

- *ACTY(Activity):* In general terms, it covers the GitHub developers' contributions such as coding history, comments, like/star, developer performances, and other past activities.
- *INTR (Interaction):* It is related to users' interactions both within the GitHub environment and on other platforms such as Stackoverflow and Twitter. Events such as following or watching among users, forking projects, etc. come under this topic.
- *REVI (Revision-Assignment):* The studies about pull request reviewer, issue or bug assignment problems are in this topic.
- *CHAR(Characterization):* Out of the topics above, the studies interest in behavior of user's emotional activity, classifying the developers according to features such as gender, activity, tenure/ volunteer were analyzed under this title.

The most studied challenges in the user domain are activity and interaction, as seen in Table 8. This trend can be interpreted as a natural consequence of GitHub being an open-source, community-oriented project repository service.

Development

The basic activity that affects the performance of its targeted product in software projects can be considered as the development process. The challenges in the development domain were divided into four topics, pull request, source code, continuous integration, and quality (Table \ref{tab:dev}).

- *PREQ (Pull Request (PR)):* It covers some problems about PR classifications or prioritization, PR description and comment contents, and PR acceptance/rejection and reasons for them.
- *CODE (Source Code):* It is about topics such as the programming languages of projects, connections between codes (referring to original source code, code cloning), refactoring, tactic codes, and code conflict on PR.
- *CONT (Continuous Integration (CI)):* It is related to the use of CI, the effect of CI quality, build breakage problems, test cases, automatizations of CI process.
- *QUAL (Quality):* It contains all studies which aim at increasing software quality as the main purpose.

In this domain, most studies are about source code. GHTorrent does not contain features directly related to source code. However, the other datasets used with GHTorrent, such as StackOverflow, give rise to this result.

Table 8. Challenges in the USER domain

References of Studies	Amount	ACTV	INTR	REVI	CHAR
(Cosentino, Izquierdo, & Cabot, 2014; Horschig, Mattis, & Hirschfeld, 2018; Rahman & Roy, 2014; Saito, Fujiwara, Igaki, Yoshida, & Iida, 2016)	4	x			
(Abdalkareem, Shihab, & Rilling, 2017; Alves, Brandão, Santana, Silva, & Moro, 2016; Batista, Brandão, Alves, da Silva, & Moro, 2017; Calefato, Lanubile, & Novielli, 2017; Komamizu, Hayase, Amagasa, & Kitagawa, 2017; Kopczyński & Celińska-Kopczyńska, 2017; J. Liu, Li, Wang, Yu, & Yin, 2018; Sheoran, Blincoe, Kalliamvakou, Damian, & Eli, 2014; Silvestri, Yang, Bozzon, & Tagarelli, 2015; Yan & Wang, 2017; Yang, Martins, Saini, & Lopes, 2017; Yu, Yin, Wang, & Wang, 2014)	12		x		
(Badashian, Hindle, & Stroulia, 2015; de Lima Júnior, Soares, Plastino, & Murta, 2015)	2			x	
(Bayati, 2018; Brokmeier, 2017; Cassee, Pinto, Castor, & Serebrenik, 2018; Hauff & Gousios, 2015; Lu et al., 2019; Ortu, Hall, et al., 2018; Ortu, Pinna, et al., 2018; Qiu, Nolte, Brown, Serebrenik, & Vasilescu, 2019; Saha, Muradul Bashir, Raihan Talukder, Karmaker, & Saiful Islam, 2018; Terrell et al., 2017)	10				x
(Badashian, Esteki, Gholipour, Hindle, & Stroulia, 2014; Baltes, Knack, Anastasiou, Tymann, & Diehl, 2018; Constantinou & Kapitsaki, 2016b; Constantinou & Mens, 2017a; Destefanis, Ortu, Bowes, Marchesi, & Tonelli, 2018; Y. Hu, Wang, Ren, & Choo, 2018; Jiang, Feng, Lian, & Zhang, 2016; Lee & Lo, 2018; Manes & Baysal, 2019; Vasilescu, Filkov, & Serebrenik, 2013)	10	x	x		
(Jarczyk, Jaroszewicz, Wierzbicki, Pawlak, & Jankowski-Lorek, 2018; Júnior, Soares, Plastino, & Murta, 2018; Xavier, Macedo, & Maia, 2014)	3	x		x	
(Baltes & Diehl, 2018a, 2018b; Brunet, Murphy, Terra, Figueiredo, & Serey, 2014; Burlet & Hindle, 2015; Jaruchotrattanasakul, Yang, Makihara, Fujiwara, & Iida, 2016; C. Liu, Yang, Zhang, Ray, & Rahman, 2018; Sayagh, Kerzazi, Adams, & Petrillo, 2018; Vasilescu, Filkov, & Serebrenik, 2015; Yamashita, McIntosh, Kamei, Hassan, & Ubayashi, 2015; Yan, Wei, Han, & Wang, 2017; P. Zhang, Xiong, Leung, & Song, 2018)	11	x			x
(Blincoe, Sheoran, Goggins, Petakovic, & Damian, 2016; Middleton et al., 2018; Rastogi & Nagappan, 2016b; Sun, Xu, Xia, Chen, & Li, 2018; Wisse & Veenman, 2015; Yan, Li, & Wang, 2017)	6		x		x
(Ying, Chen, Liang, & Wu, 2016; Yu, Wang, Yin, & Ling, 2014; Yu, Wang, Yin, & Wang, 2016)	3	x	x	x	
(Bao, Xia, Lo, & Murphy, 2019; Bayati, 2019; Casalnuovo, Vasilescu, Devanbu, & Filkov, 2015; Constantinou & Kapitsaki, 2016a; Jiang, Lo, Yang, Li, & Zhang, 2019; Nielek et al., 2016; Z. Wang, Wang, Wang, & Redmiles, 2018)	7	x	x		x
(Daricélio M. Soares, de Lima Júnior, Plastino, & Murta, 2018)	1	x	x	x	x

Table 9. Challenges in the DEVELOPMENT domain

References of Studies	Amount	PREQ	CODE	CONT	QUAL
(Brokmeier, 2017; Calefato et al., 2017; Chen, Stolee, & Menzies, 2017; El Mezouar, Zhang, & Zou, 2019; Pletea, Vasilescu, & Serebrenik, 2014; Rahman & Roy, 2014; Saito et al., 2016; Daricélio M. Soares et al., 2018; Daricélio Moreira Soares, de Lima Júnior, Murta, & Plastino, 2015; Daricélio Moreira Soares, Junior, Murta, & Plastino, 2015; Terrell et al., 2017; Y. Zhang, Yin, Yu, & Wang, 2014)	12	x			
(Cassee et al., 2018; Celińska & Kopczyński, 2017; Coelho, Almeida, Gousios, Deursen, & Treude, 2017; Coelho, Almeida, Gousios, & Van Deursen, 2015; Constantinou & Mens 2017a; Gharehyazie, Ray, & Filkov, 2014; Gharehyazie et al. 2019; Gonzalez, Prentice, & Mirakhorli, 2018; Guzman, Azócar, & Li, 2014; Horschig et al. 2018; D. Li et al. 2016; X. Liu, Shen, Zhong, & Zhu, 2016; Lopes et al., 2017; Martins, Achar, & Lopes, 2018a; Saha et al., 2018; Wisse & Veenman, 2015; Wittern, Suter, & Rajagopalan, 2016; Yang et al., 2017)	18		x		
(Baltes, Knack, et al., 2018; Beller, Gousios, & Zaidman, 2017b; Hilton, Tunnell, Huang, Marinov, & Dig, 2016; Madeyski & Kawalerowicz, 2017; Ortu, Pinna, et al., 2018; Vassallo, Proksch, Gall, & Di Penta, 2019; Xia & Li, 2017)	7			x	
(Hata, Treude, Kula, & Ishio, 2019; Flávio Medeiros et al., 2018; Veen, Gousios, & Zaidman, 2015)	3	x	x		
(Yu, Yin, Wang, Yang, & Wang, 2016; Zhao, da Costa, & Zou, 2019)	2	x			x
(Beller, Gousios, & Zaidman, 2017a; Dimitropoulos, Aung, & Svetinovic, 2017; Gonzalez, Santos, Popovich, Mirakhorli, & Nagappan, 2017; Luo, Zhao, Ma, & Chen, 2017; Muylaert & De Roover, 2017; Muylaert, Meuter, & Roover, 2016)	6		x	x	
(Baltes & Diehl, 2018b; Kikas, Gousios, Dumas, & Pfahl, 2017; Flavio Medeiros et al., 2018; Mujhid, S. Santos, Gopalakrishnan, & Mirakhorli, 2017; Santos, Campbell, Hindle, & Amaral, 2017; Sharma, Fragkoulis, & Spinellis, 2016; Tomasdottir, Aniche, & Van Deursen, 2018)	7		x		x
(Urli, Yu, Seinturier, & Monperrus, 2018; Vasilescu, Van Schuylenburg, Wulms, Serebrenik, & van den Brand, 2014; Vasilescu, Yu, Wang, Devanbu, & Filkov, 2015)	3		x	x	x
(Yu, Wang, Filkov, Devanbu, & Vasilescu, 2015)	1	x	x	x	

Project

The essential motivation of distributed version control systems is the development of targeted products on the basis of public projects. The project domain challenges were divided into four topics, issue/bug, team/ members, dependency, and characterization (Table 10).

- *ISSU (Issue/bug):* It includes topics such as open and closed issues (commits, tasks) in a project, bugs occurrence, and bug triaging. Moreover, the differences, characterization, and classification of the trio of issue-bug-feature are under this topic.
- *TEAM (Team/member):* It contains the challenges about the team diversity in terms of some features (location, gender, tenure, permanence, etc.), the actions as a team, joining or leaving behaviors, core and other members, and the effect of teams on software quality.
- *DEPE (Dependency):* It includes topics about project dependencies. Varied types of dependencies in GitHub projects were examined with regards to programming languages, codes, problems, forking cases, and code clones. In addition, the relationships between projects and the parameters related to project survival are other challenges under this topic.
- *CHAR (Characterization):* It involves some topics such as GitHub repository features, the unique parts of projects, the diversity of projects in terms of some parameters such as language or design, features of public projects, matters about the GitHub ecosystem, repository artifacts, forking, and branching.

Most studies under the project domain were related to characterization. The rich features of the GHTorrent about projects are thought to have a positive impression on this result.

Dataset

Apart from using the dataset, some extended datasets were generated by adding various features to GHTorrent. In the dataset domain, there were four sub-topics such as; definition, usage, extended-sub datasets, and helper (Table 11).

- *DEFI (Definition-Usage):* It is about the description of GHTorrent dataset. Besides, it covers the studies that contain dataset obtaining methods, dataset usage tips and tools.
- *SUBS (Subsets):* It is about the studies that created by some filtering process on GHTorrent. Most of studies filter dataset according to features of developers or projects.
- *AUGM (Augments-Derivatives):* It covers the studies that produce new datasets based upon GHTorrent (TravisTorrent, SOTorrent, etc.) and extended datasets created via data fusion from social media data.
- *HELP (Helper):* Apart from above, some papers interest in dissimilar problems via only a few features (user mail, project language, etc.) extracted from GHTorrent. These studies were brought together under this title.

Many datasets have been created by using GHTorrent. Besides, there is a lot of software engineering studies that benefit from some features of GHTorrent. It is clearly understood from the studies under this topic that GHTorrent (hence GitHub data) how has rich features.

Table 10. Challenges in the PROJECT domain

References of Studies	Amount	ISSU	TEAM	DEPE	CHAR
(Abdalkareem et al., 2017; Alonso-Abad, López-Nozal, Maudes-Raedo, & Marizorena-Sánchez, 2019; Badashian, Hindle, et al., 2015; Cabot, Canovas Izquierdo, Cosentino, & Rolandi, 2015; Destefanis et al., 2018; Fan, Yu, Yin, Wang, & Wang, 2017; Guzman et al., 2014; D. Hu, Wang, Chang, Zhang, & Yin, 2018; Jarczyk et al., 2018; Karampatsis & Sutton, 2019; Kikas, Dumas, & Pfahl, 2016; D. Li et al., 2016; X. Liu et al., 2016; Murgia et al., 2014; Pletea et al., 2014; Saha et al., 2018; Werder & Brinkkemper, 2018)	17	x			
(El Mezouar et al., 2019; Middleton et al., 2018; Qiu et al., 2019; Vasilescu, Filkov, et al., 2015; Vasilescu, Serebrenik, & Filkov, 2015)	5		x		
(Gharehyazie et al., 2017)	1			x	
(Aggarwal, Hindle, & Stroulia, 2014; Bayati, 2019; Burlet & Hindle, 2015; Cheng, Li, Li, & Liang, 2018; Constantinou & Mens, 2017b; Cosentino et al., 2014; Eck & Uebernickel, 2016; Fernández, Robles, Libresoft, Rey, & Carlos, 2017; Gharehyazie et al., 2019; Knauss, Damian, Cleland-Huang, & Helms, 2015; Kovalenko, Palomba, & Bacchelli, 2018; Lakkundi, Agrahari, & Chimalakonda, 2019; C. Liu et al., 2018; J. Liu et al., 2019; Lu et al., 2019; Ma et al., 2018; Miranda, Lins, Klosowski, & Silva, 2018; Onoue, Hata, & Matsumoto, 2014; Onoue, Kula, Hata, & Matsumoto, 2017; Raghuraman, Ho-Quang, V Chaudron Chalmers, Serebrenik, & Vasilescu, 2019; Rastogi & Nagappan, 2016a; Robles, Ho-Quang, Hebig, Chaudron, & Fernandez, 2017; W. Wang, Poo-Caamano, Wilde, & German, 2015; Yamashita, McIntosh, Kamei, & Ubayashi, 2014)	24				x
(Ortu et al., 2017; Ortu, Hall, et al., 2018)	2	x	x		
(Blincoe, Harrison, Kaur, & Damian, 2019; Izquierdo, Cosentino, Rolandi, Bergel, & Cabot, 2015)	2	x		x	
(Kalliamvakou et al., 2014; P. Zhang et al., 2018)	2	x			x
(Constantinou & Mens, 2016; Low, Yathog, & Svetinovic, 2015; Matragkas, Williams, Kolovos, & Paige, 2014; Werder, 2018)	4		x		x
(Aue, Haisma, Tomasdottir, & Bacchelli, 2016; Hata, Todo, Onoue, & Matsumoto, 2015; Liao et al., 2019; Padhye, Mani, & Sinha, 2014; Yamashita, Kamei, McIntosh, Hassan, & Ubayashi, 2016)	5			x	x
(Blincoe, Harrison, & Damian, 2015)	1	x		x	x

Table 11. Papers about the dataset

References of Studies	Amount	DEFI	SUBS	AUGM	HELP
(Badashian, Shah, et al., 2015; Gousios, Pinzger, & Deursen, 2014; Gousios & Spinellis, 2012; Markovtsev & Long, 2018)	4	x			
(Cheng et al., 2018; Gousios & Zaidman, 2014; Karampatsis & Sutton, 2019; Lakkundi et al., 2019; Martins et al., 2018a; Robles et al., 2017; Vasilescu, Serebrenik, et al., 2015)	7		x		
(Baltes, Dumani, Treude, & Diehl, 2018; Batista et al., 2017; Beller et al., 2017b; Komamizu et al., 2017)	4			x	
(Baltes & Diehl, 2016; Filippova & Cho, 2016; Gousios, Storey, & Bacchelli, 2016; Gousios, Zaidman, Storey, & Deursen, 2015; Jaffe, Lacomis, Schwartz, Goues, & Vasilescu, 2018; Y. Li, Katsipoulakis, Chandramouli, Goldstein, & Kossmann, 2017; Martins, Achar, & Lopes, 2018b; Munaiah, Kroh, Cabrey, & Nagappan, 2017; Sawant, Robbes, & Bacchelli, 2016, 2018; van der Bent, Hage, Visser, & Gousios, 2018; Vasilescu, 2014; Vasilescu, Posnett, et al., 2015)	13				x

RQ2: What are the handicaps/cons of GHTorrent?

GitHub data retrieves with the GitHub API as fast response and consistent data. However, its 5000 requests per hour limit is a crucial problem when retrieving large data[4]. Thereagainst, GHTorrent presents up to date data thanks to downloadable dumps without any restriction.

GHTorrent provides flexibility by presenting data in different types. It presents raw JSON data in MongoDB database and relational tables in MySQL database. You can use whichever format that suitable for your environment.

MongoDB Format

1. You can download previous bi-monthly MongoDB collections from the website (until 2015 / by collections.).
2. You can download daily collections from the website (from 2015/ all collections are included.)
3. You can connect to the remote MongoDB server with the instructions on the website. The remote MongoDB server's data may not up to date.

MySQL Format

1. You can download all relational tables in a single MySQL dump file. (until 2015).
2. You can download all relational tables as separate CSV files containing a table in each. (from 2015).
3. You can query the online SQLite tool from the latest dump of MySQL database. (We couldn't try this because of login problem.)

Although the GHTorrent publishes as up to date, it is seen from our review that most of the researchers (including in recent years) use the older versions of the dataset (Table 12). In this table, it is given that the dates of dataset dump which studies published in the last two years. In 25 of 55 studies, it was not explicitly stated which dump was used.

Table 12. Older dumps usages

Dataset Dumps	2019 Studies	2018 Studies
2016 and older	5	5
2017	5	4
2018	4	1
2019	1	0
unknown	6	19

In order to use up to date data, there is two possible option.

- Download huge MySQL dumps and import all CSV files to local database environments.
- Download all daily MongoDB dumps and restore them to local environments according to instructions on the website.

In both of the above two options, processing and transferring these large files is taken serious time and effort (Badashian, Shah, et al., 2015). We think that this situation prompts researchers to use older and smaller dumps. This may not a problem, however, it is a matter of curiosity why they use older data.

Besides the advantages, GHTorrent has some cons and problems. The problems reported from reviewed studies and experienced by us are given below list.

- It is reported in some studies that GHTorrent have duplicated data (Martins et al., 2018a; Werder & Brinkkemper, 2018). We noticed this problem in the collections of *repos* and *users*, too. (There are several docs have same *id* and *url* field.)
- Another problem is that some fields that can be used as a linkage between data are missing. For instance, there is no *repo id* or *full name* in *commits* and *commits comments* collections. You have to parse the *url* field to generate them.
- It is reported that GHTorrent does not provide correct data on whether developer accounts are members of teams on GitHub (Middleton et al., 2018).
- Sun et al. have also stated that GHTorrent did not have data on who edited what file (Sun et al., 2018).

It is thought that a topic is also missing about the dataset. We have also extracted dataset usage criteria from studies. Except studies that few related to data visualization or extending the dataset, almost all them use data by applying particular filters to the dataset. Commonly they use filters based on user or project metrics (number of commit/pull request/followers, code language, etc.) However, since each study has its own subset, it is not possible to compare success-even on similar subjects. In this context, it is also important to publish domain-based subsets that can be used for specific challenges. Actually, this is necessary for software engineering challenge studies that use not only GHTorrent but also all GitHub dataset.

RQ3: What are the open challenges that have not yet been studied with this dataset?

We extract top-10 studies according to citations on Google Scholar to find attention-grabbing publications. As seen Table 13, the prominent domain is Development (DEV). Besides, the studies about the dataset (DAT) domain are among to influential ones. Starting from this point of view, we aimed to find open challenges under these domains.

Table 13. Top 10 studies according to citation count

Title	Citation	Year	Domain
The promises and perils of mining GitHub	442	2014	PRO
Work practices and challenges in pull-based development: the integrator's perspective	217	2015	DAT
Quality and productivity outcomes relating to continuous integration in GitHub	212	2015	DEV
Gender and tenure diversity in GitHub teams	188	2015	DAT
Usage, costs, and benefits of continuous integration in open-source projects	169	2016	DEV
Sentiment analysis of commit comments in GitHub: an empirical study	169	2014	DEV
Work practices and challenges in pull-based development: the contributor's perspective	142	2016	DAT
Reviewer recommendation for pull-requests in GitHub: What can we learn from code review and bug assignment?	120	2016	USR
Wait for it: Determinants of pull request evaluation latency on GitHub	113	2015	DEV
Curating GitHub for engineered software projects	111	2017	DAT

Assignee feature used for assign to pull requests or issues to someone in Git-based platforms such as GitHub, GitLab, Bitbucket, etc. Much as some projects don't use this feature effectively, this is crucial for project management (Jiang, Lo, Ma, Feng, & Zhang, 2017). To automate the assigning process, issues are classified with some labels or tags, then match to suitable developers. It is seen in Table 8 that only 12% of the studies in the user domain are related to revision/assignee problems. However, it is expected that more studies can be done with GHTorrent about task or reviewer assignment, which is one of the major challenges of software engineering (Hoda & Murugesan, 2016).

New trends in software developments are aimed at automating everything from issue assignment to test and deploy. DevOps is used for this purpose. DevOps process means that to integrates developments and operations via increasing communications and automatizations. All processes such as continuous integrity, automated testing or deploying, performance managements, etc. can handle with DevOps pipelines. In the studies we reviewed, it was observed that the researchers focused on a few of the DevOps processes such as continuous integrity, testing or revision. The data provided by GHTorrent has the necessary elements to contribute to all these steps.

Due to the rapid increase of open-source software projects, developers miss some of the projects in their areas of interest. This led to the need to recommend projects to users in environments such as GitHub. In this context, one of the recent studied hot topics related to project dependency is project recommendation to users (for following or contribution) (C. Liu et al., 2018; Nielek et al., 2016; Sun et al., 2018). New recommend models and metrics can develop with GHTorrent.

CONCLUSION

Most of the studies that focus on software engineering, use GitHub as a data source because of easy to access, amount of data, and diversity of features. Thanks to the great variety of features, researchers benefit from GitHub to solve a wide range of open-source software development challenges. In this context, we thought that is important to conduct a literature review on studies that used GitHub data. In conclusion, we constructed this study in light of three research questions. Firstly, we explored trend challenges in open-source software development, and we found the most popular challenge is related to characterizing developers (users) and projects. Secondly, we analyzed the most common GitHub dataset and we put forward some issues and problems. Lastly, we investigated whether is there any challenges that have not yet been studied much yet and we discovered some open challenges such as GitHub project recommendation, and automatic assignment to pull requests or issues reviewer.

In this SLR study, we classified the open-source software development studies under 4 domains and 16 challenges via the information that we extract from words in abstracts. Unlike the existing SLR, we used the dataset citation-based review method owing to some problems may occur text-based search such a wide range of field. Hereby, we presented a filtered and classified SLR to researchers who interest in open-source software development challenges.

Our results showed that most of the studies swarm to the user and project domains. The researchers specifically focused on the *characterization* challenges under both of the two domains. In the user domain, one of the trending topics is classifying users according to some features and activities to use for other challenges. Besides, analyzing users' past activities and their relationships with each other (in GitHub or other social networks) stood out as other challenges. The topics such as features of repositories, diversity, and relations are prominent ones in project *characterization* challenges. The great majority of studies related to the development domain directed to the *source codes* of projects in order to used extract some metrics such as number of code lines in a commit, programming languages, number of contributors per code line, etc. Lastly, in the dataset domain, most studies under the *helper* challenge focus on dissimilar problems via only a few features (user mail, project language, etc.) extracted from the dataset.

We presented some issues about GHTorrent as another contribution. Missing and duplicate data should be fixed by the creators of the dataset. Besides, we showed that each researcher uses an ad-hoc sub-dataset (filtering data in a different way in each study) in their studies. This situation makes comparing studies with each other difficult. In this regard, we want to cooperate with the creators of GHTorrent to take the whole dataset and present common domain-based datasets for specific challenges.

In another result of this study, we explored that some challenges are rarely studied although they are crucial for open-source software development. For instance, in terms of distributed development, assigning a reviewer to "pull requests" or "issues" fast as possible to maintain software projects is very important. In this context, we think that revision is a crucial challenge to focus on. Moreover, the project recommendation is another important challenge in GitHub. In early this year, GitHub released the "Explore" page to recommend the project to developers based on their activities. We realized that also there are only a few studies about the project recommendation. We encourage the researchers to focus on this challenge.

Lastly, when we analyzed the methods of studies, we noticed that mostly the researchers used surveys (questionnaire, crowdsourcing, manual labeling, etc.) to evaluate their results. We think that the researchers refer to this method due to there is no labeled data on most challenges.

We plan to conduct other SLR's specific to the most studied challenges in future works. Besides, we want to research the methods of reviewed studies comprehensively to analyze which methods used why.

REFERENCES

Abdalkareem, R., Shihab, E., & Rilling, J. (2017). What Do Developers Use the Crowd For? A Study Using Stack Overflow. *IEEE Software, 34*(2), 53–60. doi:10.1109/MS.2017.31

Aggarwal, K., Hindle, A., & Stroulia, E. (2014). Co-evolution of project documentation and popularity within github. *Proceedings of the 11th Working Conference on Mining Software Repositories - MSR 2014*, 360–363. 10.1145/2597073.2597120

Alonso-Abad, J. M., López-Nozal, C., Maudes-Raedo, J. M., & Marticorena-Sánchez, R. (2019). Label prediction on issue tracking systems using text mining. *Progress in Artificial Intelligence, 8*(3), 325–342. doi:10.100713748-019-00182-2

Alves, G. B., Brandão, M. A., Santana, D. M., da Silva, A. P. C., & Moro, M. M. (2016). The Strength of Social Coding Collaboration on GitHub. *SBBD 2016*. Retrieved from https://www.semanticscholar. org/paper/The-Strength-of-Social-Coding-Collaboration-on-Alves-Brandão/15dc574702e4e61233e04 b1e8ea3f5ad38dc0cc6

Aue, J., Haisma, M., Tomasdottir, K. F., & Bacchelli, A. (2016). Social Diversity and Growth Levels of Open Source Software Projects on GitHub. *Proceedings of the 10th ACM/IEEE International Symposium on Empirical Software Engineering and Measurement - ESEM '16*, 1–6. 10.1145/2961111.2962633

Badashian, A. S., Esteki, A., Gholipour, A., Hindle, A., & Stroulia, E. (2014). Involvement, contribution and influence in GitHub and stack overflow. *Proceedings of 24th Annual International Conference on Computer Science and Software Engineering*, 19–33. Retrieved from https://dl.acm.org/citation. cfm?id=2735527

Badashian, A. S., Hindle, A., & Stroulia, E. (2015). Crowdsourced bug triaging. *2015 IEEE 31st International Conference on Software Maintenance and Evolution, ICSME 2015 - Proceedings*, 506–510. 10.1109/ICSM.2015.7332503

Badashian, A. S., Shah, V., & Stroulia, E. (2015). GitHub's big data adaptor: an eclipse plugin. *CASCON 15*, 265–268. Retrieved from https://dl.acm.org/citation.cfm?id=2886490

Baltes, S., & Diehl, S. (2016). Worse Than Spam: Issues In Sampling Software Developers. *Proceedings of the 10th ACM/IEEE International Symposium on Empirical Software Engineering and Measurement - ESEM '16*, 1–6. 10.1145/2961111.2962628

Baltes, S., & Diehl, S. (2018a). Towards a theory of software development expertise. *Proceedings of the 2018 26th ACM Joint Meeting on European Software Engineering Conference and Symposium on the Foundations of Software Engineering - ESEC/FSE 2018*, 187–200. 10.1145/3236024.3236061

Baltes, S., & Diehl, S. (2018b). Usage and attribution of Stack Overflow code snippets in GitHub projects. *Empirical Software Engineering*, 1–37. doi:10.100710664-018-9650-5

Baltes, S., Dumani, L., Treude, C., & Diehl, S. (2018). *The Evolution of Stack Overflow Posts: Reconstruction and Analysis.* Retrieved from https://arxiv.org/abs/1811.00804

Baltes, S., Knack, J., Anastasiou, D., Tymann, R., & Diehl, S. (2018). (No) influence of continuous integration on the commit activity in GitHub projects. *Proceedings of the 4th ACM SIGSOFT International Workshop on Software Analytics - SWAN 2018*, 1–7. 10.1145/3278142.3278143

Bao, L., Xia, X., Lo, D., & Murphy, G. C. (2019). A Large Scale Study of Long-Time Contributor Prediction for GitHub Projects. *IEEE Transactions on Software Engineering*, 1–1. doi:10.1109/TSE.2019.2918536

Batista, N. A., Brandão, M. A., Alves, G. B., da Silva, A. P. C., & Moro, M. M. (2017). Collaboration strength metrics and analyses on GitHub. Proceedings of the International Conference on Web Intelligence - WI '17, 170–178. 10.1145/3106426.3106480

Bayati, S. (2018). Understanding newcomers success in open source community. *Proceedings of the 40th International Conference on Software Engineering Companion Proceeedings - ICSE '18*, 224–225. 10.1145/3183440.3195073

Bayati, S. (2019). Effect of newcomers supportive strategies on open source projects socio-technical activities. *Proceedings of the 12th International Workshop on Cooperative and Human Aspects of Software Engineering CHASE*, 49–50. 10.1109/CHASE.2019.00020

Beller, M., Gousios, G., & Zaidman, A. (2017a). Oops, My Tests Broke the Build: An Explorative Analysis of Travis CI with GitHub. *2017 IEEE/ACM 14th International Conference on Mining Software Repositories (MSR)*, 356–367. 10.1109/MSR.2017.62

Beller, M., Gousios, G., & Zaidman, A. (2017b). TravisTorrent: Synthesizing Travis CI and GitHub for Full-Stack Research on Continuous Integration. *2017 IEEE/ACM 14th International Conference on Mining Software Repositories (MSR)*, 447–450. 10.1109/MSR.2017.24

Blincoe, K., Harrison, F., & Damian, D. (2015). Ecosystems in GitHub and a Method for Ecosystem Identification Using Reference Coupling. *2015 IEEE/ACM 12th Working Conference on Mining Software Repositories*, 202–211. 10.1109/MSR.2015.26

Blincoe, K., Harrison, F., Kaur, N., & Damian, D. (2019). Reference Coupling: An exploration of inter-project technical dependencies and their characteristics within large software ecosystems. *Information and Software Technology*, *110*, 174–189. doi:10.1016/j.infsof.2019.03.005

Blincoe, K., Sheoran, J., Goggins, S., Petakovic, E., & Damian, D. (2016). Understanding the popular users: Following, affiliation influence and leadership on GitHub. *Information and Software Technology*, *70*, 30–39. doi:10.1016/j.infsof.2015.10.002

Brereton, P., Kitchenham, B. A., Budgen, D., Turner, M., & Khalil, M. (2007). Lessons from applying the systematic literature review process within the software engineering domain. *Journal of Systems and Software*, *80*(4), 571–583. doi:10.1016/j.jss.2006.07.009

Brokmeier, P. (2017). Project level effects of gender on contribution evaluation on GitHub. *PeerJ* PrePrints, *5*(e2989v1). doi:10.7287/peerj.preprints.2989v1

Brunet, J., Murphy, G. C., Terra, R., Figueiredo, J., & Serey, D. (2014). Do developers discuss design? *Proceedings of the 11th Working Conference on Mining Software Repositories - MSR 2014*, 340–343. 10.1145/2597073.2597115

Burlet, G., & Hindle, A. (2015). An Empirical Study of End-User Programmers in the Computer Music Community. *2015 IEEE/ACM 12th Working Conference on Mining Software Repositories*, 292–302. 10.1109/MSR.2015.34

Cabot, J., Canovas Izquierdo, J. L., Cosentino, V., & Rolandi, B. (2015). Exploring the use of labels to categorize issues in Open-Source Software projects. *2015 IEEE 22nd International Conference on Software Analysis, Evolution, and Reengineering (SANER)*, 550–554. 10.1109/SANER.2015.7081875

Calefato, F., Lanubile, F., & Novielli, N. (2017). A Preliminary Analysis on the Effects of Propensity to Trust in Distributed Software Development. *2017 IEEE 12th International Conference on Global Software Engineering (ICGSE)*, 56–60. 10.1109/ICGSE.2017.1

Casalnuovo, C., Vasilescu, B., Devanbu, P., & Filkov, V. (2015). Developer Onboarding in GitHub: The Role of Prior Social Links and Language Experience. *2015 10th Joint Meeting of the European Software Engineering Conference and the ACM SIGSOFT Symposium on the Foundations of Software Engineering, ESEC/FSE 2015 - Proceedings*, 817–828. 10.1145/2786805.2786854

Cassee, N., Pinto, G., Castor, F., & Serebrenik, A. (2018). How swift developers handle errors. *Proceedings of the 15th International Conference on Mining Software Repositories - MSR '18*, 292–302. 10.1145/3196398.3196428

Celińska, D., & Kopczyński, E. (2017). Programming Languages in GitHub: A Visualization in Hyperbolic Plane. *11. International AAAI Conference on Web and Social Media*. Retrieved from https://www.aaai.org/ocs/index.php/ICWSM/ICWSM17/paper/viewPaper/15583

Chen, D., Stolee, K. T., & Menzies, T. (2017). *Replicating and Scaling up Qualitative Analysis using Crowdsourcing: A Github-based Case Study*. Retrieved from https://arxiv.org/abs/1702.08571

Cheng, C., Li, B., Li, Z., & Liang, P. (2018). *Automatic Detection of Public Development Projects in Large Open Source Ecosystems: An Exploratory Study on GitHub*. doi:10.18293/SEKE2018-085

Coelho, R., Almeida, L., Gousios, G., van Deursen, A., & Treude, C. (2017). Exception handling bug hazards in Android Results from a mining study and an exploratory survey. *Empirical Software Engineering*, 22(3), 1264–1304. doi:10.100710664-016-9443-7

Coelho, R., Almeida, L., Gousios, G., & Van Deursen, A. (2015). Unveiling exception handling bug hazards in android based on GitHub and Google code issues. *IEEE International Working Conference on Mining Software Repositories*. 10.1109/MSR.2015.20

Constantinou, E., & Kapitsaki, G. M. (2016a). Developers Expertise and Roles on Software Technologies. *2016 23rd Asia-Pacific Software Engineering Conference (APSEC)*, 365–368. 10.1109/APSEC.2016.061

Constantinou, E., & Kapitsaki, G. M. (2016b). Identifying Developers' Expertise in Social Coding Platforms. *2016 42th Euromicro Conference on Software Engineering and Advanced Applications (SEAA)*, 63–67. 10.1109/SEAA.2016.18

Constantinou, E., & Mens, T. (2016). Social and technical evolution of software ecosystems: A Case Study of Rails. *Proceedings of the 10th European Conference on Software Architecture Workshops - ECSAW '16*, 1–4. 10.1145/2993412.3003384

Constantinou, E., & Mens, T. (2017a). An empirical comparison of developer retention in the RubyGems and npm software ecosystems. *Innovations in Systems and Software Engineering, 13*(2–3), 101–115. doi:10.100711334-017-0303-4

Constantinou, E., & Mens, T. (2017b). Socio-technical evolution of the Ruby ecosystem in GitHub. *2017 IEEE 24th International Conference on Software Analysis, Evolution and Reengineering (SANER)*, 34–44. 10.1109/SANER.2017.7884607

Cosentino, V., Canovas Izquierdo, J. L., & Cabot, J. (2017). A Systematic Mapping Study of Software Development With GitHub. *IEEE Access: Practical Innovations, Open Solutions, 5*, 7173–7192. doi:10.1109/ACCESS.2017.2682323

Cosentino, V., Izquierdo, J. L. C., & Cabot, J. (2014). *Three Metrics to Explore the Openness of GitHub projects*. Retrieved from https://arxiv.org/abs/1409.4253

Cosentino, V., Luis, J., & Cabot, J. (2016). Findings from GitHub: methods, datasets and limitations. *Proceedings of the 13th International Workshop on Mining Software Repositories*, 137–141. 10.1145/2901739.2901776

de Lima Júnior, M. L., Soares, D. M., Plastino, A., & Murta, L. (2015). Developers assignment for analyzing pull requests. *Proceedings of the 30th Annual ACM Symposium on Applied Computing - SAC '15*, 1567–1572. 10.1145/2695664.2695884

Destefanis, G., Ortu, M., Bowes, D., Marchesi, M., & Tonelli, R. (2018). On measuring affects of github issues' commenters. *Proceedings of the 3rd International Workshop on Emotion Awareness in Software Engineering - SEmotion '18*, 14–19. 10.1145/3194932.3194936

Dimitropoulos, P., Aung, Z., & Svetinovic, D. (2017). Continuous integration build breakage rationale: Travis data case study. *2017 International Conference on Infocom Technologies and Unmanned Systems (Trends and Future Directions) (ICTUS)*, 639–645. 10.1109/ICTUS.2017.8286087

Eck, A., & Uebernickel, F. (2016). Reconstructing Open Source Software Ecosystems: Finding Structure in Digital Traces. *ICIS*. Retrieved from https://www.semanticscholar.org/paper/Reconstructing-Open-Source-Software-Ecosystems%3A-in-Eck-Uebernickel/60ace7d37a292da6b40e0ac468b326f2e0f524af

El Mezouar, M., Zhang, F., & Zou, Y. (2019). An empirical study on the teams structures in social coding using GitHub projects. *Empirical Software Engineering, 24*(6), 1–34. doi:10.100710664-019-09700-1

Fan, Q., Yu, Y., Yin, G., Wang, T., & Wang, H. (2017). Where Is the Road for Issue Reports Classification Based on Text Mining? *2017 ACM/IEEE International Symposium on Empirical Software Engineering and Measurement (ESEM)*, 121–130. 10.1109/ESEM.2017.19

Fernández, M. A., Robles, G., Libresoft, G., Rey, U., & Carlos, J. (2017). Extracting software development information from FLOSS Projects in GitHub. *SATToSE*. Retrieved from http://ghtorrent.org/

Filippova, A., & Cho, H. (2016). The Effects and Antecedents of Conflict in Free and Open Source Software Development. *Proceedings of the 19th ACM Conference on Computer-Supported Cooperative Work & Social Computing - CSCW '16*, 703–714. 10.1145/2818048.2820018

Gharehyazie, M., Ray, B., & Filkov, V. (2017). Some from Here, Some from There: Cross-Project Code Reuse in GitHub. *2017 IEEE/ACM 14th International Conference on Mining Software Repositories (MSR)*, 291–301. 10.1109/MSR.2017.15

Gharehyazie, M., Ray, B., Keshani, M., Zavosht, M. S., Heydarnoori, A., & Filkov, V. (2019). Cross-project code clones in GitHub. *Empirical Software Engineering, 24*(3), 1538–1573. doi:10.100710664-018-9648-z

Gonzalez, D., Prentice, S., & Mirakhorli, M. (2018). A fine-grained approach for automated conversion of JUnit assertions to English. *Proceedings of the 4th ACM SIGSOFT International Workshop on NLP for Software Engineering - NL4SE 2018*, 14–17. 10.1145/3283812.3283819

Gonzalez, D., Santos, J. C. S., Popovich, A., Mirakhorli, M., & Nagappan, M. (2017). A Large-Scale Study on the Usage of Testing Patterns That Address Maintainability Attributes: Patterns for Ease of Modification, Diagnoses, and Comprehension. *2017 IEEE/ACM 14th International Conference on Mining Software Repositories (MSR)*, 391–401. 10.1109/MSR.2017.8

Gousios, G. (2013). The GHTorrent dataset and tool suite. *Proceedings of the 10th Working Conference on Mining Software Repositories*, 233–236. 10.1109/MSR.2013.6624034

Gousios, G., Pinzger, M., & Van Deursen, A. (2014). An exploratory study of the pull-based software development model. *Proceedings - International Conference on Software Engineering*, (1), 345–355. 10.1145/2568225.2568260

Gousios, G., & Spinellis, D. (2012). GHTorrent: Github's data from a firehose. *2012 9th IEEE Working Conference on Mining Software Repositories (MSR)*, 12–21. 10.1109/MSR.2012.6224294

Gousios, G., Storey, M.-A., & Bacchelli, A. (2016). Work practices and challenges in pull-based development: The Contributor's Perspective. *Proceedings of the 38th International Conference on Software Engineering - ICSE '16*, 285–296. 10.1145/2884781.2884826

Gousios, G., & Zaidman, A. (2014). A dataset for pull-based development research. *Proceedings of the 11th Working Conference on Mining Software Repositories - MSR 2014*, 368–371. 10.1145/2597073.2597122

Gousios, G., Zaidman, A., Storey, M.-A., & van Deursen, A. (2015). Work Practices and Challenges in Pull-Based Development: The Integrator's Perspective. *2015 IEEE/ACM 37th IEEE International Conference on Software Engineering*, 358–368. 10.1109/ICSE.2015.55

Guzman, E., Azócar, D., & Li, Y. (2014, May 31). Sentiment Analysis of Commit Comments in GitHub. *An Empirical Study, 352–355*, 352–355. Advance online publication. doi:10.1145/2597073.2597118

Hata, H., Todo, T., Onoue, S., & Matsumoto, K. (2015). Characteristics of Sustainable OSS Projects: A Theoretical and Empirical Study. *2015 IEEE/ACM 8th International Workshop on Cooperative and Human Aspects of Software Engineering*, 15–21. 10.1109/CHASE.2015.9

Hata, H., Treude, C., Kula, R. G., & Ishio, T. (2019). 9.6 Million Links in Source Code Comments: Purpose, Evolution, and Decay. *International Conference on Software Engineering*. 10.1109/ICSE.2019.00123

Hauff, C., & Gousios, G. (2015). Matching GitHub Developer Profiles to Job Advertisements. *2015 IEEE/ACM 12th Working Conference on Mining Software Repositories*, 362–366. 10.1109/MSR.2015.41

Hilton, M., Tunnell, T., Huang, K., Marinov, D., & Dig, D. (2016). Usage, costs, and benefits of continuous integration in open-source projects. *Proceedings of the 31st IEEE/ACM International Conference on Automated Software Engineering - ASE 2016*, 426–437. 10.1145/2970276.2970358

Hoda, R., & Murugesan, L. K. (2016). Multi-level agile project management challenges: A self-organizing team perspective. *Journal of Systems and Software, 117*, 245–257. doi:10.1016/j.jss.2016.02.049

Horschig, S., Mattis, T., & Hirschfeld, R. (2018). Do Java programmers write better Python? Studying off-language code quality on GitHub. *Conference Companion of the 2nd International Conference on Art, Science, and Engineering of Programming - Programming'18 Companion*, 127–134. 10.1145/3191697.3214341

Hu, D., Wang, T., Chang, J., Zhang, Y., & Yin, G. (2018). Bugs and features, do developers treat them differently? *2018 International Conference on Artificial Intelligence and Big Data (ICAIBD)*, 250–255. 10.1109/ICAIBD.2018.8396204

Hu, Y., Wang, S., Ren, Y., & Choo, K.-K. R. (2018). User influence analysis for Github developer social networks. *Expert Systems with Applications, 108*, 108–118. doi:10.1016/j.eswa.2018.05.002

Izquierdo, J. L. C., Cosentino, V., Rolandi, B., Bergel, A., & Cabot, J. (2015). GiLA: GitHub label analyzer. *2015 IEEE 22nd International Conference on Software Analysis, Evolution, and Reengineering, SANER 2015 - Proceedings*. 10.1109/SANER.2015.7081860

Jaffe, A., Lacomis, J., Schwartz, E. J., Le Goues, C., & Vasilescu, B. (2018). Meaningful variable names for decompiled code: a machine translation approach. *Proceedings of the 26th Conference on Program Comprehension - ICPC '18*, 20–30. 10.1145/3196321.3196330

Jarczyk, O., Jaroszewicz, S., Wierzbicki, A., Pawlak, K., & Jankowski-Lorek, M. (2018). Surgical teams on GitHub: Modeling performance of GitHub project development processes. *Information and Software Technology, 100*, 32–46. doi:10.1016/j.infsof.2018.03.010

Jaruchotrattanasakul, T., Yang, X., Makihara, E., Fujiwara, K., & Iida, H. (2016). Open Source Resume (OSR): A Visualization Tool for Presenting OSS Biographies of Developers. *2016 7th International Workshop on Empirical Software Engineering in Practice (IWESEP)*, 57–62. 10.1109/IWESEP.2016.17

Jiang, J., Feng, F., Lian, X., & Zhang, L. (2016). Long-Term Active Integrator Prediction in the Evaluation of Code Contributions. *International Conference on Software Engineering and Knowledge Engineering (SEKE)*, 177–182. 10.18293/SEKE2016-030

Jiang, J., Lo, D., Ma, X., Feng, F., & Zhang, L. (2017). Understanding inactive yet available assignees in GitHub. *Information and Software Technology, 91*, 44–55. doi:10.1016/j.infsof.2017.06.005

Jiang, J., Lo, D., Yang, Y., Li, J., & Zhang, L. (2019). A first look at unfollowing behavior on GitHub. *Information and Software Technology, 105*, 150–160. doi:10.1016/j.infsof.2018.08.012

Júnior, M. L. de L., Soares, D. M., Plastino, A., & Murta, L. (2018). Automatic assignment of integrators to pull requests: The importance of selecting appropriate attributes. *Journal of Systems and Software*, *144*, 181–196. doi:10.1016/j.jss.2018.05.065

Kalliamvakou, E., Gousios, G., Blincoe, K., Singer, L., German, D. M., & Damian, D. (2014). The promises and perils of mining GitHub. *Proceedings of the 11th Working Conference on Mining Software Repositories - MSR 2014*, 92–101. 10.1145/2597073.2597074

Karampatsis, R.-M., & Sutton, C. (2019). *How Often Do Single-Statement Bugs Occur? The ManyS-StuBs4J Dataset.* Retrieved from https://arxiv.org/abs/1905.13334

Khan, A. A., & Keung, J. (2016, October 1). Systematic review of success factors and barriers for software process improvement in global software development. *IET Software*, *10*(5), 125–135. doi:10.1049/iet-sen.2015.0038

Kikas, R., Dumas, M., & Pfahl, D. (2016). Using dynamic and contextual features to predict issue lifetime in GitHub projects. *Proceedings of the 13th International Workshop on Mining Software Repositories - MSR '16*, 291–302. 10.1145/2901739.2901751

Kikas, R., Gousios, G., Dumas, M., & Pfahl, D. (2017). Structure and Evolution of Package Dependency Networks. *2017 IEEE/ACM 14th International Conference on Mining Software Repositories (MSR)*, 102–112. 10.1109/MSR.2017.55

Knauss, E., Damian, D., Cleland-Huang, J., & Helms, R. (2015). Patterns of continuous requirements clarification. *Requirements Engineering*, *20*(4), 383–403. doi:10.100700766-014-0205-z

Komamizu, T., Hayase, Y., Amagasa, T., & Kitagawa, H. (2017). Exploring Identical Users on GitHub and Stack Overflow. *SEKE*, 584–589. doi:10.18293/SEKE2017-109

Kopczyński, E., & Celińska-Kopczyńska, D. (2017). *Hyperbolic triangulations and discrete random graphs.* Retrieved from https://arxiv.org/abs/1707.01124

Kotti, Z., & Spinellis, D. (2019). Standing on shoulders or feet?: the usage of the MSR data papers. *Proceedings of the 16th International Conference on Mining Software Repositories*, 565–576. 10.1109/MSR.2019.00085

Kovalenko, V., Palomba, F., & Bacchelli, A. (2018). Mining file histories: should we consider branches? *Proceedings of the 33rd ACM/IEEE International Conference on Automated Software Engineering - ASE 2018*, 202–213. 10.1145/3238147.3238169

Lakkundi, C. S., Agrahari, V., & Chimalakonda, S. (2019). *GE852: A Dataset of 852 Game Engines.* Retrieved from https://arxiv.org/abs/1905.04482

Lee, R. K.-W., & Lo, D. (2018). Wisdom in Sum of Parts: Multi-Platform Activity Prediction in Social Collaborative Sites. *Proceedings of the 10th ACM Conference on Web Science - WebSci '18*, 77–86. 10.1145/3201064.3201067

Li, D., Li, L., Kim, D., Bissyandé, T. F., Lo, D., & Le Traon, Y. (2016). *Watch out for This Commit! A Study of Influential Software Changes.* Retrieved from https://arxiv.org/abs/1606.03266

Li, Y., Katsipoulakis, N. R., Chandramouli, B., Goldstein, J., & Kossmann, D. (2017). Mison: A Fast JSON Parser for Data Analytics. *Proceedings of the VLDB Endowment International Conference on Very Large Data Bases, 10*(10), 1118–1129. doi:10.14778/3115404.3115416

Liao, Z., Wang, N., Liu, S., Zhang, Y., Liu, H., & Zhang, Q. (2019). Identification-Method Research for Open-Source Software Ecosystems. *Symmetry, 11*(2), 182. doi:10.3390ym11020182

Liu, C., Yang, D., Zhang, X., Ray, B., & Rahman, M. M. (2018). Recommending GitHub Projects for Developer Onboarding. *IEEE Access: Practical Innovations, Open Solutions, 6*, 52082–52094. doi:10.1109/ACCESS.2018.2869207

Liu, J., Li, Z., Wang, T., Yu, Y., & Yin, G. (2018). Adaptive software search toward users' customized requirements in GitHub. *SEKE*, 143–181. doi:10.18293/SEKE2018-064

Liu, X., Shen, B., Zhong, H., & Zhu, J. (2016). EXPSOL: Recommending Online Threads for Exception-Related Bug Reports. *2016 23rd Asia-Pacific Software Engineering Conference (APSEC)*, 25–32. 10.1109/APSEC.2016.015

Lopes, C. V., Maj, P., Martins, P., Saini, V., Yang, D., Zitny, J., ... Vitek, J. (2017). DéjàVu: a map of code duplicates on GitHub. *Proceedings of the ACM on Programming Languages, 1*, 1–28. 10.1145/3133908

Low, J. F., Yathog, T., & Svetinovic, D. (2015). Software analytics study of Open-Source system survivability through social contagion. *2015 IEEE International Conference on Industrial Engineering and Engineering Management (IEEM)*, 1213–1217. 10.1109/IEEM.2015.7385840

Lu, Y., Mao, X., Wang, T., Yin, G., Li, Z., & Wang, W. (2019). Studying in the "Bazaar": An Exploratory Study of Crowdsourced Learning in GitHub. *IEEE Access: Practical Innovations, Open Solutions, 7*, 1–1. doi:10.1109/ACCESS.2019.2915247

Luo, Y., Zhao, Y., Ma, W., & Chen, L. (2017). What are the Factors Impacting Build Breakage? *2017 14th Web Information Systems and Applications Conference (WISA)*, 139–142. 10.1109/WISA.2017.17

Ma, Y., Fakhoury, S., Christensen, M., Arnaoudova, V., Zogaan, W., & Mirakhorli, M. (2018). Automatic classification of software artifacts in open-source applications. *Proceedings of the 15th International Conference on Mining Software Repositories - MSR '18*, 414–425. 10.1145/3196398.3196446

Madeyski, L., & Kawalerowicz, M. (2017). Continuous Defect Prediction: The Idea and a Related Dataset. *2017 IEEE/ACM 14th International Conference on Mining Software Repositories (MSR)*, 515–518. 10.1109/MSR.2017.46

Manes, S. S., & Baysal, O. (2019). How often and what StackOverflow posts do developers reference in their GitHub projects? *Proceedings of the 16th International Conference on Mining Software Repositories*, 235–239. 10.1109/MSR.2019.00047

Markovtsev, V., & Long, W. (2018). Public git archive: a big code dataset for all. *15th International Conference on Mining Software Repositories*, 34–37. Retrieved from https://dl.acm.org/citation.cfm?id=3196464

Martins, P., Achar, R., & Lopes, C. V. (2018a). 50K-C a dataset of compilable, and compiled, Java projects. *Proceedings of the 15th International Conference on Mining Software Repositories - MSR '18*, 1–5. 10.1145/3196398.3196450

Martins, P., Achar, R., & Lopes, C. V. (2018b). *The Java Build Framework: Large Scale Compilation.* Retrieved from https://arxiv.org/abs/1804.04621

Matragkas, N., Williams, J. R., Kolovos, D. S., & Paige, R. F. (2014). Analysing the "biodiversity" of open source ecosystems: the GitHub case. *Proceedings of the 11th Working Conference on Mining Software Repositories - MSR 2014*, 356–359. 10.1145/2597073.2597119

Medeiros, F., Lima, G., Amaral, G., Apel, S., Kästner, C., Ribeiro, M., & Gheyi, R. (2018). An investigation of misunderstanding code patterns in C open-source software projects. *Empirical Software Engineering*, 1–34. doi:10.100710664-018-9666-x

Medeiros, F., Ribeiro, M., Gheyi, R., Apel, S., Kastner, C., Ferreira, B., Carvalho, L., & Fonseca, B. (2018). Discipline Matters: Refactoring of Preprocessor Directives in the #ifdef Hell. *IEEE Transactions on Software Engineering*, 44(5), 453–469. doi:10.1109/TSE.2017.2688333

Middleton, J., Murphy-Hill, E., Green, D., Meade, A., Mayer, R., White, D., & McDonald, S. (2018). Which contributions predict whether developers are accepted into github teams. *Proceedings of the 15th International Conference on Mining Software Repositories - MSR '18*, 403–413. 10.1145/3196398.3196429

Miranda, F., Lins, L., Klosowski, J. T., & Silva, C. T. (2018). TopKube: A Rank-Aware Data Cube for Real-Time Exploration of Spatiotemporal Data. *IEEE Transactions on Visualization and Computer Graphics*, 24(3), 1394–1407. doi:10.1109/TVCG.2017.2671341 PMID:28221997

Mujhid, I. J. S., Santos, J. C., Gopalakrishnan, R., & Mirakhorli, M. (2017). A search engine for finding and reusing architecturally significant code. *Journal of Systems and Software*, 130, 81–93. doi:10.1016/j.jss.2016.11.034

Munaiah, N., Kroh, S., Cabrey, C., & Nagappan, M. (2017). Curating GitHub for engineered software projects. *Empirical Software Engineering*, 22(6), 3219–3253. doi:10.100710664-017-9512-6

Murgia, A., Concas, G., Tonelli, R., Ortu, M., Demeyer, S., & Marchesi, M. (2014). On the influence of maintenance activity types on the issue resolution time. *Proceedings of the 10th International Conference on Predictive Models in Software Engineering - PROMISE '14*, 12–21. 10.1145/2639490.2639506

Muylaert, W., & De Roover, C. (2017). Prevalence of Botched Code Integrations. *2017 IEEE/ACM 14th International Conference on Mining Software Repositories (MSR)*, 503–506. 10.1109/MSR.2017.40

Muylaert, W., De Meuter, W., & De Roover, C. (2016). An Exploratory Study Into the Prevalence of Botched Code Integrations. *SATToSE*. Retrieved from http://sattose.wdfiles.com/local--files/2016:alltalks/SATTOSE2016_paper_8.pdf

Nielek, R., Jarczyk, O., Pawlak, K., Bukowski, L., Bartusiak, R., & Wierzbicki, A. (2016). Choose a Job You Love: Predicting Choices of GitHub Developers. *2016 IEEE/WIC/ACM International Conference on Web Intelligence (WI)*, 200–207. 10.1109/WI.2016.0037

Onoue, S., Hata, H., & Matsumoto, K. (2014). Software population pyramids: The Current and the Future of OSS Development Communities. *Proceedings of the 8th ACM/IEEE International Symposium on Empirical Software Engineering and Measurement - ESEM '14*, 1–4. 10.1145/2652524.2652565

Onoue, S., Kula, R. G., Hata, H., & Matsumoto, K. (2017). *The Health and Wealth of OSS Projects: Evidence from Community Activities and Product Evolution.* Retrieved from https://arxiv.org/abs/1709.10324

Ortu, M., Destefanis, G., Counsell, S., Swift, S., Tonelli, R., & Marchesi, M. (2017). How diverse is your team? Investigating gender and nationality diversity in GitHub teams. *Journal of Software Engineering Research and Development, 5*(1), 9. doi:10.118640411-017-0044-y

Ortu, M., Hall, T., Marchesi, M., Tonelli, R., Bowes, D., & Destefanis, G. (2018). Mining Communication Patterns in Software Development: A GitHub Analysis. *Proceedings of the 14th International Conference on Predictive Models and Data Analytics in Software Engineering - PROMISE'18*, 70–79. 10.1145/3273934.3273943

Ortu, M., Pinna, A., Tonelli, R., Marchesi, M., Bowes, D., & Destefanis, G. (2018). Angry-builds: An Empirical Study Of Affect Metrics and Builds Success on GitHub Ecosystem. *Proceedings of the 19th International Conference on Agile Software Development Companion - XP '18*, 1–2. 10.1145/3234152.3234160

Padhye, R., Mani, S., & Sinha, V. S. (2014). A study of external community contribution to open-source projects on GitHub. *Proceedings of the 11th Working Conference on Mining Software Repositories - MSR 2014*, 332–335. 10.1145/2597073.2597113

Pletea, D., Vasilescu, B., & Serebrenik, A. (2014). Security and emotion: sentiment analysis of security discussions on GitHub. *Proceedings of the 11th Working Conference on Mining Software Repositories - MSR 2014*, 348–351. 10.1145/2597073.2597117

Qiu, H. S., Nolte, A., Brown, A., Serebrenik, A., & Vasilescu, B. (2019). Going farther together: the impact of social capital on sustained participation in open source. *41st ACM/IEEE International Conference on Software Engineering, (ICSE2019)*, 688–699. Retrieved from https://research.tue.nl/en/publications/going-farther-together-the-impact-of-social-capital-on-sustained-

Raghuraman, A., Ho-Quang, T. V., Chaudron Chalmers, M. R., Serebrenik, A., & Vasilescu, B. (2019). Does UML Modeling Associate with Lower Defect Proneness? A Preliminary Empirical Investigation. *16th International Conference on Mining Software Repositories.* Retrieved from https://pypi.org/project/langdetect/

Rahman, M. M., & Roy, C. K. (2014). An insight into the pull requests of GitHub. *Proceedings of the 11th Working Conference on Mining Software Repositories - MSR 2014*, 364–367. 10.1145/2597073.2597121

Rastogi, A., & Nagappan, N. (2016a). Forking and the Sustainability of the Developer Community Participation -- An Empirical Investigation on Outcomes and Reasons. *2016 IEEE 23rd International Conference on Software Analysis, Evolution, and Reengineering (SANER)*, 102–111. 10.1109/SANER.2016.27

Rastogi, A., & Nagappan, N. (2016b). On the Personality Traits of GitHub Contributors. *2016 IEEE 27th International Symposium on Software Reliability Engineering (ISSRE)*, 77–86. 10.1109/ISSRE.2016.43

Robles, G., Ho-Quang, T., Hebig, R., Chaudron, M. R. V., & Fernandez, M. A. (2017). An Extensive Dataset of UML Models in GitHub. *2017 IEEE/ACM 14th International Conference on Mining Software Repositories (MSR)*, 519–522. 10.1109/MSR.2017.48

Saha, S., Muradul Bashir, G. M., Raihan Talukder, M., Karmaker, J., & Saiful Islam, M. (2018). Which Programming Language and Platform Developers Prefer for the Development? A Study Using Stack Overflow. *2018 International Conference on Innovations in Science, Engineering and Technology (ICISET)*, 305–310. 10.1109/ICISET.2018.8745630

Saito, Y., Fujiwara, K., Igaki, H., Yoshida, N., & Iida, H. (2016). How do GitHub Users Feel with Pull-Based Development? *2016 7th International Workshop on Empirical Software Engineering in Practice (IWESEP)*, 7–11. 10.1109/IWESEP.2016.19

Santos, E. A., Campbell, J. C., Hindle, A., & Amaral, J. N. (2017). Finding and correcting syntax errors using recurrent neural networks. *PeerJ* Preprints. doi:10.7287/peerj.preprints.3123v1

Sawant, A. A., Robbes, R., & Bacchelli, A. (2016). On the Reaction to Deprecation of 25,357 Clients of 4+1 Popular Java APIs. *2016 IEEE International Conference on Software Maintenance and Evolution (ICSME)*, 400–410. 10.1109/ICSME.2016.64

Sawant, A. A., Robbes, R., & Bacchelli, A. (2018). On the reaction to deprecation of clients of 4 + 1 popular Java APIs and the JDK. *Empirical Software Engineering*, 23(4), 2158–2197. doi:10.100710664-017-9554-9

Sayagh, M., Kerzazi, N., Adams, B., & Petrillo, F. (2018). Software Configuration Engineering in Practice: Interviews, Survey, and Systematic Literature Review. *IEEE Transactions on Software Engineering*, 1–1. doi:10.1109/TSE.2018.2867847

Schreiber, R. R., & Zylka, M. P. (2020, March 1). Social Network Analysis in Software Development Projects: A Systematic Literature Review. *International Journal of Software Engineering and Knowledge Engineering*, 30(03), 321–362. doi:10.1142/S021819402050014X

Sharma, T., Fragkoulis, M., & Spinellis, D. (2016). Does your configuration code smell? *Proceedings of the 13th International Workshop on Mining Software Repositories - MSR '16*, 189–200. 10.1145/2901739.2901761

Sheoran, J., Blincoe, K., Kalliamvakou, E., Damian, D., & Ell, J. (2014). Understanding watchers on GitHub. *Proceedings of the 11th Working Conference on Mining Software Repositories - MSR 2014*, 336–339. 10.1145/2597073.2597114

Silvestri, G., Yang, J., Bozzon, A., & Tagarelli, A. (2015). Linking Accounts across Social Networks: the Case of StackOverflow, Github and Twitter. *KDWeb*. Retrieved from https://www.semanticscholar.org/paper/Linking-Accounts-across-Social-Networks%3A-the-Case-Silvestri-Yang/351b86ffc19cb02e51466522a0b4b199ac1dbd06

Soares, D. M., & de Lima, J. (2018). What factors influence the reviewer assignment to pull requests? *Information and Software Technology*, 98, 32–43. doi:10.1016/j.infsof.2018.01.015

Soares, D. M., & de Lima, J. M. L., Murta, L., & Plastino, A. (2015). Acceptance factors of pull requests in open-source projects. *Proceedings of the 30th Annual ACM Symposium on Applied Computing - SAC '15*, 1541–1546. 10.1145/2695664.2695856

Soares, D. M. Jr., Murta, L., & Plastino, A. (2015). Rejection Factors of Pull Requests Filed by Core Team Developers in Software Projects with High Acceptance Rates. *2015 IEEE 14th International Conference on Machine Learning and Applications (ICMLA)*, 960–965. 10.1109/ICMLA.2015.41

Sun, X., Xu, W., Xia, X., Chen, X., & Li, B. (2018). Personalized project recommendation on GitHub. *Science China. Information Sciences*, *61*(5), 1–14. doi:10.100711432-017-9419-x

Terrell, J., Kofink, A., Middleton, J., Rainear, C., Murphy-Hill, E., Parnin, C., & Stallings, J. (2017). Gender differences and bias in open source: Pull request acceptance of women versus men. *PeerJ. Computer Science*, *3*, e111. doi:10.7717/peerj-cs.111

Tomasdottir, K. F., Aniche, M., & Van Deursen, A. (2018). The Adoption of JavaScript Linters in Practice: A Case Study on ESLint. *IEEE Transactions on Software Engineering*, 1–1. doi:10.1109/TSE.2018.2871058

Urli, S., Yu, Z., Seinturier, L., & Monperrus, M. (2018). How to design a program repair bot? Insights from the Repairnator Project. *Proceedings of the 40th International Conference on Software Engineering Software Engineering in Practice - ICSE-SEIP '18*, 95–104. 10.1145/3183519.3183540

van der Bent, E., Hage, J., Visser, J., & Gousios, G. (2018). How good is your puppet? An empirically defined and validated quality model for puppet. *2018 IEEE 25th International Conference on Software Analysis, Evolution and Reengineering (SANER)*, 164–174. 10.1109/SANER.2018.8330206

Vasilescu, B. (2014). Human aspects, gamification, and social media in collaborative software engineering. *Companion Proceedings of the 36th International Conference on Software Engineering - ICSE Companion 2014*, 646–649. 10.1145/2591062.2591091

Vasilescu, B., Filkov, V., & Serebrenik, A. (2013). StackOverflow and GitHub: Associations between Software Development and Crowdsourced Knowledge. *2013 International Conference on Social Computing*, 188–195. 10.1109/SocialCom.2013.35

Vasilescu, B., Filkov, V., & Serebrenik, A. (2015). Perceptions of diversity on GitHub: a user survey. *Proceedings of the 8th International Workshop on Cooperative and Human Aspects of Software Engineering*, 50–56. Retrieved from https://dl.acm.org/citation.cfm?id=2819330

Vasilescu, B., Posnett, D., Ray, B., van den Brand, M. G. J., Serebrenik, A., Devanbu, P., & Filkov, V. (2015). Gender and Tenure Diversity in GitHub Teams. *Proceedings of the 33rd Annual ACM Conference on Human Factors in Computing Systems - CHI '15*, 3789–3798. 10.1145/2702123.2702549

Vasilescu, B., Serebrenik, A., & Filkov, V. (2015). A Data Set for Social Diversity Studies of GitHub Teams. *2015 IEEE/ACM 12th Working Conference on Mining Software Repositories*, 514–517. 10.1109/MSR.2015.77

Vasilescu, B., Van Schuylenburg, S., Wulms, J., Serebrenik, A., & van den Brand, M. G. J. (2014). Continuous Integration in a Social-Coding World: Empirical Evidence from GitHub. *2014 IEEE International Conference on Software Maintenance and Evolution*, 401–405. 10.1109/ICSME.2014.62

Vasilescu, B., Yu, Y., Wang, H., Devanbu, P., & Filkov, V. (2015). Quality and productivity outcomes relating to continuous integration in GitHub. *Proceedings of the 2015 10th Joint Meeting on Foundations of Software Engineering*, 805–816. 10.1145/2786805.2786850

Vassallo, C., Proksch, S., Gall, H. C., & Di Penta, M. (2019). Automated reporting of anti-patterns and decay in continuous integration. *Proceedings of the 41st International Conference on Software Engineering ICSE*, 105–115. 10.1109/ICSE.2019.00028

van der Veen, E., Gousios, G., & Zaidman, A. (2015). Automatically Prioritizing Pull Requests. *2015 IEEE/ACM 12th Working Conference on Mining Software Repositories*, 357–361. 10.1109/MSR.2015.40

Wang, W., Poo-Caamano, G., Wilde, E., & German, D. M. (2015). What Is the Gist? Understanding the Use of Public Gists on GitHub. *2015 IEEE/ACM 12th Working Conference on Mining Software Repositories*, 314–323. 10.1109/MSR.2015.36

Wang, Z., Wang, Y., & Redmiles, D. (2018). Competence-confidence gap: a threat to female developers' contribution on github. *Proceedings of the 40th International Conference on Software Engineering Software Engineering in Society - ICSE-SEIS '18*, 81–90. 10.1145/3183428.3183437

Werder, K. (2018). The evolution of emotional displays in open source software development teams: An Individual Growth Curve Analysis. *Proceedings of the 3rd International Workshop on Emotion Awareness in Software Engineering - SEmotion '18*, 1–6. 10.1145/3194932.3194934

Werder, K., & Brinkkemper, S. (2018). MEME - Toward a Method for EMotions Extraction from GitHub. *Emotion 2018 : 2018 ACM/IEEE 3rd International Workshop on Emotion Awareness in Software Engineering*. Retrieved from https://ieeexplore.ieee.org/document/8595354/keywords#keywords

Wisse, W., & Veenman, C. (2015). Scripting DNA: Identifying the JavaScript programmer. *Digital Investigation*, 15, 61–71. doi:10.1016/j.diin.2015.09.001

Wittern, E., Suter, P., & Rajagopalan, S. (2016). A look at the dynamics of the JavaScript package ecosystem. *Proceedings of the 13th International Conference on Mining Software Repositories*, 351–361. 10.1145/2901739.2901743

Xavier, J., Macedo, A., & Maia, M. de A. (2014). Understanding the popularity of reporters and assignees in the Github. *International Conference on Software Engineering and Knowledge Engineering (SEKE)*, 484–489. Retrieved from https://www.semanticscholar.org/paper/Understanding-the-popularity-of-reporters-and-in-Xavier-Macedo/a113516ff1ca5ff4ebdbb4a2b90c972158cc3763

Xia, J., & Li, Y. (2017). Could We Predict the Result of a Continuous Integration Build? An Empirical Study. *2017 IEEE International Conference on Software Quality, Reliability and Security Companion (QRS-C)*, 311–315. 10.1109/QRS-C.2017.59

Yamashita, K., Kamei, Y., McIntosh, S., Hassan, A. E., & Ubayashi, N. (2016). Magnet or Sticky? Measuring Project Characteristics from the Perspective of Developer Attraction and Retention. *Journal of Information Processing*, 24(2), 339–348. doi:10.2197/ipsjjip.24.339

Yamashita, K., McIntosh, S., Kamei, Y., Hassan, A. E., & Ubayashi, N. (2015). Revisiting the applicability of the pareto principle to core development teams in open source software projects. *Proceedings of the 14th International Workshop on Principles of Software Evolution - IWPSE 2015*, 46–55. 10.1145/2804360.2804366

Yamashita, K., McIntosh, S., Kamei, Y., & Ubayashi, N. (2014). Magnet or sticky? an OSS project-by-project typology. *Proceedings of the 11th Working Conference on Mining Software Repositories - MSR 2014*, 344–347. 10.1145/2597073.2597116

Yan, D.-C., Li, M., & Wang, B.-H. (2017). Dependence centrality similarity: Measuring the diversity of profession levels of interests. *Physica A*, *479*, 118–127. doi:10.1016/j.physa.2017.02.082

Yan, D.-C., & Wang, B.-H. (2017). *Collaborative similarity analysis of multilayer developer-project bipartite network*. Retrieved from https://arxiv.org/abs/1703.03093

Yan, D.-C., Wei, Z. W., Han, X.-P., & Wang, B.-H. (2017). Empirical analysis on the human dynamics of blogging behavior on GitHub. *Physica A*, *465*, 775–781. doi:10.1016/j.physa.2016.08.054

Yang, D., Martins, P., Saini, V., & Lopes, C. (2017). Stack Overflow in Github: Any Snippets There? *2017 IEEE/ACM 14th International Conference on Mining Software Repositories (MSR)*, 280–290. 10.1109/MSR.2017.13

Ying, H., Chen, L., Liang, T., & Wu, J. (2016). EARec: Leveraging Expertise and Authority for Pull-Request Reviewer Recommendation in GitHub. *Proceedings of the 3rd International Workshop on CrowdSourcing in Software Engineering - CSI-SE '16*, 29–35. 10.1145/2897659.2897660

Yu, Y., Wang, H., Filkov, V., Devanbu, P., & Vasilescu, B. (2015). Wait for It: Determinants of Pull Request Evaluation Latency on GitHub. *2015 IEEE/ACM 12th Working Conference on Mining Software Repositories*, 367–371. 10.1109/MSR.2015.42

Yu, Y., Wang, H., Yin, G., & Ling, C. X. (2014). Who Should Review this Pull-Request Reviewer Recommendation to Expedite Crowd Collaboration. *2014 21st Asia-Pacific Software Engineering Conference*, 335–342. 10.1109/APSEC.2014.57

Yu, Y., Wang, H., Yin, G., & Wang, T. (2016). Reviewer recommendation for pull-requests in GitHub: What can we learn from code review and bug assignment? *Information and Software Technology*, *74*, 204–218. doi:10.1016/j.infsof.2016.01.004

Yu, Y., Yin, G., Wang, H., & Wang, T. (2014). Exploring the patterns of social behavior in GitHub. *Proceedings of the 1st International Workshop on Crowd-Based Software Development Methods and Technologies - CrowdSoft 2014*, 31–36. 10.1145/2666539.2666571

Yu, Y., Yin, G., Wang, T., Yang, C., & Wang, H. (2016). Determinants of pull-based development in the context of continuous integration. *Science China. Information Sciences*, *59*(8), 080104. doi:10.100711432-016-5595-8

Zhang, P., Xiong, F., Leung, H. K. N., & Song, W. (2018). FunkR-pDAE: Personalized Project Recommendation Using Deep Learning. *IEEE Transactions on Emerging Topics in Computing*, 1–1. doi:10.1109/TETC.2018.2870734

Zhang, Y., Yin, G., Yu, Y., & Wang, H. (2014). Investigating social media in GitHub's pull-requests: a case study on Ruby on Rails. *Proceedings of the 1st International Workshop on Crowd-Based Software Development Methods and Technologies - CrowdSoft 2014*, 37–41. 10.1145/2666539.2666572

Zhao, G., da Costa, D. A., & Zou, Y. (2019). Improving the Pull Requests Review Process Using Learning-to-rank Algorithms. *Empirical Software Engineering*, 24(4), 1–31. doi:10.100710664-019-09696-8

ENDNOTES

[1]   Harzing's Publish or Perish
[2]   Last check was done on 24 July 2019
[3]   https://www.vosviewer.com
[4]   https://developer.github.com/v3/\#rate-limiting

This research was previously published in the International Journal of Open Source Software and Processes (IJOSSP), 11(4); pages 1-26, copyright year 2020 by IGI Publishing (an imprint of IGI Global).

Index

A

actionable knowledge 1297-1300, 1305, 1307, 1309, 1311-1313, 1315, 1319-1320, 1322-1324, 1327-1329, 1332

Activity Diagram 346, 399, 403, 406-408, 1526, 1832

Activity Graph 399, 408

Actual Effort 123, 136, 139, 144, 148, 163, 177, 179, 186, 821, 823, 923, 950, 960

agent-based approach 377-378, 381-382, 385-387

agile cloud 491, 501-502, 506

agile component 389

Agile Development 7, 9, 13, 15, 44, 76, 108-109, 118, 120, 248-252, 255, 257-260, 262-264, 267, 269, 271-276, 278, 280-281, 292-295, 330-332, 334, 336-338, 349, 351, 356-363, 369-374, 389, 393, 396-397, 480, 485, 489-490, 497-501, 504-507, 832, 928, 930-932, 934, 940, 943, 945-946, 950, 968, 1002-1004, 1010, 1013, 1015, 1073, 1075, 1093-1094, 1154-1158, 1161, 1163-1164, 1167-1169, 1173, 1175, 1298, 1336, 1378, 1385, 1388-1389, 1394, 1407-1408, 1417, 1419-1420, 1511-1513, 1515-1518, 1520-1521, 1525, 1529-1530, 1560, 1914, 1923, 1981, 1987, 1989-1993, 1995, 1999, 2017, 2024, 2026-2027, 2029, 2037, 2039, 2041-2042, 2068, 2107

Agile Large Project Issuees 388

Agile Manifesto 6, 13-15, 41, 44, 47, 53, 108, 110-111, 113-114, 248-249, 272-273, 332, 351, 354, 356, 358, 361, 388-389, 950, 1012, 1061, 1073, 1093, 1104, 1388-1390, 1417, 1513, 1530, 1532, 1905-1906, 1908, 1910, 1922-1923, 1959, 1981, 1988, 2080

Agile Methodologies 1, 7, 14, 43, 110-111, 113, 118-119, 248, 258, 285, 295, 298, 315, 358, 370, 372-373, 398, 932, 942-943, 948-949, 966, 1002, 1059-1063, 1074, 1090, 1093, 1158-1160, 1385-1386, 1390, 1408, 1417-1418, 1421, 1424, 1427-1428, 1432, 1440, 1845, 1853, 1895-1896,

1906-1909, 1925, 2017, 2022, 2080, 2124

Agile Practices 5-6, 9, 14-15, 102, 111, 120, 258-259, 280, 282, 294, 297, 337, 359, 361, 363-365, 370, 398, 969, 1002-1003, 1157, 1416-1437, 1440-1443, 1902-1903, 1907, 1909-1910, 1922, 1952, 1981-1982, 1987, 1990-1991, 1995, 2016-2017, 2019, 2027, 2066, 2068, 2079

Agile Process 110, 1002, 1075, 1155, 1160, 1164, 1174, 1403, 1408, 1895, 2077

Agile Project Management 9, 13, 33, 107, 114, 288, 298, 945, 1385-1388, 1393, 1395, 1428, 1607, 1913, 1924, 2079, 2155

Agile Scrum 53, 121, 388, 395, 507, 1076, 2019

Agile Software Architecture 332, 336, 351-352, 355

Agile Software Development 2, 4, 12-15, 41, 43, 53-55, 76, 80, 108, 120, 247, 249-250, 258, 262, 264, 276-279, 281-282, 284, 295-298, 331-332, 334, 351, 353-355, 357, 361, 371-374, 389, 391, 396-397, 480-482, 485-486, 489, 491, 494-495, 497, 500, 504-505, 927, 929-934, 940, 942-944, 947-949, 960-961, 965-969, 1002-1004, 1007, 1013, 1062-1063, 1068, 1073-1075, 1092-1095, 1105, 1151, 1156-1158, 1174-1176, 1360, 1386, 1388, 1390-1391, 1396, 1398, 1409-1412, 1416-1417, 1420, 1425, 1433, 1511-1513, 1522, 1529-1530, 1532-1533, 1906-1908, 1910-1911, 1913, 1916, 1919, 1921, 1923-1925, 1981, 1990, 1996-1999, 2016-2018, 2023, 2025-2027, 2033, 2039-2041, 2044, 2052, 2063, 2065-2068, 2079-2081, 2097, 2132-2133, 2159

Agile Software Development Process 264, 276, 331, 334, 354-355, 943, 1156, 1420, 1512, 1522, 1532-1533, 1907, 2041

Agile Software Engineering 280-281, 298, 1435

Agile Software Methodology 1075

Agility 2, 5, 7, 11-12, 14, 53, 120, 250-251, 266, 298, 336-337, 342, 356-361, 365, 370-374, 398, 494, 820, 832, 857, 934, 941, 1059, 1061, 1071-1073, 1155-1156, 1170, 1172-1175, 1298, 1386-1387,

F

G

H

M

N

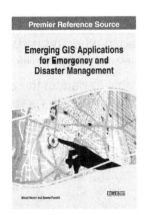
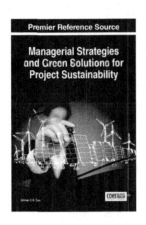

IGI Global Author Services

Providing a high-quality, affordable, and expeditious service, IGI Global's Author Services enable authors to streamline their publishing process, increase chance of acceptance, and adhere to IGI Global's publication standards.

Benefits of Author Services:

- **Professional Service:** All our editors, designers, and translators are experts in their field with years of experience and professional certifications.

- **Quality Guarantee & Certificate:** Each order is returned with a quality guarantee and certificate of professional completion.

- **Timeliness:** All editorial orders have a guaranteed return timeframe of 3-5 business days and translation orders are guaranteed in 7-10 business days.

- **Affordable Pricing:** IGI Global Author Services are competitively priced compared to other industry service providers.

- **APC Reimbursement:** IGI Global authors publishing Open Access (OA) will be able to deduct the cost of editing and other IGI Global author services from their OA APC publishing fee.

Author Services Offered:

English Language Copy Editing
Professional, native English language copy editors improve your manuscript's grammar, spelling, punctuation, terminology, semantics, consistency, flow, formatting, and more.

Scientific & Scholarly Editing
A Ph.D. level review for qualities such as originality and significance, interest to researchers, level of methodology and analysis, coverage of literature, organization, quality of writing, and strengths and weaknesses.

Figure, Table, Chart & Equation Conversions
Work with IGI Global's graphic designers before submission to enhance and design all figures and charts to IGI Global's specific standards for clarity.

Translation
Providing 70 language options, including Simplified and Traditional Chinese, Spanish, Arabic, German, French, and more.

Hear What the Experts Are Saying About IGI Global's Author Services

"Publishing with IGI Global has been *an amazing experience* for me for sharing my research. The *strong academic production* support ensures quality and timely completion." – **Prof. Margaret Niess, Oregon State University, USA**

"The service was *very fast, very thorough, and very helpful* in ensuring our chapter meets the criteria and requirements of the book's editors. I was *quite impressed and happy* with your service." – **Prof. Tom Brinthaupt, Middle Tennessee State University, USA**

Learn More or Get Started Here:

For Questions, Contact IGI Global's Customer Service Team at cust@igi-global.com or 717-533-8845

IGI Global
PUBLISHER of TIMELY KNOWLEDGE
www.igi-global.com

Printed in the United States
by Baker & Taylor Publisher Services